VALENCIA AND MURCIA
Pages 232–253

ARAGÓN
Pages 216–231

CATALONIA
Pages 196–215

Donostia
(San Sebastián)

Iruña
(Pamplona)

0 kilometers   100
0 miles   100

Zaragoza

Lleida

Barcelona

EASTERN SPAIN

BARCELONA
Pages132–185

Cuenca

THE BALEARIC ISLANDS

Palma de
Mallorca

Valencia

Albacete

Alacant
(Alicante)

Murcia

THE BALEARIC ISLANDS
Pages 482–503

mería

THE CANARY ISLANDS

THE CANARY ISLANDS
Pages 504–527

ANDALUSIA
Pages 434–477

Santa Cruz
de Tenerife

Las Palmas
de Gran Canaria

EYEWITNESS *TRAVEL GUIDES*

SPAIN

SPAIN

A DK PUBLISHING BOOK

PROJECT EDITOR Nick Inman
US EDITORS Mary Sutherland, Michael Wise
ART EDITORS Jaki Grosvenor, Janis Utton
EDITORS Catherine Day, Lesley McCave, Seán O'Connell
DESIGNERS Susan Blackburn, Dawn Davies-Cook,
Joy Fitzsimmons, Helen Westwood
MAP CO-ORDINATORS Michael Ellis, David Pugh

MANAGING EDITORS Vivien Crump, Helen Partington
MANAGING ART EDITOR Steve Knowlden
DEPUTY EDITORIAL DIRECTOR Douglas Amrine
DEPUTY ART DIRECTOR Gillian Allan

PRODUCTION Kate Hayward, David Proffit
PICTURE RESEARCHERS Monica Allende, Helen Stallion
DTP DESIGNER Ingrid Vienings

MAIN CONTRIBUTORS
John Ardagh, David Baird, Vicky Hayward, Adam Hopkins,
Lindsay Hunt, Nick Inman, Paul Richardson, Martin Symington,
Nigel Tisdall, Roger Williams

MAPS
Jennifer Skelley, Phil Rose, Jane Hanson (Lovell Johns Ltd)
Gary Bowes, Richard Toomey (ERA-Maptec Ltd)

PHOTOGRAPHERS
Max Alexander, Joe Cornish, Neil Lukas, Neil Mersh,
John Miller, Kim Sayer, Linda Whitwam, Peter Wilson

ILLUSTRATORS
Stephen Conlin, Richard Draper, Isidoro González-Adalid Cabezas
(Acanto Arquitectura y Urbanismo S.L.), Claire Littlejohn, Maltings
Partnership, Chris Orr & Assocs, John Woodcock

Text film output by Graphical Innovations (London)
Reproduced by Colourscan (Singapore)
Printed and bound by Graphicom (Italy)

First American Edition, 1996
2 4 6 8 10 9 7 5 3 1
Published in the United States by
DK Publishing, Inc., 95 Madison Avenue,
New York, New York 10016

Copyright 1996 © Dorling Kindersley Limited, London
Visit us on the World Wide Web at http://www.dk.com

Spain. -- 1st American ed.
    p.   cm. -- (Eyewitness travel guides)
    Includes index.
    ISBN 0-7894-1068-0
    1. Spain--Guidebooks. I. Series
DP14.S625 1996
914.604'83--dc20   96-14182 CIP

Every effort has been made to ensure that the information in this book is as
up-to-date as possible at the time of going to press. However, details such as
telephone numbers, opening hours, prices, gallery hanging arrangements, and
travel information are liable to change. The publishers cannot accept
responsibility for any consequences arising from the use of this book.

We would be delighted to receive any corrections and
suggestions for incorporation in the next edition. Please write to:
Deputy Editorial Director, Eyewitness Travel Guides,
Dorling Kindersley, 9 Henrietta Street, London WC2E 8PS.

THROUGHOUT THIS BOOK, FLOORS ARE REFERRED TO IN ACCORDANCE WITH EUROPEAN
USAGE, I.E. "FIRST FLOOR" IS ONE FLOOR UP.

CONTENTS

King Alfonso X the Learned

Previous pages: Pilgrimage of the Virgin of the Bridges, Belalcázar, near Córdoba in Andalusia

Grapes growing in La Mancha, the world's largest expanse of vineyards

Statue of Alfonso XII, Madrid

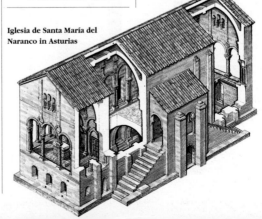

Iglesia de Santa María del Naranco in Asturias

How to Use this Guide

THIS GUIDE helps you to get the most from your visit to Spain. It provides detailed practical information and expert recommendations. *Introducing Spain* maps the country and sets it in its historical and cultural context. The five regional sections, plus *Barcelona* and *Madrid,* describe important sights using maps, photographs, and illustrations. Features cover topics from food and wine to fiestas and beaches. Restaurant and hotel recommendations can be found in *Travelers' Needs.* The *Survival Guide* has tips on everything from transportation to using the telephone system.

BARCELONA, MADRID, AND SEVILLE

These cities are divided into areas, each with its own chapter. A last chapter, *Farther Afield,* covers peripheral sights. Madrid Province, surrounding the capital, has its own chapter. All sights are numbered and plotted on the chapter's area map. Information on each sight is easy to locate as it follows the numerical order on the map.

Sights at a Glance lists the chapter's sights by category: Churches and Cathedrals, Museums and Galleries, Streets and Squares, Historic Buildings, Parks and Gardens.

2 Street-by-Street Map
This gives a bird's-eye view of the key areas in each chapter.

Stars indicate the sights that no visitor should miss.

All pages relating to Madrid have green thumb tabs. Barcelona's are pink and Seville's are red.

A locator map shows where you are in relation to other areas of the city center.

1 Area Map
For easy reference, sights are numbered and located on a map. City center sights are also marked on Street Finders: Barcelona *(pages 175–81);* Madrid *(pages 297–303);* Seville *(pages 429–33).*

A suggested route for a walk is shown in red.

3 Detailed information
The sights in the three main cities are described individually. Addresses, telephone numbers, opening hours, admission charges, tours, photography, and wheelchair access are also provided, as well as public transportation links.

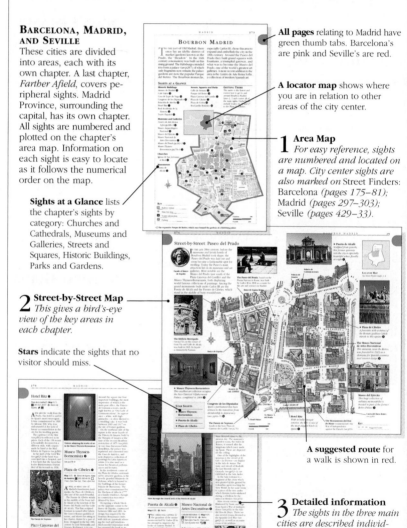

SPAIN AREA BY AREA

Apart from Barcelona, Madrid, and Seville, the country has been divided into 12 regions, each of which has a separate chapter. The most interesting cities, towns and villages, and other places to visit are numbered on a *Pictorial Map*.

1 Introduction
The landscape, history, and character of each region is outlined here, showing how the area has developed over the centuries and what it has to offer the visitor today.

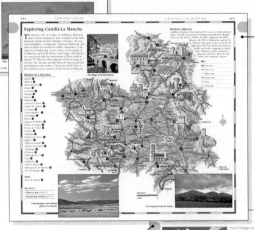

2 Pictorial Map
This shows the road network and gives an illustrated overview of the whole region. All interesting places to visit are numbered, and there are also useful tips on getting to, and around, the region by car and public transportation.

Fiesta boxes highlight the best traditional fiestas in the region.

Each area of Spain can be quickly identified by its color coding, shown on the inside front cover.

3 Detailed information
All the important towns and other places to visit are described individually. They are listed in order, following the numbering on the Pictorial Map. Within each town or city, there is detailed information on important buildings and other sights.

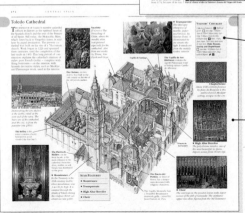

For all top sights, a Visitors' Checklist provides the practical information you will need to plan your visit.

4 Spain's top sights
These are given two or more full pages. Historic buildings are dissected to reveal their interiors. The most interesting towns or city centers are shown in a bird's-eye view, with sights picked out and described.

INTRODUCING
SPAIN

Putting Spain on the Map

S PAIN, IN SOUTHWESTERN Europe, covers the greater part
of the Iberian Peninsula. The third largest country in
Europe, it includes two island groups: the Canaries in the
Atlantic and the Balearics in the Mediterranean, and two
small territories in North Africa. Its southernmost point
faces Morocco across a strait,
making Spain a
bridge between
continents.

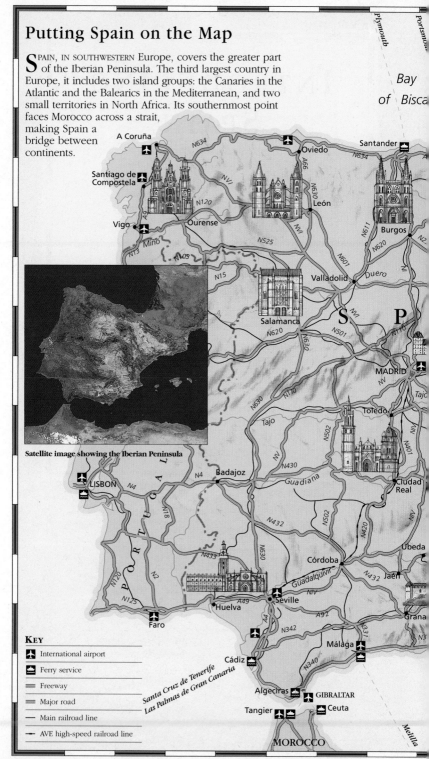

Satellite image showing the Iberian Peninsula

KEY

🛫 International airport

⚓ Ferry service

▬ Freeway

▬ Major road

— Main railroad line

-◆- AVE high-speed railroad line

◁ *Rooftops, Fortna Lux, Mallorca* (1969) by Frederick Gore

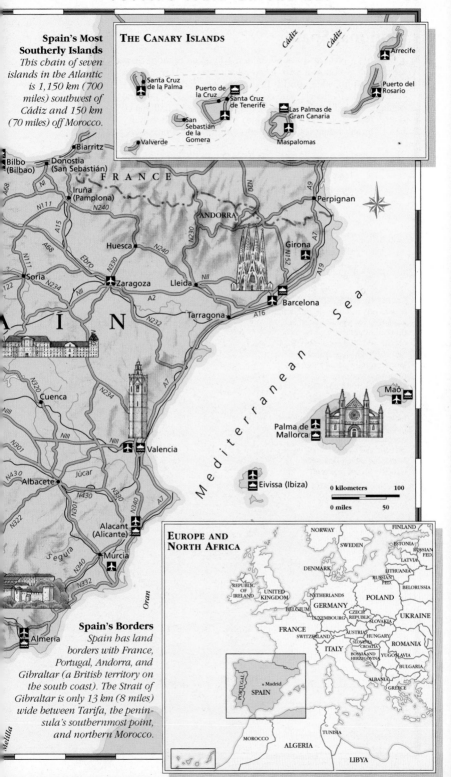

Spain's Most Southerly Islands
This chain of seven islands in the Atlantic is 1,150 km (700 miles) southwest of Cádiz and 150 km (70 miles) off Morocco.

THE CANARY ISLANDS

Cádiz   *Cádiz*

Arrecife

Santa Cruz de la Palma

Puerto de la Cruz   Santa Cruz de Tenerife

Puerto del Rosario

San Sebastián de la Gomera

Las Palmas de Gran Canaria

Valverde

Maspalomas

Biarritz

Bilbo (Bilbao)   Donostia (San Sebastián)

Iruña (Pamplona)

FRANCE

ANDORRA

Perpignan

N68

N1

N111

N240

A15

N230

A9

Huesca

N240

A68

Girona

N152

A7

Ebro

N330

Soria

N111

N234

Zaragoza

Lleida

NII

Barcelona

A2

A19

122

NII

Tarragona

A16

Mediterranean Sea

N232

Á   N

Cuenca

N234

A7

Maó

Palma de Mallorca

N320

NIII

Valencia

NIII

N301

Júcar

N330

Eivissa (Ibiza)

Albacete

N430

0 kilometers   100

N430

N322

N340

A7

0 miles   50

Alacant (Alicante)

Segura

N340

Murcia

N332

N301

Oran

EUROPE AND NORTH AFRICA

NORWAY   FINLAND

SWEDEN   ESTONIA   RUSSIAN FED.

DENMARK   LITHUANIA   LATVIA

REPUBLIC OF IRELAND   UNITED KINGDOM   RUSSIAN FED.   BELORUSSIA

NETHERLANDS   POLAND

BELGIUM   GERMANY

LUXEMBOURG   CZECH REPUBLIC   UKRAINE

SLOVAKIA

FRANCE   AUSTRIA   HUNGARY

SWITZERLAND   SLOVENIA   ROMANIA

ITALY   CROATIA   YUGOSLAVIA

BOSNIA AND HERZEGOVINA   BULGARIA

ALBANIA

PORTUGAL   SPAIN   • Madrid   GREECE

Almería

Spain's Borders
Spain has land borders with France, Portugal, Andorra, and Gibraltar (a British territory on the south coast). The Strait of Gibraltar is only 13 km (8 miles) wide between Tarifa, the peninsula's southernmost point, and northern Morocco.

Melilla

MOROCCO   TUNISIA

ALGERIA   LIBYA

Regional Spain

SPAIN HAS A POPULATION of 39 million and receives more than 57 million visitors a year. It covers an area of 504,780 sq km (194,900 sq miles). Madrid is the largest city, followed by Barcelona and Valencia. The country is dominated by a central plateau drained by the Duero, Tagus (Tajo), and Guadiana rivers. This book divides Spain into 15 areas, but officially it has 17 independent regions called *comunidades autónomas*.

GETTING AROUND

Spain's regional capitals and islands are linked by regular flights, and there is a shuttle service between Madrid and Barcelona. The TALGO and AVE high-speed trains provide fast rail services between many provincial cities and are backed up by regional and local rail networks. Some freeways have expensive tolls, but are fast. Other roads range from rapid, modern national highways to scenic, but often rough, byways. The Balearic and Canary islands are served by regular ferries from the mainland.

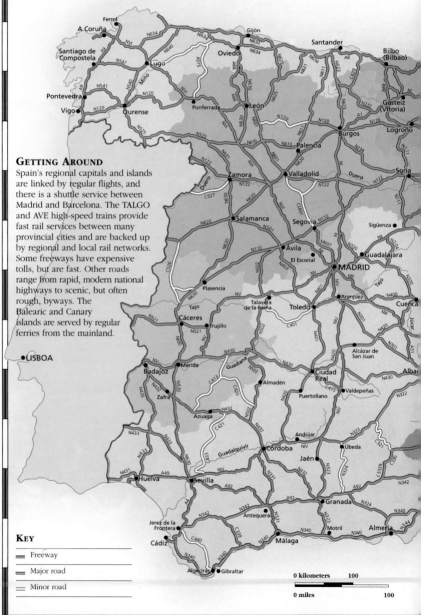

KEY

━━━ Freeway

━━━ Major road

━━━ Minor road

0 kilometers   100

0 miles   100

Eyewitness Spain Regions

Each of the chapters in this guide has a color code. The chapters are grouped into five sections: Northern, Eastern, Central, and Southern Spain, and Spain's Islands; and two cities: Madrid and Barcelona.

KEY TO COLOR CODING

Northern Spain

- Galicia
- Asturias and Cantabria
- Basque Country, Navarra, and La Rioja

Eastern Spain

- Barcelona
- Catalonia
- Aragón
- Valencia and Murcia

Central Spain

- Madrid
- Castilla y León
- Castilla-La Mancha
- Extremadura

Southern Spain

- Seville
- Andalusia

Spain's Islands

- The Balearic Islands
- The Canary Islands

...tía
(ebastián)

...ruña
(Pamplona)

N135

N240

Huesca

NA125
Tudela

N330

A125

N123

N240

N260

La Seu d'Urgell

C1313

N260

N260

N152

Figueres

N260

Vic

Girona

Zaragoza

A2

Ebro

Lleida

A2

NII

Manresa

A152

A7

Barcelona

Reus

N211

N420

N232

Tarragona

Tortosa

N232

Teruel

C580

A238

Castelló de la Plana

A7

Sagunt

Turia

N340

Valencia

N330

N430

...mansa

N344

Alcoi

Benidorm

Alacant
(Alicante)

Elx

A7

Murcia

Cartagena

THE BALEARIC ISLANDS

Ciutadella

C721

Menorca

Maó

Mallorca

Palma de Mallorca

PM13

PM27

Manacor

PM1

Ibiza

C731

Eivissa (Ibiza)

Formentera

Cabrera

THE CANARY ISLANDS

Lanzarote

Arrecife

La Palma

Santa Cruz de la Palma

Puerto de la Cruz

Santa Cruz de Tenerife

Fuerteventura

Puerto del Rosario

GC10

La Gomera

Tenerife

San Sebastián de la Gomera

Gran Canaria

GC10

Las Palmas de Gran Canaria

El Hierro

Valverde

Gran Canaria

GC1

Maspalomas

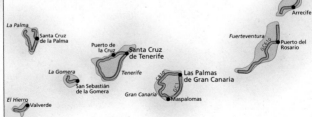

Spain's Atlantic Territories

The Canary Islands, in the Atlantic Ocean off the coast of Africa, are an integral part of Spain. They are one hour behind the rest of the country.

A PORTRAIT OF SPAIN

THE FAMILIAR IMAGES OF SPAIN – *flamenco dancing, bullfighting, tapas bars, and solemn Easter processions – do no more than hint at the diversity of the country. Spain has four official languages, two major cities of almost equal importance, and a greater range of landscapes than any other European country. These remarkable contrasts make Spain an endlessly fascinating country to visit.*

Separated from the rest of Europe by the Pyrenees, Spain reaches south to the coast of North Africa. It has both Atlantic and Mediterranean coastlines and includes two archipelagos – the Balearics and the Canary Islands.

The climate and landscape vary from snow-capped peaks in the Pyrenees, through the green meadows of Galicia and the orange groves of Valencia, to the desert of Almería. Madrid is the highest capital in Europe, and Spain its most mountainous country after Switzerland and Austria. The innumerable sierras have always hindered communications. Until railroads were built it was easier to move goods from Barcelona to South America than to Madrid.

In early times, Spain was a coveted prize for foreign conquerors, including the Phoenicians and the Romans. During the Middle Ages, much of it was ruled by the Moors, who arrived from North Africa in the 8th century. It was reconquered by Christian forces and unified at the end of the 15th century. A succession of rulers tried to impose a common culture, but Spain remains as culturally diverse as ever. Several regions have maintained a strong sense of their own independent identities. Many Basques and Catalans, in particular, do not consider themselves

Statue of Don Quixote and Sancho Panza, Madrid

Landscape with a solitary cork tree near Albacete in Castilla-La Mancha

◁ The outlandishly dressed *Peliqueiros* who take to the streets during Carnival in Laza, Galicia

Peñafiel castle in the Duero valley (Castilla y León), built between the 10th and 13th centuries

to be Spanish. Madrid may be the nominal capital but, it is closely rivaled in commerce, the arts, and sports by Barcelona, the main city of Catalonia.

THE SPANISH WAY OF LIFE

The inhabitants of this varied country have few things in common except for a natural sociability and a zest for living. Spaniards commonly put as much energy into enjoying life as they do into their work. The stereotypical *"mañana"* (leave everything until tomorrow) is a myth, but time is flexible in Spain, and many people bend their work to fit the demands

"Vinegar Face" in Pamplona's Los Sanfermines fiesta

of their social life, rather than let themselves be ruled by the clock. The day is long in Spain, and Spanish has a word, *madrugada*, for the time between midnight and dawn, when city streets are often still lively.

Spaniards are highly gregarious. In many places people still go out in the evening for the *paseo*, when the streets are crowded with strollers. Eating is invariably communal, and big groups often meet up for tapas or dinner. Not surprisingly, Spain has more bars and restaurants per head than any other country.

Underpinning Spanish society is the extended family. Traditionally, the state in Spain has been very inefficient at providing public services – although this has improved in the last 20 years. The Spanish have therefore always relied on their families and personal connections, rather than institutions, to find work or seek assistance in a crisis. This attitude has sometimes led to a disregard for general interests – such as the environment – when they have conflicted with private ones.

Most Spaniards place their family at the center of their lives. Three generations may live together under one roof, or at least see each other often. Even

Tables outside a café in Madrid's Plaza Mayor

lifelong city-dwellers refer fondly to their *pueblo* – the town or village where their family comes from and where they return whenever they can. Children are adored in Spain, and, consequently, great importance is attached to education. The family in Spain, however, is under strain as couples increasingly opt for a higher income and better lifestyle rather than a large family. One of the most striking transformations in modern Spain has been in the birth rate, from one of the highest in Europe, at 2.72 children for every woman in 1975, to one of the lowest in the world, only 1.2 in 1995.

The windmills and castle above Consuegra, La Mancha

Virgin of Guadalupe in Extremadura

Catholicism is still a pervasive influence over Spanish society, although church attendance among those under 35 has declined in recent years to below 25 percent. The images of saints watch over some shops, bars, and truck drivers' cabs. Church feast days are marked by the countless traditional fiestas that are enthusiastically maintained in modern Spain.

Sports and the Arts

Spanish cultural life has been reinvigorated in recent years. Spanish-made films – notably those of cult director Pedro Almodóvar – have been able to compete effectively with Hollywood productions for audiences. Despite the low overall level of reading (fewer than one in ten buy a daily newspaper), contemporary literature has steadily gained a wider readership. The performing arts have been restricted by a lack of facilities, but recent major investments have provided new venues, regional arts centers, and new symphony orchestras. The country has

A matador plays a bull in the Plaza de Toros de la Maestranza, Seville

Poster for a Pedro Almodóvar film

the mainstays of TV programming. Recently, Spanish sportsmen and women have been very successful – for example, tennis players Conchita Martínez and Arantxa Sánchez, cyclist Miguel Induráin, and golfer Severiano Ballesteros. Such role models have encouraged participation in sports, and new facilities have been provided to meet this demand. Most popular are basketball and, above all, soccer.

Bullfighting has enjoyed renewed popularity since the late 1980s. For aficionados, a *corrida* is a unique occasion that provides a link to Spain's roots, and the noise, color, and argumentative attitude of the crowd are as much of an attraction as the bullfight itself.

produced many remarkable opera singers, including Montserrat Caballé, Alfredo Kraus, Plácido Domingo, and José Carreras. Spain has also excelled in design, particularly evident in the interior furnishings shops of Barcelona.

Spaniards are the most avid TV-watchers in Europe after the British. In many parts of the country there are six channels: two state-owned channels, three private networks, and a regional station. Sports are one of

SPAIN TODAY

In the last 40 years Spain has undergone more social change than anywhere else in western Europe. Until the 1950s, Spain was predominantly a poor, rural country, in which only 37 percent of the population lived in towns of over 10,000 people. By the 1990s, the figure was 65 percent. As people flooded into towns and cities many rural areas became depopulated. The 1960s saw the beginning of

A farmer with his crop of corn hanging to dry on the outside of his house in the hills of Alicante

Beach near Tossa de Mar on the Costa Brava

terrorist group ETA is a constant thorn in the side of Spanish democracy.

During the 1980s Spain enjoyed an economic boom as service industries and manufacturing expanded. Even so, GDP remains below the European Union average, and growth has been very unevenly spread around the country. Agriculture is an important industry, but while it is highly developed in some regions, it is inefficient in others. Tourism provides approximately ten percent of the country's earnings. Most tourists still come for the beaches, but increasingly, foreign visitors are drawn by Spain's rich cultural heritage and spectacular countryside. Anyone who knows this country, however, will tell you that it is the Spanish people's capacity to enjoy life to the full that is Spain's biggest attraction.

spectacular economic growth, partly the result of a burgeoning tourist industry. In that decade alone the number of car owners went from 1 in 100 to 1 in 10.

After the death of the dictator General Franco in 1975 Spain became a constitutional monarchy under King Juan Carlos I. The post-Franco era, up until the mid-1990s, has been dominated by the Socialist Prime Minister Felipe González. As well as presiding over major improvements in roads, education, and health services, the Socialists increased Spain's international standing. Spain joined the European Community in 1986, triggering a spectacular increase in the country's prosperity. The country's fortunes seemed to peak in the extraordinary year of 1992, when Barcelona staged the Olympic Games and Seville hosted a world's fair, Expo '92.

King Juan Carlos I and Queen Sofía

With the establishment of democracy, the 17 autonomous regions of Spain have acquired considerable powers. Several have their own languages, which are officially given equal importance to Spanish (strictly called Castilian). A significant number of Basques favor independence for the Basque Country. The Basque

Demonstration for Catalan independence

Architecture in Spain

SPAIN HAS ALWAYS IMPORTED its styles of architecture: Moorish from North Africa, Romanesque and Gothic from France, and Renaissance from Italy. Each style, however, was interpreted in a distinctively Spanish way, with sudden and strong contrasts between light and shady areas, façades alternating between austerity and extravagant decoration, and thick walls pierced by few windows to lessen the impact of heat and sunlight. Styles vary from region to region, reflecting the division of Spain before unification. The key design of a central patio surrounded by arcades has been a strong feature of civil buildings since Moorish times.

The 15th-century Casa de Conchas in Salamanca *(see p343)*

ROMANESQUE AND EARLIER (8TH–13TH CENTURIES)

Romanesque churches were mainly built in Catalonia and along the pilgrim route to Santiago *(see p79)*. Their distinctive features include round arches, massive walls, and few windows. Earlier churches were built in Pre-Romanesque *(see 102)* or Mozarabic *(see p335)* style.

Round arch　　　**Multiple apses**

The Romanesque Sant Climent, Taüll *(p201)*

MOORISH (8TH–15TH CENTURIES)

The Moors *(see pp48–9)* reserved the most lavish decoration for the interior of buildings, where ornate designs based on geometry, calligraphy and plant motifs were created in *azulejos* (tiles) or stucco. They made extensive use of the horsehoe arch, a feature inherited from the Visigoths *(see pp46–7)*. The greatest surviving works of Moorish architecture *(see pp404–5)* are in Southern Spain.

***The Salón de Embajadores** in the Alhambra (see p466) has exquisite Moorish decoration.*

GOTHIC (12TH–16TH CENTURIES)

Gothic arched window

Gothic was imported from France in the late 12th century. The round arch was replaced by the pointed arch, which because of its greater strength, allowed for higher vaults and taller windows. External buttresses were added to prevent the walls of the nave from leaning outward. Carved decoration was at its most opulent in the Flamboyant Gothic style of the 15th century. After the fall of Granada, Isabelline, a late Gothic style, developed. Meanwhile, Moorish craftsmen working in reconquered areas created the highly decorative hybrid Christian-Islamic style Mudéjar *(see p51)*.

Rose window　　　**Tracery**

Pointed arch　　　**Flying buttress**

***The nave** of León Cathedral (see pp336–7), built in the 13th century, is supported by rib vaulting and is illuminated by the finest display of stained glass in Spain.*

***Sculptural decoration** above the doorways of León cathedral's south front depicted biblical stories for the benefit of the largely illiterate populace.*

RENAISSANCE (16TH CENTURY)

Around 1500 a new style was introduced to Spain by Italian craftsmen and Spanish artists who had studied in Italy. The Renaissance was a revival of the style of ancient Rome. It is distinguished by its sense of symmetry and the use of the round arch, and Doric, Ionic, and Corinthian columns. Early Spanish Renaissance architecture is known as Plateresque because its fine detail resembles ornate silverwork (*platero* means silversmith).

The Palacio de las Cadenas in Úbeda (see p473) has a severely Classical façade.

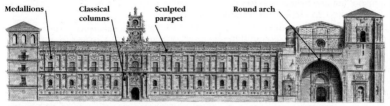

Medallions — Classical columns — Sculpted parapet — Round arch

The Hostal de San Marcos in León (*see p335*), one of Spain's finest Plateresque buildings

BAROQUE (17TH–18TH CENTURIES)

Baroque was driven by a desire for drama and movement. Decoration became extravagant, with exuberant sculpture and twisting columns. Although the excessive Baroque style of Churrigueresque is named after the Churriguera family of architects, it was their successors who were its main exponents.

The ornamentation on the Baroque façade of Valladolid University (see p348) is concentrated above the doorway.

Finials

Statues on parapet

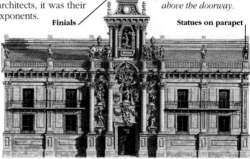

The façade of the Museo Municipal in Madrid (*pp294–5*)

MODERN (LATE 19TH CENTURY ONWARD)

Modernisme (*see pp136–7*), a Catalan interpretation of Art Nouveau, is seen at its best in Barcelona. Its architects experimented with a highly original language of ornament. In recent decades, Spain has seen an explosion of bold, functionalist architecture in which the form of a building reflects its use and decoration is sparingly used.

Torre de Picasso in Madrid

Casa Milà, in Barcelona (see p161), *was built in 1910 by Modernisme's most famous and best-loved architect, Antoni Gaudí, who drew much of his inspiration from nature.*

Curving parapet — Spiral chimney — Decorative ironwork

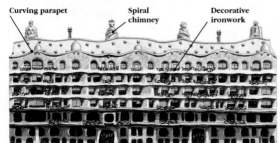

Vernacular Architecture

Window in Navarra

A S WELL AS ITS CATHEDRALS and palaces, Spain has a great variety of charming vernacular buildings. These have been constructed by local craftsmen to meet the practical needs of rural communities and to take account of local climate conditions, with little reference to formal architectural styles. Due to the high expense involved in transporting raw materials, builders used whatever stone or timber lay closest at hand. The three houses illustrated below incorporate the most common characteristics of village architecture seen in different parts of Spain.

A cave church in Artenara (see p521), on Gran Canaria

STONE HOUSE

The climate is wet in the north, and houses like this one in Carmona (see p107), in Cantabria, are built with overhanging eaves to shed the rain. Wooden balconies catch the sun.

Detail of stonework

Family and farm often share rural houses. The ground floor is used to stable animals, or to store tools and firewood.

Supporting pillar   **Large doors** accommodate carts and animals.   **The walls** are built of irregularly shaped stones.

TIMBER-FRAMED HOUSE

Spain, in general, has few large trees, and wood is in short supply. Castilla y León is one of the few regions where timber-framed houses, such as this one in Covarrubias (see p352), can be found. These houses are quick and cheap to build. The timber frame is filled in with a coarse plaster mixed from lime and sand, or adobe (bricks dried in the sun).

Half-timbered wall

The ends of the beams supporting the floorboards are visible.

Stone plinths below upright timbers provide protection from damp.

Portico   **Gently sloping roof**

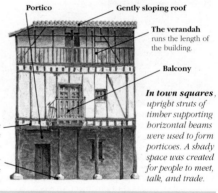

The verandah runs the length of the building.

Balcony

In town squares, upright struts of timber supporting horizontal beams were used to form porticoes. A shady space was created for people to meet, talk, and trade.

WHITEWASHED HOUSE

Houses in the south of Spain – often built of baked clay – are regularly whitewashed to deflect the sun's intense rays. Andalusia's famous white towns (see p444) exemplify this attractive form of architecture.

Clay-tiled roof

Windows are small and few in number, and deeply recessed, in order to keep the interior cool.

Irregularly shaped houses are joined together.   **Few, small windows**

Shallow-pitched roof

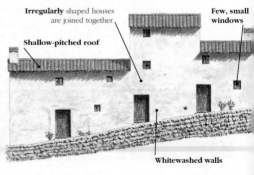

Whitewashed walls

THE PLAZA MAYOR

Almost every town in Spain centers on a main square, the *plaza mayor*, like this one in Pedraza de la Sierra *(see p347)*, near Segovia. More than a market square, it acts as a focus for local life. It is usually overlooked by the church, the town hall, shops and bars, and the mansions of aristocratic families.

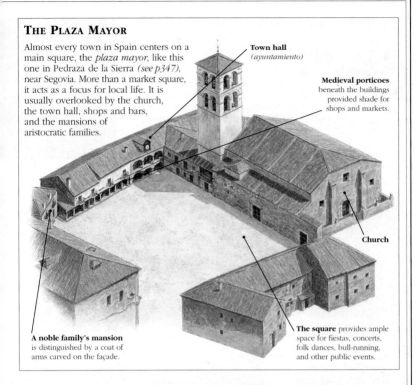

Town hall
(ayuntamiento)

Medieval porticoes
beneath the buildings provided shade for shops and markets.

Church

A noble family's mansion is distinguished by a coat of arms carved on the façade.

The square provides ample space for fiestas, concerts, folk dances, bull-running, and other public events.

RURAL ARCHITECTURE

A variety of distinctive buildings dots the countryside.

Where the rock is soft and the climate hot, subterranean dwellings have been excavated. Insulated from extremes of temperature, they provide a comfortable place to live.

Hórreos, granaries raised on stone stilts to prevent rats climbing up into the grain, are a common sight in Galicia (where they are built of stone) and Asturias (where they are made of wood). In fields you will often see shelters for livestock or storing crops, such as the *teitos* of Asturias.

Windmills provided power in parts of Spain where there was plentiful wind, like La Mancha and the Balearic Islands.

Almost everywhere in the Spanish countryside you will come across *ermitas*, isolated chapels or shrines dedicated to a local saint. An *ermita* may be opened only on the patron saint's feast day.

Cave houses in Guadix near Granada *(see p469)*

Teito in Valle de Teverga in Asturias *(see p101)*

Hórreo, a granary, on the Rías Baixas *(see p91)* **in Galicia**

Windmill above Consuegra *(see p376)* **in La Mancha**

Farming in Spain

SPAIN'S VARIED geography and climate have created a mosaic of farming patterns ranging from lush dairylands to stony hillsides where goats graze. Land is broadly divided into *secano*, or dry cultivation (used for olives, wheat, and vines), and much smaller areas of *regadío*, irrigated land (planted with citrus trees, rice, and vegetables). Farming in many parts is a family affair relying on traditional, labor-intensive methods, but it is becoming increasingly mechanized.

Donkey in Extremadura

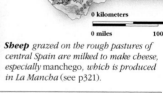

Fields of grain *make up much of the farmland of the central* meseta *of Spain. Wheat is grown in better-watered, more fertile western areas; barley is grown in the drier south.*

Cork oaks thrive in Extremadura and western Andalusia.

MADRID

SEVILLA

0 kilometers 20

0 miles 100

Sheep *grazed on the rough pastures of central Spain are milked to make cheese, especially* manchego, *which is produced in La Mancha (see p321).*

THE AGRICULTURAL YEAR

Jul–Aug Wheat harvested in central Spain	**Sep** Rice harvest in eastern Spain. Grape harvest at its height	**Oct** Corn harvested in northern Spain **Oct–Nov** Table olives picked	**Dec–Mar** Olives for making oil picked	
Spring	**Summer**	**Autumn**	**Winter**	
Mar–Apr Orange trees in blossom on Mediterranean coast		**Nov–Dec** Oranges picked	**Feb** Almond trees in blossom	
Jun–Aug Haymaking in northern Spain	**Sep** Start of wild mushroom season	**Dec** Pigs are slaughtered when cold weather arrives		

The high rainfall and mild summers of northern Spain make it suitable for dairy farming. Farms are often small, especially in Galicia, one of the country's most under-developed regions. Crops such as corn and wheat are grown in small quantities.

Wine is produced in many parts of Spain (see pp576–7). The country's best sparkling wine grapes are grown in Catalonia.

BARCELONA ●

Rice is grown mainly in the Ebro delta in Catalonia, around L'Albufera near Valencia and also at Calasparra in Murcia.

Oranges, lemons, and clementines are grown on the irrigated coastal plains beside the Mediterranean. The region of Valencia is the prime producer of oranges.

Olive trees are planted in long, straight lines across large swaths of Andalusia, especially in the province of Jaén. Spain is the world's leading producer of olive oil.

Cork oaks stripped of their bark every ten years

CROPS FROM TREES

The almond, orange, and olive create the three most characteristic landscapes of rural Spain, but several other trees provide important crops. Wine corks are made from the bark of the cork oak. Tropical species, such as avocado and cherimoya, a delicious creamy fruit little known outside Spain, have been introduced to the so-called Costa Tropical of Andalusia (see p459); bananas are a major crop of the Canary Islands. Elsewhere, peaches and loquats are also grown commercially. Figs and carobs – whose fruit is used for fodder and as a substitute for chocolate – grow semiwild.

Almonds grow on dry hillsides in many parts of Spain. The spring blossoms can be spectacular. The nut, enclosed by a fleshy green skin, is used in a variety of candies including the Christmas treat turrón (see p191).

Olive trees grow slowly and often live to a great age. The fruit is harvested in winter and either pickled in brine for eating as a tapa or pressed to extract the oil, which is widely used in Spanish cuisine.

Sweet oranges are grown in dense, well-irrigated groves near the frost free coasts. The sweet smell of orange blossom in springtime is unmistakable. Trees of the bitter orange are often planted for shade and decoration in parks and gardens.

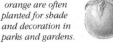

Spain's National Parks

FEW OTHER COUNTRIES in western Europe have such unspoiled scenery as Spain, or can boast tracts of wilderness where brown bears live and wolves hunt. More than 200 nature preserves protect a broad range of ecosystems. The most important areas are the 11 national parks, the first of which was established in 1918. Natural parks *(parques naturales)*, regulated by regional governments, are also vital to the task of conservation.

Giant orchid

Clear mountain river, Ordesa

Rough terrain in the Picos de Europa

MOUNTAINS

Some of Spain's finest scenery is to be found in the three national parks in the north. Rivers have carved stupendous gorges between the high peaks of the Picos de Europa. Ordesa and Aigüestortes between them share some of the most dramatic landscapes of the Pyrenees.

Eagle owls *are Europe's largest owl, easily identified by their large ear tufts. At night they hunt small mammals and birds.*

Chamois *are well adapted to climbing across slopes covered in loose stones. They live in small groups and feed mostly on grass and flowers.*

WETLANDS

Wetlands, including coastal strips and freshwater marshes, are everchanging environments. Seasonal floods rejuvenate the water, providing nutrients for animal and plant growth. These areas are rich feeding grounds for birds. Spain's best-known wetland is Doñana. Tablas de Daimiel, in La Mancha, is much smaller.

Lynx, *endangered by hunting and habitat loss, can occasionally be spotted in Doñana* (see pp440–41).

Black-winged stilts, *with their long, straight legs, are adept at stalking tiny freshwater crustaceans.*

Laguna del Acebuche, Parque Nacional de Doñana

Cabrera archipelago, Balearic Islands

ISLANDS

Cabrera, off Mallorca, is home to rare plants, reptiles, and seabirds such as Eleonara's falcon. The surrounding waters are important for their marine life.

Lizards *are often found in rocky terrain and on cliff faces.*

NATIONAL PARKS

① Mountains

④ Wetlands

⑥ Islands

⑦ Woods and Forests

⑨ Volcanic Landscapes

MOUNTAINS

① Picos de Europa *pp104–105*
② Ordesa y Monte Perdido *pp222–3*
③ Aigüestortes y Estany de Sant Maurici *p201*

WETLANDS

④ Tablas de Daimiel *p381*
⑤ Doñana *pp440–41*

ISLANDS

⑥ Archipiélago de Cabrera *p493*

WOODS AND FORESTS

⑦ Cabañeros *p369*
⑧ Garajonay *p509*

VOLCANIC LANDSCAPES

⑨ Caldera de Taburiente *p508*
⑩ Teide *pp514–15*
⑪ Timanfaya *pp524–5*

VISITORS' CHECKLIST

All but one of the national parks are managed by ICONA (Instituto para la Conservación de la Naturaleza). ☎ *(91) 347 59 71. Parque Nacional d'Aigüestortes y Estany de Sant Maurici is administered by Catalonia's Department of Agriculture.* ☎ *(973) 62 40 36. Most, but not all, of Spain's national parks have visitors' centers.*

WOODS AND FORESTS

Deciduous broad-leaved forests grow in the northwest of Spain, and stands of Aleppo and Scots pine cover many mountainous areas. On the central plateau there are stretches of open woodland of evergreen holm oak and cork oak in the Parque Nacional de Cabañeros. Dense, lush *laurasilva* woodland grows in the Parque Nacional de Garajonay, on La Gomera, one of the smaller Canary Islands.

Parque Nacional de Garajonay

Black vultures *are the largest birds of prey in Europe, with an enormous wingspan of over 2.5 m (8 ft).*

Hedgehogs, *common in woodlands, root among fallen leaves and grass to find worms and slugs.*

VOLCANIC LANDSCAPES

Three very different parks protect parts of the Canary Islands' amazing volcanic scenery. Caldera de Taburiente on La Palma is a volcanic crater surrounded by woods. Mount Teide in Tenerife has unique alpine flora, and Lanzarote's Timanfaya is composed of barren but atmospheric lava fields.

Rabbits *are highly opportunistic, quickly colonizing areas in which they can burrow. In the absence of predators, populations may increase, damaging fragile ecosystems.*

Canaries *belong to the finch family of songbirds. The popular canary has been bred from the wild serin, native to the Canaries.*

Colonizing plant species, Mount Teide (Tenerife)

Spanish Art

THREE SPANISH PAINTERS stand out as milestones in the history of Western art. Diego de Velázquez was a 17th-century court portrait painter, and his *Las Meninas* is a seminal work. Francisco de Goya depicted Spanish life during one of its most violent periods. The prolific 20th-century master, Pablo Picasso, is recognized as the founder of modern art. To these names must be added that of El Greco – who was born in Crete but who lived in Spain, where he painted religious scenes in an individualistic style. The work of these and Spain's many other great artists can be seen in world-renowned galleries, especially the Prado *(see pp282–5)*.

Self-portrait of Velázquez

The king and queen reflected in a mirror behind the painter, may be posing for their portrait

In his series, **Las Meninas** *(1957), Picasso interprets the frozen gesture of the five-year-old Infanta Margarita. Altogether, Picasso produced 44 paintings based on Velázquez's canvas. They can be seen in Barcelona's Museu de Picasso (see p149).*

RELIGIOUS ART IN SPAIN

The influence of the Catholic Church on Spanish art through the ages is reflected in the predominance of religious imagery. Many churches and museums have Romanesque altarpieces or earlier icons. El Greco *(see p373)* painted from a highly personal religious vision. Baroque religious art of the 17th century, when the Inquisition *(see p264)* was at its height, often graphically depicts physical suffering and spiritual torment.

The Burial of the Count of Orgaz by El Greco (see p372)

LAS MENINAS (1656)
In Velázquez's painting of the Infanta Margarita and her courtiers, in the Prado *(see pp282–5)*, the eye is drawn into the distance where the artist's patron, Felipe IV, is reflected in a mirror.

TIMELINE OF GREAT SPANISH ARTISTS

1285–1348 Ferrer Bassá	**1390–1410** Pere Nicolau	The Saviour *by José de Ribera*		**1598–1664** Francisco de Zurbarán
	1363–95 Jaume Serra	**1428–1460** Luis Daimau		**1591–1652** José de Ribera
1300		**1400**	**1500**	
		1388–1424 Luis Borrassa	**1474–95** Bartolomé Bermejo	**1565–1628** Francisco Ribalta
			1450–1504 Pedro Berruguete	
Virgin and Child *by* *Ferrer Bassá*		**1427–52** Bernat Martorell	**1541–1614** El Greco	**1599–1660** Diego de Velázquez

José Nieto, the queen's chamberlain, stands in the doorway in the background of the painting.

Court jester

MODERN ART

The early 20th-century artists Joan Miró *(see p168)*, Salvador Dalí *(see p205)*, and Pablo Picasso *(see p148)* all belonged to the Paris School. More recent artists of note include Antonio Saura and Antoni Tàpies *(see p160)*. Among many great Spanish art collections, the Centro de Reina Sofia in Madrid *(see pp288–9)* specializes in modern art. Contemporary artists are accorded great prestige in Spain; their work is to be seen in town halls, banks, and public squares, and many towns have a museum dedicated to a local painter.

Salvador Dalí's painting of the *Colossus of Rhodes* **(1954)**

***Collage* (1934) by Joan Miró**

The Family of King Charles IV *was painted in 1800 by Francisco de Goya (see p229), nearly 150 years after* Las Meninas. *Its debt to Velázquez's painting is evident in its frontal composition, compact grouping of figures, and in the inclusion of a self-portrait.*

The Holy Children with the Shell *by Murillo*

1893–1983 Joan Miró

1904–89 Salvador Dalí

1881–1973 Pablo Picasso

1746–1828 Francisco de Goya

1863–1923 Joaquín Sorolla

1923– Antoni Tàpies

1700　　**1800**　　**1900**

1642–93 Claudio Coello

1887–1927 Juan Gris

1618–82 Bartolomé Esteban Murillo

Jug and Glass *(1916) by Juan Gris*

1930– Antonio Saura

Literary Spain

DON QUIXOTE, considered the first modern novel, is the best-known work of Spanish literature. However, Spain has produced many major works over the last 2,000 years. The Roman writers Seneca, Lucan, and Martial were born in Spain.

The 14th-century *El Libro de Buen Amor*

Later, the Moors developed a flourishing, but now little-known, literary culture. Although Spanish (Castilian) is the national tongue, many enduring works have been written in the Galician and Catalan regional languages. Basque literature, hitherto an oral culture, is a more recent development. Many foreign writers, such as Alexandre Dumas, Ernest Hemingway, and Karel Capek, have written accounts of their travels in Spain.

MIDDLE AGES

AS THE ROMAN EMPIRE fell, Latin evolved into several Romance languages. The earliest non-Latin literature in Spain derives from an oral tradition that arose before the 10th century. It is in the form of *jarchas*, snatches of love poetry written in Mozarab, the Romance language that was spoken by Christians living under the Moors.

In the 12th century, the first poems appeared in Castilian. During the next 300 years, two separate schools of poetry developed. The best-known example of troubadour verse is the anonymous epic, *El Cantar del Mío Cid*, which tells of the heroic exploits of El Cid *(see p352)* during the Reconquest. Works of clerical poetry – for example, Gonzalo de Berceo's *Milagros de Nuestra Señora*, relating the life of the Virgin – convey a moral message.

Spanish literature evolved in the 13th century after Alfonso X the Learned *(see p51)* replaced Latin with Castilian

Alfonso X the Learned (1221–84)

Romance (later called Spanish) as the official language. Under his supervision a team of Jews, Christians, and Arabs wrote scholarly treatises. The king himself was a poet, writing in Galician Romance.

The first great prose works in Spanish appeared in the 14th and 15th centuries. *El Libro de Buen Amor*, by an ecclesiastic, Juan Ruiz, is a tale of the love affairs of a priest,

interleaved with other stories. Fernando de Rojas uses skilful characterization in *La Celestina* to tell a tragic love story about two nobles and a scheming go-between. This was an age in which tales of chivalry were also popular.

GOLDEN AGE

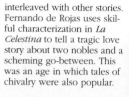

The prolific Golden Age dramatist, Félix Lope de Vega

THE 16TH CENTURY hailed the start of Spain's Golden Age of literature. But it was also a period of domestic strife. This found expression in the picaresque novel, a Spanish genre originating with the anonymous *El Lazarillo de Tormes*, a bitter reflection on the misfortunes of a blind man's guide.

Spiritual writers flourished under the austere climate of the Counter-Reformation. St John of the Cross's *Cántico Espiritual* was influenced by oriental erotic poetry and the Bible's *Song of Songs*.

The 17th century saw the emergence of more great talents. The life and work of Miguel de Cervantes *(see p315)* straddles the two centuries of the Golden Age. He published his masterpiece, *Don Quixote*, in 1605. Other important writers of the time include Francisco de Quevedo and Luis de Góngora.

Corrales (public theaters) appeared in the 17th century, opening the way for Lope de Vega *(see p280)*, Calderón de la Barca, and other dramatists.

Don Quixote's adventures portrayed by José Moreno Carbonero

18TH AND 19TH CENTURIES

INFLUENCED BY the French Enlightenment, literature in the 18th century was seen as a way to educate the people. Such was the aim, for instance, of Leandro Fernández de Moratín's comedy *El Sí de las Niñas*. This period saw the development of journalism as well as the emergence of the essay as a literary form. Romanticism had a short and late life in Spain. *Don Juan Tenorio*, a tale of the legendary irrepressible Latin lover by José Zorrilla, is the best-known Romantic play.

José Zorrilla (1817–93)

The satirical essayist Larra stands out from his contemporaries at the beginning of the 19th century. Toward the end of the century, the novel became a vehicle for realistic portrayals of Spanish society. Benito Pérez Galdós, regarded by many to be Spain's greatest novelist after Cervantes,

studied the human condition in his *Episodios Nacionales*. The heroine in Clarín's *La Regenta* is undone by the reactionary prejudices of provincial town society.

20TH CENTURY

WRITERS AT THE turn of the century, including Pío Baroja *(see p60)*, Miguel de Unamuno and Antonio Machado, described a Spain falling behind the rest of Europe. Exploring the grotesque, the only way he could describe society, led Ramón María del Valle-Inclán to lay the foundations for modern Spanish theater. In poetry, the Nobel Prize winner, Juan Ramón Jiménez, strived for pureness of form.

The so-called "Generation of 27" combined European experimental art with Spain's traditional literary subjects and forms. The best known of them is the poet and playwright Federico García Lorca

who was executed by a Fascist firing squad in 1936 *(see p63)*. He drew on the legends and stereotypes of his native Andalusia to make universal statements in his poems and plays, such as *Yerma*.

In the aftermath of the Civil War, many intellectuals who had backed the Republic were forced into exile. The Franco regime tried to create its own propagandist culture. Yet the finest literature of the period was written in spite of the prevailing political climate. Camilo José Cela's *La Colmena*, a description of everyday life in the hungry, postwar city of Madrid, set a mood of social realism that inspired other writers.

Poster for a Lorca play

The novel has had a rebirth in Spain since the 1960s, with writers like Juan Goytisolo, Joan Benet, Julio Llamazares, Antonio Muñoz Molina, José Manuel Caballero Bonald and Juan Marsé.

The 20th century has also witnessed a surge of great Spanish literature from Latin America. Prominent authors include Jorge Luis Borges and Gabriel García Márquez.

Camilo José Cela, Nobel Prize-winning novelist, by Alvaro Delgado

The Art of Bullfighting

BULLFIGHTING is a sacrificial ritual in which men (and also a few women) pit themselves against an animal bred for the ring. In this "authentic religious drama," as poet García Lorca described it, the spectator experiences vicariously the fear and exaltation felt by the matador. Although some Spaniards oppose it on grounds of its cruelty, nowadays it is as popular as ever. Many Spaniards see talk of banning bullfighting as striking at the essence of their being, for they regard the *toreo*, the art of bullfighting, as a noble part of their heritage. Bullfights today, however, are often debased by practices that weaken the bull, especially shaving its horns to make them blunt.

Plaza de Toros de la Maestranza, *Seville. This ring is regarded, with Las Ventas in Madrid, as one of the top rings for bullfighting in Spain.*

The matador wears a *traje de luces* (suit of lights), a colorful silk outfit embroidered with gold sequins.

The passes are made with a *muleta,* a scarlet cape stiffened along one side.

Well treated at the ranch, *the* toro bravo *(fighting bull) is specially bred for qualities of aggressiveness and courage. As aficionados of bullfighting point out in its defense, the young bull enjoys a full life while it is being prepared for its 15 minutes in the ring. Bulls must be at least four years old before they fight.*

THE BULLFIGHT

The *corrida* (bullfight) has three stages, called *tercios*. In the first one, the *tercio de varas*, the matador and *picadores* (horsemen with lances) are aided by *peones* (assistants). In the *tercio de banderillas*, banderilleros stick pairs of darts in the bull's back. In the *tercio de muleta* the matador makes a series of passes at the bull with a *muleta* (cape). He then executes the kill, the *estocada*, with a sword.

The matador *plays the bull with a* capa *(red cape) in the* tercio de varas. Peones *will then draw the bull toward the* picadores.

Horses are now padded.

Picadores *goad the bull with steel-pointed lances, testing its bravery. The lances weaken the animal's shoulder muscles.*

THE BULLRING

The *corrida* audience is seated in the *tendidos* (stalls) or in the *palcos* (balcony), where the *presidencia* (president's box) is situated. Opposite are the *puerta de cuadrillas*, through which the matador and team arrive, and the *arrastre de toros* (exit for bulls). Before entering the ring, the matadors wait in a corridor *(callejón)* behind *barreras* and *burladeros* (barriers). Horses are kept in the *patio de caballos* and the bulls in the *corrales*.

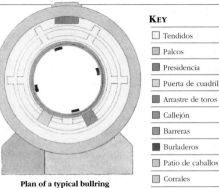

Plan of a typical bullring

KEY

- ☐ Tendidos
- ☐ Palcos
- ☐ Presidencia
- ☐ Puerta de cuadrillas
- ■ Arrastre de toros
- ☐ Callejón
- ☐ Barreras
- ■ Burladeros
- ☐ Patio de caballos
- ☐ Corrales

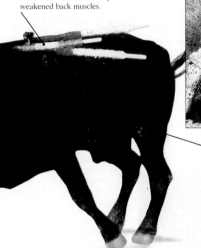

Banderillas, barbed darts, are thrust into the bull's already weakened back muscles.

Manolete is regarded by most followers of bullfighting as one of the greatest matadors ever. He was eventually gored to death by the bull Islero at Linares, Jaén, in 1947.

The bull may go free if it shows courage – spectators wave white handkerchiefs, asking the *corrida* president to let it leave the ring alive.

Joselito is one of Spain's leading matadors today. He is famous for his purist approach and for his flair and technical skill with both the capa *and the* muleta.

The bull weighs about 500 kg (1,100 lb).

Banderilleros *enter to provoke the wounded bull in the* tercio de banderillas, *sticking pairs of* banderillas *in its back.*

The matador *makes passes with the cape in the* tercio de muleta, *then lowers it and thrusts in the sword for the kill.*

The estocada recibiendo *is a difficult kill, rarely seen. The matador awaits the bull's charge rather than moving to meet it.*

The Fiestas of Spain

ON ANY DAY of the year there is a fiesta happening somewhere in Spain – usually more than one. There isn't a village, town, or city in the country that doesn't honor its patron saint, the Virgin, or the changing seasons with processions, bull-running, fireworks, reenacted battles, some ancestral rite, or a *romería* – a mass pilgrimage to a rural shrine. Whatever the excuse, a fiesta is a chance for everyone to take a break from normal life (most shops and offices close) and let off steam, with celebrations sometimes going on around the clock.

The Passion, Semana Santa

Many *romerías* wind through the countryside at Eastertime

SPRING FIESTAS

THE END OF WINTER and the start of spring are marked by Valencia's great fire festival, Las Fallas *(see p245)*, in which huge papier-mâché sculptures are set alight in a symbolic act of burning the old in order to make way for the new.

Alcoi's noisy mock battles between costumed armies of Moors and Christians in April *(see p245)* are the most spectacular of the countless fiestas that commemorate the battles of the Reconquest.

Seville's great April Fair *(see p413)* is the biggest celebration held in Andalusia.

During Los Mayos, on April 30 and the following days, crosses are decorated with flowers in parts of Spain.

EASTER

EASTER IS SPAIN'S main fiesta. Almost every community observes it in some form with pomp and solemnity.

It is heralded by the processions of Palm Sunday. The most impressive of these is in

Elx, where intricate sculptures are woven from blanched leaves cropped from the most extensive forest of palm trees in Europe *(see p251)*.

The best Semana Santa (Easter Week) processions are those held in Seville *(see p413)*, Málaga, Murcia, and Valladolid. Brotherhoods of robed men carry *pasos*, huge sculptures of the Virgin, Christ, or scenes of the Passion, through the streets. People dressed as biblical characters or penitents, in tall conical hats, accompany them. In some towns passion plays are acted out. In others, people carry heavy crosses. Sometimes the centuries-old ritual of self-flagellation can be witnessed.

SUMMER FIESTAS

THE FIRST MAJOR fiesta of the summer is Pentecost (also known as Whitsun), in May or June, and its most famous celebration is at El Rocío *(see p439)*, where many thousands of people gather in a frenzy of religious devotion.

At Corpus Christi (in May or June) the consecrated host is carried in procession through many cities in an ornate silver monstrance. The route of the procession is often covered with a carpet of flowers. The main Corpus Christi celebrations take place in Valencia, Toledo, and Granada.

On Midsummer's Eve, bonfires are lit all over Spain, especially in the areas along the Mediterranean coast, to

The Brotherhood of Candlemas, Semana Santa (Easter Week) in Seville

herald the celebration of St. John the Baptist on June 24.

St. Peter, the patron saint of fishermen, is honored in many ports with flotillas of decorated boats on June 29.

During Los Sanfermines *(see p128)* in Pamplona in July, young people run through the streets in front of six bulls.

The important Catholic holiday of Assumption Day, August 15, is marked by a huge variety of fiestas.

AUTUMN FIESTAS

THERE ARE FEW FIESTAS in autumn, but in most wine regions the grape harvest is celebrated. The annual pig slaughter has become a jubilant public event in some villages, especially in Extremadura. In Galicia chestnuts are roasted on street bonfires.

On All Saints' Day, November 1, people remember the dead by visiting cemeteries to lay flowers, especially chrysanthemums, on graves.

CHRISTMAS AND NEW YEAR

NOCHEBUENA (Christmas Eve) is the main Christmas celebration, when families gather for an evening meal before attending Midnight Mass, known as *misa del gallo* (Mass of the rooster). During the Christmas period, *belenes* (crib scenes) of painted figurines abound. You may also see a "living crib," peopled by costumed actors.

The losers end up in the harbor in Dénia's July fiesta *(see p245)*

Spain's "April Fools' Day" is December 28, the Day of the Holy Innocents, when people play practical jokes on each other. Clownlike characters may act out the role of mayor and make fun of passers-by.

To celebrate New Year's Eve *(Noche Vieja)*, crowds gather beneath the clock in Madrid's central square, the Puerta del Sol *(see p262)*.

Spanish children do not receive their Christmas presents until Epiphany, on January 6, when the Three Kings parade through large cities throwing candy into the crowds.

WINTER FIESTAS

ANIMALS HOLD center stage in a variety of fiestas on January 17, the Day of St. Anthony, patron saint of animals, when pets and livestock are blessed by priests.

St. Agatha, the patron saint of married women, is honored on February 5 when women, for once, are the protagonists of many fiestas. In Zamarramala (Segovia), for example, women take over the mayor's privileges and powers for this particular day *(see p350)*.

St. Anthony's Day in Villanueva de Alcolea (Castellón province)

CARNIVAL

CARNIVAL, in February or early March (depending on the date of Easter), brings a chance for a street party as winter comes to an end and before Lent begins. The biggest celebrations are held in Santa Cruz de Tenerife *(see p512)* – comparable with those of Rio de Janeiro – and in Cádiz *(see p439)*. Carnival was prohibited by the Franco regime because of its licentiousness and frivolity. It ends on or after Ash Wednesday with the Burial of the Sardine, a "funeral" in which a mock sardine, representing winter, is ritually burned or buried.

A spectacularly costumed choir singing during Carnival in Cádiz

SPAIN THROUGH THE YEAR

FESTIVALS, cultural events, and sports competitions crowd the calendar in Spain. Even small villages have at least one traditional fiesta, lasting a week or more, when parades, bullfights, and fireworks displays replace work *(see pp34–5)*. Many rural and coastal towns celebrate the harvest or fishing catch with a gastronomic fair at which you can sample local produce.

Matador with a cape playing a bull

Music, dance, drama, and film festivals are held in Spain's major cities throughout the year. Meanwhile, the country's favorite outdoor sports – soccer, basketball, cycling, sailing, golf, and tennis – culminate in several national and international championships.

It is a good idea to confirm specific dates of events with the local tourist board as some vary from year to year.

SPRING

LIFE IN SPAIN moves outdoors with the arrival of spring, and sidewalk cafés begin to fill with people. The countryside is at its best as wildflowers bloom before the summer heat, and irrigation channels bring water to the newly sown crops. The important Easter holiday is a time of solemn processions.

Feria de los Caballos (Festival of the Horses) in Jerez de la Frontera

MARCH

International Vintage Car Rally *(first Sun)*, from Barcelona to Sitges.
Las Fallas *(week ending Mar 19)*, Valencia *(see p245)*. A spectacular fiesta that also marks the start of the bullfighting *(see pp32–3)* season.

APRIL

Vuelta Ciclista a España *(Apr or May)*. Bicycle race around Spain.
Religious Music Week *(mid-Apr)*, Cuenca.

Trofeo Conde de Godó *(mid-Apr)*, Barcelona. Spain's premier international tennis championship.
Moors and Christians *(third week)*, Alcoi *(see p249)*. Celebration of the Christian victory over the Moors in 1276.
April Fair *(two weeks after Easter)*, Seville. Exuberant Andalusian fiesta *(see p413)*.
Feria Nacional del Queso *(late Apr/early May)*, Trujillo (Cáceres). Festival celebrating Spanish cheese *(see p389)*.

MAY

Feria de los Caballos *(first week)*, Jerez de la Frontera. Horse fair showing Andalusia at its most traditional, with fine horses, and beautiful women in flamenco dresses.
Spanish Motorcycle Grand Prix *(May)*, Jerez de la Frontera race track.
Fiesta de San Isidro *(May 8–15)*, Madrid *(see p280)*. Bullfights at Las Ventas bullring are the highlights of the taurine year.
National Flamenco Competition *(mid-May, every third year: 1998, 2001)*, Córdoba.
Peugeot Open de España *(mid-May)*, Club de Campo, Madrid. Golf tournament.
Spanish Formula One Grand Prix *(May/Jun)*, Montmeló circuit, Barcelona. International motor race.
A Rapa das Bestas *(May and Jun)*, Pontevedra (Galicia). Wild horses are rounded up so that their manes and tails can be cut *(see p94)*.

Onlookers lining the street during the Vuelta Ciclista a España

San Sebastián, one of the most popular resorts on the north coast

SUMMER

AUGUST is Spain's vacation season. The cities empty as Spaniards flock to the coast or to their second homes in the hills. Their numbers are swelled by millions of foreign tourists, and beaches and campsites are often full to bursting. As the heat starts in the center and south, entertainment often takes place only in the evening, when the temperature has dropped. In late summer the harvest begins and there are gastronomic fiestas everywhere to celebrate food and drink from the fishing catches of the north coast to the sausages of the Balearic Islands.

The pouring and tasting of cider in Asturias's Cider Festival

JUNE

International Festival of Music and Dance *(mid-Jun–early Jul)*, Granada. Many events are staged in the Alhambra or the Generalife.
Grec Arts Festival *(Jun–Jul)*, Barcelona. Theater, music and dance by Catalan, Spanish, and international performers.
Copa del Rey *(Apr–Jun)* Soccer cup final.

JULY

Classical Theater Festival *(Jul–Aug)*, Mérida. Staged in the Roman theater and amphitheater *(see p392)*.
Guitar Festival *(first two weeks)*, Córdoba. Performances range from classical to flamenco *(see pp406–7)*.
National Classical Theater Festival of Almagro *(Jul 4–28)*. Spanish and international classical repertoire in one of the oldest theaters in Europe *(see p381)*.

Cider Festival *(second Sat, even years only)*, Nava (Asturias). Includes traditional cider-pouring competitions.
International Festival of Santander *(Jul–Aug)*. Celebration of music, dance, and theater.
Pyrenean Folklore Festival *(late Jul/early Aug, odd years only)*, Jaca (Aragón). Display of folk costumes, music, and dance.
International Jazz Festivals in San Sebastián *(third week)* and Vitoria *(mid-Jul)*.

AUGUST

Certamen Internacional de Habaneras y Polifonía *(late Jul–early Aug)*, Torrevieja (Alicante). Musical competition of 19th-century seafarers' songs.
HM the King's International Cup *(first week)*, Palma de Mallorca. Sailing competition in which Juan Carlos I participates.
Descent of the Río Sella *(first Sat)*. Canoe race in Asturias from Arriondas to Ribadesella *(see p103)*.
Assumption Day *(Aug 15)* The Assumption is celebrated in cities, towns, and villages throughout the country.

Participants in the Descent of the Río Sella canoe race

Semanas Grandes *(early-mid-Aug)*, Bilbao and San Sebastián. "Great Weeks" of sports and cultural events.
Misteri d'Elx *(Aug 14–15)*, Elx *(see p251)*. Unique liturgical drama performed in a church and featuring spectacular special effects.

Vines and the village of Larouco in the Valdeorras wine region of Galicia *(see p74)* in autumn

AUTUMN

AUTUMN USUALLY brings rain after the heat of summer, and with the high tourist season over, a large number of resorts practically close down. Harvest festivities continue, however, and the most important celebrations are in honor of the grape. The first pressings are blessed and, in some places, wine is served for free.

Wild mushrooms

In woodland areas, freshly picked wild mushrooms start to appear in various dishes on local restaurant menus. The hunting season begins in the middle of October and runs until February. Autumn is also the start of the new drama and classical music seasons in the major cities of Spain.

SEPTEMBER

International Folklore Gala *(late Aug/early Sep)*, Ronda (Málaga). Music and dancing.
Grape Harvest *(first week)*, Jerez de la Frontera. Celebration of the new crop in the country's sherry capital.
Madrid Autumn Festival *(mid-Sep–mid-Nov)*. Classical and modern drama, dance, and music by national and visiting foreign companies.
San Sebastián Film Festival *(last two weeks)*. International gathering of filmmakers that includes screenings of new releases *(see p119)*.
Bienal de Arte Flamenco *(last two weeks, even years only)*, Seville. Top flamenco artists perform.

OCTOBER

Día de la Hispanidad *(Oct 12)*. Spain's national holiday marks Columbus's discovery

of America in 1492. The biggest celebration in the country is the exuberant fiesta of Día del Pilar in Zaragoza *(see p229)*, which marks the end of the bullfighting year.

Driving down the fairway in the Volvo Masters Golf Championship

IBERFLORA *(mid-Oct)*, Valencia. Flower show.
Saffron Festival *(late Oct)*, Consuegra (Toledo).
Volvo Masters Golf Championship *(late Oct)*, Valderrama (Cádiz).

NOVEMBER

All Saints' Day *(Nov 1)*. The traditional start of the *matanza* (pig slaughter) in rural areas of Spain.
Os Magostos *(Nov 11)*. Various towns in Galicia hold chestnut-harvest fairs.
Latin American Film Festival *(last two weeks)*, Huelva *(see p438)*.

Lana Turner on center stage at the San Sebastián Film Festival

PUBLIC HOLIDAYS

Besides marking the national holidays below, each region *(comunidad autónoma)* celebrates its own holiday, and every town and village has at least one other fiesta each year. If a holiday falls on a Tuesday or a Thursday shops, offices, and monuments may also be closed on the intervening Monday or Friday, making a long weekend called a *puente* ("bridge").

Año Nuevo *(New Year's Day)* (Jan 1)
Día de los Reyes *(Epiphany)* (Jan 6)
Jueves Santo *(Maundy Thursday)* (Mar/Apr)
Viernes Santo *(Good Friday)* (Mar/Apr)
Día de Pascua *(Easter Sunday)* (Mar/Apr)
Día del Trabajo *(Labor Day)* (May 1)
Asunción *(Assumption Day)* (Aug 15)
Día de la Hispanidad *(National Day)* (Oct 12)
Todos los Santos *(All Saints' Day)* (Nov 1)
Día de la Constitución *(Constitution Day)* (Dec 6)
Inmaculada Concepción *(Immaculate Conception)* (Dec 8)
Navidad *(Christmas Day)* (Dec 25)

Assumption Day in La Alberca (Salamanca)

WINTER

WINTER VARIES greatly from region to region. In the mountains, snowfalls bring skiers to the slopes; while in lower areas, olive and orange picking are in full swing. The higher parts of Central Spain can become very cold. Andalusia, the east coast and the Balearic Islands have cool nights but often sunny days. The winter warmth of the Canary Islands brings the high tourist season. Christmas is a special time of celebration – an occasion for families to re-unite, share food, and attend religious celebrations.

"El Gordo," the largest Spanish lottery prize, being drawn

Skiers in the Sierra de Guadarrama, north of Madrid *(see p311)*

DECEMBER

El Gordo *(Dec 23)*. Spain's largest lottery prize, "the Fat One," is drawn *(see p622)*.
Noche Buena *(Dec 24)* is a family Christmas Eve, followed by Midnight Mass for the devout *(see p35)*.
Santos Inocentes *(Dec 28)*, Spain's version of April Fools' Day, when people play tricks.
Noche Vieja *(Dec 31)*. New Year's Eve is most celebrated in Madrid's Puerta del Sol.

JANUARY

Canary Islands International Music Festival *(Jan–Feb)*. Classical concerts are held on all of the major islands.
Opera Season *(Jan–Apr)*, Teatro Coliseo, Bilbao.

Vigo Video Festival *(last week)*. Screenings and other events exploring all aspects of video filmmaking.

FEBRUARY

Festival of Ancient Music *(Feb–Mar)*, Seville. Early music is played on period instruments.
ARCO *(mid-Feb)*, Madrid. International contemporary art fair attracting galleries from across the world.
IMAGENMODA and **IBERMODA** *(mid-Feb)*, Madrid. Women's and men's fashion shows.
Carnival *(Feb/Mar)*. Final fiesta before Lent, with colorful costumes. Those in Santa Cruz de Tenerife and Cádiz are among the best.

The Climate of Spain

SPAIN'S LARGE LANDMASS, with its extensive high plateaus and mountain ranges, and the influences of the Mediterranean and Atlantic produce a wide range of climatic variation, especially in winter. The north is wettest year round, the eastern and southern coasts and the islands have mild winters, while winter temperatures in the interior are often below freezing. Summers everywhere are hot, except in upland areas.

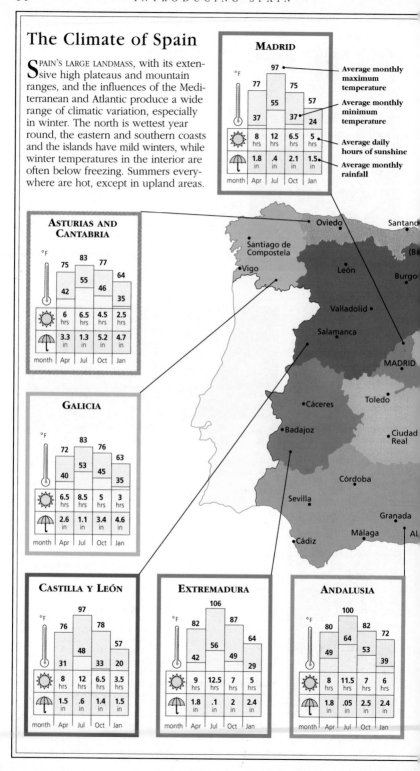

MADRID

°F			
	97		
77		75	
	55		57
37		37	24
8 hrs	12 hrs	6.5 hrs	5 hrs
1.8 in	.4 in	2.1 in	1.5 in
month Apr	Jul	Oct	Jan

Average monthly maximum temperature

Average monthly minimum temperature

Average daily hours of sunshine

Average monthly rainfall

ASTURIAS AND CANTABRIA

°F			
	83	77	
75			64
	55	46	
42			35
6 hrs	6.5 hrs	4.5 hrs	2.5 hrs
3.3 in	1.3 in	5.2 in	4.7 in
month Apr	Jul	Oct	Jan

GALICIA

°F			
	83	76	
72			63
	53	45	
40			35
6.5 hrs	8.5 hrs	5 hrs	3 hrs
2.6 in	1.1 in	3.4 in	4.6 in
month Apr	Jul	Oct	Jan

CASTILLA Y LEÓN

°F			
	97		
76		78	
	48		57
31		33	20
8 hrs	12 hrs	6.5 hrs	3.5 hrs
1.5 in	.6 in	1.4 in	1.5 in
month Apr	Jul	Oct	Jan

EXTREMADURA

°F			
	106		
82		87	
	56		64
42		49	29
9 hrs	12.5 hrs	7 hrs	5 hrs
1.8 in	.1 in	2 in	2.4 in
month Apr	Jul	Oct	Jan

ANDALUSIA

°F			
	100		
80		82	
	64		72
49		53	39
8 hrs	11.5 hrs	7 hrs	6 hrs
1.8 in	.05 in	2.5 in	2.4 in
month Apr	Jul	Oct	Jan

Oviedo
Santand
Santiago de Compostela
(B
Vigo
León
Burgo
Valladolid
Salamanca
MADRID
Cáceres
Toledo
Badajoz
Ciudad Real
Córdoba
Sevilla
Granada
Cádiz
Málaga   Al

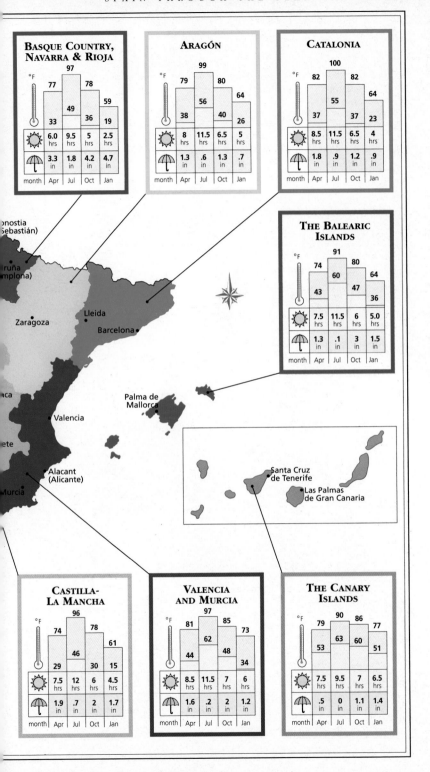

BASQUE COUNTRY, NAVARRA & RIOJA

°F			
	97		
77		78	59
	49		
33		36	19

☀	6.0 hrs	9.5 hrs	5 hrs	2.5 hrs
☂	3.3 in	1.8 in	4.2 in	4.7 in
month	Apr	Jul	Oct	Jan

ARAGÓN

°F			
	99		
79		80	64
	56		
38		40	26

☀	8 hrs	11.5 hrs	6.5 hrs	5 hrs
☂	1.3 in	.6 in	1.3 in	.7 in
month	Apr	Jul	Oct	Jan

CATALONIA

°F			
	100		
82		82	64
	55		
37		37	23

☀	8.5 hrs	11.5 hrs	6.5 hrs	4 hrs
☂	1.8 in	.9 in	1.2 in	.9 in
month	Apr	Jul	Oct	Jan

THE BALEARIC ISLANDS

°F			
	91		
74		80	64
	60		
43		47	36

☀	7.5 hrs	11.5 hrs	6 hrs	5.0 hrs
☂	1.3 in	.1 in	3 in	1.5 in
month	Apr	Jul	Oct	Jan

onostia
Sebastián)

ruña
mplona)

Zaragoza

Lleida

Barcelona

ca

Valencia

Palma de
Mallorca

ete

Alacant
(Alicante)

Murcia

Santa Cruz
de Tenerife

Las Palmas
de Gran Canaria

CASTILLA-LA MANCHA

°F			
	96		
74		78	61
	46		
29		30	15

☀	7.5 hrs	12 hrs	6 hrs	4.5 hrs
☂	1.9 in	.7 in	2 in	1.7 in
month	Apr	Jul	Oct	Jan

VALENCIA AND MURCIA

°F			
	97		
81		85	73
	62		
44		48	34

☀	8.5 hrs	11.5 hrs	7 hrs	6 hrs
☂	1.6 in	.2 in	2 in	1.2 in
month	Apr	Jul	Oct	Jan

THE CANARY ISLANDS

°F			
	90		
79		86	77
	63	60	
53			51

☀	7.5 hrs	9.5 hrs	7 hrs	6.5 hrs
☂	.5 in	0 in	1.1 in	1.4 in
month	Apr	Jul	Oct	Jan

THE HISTORY OF SPAIN

THE IBERIAN PENINSULA, first inhabited around 800,000 BC, has long been subject to foreign influences. From the 11th century BC it was colonized by sophisticated eastern Mediterranean civilizations, starting with the Phoenicians, then the Greeks and Carthaginians.

The Romans arrived in 218 BC to fight the Carthaginians, thus sparking off the Second Punic War. They harvested the peninsula's agricultural and mineral wealth and established cities with aqueducts, temples, and theaters.

Gold Aztec statue from America

With the fall of the Roman Empire in the early 5th century AD, Visigothic invaders from the north assumed power. Their poor political organization, however, made them easy prey to the Moors from North Africa. In the 8th century, the peninsula came almost entirely under Moorish rule. Europe's only major Muslim territory, the civilization of Al Andalus, excelled in mathematics, geography, astronomy, and poetry. In the 9th and 10th centuries Córdoba was Europe's leading city.

From the 11th century, northern Christian kingdoms initiated a military reconquest of Al Andalus. The marriage, in 1469, of Fernando of Aragón and Isabel of Castile, the so-called Catholic Monarchs, led to Spanish unity. They took Granada, the last Moorish kingdom, in 1492. Columbus discovered the Americas in the same year, opening the way for the Spanish conquistadors, who plundered the civilizations of the New World.

The succeeding Hapsburg dynasty spent the riches from the New World in endless foreign wars. Spain's decline was exacerbated by high inflation and religious oppression. Although the Enlightenment in the late 18th century created a climate of learning, Spain's misfortunes continued into the next century with an invasion by Napoleon's troops and the loss of her American colonies. A new radicalism began to emerge, creating a strong Anarchist movement. The political instability of the late 19th and early 20th centuries led to dictatorship in the 1920s and a republic in the 1930s, which was destroyed by the Spanish Civil War. Victorious General Franco ruled by repression until his death in 1975. Since then Spain has been a democratic state.

Bullfighting in Madrid's Plaza Mayor in the 17th century

◁ **Moors paying homage to Fernando and Isabel, the 15th-century Catholic Monarchs**

Prehistoric Spain

Helmet of Celt-iberian warrior

THE IBERIAN PENINSULA was first inhabited by hunter-gatherers around 800,000 BC. They were eclipsed by a Neolithic farming population from 5000 BC. First in a wave of settlers from over the Mediterranean, the Phoenicians landed in 1100 BC, to be followed by the Greeks and Carthaginians. Invading Celts mixed with native Iberian tribes (forming the Celtiberians). They proved a formidable force against the Romans, the next conquerors of Spain.

SPAIN IN 5000 BC

☐ *Neolithic farming settlements*

Iron Dagger *(6th century BC)*
Weapons like this dagger from Burgos represent the later Iron Age, in contrast to earlier metal objects that were for domestic use.

The 28 bracelets have perforations and molded decorations.

Small silver bottle

Stone Age Man
This skull belongs to a Paleolithic man, who hunted deer and bison with tools made of wood and stone.

Incised geometric pattern

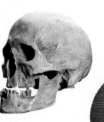

La Dama de Elche
Dating from the 4th century BC, this stone statue is a fine example of Iberian art. Her austere beauty reveals traces of Greek influence.

THE VILLENA TREASURE
Discovered in 1963 during construction in Villena, near Alicante, this Bronze Age find consists of 66 dazzling objects, including bowls, bottles, and jewelry *(see p250)*. The treasure dates from around 1000 BC.

TIMELINE

800,000 BC *Homo erectus* arrives in Iberian Peninsula	**35,000 BC** Cro-Magnon man evolves in Spain	**2500 BC** Los Millares *(p477)* is inhabited by early metalworkers with belief in the afterlife	**1800–1100 BC** Civilization of El Argar, an advanced agrarian society, flourishes in southeast Spain
300,000 BC Tribes of *Homo erectus* live in hunting camps in Soria and Madrid			
800,000 BC		**2500**	**2000**
500,000 BC Stones used as tools by hominids (probably *Homo erectus*)	**100,000–40,000 BC** Neanderthal man in Gibraltar	**5000 BC** Farming begins in Iberian Peninsula	
Bison cave drawing, Altamira		**18,000–14,000 BC** Drawings by cave dwellers at Altamira (Cantabria), near Ribadesella (Asturias), and at Nerja (Andalusia)	

Greek Ceramic Vase

The Greek colonizers brought new technology, including the potter's wheel, as well as refined artistic ideals. Ceramics, such as this 6th-century BC vase depicting the Labors of Hercules, provided sophisticated models.

The largest of the treasure's five bottles, made of silver, stands 22.5 cm (9 in) high.

Bowls of beaten gold may have originated in southwest Spain.

Brooches with separate clasps

The smaller pieces are of unknown use.

Astarte *(8th century BC)*
Worship of Phoenician deities was incorporated into local religions. One of the most popular was the fertility goddess Astarte, shown on this bronze from the kingdom of Tartessus.

WHERE TO SEE PREHISTORIC SPAIN

The most famous cave paintings in Spain are at Altamira *(see p108)*. There are dolmens in many parts of the country; among the largest are those at Antequera *(see p451)*. The Guanches – the indigenous inhabitants of the Canary Islands – left behind more recent remains *(see p523)*.

La Naveta d'es Tudons is one of the many prehistoric stone monuments scattered across the island of Menorca (see p503).

An excavated Celtic village, with its round huts, can be seen near A Guarda in Pontevedra (see p92).

 *Phoenician gold ornament*	**1100 BC** Phoenicians believed to have founded modern-day Cádiz	**600 BC** Greek colonists settle on northeast coast of Spain	**228 BC** Carthaginians occupy south-east Spain	
1500	**1000**		**500**	
1200 BC The "talaiotic" people of Menorca erect three unique types of stone building: *taulas, talaiots,* and *navetas* *Taula in Menorca*	**775 BC** Phoenicians establish colonies along the coast near Málaga	**700 BC** Semimythical kingdom of Tartessus thought to be at its height	**300 BC** *La Dama de Elche* is carved (p286)	 *Carthaginian glass necklace*

Romans and Visigoths

THE ROMANS CAME TO SPAIN to fight the Carthaginians and take possession of the Iberian Peninsula's huge mineral wealth. Later, Hispania's wheat and olive oil became mainstays of the empire. It took 200 years to subdue the peninsula, which was divided in three provinces: Tarraconensis, Lusitania, and Baetica. In time, cities with Roman infrastructure developed. The fall of the empire in the 5th century left Spain in the hands of the Visigoths, invaders from the north. Politically disorganized, they fell victim to the Moors in 711.

Roman vase

SPAIN (HISPANIA) IN 5 BC

- ☐ Tarraconensis
- ☐ Lusitania
- ☐ Baetica

Portico overlooking the gardens

Trajan *(AD 53–117)*
Trajan was the first Roman emperor (AD 98–117) from Hispania. He improved public administration and expanded the empire.

Good acoustics at every level

A Classical façade served as a backdrop for tragedies. Additional scenery was used for comedies.

Seneca *(4 BC–AD 65)*
Born in Córdoba, the Stoic philosopher Seneca lived in Rome as Nero's adviser.

The *orchestra*, a semicircular open space for the chorus

Visigothic Relief

This crude Visigothic stone carving, based on a Roman relief, is in the 7th-century church of Quintanilla de las Viñas, near Burgos (p352).

The auditorium seated over 5,000. The audience was placed according to social status.

TIMELINE

218 BC Scipio the Elder lands with a Roman army at Emporion (*p206*). The Second Punic War begins	**c.200 BC** Romans reach Gadir (modern Cádiz) after driving Carthaginians out of Hispania	**26 BC** Emerita Augusta (Mérida) is founded and soon becomes capital of Lusitania	
	155 BC Lusitanian Wars begin. Romans invade Portugal	**19 BC** Augustus takes Cantabria and Asturias, ending 200 years of war	

200 BC	100	AD 1	AD 100

| **219 BC** Hannibal takes Saguntum (*p239*) for Carthaginians — *Hannibal* | **133 BC** Celt-Iberian Wars culminate in destruction of Numantia, Soria (*p359*) | **61 BC** Julius Caesar, governor of Hispania Ulterior, begins final conquest of northern Portugal and Galicia — **82–72 BC** Roman Civil War. Pompey founds Pompaelo (Pamplona) in 75 BC | **AD 74** Emperor Vespasian grants Latin status to all towns in Hispania completing process of Romanization |

Gladiator Mosaic
Mosaics were used as decoration both indoors and out. Themes range from mythical episodes to portrayals of daily life. This 4th-century AD mosaic shows gladiators in action and has helpful labels to name the fighters and show who is dead or alive.

WHERE TO SEE ROMAN SPAIN

Like Mérida, Tarragona *(see p214)* has extensive Roman ruins and Itálica *(see p452)* is an excavated town. A magnificent Roman wall rings Lugo in Galicia *(see p95)*. Built in Trajan's rule, the bridge over the Tagus at Alcántara *(see p392)* has a temple on it.

Emporion, *a Roman town, was built next to a former Greek colony in the 3rd century BC. The ruins include grand villas and a forum* (see p206).

Segovia's Roman aqueduct (see p347), *a huge monument with 163 arches, dates from the end of the 1st century AD.*

The gardens were used as a lobby during intermissions by the Hispanic nobility, dressed in elegant togas.

Stage building in granite and marble

Scaena, the platform on which the actors performed

ROMAN THEATER, MÉRIDA
Theater was an extremely popular form of entertainment in Hispania. This reconstruction shows the theater at Mérida *(see p392)*, built in 16–15 BC.

Visigothic Cross
Although Visigothic kings seldom ruled long enough to make an impact on society, the early Christian Church grew powerful. Fortunes were spent on churches and religious art.

Mosaic from Mérida

200	300	400	500

415 Visigoths establish their court at Barcelona

409 Vandals and their allies cross Pyrenees into Tarraconensis

446 Romans attempt to win back rest of Hispania

476 Overthrow of the last Roman emperor leads to end of Western Roman Empire

258 Franks cross Pyrenees into Tarraconensis and sack Tarragona

312 Christianity officially recognized as religion under rule of Constantine, the first Christian emperor

The Codex Vigilianus, *a Christian manuscript*

589 Visigothic King Reccared converts from Arianism to Catholicism at Third Council of Toledo

Al Andalus: Muslim Spain

THE ARRIVAL OF ARAB and Berber invaders from North Africa, and their defeat of the Visigoths, gave rise to the most brilliant civilization of early medieval Europe. These Muslim settlers, often known as the Moors, called Spain "Al Andalus." A rich and powerful caliphate was established in Córdoba, and mathematics, science, architecture, and the decorative arts flourished. The caliphate eventually broke up into small kingdoms or *taifas*. Meanwhile, small Christian enclaves expanded in the north.

Alhambra Vase
(see p467)

SPAIN IN AD 750

☐ *Extent of Moorish domination*

Water Wheel
Moorish irrigation techniques, such as the water wheel, revolutionized agriculture. New crops, including oranges and rice, were introduced.

The palace, dating from the 11th century, was surrounded by patios, pools, and gardens.

Astrolabe
Perfected by the Moors around AD 800, the astrolabe was used by navigators and astronomers.

Remains of a Roman amphitheater

Silver Casket of Hisham II
In the Caliphate of Córdoba, luxury objects of brilliant craftsmanship were worked in ivory, silver, and bronze.

Fortified entrance gate

Curtain wall with watchtowers

TIMELINE

711 Moors, led by Tariq, invade Spain and defeat Visigoths at battle of Guadalete

732 Moors' advance into France is halted by Charles Martel at Poitiers

778 Charlemagne's rearguard defeated by Basques at Roncesvalles *(p130)*

785 Building of great mosque at Córdoba begins

Charlemagne (742–814)

750

800

850

722 Led by Pelayo, Christians defeat Moors at Covadonga *(p105)*

Pelayo (718–37)

756 Abd al Rahman I proclaims independent emirate in Córdoba

744 Christians under Alfonso I of Asturias take León

822 Abd al Rahman II begins 30-year rule marked by patronage of the arts and culture

c.800 Tomb of St. James (Santiago) is supposedly discovered at Santiago de Compostela

Puerta de Sabbath in Córdoba's Mezquita
Wealth and artistic brilliance were lavished on mosques, especially in Córdoba (see pp456–7). Calligraphy was a major element in decoration.

WHERE TO SEE MOORISH SPAIN

The finest Moorish buildings are found in Andalusia, especially in the cities of Córdoba *(see pp454–7)* and Granada *(see pp462–8)*. Almería *(see p477)* has a large, ruined *alcazaba* (castle). In Jaén *(see p469)* there are Moorish baths. Farther north, in Zaragoza, is the castle palace of La Aljafería *(see p227)*.

Medina Azahara (see p453), *sacked in the 11th century but partly restored, was the final residence of Córdoba's caliphs.*

Torre del Homenaje, the keep, was built by Abd al Rahman I (756–88).

Baths

Patio with Moorish decoration

ALCAZABA AT MÁLAGA

An *alcazaba* was a castle built into the ramparts of a Moorish city, often protected by massive concentric walls. In Málaga *(see p450)* – the principal port of the Moorish kingdom of Granada – the vast Alcazaba was built in the 8–11th centuries on the site of a Roman fortress and incorporated massive curtain walls and fortified gates.

Moorish Sword
A fine example of late Moorish craftsmanship, this sword has a golden pommel. The blade is inscribed with Arabic writing.

Warrior Helmet
Practical as well as ornate, this Islamic nobleman's helmet, made of iron, gold, and silver, incorporates inscriptions, a coat of arms, and chain mail.

905 Emergent Navarra becomes Christian kingdom under Sancho I

976 Al Mansur, military dictator, usurps caliphal powers and sacks Barcelona. Córdoba Mezquita finished

1010 Medina Azahara sacked by Berbers

900

950

1000

913 Christian capital is established at León

936 Building of Medina Azahara palace starts near Córdoba

Bronze stag from Medina Azahara

1013 Caliphate of Córdoba breaks up. Emergence of *taifas*: small, independent Moorish kingdoms

The Reconquest

THE INFANT CHRISTIAN KINGDOMS in the north –
León, Castile, Navarra, Aragón, and Catalonia
– advanced south gradually in the 11th
century, fighting in the name of Christianity
to regain land from the Moors. After the fall
of Toledo in 1085, the struggle became
increasingly a holy war. Militant North African
Muslims – Almoravids and Almohads – rallied
to the Moorish cause and ultimately took
over Al Andalus in the 12th century. As the
Christians pushed farther south, soon only
Granada remained under Moorish control.

Cross of the Knights of St. James

SPAIN IN 1173

☐ *Christian kingdoms*

☐ *Al Andalus*

Golden Goblet
The exquisite goblet (1063) of Doña Urraca, daughter of Alfonso VI, shows the quality of medieval Christian craftsmanship.

Armies of Castile, Aragón, and Navarra

Fernando I
Fernando formed the first Christian power bloc in 1037 by uniting León with Castile, which was emerging as a major military force.

The Almohads
fight until the bitter end, although many comrades lay slain.

LAS NAVAS DE TOLOSA

The Christian victory over the Almohads in the battle of Las Navas de Tolosa (1212) led to Moorish Spain's decline. The army of Muhammad II al Nasir was no match for the forces of Sancho VII of Navarra, Pedro II of Aragón, and Alfonso VIII of Castile. A stained-glass window in Roncesvalles *(see p130)* depicts the battle.

Alhambra, Palace of the Nasrids
Moorish art and architecture of singular beauty continued to be produced in the Nasrid kingdom of Granada. Its apogee is the exquisite Alhambra (see pp466–7).

TIMELINE

Uniforms of military orders

1037 León and Castile united for first time under Fernando I	**1065** Death of Fernando I precipitates fratricidal civil war between his sons	**1086** Almoravids respond to pleas for help from Moorish emirs by taking over *taifas* (splinter states)		**1158** Establishment of the Order of Calatrava, the first military order of knights in Spain
1050	**1100**		**1150**	**120**
1085 Toledo falls to Christians under Alfonso VI of Castile	**1137** Ramón Berenguer IV of Catalonia marries Petronila of Aragón uniting the two kingdoms under their son, Alfonso II		**1147** Almohads arrive in Al Andalus and make Seville their capital	**1212** Combined Christian forces defeat Almohads at battle of Las Navas de Tolosa
1094 The legendary El Cid *(see p352)* captures Valencia *El Cid*			**1143** Portugal becomes separate kingdom	

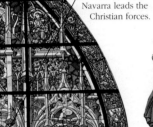

Cantigas of Alfonso X *(1252–84)*
This detail of a manuscript by Alfonxo X portrays the confrontation between Moorish and Christian cavalry. Alfonso the Learned encouraged his scholars to master Arab culture and translate ancient Greek manuscripts brought by the Moors.

Sancho VII of Navarra leads the Christian forces.

St. James (Santiago)
Known as the Moorslayer, St. James is said to have miraculously intervened at the Battle of Clavijo in 844. This powerful figurehead is the patron saint of Spain.

WHERE TO SEE MUDÉJAR SPAIN

The Mudéjares – Muslims who remained in territories under Christian occupation – created a distinctive architectural style distinguished by its ornamental work in brick, plaster, and ceramics. Aragón, particularly Zaragoza *(see pp226–7)* and Teruel *(see pp230–31)*, boasts some of the finest Mudéjar buildings. Seville's Reales Alcázares is an exquisitely harmonious collection of patios and halls built under Pedro I *(see pp422–3)*.

The Mudéjar tower *of Teruel cathedral combines both brick and colorful ceramics with highly decorative effect.*

Santa María la Blanca *(see p373), a former synagogue and church, shows the fusion of cultures in medieval Toledo.*

15 Foundation of [S]amanca University

1230 Fernando III reunites Castile and León

Crest of Castile and León

1385 Portuguese defeat Castilians at Aljubarrota, crushing King Juan's aspirations to throne of Portugal

1388–9 Treaties end Spanish phase of Hundred Years War

1250	1300	1350	1400

1250 Toledo at its height as a center of translation and learning, influenced by Alfonso X, the Learned

1232 Granada becomes capital of future Nasrid kingdom. Building of the Alhambra begins

Alfonso X

1386 Invasion of Galicia by the English ended by Bayonne Treaty

1401 Work starts in Seville on what was then the world's largest Gothic cathedral

The Catholic Monarchs

Fernando of Aragón

THE FOUNDATION of the Spanish nation-state was laid by Isabel I of Castile and Fernando II of Aragón *(see p66)*. Uniting their lands in military, diplomatic, and religious matters, the "Catholic Monarchs," as they are known, won back Granada, the last Moorish kingdom, from Boabdil. The Inquisition gave Spain a reputation for intolerance, yet in art and architecture brilliant progress was made, and the voyages of Columbus opened up the New World.

SPAIN'S EXPLORATION OF THE NEW WORLD

— *Route of Columbus's first voyage*

Tomb of El Doncel *(15th century)*
This effigy of a page who died in the fight for Granada combines ideals of military glory and learning (see p364).

Boabdil, the grief-stricken king, moves forward to hand over the keys to Granada.

Alhambra

The Inquisition
Active from 1478, the Inquisition (see p264) persecuted those suspected of heresy with increasing vigor. This member of the Brotherhood of Death took victims to the stake.

Baptizing Jews
After the Christian reconquest of Granada, Jews were forced to convert or leave Spain. The conversos (converted Jews) were often treated badly.

THE FALL OF GRANADA *(1492)*
This romantic interpretation by Francisco Pradilla (1846–1921) reflects the chivalry of Boabdil, ruler of Granada, as he surrenders the keys of the last Moorish kingdom to the Catholic Monarchs, Fernando and Isabel, following ten long years of war.

TIMELINE

1454 Enrique IV, Isabel's half-brother, accedes to throne of Castile

1465 Civil war erupts in Castile

Torquemada

1478 Papal bull authorizes Castilian Inquisition with Tomás de Torquemada as Inquisitor General

1450	1460	1470	1480

1451 Birth of Isabel of Castile

Fernando and Isabel on 15th-century gold coin

1469 Marriage of Fernando and Isabel in Valladolid unites Castile and Aragón

1474 Death of Enrique IV leads to civil war; Isabel triumphs over Juana la Beltraneja, Enrique's supposed daughter, to become queen

1479 Fernando becomes Fernando II of Aragón

Columbus Arriving in the Americas
The Catholic Monarchs financed Columbus's daring first voyage partly because they hoped for riches in return, but also because they expected him to convert infidels.

Boabdil
As the forlorn king left Granada, his mother reputedly said, "Don't cry as a child over what you could not defend as a man."

Isabel, queen of Castile, witnesses the surrender of Granada, surrounded by a glittering entourage.

ernando f Aragón

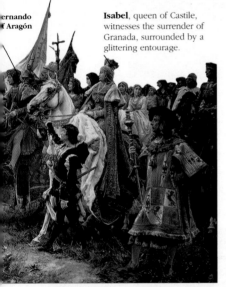

WHERE TO SEE GOTHIC ARCHITECTURE IN SPAIN

Spain has many great Gothic cathedrals, especially in Seville *(pp418–19)*, Burgos *(pp354–5)*, Barcelona *(pp144–5)*, Toledo *(pp374–5)*, and Palma de Mallorca *(pp496–7)*. Secular buildings from this era include commodity exchanges like La Lonja in Valencia *(p241)* and castles *(pp326–7)*.

León cathedral (pp336–7) has a west front covered in statuary. Here Christ is seen presiding over the Last Judgment.

Crown of Isabel
Worn at the surrender, Isabel's crown is now in her final resting place, the Capilla Real in Granada (see p462).

1494 Treaty of Tordesillas divides the New World territories between Portugal and Spain

1496 Foundation of Santo Domingo, on Hispaniola, first Spanish city in the Americas

1509 Cardinal Cisneros' troops attack Oran in Algeria and temporarily occupy it

Cardinal Cisneros

1490	1500	1510

1492 Fall of Granada after ten-year war. Columbus reaches America. Expulsion of Jews from Spain

1502 Unconverted Moors expelled from Spain

Columbus's ship, the Santa María

1504 Following death of Isabel, her daughter Juana la Loca becomes queen of Castile with Fernando as regent

1516 Death of Fernando

1512 Annexation of Navarra, leading to full unification of Spain

The Age of Discovery

Aztec god
(c.1540)

FOLLOWING COLUMBUS'S ARRIVAL in the Bahamas in 1492, the conquistadors went into Central and South America, conquering Mexico (1519), Peru (1532), and Chile (1541). In doing so, they destroyed Indian civilizations. In the 16th century, vast quantities of gold and silver flowed across the Atlantic to Spain. Carlos I and his son Felipe II spent some of it on battles to halt the spread of Protestantism in Europe, and in the Holy War against the Turks.

SPANISH EMPIRE IN 1580

☐ *Dominions of Felipe II*

Mapping the World
This 16th-century German map reflects a new world, largely unknown to Europe before the era of conquistadors.

Galleons were armed with cannons as a defense against pirates and rival conquerors.

The lookout was essential for spotting enemies and making landfall.

Forecastle

Aztec Mask
In their great greed and ignorance, the Spanish destroyed the empires and civilizations of the Aztecs in Mexico and the Incas in Peru.

Seville
Granted the trading monopoly with the Americas, Seville, on the banks of the Guadalquivir, was Europe's richest port in the early 16th century.

TIMELINE

1519 Magellan, Portuguese explorer, leaves Seville under Spanish patronage to circumnavigate the globe

1520-21 Revolt by Castilian towns when Carlos I appoints foreigner, Adrian of Utrecht, as regent

1532 Pizarro takes Peru with 180 men and destroys Inca empire

Pizarro

1554 International Catholic alliance created by marriage of future king Felipe II with Mary Tudor, Queen of England

1520	1530	1540	1550

1519 Conquest of Mexico by Cortés. Carlos I crowned Holy Roman Emperor Charles V

Conquistador Hernán Cortés

1540 Father Bartolomé de las Casas writes book denouncing the oppression of Indians

Bartolomé de las Casas

Defeat of the Spanish Armada
Spain's self-esteem suffered a hard blow when its "invincible" 133-ship fleet was destroyed in an attempt to invade Protestant England in 1588.

Armor of Felipe II
Felipe II (1556–98) was a cunning administrator, who claimed to rule the world with paper rather than military might.

Flag of Spain (until 1785)

Storage space for New World treasures

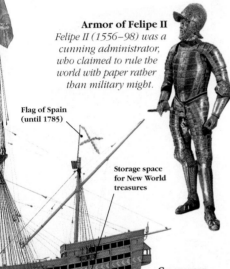

NEW WORLD CROPS

Not only did Spain profit from the gold and silver brought across the ocean from the Americas, but also from an amazing range of new crops. Some, **Cacao plant** including potatoes and corn, were introduced for cultivation in Spain while others, such as tobacco and cacao, were mainly grown in native soil. Cocoa, from cacao beans, gained favor as a drink.

Peruvian with exotic New World fruit

SPANISH GALLEON

Although sturdily built to carry New World treasure back to Spain, these ships were hard to maneuver except with the wind behind. They were often no match for smaller, swifter pirate vessels.

Carlos I *(1516–56)*
During his tumultuous 40-year reign, Carlos I (Holy Roman Emperor Charles V) often led his troops on the battlefield.

1557 First of a series of partial bankruptcies of Spain

1561 Building of El Escorial, near Madrid, begins *El Escorial (see pp312–13)*

1588 Spanish Armada fails in attack on Britain

1560	1570	1580	1590

1561 Madrid becomes capital of Spain

1568 Moriscos (converted Moors) in the Alpujarras (Granada) rebel against high taxes and persecution

1571 Spanish victory over Turks in naval battle of Lepanto

1569 Bible published for first time in Castilian

1580 Portugal unites with Spain for the next 60 years

The Golden Age

SPAIN'S GOLDEN AGE was a time of great artistic and literary achievement led by the painters – El Greco and Velázquez *(see pp28–9)* – and writers *(see pp30–31)*, especially Cervantes and the prolific dramatists, Lope de Vega and Calderón de la Barca. This brilliance occurred, however, against a background of economic deterioration and ruinous wars with the Low Countries and France. Spain was gradually losing its influence in Europe and the reigning house of Hapsburg entered irreversible decline.

THE SPANISH EMPIRE IN EUROPE IN 1647

☐ *Spanish territories*

A clock is a reminder of the inevitable passage of time.

Don Quixote and Sancho Panza
Cervantes' satire on chivalrous romance, Don Quixote, *contrasts the fantasy of the main character with his servant's realism.*

The knight is dressed in mid-17th-century fashion.

Money represents worldly wealth.

Duke of Lerma
This bronze statue depicts the Duke of Lerma (c.1550–1625), a favorite of King Felipe III.

THE KNIGHT'S DREAM *(1650)*
This painting, attributed to Antonio de Pereda, is on a familiar Golden Age theme: human vanity. A young gentleman sits asleep beside a table piled with objects symbolizing power, wealth, and mortality. The pleasures of life, we are told, are no more real than a dream.

TIMELINE

Felipe III

1600	1610	1620	1630	1640
1600 Capital temporarily moves to Valladolid	**1609** Felipe III orders the expulsion of the Moriscos	**1621** Low Countries war resumes after 12-year truce		**1643** Fall of Count-Duke Olivares. Spain heavily defeated by France at battle of Rocroi
	1619 Construction of Plaza Mayor, Madrid	**1625** Capture of Breda, Netherlands, after one-year siege		
1605 Publication of first of two parts of Cervantes' *Don Quixote*	**1609** Lope de Vega publishes poem on the art of comic drama	**1622** Velázquez moves from Seville to Madrid to become court painter the following year	**1640** Secession of Portugal, amalgamated with Spain since 1580	

Lope de Vega (1562–1635)

Fiesta in the Plaza Mayor in Madrid
This famous square (see p263) became the scene for pageants, royal celebrations, bullfights, and executions, all overlooked from the balconies.

SEVILLE SCHOOL OF ART

Seville's wealth, together with the patronage of the Church, made it a center of the arts, second only to the royal court. Velázquez, who was born in Seville, trained under the painter Pacheco. Sculptor Juan Martínez Montañés and painters Zurbarán and Murillo created great works which are displayed in the Museo de Bellas Artes *(see p412)*.

***San Diego de Alcalá Giving Food to the Poor* (c.1646) by Murillo**

An angel warns that death is near.

The banner says, "It (death) pierces perpetually, flies quickly, and kills."

A mask symbolizes the Arts.

Weapons represent power.

he skull on the book hows death triumphant ver learning.

Expulsion of the Moriscos
Although they had converted to Christianity, the last Moors were still expelled in 1609.

Surrender of Breda
Spain took the Dutch city of Breda on June 5, 1625 after a year-long siege. The event was later painted by Velázquez.

1652 Spanish troops regain Catalonia, following 12-year war with France

Calderón de la Barca

1669 Calderón de la Barca's last work, *La Estátua de Prometeo*, is published

1683–4 Louis XIV attacks Catalonia and Spanish Netherlands

1650	1660	1670	1680	1690	1700

1648 Holland achieves independence from Spain by Treaty of Westphalia, ending Thirty Years War

1659 Peace of the Pyrenees signed with France. Louis XIV marries Felipe IV's daughter María Teresa, leading to Bourbon succession in Spain

Coin from the reign of Felipe IV

1700 Death of Carlos II brings Hapsburg line to an end. Felipe V, the first Bourbon king, ascends the throne

Bourbons to First Republic

THE WAR OF THE SPANISH SUCCESSION ended in triumph for the Bourbons, who made Spain a centralized nation. Their power was at its height during the reign of the enlightened despot, Carlos III. But the 19th century was a troubled time. An invasion by revolutionary France led to the War of Independence (Peninsular War). Later came the Carlist Wars – caused by another dispute over the succession – liberal revolts, and the short-lived First Republic.

Isabel II

SPAIN IN 1714

☐ *Domain after Treaty of Utrecht*

The Enlightenment
The Enlightenment brought new learning and novel projects. On July 5, 1784 this Montgolfier balloon rose above Madrid.

Queen María Luisa
The dominating María Luisa of Parma, portrayed by Goya, forced her husband Carlos IV to appoint her lover, Manuel Godoy, prime minister in 1792.

Spanish rebel faces death in a gesture of crucifixion.

A Franciscan friar is among the innocent victims.

Battle of Trafalgar
The defeat of the Franco-Spanish fleet by the British admiral, Lord Nelson, off Cape Trafalgar in 1805 was the end of Spanish sea power.

Hundreds of lives were taken in the executions, which lasted several days

TIMELINE

1702–14 War of the Spanish Succession. Spain loses Netherlands and Gibraltar by Treaty of Utrecht

1724 Luis I (son of Felipe V) gains throne when his father abdicates, but dies within a year; Felipe V reinstated

1767 Carlos III expels Jesuits from Spain and Spanish colonies

1700	1720	1740	1760	17

1714 Siege and reduction of Barcelona by Felipe V

1762–3 English government declares war on Spanish over colonies in America

Felipe V, the first Bourbon king (1700–24)

Count of Floridablanca (1728–1808)

1782 Count of Floridablanca helps to recover Menorca from England

Carlos III Leaving Naples
When Fernando VI died without an heir in 1759, his half-brother Carlos VII of Naples was put on the Spanish throne as Carlos III. His enlightened reign saw the foundation of academies of science and art and the beginning of free trade.

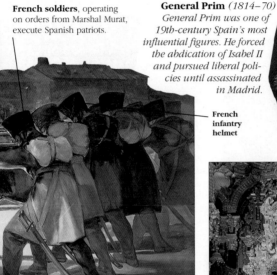

French soldiers, operating on orders from Marshal Murat, execute Spanish patriots.

General Prim *(1814–70)*
General Prim was one of 19th-century Spain's most influential figures. He forced the abdication of Isabel II and pursued liberal policies until assassinated in Madrid.

French infantry helmet

Baroque Magnificence
The sacristy of the Monasterio de la Cartuja in Granada is typical of Spanish Baroque, more sumptuous than anywhere else in Europe.

THE 3RD OF MAY BY GOYA *(1814)*
On May 2, 1808, in reaction to Napoleon's occupation of Spain, the people of Madrid rose in vain against the occupying French forces. The next day the French army took its revenge by executing hundreds of people, both rebels and bystanders. These events sparked off the War of Independence.

1805 Battle of Trafalgar. Nelson defeats French and Spanish at sea

1809 Wellington's troops join with Spanish to triumph over French at Talavera

Duke of Wellington

1841–3 María Cristina, followed by General Espartero, acts as regent for Isabel II

1868 Revolution under General Prim forces Isabel II into exile. Amadeo I is king for three years from 1870

1800	1820	1840	1860

1808–14 Joseph Bonaparte on throne. War of Independence

1812 Promulgation of liberal constitution in Cádiz leads to military uprising

1824 Peru is the last South American country to gain independence

1833–9 First Carlist War

1836 Mendizábal seizes monastic property for the Spanish state

1847–9 Second Carlist War

Carlist soldiers

Republicans and Anarchists

Primo de Rivera

SPAIN'S FIRST REPUBLIC lasted only a year (1873) and consumed four presidents. The late 19th century was a time of national decline, with Anarchism developing in reaction to rampant political corruption. The loss of Cuba, in 1898, was a low point for Spain, although there was a flurry of literary and artistic activity in the following years. The country's increasing instability was briefly checked by the dictatorship of Primo de Rivera. Spanish politics, however, were becoming polarized. Alfonso XIII was forced to abdicate and the ill-fated Second Republic was declared in 1931.

THE LEGACY OF SPANISH COLONIZATION IN 1900

☐ *Spanish-speaking territories*

Anarchist Propaganda
Anarchism was idealistic, though often violent. This poster states, "Anarchist books are weapons against Fascism."

Workers unite, calling for radical social reform.

Pío Baroja
Baroja (1872–1956) was one of the most gifted novelists of his day. He was too original to be grouped with the writers of the Generation of 1898, who tried to create a national renaissance after the loss of Spain's colonies.

POWER TO THE PEOPLE

Political protest was rife under the Second Republic, as shown by this Communist demonstration in the Basque Country in 1932. Industrial workers banded together, forming trade unions to demand better pay and working conditions, and staging strikes. The Spanish Communist Party developed later than the Anarchists, but eventually gained more support.

TIMELINE

First Republic's last president, Emilio Castelar (1832–99)

Alfonso XII and Queen María

1873 Declaration of First Republic, lasting only one year	1888 Universal Exhibition in Barcelona creates new buildings and parks, such as the Parc de la Ciutadella	1897 Prime Minister Cánovas del Castillo assassinated by an Italian Anarchist

1870	1880	1890	190

1870–75 Third Carlist War	1875 Second Bourbon restoration puts Alfonso XII on throne	1893 Anarchists bomb operagoers in the Barcelona Liceu	1898 Cuba and Philippines gain independence from Spain following the Spanish-American War

Tragic Week
Led by Anarchists and Republicans, workers in Barcelona took to the streets in 1909 to resist a military draft. The reprisals were brutal.

Universal Exhibitions
In 1929, Seville and Barcelona were transformed by exhibitions promoting art and industry. The fairs brought international recognition.

The banner
appeals for working-class solidarity.

Picasso
Born in Málaga in 1881, the artist Pablo Picasso spent his formative years as a painter in the city of Barcelona (see p148) before moving to Paris in the 1930s.

Cuban War of Independence
Cuba began its fight for freedom in 1895, led by local patriots such as Antonio Maceo. In the disastrous campaign, Spain lost 50,000 soldiers and most of its navy.

The Garrotte
Convicted Anarchists were executed by the garrotte – an iron collar that brutally strangled the victim while crushing the neck.

1912 Prime Minister José Canalejas murdered by Anarchists in Madrid

Second Republic election poster

1921 Crushing defeat of Spanish army at Anual, Morocco

1931 Proclamation of Second Republic with a two-year coalition between Socialists and Republicans

1933 General election returns right-wing government

1910	1920	1930

1909 Semana Trágica (Tragic Week) in Barcelona. Workers' revolt against conscription for Moroccan Wars quashed by Government troops

1923 Primo de Rivera stages victorious coup to become military dictator under Alfonso XIII

1930 Primo de Rivera resigns after losing military support

1931 Republicans win local elections, causing Alfonso XIII to abdicate

1934 Revolution of Asturian miners suppressed by army under General Franco

Civil War and the Franco Era

SPAIN ON JULY 31, 1936

☐ *Republican-held areas*

☐ *Nationalist-held areas*

NATIONALIST GENERALS rose against the government in 1936, starting the Spanish Civil War. The Nationalists, under General Franco, were halted by the Republicans outside Madrid, but with support from Hitler and Mussolini they inched their way to victory in the north and east. Madrid finally fell in early 1939. After the war, thousands of Republicans were executed in reprisals. Spain was internationally isolated until the 1950s, when the United States brought her into the western military alliance.

Franco

Franco's Ideal World
Under Franco, Church and State were united. This poster shows the strong influence of religion on education.

Nationalist Poster
A Nationalist poster adorned with Fascist arrows reads "Fight for the Fatherland, Bread and Justice."

Anguished mother with dead child

Composition reflecting total chaos

GUERNICA *(1937)*
On behalf of advancing Nationalists, the Nazi Condor Legion bombed the Basque town of Guernica *(see p114)* on April 26, 1937 – a busy market day. This was Europe's first air raid on civilians, and it inspired Picasso's shocking *Guernica* *(see p289)*. Painted for a Republican Government exhibition in Paris, it is full of symbols of disaster.

TIMELINE

1936 Republican Popular Front wins the general election on January 16. On July 17, Nationalist generals rise against Republicans	**1938** On January 8, Republicans lose battle for Teruel in bitter cold	**1945** By end of World War II, Spain is diplomatically and politically isolated
	1939 In March, Madrid, Valencia, and Alicante fall in quick succession to Franco's troops	**1947** Spain declared monarchy with Franco as regent

1935	1940	1945	1950

1936 Nationalists declare Franco head of state on September 29	**1939** Franco declares end of war on April 1 and demands unconditional surrender from Republicans	**1953** Deal with US permits American bases on Spanish soil in exchange for aid
1937 On April 26, Nazi planes bomb Basque town of Guernica (Gernika-Lumo)	**1938** On December 23, Nationalists bomb Barcelona	*Soldiers surrendering to Nationalist troops*

GARCÍA LORCA

Federico García Lorca (1898–1936) was Spain's most brilliant dramatist and lyric poet of the 1920s and '30s. His homosexuality and association with the left, however, made him a target for Nationalist assassins. He was shot by an ad hoc firing squad near his home town of Granada.

Scene from his play *Blood Wedding*

Anarchist Poster
Anarchists fought for the Republic, forming agricultural collectives behind the lines. Their influence waned when they were discredited by the Communist Party.

A wounded horse representing the Spanish people

Witnesses to the massacre stare in wonder and disbelief.

Crucifixion gesture

The flower is a symbol of hope in the midst of despair.

The Hungry Years
Ration cards illustrate the postwar period when Spain nearly starved. Shunned by other nations, she received aid from the US in 1953 in return for accepting military bases.

Spanish Refugees
As the Nationalists came closer to victory, thousands of artists, writers, intellectuals and other Republican supporters fled Spain into indefinite exile.

Sunbathers

1962 Tourism on the Mediterranean coast is boosted by official go-ahead

1969 Franco declares Prince Juan Carlos his successor

1973 ETA assassinates Admiral Carrero Blanco, Franco's hard-line prime minister

1955	1960	1965	1970	1975

1959 Founding of ETA, Basque separatist group

1970 "Burgos trials" of the regime's opponents outrage world opinion

1955 Spain joins United Nations

Franco's funeral, November 23, 1975

1975 Death of Franco results in third Bourbon restoration as Juan Carlos is proclaimed king

Modern Spain

Franco's death left Spain's political future hanging in the balance. But few people wanted to preserve the old regime, and the transition from dictatorship to democracy proved surprisingly swift and painless. The previously-outlawed Socialist Workers' Party, under Felipe González, won the general election in 1982 and set about modernizing Spain. Considerable power has since been devolved to the regions. A major threat facing central government has been the persistent violence of ETA, the Basque separatist organization. Spain's international relations have been strengthened by her membership in NATO and the European Union.

Contemporary Spanish fashion

SPAIN TODAY

☐ *Spain*

▨ *Other European Union states*

Coup d'Etat, February 23, 1981
Civil Guard colonel, Antonio Tejero, held parliament at gunpoint for several hours. Democracy survived because King Juan Carlos refused to support the rebels.

Anti-NATO Protest Rally
When Spain joined NATO in 1982, some saw it as a reversal of Socialist ideals. To others it represented an improvement in Spain's international standing.

Castilla and León's modern pavilion was one of EXPO's 150 pavilions built to innovative designs.

High-tech floodlight

EXPO '92
Over 100 countries were represented at the Universal Exposition which focused world attention on Seville in 1992. The many pavilions displayed scientific, technological, and cultural exhibits.

TIMELINE

1977 First free elections return centrist government under Adolfo Suárez. Political parties, including Communists, are legalized

1982 Landslide electoral victory brings Socialist Workers' Party (PSOE), under Felipe González, to power

Felipe González

	1980		1985

Spanish royal family

1981 Military officers stage attempted coup d'etat to overthrow democracy

1982 World Cup held in Spain. Spain joins NATO

1983 Semi-autonomous regional governments are established to appease Basque Country and Catalonia

1986 Spain joins EC (now EU

Felipe González Elected
In 1982 the Spanish Socialist Workers' Party (PSOE) leader was elected prime minister. González transformed Spain during his 13 years in power.

Tourism
From 1959–73 the number of annual visitors to Spain grew from 3 million to 34 million, transforming the once-quiet coasts and islands.

Ana Belén
Spanish women have enjoyed ever greater freedom and opportunity since the advent of democracy. In a 1980s opinion poll, they voted the singer and actress Ana Belén the woman they most admired.

Leaning blue tower rises above Andalusia's pavilion.

El País
Founded in Madrid in 1976, the liberal daily El País is the best-selling newspaper in Spain. During the transition to democracy it had a great influence on public opinion.

A monorail carried visitors around the site.

Barcelona Olympic Games
The opening ceremony of the Barcelona Olympics included stunning displays of music, dance, and colorful costumes.

	1992 Spain celebrates quincentenary of Columbus's voyage to America	**1995** ETA attempts to assassinate opposition leader José María Aznar	
1991 Madrid hosts Bush-Gorbachev summit		**1993** González wins third term in office	**1996** In the general election on March 3, González loses to a coalition led by Aznar
1990		**1995**	
1989 Spain holds presidency of European Community	**1994/5** Corruption scandals rock the long-serving government		
	1992 Barcelona Olympics and Seville Expo '92 place Spain firmly within community of modern European nations	*Cobi, Barcelona Olympic Mascot*	

Rulers of Spain

SPAIN BECAME A NATION-STATE under Isabel and Fernando, whose marriage eventually united Castile and Aragón. With their daughter Juana's marriage, the kingdom was delivered into Hapsburg hands. Carlos I and Felipe II were both capable rulers, but in 1700 Carlos II died without leaving an heir. After the War of the Spanish Succession, Spain came under the French Bourbons, who have ruled ever since – apart from an interregnum, two republics, and Franco's dictatorship. The current Bourbon king, Juan Carlos I, a constitutional monarch, is respected for his support of democracy.

1665–1700 Carlos II

1474–1504 Isabel, Queen of Castile

1479–1516 Fernando, King of Aragón

1516–56 Carlos I of Spain (Holy Roman Emperor Charles V)

1598–1621 Felipe III

1400	1450	1500	1550	1600	1650
INDEPENDENT KINGDOMS		**HAPSBURG DYNASTY**			
1400	1450	1500	1550	1600	1650

1469 Marriage of Isabel and Fernando leads to unification of Spain

1504–16 Juana la Loca (with Fernando as regent)

1621–65 Felipe IV

Fernando and Isabel, the Catholic Monarchs

UNIFICATION OF SPAIN

In the late 15th century the two largest kingdoms in developing Christian Spain – Castile, with its military might, and Aragón (including Barcelona and a Mediterranean empire) – were united. The marriage of Isabel of Castile and Fernando of Aragón in 1469 joined these powerful kingdoms. Together the so-called Catholic Monarchs defeated the Nasrid Kingdom of Granada, the last stronghold of the Moors (see pp52–3). With the addition of Navarra in 1512, Spain was finally unified.

1556–98 Felipe II

1843–68 Isabel II reigns following the regency of her mother María Cristina (1833–41) and General Espartero (1841–3)

1814–33 First Bourbon restoration, following French rule: Fernando VII

1871–3 Break in Bourbon rule: Amadeo I of Savoy

1939–75 General Franco Head of State

1724 Luis I reigns after Felipe V's abdication, but dies within a year

1759–88 Carlos III

1931–9 Second Republic

1875–85 Second Bourbon restoration: Alfonso XII

1700	1750	1800	1850	1900	1950	

BOURBON DYNASTY | **BOURBON** | **BOURBON**

1700	1750	1800	1850	1900	1950	

1808–13 Break in Bourbon rule: Napoleon's brother, Joseph Bonaparte, rules as José I

1746–59 Fernando VI

1788–1808 Carlos IV

1724–46 Felipe V reinstated as king upon the death of his son, Luis I

1902–31 Alfonso XIII

1886–1902 María Cristina of Hapsburg-Lorraine as regent for Alfonso XIII

1873–4 First Republic

1700–24 Felipe V

1868–70 The Septembrina Revolution

1975 Third Bourbon restoration: Juan Carlos I

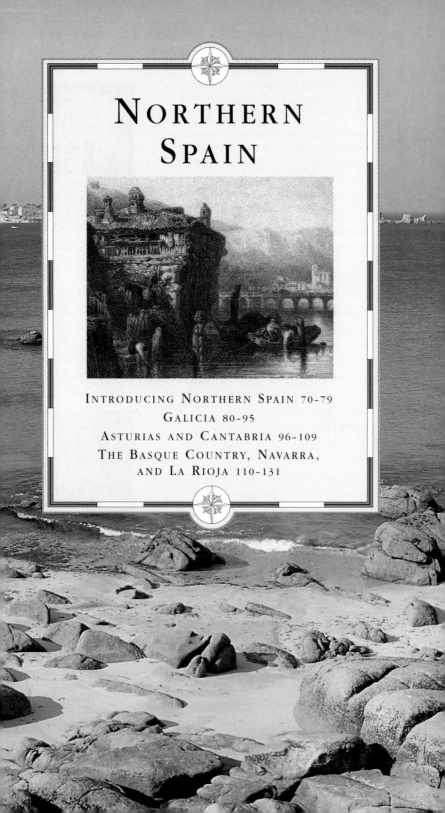

NORTHERN
SPAIN

Introducing Northern Spain

I NCREASING NUMBERS of visitors are discovering the quiet, sandy beaches and deep green landscapes of Northern Spain. The Atlantic coast, from the Pyrenees to the Portuguese border, is often scenic but at its most attractive in the cliffs and rias of Galicia. Inland, the mild, wet climate has created lush meadows and broad-leaved forests, making this area ideal for a peaceful, rural vacation. The famous medieval pilgrimage route to the city of Santiago de Compostela crosses Northern Spain, its way marked by magnificent examples of Romanesque architecture. Plentiful seafood and dairy produce, and the outstanding red wines of La Rioja, add to the pleasure of a tour through this part of Spain.

Oviedo (see p102) *has a number of Pre-Romanesque churches, most notably the graceful Santa María del Naranco, and a fine Gothic cathedral.*

GALICIA
(see pp80–95)

Lugo

A Coruña

Asturias

ASTURIAS AND CANTABRIA
(see pp96–109)

Pontevedra

Ourense

The Rías Baixas (see p91) *is one of Spain's prettiest coastlines. Scattered around its pretty towns and villages are many quaint hórreos, grain stores, raised on stone stilts.*

Santiago de Compostela (see pp86–9) *attracts thousands of pilgrims and tourists each year. Its majestic cathedral was one of the most important shrines in medieval Christendom.*

The Picos de Europa *mountain range* (see pp104–105) *dominates the landscape of Asturias and Cantabria. Rivers have carved deep gorges through the mountains, and there are many footpaths through a variety of spectacular scenery.*

0 kilometers   50

0 miles   25

Santillana del Mar (see p108), *with its well-preserved medieval streets, is one of the most picturesque towns in Spain. The Convento de Regina Coeli houses a small museum containing a collection of painted wooden figures and other works of religious art.*

San Sebastián (see p118), *the most elegant vacation resort in the Basque Country, is sited around a beautiful horseshoe bay of golden sandy beaches. The city hosts international arts events, including Spain's premier film festival.*

Vizcaya

Cantabria

Guipúzcoa

Álava

Navarra

THE BASQUE COUNTRY, NAVARRA, AND LA RIOJA
(see pp110–31)

La Rioja

Pamplona (see pp128–9), *the capital of Navarra since the 9th century, is best known for its annual fiesta, Los Sanfermines. The climax of each day of riotous celebration is the Encierro, in which bulls stampede through the streets of the city.*

The Monasterio de Leyre (see p131), *founded in the early 11th century, was built in a lonely but attractive landscape. The monastery was once the burial place of the kings of Navarra, and its crypt is among the finest examples of early Romanesque art in Spain.*

Regional Food: Northern Spain

T HE CUISINE of Northern Spain is distin-guished by abundant fish and seafood from the Atlantic. The region is also Spain's dairy and the source of some of the country's finest cheeses. Year-round rainfall yields a vari-ety of fresh vegetables, particularly potatoes, cabbages, and corn. Vast mountain ranges mean plentiful game, hams, and cured sausages, which are combined with beans to form hearty stews. The Basques, with their famous gastro-nomical societies and New Basque Cuisine, are said to produce the most sophisticated and varied food in Spain: intriguing sauces boost even salted cod to gourmet heights. Asturias is recognized for its plentiful fish, vegetables and the production of dry cider from apples; while inland Navarra is famed for its locally grown white asparagus, which it cans for the whole of Spain, as well as supplying the country with the essential, spicy, pointed pepper *pimiento piquillo.*

White asparagus

Txangurro relleno *is a Basque dish made with spider crab. The meat is cleaned, stuffed into the shell, and cooked au gratin.*

Beans are an essential element of northern cooking, and there are many specially cultivated varieties. The best, and the most expensive, are La Granja beans from Asturias. Costing double the price of lamb, they are probably the best beans in the world. Tolosa, in the Basque Country, is famous for its red and black beans.

Revuelto, *creamy scrambled egg, is served all along the north coast. It is tastiest accompanied by shrimp and turnip greens.*

Ham

Beans

Morcilla sausage

Chorizo

Empanada, *the Galician flat pie, is stuffed with salted cod or tuna. Shellfish and pork are alternative fillings.*

Fabada, *the regional dish of Asturias, is a savory stew combining pork and beans. Fat buttery fava beans are simmered with* tocino *(salt pork),* morcilla *(black sausage), smoky chorizo sausage, and* ham. *Beef is also included sometimes. The beans take on the rich flavor of the meat, especially the* tocino.

Angulas *(elvers), a winter luxury in the Basque dining clubs, are cooked lightly with oil, garlic, and chili.*

Pimientos rellenos, *from Navarra, are the local spicy pointed red pepper stuffed with fish, seafood, or meat.*

Truchas a la Navarra *are cleaned and deboned mountain trout that are stuffed with serrano ham and fried or grilled.*

Vieras de Santiago *are scallops (the symbol of St. James) in the shell, covered in a tomato and brandy sauce and grilled.*

Lacón con grelos *is the Galician national dish of cured pork shoulder with turnip greens and sausage.*

Chilindrón de cordero, *a rich dish of spicy lamb stewed with local dried or fresh peppers, is a specialty of Navarra.*

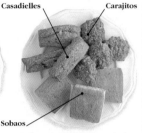

Casadielles   Carajitos

Sobaos

Cakes and biscuits include sobaos *(a Cantabrian breakfast sponge), hazelnut* carajitos, *and walnut-stuffed* casadielles.

CHEESES

From the Cantabrian mountains come the famous pungent blue Cabrales and Picón. Galicia is noted for soft cheeses, especially *tetilla*. Pear-shaped San Simón, smoked Basque Idiazábal, and Roncal are also recommended.

Idiazábal

Cabrales

Tetilla

Canned tuna

Scallops

Mussels

FISH AND SEAFOOD

Some of the most delicious seafood in Europe comes from the Atlantic coast of Spain. Specialties include mussels, scallops, lobsters, octopus, and unusual tall, black barnacles known as *percebes*. The north coast also supplies spider crabs, fat anchovies, and top quality tuna, much of which is canned. The Basques fish for cod off the coasts of Iceland and Norway. Most of the catch is salted, dried, and sold throughout Spain as the ever popular *bacalao*.

Bacalao   **Anchovies**   **Spider crab**

Wines of Northern Spain

S PAIN'S MOST PRESTIGIOUS wine region, Rioja is best known for its red wines, matured to a distinctive vanilla mellowness. Some of the most prestigious bodegas were founded by émigrés from Bordeaux, and Rioja reds are similar to claret. Rioja also produces good white and rosé wines. Navarra reds and some whites have improved dramatically, thanks to a government research program. The Basque region produces a tiny amount of the prickly, tart *txacoli (chacolí)*. Larger quantities of a similar wine are made farther west in Galicia, whose best wines are full-bodied whites.

Repairing barrels in Haro, Rioja

Ribeiro, the popular everyday wine of Galicia, is slightly fizzy. It is often served in white porcelain cups (tazas).

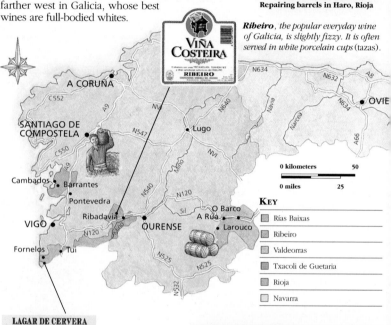

0 kilometers   50

0 miles   25

KEY

- Rías Baixas
- Ribeiro
- Valdeorras
- Txacoli de Guetaria
- Rioja
- Navarra

Lagar de Cervera is from Rías Baixas, where Spain's most fashionable whites are made from the Albariño grape.

WINE REGIONS

The wine regions of Northern Spain are widely dispersed. Cradled between the Pyrenees and the Atlantic are the important regions of Rioja and Navarra. Rioja is divided into the sub-regions of Rioja Alavesa, Rioja Alta, and Rioja Baja, divided by the Río Ebro. The river also cuts through the wine region of Navarra. To the north are the only vineyards in the Basque country: the minuscule Txacoli de Guetaria region. In the far west lie the four wine regions of rugged, wet Galicia: Rías Baixas, Ribeiro, Valdeorras, and the newly created Ribera Sacra.

Wine village of El Villar de Álava in Rioja Alta

Gathering the grape harvest in the traditional way in Navarra

Remelluri, one of the new single-estate "Château" Riojas, from the vineyards of Rioja Alavesa, is soft and not too oaky.

Chivite, from a family bodega in Navarra, is made entirely from Tempranillo and aged in the barrel, resulting in a style similar to Rioja.

Viña Ardanza is blended, as are most red Riojas. The best, like this reserva, are aged for two or more years in oak casks imported from the US.

SANTANDER

BILBO (BILBAO)

Zumaia

Getaria

DONOSTIA (SAN SEBASTIAN)

GASTEIZ (VITORIA)

IRUÑA (PAMPLONA)

Lizarra (Estella)

Haro

Logroño

Tafalla

Olite

Nájera

Calahorra

Arnedo

Alfaro

Corella

Tudela

KEY FACTS ABOUT WINES OF NORTHERN SPAIN

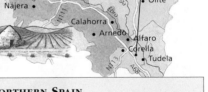

Location and Climate

Rioja and Navarra are influenced by both Mediterranean and Atlantic weather systems. The hillier, northwestern parts receive some Atlantic rain while the hot Ebro plain has a Mediterranean climate. The Basque region and Galicia are both cool, Atlantic regions with high rainfall. Soils everywhere are stony and poor, except in the Ebro plain.

Grape Varieties

The great red grape of Rioja and Navarra is Tempranillo. In Rioja it is blended with smaller quantities of Garnacha, Graciano, and Mazuelo, while in Navarra Cabernet Sauvignon is permitted and blends excitingly with Tempranillo. Garnacha, also important in Navarra, is used for the excellent *rosados* (rosés). Whites of Navarra and Rioja are made mainly from the Viura grape. Galicia has many local varieties, of which the most important are Albariño, Loureira, and Treixadura, which is now taking over from the inferior Palomino.

Good Producers

Rías Baixas: Fillaboa, Lagar de Fornelos, Morgadío, Santiago Ruiz. *Ribeiro:* Cooperativa Vinícola del Ribeiro. *Rioja:* Bodegas Riojanas (Canchales, Monte Real), CVNE (Imperial, Viña Real Oro), Faustino Martínez, Federico Paternina, Marqués de Cáceres, Marqués de Murrieta, Martínez Bujanda, Remelluri, La Rioja Alta (Viña Ardanza). *Navarra:* Bodega de Sarría, Guelbenzu, Julián Chivite (Gran Feudo), Magaña, Ochoa, Príncipe de Viana.

Forests of the North

Coniferous forest in autumn

MUCH OF SPAIN was once blanketed by a mantle of trees. Today, just ten percent of the original cover remains, mostly in the mountainous north, where rainfall is high and slopes too steep for cultivation. Large areas of mixed deciduous forest – mainly beech, Pyrenean oak, and chestnut, with some ash and lime – dominate the landscape, particularly in Cantabria and the Basque Country. The undergrowth of shrubs and flowering plants provides habitats for many insects, mammals, and birds. The forests are also the refuge of Spain's last brown bears *(see p100)*.

Purple emperor butterfly

REGENERATION OF THE FOREST

Dead materials – leaves, twigs, and the excrement and bodies of animals – are broken down by various organisms on the forest floor, especially fungi, bacteria, and ants. This process releases nutrients that are absorbed by trees and other plants, enabling them to grow.

Fly agaric mushrooms

Lichens grow slowly and are sensitive to pollution. Their presence in a forest often indicates that it is in good health.

The stag beetle takes its name from the huge antler-like mandibles of the male. Despite their ferocious appearance, these beetles are harmless to humans.

Millipede and fungus on a woodland floor

BEECH FOREST

Beech, the dominant species in the Cantabrian mountains and Pyrenees, grows in well-drained soils. Some trees retain their distinctive copper-red leaves through the winter. Beech mast (nuts) are collected to feed to pigs.

Beech leaf and mast

The thick crown shuts out light, inhibiting undergrowth.

Long, thin, orange buds

Male golden orioles, among the most colorful European birds, are hard to spot because they spend much of their time in the thick cover provided by old woodlands. Females and juveniles are a duller yellow-green with a brownish tail.

Beech martens are nocturnal. By day, they sleep in a hollow tree or another animal's abandoned nest. At night they feed on fruit, birds, and small mammals.

DISTRIBUTION OF BROAD-LEAVED FORESTS

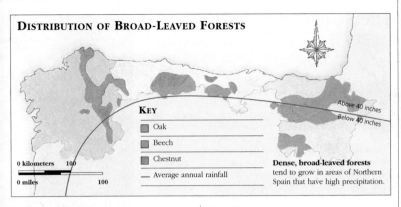

KEY

- Oak
- Beech
- Chestnut
- —— Average annual rainfall

Above 40 inches
Below 40 inches

0 kilometers 100
0 miles 100

Dense, broad-leaved forests tend to grow in areas of Northern Spain that have high precipitation.

CHESTNUT FOREST

Chestnut trees grow on well-drained acidic soils. They have slender yellow flowers and in summer produce their fruit, to be eaten by wild boar, dormice, squirrels, and mice. The wood is hard and durable but splits easily.

Leaf and chestnut

Large leaves have sharp, serrated edges.

Few massive, spreading branches

Deep spiral ridges on trunk

OAK FOREST

Three main species of oak tree – pedunculate, Pyrenean, and the evergreen holm oak – dominate the ancient woodlands of the north. Over 300 species of animal, such as wild boar, squirrels, and nuthatches, feed off oaks.

Oak leaf and acorn

Gray twigs ending in numerous buds

The pipistrelle bat is a nocturnal species common in woodlands. It catches and eats small insects in flight. Larger insects are taken to a perch. The bat hibernates in winter in a hollow tree or cave.

The lesser spotted woodpecker feeds on insects and their larvae. It detects wood-boring beetles by tapping the bark to locate their chambers. It then uses its strong beak to chisel through the bark and extract the grubs.

Blue tits feed mainly in the tree canopy of broad-leaved woods and rarely come down to the ground. The male and female have similar, distinctive plumage. They may raise the back feathers of the crown if alarmed.

Red squirrels bury large numbers of acorns during autumn to last through winter, since these diurnal creatures do not hibernate. Many of the acorns are left to sprout into seedlings.

The Road to Santiago

ACCORDING TO LEGEND, the body of Christ's apostle James was brought to Galicia. In 813 the relics were supposedly discovered at Santiago de Compostela, where a cathedral was built in his honor *(see pp88–9)*. In the Middle Ages half a million pilgrims a year flocked there from all over Europe, crossing the Pyrenees at Roncesvalles *(see p130)* or via the Somport Pass *(see p220)*. They often donned the traditional garb of cape, long staff, and curling felt hat adorned with scallop shells, the symbol of the saint. The various routes, marked by the cathedrals, churches, and hospitals built along them, are still used by travelers today.

St. James on horseback

19th-century painting of the Pórtico da Gloria of Santiago cathedral

A certificate is given to pilgrims covering at least 100 km (62 miles) of the route on foot, bicycle, or horseback.

Astorga (see p334), *once a Roman city, was an important halt on the pilgrim route in the Middle Ages. The museum inside its cathedral has a collection of gold and silver plate including a 13th-century gold filigree cross.*

O Cebreiro (see p95) has a 9th-century church and some of the ancient *pallozas* the pilgrims often used for shelter.

León *was one of the main pilgrim stops. Its cathedral* (see pp336–7) *contains one of Spain's finest collections of stained glass.*

Ponferrada's huge Templar castle stands close to the town center *(see p334)*.

Scallop shells, staffs, and gourds to carry water are symbols of the pilgrimage.

Ribadeo
A Coruña
Oviedo
SANTIAGO DE COMPOSTELA
Maritime Route
Vilar de Donas
Ligonde
Portuguese Route
PORTO
LISBOA
Vigo
Silver Route
O Cebreiro
Villafranca del Bierzo
Ponferrada
Astorga
Hospital de Orbigo
LEON
Sahagún

0 kilometers   50
0 miles   50

SALAMANCA

ROMANESQUE CHURCH ARCHITECTURE

The Romanesque style of architecture *(see p20)* was brought to Spain from France during the 10th and 11th centuries. As the pilgrimage to Santiago became more popular, many glorious religious buildings were constructed along its main routes. Massive walls, few windows, round, heavy arches, and barrel vaulting are typical features of Romanesque architecture.

Carved capital

Octagonal lantern

Twin round towers

Barrel vault

Thick walls

Round arch

Façade

Cross-section

San Martín de Frómista *(see p350), built in the 11th century, is the only complete example of the "pilgrimage" style of Romanesque. The nave and aisles are almost the same height, and there are three consecutive apses.*

Consecutive apses **Aisle** **Nave**

Floor plan

Pamplona's *(see p128) Gothic cathedral was one of the pilgrims' first stops after crossing the Pyrenees at Roncesvalles.*

Santo Domingo de la Calzada's *(see p124)* pilgrim hospital is now a parador.

Puente la Reina *(see p127) takes its name from the 11th-century humpbacked bridge (puente), built for pilgrims and still used by pedestrians.*

Frómista preserves one of the finest Romanesque churches on the French route.

Santander
Northern Route
Bilbo (Bilbao)
Donostia (San Sebastián)
PARIS
LE PUY VEZELAY
Valcarlos
Orreaga (Roncesvalles)
Iruña (Pamplona)
Lizarra (Estella)
Puente la Reina
Sangüesa
French Route
ARLES
Aragonese Route
Jaca
San Juan de la Peña
Santo Domingo de la Calzada
San Juan de Ortega
Nájera
Logroño
Frómista
BURGOS

Burgos has a magnificent Gothic cathedral *(see pp354–5).*

ROUTES TO SANTIAGO
Several traditional pilgrimage roads converge on Santiago de Compostela. The main road from the Pyrenees is known as the French Route, with the Aragonese Route as a variation.

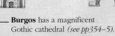

GALICIA

···

LUGO · A CORUÑA · PONTEVEDRA · OURENSE

REMOTE IN THE NORTHWEST CORNER *of the peninsula, Galicia is the country's greenest region. In its hilly interior, small farms are worked by traditional methods. Galicia is Spain's main seafaring region – three of its four provinces have an Atlantic coastline, and its cuisine is based on superb seafood. The Galicians, whose origins are Celtic, are fiercely proud of their culture and language.*

Much of Galicia still has a medieval quality. Some inland farms are divided into plots too tiny or steep for tractors to work, so oxen and horses are used for plowing. Grain is stored in quaint, pillared granaries called *hórreos*. The misty, emerald countryside abounds with old granite villages and is dotted with *pazos* – traditional stone manor houses.

The discovery of the supposed tomb of St. James the Apostle, in the 9th century, confirmed medieval Santiago de Compostela as Europe's most important religious shrine after St. Peter's in Rome. Pilgrims and tourists still follow this ancient route of pilgrimage across Northern Spain. The Galician coast is incised by many fjord-like rias; the loveliest of these are the Rías Baixas in the west. Elsewhere it juts defiantly into the Atlantic in rocky headlands, such as Cabo Fisterra, Spain's most westerly point. Many people still make a living from the sea. Vigo in Pontevedra is the most important fishing port in Spain.

Galicia's official language, used on most signs, is *gallego*. It has similarities to the language of Portugal, which borders Galicia to the south. The Celtic character of this haunting land is still evident in the Galicians' favorite traditional instrument, the bagpipes.

Staple crops – corn, cabbage, and potatoes – growing on the harsh land around Cabo Fisterra

◁ **The west façade of Santiago de Compostela's cathedral, overlooking the Praza do Obradoiro**

Exploring Galicia

Santiago de Compostela is Galicia's major tourist attraction. This beautiful city is the centerpiece of a region with many fine old towns, especially Betanzos, Mondoñedo, Lugo, and Pontevedra. The resorts along the coastline of the wild Rías Altas, with their backdrop of forest-covered hills, offer good swimming. The Rías Baixas, the southern part of Galicia's west coast, has sheltered coves and sandy beaches, and excellent seafood in abundance. Traveling through the interior, where life seems to have changed little in centuries, is an ideal way to spend a peaceful vacation.

Students in traditional dress playing music in Pontevedra

Sights at a Glance

The isolated monastery at Ribas de Sil

See Also

• *Where to Stay* pp536–8

• *Restaurants and Bars* pp578–9

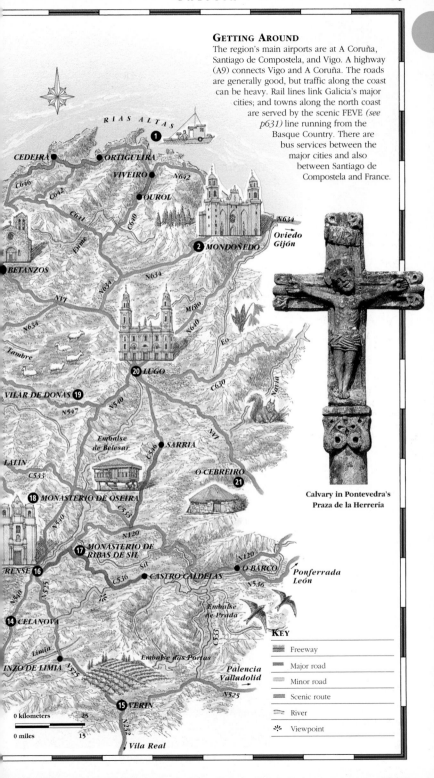

GETTING AROUND

The region's main airports are at A Coruña, Santiago de Compostela, and Vigo. A highway (A9) connects Vigo and A Coruña. The roads are generally good, but traffic along the coast can be heavy. Rail lines link Galicia's major cities; and towns along the north coast are served by the scenic FEVE *(see p631)* line running from the Basque Country. There are bus services between the major cities and also between Santiago de Compostela and France.

RIAS ALTAS

CEDEIRA

ORTIGUEIRA

VIVEIRO

OUROL   N642

❶

②MONDOÑEDO   N634

*Oviedo
Gijón*

C646

C642

C631

C640

Eume

BETANZOS

N634   N634

NVI   Miño   N640

N634   Eo

Tambre

Navia

⑳LUGO

C630

VILAR DE DONAS ⓳   N547

N540   NVI

LALIN   C533   *Embalse
de Belesar*   C546   **SARRIA**

O CEBREIRO
㉑

⑱MONASTERIO DE OSEIRA   C533

N540   N120

**⑰MONASTERIO DE
RIBAS DE SIL**   N120

RENSE ⓰   C536   **CASTRO CALDELAS**   ●O BARCO   *Ponferrada
León*   N536

Sil

A525

⓮CELANOVA

Limia   *Embalse
de Prada*   C533

INZO DE LIMIA   A525   *Embalse das Portas*   *Palencia
Valladolid*

N525

⓯VERIN

N532

Vila Real

**Calvary in Pontevedra's
Praza de la Herrería**

KEY

▬▬	Freeway
▬▬	Major road
▬▬	Minor road
▬▬	Scenic route
🌊	River
☀	Viewpoint

0 kilometers   25

0 miles   15

Carved coat of arms on a house-front in Mondoñedo

Rías Altas ❶

Lugo & A Coruña. 🚊 Ribadeo.
🚌 Viveiro. 🛈 Foz, (982) 14 00 27.

DEEP RIAS are interspersed with coves and headlands along the beautiful north coast from Ribadeo to A Coruña. Inland are hills covered with forests of pine and eucalyptus. Many of the small resorts and fishing villages are charming.

The lovely, winding **Ría de Ribadeo** forms the border with Asturias. To the west of it is the small fishing port of **Foz**, which has two good beaches. Nearby, the 10th-century Iglesia de San Martín de Mondoñedo, standing alone on a hill, contains carvings of biblical scenes on its transept capitals – note the story of Lazarus. **Viveiro**, a summer holiday resort, is a handsome old town surrounded by Renaissance walls and gateways, typically Galician glassed-in balconies or *galerías*, and a Romanesque church. Near the pretty fishing village of O Barqueiro is the headland of Estaca de Bares, with its lighthouse and wind turbines.

Westward along the coast, the lovely **Ría de Ortigueira** leads to the fishing port of the same name, characterized by neat white houses. Around this area there are also many wild and unspoiled beaches.

High cliffs rise out of the sea near the village of **San Andrés de Teixido**, whose church is the focal point for pilgrims every September 8. According to local legend, all those who fail to visit the church in their own lifetime will come back to it as an animal in the afterlife. The village of **Cedeira**, which sits in seclusion on a quiet bay, is a prosperous summer resort with neat lawns, modern houses with *galerías*, and a long, curving beach.

Mondoñedo ❷

Lugo. 👥 5,100. 🚌 🛈 Praza do Concelo, (982) 52 11 02. 🕭 Thu & Sun. 🎪 San Lucas (Oct 18).

THIS DELIGHTFUL TOWN, an old provincial capital, is set in a fertile inland valley. There are stately houses with carved coats of arms and *galerías* in the main square. This is dominated by the **cathedral**, a building of golden stone in an unusual mix of styles. It has 18th-century Baroque towers, a Romanesque portal with a 16th-century stained-glass rose window, and 17th-century cloisters. A polychromatic statue in the south ambulatory, Nuestra Señora la Inglesa, was rescued from St. Paul's cathedral in London during the Reformation. The **Museo Diocesano** contains statues, altarpieces, and works by Zurbarán and El Greco.

🏛 Museo Diocesano
Plaza de la Catedral. 📞 (982) 52 19 48. ⏲ Jun–Sep: daily. 🎟

Betanzos ❸

A Coruña. 👥 14,000. 🚌 🚉 🛈 Plaza Constitución 1, (981) 77 29 08. 🕭 Tue, Thu & Sat. 🎪 San Roque (Aug 14–25).

THE HANDSOME TOWN of Betanzos lies in a fertile valley slightly inland. Its broad main square has a replica of the Fountain of Diana at Versailles. In its steep narrow streets are some fine old houses and Gothic churches. The **Iglesia de Santiago**, built in the 15th century by the tailors' guild, has a statue of St. James on horseback above the door. The **Iglesia de San Francisco**, dated 1387, has statues of wild boars and a heraldic emblem of Count Fernán Pérez de Andrade, whose 15th-century tomb is inside the church. For centuries his family were the overlords of the region.

Ornate tomb in the Iglesia de San Francisco in Betanzos

ENVIRONS: 15 km (9 miles) north is the large, though pretty, fishing village of **Pontedeume**, with its narrow, hilly streets. Its medieval bridge still carries the main road to the large industrial town of **Ferrol**, to the north. This port became an important naval base and dockyard town in the 18th century, and its Neo-Classical buildings survive from that time. General Franco *(see pp62–3)* was born in Ferrol in 1892, and an imposing equestrian statue of him stands in the Praza de España.

Sidewalk cafés in Betanzos' Plaza de García Hermanos

Stone cross standing above the perilous waters of the Costa do Morte

A Coruña ❹

A Coruña. 🏘 *200,000.* ✈ 🚃 🚌
🛈 *Dársena de la Marina, (981) 22
18 22.* 🎉 *Fiestas de María Pita (Aug),
Semana Grande (early Aug).*

THIS PROUD CITY and busy
port has played a sizable
role in Spanish maritime
history. Felipe II's doomed
Armada sailed from here to
England in 1588 *(see p55).*
Today, the sprawling industrial
suburbs contrast with the
elegant town center that is
laid out on an isthmus leading
to a headland. The **Torre de
Hércules**, Europe's oldest
working lighthouse, is a
famous local landmark. Built
by the Romans and rebuilt in
the 18th century, it still flashes
across the deep. Climb its 242
steps for a wide ocean view.

On the large, arcaded Praza
María Pita, the city's main
square, is the handsome town
hall. The sea promenade of
La Marina is lined with tiers
of glass-enclosed balconies or
galerías. Built as protection
against the strong winds, they
explain why A Coruña is often
referred to as the City of Glass.
The peaceful, tiny Praza de
Santa Bárbara is enchanting.

A Coruña has several fine
Romanesque churches incl-
uding the **Iglesia de Santiago**,
with a carving of its saint on
horseback situated beneath

the tympanum, and the **Iglesia
de Santa María**. This church,
with its tympanum carving of
the Adoration of the Magi, is
one of the best-preserved 12th-
century buildings in Galicia.

The quiet Jardín de San
Carlos contains the tomb of the
English general Sir John Moore,
killed by the French in battle.
This old part of town is still
somewhat military, and army
jeeps are a common sight in
its narrow streets.

**The lofty Torre de Hércules
lighthouse at A Coruña**

Costa do Morte ❺

A Coruña. 🚌 *A Coruña, Malpica,
Santiago de Compostela.* 🛈 *A Coruña,
(981) 22 18 22.*

FROM MALPICA to Fisterra the
coast is wild and remote. It
is called the "Coast of Death"
because of the many ships
lost in storms or smashed on
the rocks by gales over the
centuries. But the headlands
are majestic and the sunsets
beautiful. Inland, the countryside is breezy and open. There
are no coastal towns, only simple villages, where fishermen
gather edible *percebes* (barnacles), destined for the region's
restaurants.

One of the most northerly
points of the Costa do Morte,
Malpica, has a seabird sanctuary. Laxe has good beaches
and safe swimming.
Camariñas, one of the most
appealing places on this
coast, is a fishing village
where women make bobbin-
lace in the streets. Beside the
lighthouse on nearby Cabo
Vilán, a group of futuristic
wind turbines, tall and
slender, swirl in graceful
unison – a haunting sight.

To the south is Corcubión,
exuding a faded elegance, and,
lastly, the lighthouse of **Cabo
Fisterra**, "where the land
ends," which is a good place
to watch the sun go down.

Street-by-Street: Santiago de Compostela ❻

Vegetable stall in Santiago market

IN THE MIDDLE AGES Santiago de Compostela was Christendom's third most important place of pilgrimage *(see pp78–9)*, after Jerusalem and Rome. Around the Praza do Obradoiro is an ensemble of historic buildings with few equals in Europe. The local granite gives a harmonious unity to the mixture of architectural styles. With its narrow streets and old squares, the city center is compact enough to explore on foot. Two other monuments worth seeing are the Convento de Santo Domingo de Bonaval, to the east of the center, housing a Galician folk museum, and the Colegiata del Sar, a 12th-century Romanesque church, located to the south of the city.

★ **Convento de San Martiño Pinario**
The Baroque church of this monastery has a huge double altar and an ornate Plateresque façade with carved figures of saints and bishops.

Pazo de Xelmírez

★ **Hotel de los Reyes Católicos**
Built by the Catholic Monarchs as an inn and hospital for sick pilgrims, and now a parador (see p537), this magnificent building has an elaborate Plateresque doorway.

Praza do Obradoiro
This majestic square is one of the world's finest and the focal point for pilgrims arriving in the city. The cathedral's Baroque façade dominates the square.

The Pazo de Rax with its Classical façade, was built 1772 and houses the town hall.

RUA DA TRO

RUELA DO VAL DE DEUS

RUA DE SAN FRANCISCO

PRAZA D INMAC

PRAZA OBRAD

Convento de San Paio de Antealtares
This is one of the oldest monasteries in Santiago. It was founded in the 9th century to house the tomb of St. James, now in the cathedral.

VISITORS' CHECKLIST

A Coruña. ⚄ 100,000. ✈ 10 km (6 miles) north. ⛒ Calle Hórreo, (981) 52 02 02. ⛒ Avenida Rodríguez de Viguri, (981) 58 77 00. ℹ Calle Rúa do Villar 43, (981) 58 40 81. ⛪ Thu. ⛪ Semana Santa (Easter Week), Ascensión (May), Santiago (Jul 25).

Praza da Quintana, under the cathedral clock tower, is one of the city's most elegant squares.

Praza das Praterias
The Goldsmiths' Doorway of the cathedral opens onto this charming square with a 17th-century fountain in the center.

KEY

– – – Suggested route

– – – Pilgrims' route

Rúa Nova is a handsome arcaded old street leading from the cathedral to the newer part of the city.

To tourist information

0 meters   100

0 yards   100

Colegio de San Jerónimo

STAR SIGHTS

★ **Convento de San Martiño Pinario**

★ **Hotel de los Reyes Católicos**

★ **Cathedral**

★ **Cathedral**
This grand, towering spectacle has welcomed pilgrims to Santiago for centuries. Though the exterior has been remodeled over the years, the core of the building has remained virtually unchanged since the 11th century.

Santiago Cathedral

W ITH ITS TWIN BAROQUE TOWERS soaring high
over the Praza do Obradoiro square, this
monument to St. James is a majestic sight,
as befits one of the great shrines of Christendom
(*see pp78–9*). The present building dates from
the 11th–12th centuries and stands on the
site of the original 9th-century basilica built
by Alfonso II. Through the famous carved
Pórtico da Gloria, one of the great wonders
of Christian art, is the same lofty interior
that welcomed pilgrims in medieval times.

**The gigantic
botafumeiro**

**"Passport" – proof of
a pilgrim's journey**

★ West Façade
*The richly sculpted Baroque
Obradoiro façade was added
in the 18th century.*

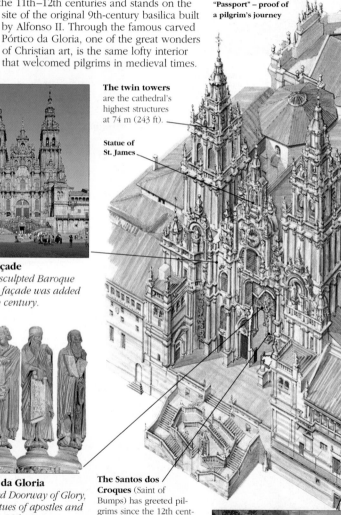

The twin towers
are the cathedral's
highest structures
at 74 m (243 ft).

**Statue of
St. James**

★ Pórtico da Gloria
*The sculpted Doorway of Glory,
with its statues of apostles and
prophets, is 12th century.*

**The Santos dos
Croques** (Saint of
Bumps) has greeted pil-
grims since the 12th century. Touching this statue
with the forehead is said
to impart luck and wisdom.

STAR FEATURES
★ West Façade
★ Pórtico da Gloria
★ Porta das Praterias

Tapestry Museum
*Tapestries dating from the
early 16th century are
displayed in the museum
above the chapterhouse and
library. Some later tapestries
are based on Goya's works.*

The *botafumeiro*, a giant censer, is swung high above the altar by eight men during important services.

Mondragon Chapel (1521) contains fine wrought-iron grilles and vaulting.

Clock Tower

High Altar
Visitors can pass behind the ornate high altar to kiss the silver mantle of the 13th-century statue of St. James.

Cloisters

★ Porta das Praterias
The 11th-century Gold-smiths' Doorway is rich in bas-relief sculptures of biblical scenes.

Crypt
The relics of St. James and two disciples are said to lie in a tomb in the crypt, under the altar, in the original 9th-century foundations.

Chapterhouse

Padrón 🏛 ❼

A Coruña. 🏛 10,700. 🚍 🚌 🏛
Calle General Franco 27, (981) 81 04
51. 🚍 Sun. 🎇 Santiago (Jul 24–5).

THIS QUIET TOWN on the Río
Ulla, known for its piquant
green peppers, was a major
seaport until it silted up. Legend has it the boat carrying
the body of St. James to Galicia
(see p78) arrived here. The
supposed mooring stone, or
padrón, lies below the altar
of the church by the bridge.

The leafy avenue beside the
church is featured in the poems
of one of Galicia's greatest writers, Rosalia de Castro (1837–
85). Her home on the edge of
town, where she spent her
final years, has been converted into a museum.

ENVIRONS: The estuary town
of Noia (Noya) lies on the
coast 20 km (12 miles) west.
Its Gothic church has a finely
carved portal. East of Padrón is
Pazo de Oca, a manor house,
with a crenelated tower, idyllic
garden and a lake.

🏛 **Museo Rosalia de Castro**
La Matanza. 📞 (981) 81 12 04.
🔲 Tue–Sun. ♿

The picturesque gardens and lake of Pazo de Oca

A Toxa ❽

Near O Grove. 🚍 🚻 Ayuntamiento,
O Grove, (986) 73 06 28.

A TINY pine-covered island
joined to the mainland by
a bridge, A Toxa (La Toja) is
one of the most stylish resorts
in Galicia. The belle époque
palace-hotel (see p537) and
luxury villas add to the island's
elegant atmosphere. A Toxa's
best-known landmark is the
small church covered with
scallop shells. Across the bridge
is O Grove (El Grove), a
thriving family resort and fishing port on a peninsula, with
vacation hotels and apartments
along glorious beaches.

Scallop-covered roof of the church on A Toxa island

Pontevedra ❾

Pontevedra. 🏛 65,000. 🚍 🚌
🚻 Calle General Mola 1, (986) 85
08 14. 🚍 Sat. 🎇 Fiestas de la
Peregrina (second week in Aug).

PONTEVEDRA lies inland, at the
head of a long ria that is
backed by green hills. The delightful old town is typically
Galician and has a network of
cobbled alleys and tiny graceful squares with granite calvaries, arcades, flower-filled balconies, and excellent tapas bars.
On the south side of the old
town is the Gothic **Convento
de Santo Domingo**. It is now
a museum containing Roman
steles and Galician coats of
arms and tombs. To the west,
the 16th-century **Iglesia de
Santa María la Mayor** contains a magnificent Plateresque
(see p21) façade that includes
richly carved figures of oars-
men and fishermen at the top.

On the **Praza de la Leña**, a
small, shaded square, two 18th-
century mansions form the
Museo de Pontevedra, one of
Galicia's best museums. The
gold bracelets, collars, and
other Celtic Bronze Age treasures found locally are superb.
Among the paintings on display are 15th-century Spanish
primitives, and canvases by
Zurbarán and Goya. On the
top floor is the museum's star
display: a collection of drawings and paintings by Alfonso
Castelao, a 20th-century Galician artist, writer, and nationalist
who forcefully depicted the
misery endured by his people
during the Spanish Civil War.

🏛 **Museo de Pontevedra**
Calle Pasandedia 10. 📞 (986) 85 14
55. 🔲 Tue–Sun.

Rías Baixas

THIS SOUTHERN PART of Galicia's west coast consists of four large rias or inlets between pine-covered hills. The beaches are good, the scenery is lovely, the swimming safe, and the climate much milder than on the wilder coast to the north. Though areas such as Vilagarcía de Arousa and Panxón have become popular resorts, much of the Rías Baixas (Rías Bajas) coastline is unspoiled, such as the quiet stretch from Muros to Noia. This part of the coastline provides some of Spain's most fertile fishing grounds. Mussel-breeding platforms are positioned in neat rows along the rias, looking like half-submerged submarines; and in November, the women harvest clams.

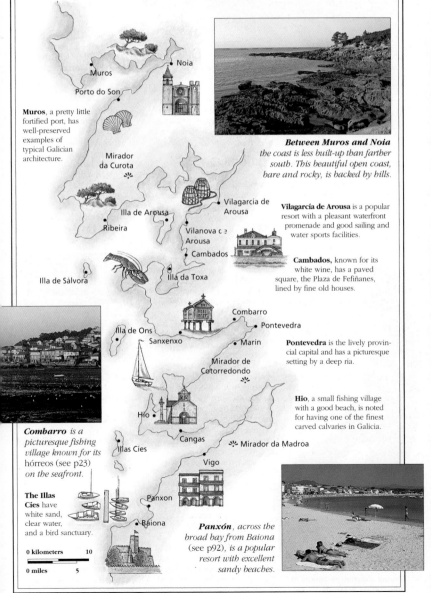

Muros, a pretty little fortified port, has well-preserved examples of typical Galician architecture.

Noia

Muros

Porto do Son

Mirador da Curota

Between Muros and Noia
the coast is less built-up than farther south. This beautiful open coast, bare and rocky, is backed by hills.

Illa de Arousa

Ribeira

Vilagarcía de Arousa

Vilanova de Arousa

Cambados

Vilagarcía de Arousa is a popular resort with a pleasant waterfront promenade and good sailing and water sports facilities.

Cambados, known for its white wine, has a paved square, the Plaza de Fefiñanes, lined by fine old houses.

Illa de Sálvora

Illá da Toxa

Combarro

Pontevedra

Illa de Ons

Sanxenxo

Marin

Mirador de Cotorredondo

Pontevedra is the lively provincial capital and has a picturesque setting by a deep ria.

Hío

Hío, a small fishing village with a good beach, is noted for having one of the finest carved calvaries in Galicia.

Cangas

❧ Mirador da Madroa

Combarro is a picturesque fishing village known for its hórreos (see p23) on the seafront.

Illas Cíes

Vigo

The Illas Cíes have white sand, clear water, and a bird sanctuary.

Panxon

Baiona

Panxón, across the broad bay from Baiona (see p92), is a popular resort with excellent sandy beaches.

0 kilometers   10

0 miles   5

Cannon on the battlements of Monterreal fortress, Baiona

Vigo ⑩

Pontevedra. 🚶 *300,000.* ✈ 🚢
🚌 🛈 *Estación Marítima, (986) 43
05 77.* 🚃 *Wed & Sun.* 🎭 *Cristo de
los Afligidos (Jul).*

G ALICIA'S LARGEST TOWN is
also the biggest fishing
port in Spain. It is situated in
an attractive setting near the
mouth of a deep ria spanned
by a high suspension bridge,
and is surrounded by wooded
hills. Vigo isn't noted for its
old buildings but does have
striking modern
sculptures such as
local artist Juan José
Oliveira's horses
statue in the Praza
de España. The
oldest part of the
town, Barrio del Berbes,
is near the port and
used to be the
sailors' quarter.
Its cobbled alleys
are teeming with
bars, and here
you can find
some of the
finest

**Bronze sculpture by Oliveira in
Vigo's Praza de España**

tapas bars, which serve mainly
seafood. The Mercado de la
Piedra, near the port, sells
reasonably priced fish and
shellfish – particularly oysters.

Baiona ⑪

Pontevedra. 🚶 *10,000.* 🚌 🛈 *Calle
Lorenzo de la Carrera 17, (986) 35 52
50.* 🚃 *Mon.* 🎭 *Santa Marina (Jul 18).*

T HE PINTA, one of the cara-
vels from the fleet of
Christopher Columbus, arrived
at this small port on March 10,
1493, bringing the first news
of the discovery of the New
World. Today Baiona (Bayona),
is a popular summer resort,
its harbor a mix of pleasure
and fishing boats. The 12th-
century **collegiate church** is
Romanesque and Gothic. Symbols such as knives, chisels,
and axes, carved on the arches,
indicate the local guilds that
helped build the church.
A royal fortress once stood
on Monterreal promontory, to
the north of town. Its huge
defensive walls remain, but the
interior has recently been
converted into a chic and
stylish parador *(see p536).* The
cannon used as protection
against pirates can still be
seen. A walk around the
battlements offers superb
views of the coast.
On the coast about 3 km
(2 miles) farther south is a
huge granite statue of the
Virgen de la Roca. During
important religious festivals,
visitors climb up inside and
onto the ship she holds.

A Guarda ⑫

Pontevedra. 🚶 *10,000.* 🚌
🛈 *Plaza de España 1, (986) 61 00
00.* 🚃 *Sat.* 🎭 *Monte de Santa Tecla
(second week of Aug).*

T HE LITTLE FISHING PORT of A
Guarda (La Guardia) has a
reputation for good seafood
and is particularly well known
for the quality of its lobsters.
On the slopes of Monte de
Santa Tecla are the remains of
a Celtic settlement of some
100 round stone dwellings
that are dated around
600–200 BC. The **Museo de
Monte de Santa Tecla** is
situated on a nearby hilltop.

ENVIRONS: About 10 km
(6 miles) north, the tiny
Baroque **Monasterio de Santa
María** stands by the beach at
Oia. Semiwild horses roam
the surrounding hills and, in
May and June, are rounded
up for branding in a series of
day-long fiestas *(see p94).*

🏛 **Museo de Monte de
Santa Tecla**
A Guarda. 📞 *(986) 61 00 00.*
🕐 *daily.*

**Circular foundations of Celtic
dwellings at A Guarda**

Tui ⑬

Pontevedra. 🚶 *16,400.* 🚌 🚃 🛈
Avda Portugal, (986) 60 17 89. 🚃 *Thu.*
🎭 *San Telmo (week after Easter),
Descent of the Río Miño (Aug).*

S PAIN'S main border town
with Portugal, Tui (Tuy)
stands on a hillside above the
Río Miño. Its graceful old
streets curve up to an old quarter and the 13th-century hilltop
cathedral. The two countries
were often at war during the
Middle Ages, and as a result
the church is built in the style

Unloading the catch in Spain's largest fishing port, Vigo

Fishing in Spain

The Spanish eat more seafood per head of population than any other European nation except Portugal. Half of this is caught by Galician fishing fleets. Some 90,000 fishermen and 20,000 boats land over a million tons of fish and shellfish a year, much of this caught offshore where sardines, tuna, lobster, and clams are plentiful. In recent years, the stocks in the seas around Spain have become depleted by overfishing, forcing deep-sea trawlers to travel as far as Canada and Iceland.

of a fortress, with towers and battlements. It has a cloister and choir stalls and a richly decorated west porch.

Nearby is the **Iglesia de San Telmo**, dedicated to the patron saint of fishermen, whose Baroque ornamentation shows a Portuguese influence. Below the cathedral is an iron bridge, the **Puente Internacional**, built by Gustave Eiffel in 1884 to stretch across the river to Valença do Minho in Portugal.

The Gothic **Iglesia de Santo Domingo**, situated beside the Parque de la Alameda, contains ivy-covered cloisters and tombs with delicately carved effigies. The church overlooks the river, which is filled with boats in August for the Descent of the Río Miño, a canoe race and fiesta.

Celanova ⓮

Ourense. 6,200. *Plaza Mayor 1, (988) 43 14 81.* *Thu.* *San Roque (Aug 15).*

On the main square of this little town is the massive **Monasterio de San Salvador**, which was formerly one of the most important monasteries in Spain. Founded during the 10th century and later rebuilt, it is mainly Baroque, though one of its two lovely cloisters is Renaissance. The enormous church of this Benedictine monastery has an ornate altarpiece and Gothic choir stalls. In the garden is the 10th-century Mozarabic **Iglesia de San Miguel**.

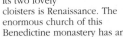

Ceramic tiled floor of the Iglesia de San Miguel

Environs: At **Santa Comba de Bande**, 26 km (16 miles) to the south, is an even older little church. The features of this Visigothic *(see pp46–7)* church, which is thought to be 7th century, include a lantern turret and a horseshoe arch that has carved marble pillars.

Verín ⓯

Ourense. *11,500.* *Plaza del Ayuntamiento, (988) 41 00 00.* *3rd, 11th & 23rd of month.* *Santa María la Mayor (Aug 15).*

Though it stands amid vineyards, Verín produces more than wine. Its thermal springs have given it a thriving bottled water industry. The town has a few 17th-century houses with arcades, *galerías*, and coats of arms. The **Castillo de Monterrei**, built during the wars with Portugal, is 4 km (2.5 miles) to the west. Inside its three rings of walls are a square 15th-century keep, an arcaded courtyard, and a 13th-century church with a delicately carved portal. The castle once housed a monastery and hospital.

The Castillo de Monterrei, standing high above the town of Verín

GALICIA'S FIESTAS

Os Peliqueiros
(Carnival, Feb/Mar), Laza
(Ourense). Dressed up in
grinning masks and out-
landish costumes, with
cowbells tied to their belts
and brandishing sticks, *Os
Peliqueiros* take to the
streets on Carnival Sunday.
They are licensed to lash
out at onlookers, who are
forbidden to retaliate. On
Carnival Monday morning
a battle takes place, with
flour, water, and live ants
used as ammunition. Laza's
carnival comes to on end
on the Tuesday with a
reading of the satirical
"Donkey's Will" and the
burning of an effigy.

The outrageous costumes of
Os Peliqueiros **in Laza**

A Rapa das Bestas
(May and Jun), Oia
(Pontevedra). Semiwild
horses are rounded up by
local farmers for their
manes and tails to be cut.
What was once a chore is
now a popular fiesta.
Flower pavements
(Corpus Christi, May/Jun),
Ponteareas (Pontevedra).
The streets of the town
along which the Corpus
Christi procession passes
are carpeted with intricate
designs made from brightly
colored flower petals.
St. James's Day *(Jul 25)*,
Santiago de Compostela.
On the night before, there
is a firework display in
the Praza do Obradoiro.
The celebrations are es-
pecially wild when July
25 falls on a Sunday.

Ourense ⑯

Ourense. 👥 *100,000.* 🚉 🚌
ℹ️ *Curros Enríquez 1, (988) 37 20 20.*
📅 *7th & 17th of each month.* 🎉
Os Maios (May 3), San Martín (Nov 11).

T HE OLD QUARTER of Ourense
was built around the city's
well-known thermal springs,
Fonte as Burgas. Even today,
these spout water at a temperature of 65°C (150°F) from
three fountains.
This old part of the town is
the most interesting, particularly the small area around the
arcaded Plaza Mayor. Here the
cathedral, founded in 572 and
rebuilt in the 12th–13th centuries, has a vast gilded reredos
by Cornelis de Holanda. On
the triple-arched doorway are
carved multicolored figures
reminiscent of the Pórtico da
Gloria at Santiago *(see p88)*.
Nearby is the elegant 14th-
century cloister, the **Claustro
de San Francisco**.
One of the city's landmarks
is the 13th-century **Puente
Romano**, a seven-arched
bridge that crosses the Río
Miño, north of the town. It is
built on Roman foundations
and still used by traffic.

ENVIRONS: Allariz, 25 km (16
miles) south, and Ribadavia,
to the west, have old Jewish
quarters with narrow streets
and Romanesque churches.
Ribadavia is also noted for its
Ribeiro wines – a dry white
and a port-like red *(see p74)*
– and has a wine museum.

**Ornate Gothic reredos in the
cathedral at Ourense**

Monasterio
de Ribas de Sil ⑰

Ribas de Sil. 🚌 *San Esteban de Sil.*
🚌 *from Ourense.* ☎ *(988) 20 10 54.*
🕐 *Tue–Sun.* ♿

N EAR ITS CONFLUENCE with the
Miño, the Río Sil carves
a deep, curving gorge in which
dams form two reservoirs of
dark green water. A hairpin
road winds to the top of the
gorge, where the Romanesque-
Gothic Monasterio de Ribas de
Sil is situated high on a crag
above the chasm. Partly dilapi-
dated, partly over-restored – it
has an enormous glass wall
in one of the three cloisters –
it nevertheless has a certain
ghostly grandeur.

The Río Sil winding its way through the gorge

The grandiose Monasterio de Oseira surrounded by the forests of the Valle de Arenteiro

Monasterio de Oseira ⑱

Oseira. 🚌 🚍 from Ourense. 📞 (988) 28 20 04. ◯ daily. 🏵

THIS MONASTERY stands on its own in a wooded valley near the village of Oseira, named after the bears (osos) that once lived in this region. It is a big, gray building with a Baroque façade dating from 1708. On the doorway is a statue of the Virgin as nurse, with St. Bernard kneeling at her feet. The interior of the 12th–13th-century church is typically Cistercian in its simplicity. The cloisters, main stairway, and vaulted chapterhouse are impressive.

Fresco of a *dona* in the monastery at Vilar de Donas

Vilar de Donas ⑲

Lugo. 🏘 80. 🛈 Ctra de Santiago 28, (982) 38 00 01. 🏵 San Antonio (Jun 13), San Salvador (Aug 6).

THIS HAMLET on the Road to Santiago (see pp78–9) has a small church situated just off the main road, with a Romanesque doorway. Inside are tombs of some of the Knights of the Order of Santiago, and 15th-century frescoes of the nuns (donas) who lived here until the 15th century and who gave the village its name. Some frescoes are on biblical themes.

The Cistercian **Monasterio Sobrado de los Monjes**, to the northwest, has a medieval kitchen and chapterhouse, and a church with attractive domes.

Lugo ⑳

Lugo. 🏘 80,000. 🚌 🚍 🛈 Praza de España 27–9, (982) 23 13 61. 🚍 Tue & Fri. 🏵 San Froilán (Oct 4–12).

CAPITAL of Galicia's largest province, Lugo was also an important center under the Romans. Attracted to the town by its thermal springs, they constructed what is now the finest surviving **Roman wall** in Spain. The wall, which encircles the city, is about 6 m (20 ft) thick and 10 m (33 ft) high with ten gateways. Six of these have stairways to the top of the wall, where there is a good view of the city.

Inside the wall, the old town is lively but dignified, with pretty squares. In the **Praza de Santo Domingo** is a black statue of a Roman eagle, built to commemorate Augustus' capture of Lugo from the Celts in the 1st century BC. The Romanesque **cathedral** is large and rambling, and modeled on that of Santiago. It features an elegant Baroque cloister and a chapel containing the alabaster statue of Nuestra Señora de los Ojos Grandes (Virgin of the Big Eyes). The **Museo Provincial** exhibits Celtic gold torques (collars), local Roman finds, a life-size model of a farm kitchen, modern Galician paintings, and a statue of a kneeling peasant woman holding a miniature priest.

ENVIRONS: The stone hamlet of **Santa Eulalia**, situated in lovely open country to the west, conceals a curious building excavated in 1924: a tiny temple, with lively, bright frescoes of birds and leaves. Though its exact purpose is unknown, it is thought to be an early Christian church and has been dated at around the 3rd century AD.

🏛 Museo Provincial
Plaza de la Soledad. 📞 (982) 24 21 12. ◯ daily. 🚻

O Cebreiro ㉑

Lugo. 🏘 16. 🚌 🛈 (982) 36 70 25. 🏵 Santo Milagro (Sep 8).

UP IN THE HILLS in the east of Galicia, close to the border with León, is one of the most unusual villages on the Road to Santiago. Its 9th-century church was supposedly the scene of a miracle in 1300 when the wine was turned into blood and the bread into flesh. Near the church there are several *pallozas*, round, thatched stone huts of a Celtic design. Some of these ancient dwellings, which often had annexes for livestock and grain, have been restored. One of them is now a folk museum.

🏛 Museo Etnográfico
O Cebreiro. ◯ Wed–Sun.

Painted gourd in O Cebreiro's museum

ASTURIAS AND CANTABRIA

ASTURIAS · CANTABRIA

THE SPECTACULAR PICOS DE EUROPA *massif sits astride the border between Asturias and Cantabria. In this rural region cottage crafts are kept alive in villages in remote mountain valleys and forested foothills. There are many ancient towns and churches, and pretty fishing ports on the coasts. Cave paintings, such as those at Altamira, were made by people living here over 10,000 years ago.*

Asturias is proud that it resisted invasion by the Moors. The Reconquest of Spain is held to have begun in 718 when a Moorish force was defeated by Christians at Covadonga in the Picos de Europa.

The Christian kingdom of Asturias was founded in the 8th century, and in the brilliant, brief artistic period that followed many churches were built around the capital, Oviedo. Some of these pre-Romanesque churches still stand. Today, Asturias is a province and a principality under the patronage of the heir to the Spanish throne. In the charming, unspoiled Asturian countryside cider is produced and a quaint dialect, *bable,* is spoken.

Cantabria centers on Santander, its capital, a port and an elegant resort. It is a mountainous province with a legacy of Romanesque churches in isolated spots. It also has well preserved towns and villages such as Santillana del Mar, Carmona, and Bárcena Mayor.

Mountains cover more than half of both provinces, so mountain sports are a major attraction. Expanses of deciduous forests remain in many parts, some sheltering Spain's last wild bears. Along the coasts are pretty fishing ports and resorts, such as Castro Urdiales, Ribadesella, and Comillas, and sandy coves for swimming. Both the coastal plains and uplands are ideal for quiet rural vacations.

Peaceful meadow around Lago de la Ercina in the Picos de Europa massif

◁ One of the pretty cobbled streets of Santillana del Mar, Cantabria

Exploring Asturias and Cantabria

THE MOST OBVIOUS ATTRACTION in this area is the group of mountains that straddles the two provinces – the Picos de Europa. These jagged peaks offer excellent rock climbing and rough hiking, and in certain parts can be explored by car or bicycle. These and several other nature preserves in the area are home to rare species of flora and fauna, including the capercaillie and brown bear. The coast offers many sandy coves for swimming. Santander and Oviedo are lively college towns with a rich cultural life. There are innumerable unspoiled villages to explore, especially the ancient town of Santillana del Mar. Some of the earliest examples of art exist in Cantabria, most notably at Altamira, where the cave drawings and engravings are among the oldest to be found in Europe.

Typical flower-covered balcony in the village of Bárcena Mayor

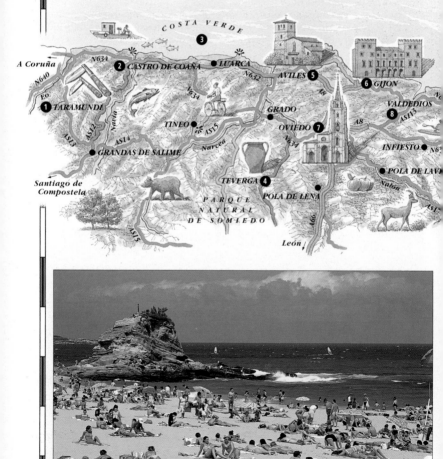

COSTA VERDE

A Coruña
N640
N634
Eo
1 TARAMUNDI
2 CASTRO DE COAÑA
LUARCA
3
N632
AVILÉS **5**
6 GIJON
A8
VALDEDIOS
8
Navia
N634
AS12
AS13
GRADO
ASI5
TINEO
Narcea
OVIEDO **7**
AS14
N634
INFIESTO
GRANDAS DE SALIME
N6?
AS15
Santiago de
Compostela
POLA DE LAV
Nalón
TEVERGA **4**
AS1?
POLA DE LENA
PARQUE
NATURAL
DE SOMIEDO
N60?
AS15
León

A view along the crowded beach of Playa del Camello, Santander

SIGHTS AT A GLANCE

Cantabrian dairy farmers loading hay onto their cart

RIBADESELLA
LLANES
NGAS DE ONIS   N634   COMILLAS ⓭
ROQUE NACIONAL   ⓰   ⓱ SANTILLANA DEL MAR
DE PICOS   ⓳ SANTANDER   ● SANTOÑA
DE EUROPA   CUEVAS DE ALTAMIRA   LAREDO ⓴
⓫   ⓲ PUENTE VIESGO   CASTRO-⓶①
⓬   ⓮ VALLE DE   URDIALES
POTES   CABUERNIGA   ● VILLACARRIEDO   A8
N621   ALTO CAMPOO ⓯   Donostia
(San Sebastián)
Bilbo (Bilbao)
REINOSA   Burgos
Embalse del Ebro

0 kilometers   25
0 miles   15

Palencia

SEE ALSO

• *Where to Stay* pp538–40

• *Restaurants and Bars* pp580–81

GETTING AROUND

The main road through the region is the N634, which is still narrow and hilly in places and often suffers from heavy truck traffic. Most other major roads follow the directions of the valleys and run north to south. Minor roads are generally good but can be slow and winding. The private FEVE railroad, which follows the coast from Bilbao to Ferrol in Galicia, is both useful and scenic. A twice-weekly Brittany Ferries service links Santander with Britain. Asturias' one international airport is near Avilés (serving Oviedo and Gijón). Parts of Cantabria are closer to Bilbao airport.

**Carved figure in the
Convento de Regina
Coeli, Santillana del Mar**

KEY

▬▬	Freeway
▬▬	Major road
▬▬	Minor road
▬▬	Scenic route
⌒	River
☼	Viewpoint

Craftsman making knife blades in a forge at Taramundi

Taramundi ●

Asturias. 🏘 *1,000.* 🚹 *Plaza del Poyo, (98) 564 67 01.* 🎊 *San José (Mar 19), Día del Turista (last Sun of Jul).*

SITUATED in the remote Los Oscos region, this small village houses a rural tourism center that organizes tours of the forests in four-wheel drive vehicles. Taramundi has a long tradition of wrought iron craftsmanship. Iron ore was first mined in the area by the Romans. There are approximately two dozen forges in and around the village, where craftsmen can still be seen making their traditional knives and penknives with attractively decorated wooden handles.

ENVIRONS: About 20 km (12 miles) to the east, at **San Martín de Oscos**, there is an 18th-century palace. At **Grandas de Salime**, 10 km (6 miles) farther southeast, the Museo Etnográfico has displays showing local crafts, traditional life, and farming.

🏛 **Museo Etnográfico**
Avenida del Ferreiro. 📞 *(98) 562 72 43.* ⏰ *Tue–Sun.* 🈺 ♿

Castro de Coaña ●

Southwest of Navia. 🚍 *from Navia.* 📞 *(98) 597 84 01.* ⏰ *Tue–Sun.* 🈺 ♿

ONE OF the most important Celtic settlements in Spain, Castro de Coaña was established in the Iron Age and later occupied by the Romans. Located on a hillside in the Navia valley are the well-preserved remains of its fortifications and the stone foundations of a number of circular dwellings, some of which stand head high. Inside the walls can be found several hollowed-out stones that may once have been used as funerary urns or for crushing corn.

The museum on the site displays many of the finds that have been unearthed at Castro de Coaña. Among the interesting remains on display are pottery, tools, and Roman coins.

Circular stone foundations of dwellings at Castro de Coaña

Costa Verde ●

Asturias. 🚇 *Avilés.* 🚌 *Oviedo, Gijón.* 🚹 *Plaza del Ayuntamiento, Castropol, (98) 563 50 01.*

THE APTLY NAMED "green coast" is a succession of attractive sandy coves and dramatic cliffs, punctuated by deep estuaries and numerous fishing villages. Inland, there are lush meadows, and pine and eucalyptus forests, backed by mountains. This stretch of coastline has been less spoiled than most in Spain; the resorts tend to be modest in size, like the hotels.

Two pretty fishing ports, **Castropol** and **Figueras**, stand by the eastern shore of the Ría de Ribadeo, forming the border with Galicia. To the east are other picturesque villages such as Tapia de Casariego and Ortiguera, in a small rocky cove. Following the coast, **Luarca** lies below a church and a quiet cemetery on a headland, and has a neat little harbor packed with red, blue, and white boats. The village of **Cudillero** is even more delightful – outdoor cafés and excellent seafood restaurants crowd the tiny plaza beside the port, all of which are squeezed into a narrow cove. Behind, white cottages are scattered over the steep hillsides.

Farther along the coast is the rocky headland of Cabo de Peñas where, in the fishing village of **Candas**, bullfights are sometimes held on the sand at low tide. East of Gijón, **Lastres** is impressively located below a cliff, and **Isla** has a broad open beach. Beyond Ribadesella is the

---

THE BROWN BEAR

The population of Spain's brown bears *(Ursus arctos)* has dwindled from about 1,000 at the beginning of the 20th century to less than 100. Hunting by man and the destruction of the bear's natural forest habitat have caused the decline. But now, protected by nature preserves such as Somiedo, where most of the bears in Asturias are found, together with new conservation laws, it is hoped this magnificent omnivore will thrive again.

One of the few remaining bears in the forests of Asturias

Church and cemetery overlooking the sea from the headland at Luarca

lively town of **Llanes**. Among the attractions of this old forti-fied seaport, with its dramatic mountain backdrop, are ruined ramparts and good beaches.

Teverga ❹

Asturias. 🚉 La Plaza. 🚶 C/ Dr Garcia Miranda, La Plaza, (98) 576 42 02.

THIS AREA, southwest of Oviedo, is rich in scenery, wildlife, and ancient churches. Near the southern end of the narrow Teverga gorge is **La Plaza**. Its 12th-century church, the Iglesia de San Pedro is a wonderful example of Romanesque architecture.

Just to the west of La Plaza is **Villanueva**, with its Roman-esque Iglesia de Santa María. To the east, the Quirós valley, with hamlets dotted around its hillsides, is picturesque.

ENVIRONS: The large **Parque Natural de Somiedo** strad-dles the mountains bordering León. Its high meadows and forests of chestnut, beech, and oak are a sanctuary for wolves, brown bears, and capercaillies, as well as a number of rare species of wildflowers.

The park has 18 glacial lakes and is peppered with herds-men's traditional thatched huts, known as *teitos (see p23)*.

Avilés ❺

Asturias. 🚉 88,000. 🚃 🚌 🚆 🚶 Plaza de España 1, (98) 512 21 00. 🗓 Mon. 🎉 San Agustín (Aug 28).

AVILÉS BECAME the capital of Asturias' steel industry dur-ing the 19th century and is still ringed by big factories. Even though it is sometimes criti-cized for having little to offer

the visitor, the town hides a medieval heart of some char-acter, especially around the Plaza de España. The **Iglesia de San Francisco** is decorat-ed with ancient frescoes and has a Renaissance cloister. The **Iglesia de San Nicolás** con-tains a fine 14th-century chapel and holds the tomb of the first governor of the US state of Florida. All around are arcaded streets with lively bars. The international airport outside Avilés serves all Asturias.

Gijón ❻

Asturias. 🚉 260,000. 🚌 🚃 🚶 Calle Marqués de San Esteban 1, (98) 534 60 46. 🗓 Sun. 🎉 San Antonio (Jun 13), La Virgen de Begoña (Aug 15).

THE PROVINCE'S largest city, this industrial port has been much rebuilt since the Civil War, when it was bombarded by the Nationalist navy. The city's most famous son is Gaspar Melchor de Jovellanos, an eminent 18th-century author, reformer, and diplomat.

Gijon's old town is on a small isthmus and headland. It centers on the arcaded Plaza Mayor and the 18th-century **Palacio de Revillagigedo**, a Neo-Renaissance folly with towers and battlements. The long sandy beach, near the city center, is popular in summer.

🏛 **Palacio de Revillagigedo**
Plaza del Marqués. 📞 (98) 534 69 21.
🕐 Tue–Sun. 🔴 public hols.

The pretty 12th-century Iglesia de San Pedro at La Plaza

Oviedo ❼

Asturias. 🏛 *180,000*. 🚌 🚇 ℹ
Plaza de la Catedral 6, (98) 521 33 85.
📧 *Fri & Sun.* 🎭 *San Mateo (Sep 21).*

OVIEDO, A COLLEGE town and
the cultural and commer-
cial capital of Asturias, stands
on a raised site on a fertile
plain. The nearby coal mines
have made it an important
industrial center since the 19th
century. It retains some of the
atmosphere of that time, as
described by Leopoldo Alas
("Clarín") in his great novel
La Regenta (see p31).

In and around Oviedo are
many Pre-Romanesque buildings. This style flourished in
the 8th–10th centuries and
was confined to a small area of
the kingdom of Asturias, one
of the few enclaves of Spain
not invaded by the Moors.

The nucleus of the medieval
city is the stately Plaza Alfonso
II, bordered by a number of
handsome old palaces. On
this square is situated the
Flamboyant Gothic *(see p20)*
cathedral with its high tower
and asymmetrical west façade.
Inside are tombs of Asturian
kings and a majestic 16th-
century gilded reredos. The
cathedral's supreme treasure is
the Cámara Santa, a restored
9th-century chapel containing
expressive statues of Christ
and the apostles. The chapel

**Cross of Angels in the treasury of
Oviedo cathedral**

also houses many sumptuous
works of 9th-century Asturian
art including two crosses and
a reliquary – all made of gold,
silver, and precious stones.

Also situated in the Plaza
Alfonso II is the **Iglesia de
San Tirso**. This church was
originally constructed in the
9th century, but subsequent
restorations have left the east
window as the only surviving
Pre-Romanesque feature.

Sited immediately behind
the cathedral is the **Museo
Arqueológico**, which is
housed in an old monastery
with fine cloisters. It contains
local prehistoric, Roman, and
Romanesque treasures.

The **Museo de Bellas Artes**,
in the handsome 18th-century
Velarde Palace, has a good
range of Asturian and Spanish
paintings, such as Carreño's
portrait of Carlos II *(see p66)*.

Two of the most magnificent
Pre-Romanesque churches are
on Mount Naranco, to the north.

SANTA MARÍA DEL NARANCO

This church, on Mount Naranco, was originally built as a
summer palace for Ramiro I in the 9th century. It is one of
the finest examples of Pre-Romanesque or Asturian
architecture, a style characterized by the
slender proportions of its buildings and
their original and graceful
ornamentation.

The Hall has an
unusually high
ceiling.

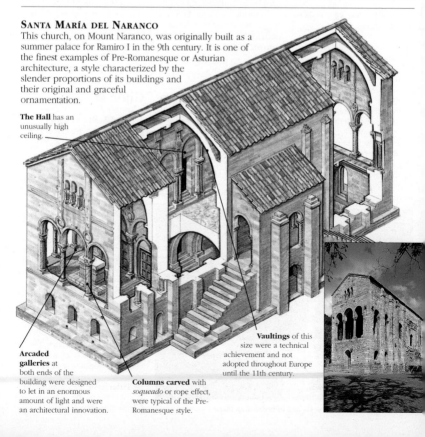

**Arcaded
galleries** at
both ends of the
building were designed
to let in an enormous
amount of light and were
an architectural innovation.

Columns carved with
soqueado or rope effect,
were typical of the Pre-
Romanesque style.

Vaultings of this
size were a technical
achievement and not
adopted throughout Europe
until the 11th century.

Chapel overlooking the sea at Ribadesella

Santa María del Naranco has a large barrel-vaulted hall on the main floor and arcaded galleries at either end. Some of the intricate reliefs on the door jambs of the nearby **San Miguel de Lillo** show acrobats and animal tamers in a circus.

The early 9th-century church of **San Julián de los Prados** stands on the road leading northeast out of Oviedo. It is the largest of all the Pre-Romanesque churches and is particularly noted for the frescoes that once covered the whole of its interior.

🏛 **Museo Arqueológico**
Calle San Vicente. 【 (98) 521 54 00.
◻ Tue–Sun.

🏛 **Museo de Bellas Artes**
Calle La Rua 8. 【 (98) 521 30 61.
◻ Tue–Sun.

Valdediós 🔞

Asturias. 🏠 150. 🛈 Villaviciosa, (98) 589 01 66.

Sᴇᴛ ᴀʟᴏɴᴇ in a field near this hamlet, the tiny 9th-century **Iglesia de San Salvador** is a jewel of Pre-Romanesque art. Its ceiling has vivid Asturian

frescoes, and by the portal are stone recesses where pilgrims slept. The church in the monastery next door is 13th-century Cistercian, with cloisters dating from the 15th century.

Environs: To the north, the graceful little resort town of **Villaviciosa** lies amid apple orchards and glorious hilly scenery, and has glass-fronted mansions on its narrow streets. In nearby **Amandi**, the hilltop Iglesia de San Juan has a 13th-century portal and delicate carvings and friezes.

Iglesia de San Salvador de Valdediós in its idyllic setting

Ribadesella 🟒

Asturias. 🏠 6,400. 🚊 🚌 🛈 Plaza Maria Cristina 1, (98) 586 02 55.
🛒 Wed. 🎉 Descent of the Río Sella (first Sat of Aug).

Tʜɪs ᴇɴᴄʜᴀɴᴛɪɴɢ little seaside town straddles a broad estuary. On one side is the lively old seaport full of tapas bars below a clifftop church. Across the estuary is a resort. A multicolored flotilla of kayaks arrives here from Arriondas (upstream) in an international regatta that is held every year on the first Saturday in August.

On the edge of town is the **Cueva de Tito Bustillo**. This cave is rich in stalactites but is best known for the many prehistoric drawings discovered in 1968, some dating from around 18,000 BC. These include red and black pictures of stags and horses. To protect the paintings only 400 visitors are allowed in per day, so in the tourist season it is advisable to arrive early. A museum on the site includes an artist's impressions of prehistoric living conditions.

⋔ **Cueva de Tito Bustillo**
Ribadesella. 【 (98) 510 55 00.
◻ Tue–Sun. ● Oct–Apr. 🖌

Cangas de Onís 🔟

Asturias. 🏠 3,300. 🚌 🛈 Avenida de Covadonga 21, (98) 584 80 43.
🛒 Sun. 🎉 Fiesta del Pastor (Jul 25).

Cᴀɴɢᴀs ᴅᴇ ᴏɴɪs, one of the gateways to the Picos de Europa *(see pp104–105)*, is where Pelayo, the 8th-century Visigothic nobleman and early hero of the Reconquest, set up his court. The town has a graceful Roman bridge and the 15th-century chapel of Santa Cruz with an engraved Bronze Age dolmen.

Environs: About 5 km (3 miles) east of Cangas de Onís is the **Cueva del Buxu**, which has rock-drawings and engravings which are over 10,000 years old. Arenas de Cabrales, some 25 km (16 miles) east of Cangas de Onís, is the home of Cabrales, a smooth but pungent cheese *(see p73)*.

Parque Nacional de los Picos de Europa ⓫

THESE BEAUTIFUL mountains were reputedly christened the "Peaks of Europe" by returning sailors for whom this was often the first sight of their homeland. The range, now Europe's biggest national park, straddles three regions – Asturias, Cantabria, and Castilla y León – and has diverse terrain. In some parts, deep winding gorges cut through craggy rocks while elsewhere verdant valleys support orchards and dairy farming. The celebrated creamy blue cheese Cabrales *(see p73)* is made here. The Picos offer rock climbing and upland hiking as well as a profusion of flora and fauna. Tourism is well organized, with good roads and many hotels and shelters.

Lefebvre's Ringlet

Covadonga
The Neo-Romanesque basilica, built between 1886 and 1901, stands on the site of Pelayo's historic victory.

Lago de la Ercina
Together with the nearby Lago Enol, this lake lies on a wild limestone plateau above Covadonga and below the peak of Peña Santa.

RIBADESELLA   Cangas de Onís   AS114

DESFILADERO DE LOS BEYOS

Sella

Covadonga

LAGO ENOL   LAGO DE LA ERCINA

N625

CA.P

Posada de Valdeón

Cares

Oseja de Sajambre   Puerto de Panderruedas   LE244

Puerto de Pontón   RIAÑO

Desfiladero de los Beyos
This deep, narrow gorge with its high limestone cliffs winds spectacularly for 10 km (6 miles) through the mountains. Tracing the route of the Río Sella below, it carries the main road from Cangas de Onís to Riaño.

KEY

▭	Major road
▭	Minor road
▪ ▪	Footpath
▬	National park boundary
ℹ	Tourist information
☀	Viewpoint

Desfiladero del Río Cares
The Cares River forms a deep gorge in the heart of the Picos. A dramatic footpath follows the gorge, passing through tunnels and across high bridges up to 1,000 m (3,280 ft) above the river.

Dramatic view of the mountains of the Picos de Europa

VISITORS' CHECKLIST

ℹ️ Cangas de Onís, (985) 84 86 14. 🚌 from Oviedo to Cangas de Onís. **Fuente Dé cable car** ⬜ Jul–Sep: 9am–8pm daily, Oct–Jun: 10am–6pm daily. ⬤ Dec.

PELAYO THE WARRIOR

A statue of this Visigothic nobleman who became king of Asturias guards the basilica at Covadonga. It was close to this site, in 722, that Pelayo and a band of men – though vastly outnumbered – are said to have defeated a Moorish army. The victory inspired Christians in the north of Spain to reconquer the peninsula (see pp48–51). The tomb of the warrior is in a cave that has since become a shrine, also containing a painted image of the Virgin.

Pelayo's statue

Naranjo de Bulnes, with its toothlike crest, is in the heart of the massif. At 2,519 m (8,264 ft) it is one of the highest summits in the Picos de Europa.

Map labels

Panes
SAN VICENTE DE LA BARQUERA
AS114
Arenas de Cabrales
AS264
Poncebos
DESFILADERO DE LA HERMIDA
Bulnes
Santa María de Lebeña
Deva
Parador de Fuente Dé
Monasterio de Santo Toribio de Liébana
Potes
de Randetrave
N621
RIAÑO
CA743
Puerto de San Glorio

0 kilometers   5

0 miles   5

Fuente Dé Cable Car
The 900-m (2950-ft) ascent from Fuente Dé takes visitors up to a wild rocky plateau pitted with craters. From here there is a spectacular panorama of the Picos' peaks and valleys.

Statue of the Virgin, San Vicente de la Barquera

ASTURIAS AND CANTABRIA'S FIESTAS

La Folía *(Apr)*, San Vicente de la Barquera (Cantabria). The statue of the Virgen de la Barquera is said to have arrived at San Vicente in a boat with no sails, oars, or crew. Once a year, it is put in a fishing boat decorated with flags and flowers, which sails at the head of a procession to bless the sea. Groups of young girls, called *picayos*, stand on the shore singing traditional songs of the region in honor of the Virgin. La Folía usually falls at the end of April, but its date is dependent on the local tides.
Fiesta del Pastor *(Jul 25)*, near Cangas de Onís (Asturias). Regional songs and dances are performed at the annual Shepherds' Festival beside the shores of Lake Enol in the Picos de Europa National Park.
Battle of the Flowers *(last Fri of Aug)*, Laredo (Cantabria). Floats adorned with flowers are paraded through this small resort. A flower-throwing free-for-all follows the procession.
Nuestra Señora de Covadonga *(Sep 8)*, Picos de Europa (Asturias). Huge crowds converge on the shrine of Covadonga *(see p104)* to pay homage to the patron saint of Asturias.

Potes ⑫

Cantabria. 🏔 *1,500.* ℹ️ *Calle de la Independencia, (942) 73 00 06.* 🚌 *Mon.* 🎭 *Santísima Cruz (Sep 15).*

A SMALL ANCIENT TOWN, with old-balconied houses lining the river, Potes is the main center of the eastern Picos de Europa. It is situated in the broad Valle de Liébana, whose fertile soil yields prime crops of walnuts, cherries, and grapes. A potent spirit called *orujo* is made in the town. The **Torre del Infantado**, in the main square, is a defensive tower built in the 15th century.

ENVIRONS: Between Potes and the coast runs a gorge, the **Desfiladero de la Hermida**. Halfway up it is **Santa María de Lebeña**, a 10th-century Mozarabic *(see p335)* church with horseshoe arches.
West of Potes is the monastery church of **Santo Toribio de Liébana**, one of the most revered spots in the Picos de Europa. Founded during the 7th century, it became known throughout Spain a century later when it received reputedly the largest fragment of the True Cross, kept in a silver reliquary. An 8th-century monk, St. Beatus of Liébana, wrote the *Commentary on the Apocalypse*, later much copied and illuminated. The restored Romanesque buildings of the monastery, which was rebuilt in the 13th century, are now occupied by Franciscan monks.

Comillas ⑬

Cantabria. 🏔 *2,500.* ℹ️ *Calle la Aldea 6, (942) 72 07 68.* 🚌 *Fri.* 🎭 *El Cristo (Jul 16).*

THIS PRETTY RESORT is known for its unusual buildings by Catalan Modernista architects *(see pp136–7)*. Antonio López y López, a shipping tycoon who became the first Marquis of Comillas, commissioned Joan Martorell to design the **Palacio Sobrellano** (1881), an enormous Neo-Gothic edifice.

Stone bridge and houses in the ancient town of Potes

Surviving Classical columns among the ruins of the Roman town of Juliobriga, near Reinosa

Comilla's best-known monument, is Antoni Gaudí's *(see p160)* **El Capricho**, now a restaurant *(see p580)*. It was designed for a rich businessman from 1883–9 by Gaudí and is a Mudéjar-inspired fantasy with a minaret-like tower covered in green and yellow tiles. Another of the town's Modernista buildings is the **Universidad Pontificia**, which overlooks the sea from a hilltop. It was designed by Joan Martorell to plans by Domènech i Montaner *(see p136)*.

Wall tile on the façade of El Capricho

ENVIRONS: The fishing port of **San Vicente de la Barquera** has arcaded streets, ramparts and the Gothic Romanesque church of Nuestra Señora de los Ángeles.

Valle de Cabuérniga ⓮

Cantabria. 🚍 *Bárcena Mayor*. 🛈 *Ayuntamiento, Ruente, (942) 70 91 04*.

TWO EXCEPTIONALLY picturesque towns, notable for their superb examples of rural architecture, draw visitors to the Cabuérniga Valley. A good road takes you to the once-remote **Bárcena Mayor**. Its cobbled streets are illuminated with old lamps and filled with boutiques and restaurants serving a range of regional dishes. The pretty houses have flower-

covered balconies, and cattle barns on the ground floor.

Carmona is an old, unspoiled village approximately 20 km (12 miles) to the northwest of Bárcena Mayor. Its solid stone houses, with tiled roofs and wooden balconies, are typically Cantabrian *(see p22)*. Woodcarving, the traditional craft of the region, is still practiced in this village, where men work outside their houses on a variety of artifacts including bowls, fiddles, *albarcas* (clogs), and chairs. The 13th-century Palacio de los Mier, a manor house in the center of the village, has been restored and is now a hotel.

The extensive, wild beech woods near **Saja** have been designated a nature preserve.

Traditional balconied houses in Bárcena Mayor

Alto Campoo ⓯

Cantabria. 🏔 *1,900*. 🚍 🚠 🕎 *Mon.* 🎿 *Nuestra Señora de las Nieves (Aug 5), San Roque (Aug 16)*.

SITED HIGH in the Cantabrian mountains, this winter resort lies below the Pico de Tres Mares (2,175 m/7,135 ft), the "Peak of the Three Seas," so called because the rivers rising near it flow into the Mediterranean, the Atlantic and the Bay of Biscay. The Río Ebro, one of Spain's longest rivers, rises in this area, and its source, at Fontibre, is a lovely spot. A road and a chair lift reach the summit of Tres Mares for a breathtaking panorama of the Picos de Europa and other mountain chains. The resort is small, with ten trails totaling 17 km (10 miles) in length, and has few facilities for apres-ski.

ENVIRONS: Reinosa, some 26 km (16 miles) to the east of Alto Campoo, is a handsome market town with old stone houses. Further southeast is Retortillo, a hamlet where the remains of **Juliobriga**, a town built by the Romans as a bastion against the wild tribes of Cantabria, can be seen.

The main road south out of Reinosa leads to **Cervatos**, where the former collegiate church has erotic carvings on its façade just below the roof. This novel device was meant as a warning to the villagers against pleasures of the flesh.

At **Arroyuelo** and **Cadalso**, to the southeast, are two churches built into rock faces in the 9th and 10th centuries.

One of the many paintings of bison at Altamira

Cuevas de Altamira ⓰

Cantabria. **C** (942) 81 80 05 **🚌**
Santillana del Mar. **Caves** ⬜ *write in advance for permission.* **Museum** ⬜
Tue–Sun. ⬤ *Dec 24, 25, 31 & Jan 1.*

THESE CAVES contain some of the world's finest examples of prehistoric art. The earliest of these engravings and drawings, which were discovered in 1869, date back to around 18,000 BC *(see p44)*. The caves' famous bison, dated around 13,000 BC, are painted in bold colors using the rock contours to emphasize shape and movement. Admission to the caves is restricted to prevent deterioration of the paintings. You should apply for permission months in advance. Displays in a museum on the site explain the significance of the paintings.

Santillana del Mar ⓱

Cantabria. **🏃** 4,000. **🚌 ℹ** *Plaza Mayor, (942) 81 80 75.* **📅** *Santa Juliana (Jun 28), San Roque (Aug 16).*

SET JUST INLAND, belying its name, this town is one of the prettiest in Spain. Its ensemble of 15th- to 17th-century golden stone houses survives largely intact despite the many tourists and souvenir shops.

The town grew up around a monastery, which was an important pilgrimage center, the Romanesque **La Colegiata**. The church houses the tomb of the local early-medieval martyr St. Juliana, and contains a 17th-century painted reredos and a carved south door. In its lovely cloisters, vivid biblical scenes have been sculpted on the capitals. On the town's two main cobbled streets there are houses built by local noblemen. These have either fine wooden galleries or iron balconies, and coats of arms inlaid into their stone façades. In the past, farmers used the open ground floors as barns for stabling their cattle.

Carved figure of Christ in the Convento de Regina Coeli

In the enchanting **Plaza Mayor**, in the center of town, is a mansion-turned-parador

(see p540). The **Museo Diocesano** is housed in the restored Convento de Regina Coeli, east of the town center, and has a collection of painted carvings of religious figures.

🏛 Museo Diocesano
Calle Le Dorat. **C** *(942) 81 80 04.*
⬜ *Thu–Tue.* 🎫

Puente Viesgo ⓲

Cantabria. **🏃** 2,500. **🚌 ℹ** *Calle Manuel Pérez Maso, (942) 59 81 05.* **📅** *San Miguel (Sep 28–9).*

THE SPA of Puente Viesgo is best known for the caves – especially **Cueva de El Castillo** – dotted around the limestone hills above the town, that were decorated by prehistoric man. It is thought the late Palaeolithic cave dwellers used the deep interior as a sanctuary. In these caves they left drawings of horses, bison, and other animals, and some 50 hand prints – almost always the left hand. The ocher and other colors used to create the images were extracted from minerals in the cave.

ENVIRONS: The lush Pas valley, to the southeast, is home to transhumant dairy farmers, the Pasiegos. In the main town of **Vega de Pas**, you can buy two Pasiego specialties – *sobaos*, or sponge cakes *(see p73)*, and *quesadas*, a sweet that is made from milk, butter, and eggs. In **Villacarriedo** there is a handsome 18th-century mansion, with two Baroque façades of carved stone hiding a medieval tower.

⋔ Cueva de El Castillo
Puente Viesgo. **C** *(942) 59 84 25.*
⬤ *Mon.*

Main façade of La Colegiata in Santillana del Mar

The Palacio de la Magdalena in El Sardinero

Santander ⑲

Cantabria. 🕭 200,000. ✈ 🚉 🚌 ⛴ ℹ Estación Marítima, (942) 31 07 08. 🗓 Mon & Thu. 🎏 Santiago (Jul 25), La Virgen la Bien Aparecida (Sep 15).

Cantabria's capital, a busy port, enjoys a splendid site near the mouth of a deep bay. The town center is modern – after being ravaged by fire in 1941 it was completely reconstructed. The **cathedral** was rebuilt in Gothic style after the 1941 fire, but retains its 12th-century crypt. Worth visiting is the **Museo de Bellas Artes**, which houses works by Goya, Zurbarán, and Mengs, as well as regional artists. The town's **Museo de Prehistoria y Arqueología** displays finds from caves in Cantabria, such as Neolithic axe heads, and Roman coins, figurines, and pottery. The **Museo Marítimo** has rare whale skeletons and 350 species of local fish.

The town extends along the coast around the Península de la Magdalena, a headland on which there is a park, a zoo, and the **Palacio de la Magdalena** – a summer palace built for Alfonso XIII in 1912, reflecting the resort's popularity at the time with the Royal Family.

The seaside suburb of **El Sardinero**, north of the headland, is a smart resort with a long graceful beach, backed by gardens, elegant cafés, and a majestic white casino. A cultured, self-confident place, in July and August El Sardinero plays host to a major theater and music festival.

🏛 **Museo de Bellas Artes**
Calle Rubio 5. ℹ (942) 23 94 85. 🗓 Mon–Sat.

🏛 **Museo de Prehistoria y Arqueología**
Calle Casimiro Saenz 4. ℹ (942) 20 71 05. 🗓 Tue–Sun.

🏛 **Museo Marítimo**
Promontorio de San Martín. ℹ (942) 27 49 62. 🗓 Tue–Sun.

Laredo ⑳

Cantabria. 🕭 14,000. 🚌 ℹ Calle Lopez Seña, (942) 61 10 96. 🎏 Batalla de Flores (last Fri of Aug), San Martín (Nov 11).

The excellent long, sandy beach of this small town has made it one of Cantabria's most popular beach resorts. The old part of the town is attractive: narrow streets with balconied houses lead up to the 13th-century **Iglesia de la Asunción**, with its Flemish altar and enormous bronze lecterns. One of the highlights of the year in Laredo is the colorful fiesta of the Battle of the Flowers (see p106).

Castro Urdiales ㉑

Cantabria. 🕭 15,500. 🚌 ℹ Plaza del Ayuntamiento, (942) 86 19 97. 🗓 Thu. 🎏 Coso Blanco (Jun 27), Santa Ana (Jul 26).

Castro Urdiales, a busy fishing town and popular vacation resort, is built around a picturesque natural harbor full of boats. Above the port, on a high promontory, stands the pinkish Gothic **Iglesia de Santa María**, as big as a cathedral. Beside it there is a half-ruined castle built by the Knights Templar, which has been converted into a lighthouse. Handsome glass-fronted houses, or *galerías*, line the elegant promenade. The small town beach often becomes crowded, but there are bigger ones to the west, such as the Playa de Ostende.

Environs: Near the village of **Ramales de la Victoria**, 20 km (12 miles) south, are prehistoric caves containing etchings and engravings, reached by a very steep mountain road.

Small boats moored in the harbor at Castro Urdiales

THE BASQUE COUNTRY, NAVARRA, AND LA RIOJA

VIZCAYA · GUIPÚZCOA · ÁLAVA · LA RIOJA · NAVARRA

GREEN HILLS MEET ATLANTIC BEACHES *in the Basque Country, land of an ancient people of mysterious origin. Navarra, also partly Basque, was a powerful medieval kingdom. The beautiful western Pyrenees form part of its charming countryside. The vineyards of La Rioja, to the south, produce many of Spain's finest wines.*

The Basques are a race apart – they will not let you forget that theirs is a culture different from any in Spain. Although the Basque regional government enjoys considerable autonomy, there is a strong separatist movement seeking to sever links with the government in Madrid.

The Basque Country (Euskadi is the Basque name) is an important industrial region. The Basques are great deep-sea fishermen, and fish has a major role in their imaginative cuisine, regarded by many as the best in Spain.

Unrelated to any other tongue, the Basque language, *Euskera,* is widely used on signs, and several towns have two names; the fashionable resort of San Sebastián, for example, is known to locals as Donostia. *Euskera* is also spoken in parts of Navarra, which is counted as part of the wider (unofficial) Basque Country. Many of its finest sights – the towns of Olite and Estella, and the monastery of Leyre – date from the Middle Ages, when Navarra was a kingdom straddling the Pyrenees. Pamplona, its capital, is best known for its daredevil bull-running fiesta, which is held in July.

As well as its vineyards and wineries, La Rioja is a region of market gardens. Among its many historic sights are the cathedral of Santo Domingo de la Calzada and the monasteries of San Millán de la Cogolla and Yuso.

Basque farmhouse near Gernika-Lumo in the Basque Country

◁ **A street in the village of Roncal, in the foothills of the Navarrese Pyrenees**

Exploring the Basque Country, Navarra, and La Rioja

THESE GREEN, HILLY REGIONS have diverse attractions. The Pyrenees in Navarra offer skiing in winter and climbing, caving, and canoeing the rest of the year. The cliffs of the Basque Country are broken by rocky coves, rias, and wide bays with beaches of fine yellow sand, interspersed with fishing villages. Inland, small roads wind through wooded hills, valleys, and gorges past lonely castles and isolated homesteads. In La Rioja, to the south, they cross vineyards, passing villages and towns clustered around venerable churches and monasteries.

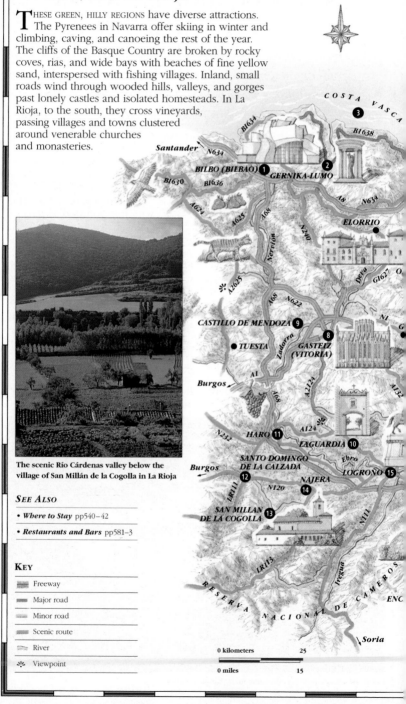

The scenic Río Cárdenas valley below the village of San Millán de la Cogolla in La Rioja

SEE ALSO

- **Where to Stay** pp540–42

- **Restaurants and Bars** pp581–3

KEY

▬▬	Freeway
▬▬	Major road
▬▬	Minor road
▬▬	Scenic route
▭▭	River
☀	Viewpoint

0 kilometers   25

0 miles   15

SIGHTS AT A GLANCE

GETTING AROUND

Highways give access to much of the area. The main road in the north, the A8, runs between Irún and Bilbao. The A68 runs southward from Bilbao via Haro and follows the Ebro Valley, the area's east–west communications corridor, past Tudela. Motorway spurs extend to Vitoria and Pamplona. The railroad network connects the cities and the larger towns, and most towns are served by bus. Bilbao has an international airport.

The fashionable Playa de Ondarreta, one of San Sebastián's three beaches

Buildings overlooking the Río Nervión in Bilbao

Bilbao ①

Vizcaya. 375,000. ✈ 🚊 🚌 ⛴
ℹ Plaza de Arriaga 1, (94) 416 02 88.
🎉 Santiago (Jul 25), San Ignacio
(Jul 31), La Asunción (Aug 15),
Semana Grande (mid-Aug).

BILBAO (BILBO) is the center of Basque industry, Spain's leading commercial port, and the largest Basque city. It is surrounded by high, bare hills. Its suburbs spread 16 km (10 miles) along the Río Nervión (Nerbioi) to its estuary. The river between Las Arenas and the fishing port of Portugalete is crossed via the **Puente Colgante**. This iron transporter bridge, built in 1893, has a suspended cabin for cars and passengers. On the east bank of the estuary is Santurtzi (Santurce), from which ferries sail to the UK (see p628).

Bilbao has flourished as an industrial city since the mid-19th century, when iron ore began to be extracted from deposits northwest of the city. Soon, steelworks and chemical factories became a major part of the local landscape.

The city is not beautiful, but it is prosperous, and its once heavy pollution is now much reduced. An urban development plan includes a new metro system and a European branch of the Guggenheim Museum, a gallery of modern art. The airport and the harbor are soon to be extended.

The *casco viejo* (old town) by the river, built in the 14th century, is the most attractive district. Here, amid alleys lively with tapas bars, is the arcaded Plaza Nueva and the **Catedral Basílica de Santiago**. The **Museo Arqueológico, Etnográfico, e Histórico Vasco** displays Basque art, folk artifacts, and photographs and *tableaux vivants* of Basque life. In the cloister is the Idol of Mikeldi, an animal-like carving from the 3rd–2nd century BC.

In the newer town is the large **Museo de Bellas Artes** (Museum of Fine Art), one of Spain's best art museums. It displays art ranging from 12th-century Catalan masterpieces to works by modern artists of international fame, including Vasarely, Kokoschka, Bacon, Delaunay, and Léger. Spanish art is represented, among others, by Murillo, Zurbarán, El Greco, three Goyas, and Ribera's fine *St. Sebastian*. There are also several rooms of paintings by Basque artists.

West of the city, a road and a funicular railway ascend to the village of La Reineta, from which there is a wide urban panorama across the old dockyards. On the estuary's east bank is Algorta, a beach resort with vacation cottages.

🏛 **Museo Arqueológico, Etnográfico e Histórico Vasco**
Calle Cruz 4. [(94) 415 54 23.
○ Tue–Sun. ● public hols. ♿
🏛 **Museo de Bellas Artes**
Plaza del Museo 2. [(94) 441
01 54. ○ Tue–Sun. ● public hols.

The historic Oak of Gernika, the symbol of Basque nationalism

Gernika-Lumo ②

Vizcaya. 15,400. 🚌 🚉
ℹ Arte Calle 8, (94) 625 58 92.
🗓 Mon. 🎉 Aniversario del
Bombardeo de Guernica (Apr 26).

THIS LITTLE TOWN is of great symbolic significance to the Basques. For centuries, Basque leaders met in democratic assembly under an oak on a hillside here. On April 26, 1937, Gernika-Lumo (Guernica) was the target of the world's first saturation bombing raid, carried out by Nazi aircraft at the request of General Franco. Picasso's powerful painting (see pp62–3) of this outrage can be seen in Madrid (see p289).

The town has since been rebuilt and is rather dull. But in a garden, inside a pavilion and closely guarded, is the 300-year-old petrified trunk of the oak tree, the *Gernikako Arbola*, or Oak of Gernika, symbol of the ancient roots of the Basque people. A younger oak, its successor, is planted beside it. The Basque people make visits to this ancient tree as if on a pilgrimage.

Zuloaga's *Condesa Mathieu de Noailles* (1913), Bilbao Museum of Fine Art

Basque fishermen depicted in the stained-glass ceiling of the Casa de Juntas in Gernika-Lumo

The **Casa de Juntas**, nearby, is a former chapel where the parliament of the province of Vizcaya has convened since 1979, when the Basque provinces regained their autonomy. In one room a stained-glass ceiling depicts the Oak of Gernika with Basque citizens debating their rights.

The Europa Park, next door, has peace sculptures by Henry Moore and Eduardo Chillida.

ENVIRONS: Five km (3 miles) northeast of Gernika, near Kortézubi (Cortézubi), are the **Cuevas de Santimamiñe**. On the walls of a small chamber are drawings in charcoal of bison and other animals made by Cro-Magnon cave dwellers around 11,000 BC. They were discovered in 1917. A guide shows visitors these ancient drawings and then leads them down the Long Gallery, an underground passage full of oddly shaped stalagmites and stalactites, some of them shot through with brilliant colors. Santimamiñe is one of several huge cave complexes in this mountain area, but most are closed to the public.

🏛 **Casa de Juntas**
C/ Karmelo Etxegarai. 【 (94) 625 11 38. ◯ daily. ◯ Aug 15 & Dec 25. ♿
⋒ **Cuevas de Santimamiñe**
Barrio Basondo, Kortézubi. 【 (94) 625 29 75. ◯ Mon–Fri. ◯ public hols.

Costa Vasca ❸

Vizcaya & Guipúzcoa. ▤ Bilbao.
▤ Bilbao. ℹ Getxo, (94) 491 08 00.

THE BASQUE COUNTRY'S 176 km (110 miles) of coastline is heavily indented: rugged cliffs alternate with inlets and coves, the whole backed by wooded hills. Some of the fishing villages are overdeveloped, but the scenery inland is attractive.

There are good beaches north of Algorta (near Bilbao). Plentzia is a pleasant estuary town with a marina. Eastward on the coast is Bakio, a large fishing village also known for its beaches. Beyond it the BI3101, a dramatic cliffside road, winds high above the sea past the tiny island hermitage,

Anglers on the quayside at Lekeitio, a port on the Costa Vasca

San Juan de Gaztelugatxe, and Matxitxaco, a headland light-house. It passes Bermeo, a port with a fishery museum, the **Museo del Pescador**, and Mundaka, a small surfing resort. On the serene Ría de Guernica there are two sandy beaches, Laida and Laga.

Lekeitio, a fishing port to the east, has a pretty shore-line. Old Basque houses line the seafront below the 15th-century church of Santa María. One long beach, good for swimming, sweeps around the village of **Saturrarán** and the old port of **Ondarroa**. The Lekeitio–Ondarroa road is pleasantly planted with pines.

Zumaia is a beach resort with an old quarter. In the **Museo de Ignacio Zuloaga**, the former home of the well-known Basque painter who lived from 1870–1945, color-ful studies of Basque rural and maritime life are on display. **Getaria**, along the coast, is a trawler port with lively cafés and the 14th-century Iglesia de San Salvador. **Zarautz**, once a fashionable resort, has sizeable beaches and elegant mansions.

🏛 **Museo del Pescador**
Plaza Torrontero 1. 【 (94) 688 11 71. ◯ Tue–Sun. ◯ public hols. ♿
🏛 **Museo de Ignacio Zuloaga**
Casa Santiago Zumaya, Carretera de San Sebastián. 【 (94) 386 10 15.
◯ Jan–Sep: Wed–Sun.

San Sebastián's Playa de Ondarreta, with its view across the bay

San Sebastián ❹

Guipúzcoa. 🏙 180,000. 🚉 🚌 🛈
Paseo de los Fueros 1, (94) 342 62 82.
🚢 *Sun.* 🎭 *San Sebastián (Jan 20),
Semana Grande (around Aug 15 for
one week), Regatta (early Sep).*

GLORIOUSLY SITUATED on a neat, shell-shaped bay, San Sebastián (Donostia) is the most elegant and fashionable Spanish seaside resort. At either end of the bay is a tower-topped hill – Monte Urgull in the east and Monte Igueldo in the west. Between the two, in the mouth of the bay, lies a small island, the Isla de Santa Clara.

San Sebastián became a stylish resort in the late 19th century and has been popular with the Spanish aristocracy ever since, although it no longer has quite the allure it held in decades past. It still has many fashionable shops and one of Spain's grandest luxury hotels, the María Cristina *(see p542)*, but San Sebastián is now primarily a family resort.

The city is renowned for its great summer arts festivals. A jazz festival is held in July, a classical music festival in late August, and the San Sebastián International Film Festival in September. The Semana Grande in August focuses on traditional Basque folk culture.

Cuisine also plays a huge part in local life: many Basque men in San Sebastián belong to gastronomic clubs where they gather to cook, eat, drink, and talk. Even these days, women are seldom invited to such gatherings.

The Old Town
San Sebastián's fascinating old town, called the Parte Vieja, is wedged between the bay and the Río Urumea. Although few of its buildings predate 1813, when it was rebuilt after a devastating fire, it still has plenty of character. The alleys of the old town, packed with restaurants and tapas bars, are intensely animated at night. In the large local fish market, stalls piled high with delicacies such as *kokotxa* (cheek of hake) testify to the key role of fish in the life of the town.

The heart of the old town is the **Plaza de la Constitución**, a handsome, arcaded square with blue and orange shutters. The numbers on the balconies date from when the square was used as a bullring – organizers sold a ticket for each numbered place. The church of **Santa María del Coro**, nearby, has a rich Baroque portal.

Monte Urgull rises behind the old town. It is well worth climbing up to the top for a panorama of the coast and the city encircled by knobbly hills. On the summit are a statue of Christ and the ruined **Castillo de Santa Cruz de la Mota**, with old cannons.

Beaches
San Sebastián's two principal beaches follow the bay around to **Monte Igueldo**. The **Playa de Ondarreta** is the more fashionable of the two while the **Playa de la Concha** is the larger. They are separated by a rocky outcrop. Between them is the **Palacio Miramar**, built in 1889 by the Basque architect, José Goicoa, to designs by Selden Wornum, a British architect. The palace, built for Queen María Cristina as a summer residence, helped to establish San Sebastián as an aristocratic resort. The gardens are open to the public, and events are occasionally held in the palace.

At the water's edge near the Playa de Ondarreta is a striking modern iron sculpture *The Comb of the Winds* by Eduardo Chillida. A road and a funicular railroad lead to the top of Monte Igueldo, where there is an amusement park.

To the east of the Playa de la Concha is another beach, the **Playa de la Zurriola**, which is overlooked by the resort's third hill, **Monte Ulía**.

The Comb of the Winds by Eduardo Chillida

◁ The russet and green hills of Guipúzcoa province in the Basque Country, south of the Río Oyarzun

Josep Maria Sert's murals of Basque life in the Museo de San Telmo

🏛 Museo de San Telmo

Plaza Zuloaga. 📞 (94) 342 49 70.
🕐 Tue–Sun. ♿

This is a large museum in a 16th-century monastery below Monte Urgull. In the cloister is a collection of Basque tombstones: rounded, inscribed funerary columns dating from the 15th to the 17th centuries.

The museum also contains displays of headdresses worn by women of the region, furniture, tools, and other artifacts, and paintings by several local Basque artists. Among them are vivid 19th-century works by Antonio Ortiz Echagüe and modern paintings by Ignacio Zuloaga. There are also portraits by Vicente López and masterpieces by El Greco and other classic Spanish artists. In the chapel are 16 murals in sepia and gold by the Catalan artist Josep Maria Sert depicting Basque legends, culture, and the region's seafaring life.

🚢 Palacio del Mar

Po de Muelle 34. 📞 (94) 342 19 05.
🕐 Tue–Sun. ⬛ Jan 1 & Dec 25. 📷

A local architect, Juan Carlos Guerra, incorporated traditional Basque architectural styles in the design of this building. It opened in 1828 as the headquarters of the Guipúzcoa Oceanographic Society. The Aquarium features a unique collection of marine life from the local coastal waters. The museum contains exhibits of Basque maritime life, ranging from shipbuilding to profiles of Basque sailors.

ENVIRONS: Approximately 5 km (3 miles) east of San Sebastián is **Pasaia Donibane** (Pasajes de San Juan), a picturesque fishing village consisting of a jumble of houses with pretty painted balconies and a cobbled main street which has some good fish restaurants.

The waterfront of the tiny fishing village of Pasaia Donibane

SAN SEBASTIÁN FILM FESTIVAL

This festival, founded in 1953, is one of the five leading European annual film festivals. It is held in late September, drawing more than 100,000 spectators. The special Donostia Prize is awarded as a tribute to the career of a star or director: it went to Lana Turner in 1994, and Susan Sarandon in 1995. Other visitors have included Quentin Tarantino, Greta Scacchi, and William Hurt. Prizes also go to individual new films. An early winner was Hitchcock's *Vertigo*. The festival is strongly international, representing film from many countries.

Lauren Bacall receiving an award

Old balconied houses in the upper town, Hondarribia

Hondarribia ❺

Guipúzcoa. 🏘 14,000. 🛈 Calle Javier Ugarte 6, (94) 364 54 58.
🎉 La Kutxa Entrega (Jul 25), Alarde (Sep 6–8).

H ONDARRIBIA (Fuenterrabia), the historic town at the mouth of the Río Bidasoa, was attacked by the French over many centuries. The upper town is protected by 15th-century walls and entered via their original gateway, the handsome **Puerta de Santa María**. They enclose alleys of old houses with carved eaves, balconies, and coats of arms.

The streets cluster around the church of **Santa María de la Asunción**, with its massive buttresses, tall Baroque tower, and, inside, a gold reredos. At the town's highest point is the **castle**, which was founded in the 10th century and is now a parador *(see p541)*.

Hondarribia is a fishing port, and there are seafront cafés in La Marina, the lively fishermen's quarter. It is also a seaside resort, with beaches stretching to the north.

ENVIRONS: A hill road climbs westward to the shrine of the Virgin of Guadalupe. Further along this road are panoramic views of the coast and the mountains. From the **Ermita de San Marcial**, which stands on a hill 9 km (6 miles) to the south, there are views of the Bidasoa plain straddling the border – the French towns are neatly white, the Spanish ones are grayer.

The Renaissance façade of the former Basque university in Oñati

Santuario de Loiola ❻

Loiola (Guipúzcoa). 【 (94) 381 65 08. 🚌 🅿 daily.

SAINT IGNATIUS OF LOYOLA (San Ignacio de Loyola), founder of the Jesuits, was born in the 1490s in the Santa Casa (holy house), a stone manor near Azpeitia. In the 17th century it was enclosed by the Basílica de San Ignacio, and the rooms in which the aristocratic Loyola family lived were converted into chapels. The Chapel of the Conversion is the room in which Ignatius, as a young soldier, recovered from a war injury and had a profound religious experience.

A diorama depicts episodes in the saint's life: dedicating his life to Christ at the Monastery of Montserrat *(see pp208–209)*; writing his *Spiritual Exercises* in a cave at Manresa; his imprisonment by the Inquisition; and his pilgrimage to the Holy Land. The basilica, built from 1681–1738, has a Churrigueresque dome and a circular nave, in which almost every surface is richly carved.

Oñati ❼

Guipúzcoa. 🏠 10,000. 🚌 🚻 Plaza de los Fueros 4, (94) 378 34 53. 🚌 Sat. 🎭 Corpus Christi (May/Jun), San Miguel (Sep 29).

THE HISTORIC TOWN of Oñati (Oñate) in the Udana Valley has a distinguished past. In the First Carlist War, 1833–9 *(see p59)*, it was a seat of the court of Don Carlos, brother of King Fernando VII and pretender to the throne. Its former **university**, built in about 1540, was for centuries the only one in the Basque Country. It has a Renaissance façade decorated with statues of saints, and an elegant patio.

In the Plaza de los Fueros is the **Iglesia de San Miguel**, a Gothic church with a stone cloister in Plateresque *(see p21)* style. It contains the tomb of Bishop Zuázola of Ávila, the founder of the university. Opposite is the Baroque **town hall** *(ayuntamiento)*.

ENVIRONS: A mountain road ascends to the **Santuario de Arantzazu**, overshadowed by the high peak of Aitzgorri. In 1469 a shepherd reported seeing a vision of the Virgin here. The church, built in the 1950s, has a high bell tower and a huge wooden altarpiece.

🏛 Universidad de Sancti Spiritus
Avenida de la Universidad. 【 (94) 378 34 53. ☐ Mon–Fri for guided tours (phone in advance). 🚫

The imposing Santuario de Loiola, with its Churrigueresque cupola

---

THE FOUNDING OF THE JESUIT ORDER

The Society of Jesus was founded in Rome in 1539 by Saint Ignatius and a group of priests who were dedicated to helping the poor. Pope Paul III soon approved the order's establishment, with Ignatius as Superior General. The order, which grew wealthy, vowed military obedience to the Pope and became his most powerful weapon against the Reformation. Today, there are approximately 24,000 Jesuits working, mainly in education, in 110 countries.

Saint Ignatius of Loyola

Basque Culture

THE BASQUES may be Europe's oldest race. Anthropologists think they could be descended from Cro-Magnon people, who lived in the Pyrenees 40,000 years ago. The dolmens and carved stones of their ancestors are evidence of the Basques' pagan roots.

Long isolated in their mountain valleys, the Basques preserved their unique language, myths, and art for millennia, almost untouched by other influences.

Many families still live in the isolated, chalet-style stone *caseríos*, or farmhouses, built by their forebears. Their music and high-bounding dances are unlike those of any other culture, and their cuisine is varied and imaginative.

The *fueros* or ancient Basque laws and rights were suppressed under General Franco, but since the arrival of democracy in 1975 the Basques have had their own parliament and police force, having won great autonomy over their own affairs.

Basque policeman

THE BASQUE REGION

☐ *Areas of Basque culture*

The national identity *is symbolized by the region's flag:* La Ikurriña. *The white cross symbolizes Christianity. The green St. Andrew's Cross commemorates a battle won on his feast day.*

Bertsolaris *are bards. They improvise witty, sometimes humorous, songs whose verses relate current events or legends. Bertsolaris sing, unaccompanied, to gatherings in public places such as bars and squares, often in competition. This oral tradition has preserved Basque folklore, legends, and history. No texts were written in* Euskera *(Basque) until the 16th century.*

The Basque economy *has always relied on fishing and associated industries, such as shipbuilding and agriculture. In recent history, heavy industries have made this region prosperous.*

Traditional sports *are highly respected in Basque culture. In pelota (frontón), teams hit a ball at a wall then catch it with a wicker scoop or their hands. Sports involving strength, such as log-splitting and weightlifting, are the most popular.*

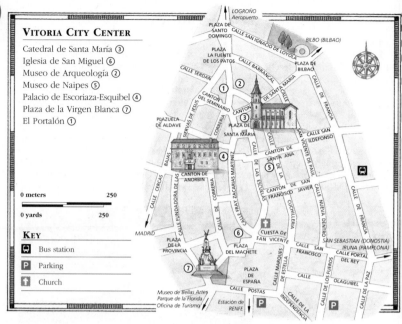

VITORIA CITY CENTER

Catedral de Santa María ③
Iglesia de San Miguel ⑥
Museo de Arqueología ②
Museo de Naipes ⑤
Palacio de Escoriaza-Esquibel ④
Plaza de la Virgen Blanca ⑦
El Portalón ①

0 meters 250
0 yards 250

KEY

🚌 Bus station

🅿 Parking

⛪ Church

Vitoria ❽

Álava. 🏙 *210,000.* ✈ 🚌 🚆
ℹ *Parque de la Florida, (94) 513 13
21.* 🗓 *Thu.* 🎉 *Romería de San
Prudencio (Apr 28), Fiestas de la Virgen
Blanca (Aug 4–9), Romería de Olárizu
(second Mon of Sep).*

VITORIA (GASTEIZ), the seat
of the Basque government,
was founded on a hill – the
province's highest point and
the site of an ancient Basque
town, Gasteiz. Vitoria's oldest
part, El Campo Suso, was rebuilt after a victory over the
Moors. The city later grew rich
on the iron and wool trades.
  The old town focuses on the
Plaza de la Virgen Blanca,
with its monument to a battle

fought nearby in 1813, when
the British Duke of Wellington
defeated the French. Around
the plaza are old houses with
miradores (glazed balconies).
  On the hillside above the
plaza is the Gothic **Iglesia de
San Miguel**. An outside niche
contains a statue of the Virgen
Blanca (White Virgin), Vitoria's
patron saint. A big festival *(see
p128)* begins on her feast day,
August 4. On the wall of San
Miguel facing the **Plaza del
Machete** there is a recess that
once held a machete on which
the city's rulers swore to up-
hold the laws or be slain.
  The old town has several
Renaissance palaces, including
the 16th-century **Palacio de
Escoriaza-Esquibel**, which

has a Plateresque *(see p21)*
patio. Around it is a charming
area of old alleys linked by
steep steps. Young people
throng the bars at night.
  The city has two cathedrals.
The oldest, on the old town's
limit, is the Gothic **Catedral
de Santa María**, with a sculpted west porch. Close by, in
Calle Correría, a street of old
houses, is the enchanting **El
Portalón**, a merchant's house
and hostel from the 15th century. The building, which is full
of Basque country furniture
and art, is now a restaurant.
  Among the city's later architectural gems are an arcaded
street, **Los Arquillos**, and the
adjoining **Plaza de España**,
also arcaded. They were built
in the late 18th century to link
the old town with the new
quarter then being built. South
of the old town is the Neo-
Gothic **Catedral de la Virgen
Inmaculada**, begun in 1907
and in use, though unfinished.

🏛 Museo de Arqueología

Calle Correría 116. 📞 *(94) 514
23 10.* 🕐 *Tue–Sun.*
The exhibits in this museum, in
a 16th-century half-timbered
house, include dolmens erected more than 4,000 years ago,
Roman sculptures found in
Álava, and medieval artifacts.

The quiet Plaza de España in the center of Vitoria

The Gothic west door of Vitoria's Catedral de Santa María

🏛 Museo de Naipes

Palacio de Vendaña, C/ Cuchillería 54.
📞 (94) 523 17 77. ⏰ Tue–Sun. ♿
The grandson of Heraclio Fournier, who founded a playing card factory in Vitoria in 1868, displays his collection of more than 6,000 items in this museum. The oldest exhibits are late 14th-century Italian cards. Among the many sets of tarot cards are some designed by Salvador Dalí in the 1980s.

🏛 Museo de Armería

Paseo Fray Francisco 3. 📞 (94) 523 17 77. ⏰ Tue–Sun.
The weapons exhibited in this museum range in age from prehistoric axes to 20th-century pistols. There are also displays of medieval armor and an exhibit tracing the events of the 1813 Battle of Vitoria.

🏛 Museo de Bellas Artes

Paseo Fray Francisco 8. 📞 (94) 523 17 77. ⏰ Tue–Sun.
Exhibits in this art gallery, in a Neo-Renaissance mansion, range in date from ancient to modern times. They include 14th-century wood sculptures, 16th-century Flemish triptychs, paintings by Spanish masters such as Ribera, and modern Basque and Spanish works by Zuloaga, Picasso, and others.

Castillo de Mendoza ❾

Mendoza (Álava). 📞 (94) 524 00 30. ⏰ Tue–Sun.

IN THE CENTER of Mendoza village, 8 km (5 miles) west of Vitoria, stands this small, square, much re-stored fortress dating from the 13th century. There are marvelous views from the tops of the four towers. Once a ducal residence, the thick-walled castle now houses the **Museo Heráldica**. In it are displayed the coats of arms of noble Basque families and items relating to them.

ENVIRONS: On the A2622 Pobes–Tuesta road are the **Salinas de Añana**, a group of tiered saltpans that are fed by mineral springs. The nearby village of **Tuesta** boasts a Romanesque church with a decorated portal. Inside are capitals carved with historical scenes, and a medieval wood sculpture of St. Sebastian.

Laguardia ❿

Álava. 🏘 1,500. 🛈 Paseo Sancho Abarca, (94) 110 08 45. 🚌 Tue. 🎉 San Juan and San Pedro (Jun 24).

THIS LITTLE WINE TOWN is the capital of La Rioja Alavesa, a part of southern Álava province where Rioja wines (see pp74–5) have been produced for centuries. It is a fertile, vine-clad plain, sheltered by high hills to the north. There are fine panoramic views from the road that climbs up to the Herrera pass. Laguardia is a medieval hill town, its encircling ramparts, towers, and fortified gateways visible from afar. Along its steep, narrow, cobbled streets there are many **bodegas** (wine cellars), offering wine tastings and tours throughout the year. It is usually necessary to make a booking in advance.
The Gothic **Iglesia de Santa María de los Reyes** has an austere façade and unusual portal. A delicate statue of the Virgin and Child is displayed inside the church.

Virgin and child statue in Laguardia

Vineyards near Laguardia, capital of La Rioja Alavesa, a wine-producing region since the Middle Ages

Haro

La Rioja. 🚶 9,000. 🚌 🚍 🛈 Plaza de la Paz 1, (941) 31 01 05. 🛥 Tue & Sat. 🍇 Wine Battle (Jun 29), Virgen de la Vega (Sep 8).

A GRACEFUL TOWN on the Río Ebro, Haro has a lively old quarter with wine taverns and mansions. It is crowned by the hilltop **Iglesia de Santo Tomás**, a Gothic church with a Plateresque (see p21) portal.

Haro is the center for the vineyards and bodegas of the Rioja Alta wine region, which is higher and cooler than the Rioja Baja (see pp74–5). The clay soil and the climate – Haro is sheltered by a sierra to the north – create the conditions in which the famous regional wines are produced. Many bodegas run tours of their cellars, including tastings. To join one, you usually need to book ahead at the bodega or the tourist office. There is sometimes a small charge.

The cafés in the main square offer local wines at low prices and a convivial atmosphere, especially in the evenings.

A wine-throwing orgy is the climax of the town's fiesta (see p128) held every June.

Tomb of St. Dominic in the cathedral of Santo Domingo de la Calzada

Rows of Rioja vines on the rolling hills near Haro

Santo Domingo de la Calzada

La Rioja. 🚶 5,800. 🚍 🛈 Plaza de España 4, (941) 34 00 07. 🛥 Sat. 🍇 Día del Patron (May 12), San Jerónimo Hermosilla (Sep 19).

T HIS TOWN on the Road to Santiago de Compostela (see pp78–9) is named after the 11th-century saint who built bridges and roads (calzadas) to help pilgrims. To tend sick travelers, St. Dominic also built a hospital, which now serves as a parador (see p542).

Miracles performed by the saint are recorded in carvings on his tomb in the town's part-Romanesque, part-Gothic **cathedral**, and in paintings on the wall of the choir. The most obvious and bizarre record is a sumptuously decorated cage set in a wall in which, for centuries, a live cock and hen have been kept. The cathedral has a carved walnut reredos at the high altar, the last work, in 1541, of the artist Damià Forment. The restored 14th-century ramparts of the town are also well worth seeing.

THE COCK AND HEN OF ST. DOMINIC

A live cock and hen are kept in the cathedral of Santo Domingo de la Calzada as a tribute to the saint's miraculous life-giving powers. Centuries ago, it is said, a German pilgrim refused the advances of a local girl, who denounced him as a thief. He was hanged as a consequence, but later his parents found him alive on the gallows. They rushed to a judge, who said, dismissively, "Nonsense, he's no more alive than this roast chicken on my plate." Whereupon, the chicken stood up on the plate and crowed.

The cock and hen in their decorated cage

San Millán de la Cogolla ⓭

La Rioja. 🏠 *300*. 🚹 *Calle Mayor 59, (941) 37 30 35.* 🎪 *Traslación de las Reliquias (Sep 26), San Millán (Nov 12).*

THIS VILLAGE grew up around two monasteries. On a hillside above the village is the **Monasterio de San Millán de Suso**. It was built in the 10th century on the site of a community founded by St. Emilian, a hermit shepherd, in 537. The church, hollowed out of pink sandstone, has Romanesque and Mozarabic features. It contains the carved alabaster tomb of St. Emilian and also the tomb of the 13th-century writer, Gonzalo de Berceo *(see p30)*, who was a monk here.

The **Monasterio de San Millán de Yuso** is below it, in the Cárdenas Valley. It was built between the 16th and 18th centuries on the site of an earlier monastery. The part-Renaissance church has Baroque golden doors and a rococo sacristy, where 17th-century paintings are hung.

In the treasury there is a collection of ivory plaques. They were once part of two 11th-century jeweled reliquaries that were plundered by French troops in 1813.

Medieval manuscripts are also displayed in the treasury. Among them is a facsimile of one of the earliest known texts in Castilian Romance. It is a commentary on a work by St. Augustine, the *Glosas Emilianenses,* written in the 10th century by a Suso monk.

The Monasterio de San Millán de Yuso in the Cárdenas valley

Cloister of the Monasterio de Santa María la Real, Nájera

Nájera ⓮

La Rioja. 🏠 *7,200*. 🚌 🚹 *Plaza de España 1, (941) 36 36 66.* 🅰 *Thu.* 🎪 *Fiestas de Nájera (Jun 24), Santa María la Real (Sep 16, 17).*

THE OLD TOWN of Nájera, west of Logroño, was the capital of La Rioja and Navarra until 1076, when La Rioja was incorporated into Castile. The royal families of Navarra, León, and Castile are buried in the **Monasterio de Santa María la Real**. It was founded in the 11th century beside a sandstone cliff where a statue of the Virgin was found in a cave. A 13th-century Madonna can be seen in the cave, beneath the carved choir stalls of the 15th-century church.

The 12th-century carved tomb of Blanca of Navarra, the wife of Sancho III, is the finest of many royal sarcophagi.

🏛 **Monasterio de Santa María la Real**
Nájera. 📞 *(941) 36 36 50.* ⏰ *Tue–Sun.* ⬤ *public hols.* 🎫 ♿

Logroño ⓯

La Rioja. 🏠 *130,000.* 🚌 🚆 🚹 *Calle Miguel Villanueva 10, (941) 29 12 60.* 🎪 *San Bernabé (Jun 11), Grape Harvest (Sep 21).*

THE CAPITAL OF LA RIOJA is a tidy, modern city of wide boulevards and fashionable shops. It is the commercial center of a fertile plain where vegetables are produced, in addition to Rioja wines.

In Logroño's pleasant old quarter of narrow streets abutting the Río Ebro is the Gothic **cathedral**, with twin towers. Above the south portal of the nearby **Iglesia de Santiago el Real** is a Baroque equestrian statue of St. James in his role as Moorslayer *(see p51)*.

ENVIRONS: About 50 km (30 miles) south of Logroño, the N111 winds through the dramatic **Iregua Valley**, through tunnels and gorges and under twisted crags, before climbing into the Sierra de Cameros.

The ornate Baroque west door of Logroño cathedral

Enciso ⓰

La Rioja. 🏠 *220.* 🚌 *from Logroño.* 🚹 *Plaza Mayor, (941) 39 60 05.* 🎪 *San Roque (Aug 16).*

NEAR THIS REMOTE hill village west of Calahorra is Spain's "Jurassic Park." Signs point to the *huellas de dinosaurios* (dinosaur footprints). Embedded in rocks overhanging a stream are the prints of many giant, three-toed feet, up to 30 cm (1 ft) long. They were made around 150 million years ago, when dinosaurs moved between the marshes of the Ebro valley, at that time a sea, and these hills. Prints can also be seen at other locations in the area.

ENVIRONS: **Arnedillo**, 10 km (6 miles) to the north, is a spa with thermal baths. In **Autol**, to the east, there are two unusual limestone peaks.

The intricately carved portal of
Tudela cathedral

Tudela ⑰

Navarra. 👥 25,600. 🚉 🚌
ℹ️ Plaza Vieja 1, (948) 82 15 39.
🗓️ Sat. 🎪 Santa Ana (Jul 26).

NAVARRA'S SECOND CITY is the
great commercial center
of the vast agricultural lands
of the Ebro valley in Navarra,
the Ribera. Although much of
Tudela consists of modern
developments, its origins are
ancient. Spanning the Ebro is
a 13th-century bridge with 17
irregular arches. The old town
has well-preserved Mudéjar
and Jewish districts.

The delightful **Plaza de los
Fueros** is old Tudela's main
square. It is surrounded by
houses with wrought-iron balconies. On their façades are
paintings of bullfights, a reminder that the plaza was
formerly used as a bullring.

The **cathedral**, begun in
1194, exemplifies the religious
toleration under which Tudela
was governed after the Reconquest. It is Early Gothic, with a
carved portal depicting the Last
Judgement. The Romanesque
cloister encloses the ruins of
a 9th-century mosque, and a
Mudéjar chapel that may have
been a synagogue.

ENVIRONS: To the north is the
Bárdenas Reales, an arid area
of limestone cliffs and crags.
About 20 km (12 miles) west
of Tudela is the spa town of
Fitero, with the 12th-century
Monasterio de Santa María.

Monasterio de La Oliva ⑱

Carcastillo (Navarra). 📞 (948) 72
55 97. 🚌 from Pamplona. 🕐 daily.

FRENCH CISTERCIAN MONKS built
this small monastery on a
remote plain in the 12th century. The church is simple, in
typical Cistercian style, but
adorned with rose windows.

One of the cloisters in the
Monasterio de La Oliva

The serene cloister, dating
from the 15th-century, adjoins
a 13th-century chapterhouse.
The church also has a tower
erected in the 17th century.

Today, the monks survive
by selling their honey, cheese,
and wine, and by accepting
paying guests (see p532).

Ujué ⑲

Navarra. 👥 280. ℹ️ Plaza Municipal,
(948) 73 90 23. 🎪 Virgen de Ujué
(Sep 8).

ONE OF SPAIN'S least spoiled
hill villages, Ujué com-
mands a high spur at the end
of a winding road. It has quaint
façades, cobbled alleys, and
steep steps. The **Iglesia de
Santa María** is in Gothic style
with a Romanesque chancel
and an exterior lookout gallery.
Beside the church is a ruined
fortress. From its terrace there
are views of the Pyrenees.

On April 25 every year, pilgrims in black capes come
here to visit the Virgin of Ujué,
whose Romanesque image is
displayed in the church.

Olite ⑳

Navarra. 👥 3,000. 🚉 ℹ️ Galerias
de la Plaza Carlos III el Noble, (948)
71 24 34. 🗓️ Wed. 🎪 Exaltación de
la Santa Cruz (Sep 14–20).

THE HISTORIC TOWN of Olite
was founded by the Ro-
mans and later chosen as a
royal residence by the kings
of Navarra. Part of the town's
old walls can be seen. They

THE KINGDOM OF NAVARRA

Navarra emerged as an independent Christian
kingdom in the 10th century, after Sancho I
Garcés became king of Pamplona. Sancho III
the Great expanded the kingdom, and at his
death, in 1035, Navarra stretched all the way
from Ribagorza in Aragón to Valladolid. Sancho
VI the Wise, who reigned 1150–94, recognized
the independent rights (fueros) of many towns. In
1234, Navarra passed by marriage to a line of
French rulers. One, Carlos III the Noble, built
Olite castle. His grandson, Carlos de Viana, wrote
the Chronicle of the Kings of Navarra in 1455.
In 1512 Navarra was annexed by Fernando II
of Castile, as part of united Spain, but it kept its
own laws and currency until the 1800s.

**Prince Carlos de Viana,
Carlos III's grandson**

enclose a delightful jumble of steep, narrow streets and little squares, churches, and the **Monasterio de las Clarisas**, begun in the 13th century. The houses along the Rúa Cerco de Fuera and the Rúa Mayor were built between the 16th and 18th centuries.

The castle, the **Palacio Real de Olite**, was built about 1406 by Carlos III, and has earned Olite its nickname "the Gothic town." It was heavily fortified, but was brilliantly decorated inside by Mudéjar artists with *azulejos* (ceramic tiles) and marquetry ceilings. The walkways were planted with vines and orange trees, and there was an aviary and a lions' den.

In the 19th century the castle was sacked by Carlists *(see pp58–9)* and the French. Since the 1920s, however, it has been restored to a semblance of its former glory. Part of it houses a parador *(see p541)*.

Today, the castle is a complex of courtyards, passages, steep stairs, large halls, royal chambers, battlements, towers, and turrets. From the "windy tower" monarchs were able to watch tournaments.

Adjoining the castle is a 13th-century former royal chapel, the **Iglesia de Santa María la Real**, with a richly carved Gothic portal. Inside there is a 16th-century reredos.

Olite is in the Navarra wine region *(see pp74–5)* and the town has several bodegas.

♦ **Palacio Real de Olite**
Plaza de Carlos III. 【 *(948) 74 00 35.*
◯ *daily.* ▦

The battlements and towers of the Palacio Real de Olite

The five-arched, medieval pilgrims' bridge at Puente la Reina

Puente la Reina ㉑

Navarra. ▦ *2,200.* ▯ *Plaza de Mena 1, (948) 34 00 07.* ▤ *Sat.*
▨ *Santiago (Jul 25).*

Few towns along the Road to Santiago de Compostela *(see pp78–9)* evoke the past as vividly as Puente la Reina. The town takes its name from the graceful, humpbacked pedestrian bridge over the Río Arga. The bridge was built for pilgrims during the 11th century by royal command.

On Puente la Reina's narrow main street is the **Iglesia de Santiago**, which has a gilded statue by the west door showing the saint as a pilgrim. On the edge of town is the **Iglesia del Crucifijo**, another pilgrim church that was built in the 12th century by the Knights Templar. Contained within the church is a Y-shaped wooden crucifix of a sorrowful Christ with arms upraised, which is said to have been a gift from a German pilgrim in the 14th century.

Distinctive crucifix in Puente la Reina

ENVIRONS: Isolated in the fields about 5 km (3 miles) to the east is the 12th-century **Iglesia de Santa María de Eunate**. This octagonal Romanesque church may once have been a cemetery church for pilgrims, as human bones have been unearthed here. Pilgrims would shelter beneath the church's external arcade. West of Puenta la Reina is the showpiece hill village of **Cirauqui**. It is also charming, if rather overrestored. Chic little balconied houses line tortuously twisting alleys linked by steps. The Iglesia de San Román, built in the 13th century on top of the hill, has a sculpted west door.

BASQUE COUNTRY, NAVARRA, AND LA RIOJA'S FIESTAS

Los Sanfermines *(Jul 6–14)*, Pamplona (Navarra). In the famous *encierro* (bull running) six bulls are released early each morning to run from their corral through the narrow, cobbled streets of the old town. On the last night of this week-long, non-stop party, crowds with candles sing Basque songs in the main square. The event gained worldwide fame after Ernest Hemingway described it in his novel *The Sun Also Rises*.

Bulls scattering the runners in Pamplona

Wine Battle *(Jun 29)*, Haro (La Rioja). People dressed in white clothes squirt each other with wine from leather drinking bottles in the capital of the Rioja Alta wine region.
Danza de los Zancos *(Jul 22 and last Sat of Sep)*, Anguiano (La Rioja). Dancers on stilts, wearing ornate waistcoats and yellow skirts, hurtle down the stepped alley from the church to the main square.
L: Virgen Blanca *(Aug 4)*, Vitoria (Álava). A dummy holding an umbrella (the *celedón*) is lowered from San Miguel church to a house below – from which a man in similar dress emerges. The mayor fires a rocket and the crowds in the square light cigars.

Pilgrims drinking from the wine tap near the monastery at Irache

Estella ❷

Navarra. 🏠 *13,000.* 🚌 🛈 *Calle de San Nicolás 1, (948) 55 40 11.* 🕐 *Thu.* 🎎 *San Andrés (early Aug).*

IN THE MIDDLE AGES Estella (Lizarra) was the center of the royal court of Navarra and a major stopping point on the pilgrims' Road to Santiago de Compostela *(see pp78–9)*. The town was a stronghold of the Carlists *(see p59)* in the 19th century. A memorial rally is held here on the first Sunday of May every year.

The most important monuments in Estella are sited on the edge of town, across the bridge over the Río Ega. Steps climb steeply from the arcaded Plaza de San Martín to the remarkable 12th-century **Iglesia de San Pedro de la Rúa**, built on top of a cliff. It features a a Mudéjar-influenced, sculpted doorway. The carved capitals are all that now remain of the Romanesque cloister, which was destroyed when a castle overlooking the church was blown up in 1592. The **Palacio de los Reyes de Navarra**, on the other side of the Plaza de San Martín, is a rare example of civil Romanesque architecture. It also houses a gallery of Navarrese art.

In the town center, on the arcaded Plaza de los Fueros, the **Iglesia de San Juan Bautista** has a Romanesque porch. The north portal of the **Iglesia de San Miguel** has Romanesque carvings of St. Michael slaying a dragon.

ENVIRONS: The **Monasterio de Nuestra Señora de Irache**, 3 km (2 miles) southwest of Estella, was built by Cistercian monks, who sheltered pilgrims on their way to Santiago. The church is mainly Transitional Gothic in style, but it has Romanesque apses and a cloister in Plateresque style. It is capped by a remarkable dome.

A bodega next to the monastery provides pilgrims with wine from a tap in a wall.

A small road branches off the NA120 north of Estella and winds through a wooded gorge to reach the **Monasterio de Iranzu**, built in the 12th century. The graceful austerity of its church and cloisters are typically Cistercian features.

The Lizarraga Pass, further up the NA120, offers views of attractive beech woods.

Pamplona ❷

Navarra. 🏠 *183,000.* ✈ 🚌 🚍 🛈 *Calle Duque de Ahumada 3, (948) 22 07 41.* 🎎 *Sanfermines (Jul 6–14), San Saturnino (Nov 29).*

THE OLD FORTRESS city of Pamplona (Iruña) is said to have been founded by the Roman general Pompey. In the 9th century it became the capital of Navarra. This otherwise quiet city explodes into life in July during the fiesta of Los Sanfermines, with its daredevil bull running.

From the old **city walls** *(murallas)* you can get a good overview of Pamplona. The nearby **cathedral**, which is

Sumptuous interior of the Palacio de Navarra, Pamplona

Stone tracery in the elegant cloister of Pamplona's cathedral

de la Preciosa. The cathedral priests would gather here to sing an antiphon (hymn) to La Preciosa (Precious Virgin) before the night service.

The Museo Diocesano in the cathedral's 14th-century kitchen and refectory (closed for restoration) displays Gothic altarpieces, polychrome wood statues from all over Navarra, and a French 13th-century reliquary of the Holy Sepulchre.

West of the cathedral is the old town, the former Jewish quarter, cut through with many alleys. The Baroque **Palacio de Navarra** is near the Plaza del Castillo. Its opulent throne room of the kings of Navarra contains a portrait of King Fernando VII by Goya. Outside, a statue of 1903 shows a symbolic queen upholding the *fueros* (historic laws) of Navarra (*see*

built in ocher-colored stone, looks down on a loop in the Río Arga. It was built on the foundations of its 12th-century predecessor and is mainly Gothic in style, with twin towers and an 18th-century façade. Inside there are lovely choir stalls and the alabaster tomb of Carlos III and Queen Leonor.

The southern entrance to the cloister is the beautifully carved, medieval Puerta

p126). North of the palace are the medieval **Iglesia de San Saturnino**, built on the site where St. Saturninus is said to have baptized some 40,000 pagan townspeople, and the Baroque **town hall** (*ayuntamiento*).

Beneath the old town wall, in a 16th-century hospital with a Plateresque doorway, is the **Museo de Navarra**. This is a museum of regional archaeology, history, and art. Exhibits include Roman mosaics and an 11th-century, Islam-inspired ivory casket. There are murals painted during the 14th–16th centuries, a portrait by Goya, and a collection of paintings by Basque artists.

To the southeast is the city's massive 16th-century **citadel**, erected in Felipe II's reign. It is designed with five bastions in a star shape. Beyond it are the spacious boulevards of the new town and also the university's green campus.

🏛 **Museo de Navarra**
Calle Santo Domingo. 📞 (948) 10 64 92. ⬜ Tue–Sun. 📷 ♿
🏛 **Palacio de Navarra**
Avenida Carlos III 2. 📞 (948) 10 70 00. ⬜ by appointment. ♿

Sculpture in Pamplona depicting the *encierro*

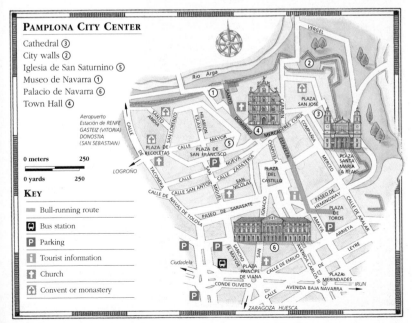

PAMPLONA CITY CENTER

Cathedral ③
City walls ②
Iglesia de San Saturnino ⑤
Museo de Navarra ①
Palacio de Navarra ⑥
Town Hall ④

Aeropuerto
Estación de RENFE
GASTEIZ (VITORIA)
DONOSTIA
(SAN SEBASTIAN)

0 meters   250
0 yards   250

LOGROÑO

KEY

━━ Bull-running route
🚌 Bus station
🅿 Parking
ℹ Tourist information
✝ Church
✝ Convent or monastery

Basque houses in the picturesque town of Etxalar, Regata de Bidasoa

Regata de Bidasoa 24

Navarra. 🚍 Pamplona, San Sebastián. 🛈 Oieregi, (948) 59 22 36.

FIVE ATTRACTIVE Basque towns lie in or near this valley, the most northerly being **Bera** (Vera). The houses in **Lesaka** have wooden balconies under deep eaves. The road south passes hills dotted with white farmsteads to reach **Igantzi**, (Yanci), with its red-and-white half-timbered houses. **Arantza**, farther south, is the most remote town. Since the 12th century, pigeons have been caught in huge nets strung across a pass above **Etxalar** (Echalar). From the summit of La Rhune, on the French border above the valley, there is a great view of the Pyrenees.

Elizondo 25

Navarra. 👥 3,000. 🚍 🛈 Plaza de los Fueros, (948) 58 00 06. 🕭 Thu. Santiago (Jul 25), Feria (late Oct).

THIS IS THE BIGGEST of a string of typical Basque villages in the very beautiful valley of Baztán. By the river are noble houses bearing coats of arms.

Arizkun, farther up the valley, has old fortified houses and a 17th-century convent. The **Cueva de Brujas**, near Zugarramurdi, was once a meeting place for witches.

Canopy over the Virgin and Child in the Colegiata Real

Roncesvalles 26

Navarra. 👥 20. 🛈 Roncesvalles, (948) 76 01 93. 🕭 Día de la Virgen de Roncesvalles (Sep 8).

RONCESVALLES (ORREAGA), on the Spanish side of a pass through the Pyrenees, is a major stop on the Road to Santiago (see pp78–9). Before it became associated with the pilgrim's way, Roncesvalles was the site of a major battle in 778, in which the Basques of Navarra slew the rear guard of Charlemagne's army as it marched homeward. This event is described in the 12th-century French epic poem, *The Song of Roland*.

The 13th-century **Colegiata Real**, which has served travelers down the centuries, has a silver-plated Virgin and Child below a high canopy. In the graceful chapterhouse, off the cloister, is the white tomb of Sancho VII the Strong (1154–1234), sitting under a stained-glass window of his great victory, the Battle of Las Navas de Tolosa (see pp50–51). Exhibits in the church museum include "Charlemagne's chessboard," an enameled reliquary which is so-called because of its checkered design.

Valle de Roncal 27

Navarra. 🚍 from Pamplona. 🛈 Roncal, (948) 47 51 36.

RUNNING perpendicular to the Pyrenees, this valley is still largely reliant on sheep, and the village of **Roncal** is known for its cheeses. Because of the relative isolation of the valley, the inhabitants have preserved their own identity, and local costumes are worn

The forested countryside around Roncesvalles

during fiestas. The ski resort of **Isaba**, farther up the valley, has a museum of local life and history. A spectacular road winds from Isaba to the tree-lined village of Ochagavia in the parallel **Valle de Salazar**. To the north, the pines and beeches of the **Bosque de Irati**, one of Europe's largest woodlands, spread over the Pyrenees into France, below the snowy summit of Monte Ori at 2,017 m (6,617 ft).

Colorful balconies of houses in the village of Roncal

Monasterio de Leyre 28

Yesa (Navarra). [(948) 88 40 11. ☐ Yesa. ☐ daily. 🎨 ⚄

T HE MONASTERY of San Salvador de Leyre is situated high above a reservoir, alone amid grand scenery, backed by limestone cliffs. The abbey has been here since the 11th century, when it was a great spiritual center. Sancho III and his successors made it the royal pantheon of Navarra.

The monastery began to decline in the 12th century. It was abandoned from the 19th century until 1954, when it was restored by Benedictines. They turned part of it into a modestly priced hotel (see p542). To see the monastery you must join one of the tours run by the monks every morning and afternoon.

The big church, unadorned in the Cistercian manner, has three lofty apses. On its west portal are weatherworn carvings of strange beasts, as well as biblical figures. The 11th-century crypt has unusually short columns with chunky capitals. The monks' Gregorian chant (see p358) during services is wonderful to hear.

Castillo de Javier 29

Javier (Navarra). [(948) 88 40 24. ☐ from Pamplona. ☐ daily. ⚄

S T. FRANCIS XAVIER, the patron saint of Navarra, a missionary and a co-founder of the Jesuit order (see p120), was born in this romantic-looking 13th-century castle in 1506. It has since been completely restored and is now used by the Jesuits as a college. Visitors can see the saint's bedroom and a museum in the keep devoted to his life. In the oratory is a 13th-century polychrome Christ and a macabre 15th-century mural of grinning skeletons titled *The Dance of Death*.

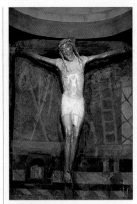

Crucifix in the oratory of the Castillo de Javier

Sangüesa 30

Navarra. 🏠 4,500. ☐ 🛈 Calle Alfonso el Batallador 20, (948) 87 03 29. ☐ Fri. 🎨 San Sebastián (Sep 11).

S INCE MEDIEVAL TIMES this small town beside a bridge over the Río Aragón has been a stop on the Aragonese pilgrimage route to Santiago (see pp78–9).

The richly sculpted south portal of the **Iglesia de Santa María la Real** is a 13th-century treasure of Romanesque art (see p20). It is crammed with figures and details. Above the door, God is shown rejecting sinners and welcoming the chosen. This scene is surrounded by angels, musicians, warriors, artisans, geometric motifs, and mythical animals.

The Romanesque **Iglesia de Santiago** and the 14th-century Gothic **Iglesia de San Francisco** are also worth seeing. On the main street is the **town hall** (ayuntamiento), formerly the palace of the Prince of Viana and a residence of the kings of Navarra. The interior is not open to visitors, but the Gothic and Baroque façades can be seen.

ENVIRONS: To the north of Sangüesa there are two deep, narrow gorges. The most impressive of them is the **Hoz de Arbayún**, whose limestone cliffs are inhabited by colonies of vultures. It is best seen from the NA178 north of Domeño. The **Hoz de Lumbier** can be seen from a point on the N240.

The roughly carved columns in the crypt of the Monasterio de Leyre

BARCELONA

Introducing Barcelona

BARCELONA, one of the Mediterranean's busiest ports, is more than the capital of Catalonia. In culture, commerce, and sports it not only rivals Madrid, but also considers itself on a par with the greatest European cities. The success of the 1992 Olympic Games, staged in the Parc de Montjuïc, confirmed this to the world. Although there are plenty of historical monuments in the Old Town (Ciutat Vella), Barcelona is best known for the scores of buildings in the Eixample left by the artistic explosion of Modernisme *(see pp136–7)* in the decades around 1900. Always open to outside influences because of its location on the coast, not too far from the French border, Barcelona continues to sizzle with creativity: its bars and the public parks speak more of bold contemporary design than of tradition.

Casa Milà *(see p161) is the most avant-garde of all the works of Antoni Gaudí (see p160). Barcelona has more Modernista buildings than any other city in the world.*

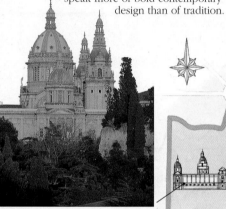

Palau Nacional *(see p168), on the hill of Montjuïc, dominates the monumental halls and fountain-filled avenue built for the 1929 International Exhibition. It now houses the Museu Nacional d'Art de Catalunya, an exceptional collection of medieval art, rich in Romanesque frescoes.*

MONTJUIC
(see pp164–9)

Christopher Columbus *surveys the waterfront from the top of a 60-m (200-ft) column (see p152) in the heart of the Port Vell (Old Port). From the top, visitors can look out over the new promenades and wharves that have revitalized the area.*

Montjuïc Castle *(see p169) is a massive fortification dating from the 17th century. Sited on the crest of the hill of Montjuïc, it offers panoramic views of the city and port, and forms a sharp contrast to the ultramodern facilities built nearby for the 1992 Olympic Games.*

0 kilometers   1

0 miles   0.5

◁ **The Ramblas and the Old Town stretching out behind Barcelona's monument to Columbus**

The Sagrada Família (see pp162–3), Gaudí's unfinished masterpiece, begun in 1882, rises above the streets of the Eixample. Its polychrome ceramic mosaics and sculptural forms inspired by nature are typical of his work.

EIXAMPLE
(see pp154–63)

Barcelona cathedral (see pp144–5) is a magnificent 14th-century building in the heart of the Barri Gòtic (Gothic Quarter). It has 28 side chapels that encircle the nave and contain some splendid Baroque altarpieces. The keeping of white geese in the cloisters is a centuries-old tradition.

OLD TOWN
(see pp138–53)

Parc de la Ciutadella (see p150), between the Old Town and the Vila Olímpica, has something for everyone. The gardens full of statuary offer relaxation, the boating lake and the zoo are fun, and the three museums within its gates cover art, geology, and zoology.

Las Ramblas (see pp146–7) is the most famous street in Spain, alive at all hours of the day and night. A stroll down its length to the waterfront, taking in its palatial buildings, shops, cafés, and street vendors, makes a perfect introduction to Barcelona life.

Gaudí and Modernisme

Chimney,
Casa Vicens

Toward the end of the 19th century a new style of art and architecture, Modernisme, a variant of Art Nouveau, was born in Barcelona. It became a means of self-expression for Catalan nationalism and counted Josep Puig i Cadafalch, Lluís Domènech i Montaner, and, above all, Antoni Gaudí i Cornet *(see p160)* among its major exponents. Barcelona's Eixample district *(see pp154–63)* is full of the highly original buildings they created for their wealthy clients.

All aspects of decoration in a Modernista building, even interior design, were planned by the architect. This door and its tiled surround are in Gaudí's 1906 Casa Batlló (see p160).

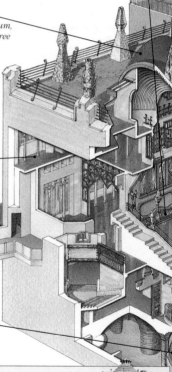

A dramatic cupola covers the central atrium, which rises through three floors. It is pierced by small round holes, inspired by Islamic architecture, giving the illusion of stars.

Upper galleries are richly decorated with carved wood and cofferwork.

The spiral carriage ramp is an early sign of Gaudí's predilection for curved lines. He would later exploit this to the full in the wavy façade of his masterpiece, the Casa Milà (see p161).

THE EVOLUTION OF MODERNISME

1850	1865	1880	1895	1910	1925

1859 Civil Engineer Ildefons Cerdà i Sunyer submits proposals for expansion of Barcelona

1878 Gaudí graduates as an architect

1883 Gaudí takes over design of Neo-Gothic Sagrada Família *(see pp162–3)*

Detail of Sagrada Família

1888 Barcelona Universal Exhibition gives impetus to Modernisme

1900 Josep Puig i Cadafalch builds Casa Amatller *(see p160)*

1903 Lluís Domènech i Montaner builds Hospital de la Santa Creu i de Sant Pau *(see p161)*

Hospital detail

1905 Domènech i Montaner builds Casa Lleó Morera *(see p160)*. Puig i Cadafalch builds Casa Terrades *(see p161)*

1910 Casa Milà completed

1926 Gaudí dies

Bizarrely decorated chimneys became one of the trademarks of Gaudí's later work. They reach a fantastic extreme on the gleaming, hump-backed roof of the Casa Batlló.

Elaborate wrought iron lamps light the grand hall.

Ceramic tiles decorate the chimneys.

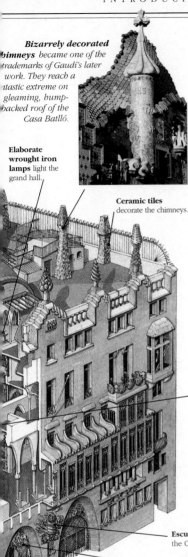

GAUDÍ'S MATERIALS

Gaudí designed, or collaborated on designs, for almost every known media. He combined bare, undecorated materials – wood, rough-hewn stone, rubble, and brickwork – with meticulous craftwork in wrought iron and stained glass. Mosaics of ceramic tiles were used to cover his fluid, uneven forms.

Stained-glass window in the Sagrada Família

Mosaic of ceramic tiles, Parc Güell *(see p174)*

Detail of iron gate, Casa Vicens *(see p160)*

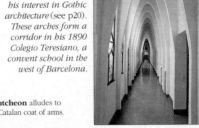

Ceramic tiles on El Capricho *(see p107)*

Parabolic arches, used extensively by Gaudí, beginning in the Palau Güell, show his interest in Gothic architecture (see p20). These arches form a corridor in his 1890 Colegio Teresiano, a convent school in the west of Barcelona.

Escutcheon alludes to the Catalan coat of arms.

PALAU GÜELL *(1889)*

Gaudí's first major building in the center of the city *(see p147)* established his international reputation for outstandingly original architecture. Built for his life-long patron, the industrialist Eusebi Güell, the mansion stands on a small plot of land in a narrow street, making the façade difficult to view. Inside, Gaudí creates a sense of space by using carved screens, galleries, and recesses. His unique furniture is also on display.

Organic forms inspired the wrought iron around the gates to the palace. Gaudí's later work teems with wildlife, such as this dragon, covered with brightly colored tiles, that guards the steps in the Parc Güell.

OLD TOWN

THE OLD TOWN, traversed by Barcelona's most famous avenue, the Ramblas, is one of the most extensive and harmonious medieval city centers in Europe. The Barri Gòtic (Gothic Quarter) contains the cathedral and ancient royal palace. Adjoining it is La Ribera, full of 14th-century mansions, one of which is occupied by the Museu Picasso. This area is bounded by the beautiful Parc de la Ciutadella, which contains the Museu d'Art Modern and the zoo. The revitalized seafront has several kilometers of reclaimed beaches, stretching from the modern Olympic Village to the Old Port, where there are historic shipyards, a fashionable marina, and a promenade.

SIGHTS AT A GLANCE

Museums and Galleries
Museu d'Art Modern ⑳
Museu Frederic Marès ②
Museu de Geologia ⑱
Museu d'Història de la
   Ciutat ④
Museu Marítim and
   Drassanes ㉗
Museu Picasso ⑬
Museu de Zoologia ⑰

Streets and Districts
Barceloneta ㉓
Carrer Montcada ⑫
Las Ramblas ⑨
El Raval and Barri Xinès ⑧

Harbor Sights
Golondrinas ㉖
Port Vell ㉔

Churches
Basílica de Santa Maria
   del Mar ⑪
Cathedral (pp144–5) ⑦

Historic Buildings
Casa de l'Ardiaca ①
Casa de la Ciutat ⑤
La Llotja ⑩
Palau de la Generalitat ⑥
Palau de la Música Catalana ⑭
Palau Reial Major ③

Modern Architecture
Vila Olímpica ㉒

Monuments
Arc del Triomf ⑮
Homenatge a Picasso ⑲
Monument a Colom ㉕

Parks and Gardens
Parc de la Ciutadella ⑯
Parc Zoològic ㉑

GETTING THERE
The area is well served by metro lines 1, 3, and 4; Jaume I station is in the heart of the Barri Gòtic. Many buses pass the Plaça de Catalunya, the center of the modern city.

KEY

Street-by-Street map *pp140–41*

Ⓜ Metro station

🚇 Railroad station

🚌 Main bus stop

ℹ Tourist information

🅿 Parking

0 meters   500
0 yards   500

◁ **Stunning floral mosaic pillars in the Palau de la Música Catalana**

Street-by-Street: Barri Gòtic

THE BARRI GOTIC (Gothic Quarter) is the true heart of Barcelona. The oldest part of the city, it was the site chosen by the Romans in the reign of Augustus (27 BC–AD 14) on which to found a new *colonia* (town), and has been the location of the city's administrative buildings ever since. The Roman forum was on the Plaça de Sant Jaume, where now stand the medieval Palau de la Generalitat, Catalonia's parliament, and the Casa de la Ciutat,

Wax candle, Barcelona's town hall. Close
Cereria by are the Gothic cathedral
Subirà and royal palace, where
Columbus was received by Fernando and Isabel on his return from his voyage to the New World in 1492 *(see p53).*

Casa de l'Ardiaca
Built on the Roman city wall, the Gothic-Renaissance archdeacon's residence now houses Barcelona's historical archives **1**

To Plaça de Catalunya

★ **Cathedral**
The façade and spire are 19th-century additions to the original Gothic building. Among the artistic treasures inside are medieval Catalan paintings **7**

Palau de la Generalitat
Catalonia's parliament retains superb Gothic features, which include the chapel and a stone staircase rising to an open-air, arcaded gallery **6**

CARRER DE FERRAN

PLAÇA DE SANT JAUME

To Las Ramblas

Casa de la Ciutat
Barcelona's town hall was built in the 14th and 15th centuries. The façade is a Neo-Classical addition. In the entrance hall stands Three Gypsy Boys *by Joan Rebull (1899–1981), a 1976 copy of a sculpture he originally created in 1946* **5**

KEY

– – – Suggested route

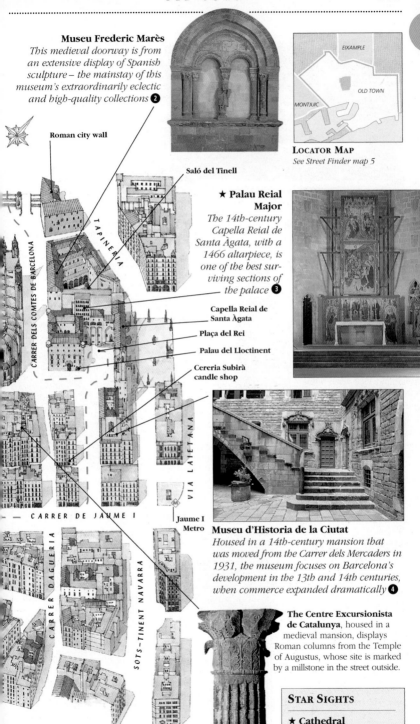

Museu Frederic Marès
This medieval doorway is from an extensive display of Spanish sculpture – the mainstay of this museum's extraordinarily eclectic and high-quality collections ❷

Roman city wall

LOCATOR MAP
See Street Finder map 5

EIXAMPLE

OLD TOWN

MONTJUIC

Saló del Tinell

★ Palau Reial Major
The 14th-century Capella Reial de Santa Àgata, with a 1466 altarpiece, is one of the best surviving sections of the palace ❸

Capella Reial de Santa Àgata

Plaça del Rei

Palau del Lloctinent

Cereria Subirà candle shop

TAPINERIA

CARRER DELS COMTES DE BARCELONA

VIA LAIETANA

CARRER DE JAUME I

Jaume I
Metro

Museu d'Historia de la Ciutat
Housed in a 14th-century mansion that was moved from the Carrer dels Mercaders in 1931, the museum focuses on Barcelona's development in the 13th and 14th centuries, when commerce expanded dramatically ❹

CARRER DAGUERIA

SOTS–TINENT NAVARRA

The Centre Excursionista de Catalunya, housed in a medieval mansion, displays Roman columns from the Temple of Augustus, whose site is marked by a millstone in the street outside.

STAR SIGHTS

★ **Cathedral**

★ **Palau Reial Major**

0 meters   100
0 yards   100

Decorated marble letterbox, Casa de l'Ardiaca

Casa de l'Ardiaca ❶

Carrer de Santa Llúcia 1. **Map** 5 B2.
🅒 (93) 318 11 95. Ⓜ Jaume I.
🕐 Sep–Jul: 9am–8:45pm Mon–Fri,
9am–2pm Sat; Aug: 9am–2pm
Mon–Fri. ⬤ public hols.

STANDING BESIDE what was originally the Bishop's Gate in the Roman wall is the Archdeacon's House. It was built in the 12th century, but its present appearance dates from around 1500 when it was remodeled and a colonnade added. In 1870 this was extended to form the Flamboyant Gothic (*see p20*) patio around a fountain. The Modernista architect Domènech i Montaner (1850–1923) added the fanciful marble letterbox, carved with three swallows and a tortoise, beside the Renaissance portal. The Municipal Institute of Barcelona History is upstairs.

Museu Frederic Marès ❷

Plaça de Sant Iu 5. **Map** 5 B2.
🅒 (93) 310 58 00. Ⓜ Jaume I.
🕐 10am–5pm Tue–Sat, 10am–2pm
Sun & public hols. ⬤ Jan 1, Good
Fri, May 1, Dec 25.

THE SCULPTOR Frederic Marès i Deulovol (1893–1991) was also a traveler and collector, and this extraordinary museum is a monument to his eclectic taste. The building is part of the Royal Palace complex and was occupied by 13th-century bishops, 14th-century counts of Barcelona, 15th-century judges, and 18th-century

nuns, who lived here until they were expelled in 1936. Marès, who had a small apartment in the building, opened his museum in 1948. It is one of the most fascinating in the city and has an outstanding collection of Romanesque and Gothic religious art. In the crypt there is an extensive assemblage of stone sculpture and two complete Romanesque portals. Exhibits on the three floors above range through clocks, crucifixes, costumes, antique cameras, pipes, tobacco jars, and pin-up postcards to an amusement room full of children's toys.

Virgin, Museu Frederic Marès

Palau Reial Major ❸

Plaça del Rei. **Map** 5 B2. 🅒 (93) 315
11 11. Ⓜ Jaume I. 🕐 10am–2pm,
4–8pm Tue–Sat, 10am–2pm Sun.
⬤ Jan 1, Good Fri, Dec 25 & 26. 📷

THE ROYAL PALACE was the residence of the count-kings of Barcelona from its foundation in the 13th century. The complex includes the 14th-century Gothic Saló del Tinell, a massive room with semicircular arches spanning 17 m (56 ft). This is where Isabel and Fernando (*see p66*) received Columbus after his triumphal return from America. It is also where the Inquisition (*see p264*) sat, believing the walls would move if lies were told.

On the right, built into the Roman city wall, is the royal chapel, the Capella de Santa Àgata, with a painted wood

Gothic nave of the Capella de Santa Àgata, Palau Reial

BARCELONA'S EARLY JEWISH COMMUNITY

Hebrew tablet

From the 11th to the 13th centuries Jews dominated Barcelona's commerce and culture, providing doctors and founding the first seat of learning. But in 1243, 354 years after they were first documented in the city, violent anti-Semitism led to the Jews being consigned to a ghetto, El Call. Ostensibly to provide protection, the ghetto had only one entrance, which led into the Plaça de Sant Jaume. Jews were heavily taxed by the monarch, who

viewed them as "royal serfs," but in return they also received privileges, as they handled most of Catalonia's lucrative trade with North Africa. However, official and popular persecution finally led to the disappearance of the ghetto in 1401, 91 years before Judaism was fully outlawed in Spain (*see p53*).

Originally there were three synagogues, the main one being in Carrer Sant Domènec del Call, but only the foundations are left. A 14th-century Hebrew tablet is embedded in the wall at No. 1 Carrer de Martlet, which reads: "Holy Foundation of Rabbi Samuel Hassardi, for whom life never ends."

ceiling and an altarpiece (1466) by Jaume Huguet. Its bell tower is formed by part of a watchtower on the Roman wall. Stairs through a small door on the right of the altar lead to the 16th-century tower of Martí the Humane (who reigned from 1396–1410), the last ruler of the 500-year dynasty of the count-kings of Barcelona. From the top of the tower there are fine views over the royal complex.

Museu d'Història de la Ciutat ❹

Plaça del Rei. **Map** 5 B2. ☎ (93) 315 11 11. Ⓜ Jaume I. ☐ 10am–2pm, 4–8pm Tue–Sat, 10am–2pm Sun. ☐ Jan 1, Good Fri, Dec 25 & 26.

T HE CITY MUSEUM occupies the Casa Clariana-Padellàs, a Gothic building that was brought here stone by stone in 1931 from its original site in Carrer dels Mercaders. During excavation of its new site, the remains of Roman water and drainage systems, baths, mosaic floors, and a road were found. These can be seen in the basement, which extends beneath the Plaça de l'Angel. A short stretch of the Roman city wall is accessible from the upper floors, which are devoted to Barcelona's post-Roman development.

Casa de la Ciutat ❺

Plaça de Sant Jaume. **Map** 5 A2. ☎ (93) 402 73 62. Ⓜ Jaume I. ☐ write in advance for permission. ☑

T HE MAGNIFICENT city hall *(ajuntament)*, dating from the 14th century, faces the Palau de la Generalitat across the Plaça de Sant Jaume. Flanking the entrance of the Casa de la Ciutat are statues of Jaime (Jaume) I, who granted the city rights to elect councillors in 1249, and Joan Fiveller, who in the 1500s successfully levied taxes on members of the court.

Inside is the huge council chamber, the 14th-century Saló de Cent, built for the city's 100 councillors. The Saló de les Cròniques, on the first floor, was commissioned for the 1929 International Exhibition and decorated by Josep-Marià Sert with murals of momentous events in Catalan history.

Palau de la Generalitat ❻

Plaça de Sant Jaume. **Map** 5 A2. ☎ (93) 402 73 62. Ⓜ Jaume I. ☐ Apr 23 for groups only (write in advance for permission). ☐ ☑

S INCE 1403, the Generalitat has been the seat of the Catalonian Government. Above the entrance, in its Renaissance

The Italianate façade of the Palau de la Generalitat

façade, is a statue of Sant Jordi (St. George) – the patron saint of Catalonia – and the Dragon. The late Catalan-Gothic courtyard is by Marc Safont (1416).

Among the fine interiors are the Gothic chapel of Sant Jordi, also by Safont, and Pere Blai's Italianate Saló de Sant Jordi. The building is open to the public only on the saint's feast day. At the back, one floor above street level, lies the *Pati dels Tarongers*, the Orange Tree Patio, by Pau Mateu, which has a bell tower built by Pere Ferrer in 1568.

The Catalan president has offices here as well as in the Casa dels Canonges. The two buildings are connected by a bridge across Carrer del Bisbe, built in 1928 and modeled on the Bridge of Sighs in Venice.

The magnificent council chamber, the Saló de Cent, in Casa de la Ciutat

Barcelona Cathedral ❼

T HIS COMPACT GOTHIC CATHEDRAL, with a Romanesque chapel (Capella de Santa Llúcia) and beautiful cloister, was begun in 1298 under Jaime (Jaume) II, on the foundations of a Roman temple and Moorish mosque. It was not finished until the late 19th century, when the main façade was completed. A white marble choir screen, sculpted in the 16th century, depicts the martyrdom of St. Eulalia, the city's patron. Next to the font, a plaque records the baptism of six Caribbean Indians, whom Columbus brought back from the Americas in 1493.

Statue of St. Eulalia

The twin octagonal bell towers date from 1386–93. The bells were installed in this tower in 1545.

The main façade was not completed until 1889, and the central spire until 1913. It was based on the original 1408 plans of the French architect Charles Galtés.

Nave Interior
The Catalan-style Gothic interior has a single wide nave with 28 side chapels. These are set between the columns supporting the vaulted ceiling, which rises to 26 m (85 ft).

★ Choir Stalls
The top tier of the beautifully carved 15th-century stalls contains painted coats of arms (1518) of several European kings.

Capella del Santíssim Sagrament
This small chapel houses the 16th-century Christ of Lepanto crucifix.

Capella de Sant Benet
This chapel, dedicated to the founder of the Benedictine Order and patron saint of Europe, houses a magnificent altarpiece showing The Transfiguration *by Bernat Martorell (1452).*

VISITORS' CHECKLIST

Plaça de la Seu. **Map** 5 A2. ☎ (93) 315 15 54. 🚇 *Urquinaona, Liceu.* 🚌 *17, 19, 45.* ⬜ *8am–1:30pm, 4–7:30pm daily.* 📷 ✝ *9am, noon, 7pm daily.* ♿ **Sacristy Museum** ⬜ *10am–1pm daily.* 📷 **Choir** ⬜ *9am–1:30pm, 4–7 pm Mon–Fri, 9am–1pm Sat.* 📷

★ Crypt
In the crypt, beneath the main altar, is the alabaster sarcophagus (1339) of St. Eulalia, martyred for her beliefs by the Romans during the 4th century AD.

★ Cloisters
The fountain, set in a corner of the Gothic cloisters and decorated with a statue of St. George, provided fresh water.

Porta de Sta Eulàlia, entrance to Cloisters

The Sacristy Museum has a small treasury. Pieces include tapestries, an 11th-century font, and liturgical artifacts.

Capella de Santa Llúcia

STAR FEATURES

★ Choir Stalls

★ Crypt

★ Cloisters

TIMELINE

559 Basilica dedicated to St. Eulalia and Holy Cross		**1339** St. Eulalia's relics transferred to alabaster sarcophagus		**1913** Central spire completed	
877 St. Eulalia's remains brought from Santa Maria del Mar		**1046–58** Romanesque cathedral built under Ramon Berenguer I		**1889** Main façade completed, based on plans by architect Charles Galtés dating from 1408	

400	700	1000	1300	1600	1900

4th century Original Roman (paleo-Christian) basilica built	**985** Building destroyed by the Moors	**1257–68** Romanesque Capella de Santa Llúcia built	**1493** Indians brought back from the Americas are baptized	
		1298 Gothic cathedral begun under Jaime II		*Plaque of the Indians' baptism*

The former dissecting room of the Antic Hospital de la Santa Creu

El Raval and the Barri Xinès ➑

Map 2 E3. ⊛ *Catalunya, Liceu.*
Museu d'Art Contemporani Pl dels
Angeles 1. ☎ *(93) 412 08 10.* ◯
*noon–8pm Tue–Fri, 10am–8pm Sat,
10am–3pm Sun & public hols.* 📷 ♿

THE DISTRICTS of El Raval and
the Barri Xinès occupy the
streets south of the Ramblas.
Having grown up outside the
city walls, they may lack the
Barri Gòtic's architecture, but
they are full of atmosphere and
have some grand buildings.
     The huge 14th-century Casa
de la Caritat (Charity House) is
now a cultural center. Next to
it stands the stunning, white
Museu d'Art Contemporani,
which opened in 1995. Close
by, off the Carrer de l'Hospital,
which has some of Barcelona's
most intriguing shops, is the
15th-century Hospital de la
Santa Creu, now housing the
city's main library.
     The Barri Xinès (Chinese
Quarter), toward the port, is
Barcelona's red light district.
There is, in fact, nothing at all
Chinese about it except its
name, which was given to it in
the 1920s by a local journalist
after he had seen a film about
San Francisco's Chinatown.
     On Carrer Nou de la Rambla
are Gaudí's Palau Güell *(see
p137)*; the Hotel Espanya *(see
p543)*, with its superb Modernista interior by Domènech i
Montaner; and the city's most
complete Romanesque church,
Sant Pau del Camp, where
Franciscans still sing Mass.

Las Ramblas ➒

THE HISTORIC AVENUE of Las Ramblas (Les Rambles in
Catalan) is busy around the clock, especially in the
evenings and on weekends. Newsstands, caged bird and
flower stalls, tarot readers, musicians, and mime artists
throng the wide, tree-shaded central walkway. Among
its famous buildings are the Liceu Opera House, the
huge Boqueria food market, and some grand mansions.

Exploring Las Ramblas
The name of this long avenue,
also more simply known as
La Rambla, comes from the
Arabic *ramla*, meaning the
dried-up bed of a seasonal
river. Barcelona's 13th-century
city wall followed the left
bank of one such river that
flowed from the Collserola
hills down to the sea.
     Convents, monasteries, and
the university were built on
the opposite bank in the 16th
century. As time passed, the
riverbed was filled in and
those buildings demolished,
but they are remembered in
the names of the five Ramblas
that make up the great avenue
between the Plaça de Catalunya and Port Vell (Old Port).
Today, it is lined with hotels,
mansions, shops, and cafés.

Palau Güell C/ Nou de la Rambla 3.
Map 2 F3. ☎ *(93) 317 39 74.* ⊛
Liceu. ◯ *10am–2pm, 4–8pm Mon–
Sat.* ⬤ *public hols.* 📷 **Museu de
Cera** Pg de la Banca 7. **Map** 2 F4.
☎ *(93) 317 26 49.* ⊛ *Drassanes.*
◯ *10am–1:30pm, 4–7:30pm
Mon–Fri, 10am–1:30pm, 4:30–8pm
Sat, Sun & public hols* 📷 ♿

The monument to Columbus at the bottom of the tree-lined Ramblas

Font de Canaletes ①
Saying that someone "drinks the waters of Canaletes" – from this 19th-century fountain – indicates he or she is from Barcelona.

Reial Acadèmia de Ciències i Arts ②
Converted to a theater in 1910, this building has Barcelona's first official public clock.

Palau de la Virreina ④
The first occupant of this great palace, in 1777, was the *virreina* (viceroy's wife) of Spain in Peru.

Mercat de Sant Josep ⑤
Popularly known as "La Boqueria," this is Barcelona's most colorful food market.

Gran Teatre del Liceu ⑦
The opera house has had to be restored twice after fires – in 1861 and 1994.

Palau Güell ⑨
This Neo-Gothic palace is considered to be one of Gaudí's most important works (*see p137*).

Palau Moja ③
The Baroque first-floor salon of this Classical building of 1790 is used for exhibitions.

Plaça de la Boqueria ⑥
This square features a mosaic pavement by Miró and an Art Deco dragon designed for a former umbrella shop.

Plaça Reial ⑧
Barcelona's most lively square was built in the 1850s. The Neo-Classical lampposts were designed by Gaudí.

Museu de Cera ⑩
This waxwork museum, in an atmospheric 19th-century building, contains about 300 exhibits.

KEY

🔄 FF CC railroad station

◈ Metro station

🅿 Parking

✝ Church

0 meters 100
0 yards 100

Monument a Colom
Plaça del Portal de la Pau

Statue of Poseidon in the courtyard of La Llotja

La Llotja ⓾

Carrer de Consolat del Mar 2. **Map** 5 B3. 🛈 *(93) 401 35 55.* Ⓜ *Jaume I.* 🕐 *10am–12:30pm Mon–Fri.*

Oᴿɪɢɪɴᴀʟʟʏ ʙᴜɪʟᴛ in the 14th century as the customs house for Barcelona's busy port, the Stock Exchange's Classical appearance dates from a complete remodeling in the 18th century. The main trading room, however, which can be glimpsed through the large ground-floor windows, is an impressive three-aisled Gothic room which has been beautifully preserved.

The Barcelona School of Fine Arts occupied the upper floors between 1849 and 1970. It was attended by the young Picasso *(see p28)*, whose father taught there, and also by Joan Miró (1893–1983) *(see p168).*

Basílica de Santa Maria del Mar ⓫

Passeig del Born 1. **Map** 5 B3. 🛈 *(93) 310 23 90.* Ⓜ *Jaume I.* 🕐 *9am–noon, 4:30–8:15pm daily.*

Tʜɪs ʙᴇᴀᴜᴛɪꜰᴜʟ building, the city's favorite church with superb acoustics for concerts, is the only example of a church entirely in the Catalan Gothic style. It took just 55 years to build, with money donated by merchants and shipbuilders. The speed – unrivaled in the Middle Ages – gave it a unity of style both inside and out. The west front has a 15th-century rose window of the Coronation of the Virgin. More stained glass, dating from the 15th to the 18th centuries, lights the wide nave and high aisles.

The choir and furnishings were burned in the Civil War *(see p63)*, adding to the sense of space and simplicity.

Carrer Montcada ⓬

Map 5 B3. Ⓜ *Jaume I.* **Museu Tèxtil i de la Indumentària** 🛈 *(93) 310 45 16.* 🕐 *10am–5pm Tue–Sat, 10am–2pm Sun & public hols.* ⬤ *Jan 1 & 5, Dec 25.* 🈂

Tʜᴇ ᴍᴏsᴛ ᴀᴜᴛʜᴇɴᴛɪᴄ medieval street in Barcelona is a narrow lane overshadowed by gargoyles and protruding roofs that almost touch overhead. The Gothic palaces that line it, entered through great wooden doors and built around magnificent courtyards, date back to the expansion of Catalonia in the 13th century. A mural of the conquest of Mallorca, a rare secular Romanesque painting once in the 13th–15th century Palau Berenguer d'Aguilar, is now in the Museu Nacional d'Art de Catalunya *(see p168).*

Carrer Montcada's buildings were all modified over the years, particularly in the 17th

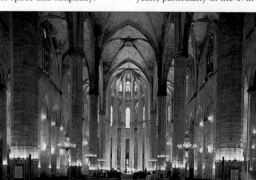

A wedding service in the Gothic interior of Santa Maria del Mar

Pablo Picasso, *Self-Portrait* in charcoal (1899–1900)

Pᴀʙʟᴏ Pɪᴄᴀssᴏ ɪɴ Bᴀʀᴄᴇʟᴏɴᴀ

Picasso (1881–1973) was born in Málaga and was almost 14 when he came to Barcelona, where his father had found a job in the city's art academy. Picasso enrolled and was a precocious talent among his contemporaries. He was a regular visitor to Els Quatre Gats, an artists' café still in existence in Carrer Montsió, where he held his first exhibition. He also exhibited in Sala Parks, a gallery still functioning in Carrer Petritxol. The family lived in Carrer Mercé, and Picasso had a studio in Carrer Nou de la Rambla. It was among the prostitutes of Carrer d'Avinyò that he found inspiration for the work that many art historians see as the wellspring of modern art, *Les Demoiselles d'Avignon* (1906–7). Picasso left Barcelona for Paris in his early twenties and initially returned several times. After the Civil War his opposition to Franco kept him in France, but he designed a frieze for Barcelona's College of Architects in 1962 and was persuaded to allow the city to open a museum of his work, which it did the following year.

century when the Renaissance style prevailed. The only one to retain its original façade is the Casa Cervelló-Guidice at No. 25. The **Museu Tèxtil i de la Indumentària** in the Palau dels Marquesos de Lló at No. 12 (also called the Palau Mora) displays textiles and clothing from the 4th century onward. The street also has the city's best known champagne bar, *El Xampanyet (see p185).*

Museu Picasso ⑬

Carrer Montcada 15–19. **Map** 5 B1.
[(93) 319 63 10. ⚇ *Jaume I.*
◯ *10am–8pm Tue–Sat & public hols,*
10am–3pm Sun. 🖼

O NE OF BARCELONA'S most popular attractions, the Picasso Museum, is housed in three palaces on the Carrer Montcada: the Baroque Meca, and the medieval Berenguer d'Aguilar, and Baró de Castellet.
  The museum opened in 1963 using works donated by Jaime Sabartes, a great friend of Picasso. Following Sabartes' death in 1968, Picasso himself donated paintings, including early examples which had been kept by his sister. These were complemented by graphic works, left in his will, and 141 ceramic pieces given by his widow, Jacqueline.
  The works are divided into three sections: paintings and drawings, engravings, and ceramics. But the strength of the 3,000-piece collection is in Picasso's early drawings and paintings. These demonstrate that even as a teenager he was painting major works,

Glorious stained-glass dome, Palau de la Música Catalana

such as *The First Communion* (1896). There are only a few pictures from his Blue and Rose periods. The most famous work is his series *Las Meninas* – based on Velázquez's master-piece *(see p28)* – which is displayed in its entirety.

Palau de la Música Catalana ⑭

Carrer de Sant Francesc de Paula 2.
Map 5 B1. [(93) 268 10 00.
⚇ *Catalunya, Urquinaona.* ◯ *for concerts, or by appointment 3–4:30pm Tue & Thu, 10am–noon Sat.*
● *Aug.* 🖼

T HIS IS a real palace of music, a Modernista celebration of tile work, sculpture, and glorious stained glass. It is the only concert hall in Europe lit by natural light. Designed by Lluís Domènech i Montaner, it was completed in 1908 on the site of a monastery dissolved in the 19th century. Although a few extensions have been

added, the building still retains its original appearance. The elaborate red brick façade is hard to appreciate fully in the confines of the narrow street. It is lined with mosaic-covered pillars topped by busts of Palestrina, Bach, and Beethoven. The large stone sculpture of St. George and other figures at the corner of the building is an allegory of Catalan folk-song by Miquel Blay.
  But it is the interior of the building which is truly inspiring. The auditorium on the first floor is lit by a huge inverted dome of stained glass depicting angelic choristers.
  The sculptures of the com-posers Wagner and Clavé on the proscenium arch were de-signed by Domènech but fin-ished by Pablo Gargallo. Josep Anselm Clavé's (1824–74) work in promoting Catalan song led to the creation of the Orfeó Català choral society in 1891, which became a focus of Catalan nationalism and the inspiration behind the Palau.

Painting in Picasso's series *Las Meninas* (1957), Museu Picasso

The pink brick façade of the late 19th-century Arc del Triomf

Arc del Triomf ⓯

Passeig Lluís Companys. **Map** 5 C1.
Ⓜ *Arc de Triomf.*

THE MAIN GATEWAY to the 1888 Universal Exhibition, which filled the Parc de la Ciutadella, was designed by Josep Vilaseca i Casanovas. It is built of brick in the Mudéjar style *(see p51)*, with sculptured allegories of crafts, industry, and business. The frieze by Josep Reynés on the main façade represents the city of Barcelona welcoming foreign visitors. The one at the rear by Josep Llimona is of a prize-giving ceremony.

Parc de la Ciutadella ⓰

Avda del Marqués de l'Argentera. **Map** 6 D2. Ⓜ *Barceloneta, Ciutadella-Vila Olímpica.* ◯ *9am–9pm daily.* ♿

THIS POPULAR park has a large boating lake, orange groves, and scores of naturalized parrots living in the palm trees. The 75-acre park was previously

the site of a massive star-shaped citadel. Designed by Prosper Verboom, this was built for Felipe V between 1715 and 1720 following a 13-month siege of the city, brought about by Barcelona's opposition to the Bourbon succession *(see p58)*. The fortress was intended to house soldiers to help keep law and order, but was never used for this purpose. It was converted into a prison that became particularly notorious during the Napoleonic occupation *(see p59)*, and during the 19th-century liberal repressions, when it was hated as a symbol of centralized power.

In 1878, under the enlightened dictator General Prim, whose statue stands in the middle of the park, the citadel was pulled down and the park was given to the city, to become, in 1888, the venue of the Universal Exhibition.

Three buildings, however, survived: the arsenal, which was redesigned in 1932 for use by the Catalan parliament and is today shared with the Museu d'Art Modern; the Governor's Palace, which is now a school; and the chapel, still sometimes used by the military.

The gardens in the Plaça de Armes were laid out by the French landscape gardener Jean Forestier. They center on a cascade based around a triumphal arch and partly inspired by the Trevi Fountain in Rome. It was designed by architect Josep Fontseré, with the help of Antoni Gaudí, who was then still a young student.

One of the galleries inside the spacious Museu de Zoologia

Museu de Zoologia ⓱

Passeig de Picasso. **Map** 5 C2. 🚻 *(93) 319 69 12.* Ⓜ *Arc de Triomf.* ◯ *10am–2pm Tue–Sun & public hols.* 🈲

AT THE ENTRANCE to the Parc de la Ciutadella is the fortresslike Castell dels Tres Dragons (Castle of the Three Dragons), named after a play by Frederic Soler that was popular at the time it was built.

This brick edifice, crenellated and decorated with a frieze of ceramic shields, was built as a café-restaurant for the 1888 Universal Exhibition. The architect Lluís Domènech i Montaner modeled it on Valencia's Lonja *(see p241)*. He later used it as a workshop for Modernista design, and it became a focus of the movement. It has housed the city's Zoological Museum since 1937.

Ornamental cascade in the Parc de la Ciutadella designed by Josep Fontseré and Antoni Gaudí

Museu de Geologia ⑱

Parc de la Ciutadella. **Map** 5 C3.
📞 *(93) 319 68 95.* 🚇 *Arc de Triomf, Jaume I.* 🕐 *9am–2pm Tue–Sun & public hols.* ⬤ *May1, Dec 25.* 🈳

BARCELONA'S OLDEST MUSEUM opened in 1882, the same year the Parc de la Ciutadella became a public space for the city. It has a large collection of fossils and minerals, including specimens from Catalonia and around the country.

Beside it is the Hivernacle, an iron-framed glass building by Josep Amargós that is often used for concerts. Nearby is the Umbracle, a brick and wood conservatory built by the park's architect, Josep Fontseré, to shelter tropical plants.

Glass cube of the *Homenatge a Picasso*, Parc de la Ciutadella

Homenatge a Picasso ⑲

Passeig de Picasso. **Map** 5 C3.
🚇 *Barceloneta.*

AT THE EDGE OF THE Parc de la Ciutadella, opposite the Avinguda del Marqués de l'Argentera, is Catalan sculptor Antoni Tàpies' intriguing 1983 work, *Homage to Picasso.*

Built to pay homage to Picasso's Cubist works, it is an intellectual sculpture that does not immediately suggest its title. A large, plain glass cube sits in a square pond, with water streaming down the sides. The cube contains an old sofa, chairs, and a sideboard skewered by metal poles and draped with a blanket. The elements have not treated it kindly, and an air-conditioning system has had to be installed to prevent the glass from cracking.

***Dusk on the River Loing* by Alfred Sisley (1839–99)**

Museu d'Art Modern ⑳

Parc de la Ciutadella. **Map** 6 D3.
📞 *(93) 319 50 23.* 🚇 *Arc de Triomf.* 🕐 *10am–7pm Tue–Sat & public hols, 10am–2pm Sun.* 🈳

THE NAME OF THIS MUSEUM is slightly misleading, as it really houses a collection of 19th- and 20th-century Catalan art, in which the main players – Miró, Picasso, Dalí, and Tàpies – are under-represented as they have museums of their own. This should not put potential visitors off, as much of the work is excellent and of great help in understanding Catalan life and culture.

In particular there are works by Catalonia's two main early 20th-century painters, Santiago Rusiñol (1861–1931) and Ramón Casas (1866–1932), considered to be the region's first Impressionist. Casas' line drawings record the faces of the great men of his day. Chief among them is a picture of Pablo Picasso newly arrived in Montmartre in Paris. There is also a painting of Casas himself on a tandem bicycle with Pere Romeu; they were founders of Barcelona's Els Quatre Gats café *(see p148)*, where the painting originally hung.

Picasso's contemporaries, the painters Joaquim Mir (1873–1940) and Isidre Nonell (1873–1911), are represented here, and there are some sculptures by Miquel Blay (1866–1936). There is also a landscape by Alfred Sisley (1839–99), *Dusk on the River Loing.*

The museum has a few excellent examples of Modernista furniture from homes around the Eixample, including an entire private altar.

Parc Zoològic ㉑

Parc de la Ciutadella. **Map** 6 D3.
📞 *(93) 221 25 06.* 🚇 *Ciutadella-Vila Olímpica.* 🕐 *Mar: 10am–6pm, Apr & Sep: 10am–7pm, May–Aug: 9:30am–7:30pm, Oct–Feb: 10am–5pm.* 🈳

BARCELONA'S ZOO was laid out in the 1940s to a relatively enlightened design in which the animals are separated by moats instead of iron bars. The zoo is strong on primates, and for years its mascot has been Floquet de Neu (Snowflake), a rare white gorilla. Dolphin and whale shows are held in one of the aquariums. By the entrance is Roig i Soler's romantic 1885 fountain sculpture, *The Lady with the Umbrella*, so well loved that it has become a symbol of Barcelona.

Floquet de Neu, Barcelona zoo's rare white gorilla

Tree lined beach, Vila Olímpica

Vila Olímpica ㉒

Map 6 F4. 🚇 *Ciutadella-Vila Olímpica.*

THE MOST DRAMATIC rebuilding for the 1992 Olympics took place along the old industrial waterfront of Poble Nou, an area now known as the Vila Olímpica. A promenade and ring road were built to replace old shacks and shunting yards. Running parallel are 4 km (2 miles) of rehabilitated sandy beaches that are packed with locals during the summer.

The factory district behind was replaced by a new 160-acre town of 2,000 apartments and parks that cover nearly as much land again. The apartments accommodated thousands of athletes during the Games and were afterward put to normal residential use.

Two 44-floor skyscrapers were also built, one for offices and one for a hotel and apartments. At their feet is a new marina (Port Olímpic), lined with cafés and restaurants.

Barceloneta ㉓

Map 5 B5. 🚇 *Barceloneta.*

BARCELONA'S fishing "village," which lies on a triangular tongue of land jutting into the sea just below the city center, is renowned for its seafood restaurants and portside cafés.

Barceloneta was built by the architect and military engineer Juan Martín de Cermeño in 1753 to rehouse people made homeless by the construction, just inland, of a large fortress, La Ciutadella *(see p150)*. The area was later inhabited largely by fishermen and workers.

Its last remaining warehouse, built by Elies Rogent in the 1880s, was remodeled in 1992 to become the Palau de Mar. This is a complex of bars, cafés, and restaurants specializing in seafood dishes. Upstairs there is a museum of Catalan history.

Barceloneta's short streets, laid out in a grid system, and the low, balconied houses have a friendly air and seem far removed from the city. In the small Plaça de la Barceloneta, at the center of the district, is the Baroque church of Sant Miquel del Port, also designed by Cermeño. A market is often held in the square in front of it.

Port Vell ㉔

Map 5 A4. 🚇 *Barceloneta, Drassanes.* **Aquàrium** ⬛ *(93) 221 74 74.* ◯ *10am–8pm daily.* 🔯

THE CITY'S NEW leisure port lies at the foot of the Ramblas, which is connected by a pedestrian jetty across to the yacht clubs on the far Moll d'Espanya (*moll* meaning wharf). A swing bridge allows vessels through. At the end of this wharf is Maremagnum, a large complex of restaurants, shops, and movie houses, and Europe's largest aquarium.

The Moll de la Fusta (Timber Wharf) includes red bridges inspired by Van Gogh's bridge at Arles. It is built on two levels – the upper level dotted with terrace cafés giving a good view of the port. Nearby is the restaurant Gambrinus *(see p173)*, identified by a giant lobster designed by Alfredo Arribas and Javier Mariscal. At the end of the wharf stands *El Cap de Barcelona (Barcelona Head)*, a strikingly colorful, columnar, 20-m (66-ft) tall sculpture by American Pop artist Roy Lichtenstein.

The popular cable car passing dramatically over Port Vell from Montjuïc to Barceloneta was closed in 1995, pending a future decision on whether to rebuild it or demolish it.

Monument a Colom ㉕

Plaça del Portal de la Pau. **Map** 2 F4. ⬛ *(93) 302 52 24.* 🚇 *Drassanes.* ◯ *Oct–May: 10am–2pm, 3:30–6:30pm Tue–Sun; Jun–Sep: 9am–8:30pm daily.* 🔯

THE COLUMBUS monument in the Portal de la Pau (the "Gate of Peace") was designed by Gaietà Buigas for the 1888 Universal Exhibition.

The 60-m (200-ft) monument – a cast iron column on a stone plinth – marks the spot where Columbus stepped ashore in 1493 after discovering America, bringing with him six Caribbean Indians. He was accorded a state welcome by the Catholic Monarchs in the Saló del Tinell *(see p142)*. The Indians' subsequent conversion to Christianity is commemorated in the cathedral *(see pp144–5)*.

An elevator reaches a viewing platform at the top of the monument. The bronze statue, pointing out to sea, was designed by Rafael Arché.

Fishing boat moored at the wharf in Barceloneta

A *golondrina* departing from the Plaça del Portal de la Pau

Golondrinas 🕹

Plaça del Portal de la Pau. **Map** 2 F5.
📞 *(93) 442 31 06.* 🚇 *Drassanes.*
🕐 *Jun – Sep: 11am – 8pm daily; Oct – May: 10am – 1pm Mon – Fri, 11am – 5:30pm Sat & Sun.* 📷

Sightseeing trips around Barcelona's harbor can be made on small double-decker boats called *golondrinas* (literally "swallows"). They dock beside the steps of the Plaça del Portal de la Pau at the bottom of Las Ramblas.

Tours last around half an hour. The boats go out beneath the steep, castle-topped hill of Montjuïc toward the industrial port. They usually stop off at the breakwater, which reaches out to sea from Barceloneta, to allow passengers to disembark for a stroll.

An alternative, commentated, two-hour trip takes in the commercial port and beaches and stops off at the Port Olímpic.

Museu Marítim and Drassanes 🕹

Avinguda de les Drassanes. **Map** 2 F4.
📞 *(93) 301 18 71.* 🚇 *Drassanes.*
🕐 *10am – 7pm Tue – Sun; Oct 12, Nov 1, Dec 6 & 8: 10am – 2pm.*
⚫ *some public hols.* 📷 ♿ 📷

The great galleys that made Barcelona a major seafaring power were built in the sheds of the Drassanes (shipyards) that now house the maritime museum. These royal dry docks are the largest and most complete surviving medieval complex of their kind in the world. They were founded in the mid-13th century, when dynastic marriages uniting the kingdoms of Sicily and Aragón meant that better maritime communications between the two became a priority. Three of the yards' four original corner towers survive.

Among the vessels to slip from the Drassanes' vaulted halls was the *Real*, flagship of Don Juan of Austria, Charles V's illegitimate son, who led the Christian fleet to victory against the Turks at Lepanto in 1571 *(see p55)*. The museum's showpiece is a full-scale replica decorated in red and gold.

The *Llibre del Consulat de Mar*, a book of nautical codes and practice, serves as a reminder that Catalonia was once the arbiter of maritime law in the Mediterranean. The expertise of its sailors is also evident in the museum's collection of pre-Columbian charts and maps, including one of 1439 which was used by the navigator Amerigo Vespucci.

Stained-glass window in the Museu Marítim

BARCELONA'S FIESTAS

La Mercè *(Sep 24)*. The patroness of Barcelona, Nostra Senyora de la Mercè (Our Lady of Mercy), whose church is near the port, is honored for a week around September 24 with masses, concerts, and dances. The biggest events are the *carrefoc* – a procession of people dressed as devils and monsters, illuminated by fireworks – and the *piro musical* – a fireworks display with music held at the Font Màgica in Montjuïc.

Fireworks display during the fiesta of La Mercè

Els Tres Tombs *(Jan 17)*. Horsemen, dressed in top hats and tails, ride three times through the streets in honor of St. Anthony, the patron saint of animals.
La Diada *(Sep 11)*. Catalonia's "national" day is an occasion for singing the Catalan anthem and separatist demonstrations.
Dia de Sant Ponç *(May 11)*. Stalls along Carrer Hospital sell herbs, honey, and candied fruit on the day of the patron saint of beekeepers and herbalists.
Festa Major *(mid-Aug)*. Each district hosts its own *festa* in which streets compete to outdo each other in the inventiveness and beauty of their decorations. The most spectacular displays take place in the old district of Gràcia.

Eixample

BARCELONA CLAIMS to have the greatest collection of Art Nouveau buildings of any city in Europe. The style, known in Catalonia as Modernisme, flourished after 1854, when it was decided to tear down the medieval walls to allow the city to develop into what had previously been a construction-free military zone.

The designs of the civil engineer Ildefons Cerdà i Sunyer (1815–76) were chosen for the new expansion *(eixample)* inland. These plans called for a rigid grid system of streets, but at each intersection the corners were chamfered to allow the buildings there to overlook the junctions or squares. The few exceptions

Jesus of the Column,
Sagrada Família

to this grid system include the Diagonal, a main avenue running from the wealthy area of Pedralbes down to the sea, and the Hospital de la Santa Creu i de Sant Pau by Modernista architect Domènech i Montaner (1850–1923). He hated the grid system and deliberately angled the hospital to look down the diagonal Avinguda de Gaudí toward Antoni Gaudí's church of the Sagrada Família, the city's most spectacular Modernista building *(see pp162–3).* The wealth of Barcelona's commercial elite, and their passion for all things new, allowed them to give free rein to the age's most innovative architects in designing their residences as well as public buildings.

SIGHTS AT A GLANCE

Museums and Galleries
Fundació Antoni Tàpies ❷

Churches
Sagrada Família ❻

Modernista Buildings
Casa Milà, "La Pedrera" ❸
Casa Terrades, "Casa de les Punxes" ❹
Hospital de la Santa Creu i de Sant Pau ❺
Illa de la Discòrdia ❶

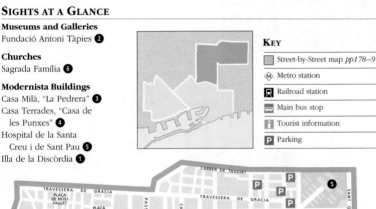

KEY

▨	Street-by-Street map *pp178–9*
Ⓜ	Metro station
🚆	Railroad station
🚍	Main bus stop
ℹ	Tourist information
🅿	Parking

GETTING THERE

Metro line 1 has stations at both ends of the Passeig de Gràcia (Catalunya and Diagonal), and one in the middle, at the Illa de la Discòrdia (Passeig de Gràcia). Metro line 5 takes you straight to the Sagrada Família and Hospital de Sant Pau (a long walk from other sights).

0 meters	500
0 yards	500

◁ **Nativity façade of the Sagrada Família – the only façade to be more or less completed in Gaudí's lifetime**

Street-by-Street: Quadrat d'Or

Tᴴᴇ ʜᴜɴᴅʀᴇᴅ ᴏʀ so city blocks centering on the Passeig de Gràcia are known as the Quadrat d'Or, "Golden Square," because they contain so many of Barcelona's best Modernista buildings *(see pp136–7)*. This was the area within the Eixample favored by the wealthy bourgeoisie, who embraced the new artistic and architectural style with enthusiasm, not only for their residences, but also for commercial buildings. Most remarkable is the Illa de la Discòrdia, a single block containing houses by Modernisme's most illustrious exponents. Many interiors can be visited by the public, revealing a feast of stained glass, ceramics, and ornamental ironwork.

Perfume bottle, Museu del Perfum

Diagonal Metro

Passeig de Gràcia, the Eixample's main avenue, is a showcase of highly original buildings and stylish shops. The graceful street lamps are by Pere Falqués (1850–1916).

R A M B L A   D E   C A T A L U N Y A

Vinçon home decorating store *(see p183)*

P A S S E I G   D E   G R A C I A

Fundació Tàpies
Topped by Antoni Tàpies' wire sculpture Cloud and Chair, *this 1879 building by Domènech i Montaner houses a wide variety of Tàpies' paintings, graphics, and sculptures* ❷

Casa Amatller

Museo del Perfum

Casa Ramon Mulleras

★ Illa de la Discòrdia
In this city block, four of Barcelona's most famous Modernista houses vie for attention. All were created between 1900 and 1910. This ornate tower graces the Casa Lleó Morera by Domènech i Montaner ❶

To Plaça de Catalunya

Casa Batlló

Casa Lleó Morera

Passeig de Gràcia Metro

Museu de la Música is housed in the Palau Baró de Quadras designed by Puig i Cadafalch in 1904. This carving adorns the doorway. The museum has displays of historical instruments collected from around the world.

LOCATOR MAP
See Street Finder map 3

EIXAMPLE

OLD TOWN

AVINGUDA DIAGONAL

CARRER DE PAU CLARIS

CARRER DE PROVENÇA

CARRER DE MALLORCA

CARRER DE ROGER DE LLURIA

ARRER DE VALENCIA

CARRER DEL BRUC

CARRER D'ARAGO

Casa Thomas

To Sagrada Família

Palau Ramon de Montaner

Casa Terrades
Built in red brick with carved stone ornamentation, this 1905 house by Puig i Cadafalch echoes the Gothic buildings of northern Europe ❹

★ Casa Milà "La Pedrera"
Gaudí put all his architectural daring into this, his most famous house. The result is a remarkable wavelike façade and a roofscape of chimneys and vents resembling abstract sculptures ❸

0 meters   100
0 yards   100

KEY

— — — Suggested route

STAR SIGHTS

★ Illa de la Discòrdia

★ Casa Milà "La Pedrera"

Sumptuous interior of the Casa Lleó Morera, Illa de la Discòrdia

Illa de la Discòrdia ❶

Passeig de Gràcia, between Carrer d'Aragó and Carrer del Consell de Cent. **Map** 3 A4. Ⓜ *Passeig de Gràcia.*

THE MOST famous group of Modernista *(see pp136–7)* buildings in Barcelona amply illustrates the range of styles involved in the movement. The city block in which they stand has been dubbed the Illa de la Discòrdia, "Block of Discord," owing to the startling visual argument between them.

The three most famous houses, on Passeig de Gràcia, were remodeled in Modernista style from existing houses early in the 20th century, but named after their original owners.

No. 35 is Casa Lleó Morera (1902–6), the first residential work of Lluís Domènech i Montaner. The ground floor was gutted to create a shop in 1943, but the sumptuous Modernista interiors upstairs still exist, and the first floor may in future be opened to the public.

Beyond the next two houses, one of which is a beauty shop containing a perfume museum,

is Casa Amatller, designed by Puig i Cadafalch in 1898. Its façade is a harmonious blend of styles, featuring Moorish and Gothic windows encased in iron grilles. The stepped gable roof is dotted with tiles. Inside the wrought-iron main doors is a fine stone staircase beneath a stained-glass roof. The building, now used by the Institut Amatller d'Art

Hispànic, has a beautiful wood-paneled library. Next door is Antoni Gaudí's Casa Batlló (1904–6). Its façade is typically liquid, with heavily tiled walls and curving iron balconies pierced with holes to look like masks or skulls. The hump-backed, scaly-looking roof is thought to represent a dragon, with St. George (the patron saint of Catalonia) as a chimney. Step inside to see the blue-tiled entrance hall.

Fundaciò Antoni Tàpies ❷

Carrer d'Aragó 255. **Map** 3 A1. Ⓒ (93) 487 03 15. Ⓜ *Passeig de Gràcia.* ◯ *11am–8pm Tue–Sun & public hols (Sun in Aug: 11am–3pm).* ● *Jan 1 & 6, Dec 25 & 26.* 🈂 ♿

ANTONI TAPIES, born in 1923, is Barcelona's best-known living artist. Inspired by Surrealism, his abstract work is executed in a variety of materials, including concrete and metal *(see p156)*. It is not easy to appreciate at first, but the exhibits should help those interested obtain a clearer perspective, even if there are not enough here to gain a full understanding of the artist's work. They are housed in the first domestic building in Barcelona to be built with iron (1880), designed by Domènech i Montaner for his brother's publishing firm.

ANTONI GAUDÍ (1852–1926)

Born in Reus (Tarragona) into a family of artisans, Gaudí was the leading exponent of Catalan Modernisme. Following a stint as a blacksmith's apprentice, he studied at Barcelona's School of Architecture. Inspired by a nationalistic search for a romantic medieval past, his work was supremely original. His first major achievement was the Casa Vicens (1888) at No. 24 Carrer de les Carolines, but his most celebrated building is the extravagant church of the Sagrada Família *(see pp162–3)*, to which he devoted his life from 1914. He gave all his money to the project and often went from house to house begging for more, until his death a few days after being run over by a trolley.

Decorated chimney pot, Casa Vicens

◁ **Extraordinary sculptured and ceramic-encrusted chimneys of Gaudí's Casa Milà**

The rippled façade of Gaudí's apartment building, Casa Milà

Casa Milà ❸

Passeig de Gràcia 92. **Map** 3 B3.
(93) 484 59 80. Diagonal.
guided tours only: Tue–Sat 10am,
11am, noon, 1pm. public hols.

Usually called "La Pedrera" ("the stone quarry"), the Casa Milà is Gaudí's greatest contribution to Barcelona's civic architecture, and his last work before he devoted himself entirely to the Sagrada Família *(see pp162–3)*.

Built between 1906 and 1910, "La Pedrera" completely departed from the established construction principles of the time and, as a result, was ridiculed and strongly attacked by Barcelona's intellectuals.

Gaudí designed this corner apartment building, eight stories high, around two circular courtyards. In the basement he incorporated the city's first underground parking lot. The intricate ironwork balconies, by Josep Maria Jujol, are like seaweed against the wave-like walls of white undressed stone. There are no straight walls anyhere in the building.

The Milà family had an apartment on the first floor. Regular guided tours from an office on the ground floor take in the extraordinary roof, where the multitude of sculpted air ducts and chimneys look so threatening they have been dubbed the *espantabruixas*, the witch-scarers.

Casa Terrades ❹

Avinguda Diagonal 416. **Map** 3 B3.
Diagonal. to public.

This freestanding, six-sided apartment building designed by the Modernista architect Puig i Cadafalch gets its nickname, *Casa de les Punxes* (House of the Points), from the spires on its six corner turrets. It was built between 1903 and 1905 by converting three existing houses on the site and was Cadafalch's largest work. It is an eclectic mixture of medieval and

Spire on the main tower, Casa Terrades

Renaissance styles. The towers and gables are influenced in particular by north European Gothic architecture. However, the deeply carved, floral stone ornament of the exterior, along with red brick used as the main building material, are typically Modernista.

Hospital de la Santa Creu i de Sant Pau ❺

Carrer de Sant Antoni Maria Claret 167.
Map 4 F1. *(93) 291 90 00.*
Hospital de Sant Pau. **Grounds**
daily; write in advance for permission to
visit pavilions not in medical use.

Lluis Domenech i Montaner began designing a new city hospital in 1902. Totally innovative in concept, his plan consisted of 26 attractive Mudéjar-style pavilions set in large gardens, as he strongly disliked huge wards and believed that patients would recover better amid fresh air and trees. All the connecting corridors and service areas were hidden underground.

Also believing art and color to be therapeutic, he decorated the pavilions profusely. The turreted roofs were tiled with ceramics, and the admitting pavilion embellished with sculptures by Pau Gargallo and mosaic murals. The vast project was completed in 1930, after Domènech's death, by his son, Pere.

Statue of the Virgin, Hospital de la Santa Creu i de Sant Pau

Sagrada Família ⑥

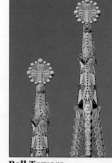

Bell Towers
Eight of the 12 spires, one for each apostle, have been built. Each is topped by Venetian mosaics.

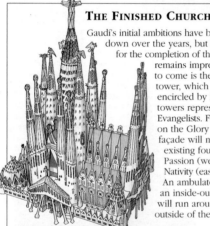

A carved whelk

E UROPE'S MOST unconventional church, the Temple Expiatori de la Sagrada Família, is an emblem of a city that likes to think of itself as individualistic. Crammed with symbolism inspired by nature and striving for originality, it is Gaudí's *(see pp136 –7)* greatest work. In 1883, a year after work had begun on a Neo-Gothic church on the site, the task of completing it was given to Gaudí, who changed everything, extemporizing as he went along. It became his life's work and he lived like a recluse on the site for 16 years. He is buried in the crypt. At his death only one tower on the Nativity façade had been completed, but several more have been finished to his original plans. After the Civil War, work resumed and continues today, financed by public donations.

THE FINISHED CHURCH

Gaudí's initial ambitions have been scaled down over the years, but the design for the completion of the building remains impressive. Still to come is the central tower, which is to be encircled by four large towers representing the Evangelists. Four towers on the Glory (south) façade will match the existing four on the Passion (west) and Nativity (east) façades. An ambulatory – like an inside-out cloister – will run around the outside of the building.

Tower with elevator

The apse was the first part of the church Gaudí completed. Stairs lead down from here to the crypt below.

The altar canopy, designed by Gaudí, is still waiting for the altar.

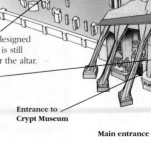

Entrance to Crypt Museum

Main entrance

★ **Passion Façade**
This bleak façade was completed in the late 1980s by artist Josep Maria Subirachs. A controversial work, its sculpted figures are angular and often sinister.

Spiral Staircases
400 steep stone steps allow access to the towers and upper galleries. Majestic views reward those who climb or take the elevator.

VISITORS' CHECKLIST

Carrer de Mallorca 401. **Map** 4 E3.
(93) 455 02 47. Sagrada Familia. 19, 34, 43, 50, 51, 54.
Apr–Aug: 9am–8pm daily; Sep: 9am–7pm daily; Oct–Mar: 9am–6pm daily. Jan 1, Dec 25 (pm). 9am, 8:15pm Mon–Sat; 9am, 10:30am, 11:45am, 1pm, 8:15pm Sun.

Tower with elevator

★ **Nativity Façade**
The most complete part of Gaudí's church, finished in 1904, has doorways that represent Faith, Hope, and Charity. Scenes of the Nativity and Christ's childhood are embellished with symbolism such as white doves, which represent the congregation.

★ **Crypt**
The crypt, where Gaudí is buried, was built by the original architect, Francesc de Paula Villar i Lozano, in 1882. This is where services are currently held. The lower floor contains a small museum tracing the careers of both architects and the church's complicated history.

The final parts of the structure to be built will be the nave and the south (Glory) façade – which was originally planned as the main entrance. The finished building will be in the form of a Latin cross. A forest of intricately fluted pillars will support four galleries above the side aisles.

STAR FEATURES

★ **Passion Façade**

★ **Nativity Façade**

★ **Crypt**

MONTJUÏC

THE HILL OF MONTJUIC, rising to 213 m (699 ft) above the commercial port on the south side of the city, is Barcelona's biggest recreation area. Its museums, art galleries, amusement park, and nightclubs make it a popular place both day and night.

There was probably a Celt-iberian settlement here before the Romans built a temple to Jupiter on their Mons Jovis, which may have given Montjuïc its name – though another theory suggests that a Jewish cemetery on the hill inspired the name Mount of the Jews.

The absence of a water supply meant that there were few buildings on Montjuïc until the castle was erected on the top in 1640.

Statue, gardens of the Palau Nacional

The hill finally came into its own as the site of the 1929 International Fair. With great energy and flair, buildings were erected all over the north side, with the grand Avinguda de la Reina María Cristina, lined with huge exhibition halls, leading into it from the Plaça d'Espanya. In the middle of the avenue is the Font Màgica (Magic Fountain), which is sometimes illuminated in color. Above it is the Palau Nacional, home of the city's great art collection. The Poble Espanyol is a crafts center housed in copies of buildings from all over Spain. The last great surge of building on Montjuïc was for the 1992 Olympic Games, which have left Barcelona with international-class sports facilities.

SIGHTS AT A GLANCE

Historic Buildings
Castell de Montjuïc ❼

Modern Architecture
Estadi Olímpic de Montjuïc ❽
Pavelló Mies van der Rohe ❹

Museums and Galleries
Fundació Joan Miró ❶
Museu Arqueològic ❷
Museu Nacional d'Art de Catalunya ❸

Squares
Plaça d'Espanya ❻

Theme Parks
Poble Espanyol ❺

GETTING THERE
Apart from the exhibition halls near Espanya metro station, reaching most of Montjuïc's attractions on foot involves a steep climb. However, buses 13 and 61 will take you up the hill from Plaça d'Espanya. For the amusement park and castle, take the funicular from metro Paral·lel, then the cable car. Both run from 11am–7:30/8pm weekends, and daily in summer.

PARC DE MONTJUIC

0 meters   500
0 yards   500

KEY

▦	Street-by-Street map pp166–7
Ⓜ	Metro station
🚡	Cable car station
🚞	Funicular railway station
Ⓟ	Parking

◁ Changing colors of the Font Màgica (Magic Fountain) on the grand avenue leading up to Montjuïc

Street-by-Street: Montjuïc

MONTJUIC IS A SPECTACULAR vantage point
from which to view the city. It has art
galleries and museums, an amusement park,
and an open-air theater adjoining a rose
garden. The most interesting buildings lie
around the Palau Nacional, where Europe's
greatest Romanesque art collection is housed.
Montjuïc is approached from the Plaça
d'Espanya between brick pillars based on
the campanile of St. Mark's in Venice, which
give a foretaste of the eclec-
ticism of building styles.
The Poble Espanyol
illustrates the traditional
Spanish architecture,
while the Fundació Joan
Miró is boldly modern.

Pavelló Mies va
der Rohe
*This statue by Ge
Kolbe (see p169)
stands serenely i
the steel, glass, st
and onyx pavilio
built in the Bauh
style as the Germ
contribution to th
1929 Internation
Exhibition* ❹

AVINGUDA DEL MARQUES DE COMILLAS

AVINGUDA DELS MONTANYANS

PASSEIG DE LES

AVINGUDA DEL ESTADI

★ Poble
Espanyol
*Containing
replicas of build-
ings from many
regions, this "village" provides a fascinating glimpse
of vernacular styles* ❺

**To Montjuïc castle
and Olympic stadium**

★ Museu Nacional
d'Art de Catalunya
*Displayed in the
National Palace, the
main building of the
1929 International
Exhibition, is Europe's
finest collection of
early medieval
frescoes. These were
a great source of
inspiration for Joan
Miró (see p168)* ❸

STAR SIGHTS

★ Poble Espanyol

★ Museu Nacional
d'Art de Catalunya

★ Fundació Joan Miró

Fountains and cascades descend in terraces from the Palau Nacional. Below them is the Font Màgica (Magic Fountain). On summer evenings, from Thursday to Sunday, its jets are programmed to a multicolored music and light show. This marvel of water-and-electrical engineering was originally built by Carles Buigas (1898–1979) for the 1929 International Exhibition.

LOCATOR MAP
See Street Finder map 1

ça d'Espanya

Museu Arqueològic
The museum displays important finds from prehistoric cultures in Catalonia and the Balearic Islands. The Dama de Ibiza, *a 4th-century sculpture, was found in Ibiza's Carthaginian necropolis (see p487)* ❷

Museu Etnològic displays artifacts from Oceania, Africa, Asia, and Latin America.

Mercat de les Flors theater *(see p185)*

Teatre Grec is an open-air theater set among gardens.

★ Fundació Joan Miró
This tapestry by Joan Miró hangs in the center he created for the study of modern art. In addition to Miró's works in various media, the modern building by Josep Lluís Sert is of architectural interest ❶

To amusement park, Montjuïc castle, and cable car

KEY

– – – Suggested route

0 meters	100
0 yards	100

Flame in Space and Naked Woman (1932) by Joan Miró

Fundació Joan Miró ❶

Parc de Montjuïc. **Map** 1 B3. 【 *(93) 329 19 08.* 🚇 *Espanya, then bus 61.* ⬜ *Jul–Sep: 10am–8pm Tue–Sat, Oct–Jun: 11am–7pm Tue, Wed, Fri & Sat, 11am–9:30pm Thu, 10:30am– 2:30pm Sun & public hols.* 🎨 ♿

THE SON OF A GOLDSMITH, Joan Miró (1893–1983) studied at the fine art school at La Llotja *(see p148)*. From 1919, he spent much of his time in Paris. Though opposed to Franco, he returned to Spain in 1940 and from then on lived mainly in Mallorca, where he died.

An admirer of primitive Catalan art and Gaudí's Modernisme *(see p136)*, Miró always remained a Catalan painter but invented and developed a Surrealistic style, with vivid colors and fantastical forms suggesting dreamlike situations. During the 1950s he concentrated on ceramics.

In 1975, after the return of democracy to Spain *(see p64)*, his friend, the architect Josep Lluís Sert, designed the stark, white building to house a permanent collection of graphics, paintings, sculptures, and tapestries lit by natural light. Miró himself donated the works, and some of the best pieces on display include his *Barcelona Series* (1939–44), a set of 50 black-and-white lithographs. Periodic exhibitions of other artists' work are also held.

Museu Arqueològic ❷

Passeig Santa Madrona 39. **Map** 1 B3. 【 *(93) 423 21 49.* 🚇 *Espanya, Poble Sec.* ⬜ *9:30am–1:30pm & 3:30–7pm Tue–Sat, 9am–2pm Sun.* ⬛ *public hols.* 🎨 *except Sun.* ♿

HOUSED IN the Renaissance-inspired 1929 Palace of Graphic Arts, the museum shows artifacts from prehistory to the Visigothic period (415–711 AD). Highlights are finds from the Greco-Roman town of Empúries *(see p206)*, Hellenistic Mallorcan jewels, and Iberian silver treasure. There is also a splendid collection of Visigothic jewelry.

Museu Nacional d'Art de Catalunya ❸

Parc de Montjuïc. **Map** 1 A2. 【 *(93) 423 71 99.* 🚇 *Espanya.* ⬜ *10am– 7pm Tue–Sat, 10am–9pm Thu, 10am– 2:30pm Sun.* 🎨 🚫 ♿ 🎨

THE AUSTERE Palau Nacional was built for the 1929 International Exhibition, but in 1934 it was used to house an art collection that has since become the most important in the city.

The museum includes what is probably the greatest display of Romanesque items in the world, centered around a series of magnificent 12th-century frescoes. These have been peeled from a number of Catalan Pyrenean churches and repasted onto replicas of the original vaulted ceilings and apses they decorated, to save them from plunder and the ravages of time. The most remarkable are the wall paintings from Santa Maria de Taüll *(see p201)* and from Sant Climent de Taüll *(see p20)*.

There is also an impressive Gothic collection, covering the whole of Spain but particularly good on Catalonia. Notable artists of the time are exhibited, including the 15th-century Spanish artists Lluís Dalmau and Jaume Huguet.

Other items include a large number of wooden and stone sculptures, and altarpieces. An outstanding example is the massive 14th-century *Altar to Our Lady* by the Serra brothers.

12th-century *Christ in Majesty*, **Museu Nacional d'Art de Catalunya**

Morning by Georg Kolbe (1877–1945), Pavelló Mies van der Rohe

Pavelló Mies van der Rohe ❹

Avinguda del Marqués de Comillas. **Map** 1 B2. (93) 423 40 16. Espanya. Apr–Oct: 10am–8pm daily, Nov–Mar: 10am–6pm daily.

I F THE ELEGANTLY simple lines of the glass and polished stone German Pavilion look modern today, they must have shocked visitors to the International Exhibition in 1929. Designed by Ludwig Mies van der Rohe (1886–1969), director of the avant-garde Bauhaus school, it includes his famous *Barcelona Chair*. The building was demolished after the exhibition, but a replica was built on the centenary of his birth.

Poble Espanyol ❺

Avinguda del Marqués de Comillas. **Map** 1 A2. (93) 325 78 66. Espanya. 9am–2am Tue–Thu, 9am–3am Fri & Sat, 9am–midnight Sun.

T HE IDEA BEHIND the Poble Espanyol (Spanish Village) was to illustrate and display local Spanish architectural styles and crafts. It was laid out for the 1929 International Exhibition, but has proved to be enduringly popular.

Building styles from all over Spain are illustrated by 116 houses. These are arranged on streets radiating from a main square and were created by many well-known architects

and artists of the time. The village was refurbished at the end of the 1980s and is now a favorite place to visit for both tourists and *Barcelonins*.

Resident artisans produce a wide range of crafts including hand-blown glass, ceramics, sculpture, Toledo damascene *(see p372)*, and Catalan canvas sandals. The Torres de Ávila *(see p185)*, which form the huge main entrance, have been converted into one of the city's most popular nightspots, with an interior by designers Alfredo Arribas and Javier Mariscal. There are also shops, cafés, bars, and a children's theater.

View from Palau Nacional downhill toward the Plaça d'Espanya

Plaça d'Espanya ❻

Avinguda de la Gran Via de les Corts Catalanes. **Map** 1 B1. Espanya.

T HE FOUNTAIN in the middle of this intersection, the site of public gallows until they were transferred to Ciutadella in 1715, is by Josep Maria Jujol, one of Gaudí's followers. The sculptures are by Miquel Blay. The 1899 bullring to one side is by Font i Carreras, but Catalans have never taken to bullfighting and the arena is now used as a music venue.

On the Montjuïc side of the traffic circle is the Avinguda de la Reina María Cristina. This is flanked by two 47-m (154-ft) high brick campaniles by Ramon Raventós, modeled on the bell towers of St. Mark's in Venice and built as the entrance way to the 1929 International Exhibition. The avenue, lined with exhibition buildings, leads up to Carles Buigas's illuminated *Font Màgica* (Magic Fountain) in front of the Palau Nacional.

Castell de Montjuïc ❼

Parc de Montjuïc. **Map** 1 B5. (93) 329 86 13. Paral·lel, then funicular & cable car. **Museum** 9:30am–7:30pm Tue–Sun.

T HE WHOLE OF THE summit of Montjuïc is occupied by a huge, 18th-century castle with fabulous views over the port.

The first castle was built in 1640, but was destroyed by Felipe V in 1705. The present star-shaped fortress was built on the ruins for the Bourbon family. During the War of Independence it was captured by French troops. After the Civil War it became a prison, in which the defeated Catalan leader Lluís Companys was executed in 1940.

The castle is now a military museum with an extensive display of ancient weaponry and models of Catalan castles.

Estadi Olímpic de Montjuïc ❽

Passeig Olímpic 17–19. **Map** 1 A3. (93) 426 20 89. Espanya, Poble Sec. 10am–6pm daily.

T HE NEO-CLASSICAL FAÇADE has been preserved from the original stadium, built by Pere Domènech i Roura for the 1936 "Alternative" Olympics. However, these were canceled at the outbreak of the Civil War in 1936. The arena was refitted to increase its capacity to 70,000 for the 1992 Olympics.

Nearby are the steel-and-glass **Palau Sant Jordi** indoor stadium, by Japanese architect Irata Isozaki, and swimming pools by Ricardo Bofill.

Entrance to the refurbished 1992 Olympic Stadium

FARTHER AFIELD

THE RADICAL redevelopment of Barcelona's outskirts in the late 1980s and early 1990s gave it a wealth of new buildings, parks, and squares. The city's main station, Sants, was rebuilt, and the neighboring Parc de l'Espanya Industrial and Parc Joan Miró were created, containing lakes, modern sculpture, and futuristic architecture. The Parc de Clot, beyond the new national theater *(see p184)*, is also of striking modern design. In the west of the city, where

**Parc Güell
gateway signs**

the streets start to climb steeply, are the historic royal palace and monastery of Pedralbes, and Gaudí's famous Parc Güell, dating from 1910. Beyond is the Serra de Collserola, the city's closest rural area. Two funiculars provide an exciting way of reaching its heights, which offer views of the city. Tibidabo, the highest point, with an amusement park, the Neo-Gothic church of the Sagrat Cor, and a modern steel-and-glass communications tower, is a favorite place among *Barcelonins* for a day out.

SIGHTS AT A GLANCE

Museums and Galleries
Museu de la Ciència ❽
Museu del Futbol Club
　Barcelona ❸

Historic Buildings
Monestir de Pedralbes ❺
Palau Reial de Pedralbes ❹

Modern Buildings
Torre de Collserola ❻

Parks and Gardens
Parc de l'Espanya Industrial ❷
Parc Güell ❾
Parc de Joan Miró ❶

Theme Parks
Tibidabo ❼

0 meters 　　500
0 yards 　　500

KEY

▨	Street-by-Street map
▢	Built-up area
🚉	Railroad station
🚟	Funicular railroad station
▬	Freeway
▬	Major road
▬	Minor road

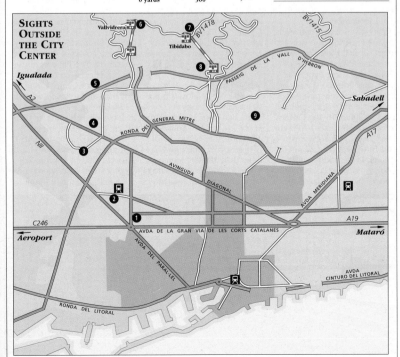

SIGHTS
OUTSIDE
THE CITY
CENTER

Vallvidrera
Tibidabo
Igualada
Sabadell
PASSEIG DE LA VALL D'HEBRON
RONDA DEL GENERAL MITRE
AVINGUDA DIAGONAL
AVDA MERIDIANA
C246
Aeroport
AVDA DE LA GRAN VIA DE LES CORTS CATALANES
A19
Mataró
AVDA DEL PARAL·LEL
AVDA CINTURO DEL LITORAL
RONDA DEL LITORAL

◁ **The Neo-Gothic Temple Expiatori del Sagrat Cor, dominating Barcelona from the summit of Tibidabo**

Dona i Ocell (1983) by Joan Miró
in the Parc de Joan Miró

Parc de Joan Miró ❶

Carrer d'Aragó 1.   Tarragona.

BARCELONA'S 19th-century slaughterhouse *(escorxador)* was transformed in the 1980s into this unusual park, hence its alternative name, Parc de l'Escorxador.

It is constructed on two levels, the lower of which is devoted to soccer fields interspersed with landscaped sections of palms, pines, eucalyptus trees, and flowers. The upper level is completely paved and is dominated by a magnificent 1983 sculpture by the Catalan artist Joan Miró *(see p168)* entitled *Dona i Ocell* (Woman and Bird). Standing 22 m (72 ft) high in the middle of a pool, its surface is coated with colorful pieces of glazed tile.

Parc de l'Espanya Industrial ❷

Plaça de Joan Peiró.   Sants-Estació.

THIS DISTINCTIVE modern park, designed by the Basque architect Luis Peña Ganchegui, owes its name to the textile mill that used to stand on the 12-acre site.

Laid out in 1986 as part of Barcelona's policy to provide more open spaces within the city, the park has canals and a rowing lake – with a Classical statue of Neptune at its center. Tiers of steps rise around the lake like an amphitheater and on one side a row of ten futuristic watchtowers dominates the entire area. Their only function is to serve as public viewing platforms and lamp standards.

Six contemporary sculptors are represented in the park, among them Andrés Nagel, whose huge metal dragon incorporates a children's slide.

Museu del Futbol Club Barcelona ❸

Avda de Aristides Maillol.   (93) 496 36 00.   Maria Cristina, Les Cortes.   Apr–Oct: 10am–1pm, 3–6pm Mon–Sat, 10am–2pm public hols; Nov–Mar: 10am–1pm, 3–6:30pm Tue–Fri, 10am–2pm Sat & Sun.

CAMP NOU, Europe's largest soccer stadium, is home to the city's famous soccer team, Barcelona FC (Barça, as it is known locally). Founded in 1899, it is one of the world's richest soccer clubs, and has more than 100,000 members.

The stadium is a magnificent, sweeping structure, built in 1957

Line of watchtowers in the Parc de l'Espanya Industrial

to a design by Francesc Mitjans. An extension was added in 1982 and it can now comfortably seat 98,000 fans, with standing room for 17,000 more.

The club's museum, which displays club memorabilia and trophies on two floors, and has a souvenir shop, is one of the most popular in Barcelona. There are also paintings and sculptures of famous club players commissioned for the Blau-grana Biennial, an exhibition held in celebration of the club in 1985 and 1987. *Blau-grana* (blue-burgundy) are the colors of Barça's uniform. The flags were used as an expression of local nationalist feelings during the Franco dictatorship, when the Catalan flag was banned.

As well as hosting its own high-profile games (mainly on weekends), Camp Nou also accommodates affiliated local soccer clubs and promotes other sports in its sports center, ice rink, and ministadium.

View across Camp Nou stadium, prestigious home of the Futbol Club Barcelona

Palau Reial de Pedralbes ❹

Avinguda Diagonal 686. **℃** *(93) 280 16 21.* **Ⓜ** *Palau Reial.* **⊟** *10am–3pm Tue–Sun.* **⊙** *Jan 1, Good Fri, May, Jun 24, Dec 25 & 26.* 🖼 🅰 🖼

THE PALACE OF PEDRALBES was once the main house on the estate of Count Eusebi Güell. In 1919 he offered it to the royal family to use when they visited Barcelona. The first visit was from Alfonso XIII in 1926, before which it was refurbished to be fit for a king. Visitors can still see the throne, supported by golden lions, created for him.

The building was opened to the public in 1937 and a decorative arts museum installed. Among the exhibits are items of period furniture brought here from other great houses in the city. A genealogical tree traces the 500-year dynasty of the count-kings of Barcelona, showing Catalonia's union by marriage with the kingdom of Aragón in 1137 *(see p217)*.

The palace also houses a ceramics museum that has displays of historic Catalan and Moorish pottery and modern ceramics, including works by Miró and Picasso *(see p148)*.

The palace gardens are well laid out with small ponds and paths. Just behind the gardens, in Avinguda de Pedralbes, is the entrance to the original Güell estate. It is guarded by a black wrought-iron gate, its top forged into a great, open-jawed dragon, and two gate houses, all by Gaudí *(see pp136–7)*.

***Madonna of Humility*, Monestir de Santa Maria de Pedralbes**

Monestir de Santa Maria de Pedralbes ❺

Baixada del Monestir 9. **℃** *(93) 203 92 82 (Monastery), (93) 280 14 34 (Thyssen-Bornemisza Collection).* 🖼 *Reina Elisenda.* **⊟** *10am–2pm Tue–Sun, 10am–5pm Sat.* 🖼

APPROACHED through an arch in its ancient walls, the monastery of Pedralbes still retains the air of a lived-in, enclosed community. This is heightened by the good state of preservation of its furnished cells, kitchens, infirmary, and refectory. But the nuns of the Order of St. Clare moved to an adjoining building in 1983. The monastery was founded in 1326 by Elisenda de Montcada de Piños, fourth wife of Jaime II of Gatalonia and Aragón. Her alabaster tomb lies in the wall between the church and the cloister. On the church side her effigy is dressed in royal robes; on the other as a nun.

The most important room in the monastery is the Capella (chapel) de Sant Miquel, with murals of the *Passion* and the *Life of the Virgin*, both painted by Ferrer Bassa in 1346, when Elisenda's niece, Francesca Saportella, was abbess.

In 1989, some 60 paintings forming part of the Thyssen-Bornemisza Collection (most of which is in Madrid – *see pp278–9*) were donated to the monastery. They now hang in the former dormitory and are mainly religious in theme. The collection is strong in Italian and Spanish works, including examples by Fra Angelico, Tiepolo, Canaletto, Veronese, Velázquez, and Zurbarán.

Torre de Collserola ❻

Carretera de Vallvidrera al Tibidabo. **℃** *(93) 211 79 42.* 🖼 *Avda del Tibidabo, then Tramvia Blau & Funicular.* **⊟** *Jan & Jul–Sep 15: 11am–7pm Tue–Sun; Feb–Apr: 11am–7pm Sat, Sun & Easter; May–Jun: 11am–8pm Wed–Sun & public hols.* 🖼 🅰

IN A CITY that enjoys thrills, the ultimate ride is offered by the communications tower near Tibidabo mountain *(see p174)*. A glass elevator takes less than two minutes to reach the top of this 288-m (945-ft) tall structure standing on the summit of a 445-m (1,460-ft) hill – not a pleasant experience for those who fear heights.

The tower was designed by English architect Norman Foster for the 1992 Olympic Games. Needlelike in form, it is a tubular steel mast on a concrete pillar. There are 13 levels. The top one has an observatory with a powerful telescope, and a public viewing platform with a 360° view encompassing Barcelona, the sea, and the mountain chain on which Tibidabo sits.

BARCELONA V REAL MADRID

FC Barcelona

Més que un club is the motto of Barcelona FC (soccer team): "More than a club." Above all it has been a symbol of the struggle of Catalan nationalism against the central government in Madrid. To fail to win the league is one thing. To come in behind Real Madrid is a complete disaster. Each season the big question is which of the two teams will win the title. Under the Franco regime in a memorable episode in 1941, Barça won 3–0 at home. At the return match in Madrid, the crowd was so hostile that the police and referee "advised" Barça to prevent trouble. Demoralized by the intimidation, they lost 11–1. Loyalty is paramount: one Barça player who left to join Real Madrid received death threats.

Real Madrid

Merry-go-round, Tibidabo

Tibidabo **7**

Plaça del Tibidabo. 🛈 *(93) 211 79 42.* 🚋 *Avda Tibidabo, then Tramvia Blau & Funicular.* **Funfair** 🕐 *May: noon–8pm Wed–Sun; Jun: noon–8pm Tue–Sun; Jul–mid-Sep: noon–10pm Tue–Sun; mid-Sep–Apr: noon–7pm weekends & public hols.* 🔴 *Apr 1, Nov.* 🔧
Temple del Sagrat Cor 🕐 *10am–7pm daily.*

THE HEIGHTS OF TIBIDABO are reached by the Tramvia Blau (Blue Trolley), Barcelona's last trolley, and a funicular railroad. The name, inspired by Tibidabo's views of the city, comes from the Latin *tibi dabo* (I shall give you) – a reference to the Temptation of Christ when Satan took him up a mountain and offered him the world spread at his feet.

The hugely popular Parc d'Atraccions (amusement park, *see p185*) first opened in 1908. The rides were completely renovated in the 1980s. While the old ones retain their charm, the newer ones provide the latest in vertiginous experiences. Their hilltop location at 517 m (1,696 ft) adds to the thrill. Also in the park is the Museu d'Automates, displaying automated toys, juke boxes, and gaming machines.

Tibidabo is crowned by the Temple Expiatori del Sagrat Cor (Church of the Sacred Heart), built by Enric Sagnier between 1902 and 1911. An elevator takes you to the feet of a huge figure of Christ.

Just a short bus ride away is another viewpoint – the Torre de Collserola *(see p173)*.

Museu de la Ciència **8**

Carrer Teodor Roviralta 55. 🛈 *(93) 212 60 50.* 🚋 *Avinguda del Tibidabo, then Tramvia Blau.* 🕐 *10am–8pm Tue–Sun.* 🔧🔧

THE CITY'S science museum provides some excellent hands-on experiences. Here you can test your senses and physical abilities and learn about world ecology. Separate floors are devoted to sound and light. There is a weather station and a planetarium that stages 30-minute shows. Outside is a full-size submarine that you can enter through holes cut in the hull.

Parc Güell **9**

Carrer d'Olot. 🛈 *(93) 213 04 88.* Ⓜ *Lesseps.* 🕐 *10am–8pm daily.* 🔧🔧

DESIGNATED a World Heritage Site by UNESCO, the Parc Güell is Antoni Gaudí's *(see pp136–7)* most colourful creation. He was commissioned in the 1890s by Count Eusebi Güell to design a garden city on 50 acres of the family estate. In the end, little of the grand design for decorative public buildings and 60 houses among landscaped gardens became reality. What we see today was completed between 1910 and 1914, and the park opened in 1922.

Most atmospheric is the Room of a Hundred Columns, a cavernous covered market hall of 84 crooked pillars, which is brightened by glass and ceramic mosaics. Above it, reached by a flight of steps flanked by ceramic animals, is the Gran Plaça Circular, an open space with a snaking balcony of colored mosaics, said to have the longest bench in the world. It was executed by Josep Jujol, one of Gaudí's chief collaborators. The view from here is panoramic.

The two mosaic-decorated pavilions at the entrance are by Gaudí, but the Casa-Museu Gaudí, a gingerbread-style house where Gaudí lived from 1906–26, was built by Francesc Berenguer. It contains drawings and furniture by Gaudí.

Mosaic-encrusted chimney by Gaudí at the entrance of the Parc Güell

BARCELONA STREET FINDER

THE MAP REFERENCES given with the sights, shops, and entertainment venues described in the Barcelona section of the guide refer to the street maps on the following pages. Map references are also given for Barcelona hotels (see *pp543–5*), and for bars and restaurants (see *pp584–6*). The schematic map below shows the area of Barcelona covered by the *Street Finder*. The symbols used for sights and other features and services are listed in the key at the foot of the page.

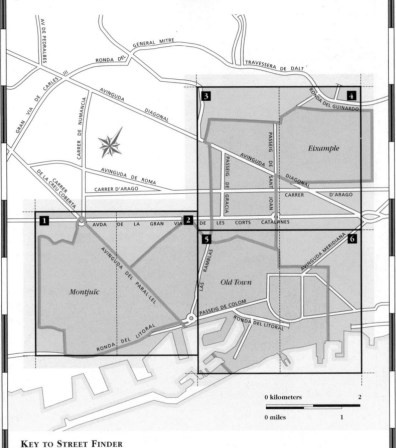

KEY TO STREET FINDER		
▉ Major sight	▦ Golondrina boarding point	✠ Church
▦ Place of interest	▦ Cable car	⊠ Post office
▦ Other building	▦ Funicular railroad station	═ Railroad line
⇌ Main railroad station	▦ Taxi stand	→ One way street
Ⓢ Local (FF CC) railroad station	Ⓟ Parking	▬ Pedestrianized street
Ⓜ Metro station	ⓘ Tourist information	**SCALE OF MAP PAGES**
▦ Main bus stop	✚ Hospital with emergency room	0 meters 250
▦ Bus station	▦ Police station	0 yards 250

0 kilometers   2
0 miles   1

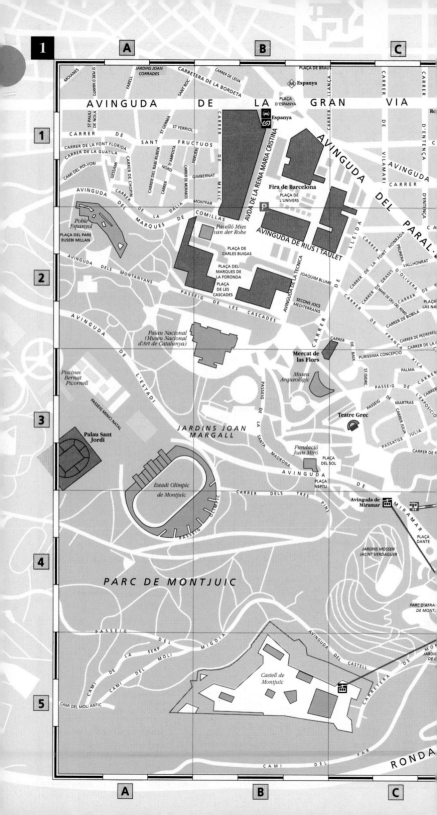

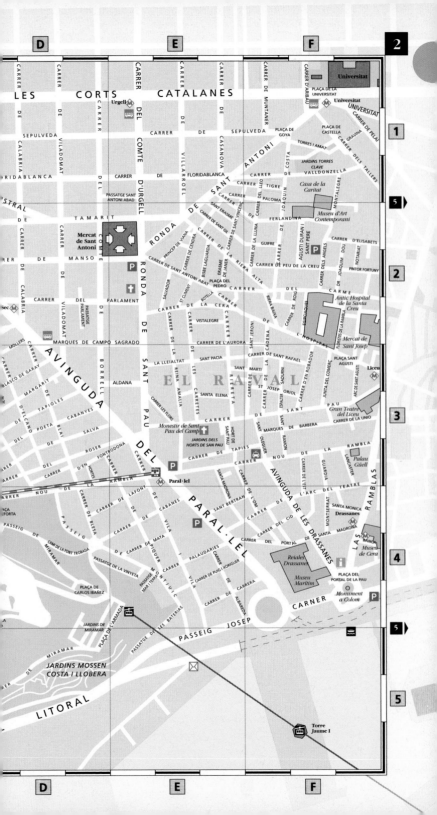

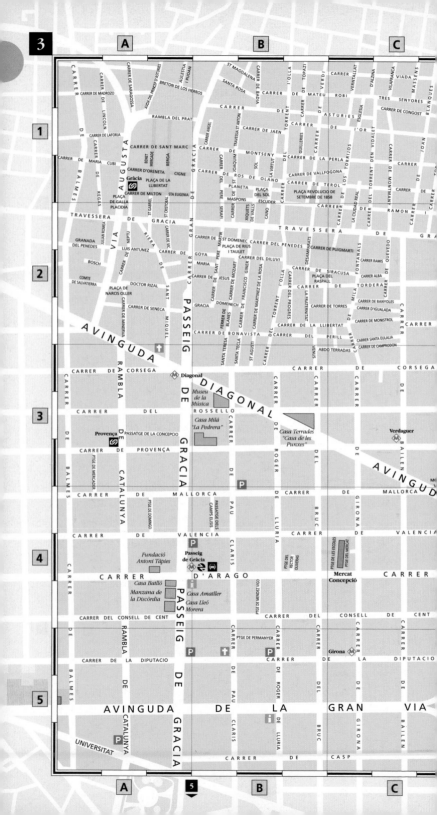

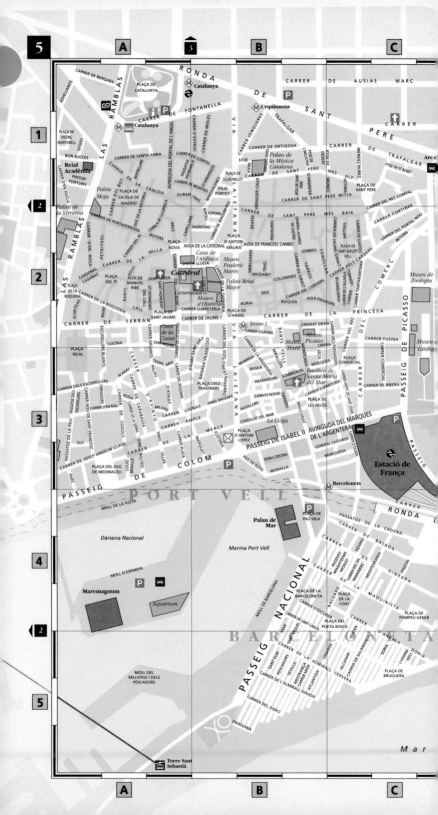

SHOPPING IN BARCELONA

A CITY WITH impeccable style, Barcelona is where you'll find the best in Catalan, Spanish, and international design. For those in search of fashion, a good place to begin a tour of Barcelona is on the streets around the Passeig de Gràcia, which make up the most important shopping area, and where crowds browse among the well-known fashion and design stores. In this area there are also many interesting

Wall tile outside La Manual Alpargatera

old shops such as food stores, herbalists, and pharmacies – some displaying beautiful Modernista frontages. For those who enjoy the hustle and bustle of small crowded streets, the Barri Gòtic, in the heart of the city, has something for everyone. Particularly interesting are the antique dealers and the shops specializing in traditional crafts such as carnival masks, ceramics, and handmade espadrilles.

Some of the beautifully displayed confectionery at Escribà

FOOD AND DRINK

B ARCELONA'S cake shops are sights in themselves and, with its displays of chocolate sculptures, no *pastisseria* is more enticing or spectacular than **Escribà**. Other food shops also have a great deal of character, none more so than **Colmado Quilez** in the Eixample. This wonderful old store stocks a huge range of hams, cheeses, and preserves, in addition to a comprehensive selection of Spanish and foreign wines and spirits.

DEPARTMENT STORES AND GALERÍAS

T HE BRANCH of **El Corte Inglés**, Spain's largest department store chain, on Plaça Catalunya, is a Barcelona landmark and a handy place to find everything under one roof, including plug adaptors and services like key-cutting. Other branches are located around the city. Barcelona's hypermarkets also sell a wide

range of goods. As they are on the outskirts of the city – south along the Gran Via toward the airport, and on the Avinguda Meridiana to the north – a car is the best way to reach them.

The fashion malls or *galerías*, built mostly during the affluent 1980s, are hugely popular. Both branches of **Bulevard Rosa**, on the Passeig de Gràcia and the Avinguda Diagonal, have hundreds of shops selling clothes and accessories. Also on the Avinguda Diagonal is **La Illa**, a large, lively shopping mall containing chain stores as well as specialty retailers.

FASHION

I NTERNATIONAL fashion labels are found alongside clothes by young designers on and around the Passeig de Gràcia. **Adolfo Domínguez** stocks classically styled clothes for men and women; **Armand Basi** sells quality leisure and sportswear; and discount designer fashion is available at

Contribuciones. Many shops offer traditional, fine-quality tailoring skills, and **Calzados E Solé**, which is situated in the Old Town, specializes in classic handmade shoes and boots.

SPECIALTY SHOPS

A WALK AROUND Barcelona can reveal a wonderful choice of shops selling traditional craft items and handmade goods that in most places have now been largely replaced by the production line. **La Caixa de Fang** has a good variety of Catalan and Spanish ceramics, among them traditional Catalan cooking pots and colorful tiles. **L'Estanc** has everything for the smoker, including the best Havana cigars. **La Manual Alpargatera** is an old shoe store that specializes in Catalan-style espadrilles. These are handmade on the premises and come in all colors. The city's oldest shop, **Cereria Subirà** *(see pp140–41)*, sells candles in every imaginable form.

Menswear department in Adolfo Domínguez

Design, Art, and Antiques

If you are interested in modern design, or just looking for gifts, you should pay a visit to **Vinçon**, the city's most famous design emporium. Situated on the Passeig de Gràcia, it has everything for the home, including beautiful fabrics and furniture. A must is **BD-Ediciones de Diseño**, which has the feel of an art gallery. Housed in a building designed by Domènech i Montaner, the shop has furniture based on designs by Gaudí and Charles Rennie Mackintosh, and sells wonderful contemporary furniture and accessories.

Most of the commercial art galleries and print shops are found on Carrer Consell de

Mouthwatering fruit stalls in La Boqueria market

The stylishly sparse display of furniture at Vinçon

Cent, in the Eixample, while the Barri Gòtic – especially the Carrer de la Palla and Carrer del Pi – is the best place to browse around small but fascinating antique shops. As well as fine furniture and old dolls, **L'Arca de l'Avia** sells antique silks and lace, all of which are set out in pretty displays.

Books and Newspapers

Most city-center newsstands stock English-language newspapers, but the most comprehensive stock of foreign newspapers and magazines is in **Crisol**, which also sells books, videos, CDs, and photographic equipment.

Markets

No one should miss the chance to look around **La Boqueria** on the Ramblas, one of the most spectacular food markets in Europe. It has every kind of food: fresh fruit, fine meats, and all types of seafood. There is an antique market in the Plaça del Pi on Thursdays. On Sunday mornings coin, stamp, and book collectors set up stalls in the Plaça Reial, and a craft market is held near the Sagrada Família. The city's traditional flea market, **Els Encants**, takes place on Mondays, Wednesdays, Fridays, and Saturdays. It offers a variety of jewelry and clothes.

DIRECTORY

FOOD AND DRINK

Colmado Quilez
Rambla de Catalunya 63.
Map 3 A4.
[(93) 215 23 56.

Escribà Pastisseries
Gran Via de les Corts
Catalanes 546. **Map** 2 E1.
[(93) 454 75 35.

DEPARTMENT STORES AND GALERÍAS

Bulevard Rosa
Passeig de Gràcia 55.
Map 3 A4.
[(93) 309 06 50.

El Corte Inglés
Pl Catalunya 14. **Map** 5 B1.
[(93) 302 12 12.

La Illa
Avinguda Diagonal 557.
[(93) 444 00 00.

FASHION

Adolfo Domínguez
Passeig de Gràcia 89.
Map 3 A3.
[(93) 215 13 39.

Armand Basi
Centre Comercial
Maremàgnum, Moll
d'Espanya.
Map 5 A4.
[(93) 225 80 58.

Calzados E Solé
Carrer Ample 7.
Map 5 A3.
[(93) 301 69 84.

Contribuciones
Riera de Sant Miquel 30.
Map 3 A2.
[(93) 237 47 49.

SPECIALTY SHOPS

La Caixa de Fang
C/ Freneria 1. **Map** 5 B2.
[(93) 315 17 04.

Cereria Subirà
C/ Llibreteria 7. **Map** 5 B2.
[(93) 315 26 06.

L'Estanc
Via Laietana 4. **Map** 5 B3.
[(93) 310 10 34.

La Manual Alpargatera
C/ d'Avinyó 7. **Map** 5 A3.
[(93) 301 01 72.

DESIGN, ART, AND ANTIQUES

L'Arca de l'Avia
Carrer dels Banys Nous 20.
Map 5 A2.
[(93) 302 15 98.

BD-Ediciones de Diseño
Carrer de Mallorca 291–3.
Map 3 B4.
[(93) 458 69 09.

Vinçon
Pg Gràcia 96. **Map** 3 B3.
[(93) 215 60 50.

BOOKS AND NEWSPAPERS

Crisol
Carrer Consell de Cent
341. **Map** 3 A4.
[(93) 215 31 21.

MARKETS

La Boqueria
Ramblas 100. **Map** 5 A2.

Els Encants
Plaça de les Glòries.
Map 4 F5.

ENTERTAINMENT IN BARCELONA

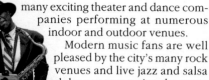

Musician in
the Barri Gòtic

FEW CITIES CAN MATCH the vitality of Barcelona, and nowhere is this more evident than in its live arts scene. The stunning Palau de la Música Catalana has enthusiastic and critical audiences. It regularly hosts some of the world's greatest classical musicians, including Montserrat Caballé and José Carreras, who are both *Barcelonins*. Equally dynamic are the many exciting theater and dance companies performing at numerous indoor and outdoor venues.

Modern music fans are well pleased by the city's many rock venues and live jazz and salsa clubs, not to mention the street musicians on the Ramblas or in the squares of the Barri Gòtic. A vibrant and thriving tradition of old Barcelona is its brash, glittering music halls.

The magnificent interior of the Palau de la Música Catalana

ENTERTAINMENT GUIDES

THE MOST COMPLETE guide to what's on each week in Barcelona is the *Guía del Ocio*, out every Thursday. It includes a movie listings section. The Friday *El País* also has an entertainment supplement.

SEASONS AND TICKETS

THEATER and concert seasons for the main venues run from September to June, with limited programs at other times. In summer the city hosts the Festival del Grec, a showcase of international music, theater, and dance, in open air venues such as the Teatre Grec in Montjuïc and the Plaça del Rei in the Barri Gòtic. There is also a varied menu of concerts during the Festa de la Mercé *(see p153)* in September.

The simplest way to get theater and concert tickets is to buy them at the box office of the relevant venue, although tickets for many theaters can also be bought from branches of the Caixa de Catalunya or La Caixa savings banks. Tickets for the Festival should be obtained from tourist offices.

CLASSICAL MUSIC

BARCELONA's **Palau de la Música Catalana** *(see p149)* is one of the world's most beautiful concert halls. The Orquestra Simfònica de Barcelona performs there throughout the season.

Barcelona's status as the opera capital of Spain took a knock when the Liceu opera house burned down in 1994, but restoration is due to be completed in 1999. Meanwhile, opera goers can see productions staged at the Palau de la Música Catalana and other theaters around the city. Check with tourist offices for details.

THEATER AND DANCE

WORTH SEEING are Catalan contemporary theater groups such as Els Comediants or La Cubana, whose original style combines theater, music, mime, and elements from traditional Mediterranean fiestas.

The **Mercat de les Flors** *(see p167)*, a converted former flower market in Montjuïc, is an exciting theater presenting quality productions of classic and modern plays in Catalan. The new **Teatre Nacional de Catalunya**, near the Plaza de Toros Monumental, is another showcase for Catalan drama.

Although classical ballet has suffered from a lack of venues since the loss of the Liceu, there are many contemporary dance companies and regular performances are staged at the Mercat de les Flors in Montjuïc.

MUSIC HALL

A STAGE SHOW that is camp and tacky with extremely vulgar jokes may not appeal to everyone, but the music halls along the Avinguda del Paral·lel take you back in time to the golden age of variety. The legendary 1920s **El Molino** (The Windmill) is still the most popular place for a noisy night out.

Outrageous stage show at one of Barcelona's many clubs

Gambrinus bar and restaurant, identified by its looming lobster

CAFÉS, BARS, AND CLUBS

AMONG BARCELONA'S most famous modern sights are the high-tech design bars built in the prosperous 1980s. The **Mirablau** looks over the city and **Gambrinus** *(see p152)* is on the harbor. The **Torres de Ávila**, in the Poble Espanyol *(see p169)*, is the height of post-modernism. The **Universal** and **Otto Zutz** have live music. Less chic, but still fun, are the **Apolo**, and **La Paloma**, a fine dance hall with a 1904 interior where the paso doble rules.

Two of the best-known champagne and cocktail bars are in the old city: **Boadas** and **El Xampanyet**. The **Bar Velódromo** is a friendly Art Deco café. The cafés on the secluded Plaça del Sol in the Gràcia district are an ideal place for a quiet drink.

ROCK, JAZZ, AND WORLD MUSIC

BIG NAMES like David Byrne and Paul McCartney have performed at **Zeleste**, while **La Boîte** has live folk and blues. In summer, festivals and open-air concerts are held around the city. Jazz venues include the **Harlem Jazz Club**, while Latin music fans can enjoy live salsa at **Antilla Cosmopolita**.

AMUSEMENT PARKS

IN SUMMER, Barcelona's giant amusement parks open till the early hours and are full until closing time. **Tibidabo** *(see p174)* and the older **Montjuïc** fairgrounds are even more enjoyable if you go by tram, funicular, or cable car.

SPORTS

THE UNDOUBTED KINGS of sports in this city are **FC Barcelona**. They boast the largest soccer stadium in Europe, the Nou Camp *(see p173)*, and have a fanatical following. Barcelona also has a high-ranking basketball team.

Packed house at the gigantic Nou Camp stadium

DIRECTORY

CLASSICAL MUSIC

Palau de la Música Catalana
Carrer de Sant Francesc de Paula 2. **Map** 5 B1.
(93) 268 10 00.

THEATER AND DANCE

Mercat de les Flors
Carrer de Lleida 59.
Map 1 B3.
(93) 426 18 75.

Teatre Nacional de Catalunya
Pl de les Artes. **Map** 4 F5.

MUSIC HALL

El Molino
Carrer de Vila i Vilà 99.
Map 2 E3.
(93) 441 63 83.

CAFÉS, BARS, AND CLUBS

Gambrinus
Moll de la Fusta. **Map** 6 F4.
(93) 221 50 14.

Apolo
Carrer Nou de la Rambla 113.
Map 2 E3.
(93) 441 90 06.

Bar Velódromo
Carrer de Muntaner 213.
(93) 430 51 98.

Boadas
Carrer dels Tallers 1.
Map 5 A1.
(93) 318 95 92.

Mirablau
Plaça Doctor Andreu.
(93) 418 58 79.

Otto Zutz
Carrer de Lincoln 15.
Map 3 A1.
(93) 238 07 22.

La Paloma
C/ Tigre 27. **Map** 2 F1.
(93) 301 68 97.

Torres de Ávila
Poble Espanyol, Avinguda M de Comillas. **Map** 1 A1.
(93) 424 93 09.

Universal
C/ Marià Cubí 182–4.
(93) 201 46 58.

El Xampanyet
Carrer Montcada 22.
Map 5 B2.
(93) 319 70 03.

ROCK, JAZZ AND WORLD MUSIC

Antilla Cosmopolita
Carrer de Muntaner 244.
(93) 200 77 14.

La Boîte
Avinguda Diagonal 477.
(93) 419 55 50.

Harlem Jazz Club
Carrer de la Comtessa de Sobradiel 8.
(93) 310 07 55.

Zeleste
Carrer de Almogàvers 122.
Map 6 F2.
(93) 309 12 04.

AMUSEMENT PARKS

Parc d'Atraccions de Montjuïc
Map 1 C4.
(93) 441 70 24.

Tibidabo
(93) 211 79 42.

SPORTS

FC Barcelona
Nou Camp, Avinguda Aristides Maillol.
(93) 496 36 00.

EASTERN SPAIN

Introducing Eastern Spain

EASTERN SPAIN covers an extraordinary range of climates and landscapes, from the snowbound peaks of the Pyrenees in Aragón to the beaches of the Costa Blanca and Costa Cálida, popular for their winter warmth and sunshine. The region has a wealth of historical sights including ancient monasteries near Barcelona, magnificent Roman ruins in Tarragona, Mudéjar churches and towers in Aragón, and the great cathedrals of Valencia and Murcia. Away from the busy coasts, the countryside is often attractive but little visited.

Zaragoza

ARAGON
(see pp216–31)

Teruel

Ordesa National Park (see pp222–3)
*in the Pyrenees has some of the most
dramatic mountain scenery in Spain.
It makes excellent walking country.*

Zaragoza (see pp226–7)
*has many striking
churches, especially the
cathedral, the Basílica de
Nuestra Señora del Pilar,
and the Mudéjar-style
Iglesia de la Magdalena.*

Valencia (see pp240–43) is
*Spain's third largest city. It
has an old center of narrow
streets overlooked by venerable
houses and monuments, such
as El Miguelete, the cathedral's
conspicuous bell tower. The
city hosts a spectacular festival,
Las Fallas, in March.*

VALEN
AND MU
(see pp232

Valer

Murcia cathedral (see p252),
*built in the 14th century, has a
Baroque façade and belfry, and
two ornate side chapels – one in
late-Gothic style and the other
Renaissance. In Murcia, you
can also visit an elegant
19th-century gentlemen's
club, the Casino.*

Alia

| 0 kilometers | 50 |
| 0 miles | 50 |

Murcia

◁ **The 12th-century monastery at Gerri de la Sal in Catalonia**

Lleida

CATALONIA
(see pp196–215)

Girona

Barcelona

Tarragona

ellón

The Costa Brava (see pp206–207), *stretching south from the French border, is a mix of cliffs, wooded coves, and pretty beaches. Lloret de Mar is the busiest, most popular tourist resort on the coast.*

Poblet (see pp212–13), *enclosed by triple walls, is one of the most interesting medieval Cistercian monasteries in Catalonia. It contains a royal pantheon with the carved tombs of six of the kings of Aragón.*

Tarragona (see pp214–15) *was one of the most important cities in Roman Spain. Among its remains are a theater and an aqueduct. A statue of Roger de Llúria, the great 13th-century Catalan naval commander, overlooks the beach.*

The Costa Blanca (see pp248–51) *is an attractive coast, as well as a popular vacation spot. Calp is overshadowed by a huge rock, the Penyal d'Ifach. In La Vila Joiosa, a line of houses has been painted in striking colors to make them visible to sailors at sea.*

Regional Food: Eastern Spain

THE MEDITERRANEAN CUISINE of the east coast has been enriched by centuries of foreign influence, from the Romans and the Moors especially. Olives, rice, oranges, almonds, and saffron are combined with produce from the sea and the mountains. The varied cooking of Catalonia embraces sweet and savory combinations, fish stews, snails, and several classic sauces, like spicy *romesco* made from red peppers, tomatoes, and chilies. High-quality fruit and vegetables, such as ñora peppers, grow on the fertile coastal plains of Valencia and Murcia. Paella is the best known of the many rice dishes of these two regions. The cold, dry, mountain air of Aragón is ideal for curing hams.

Ñora peppers

Amanida *is a Catalan salad that combines vegetables with cured meat or cheese, or some kind of fish or shellfish.*

Oranges *are the main crop of Valencia and Alicante. These two provinces are the world's biggest orange exporters; they also grow three-quarters of Spain's lemons. The tangy Valencia orange is used mainly for its juice; the sweet navel orange, which is easier to peel, is usually grown for eating. Many varieties of satsuma and clementine are also grown.*

Parrillada de mariscos *is an assortment of shellfish grilled on a barbecue and served with allioli (garlic mayonnaise).*

Shrimp

Saffron rice

Mussels

Peppers

Suquet, *one of the famous fish and shellfish stews of Catalonia, is made with saffron, wine, tomatoes, and potatoes.*

Paella, *a Valencian rice dish known the world over, is cooked in a large, shallow, two-handled pan, traditionally over an open fire. Short-grain Spanish rice, flavored and perfumed with saffron, is simmered with a variety of colorful ingredients: seafood, chicken, rabbit, pork, tomatoes, peppers, and fresh and dried beans.*

Fideus a la cassola *is a dish of fideus (a kind of noodle) with red peppers, pork chops or fillet, and sausages.*

Butifarra amb mongetes *is a traditional Catalan dish of grilled black sausage with dried white beans.*

Cochifrito, *a simple peasant dish from Aragón, is prepared from lamb fried with lemon, garlic, and paprika.*

Pollo al ajillo *is chicken grilled with garlic. It is served with a white wine or sherry sauce made with the juices of the chicken.*

Pastel de carne, *a Murcian pie of Middle Eastern origin, consists of minced meat and chopped boiled eggs in a puff pastry case.*

Llagosta i pollastre *is a typical Catalan combination of lobster with chicken in a tomato and hazelnut sauce.*

Crema catalana *is a rich egg custard with a golden brown layer of grilled sugar on top. It is served very cold.*

Pear

Apple

Cherry

Orange

Pumpkin

Candied fruits (frutas escarchadas) *are a popular way of preserving the abundant produce of the region. In Aragón they are often chocolate coated.*

Almendras
garrapiñadas

Torta
imperial

Almond sweets, like almendras garrapiñadas *(almonds coated in a crunchy sugar) and* torta imperial *(containing toasted almonds), were introduced to Spain by the Moors.* Turrón *comes in two main varieties: one white and hard and studded with whole nuts; the other made from a soft paste of ground almonds.*

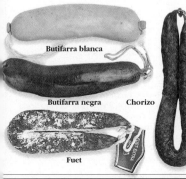

Butifarra blanca

Butifarra negra   Chorizo

Fuet

SAUSAGES

Catalan sausages, especially those from the mountain town of Vic, are renowned. The white *butifarra* sausage contains pork, tripe, and pine nuts, while the black variety uses blood, pork belly, and spices. Both can be grilled or served with beans. The region produces many types of cured sausage, such as the firm, finely textured *llangonisseta,* and the long, dry *fuet.* The coarser, scarlet-colored chorizo, particularly beloved of Aragón and Murcia, contains paprika, and can be sliced finely and eaten with bread, perhaps as a tapa, or served in stew or soup.

Wines of Eastern Spain

SPAIN'S EASTERN SEABOARD offers a wide spread of wines of different styles. Catalonia stands in first place, and here the most important region is Penedès, home of *cava* (traditional-method sparkling wine) and some high quality still wine. In Aragón, Cariñena reds can be good, and Somontano, in the Pyrenees, has fine, international-style varietals. Valencia and Murcia provide large quantities of easy-drinking reds, whites, and *rosados* (rosés). Most notable among these are the rosés of Utiel-Requena, the Valencian Muscatels, and the strong, full-bodied reds made in Jumilla.

Cabernet Sauvignon vines

Somontano has had remarkable success because of the COVISA company's cultivation of international grape varieties such as Chardonnay and Pinot Noir.

Monastery of Poblet and Las Murallas vineyards in Catalonia

0 kilometers   100

0 miles   50

KEY FACTS ABOUT WINES OF EASTERN SPAIN

Location and Climate
The climate of eastern Spain varies mainly with altitude – low-lying parts are hot and dry; it also gets hotter the farther south you go. The wine regions of Catalonia have a Mediterranean climate along the coast, which becomes drier futher inland. The middle Penedès is a favored location with a range of climates that suits many grape varieties. Somontano has a cooler, altitude-tempered climate. Valencia and Murcia can be, in contrast, unrelentingly hot.

Grape Varieties
The most common native red grape varieties planted in much of eastern Spain are Garnacha, Tempranillo – which is called Ull de Llebre in Catalonia – Monastrell, and Cariñena. Bobal makes both reds and, to a greater extent, rosés in Utiel-Requena. For whites, Catalonia has Parellada, Macabeo,

and Xarel·lo (the trio most commonly used for *cava*), while in Valencia, Merseguera and Muscatel predominate. In the regions farthest to the southeast, Airén and Pedro Ximénez are sometimes found. French grape varieties, such as Chardonnay, Merlot, Cabernet Sauvignon, and Sauvignon Blanc, flourish in the regions of Penedès, Costers del Segre, and Somontano.

Good Producers
Somontano: COVISA (Viñas del Vero), Viñedos del Altoaragón. **Alella:** Marqués de Alella, Parxet. **Penedès:** Codorníu, Conde de Caralt, Freixenet, Juvé y Camps, Masía Bach, Mont-Marçal, René Barbier, Miguel Torres. **Costers del Segre:** Castell del Remei, Raimat. **Priorato:** Cellers Scala Dei, Masía Barril. **Valencia:** Vicente Gandía. **Utiel-Requena:** C. Augusto Egli. **Alicante:** Gutiérrez de la Vega. **Jumilla:** Asensio Carcelén (Sol y Luna), Bodegas Vitivino.

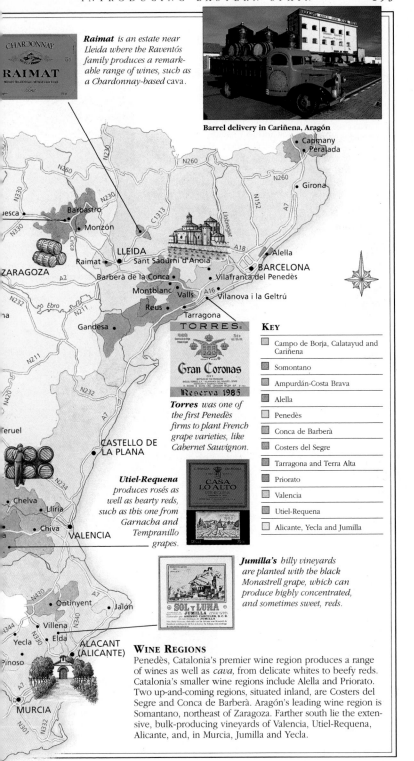

Raimat *is an estate near Lleida where the Raventós family produces a remarkable range of wines, such as a Chardonnay-based* cava.

Barrel delivery in Cariñena, Aragón

TORRES

Gran Coronas

Reserva 1985

Torres *was one of the first Penedès firms to plant French grape varieties, like Cabernet Sauvignon.*

Utiel-Requena *produces rosés as well as hearty reds, such as this one from Garnacha and Tempranillo grapes.*

CASA LO ALTO

Jumilla's *hilly vineyards are planted with the black Monastrell grape, which can produce highly concentrated, and sometimes sweet, reds.*

SOL y LUNA

KEY

- Campo de Borja, Calatayud and Cariñena
- Somontano
- Ampurdán-Costa Brava
- Alella
- Penedès
- Conca de Barberà
- Costers del Segre
- Tarragona and Terra Alta
- Priorato
- Valencia
- Utiel-Requena
- Alicante, Yecla and Jumilla

WINE REGIONS

Penedès, Catalonia's premier wine region produces a range of wines as well as *cava,* from delicate whites to beefy reds. Catalonia's smaller wine regions include Alella and Priorato. Two up-and-coming regions, situated inland, are Costers del Segre and Conca de Barberà. Aragón's leading wine region is Somantano, northeast of Zaragoza. Farther south lie the extensive, bulk-producing vineyards of Valencia, Utiel-Requena, Alicante, and, in Murcia, Jumilla and Yecla.

Flowers of the Matorral

THE MATORRAL, a scrubland rich in wildflowers, is the distinctive landscape of Spain's eastern Mediterranean coast. It is the result of centuries of woodland clearance, during which the native holm oak was felled for timber and to provide land for grazing and cultivation. Many colorful plants have adapted to the extremes of climate here. Most flower in spring, when hillsides are daubed with pink and white cistuses and yellow broom, and the air is perfumed by aromatic herbs such as rosemary, lavender, and thyme. Buzzing insects feed on the abundance of nectar and pollen.

Yellow bee orchid

The century plant's flower stalk can reach 10 m (32 ft).

Spanish broom *is a small bush with yellow flowers on slender branches. The black seed pods split when dry, scattering the seeds on the ground.*

Rosemary

Jerusalem sage*, an attractive shrub that is often grown in gardens, has tall stems surrounded by bunches of showy yellow flowers. Its leaves are grayish-white and woolly.*

Rose garlic *has round clusters of violet or pink flowers at the end of a single stalk. It survives the summer as the bulb familiar to all cooks.*

FOREIGN INVADERS

Several plants from the New World have managed to colonize the bare ground of the *matorral*. The prickly pear, thought to have been brought back by Christopher Columbus, produces a delicious fruit that can be picked only with thickly gloved hands. The rapidly growing century plant, a native of Mexico, has tough spiny leaves and sends up a tall flower shoot only when it is 10–15 years old, after which it dies.

Prickly pear in bloom

Flowering shoots of the century plant

Common thyme *is a low-growing aromatic herb that is widely cultivated for in the kitchen*

The mirror orchid*, a small plant that grows on grassy sites, is easily distinguished from other orchids by the brilliant metallic blue patch inside the lip, fringed by brown hairs.*

CLIMATE CHART

Most plants found in the *matorral* come into bloom in the warm, moist spring. The plants protect themselves from losing water during the dry summer heat with thick leaves or waxy secretions, or by storing moisture in bulbs or tubers.

| mp | Rainfall |
| (F) | (in) |

J F M A M J J A S O N D

— Temperature   ▨ Rainfall

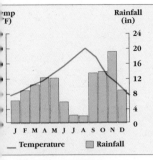

Holm oaks *are very common in Eastern Spain. The leaves are tough and rubbery to prevent water loss.*

The strawberry tree *is an evergreen shrub with glossy serrated leaves. Its inedible strawberry-like fruit turns red when ripe.*

Tree heather

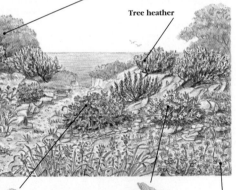

Gray-leaved cistus, *growing on sunny sites, has crumpled petals and bright yellow anthers.*

Narrow-leaved cistus *exudes a sticky aromatic gum used in perfumes.*

Star clover *is a low-growing annual whose fruit develops into a star-shaped seed head. Its flowers are often pale pink.*

WILDLIFE OF THE MATORRAL

The animals that live in the *matorral* are most often seen early in the morning, before the temperature is high. Countless insects fly from flower to flower, providing a source of food for birds. Smaller mammals, such as mice and voles, are active only at night when it is cooler and there are few predators around.

Ladder snakes *feed on small mammals, birds, and insects. The young are identified by a black pattern like the rungs of a ladder, but adults are marked with two simple stripes.*

Scorpions *hide under rocks or wood by day. When disturbed, the tail is curled quickly over the body in a threatening gesture. The sting, lethal to small animals, can cause some irritation to humans.*

The Dartford warbler, *a skulking bird that has a dark plumage and a cocked tail, sings melodiously during its mating display. Males are more vividly colored than females.*

The swallow-tail butterfly *is one of the most conspicuous of the great many insects living in the* matorral. *Bees, ants, and grasshoppers are also extremely common.*

CATALONIA

LLEIDA · ANDORRA · GIRONA
BARCELONA PROVINCE · TARRAGONA

C ATALONIA *is a proud nation-within-a-nation that was once, under the count-kings of Barcelona-Aragón, one of the Mediterranean's great sea powers. It has its own semiautonomous regional government and its own language, Catalan, which has all but replaced Spanish in place names and on road signs throughout the region.*

The Romans first set foot on the Iberian Peninsula at Empúries on Catalonia's Costa Brava ("wild coast"). They left behind them great monuments, especially in and around Tarragona, the capital of their vast province of Tarraconensis. Later, Barcelona emerged as the region's capital, economically and culturally important enough to rival Madrid.

In the 1960s the Costa Brava became one of Europe's first mass package vacation destinations. Although resorts such as Lloret de Mar continue to draw the crowds, former fishing villages such as Cadaqués remain relatively unspoiled on this naturally attractive coast.

Inland, there is a rich artistic heritage to be explored. Catalonia has several spectacular monasteries, especially Montserrat, its spiritual heart, and Poblet. There are also many medieval towns, such as Montblanc, Besalú, and Girona – which contain a wealth of monuments and museums.

In the countryside there is a lot to seek out, from the wetland wildlife of the Río Ebro delta to the vineyards of Penedès (where most of Spain's sparkling wine is made). In the high Pyrenees rare butterflies brighten remote mountain valleys, and little hidden villages encircle exquisite Romanesque churches.

Fruit trees in bloom near Balaguer, in the province of Lleida

◁ **A fisherman inspects his nets in Cadaqués on the Costa Brava**

Exploring Catalonia

CATALONIA INCLUDES a long stretch of the Spanish Pyrenees, whose green, flower-filled valleys hide picturesque villages with Romanesque churches. The Parc Nacional d'Aigüestortes and Vall d'Aran are paradises for naturalists, and Baqueira-Beret offers skiers reliable snow. Sun-lovers can choose between the rugged Costa Brava or the long sandy stretches of the Costa Daurada. Tarragona is rich in Roman monuments. Inland are the monasteries of Poblet and Santes Creus and the well-known vineyards of Penedès.

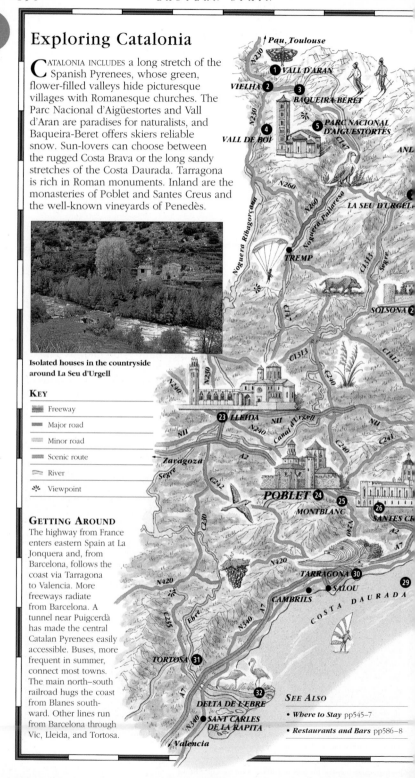

Isolated houses in the countryside around La Seu d'Urgell

KEY

▬▬	Freeway
▬▬	Major road
▬▬	Minor road
▬▬	Scenic route
▭	River
☀	Viewpoint

GETTING AROUND

The highway from France enters eastern Spain at La Jonquera and, from Barcelona, follows the coast via Tarragona to Valencia. More freeways radiate from Barcelona. A tunnel near Puigcerdà has made the central Catalan Pyrenees easily accessible. Buses, more frequent in summer, connect most towns. The main north–south railroad hugs the coast from Blanes south-ward. Other lines run from Barcelona through Vic, Lleida, and Tortosa.

Map labels:
Pau, Toulouse
N230
① VALL D'ARAN
VIELHA ②
③ BAQUEIRA-BERET
④ VALL DE BOÍ
⑤ PARC NACIONAL D'AIGÜESTORTES
C147
ANL
N260
N260
Noguera Ribagorçana
Noguera Pallaresa
LA SEU D'URGELL
C1313
Segre
TREMP
C137
SOLSONA ②
C1313
C241
C1412
C240
N230
N240
N240
NII
②③ LLEIDA
NII
NII
Canal d'Urgell
C230
C241
Zaragoza
Segre
A2
C242
C230
POBLET ②④
②⑤
②⑥
MONTBLANC
SANTES CR
N420
A2
A7
N420
TARRAGONA ③⓪
②⑨
SALOU
CAMBRILS
COSTA DAURADA
C235
Ebre
N340
A7
N340
TORTOSA ③①
③②
DELTA DE L'EBRE
SANT CARLES DE LA RÀPITA
N340
A7
Valencia

SEE ALSO
• Where to Stay pp545–7
• Restaurants and Bars pp586–8

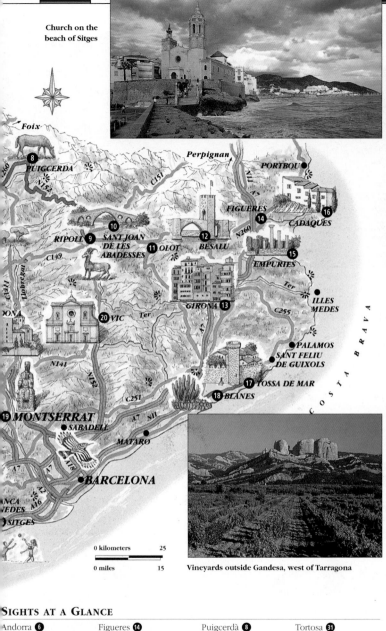

Church on the beach of Sitges

Vineyards outside Gandesa, west of Tarragona

SIGHTS AT A GLANCE

The Vall d'Aran, surrounded by the snow-capped mountains of the Pyrenees

BUTTERFLIES OF THE VALL D'ARAN

A huge variety of butterflies and moths can be found high in the mountains and valleys of the Pyrenees. In particular, the isolated Vall d'Aran is the home of several unique and rare subspecies. The best time of year to see the butterflies is between May and July.

Grizzled Skipper
(Pyrgus malvae)

Checkered Skipper
(Carterocephalus palaemon)

Clouded Apollo
(Parnassius mnemosyne)

Vall d'Aran ❶

Lleida. 🚌 Vielha. 🛈 Vielha (973) 64 01 10.

THIS VALLEY OF VALLEYS – *aran* means valley – is a beautiful 600-sq km (230-sq mile) haven of forests and flower-filled meadows surrounded by towering mountain peaks.

The Vall d'Aran was formed by the Riu Garona, which rises in the area and flows out to France as the Garonne. With no proper link to the outside world until 1924, when a road was built over the Bonaigua Pass, the valley was cut off from the rest of Spain for most of the winter. Snow still blocks the narrow pass from November to April, but today access is easy through the Túnel de Vielha from El Pont de Suert.

The fact that the Vall d'Aran faces north means that it has a climate similar to that found on the Atlantic coast. Many rare wild flowers and butterflies flourish in the perfect conditions created by the damp breezes and shady slopes. It is also a noted habitat for many species of narcissus.

Tiny villages have grown up beside the Riu Garona, often around Romanesque churches, notably at **Bossòst**, **Salardú**, **Escunhau**, and **Arties**. The valley is also ideal for outdoor sports like skiing and is popular with walkers.

Vielha ❷

Lleida. 👥 2,300. 🚌 🛈 Carrer Sarriulera 10, (973) 64 01 10. 🛒 Thu. 🎉 Fiesta de Vielha (Sep 8).

NOW A modern ski resort, the capital of the Vall d'Aran preserves relics of its medieval past. The Romanesque church of **Sant Miquel** has an octagonal bell tower, a tall, pointed roof, and a superb wooden 12th-century crucifix, the *Mig Aran Christ*. It once formed part of a larger carving, since lost, that represented the Descent from the Cross. The **Museu de la Vall d'Aran** is a museum devoted to Aranese history and folklore.

🏛 **Museu de la Vall d'Aran**
Carrer Major 26. 📞 (973) 64 18 15. 🕐 Jul – mid-Sep: daily; mid-Sep – Jun: Tue – Sun. 🔴 public hols. ♿ 📷

Mig Aran Christ (12th-century), Sant Miquel church, Vielha

Baqueira-Beret ❸

Lleida. 🏂 *100.* 🚌 🚹 *Baqueira, (973) 64 44 55.* 🎭 *Romería de Nuestra Señora de Montgarri (Jul 2).*

THIS EXTENSIVE ski resort, one of the best in Spain, is popular with both the public and the Spanish royal family. There is reliable winter snow cover and a choice of over 40 trails at altitudes from 1,520 m to 2,470 m (4,987 ft to 8,104 ft).

Baqueira and Beret were separate mountain villages – before skiing became popular, but they have now merged to form a single resort. The Romans took full advantage of the thermal springs located here, which are nowadays appreciated by tired skiers.

Vall de Boí ❹

Lleida. 🚌 *La Pobla de Segur.* 🚌 *El Pont de Suert.* 🚹 *Barruera, (973) 69 40 18.*

THIS SMALL VALLEY on the edge of the Parc Nacional d'Aigüestortes is dotted with tiny villages, many of which are built around magnificent Catalan Romanesque churches.

Dating from the 11th and 12th centuries, these churches are distinguished by their tall belfries, such as the six-story bell tower of the **Església de Santa Eulàlia** at Erill-la-Vall.

The two churches at Taüll, **Sant Climent** *(see p20)* and **Santa Maria**, have superb frescoes. Between 1919 and 1923 the originals were taken for safekeeping to the Museu Nacional d'Art de Catalunya in Barcelona *(see p168),* and replicas now stand in their place. You can climb the towers of Sant Climent for superb views of the surrounding countryside.

Other churches in the area worth visiting include those at **Coll**, for its fine ironwork, **Barruera**, and **Durro**, which has another massive bell tower.

At the head of the valley is the hamlet of **Caldes de Boí**, popular for its thermal springs and ski facilities. It is also a good base for exploring the Parc Nacional d'Aigüestortes, the entrance to which is only 5 km (3 miles) from here.

The tall belfry of Sant Climent church at Taüll in the Vall de Boí

Parc Nacional d'Aigüestortes ❺

Lleida. 🚌 *La Pobla de Segur.* 🚌 *El Pont de Suert, La Pobla de Segur.* 🚹 *Barruera, (973) 69 40 18.*

THE PRISTINE mountain scenery of Catalonia's only national park *(see pp26–7)* is among the most scenically spectacular in the Pyrenees.

Established in 1955, the park covers 10,230 hectares (25,280 acres). Its full title is Parc Nacional d'Aigüestortes i Estany de Sant Maurici, named after the lake *(estany)* of Sant Maurici in the east and the Aigüestortes (literally, twisted waters) area in the west. The main village is the mountain settlement of Espot, on the park's eastern edge. Dotted around the park are waterfalls and the sparkling, clear waters of around 150 lakes and tarns which, in an earlier era, were scoured by glaciers to depths of up to 50 m (164 ft).

The finest scenery is around Sant Maurici lake, which lies beneath the twin shards of the Sierra dels Encantats, (Mountains of the Enchanted). From here, there is a variety of walks, particularly along the string of lakes that lead north to the towering peaks of Agulles d'Amitges. To the south is the dramatic vista of Estany Negre, the highest and deepest tarn in the park.

Early summer in the lower valleys is marked by a mass of pink and red rhododendron, and later in the year wild lilies bloom in the forests of fir, beech, and silver birch.

The park is also home to a variety of wildlife. Chamois (also known as *izards*) live on the mountain scree and in the meadows, while beaver and otters can be spotted by the lakes. Golden eagles nest on mountain ledges, and grouse and capercaillie are found in the woods.

During the summer the park is popular with walkers, while in winter, the snow-covered mountains are ideal for cross-country skiing.

A crystal-clear stream, Parc Nacional d'Aigüestortes

THE CATALAN LANGUAGE

Catalonia's national emblem

Catalan has now fully recovered from the ban it suffered under Franco's dictatorship and has supplanted Castilian (Spanish) as the language in everyday use all over Catalonia. Spoken by more than eight million people, it is a Romance language akin to the Provençal of France. Previously it was suppressed by Felipe V in 1717 and only officially resurfaced in the 19th century, when the Jocs Florals (medieval poetry contests) were revived during the rebirth of Catalan literature. A leading figure of the movement was the poet Jacint Verdaguer (1845–1902).

Andorra ❻

Principality of Andorra. 🚶 58,000. 🚌
Andorra la Vella. 🛈 Pl de la Rotonda,
Andorra la Vella, (07-376) 82 71 17.

ANDORRA OCCUPIES 464 sq km (179 sq miles) of the Pyrenees between France and Spain. In 1993, it became fully independent and held its first ever democratic elections. Since 1278 it had been an autonomous feudal state under the jurisdiction of the Spanish bishop of La Seu d'Urgell and the French Count of Foix (a title adopted by the President of France). These are still the ceremonial joint heads of state.

Andorra's official language is Catalan and its currency the peseta, though French and Castilian are also spoken and French francs are accepted.

For many years Andorra has been a tax-free paradise for shoppers, a fact reflected in the crowded shops and supermarkets of the capital **Andorra la Vella**. Les Escaldes (near the capital), as well as Sant Julià de Lòria and El Pas de la Casa, (the towns nearest the Spanish and French borders), have also become shopping meccas.

Most visitors never see Andorra's rural charms, which match those of other parts of the Pyrenees. The region is excellent for walkers. One of the main routes leads to the **Cercle de Pessons**, a bowl of lakes in the east, and past Romanesque chapels such as **Sant Martí** at La Cortinada. In the north is the picturesque Sorteny valley, where traditional farmhouses have been made into snug restaurants.

La Seu d'Urgell ❼

Lleida. 🚶 11,000. 🚌 🛈 Parc del
Segre, (973) 36 00 92. 🏪 Tue & Sat.
🎺 Fiesta Mayor (last week of Aug).

THIS ANCIENT Pyrenean town was made a bishopric by the Visigoths in the 6th century. Feuds between the bishops of Urgell and the Counts of Foix over land ownership led to the emergence of Andorra in the 13th century.

The 12th-century **cathedral** has a much venerated Romanesque statue of Santa Maria d'Urgell. The **Museu Diocesà** contains medieval works of art and manuscripts, including a 10th-century copy of St. Beatus of Liébana's *Commentary on the Apocalypse (see p106).*

𝕞 Museu Diocesà
Bisbe 1. 📞 (973) 26 86 28.
🔲 Mon–Sat. 🔴 public hols. 🖼

Carving, La Seu d'Urgell cathedral

Puigcerdà ❽

Girona. 🚶 6,500. 🚌 🚐 🛈 Pl de
l'Ajuntament, (972) 88 05 42. 🏪 Sun.
🎺 Fiesta del Lago (third Sun of Aug).

PUIG IS CATALAN for hill. Although Puigcerdà sits on a relatively small hill compared with the encircling mountains, which rise to 2,900 m (9,500 ft), it nevertheless has a fine

view right down the beautiful Cerdanya valley, watered by the trout-filled Riu Segre.

Puigcerdà, very close to the French border, was founded in 1177 by Alfonso II as the capital of Cerdanya, an important agricultural region that shares a past and its culture with the French Cerdagne. The Spanish enclave of **Llívia**, an attractive little town with a medieval pharmacy, lies 6 km (3.5 miles) inside France.

Cerdanya is the largest valley in the Pyrenees. At its edge is the nature preserve of **Cadí-Moixeró**, which has a population of alpine choughs.

Portal of Monestir de Santa Maria

Ripoll ❾

Girona. 🚶 12,000. 🚌 🚐 🛈 Plaça
Abat Oliva, (972) 70 23 51. 🏪 Sat.
🎺 Sant Eudald (May 11–12).

ONCE A TINY mountain base from which raids against the Moors were made, Ripoll is now best known for the **Monestir de Santa Maria**, built in AD 888. The town has been called "the cradle of Catalonia" as the monastery was both the power base and cultural center of Guifré el Pilós (Wilfred the Hairy), founder of the 500-year dynasty of the House of Barcelona. He is buried in the monastery.

In 1032, under Abbot Oliva, the huge west portal gained a superb series of intricate carvings that are perhaps the finest Romanesque carvings in Spain. They depict historical and evangelical tales as well as biblical scenes. The two-story cloister is the only other part of the original monastery to have survived wars and anti-clerical purges. The rest is a 19th-century reconstruction.

The medieval town of Besalú on the banks of the Riu Fluvià

Sant Joan de les Abadesses ⑩

Girona. 🏠 3,800. 🚉 🛈 Passeig Comte Guifré, (972) 72 05 99. 🚌 Sun. 🎉 Fiesta Mayor (second week of Sep).

A FINE 12th-century Gothic bridge arches over the Riu Ter to this unassuming market town, whose main attraction is its **monastery**.

Founded in AD 885, it was a gift from Guifré, first count of Barcelona, to his daughter, the first abbess. The peaceful church is unadorned except for a superb wooden calvary, *The Descent from the Cross*. Made in 1150, it looks almost modern; part of it, a thief, was burned in the Civil War and replaced with such skill that it is hard to tell which section is new. The monastery's museum has a series of Baroque and Renaissance altarpieces.

12th-century calvary, Sant Joan de les Abadesses monastery

ENVIRONS: To the north is **Camprodon**, a small town full of grand houses, and shops selling local produce. The region is especially noted for its *llonganisses* (sausages).

Olot ⑪

Girona. 🏠 2,700. 🚉 🛈 Bisbe Lorenzana 15, (972) 26 01 41. 🚌 Mon. 🎉 Corpus Christi (May/ Jun), Fiesta del Tura (Sep 8).

T HIS SMALL MARKET TOWN is at the center of a landscape pockmarked with the conical hills of extinct volcanoes. But it was an earthquake in 1474 that last disturbed the town, destroying its medieval past.

During the 18th century the town's textile industry spawned the "Olot School" of art: finished cotton fabrics were printed with drawings, and in 1783 the Public School of Drawing was founded.

Much of the school's work, which includes sculpted saints and paintings such as Joaquim Vayreda's *Les Falgueres,* is in the **Museu Comarcal de la Garrotxa**, housed in an 18th-century hospice. There are also pieces by *Modernista* sculptor Miquel Blay, whose damsels support the balcony at No. 38 Passeig Miquel Blay.

🏛 **Museu Comarcal de la Garrotxa**
Hospici 8. 📞 (972) 27 91 30. 🕐 Wed–Mon. 🈲 ⚒

Besalú ⑫

Girona. 🏠 2,100. 🚉 🛈 Plaça de la Llibertat 1, (972) 59 12 40. 🚌 Tue. 🎉 Sant Vicenç (Jan 22), Fiesta Mayor (last weekend of Sep).

A MAGNIFICENT medieval town, with a striking approach across a fortified bridge over the Riu Fluvià, Besalú has two fine churches. These are the Romanesque **Sant Vicenç** and **Sant Pere**, the sole remnant of Besalú's Benedictine monastery, which was founded in AD 948, but torn down in 1835 leaving an empty square.

In 1964 a **mikvah**, a ritual Jewish bath, was discovered by chance. It was built in 1264 and is one of only three of that period to survive in Europe. The tourist office has the keys to all the town's attractions.

To the south, the sky-blue lake of **Banyoles**, where the 1992 Olympic rowing contests were held, is ideal for picnics.

Sausage shop in the mountain town of Camprodon

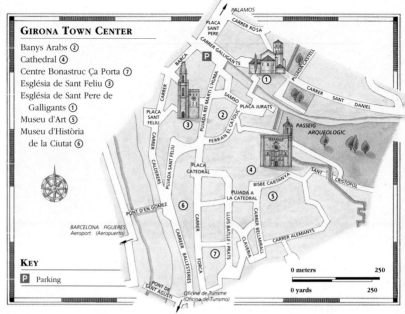

GIRONA TOWN CENTER

Banys Arabs ②
Cathedral ④
Centre Bonastruc Ça Porta ⑦
Església de Sant Feliu ③
Església de Sant Pere de
  Galligants ①
Museu d'Art ⑤
Museu d'Història
  de la Ciutat ⑥

KEY

P Parking

0 meters 250
0 yards 250

Girona ⑬

Girona. 🏛 *75,000.* ✈ 🚌 🚉 🛈
*Rambla de la Llibertat 1, (972) 22 65
75.* 🛒 *Tue, Sat.* 🎪 *El Pedal (last fort-
night of Sep), San Narciso (Oct 29).*

THIS HANDSOME TOWN puts
on its best face beside the
Riu Onyar, where tall, pastel-
colored buildings rise above
the water. Behind them, in
the old town, the Rambla de
la Llibertat is lined with busy
shops and street cafés.

The houses were built in the
19th century to replace sections of the city wall damaged
during a seven-month siege
by French troops in 1809. Most
of the rest of the ramparts, first
raised by the Romans, are still
intact and have been turned
into the **Passeig Arqueològic**
(Archaeological Walk) that
runs around the city.

The starting point of the
walk is on the north side of
the town, near the **Església
de Sant Pere de Galligants**
(St. Peter of the Cock Crows).
The church now houses the
city's archaeological collection.

From here a narrow street into the old part of town passes
through the north gate, where
huge Roman foundation stones
are still visible. They mark the
route of the Via Augusta, the
important road that originally
ran from Tarragona to Rome.
The most popular place of
devotion for the people of
Girona is the **Església de
Sant Feliu**, which brims with
history. The church, begun in
the 14th century, was built
over the tombs of St. Felix and
St. Narcissus, both patrons of
the city. Next to the high altar
are eight Roman sarcophagi
embedded in the apse wall.

Despite their name, the
nearby **Banys Arabs** (Arab
Baths), lit by a fine octagonal
lantern, were built in the late
12th century, about 300 years
after the Moors had left.

🏛 Centre Bonastruc Ça Porta
Carrer de Sant Llorenç. **(** *(972) 21
67 61.* 🛒 *Tue–Sun.* 🎫
Amid the maze of alleyways
and steps in the old town is
the former, partially restored,
Jewish quarter of El Call. The
Centre Bonastruc Ça Porta
gives a history of Girona's
Jews, who were expelled in
the late 15th century after
being forced into a ghetto.

🔒 Cathedral
The style of Girona Cathedral's
solid west face is pure Catalan
Baroque, but the rest of the
building is Gothic. The single
nave, built in 1416 by Guillem
Bofill, is the widest Gothic
span in Christendom. Behind
the altar is a marble throne
known as "Charlemagne's
Chair" after the Frankish king

Painted houses crowded along the bank of the Riu Onyar in Girona

whose troops took Girona in 785. In the chancel is a 14th-century jewel-encrusted silver and enamel altarpiece, the best example in Catalonia. Among the fine Romanesque paintings and statues in the cathedral's museum are a 10th-century illuminated copy of St. Beatus of Liébana's *Commentary on the Apocalypse*, and a 14th-century statue of the Catalan king Pere the Ceremonious.

The collection's most famous item is a tapestry, called *The Creation*, decorated with lively figures. The rich colors of this large 11th- to 12th-century work are well preserved.

Tapestry of *The Creation*

🏛 Museu d'Art
Pujada de la Catedral 12. 【 (972) 20 95 36. 🔲 *Tue–Sun.* 🌚 🔖
This former episcopal palace is one of Catalonia's best art galleries, with works ranging from the Romanesque period to the 20th century. The many items from churches destroyed through war or neglect give an idea of the richness of church interiors long ago. Highlights are carvings and a silver-clad altar of the 10th-century from the church at Sant Pere de Rodes. A 12th-century beam from Cruïlles is painted with humorous figures of monks.

🏛 Museu d'Història de la Ciutat
Carrer de la Força 27. 【 (972) 22 22 29. 🔲 *Tue–Sun.*
The city's history museum is housed in an 18th-century former convent. Parts of the convent's cemetery are preserved, including the recesses where the deceased nuns of the Capuchin Order were placed while decomposing. The collection includes scientific items and old *sardana (see p215)* instruments.

Figueres ⑭

Girona. 👥 35,000. 🚇 🚌 ℹ *Plaça del Sol, (972) 50 31 55.* 🏪 *Thu.* 🎉 *Santa Cruz (May 3), San Pedro (Jun 29).*

FIGUERES is in the north of the Empordà (Ampurdán) region, the fertile plain that sweeps inland from the Gulf of Roses. Every Thursday, the market here fills with fruit and vegetables from the area.

The **Museu de Joguets** (Toy Museum) is housed on the top floor of the old Hotel de Paris, on the Rambla, Figueres' main street. Inside are exhibits from all over Catalonia. At the lower end of the Rambla is a statue of Narcís Monturiol i Estarriol (1819–85), claimed to be the inventor of the submarine.

A much better-known son of the town is Salvador Dalí, who founded the **Teatro-Museo Dalí** in 1974. The most visited museum in Spain after the Prado, it is an entertaining place occupying Figueras's old main theater. Its roof has an eye-catching glass dome. Not all the work shown is by Dalí, and none of his best-known works are here. But the whole

***Rainy Taxi,* a monument in the garden of the Teatro-Museu Dalí**

place, ranging from *Rainy Taxi* – a black Cadillac being sprayed by a fountain – to the Mae West Room, with furnishings made to look like a huge face, is a monument to the man who, fittingly, is buried here.

🏛 Museu de Joguets
Rambla. 【 (972) 50 45 85. 🔲 *Wed–Mon.* ● *Feb.* 🌚
🏛 Teatro-Museu Dalí
Plaça Gala-Salvador Dalí. 【 (972) 51 18 00. 🔲 *Tue–Sun.* ● *Jan 1, Dec 25.* 🌚 🔖

THE ART OF DALÍ

Salvador Dalí e Domènech was born in Figueres in 1904 and mounted his first exhibition at the age of 15. After studying at the Escuela de Bellas Artes in Madrid, and dabbling with Cubism, Futurism, and Metaphysical painting, the young artist embraced Surrealism in 1929, becoming the movement's best-known painter. Never far from controversy, the self-publicist Dalí became famous for his hallucinatory images – such as *Woman-Animal Symbiosis* – which he described as "hand-painted dream photographs." Dalí's career also included writing and film-making and established him as one of the 20th century's greatest artists. He died in his home town in 1989.

Ceiling fresco in the Wind Palace Room, Teatro-Museu Dalí

Empúries **⓯**

Girona. 🚌 *L'Escala.* **ℂ** *(972) 77 02 08.* 🕐 *daily.* 🎟️ *for ruins.*

THE EXTENSIVE ruins of the Greco-Roman town of Empúries (Ampurias) occupy an imposing site beside the sea. Three separate settlements were built between the 7th and 3rd centuries BC: the old town (known to archaeologists as Palaiapolis); the new town (Neapolis), and the Roman town, which was founded by Julius Caesar in 49 BC.

The **old town** (Palaiapolis) was founded by the Greeks in 600 BC as a trading port. It was built on what was then a small offshore island, and is now the site of the tiny walled hamlet of Sant Martí de Empúries.

Around 550 BC this was replaced by a larger colony on the shore – the new town – which the Greeks named Emporion ("trading place"). In 218 BC, the Romans landed at Empúries and built a city next to the new town. From here they began their subjugation of the peninsula *(see p46).*

Excavations in the **Greek new town** have uncovered several temples, including one to Asklepios, the god of healing. On the main street are the remains of the agora (meeting place), and floor mosaics. A museum nearby exhibits some finds from the site, although the best are now in the Museu Arqueològic of Barcelona *(see p168).* The extensive **Roman town** was located on the hill behind the museum. So far excavations have revealed the ruins of two villas and a forum.

Looking south along the Costa Brava from Tossa de Mar

An excavated Roman pillar in the ruins of Empúries

Cadaqués **⓰**

Girona. 👥 *2,000.* 🚌 **ℹ️** *Carrer Cotxe 2, (972) 25 83 15.* 🚌 *Mon.* 🎎 *Santa Esperanza (Dec 18).*

THIS PRETTY, whitewashed resort, overlooked by the large Baroque **Església de Santa Maria**, is the most easterly in the country. In the 1960s it was dubbed "Spain's St. Tropez," largely because of the young crowd that sought out Salvador Dalí in the nearby unspoiled bay of Portlligat.

The **Centre d'Art Perrot-Moore** contains fine examples of Dalí's work, some excellent Picassos, and a room dedicated to contemporary artists.

🏛 **Centre d'Art Perrot-Moore**
Carrer Vigilant 1. **ℂ** *(972) 25 82 31.* 🕐 *daily.* 🎟️ 👌

Tossa de Mar **⓱**

Girona. 👥 *3,500.* 🚌 **ℹ️** *Avinguda Pelegrí 25, (972) 34 01 08.* 🚌 *Thu.* 🎎 *Fiesta de Verano (Jun 29).*

AT THE END of a tortuous corniche, the Roman town of Turissa is one of the prettiest places along the Costa Brava. Above the modern town is the **Vila Vella** (old town), a protected national monument. The medieval walls, which have three towers, enclose fishermen's cottages, a 14th-century church and countless bars.

Within the old town is the **Museu Municipal**. This collection of local archaeological finds and modern art includes *The Flying Violinist,* by the 20th-century Russian artist Marc Chagall.

🏛 **Museu Municipal**
Plaça Roig y Soler. **ℂ** *(972) 34 07 09.* 🕐 *Tue–Sun.* ● *Dec 25.* 🎟️

Blanes **⓲**

Girona. 👥 *26,000.* 🚌 **ℹ️** *Plaça de Catalunya 21, (972) 33 03 48.* 🚌 *Mon.* 🎎 *Santa Ana (Jul 24–6).*

THE WORKING PORT of Blanes has one of the longest beaches on the Costa Brava, but the highlight of the town is the **Jardí Botànic Mar i Murtra**. These fine gardens, designed by the German Karl Faust in 1928, are spectacularly located above cliffs. There are 7,000 species of Mediterranean and tropical plants here, in particular African cacti.

🌿 **Jardí Botànic Mar i Murtra**
Passeig Karl Faust 10. **ℂ** *(972) 33 08 26.* 🕐 *daily.* ● *Sat before Easter & Dec 24.* 🎟️

A few of the many species of cactus, in the Jardí Botànic

The Costa Brava

THE COSTA BRAVA ("wild coast") runs for some 200 km (125 miles) from Blanes northward to the region of Empordà (Ampurdán) bordering France. It is a mix of pine-backed sandy coves, golden beaches, and crowded, modern resorts. The busiest resorts – Lloret de Mar, Tossa de Mar, and La Platja d'Aro – are to the south. Sant Feliu de Guíxols and Palamós are still working towns behind the summer rush. Just inland there are medieval villages to explore, such as Peralada, Peratallada, and Pals. Wine, olives, and fishing were the mainstays of the area before the tourists came in the 1960s.

Cadaqués retains an air of seclusion as it is accessible only by a steep road. It has an arty air and its small, stony beaches remain unspoiled and less crowded than others.

L'Estartit is a good base for the Illes Medes, a former pirates' lair that now forms a marine reserve with clear waters perfect for skin diving.

Palamós is a working port with modern hotels to the south, and secluded beaches and coves lapped by clear water to the north.

La Platja d'Aro's long and sandy beach is lined with modern hotels. It is one of the most popular resorts on the coast.

Tossa de Mar has a golden beach and a small cove beneath the fortified old town.

Cadaqués

Roses

L'Escala

L'Estartit
Illes Medes

Begur

Llafranc
Calella de
Palafrugell

Palamós

La Platja d'Aro

S'Agaró

Sant Feliu de Guíxols

Tossa de Mar

Lloret de Mar

Blanes

Roses lies at the head of a sweeping bay. Its sandy beach, the longest on the Costa Brava, has become a mecca for lovers of water sports.

L'Escala is a small resort, popular mainly with local tourists. It has fine beaches and a small port where fishing nets dry in the sun.

Begur is a hilltop town just inland. It has good views of the coast, and small coves are tucked at its feet.

Lafranc, a whitewashed resort with a promenade leading to neighboring Calella, is one of the coast's most pleasant resorts.

Lloret de Mar has more hotels than anywhere else on the coast. But there are unspoiled beaches nearby, such as Santa Cristina.

0 kilometers   10

0 miles   5

Monestir de Montserrat ⑲

THE "SERRATED MOUNTAIN" (*mont serrat*), its highest peak rising to 1,236 m (4,055 ft), is a magnificent setting for Catalonia's holiest place, the Monastery of Montserrat, which is surrounded by chapels and hermits' caves. The monastery was first mentioned in the 9th century, enlarged in the 11th century, and in 1409 became independent of Rome. In 1811, when the French attacked Catalonia in the War of Independence *(see p59)*, the monastery was destroyed and the monks killed. Rebuilt and repopulated in 1844, it was a beacon of Catalan culture during the Franco years. Today Benedictine monks live here.

A Benedictine monk

The Old Museum displays a collection of liturgical items brought from the Holy Land.

Plaça de Santa Maria
The focal points of the square are two wings of the Gothic cloister built in 1477. The modern monastery façade is by Françesc Folguera.

Plaça de la Creu   **Gothic cloister**

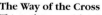

The New Museum has a collection of 19th- and 20th-century Catalan paintings and many Italian works.

The Way of the Cross
This path passes 14 statues representing the stations of the Cross. It begins near the Plaça de l'Abat Oliba.

STAR FEATURES

★ **Basilica Façade**

★ **Black Virgin**

View of Montserrat
The complex includes shops, cafés, and a hotel. Funicular railroads take visitors from the Plaça de la Creu to the Cova Santa and the hermitage of Sant Joan.

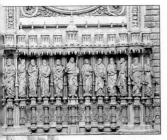

★ Basilica Façade
Agapit and Venanci Vallmitjana sculpted Christ and the apostles on the basilica's Neo-Renaissance façade. It was built in 1900 to replace the Plateresque façade of the original church, consecrated in 1592.

VISITORS' CHECKLIST

Montserrat (Barcelona province). **(** (93) 835 02 51. **☒** *Aerí de Montserrat, then cable car.* **☒** *from Barcelona.* **Basilica** **◯** 9am–7:30pm Mon–Sat, 8am–7:30pm Sun. **✝** *throughout the day, from 9am Mon–Fri, from 7:30am Sat, from 8am Sun & religious hols.* **☒ Old Museum** **◯** 10:30am–2pm daily. **●** *Jan 6–31.* **New Museum** **◯** 3–6pm daily. **●** *Jan 6–31.* **✍ ☒ ◻**

★ Black Virgin
La Moreneta looks down from behind the altar. Protected behind glass, her wooden orb protrudes for pilgrims to touch.

Basilica Interior
The sanctuary in the domed basilica is adorned by a richly enameled altar and paintings by Catalan artists.

The Escolania is the famous choir of 50 boy choristers, who sing twice a day in the basilica.

Terminal for cable car from Aerí de Montserrat railroad station

THE VIRGIN OF MONTSERRAT

The small wooden statue of La Moreneta (the dark one) is the soul of Montserrat. It is said to have been made by St. Luke and brought here by St. Peter in AD 50. Centuries later, the statue is believed to have been hidden from the Moors in the nearby Santa Cova (Holy Cave). Carbon dating suggests, however, that the statue was carved around the 12th century. In 1881 Montserrat's Black Virgin became patroness of Catalonia.

The blackened Virgin of Montserrat

Inner Courtyard
On one side of the courtyard is the baptistry (1902), with sculptures by Charles Collet. Pilgrims may approach the Virgin through a door to the right.

Vic ⑳

Barcelona. 🏠 30,000. ☒ ☒
ℹ️ Plaça Major 1, (93) 886 20 91.
☒ Tue & Sat. 🎪 Mercat del Ram (Sat
before Easter), Sant Miquel (Jul 5–15).

MARKET DAYS – Tuesdays and Saturdays – are the best time to go to this small country town. This is when the excellent local sausages *(embotits)*, for which the area is renowned, are piled high in the large Gothic Plaça Major, along with other produce from the surrounding plains.

In the 3rd century BC Vic was the capital of an ancient Iberian tribe, the Ausetans. The town was then colonized by the Romans – the remains of a Roman temple survive today. Since the 6th century the town has been a bishop's see. In the 11th century, Abbot Oliva commissioned the El Cloquer tower, around which the cathedral was built in the 18th century. The interior of the cathedral is covered with vast murals by Josep Maria Sert (1876–1945). They are painted in reds and golds, and represent scenes from the Bible.

Adjacent to the cathedral is the **Museu Episcopal de Vic**, which has one of the best collections of Romanesque artifacts in Catalonia. Its large display of mainly religious art and relics includes bright, simple murals and wooden sculptures from rural churches. Also on display are 11th- and 12th-century frescoes and some superb altar frontals.

Cardona dominating the surrounding area from its hilltop site

🏛 **Museu Episcopal**
Plaça Bisbe Oliva. 📞 (93) 886 22 14.
⭕ daily. 🎫

Cardona ㉑

Barcelona. 🏠 6,200. ☒ ℹ️ Avinguda
Rastrillo, (93) 869 27 98. ☒ Sun.
🎪 Fiesta Mayor (second Sun of Sep).

THE 13TH-CENTURY ruddy-stoned castle of the Dukes of Cardona, constables to the crown of Aragón, is set on the top of a hill. The castle was rebuilt in the 18th century and is now a luxurious parador *(see p534).* Beside the castle is an elegant early 11th-century church, the **Església de Sant Vicenç**, where the Dukes of Cardona are buried.

The castle gives views of the town below and of the Montanya de Sal (Salt Mountain), a huge salt deposit beside the Riu Cardener that has been mined since Roman times.

Twelfth-century altar frontal, Museu Episcopal de Vic

Solsona ㉒

Lleida. 🏠 6,500. ☒ ℹ️ Avinguda
Pont, (973) 48 23 10. ☒ Tue & Fri.
🎪 Carnival (late Feb), Corpus Christi
(May/Jun), Fiesta Mayor (Sep 8–10).

NINE TOWERS and three gateways remain of Solsona's moated fortifications. Inside the walls is an ancient town of noble mansions. The cathedral houses a beautiful black stone Virgin. The adjoining **Museu Diocesà i Comarcal** contains Romanesque paintings and local archaeological finds.

🏛 **Museu Diocesà i Comarcal**
Plaça Palau 1. 📞 (973) 48 21 01.
⭕ Tue–Sun. ⬤ Jan 1 & Dec 25. ♿

Lleida ㉓

Lleida. 🏠 120,000. ☒ ☒ ℹ️
Avinguda de Madrid 36, (973) 27 09
97. ☒ Thu & Sat. 🎪 Sant Anastasi
(May 11), Sant Miquel (Sep 29).

DOMINATING Lleida (Lérida), the capital of Catalonia's only landlocked province, is **La Suda**, a large, ruined fort taken from the Moors in 1149. The old cathedral, **La Seu Vella**, founded in 1203, is situated within the walls of the fort, high above the town. It was transformed into barracks by Felipe V in 1707 but today, sadly, is desolate, the haunt of pigeons. It remains imposing, however, with magnificent Gothic windows in the cloister.

An elevator descends from the Seu Vella to the Plaça de Sant Joan in the town. This square is at the mid-point of a pedestrianized shopping street that sweeps around the foot of the hill. The new cathedral is here, as are manorial buildings such as the reconstructed 13th-century town hall, the **Paeria**.

Poblet ㉔

See pp212–13.

Montblanc ㉕

Tarragona. 🏘 *6,000.* 🚉 🚌 ℹ *Muralla Santa Tecla 24, (977) 86 12 32.* 🛒 *Fri.* 🎉 *Fiesta Mayor (Sep 8).*

THE MEDIEVAL grandeur of Montblanc lives on within its walls, which are considered to be Catalonia's finest piece of military architecture. At the **Sant Jordi** gate, St. George allegedly slew the dragon. The **Museu Comarcal de la Conca de Barberà** has interesting displays on local crafts.

🏛 **Museu Comarcal de la Conca de Barberà**
Carrer Josa 6. 📞 *(977) 86 03 49.* 🕐 *Tue–Sun.* 🌐

Santes Creus ㉖

Tarragona. 🏘 *100.* 🚉 ℹ *Plaça de Sant Bernard, (977) 63 83 01.* 🛒 *every other Sat & Sun.* 🎉 *Sta Llúcia (Dec 13).*

HOME TO THE the prettiest of the "Cistercian triangle" monasteries is the tiny village of Santes Creus. The other

two, Vallbona de les Monges and Poblet *(see pp212–13)*, are nearby. The **Monestir de Santes Creus** was founded in 1150 by Ramon Berenguer IV *(see p50)* during his reconquest of Catalonia. The Gothic cloisters are decorated with figurative sculptures, a style first permitted by Jaime II, who ruled from 1291 to 1327. His finely carved tomb, along with that of other nobles, is in the 12th-century church. The austerity of the interior is relieved by a beautiful rose window.

🏛 **Monestir de Santes Creus**
📞 *(977) 63 83 29.* 🕐 *Tue–Sun.* 🌐

Vilafranca del Penedès ㉗

Barcelona. 🏘 *28,500.* 🚉 🚌 ℹ *Carrer Cort 14, (93) 892 03 58.* 🛒 *Sat.* 🎉 *Fiesta Mayor (Aug 29–31).*

THIS BUSY MARKET town is set in the heart of Catalonia's main wine-producing region *(see pp192–3)*. The **Museu del Vi** (Wine Museum), in the 14th-century palace of the kings of Aragón, documents the long history of the area's wine trade. Local bodegas can be visited for wine tasting.

Eight km (5 miles) to the north is **Sant Sadurní**, the capital of Spain's sparkling wine, *cava (see pp576–7)*.

🏛 **Museu del Vi**
Plaça Jaume I. 📞 *(93) 890 05 82.* 🕐 *Tue–Sun.* 🌐

Anxaneta climbing to the top of a tower of *castellers*

CATALONIA'S FIESTAS

Human Towers *(various dates and locations).* The province of Tarragona is famous for its *castellers* festivals, where teams of men stand on each others' shoulders in an effort to build the highest human tower. Each tower, which can be up to seven stories high, is topped by a small boy called the *anxaneta*. *Castellers* can be seen in action in many towns, especially Vilafranca del Penedès and Valls.

Dance of Death *(Maundy Thu),* Verges (Girona). Men dressed as skeletons perform a macabre dance.

St. George's Day *(Apr 23).* Lovers give each other a rose and a book on the day of Catalonia's patron saint. The book is in memory of Cervantes, who died on this day in 1616.

La Patum *(Corpus Christi, May/Jun),* Berga (Barcelona province). Bizarre monsters, giants, and devils parade through the town.

Midsummer's Eve *(Jun 23).* Celebrated all over Catalonia with bonfires and fireworks.

Monestir de Santes Creus, surrounded by poplar and hazel trees

Monestir de Poblet ❷⁴

THE MONASTERY OF SANTA MARIA DE POBLET is a haven of tranquility and a resting place of kings. It was the first and most important of three sister monasteries, known as the "Cistercian triangle" *(see p211)*, that helped to consolidate power in Catalonia after it had been recaptured from the Moors by Ramon Berenguer IV. During the 1835 Carlist revolution, the abbey was plundered and seriously damaged by fire. Restoration of the impressive ruins, now largely complete, began in 1930 and monks returned in 1940.

The dormitory is reached by stairs from the church. The vast 87-m (285-ft) gallery dates from the 18th century. Half of it is still in use by the monks.

The 13th-century refectory is a vaulted hall with an octagonal fountain and a pulpit.

View of Poblet
The abbey, its buildings enclosed by fortified walls that have hardly changed since the Middle Ages, is in an isolated valley near the Riu Francolí's source.

Museum

Wine cellar

Library
The Gothic scriptorium was converted into a library in the 17th century, when the Duke of Cardona donated his book collection.

Former kitchen

Royal doorway   Royal palace

TIMELINE

Royal tombs

1157 Founding of sister monastery at Vallbona de les Monges						**1812** Poblet desecrated by French troops	**1940** Monks return	
1168 Santes Creus founded – third abbey in Cistercian triangle	**14th century** Main cloister finished		**1479** Juan II, last king of Aragón, buried here					

1100	1300	1500	1700	1900

1196 Alfonso II is the first king to be buried here	**1336–87** Reign of Pere the Ceremonious, who designates Poblet a royal pantheon			**1953** Tombs reconstructed. Royal remains returned
1151 Poblet monastery founded by Ramon Berenguer IV		**1788–1808** Reign of Carlos IV, who has main reredos installed	**1835** Disentailment *(p59)* of monasteries. Poblet ravaged	

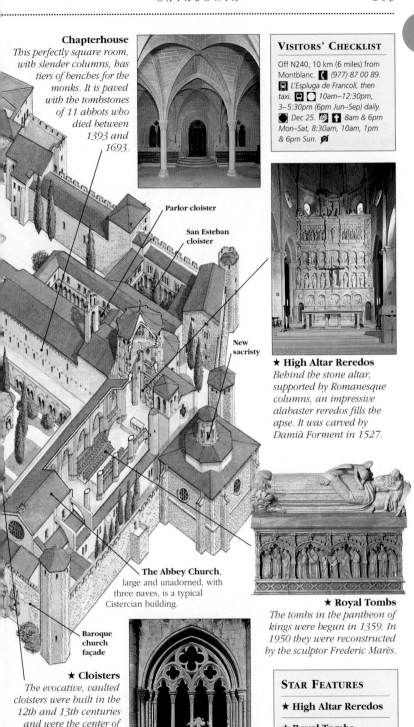

Chapterhouse
This perfectly square room, with slender columns, has tiers of benches for the monks. It is paved with the tombstones of 11 abbots who died between 1393 and 1693.

Parlor cloister

San Esteban cloister

New sacristy

The Abbey Church, large and unadorned, with three naves, is a typical Cistercian building.

Baroque church façade

VISITORS' CHECKLIST

Off N240, 10 km (6 miles) from Montblanc. (977) 87 00 89. L'Espluga de Francolí, then taxi. 10am–12:30pm, 3–5:30pm (6pm Jun–Sep) daily. Dec 25. 8am & 6pm Mon–Sat, 8:30am, 10am, 1pm & 6pm Sun.

★ High Altar Reredos
Behind the stone altar, supported by Romanesque columns, an impressive alabaster reredos fills the apse. It was carved by Damià Forment in 1527.

★ Royal Tombs
The tombs in the pantheon of kings were begun in 1359. In 1950 they were reconstructed by the sculptor Frederic Marès.

★ Cloisters
The evocative, vaulted cloisters were built in the 12th and 13th centuries and were the center of monastic life. The capitals are beautifully decorated with carved scrollwork.

STAR FEATURES

★ High Altar Reredos

★ Royal Tombs

★ Cloisters

Palm trees lining the waterfront at Sitges

Sitges ❷❽

Barcelona. 🚶 *15,000.* 🚌 🚉 🛈
Carrer Sinia Morera 1, (93) 811 76 30.
🚢 *Thu.* 🎉 *Fiesta Mayor (Aug 23–24).*

L IVELY BARS line the seafront at
Sitges, which, as Barcelona
province's premier resort, is
popular with both locals and
foreigners. Modernista artist
Santiago Rusiñol (1861–1931)
spent much time here. He
bequeathed his eclectic collection of wrought-iron ceramics,
sculptures, and paintings to
the **Museu Cau Ferrat**, which
also has works by El Greco.

🏛 Museu Cau Ferrat
Carrer Fonollar. 📞 *(93) 894 03 64.*
🔲 *Tue–Sun.* ⬤ *public hols.* 🚫

Costa Daurada ❷❾

Tarragona. 🚉 🚢 *Calafell, San Vicente,*
Salou. 🛈 *Tarragona, (977) 23 34 15.*

T HE ENTIRE coast of Tarragona
province is known as the
Costa Daurada, the Golden
Coast, because of its long,
sandy beaches. **Vilanova i la
Geltrú** and **El Vendrell** are
two of the many ports along it
that are still active. The **Museu
Pau Casals** in El Vendrell is
dedicated to the famous cellist.
   Port Aventura, south of
Tarragona, is one of Europe's
largest theme parks. Its exoti-
cally inspired attractions are
named Mediterrània, México,

China, Polynesia, and Wild
West. **Salou** and **Cambrils** to
the south are the liveliest resorts – the others are mostly
low-key, family holiday places.

🏛 Museu Pau Casals
Avinguda Palfuriana 59–61. 📞 *(977)*
68 01 17. 🔲 *Tue–Sun.* 🚫 ♿
🎢 Port Aventura
Autovia Salou–Vila-seca. 📞 *(977) 77*
90 00. 🔲 *Apr–Oct.* 🚫 ♿

Tarragona ❸⓪

Tarragona. 🚶 *75,000.* ✈ 🚉 🚢
🛈 *Carrer Fortuny 4, (977) 23 34 15.*
🚢 *Tue & Thu.* 🎉 *Santa Tecla (Sep 23).*

T ARRAGONA IS NOW a major
industrial port with a large
petrochemical industry, but it
also preserves many remnants
of its Roman past. It was then
the capital of Tarraconensis.
The Romans chose it as their
base for the conquest of the
peninsula, which began in the
3rd century BC *(see pp46–7).*
   The avenue of Rambla Nova
ends abruptly above the sea on
the clifftop Balcó de Europa,
from which the extensive ruins
of the **Anfiteatro Romano** can
be seen. Within them is the
ruined 12th-century church of
Santa Maria the Miracle.
   Nearby is the Praetorium,
a Roman tower that was converted into a palace in medieval times. It is sometimes
known as the Castell de Pilato
(named after Pontius Pilate),
and it now houses the **Museu
de la Romanitat**. This displays Roman and medieval
finds and gives access to the
cavernous passageways of the
excavated Roman circus, built

The remains of the Roman amphitheater, Tarragona

In the 1st century AD. Adjoining the Praetorium is the **Museu Nacional Arqueològic,** containing the most important collection of Roman artifacts in Catalonia. It has a large collection of bronze implements, stone busts, and beautiful mosaics, including the *Head of Medusa.*

Among the most impressive Roman remains in the city are the gigantic stones built into the Roman wall. An archaeological walk runs along a 1-km (1,100-yds) long stretch of the wall and its towers.

Behind it is the 12th-century **cathedral**, built on the site of a Roman temple to Jupiter and a subsequent Arab mosque. The structure evolved over many centuries, as seen from the harmonious blend of styles of the exterior. Inside is an alabaster altarpiece of St. Tecla carved by Pere Johan in 1434. The large 13th-century cloister, which is filled with orange trees, has early Gothic vaulting, but the doorway is Romanesque in its geometric decoration.

In the west of town is a 3rd- to 6th-century Christian cemetery (ask about opening times in the archaeological museum). Some of the carved sarcophagi, in the site museum were originally used as pagan tombs.

ENVIRONS: The well-preserved **Aqüeducte de les Ferreres** lies just outside the city, next to the A7 highway. (There is a scenic viewpoint.) This 2nd-century aqueduct was built to bring water to the city from the Riu Gaià, 30 km (19 miles) to the north. The **Arc de Berà**, a 1st-century triumphal arch on the Via Augusta, is 20 km (12 miles) northeast on the N340.

🏛 **Museu Nacional Arqueològic de Tarragona**
Plaça del Rei 5. ☎ (977) 23 62 09.
◯ Tue –Sun. 🖾 🕭
🏛 **Museu de la Romanitat**
Plaça del Rei. ☎ (977) 24 19 52.
◯ Tue –Sun. 🖾

Tortosa ❸

Tarragona. 🏘 30,000. 🚆 Plaça Bimil·lenari, (977) 51 08 22. 🚌 Mon. 🎉 Nuestra Señora de la Cinta (first week of Sep).

A RUINED CASTLE and medieval walls are clues to Tortosa's historical importance. Sited at the lowest crossing point on the Riu Ebre (Río Ebro), it has been strategically significant since Iberian times. The Moors held the city from the 8th century until 1148. The old Moorish castle, known as La Zuda, is all that remains of their defenses. It has now been renovated as a parador *(see p547)*. The Moors also built a mosque in 914. Its foundations were

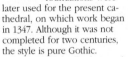

Ruins of the Palaeo-Christian Necropolis

later used for the present cathedral, on which work began in 1347. Although it was not completed for two centuries, the style is pure Gothic.

Tortosa was badly damaged in 1938–39 during one of the fiercest battles of the Civil War *(see pp62–3)*, when the Ebre formed the front line between the opposing forces.

Delta de L'Ebre ❸

Tarragona. 🚆 Aldea. 🚌 Deltebre, Aldea. 🚆 Deltebre (977) 48 96 79.

T HE DELTA of the Riu Ebre is a prosperous rice-growing region and wildlife haven. Some 70 sq km (27 sq miles) have been turned into a nature preserve, the **Parc Natural del Delta de L'Ebre**. In Deltebre there is an information center and an interesting **Eco-Museu**, with an aquarium containing species found in the delta.

The main towns in the area are **Amposta** and **Sant Carles de la Ràpita**, both of which serve as good bases for exploring the preserve.

The best sites for seeing the huge variety of wildlife are along the shore, from the Punta del Fangar in the north to the Punta de la Banya in the south. Everywhere is accessible by car except Illa de Buda. Flamingoes breed on this island and, along with other water birds such as black-winged stilts, herons, and avocets, can be seen from tourist boats that leave from Riumar and Deltebre.

🏛 **Eco-Museu**
Carrer Martí Buera 22. ☎ (977) 48 96 79. ◯ daily. ● Dec 25. 🖾 🕭

THE SARDANA

Catalonia's national dance is more complicated than it appears. The success of the Sardana depends on all of the dancers accurately counting the complicated short- and long-step skips and jumps, which accounts for their serious faces. Music is provided by a *cobla*, an 11-person band consisting of a leader playing a three-holed flute *(flabiol)* and a little drum *(tabal)*, five woodwind players, and five brass players. When the music starts dancers join hands and form circles. The Sardana is performed during most local fiestas *(see p211)* and at special day-long gatherings called *aplecs*.

A group of Sardana dancers captured in stone

ARAGÓN

STRETCHING ALMOST HALF the length of Spain, and bisected by the Ebro, one of the country's longest rivers, Aragón takes in a wide variety of scenery, from the snow-capped summits of Ordesa National Park in the Pyrenees to the dry plains of the Spanish interior. This largely unsung and undervisited region contains magnificent Mudéjar architecture and many unspoiled medieval towns.

From the 12th–15th centuries Aragón was a powerful kingdom, or, more accurately, a federation of states, including Catalonia. In its heyday, in the 13th century, its dominions stretched across the Mediterranean as far as Sicily. By his marriage to Isabel of Castile and León in 1469, Fernando II of Aragón paved the way for the unification of Spain.

After the Reconquest, Muslim architects and craftsmen were treated more tolerantly here than elsewhere, and they continued their work in the distinctive Mudéjar style, building with elaborate brickwork and patterned ceramic decoration. Their work can be seen in churches all over Aragón and there are outstanding examples in the cities of Teruel and the capital, Zaragoza, Spain's fifth largest city, which stands on the banks of the Ebro.

The highest peaks of the Pyrenees lie in Huesca province. Some of the region's finest sights are in the Pyrenean foothills, which are crossed by the Aragonese variation of the pilgrims' route to Santiago de Compostela. Probably the most spectacular of them is the monastery of San Juan de la Peña – half concealed beneath a rock overhang – which was founded in the 9th century.

The climate of the region varies as much as the landscape: winters can be long and harsh and summers hot.

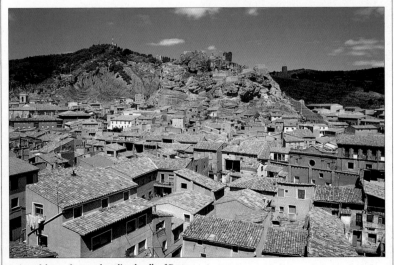

A view of the rooftops and medieval walls of Daroca

◁ Torla village church, on the edge of Ordesa National Park

Exploring Aragón

Stone carving, San Juan de la Peña

THE LANDSCAPES OF ARAGÓN range from the high Pyrenees, north of Huesca, through the desiccated terrain around Zaragoza to the forested hills of Teruel province. The cities of Teruel and Zaragoza have some of the most striking Mudéjar monuments in Spain. There are many small, picturesque preserved towns in the region. Ordesa National Park contains stunning mountain scenery, but it can be fully visited only after the snow melts in spring, and even then much of it has to be explored on foot. Pretty Los Valles offers less dramatic but equally enjoyable landscapes and is a popular tourist destination. Other attractive places include the impressively sited Castillo de Loarre and Monasterio de San Juan de la Peña, and the waterfalls of Monasterio de Piedra.

The Puerto de Somport, near Panticosa.

SIGHTS AT A GLANCE

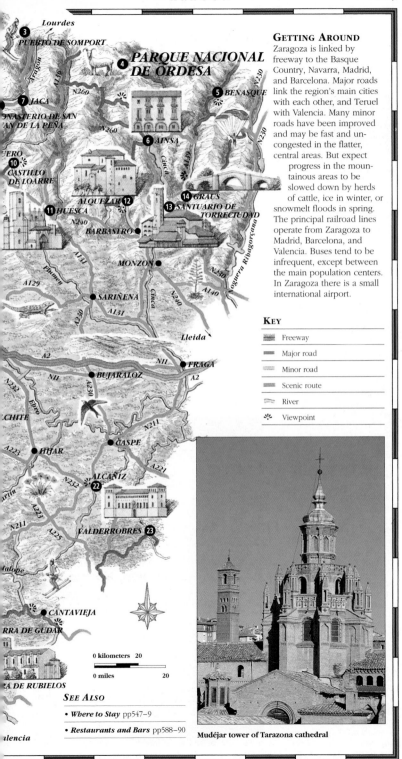

Lourdes

❸ **PUERTO DE SOMPORT**

PARQUE NACIONAL DE ORDESA ❹

❺ **BENASQUE**

❼ **JACA**

Aragón N330

N260

N260

ONASTERIO DE SAN AN DE LA PEÑA

❻ **AINSA**

Cinca A139

ERO N240

❿ **CASTILLO DE LOARRE**

ALQUÉZAR ❶❷

❶❸ **SANTUARIO DE TORRECIUDAD**

❶❹ **GRAUS**

❶❶ **HUESCA**

Noguera Ribagorçana N230

N240

BARBASTRO

A131

Flumen

MONZÓN

A129

SARIÑENA

A231

A140

A230

A131

Cinca

N230

Lleida

A2

N II

FRAGA

Ebro

N232

N II

A230

BUJARALOZ

A2

A221

.CHITE

A223

HIJAR

N232

CASPE

N211

Martín

A223

ALCAÑIZ ❷❷

N211

A225

VALDERROBRES ❷❸

alope

CANTAVIEJA

RRA DE GUDAR

RA DE RUBIELOS

alencia

GETTING AROUND

Zaragoza is linked by freeway to the Basque Country, Navarra, Madrid, and Barcelona. Major roads link the region's main cities with each other, and Teruel with Valencia. Many minor roads have been improved and may be fast and un-congested in the flatter, central areas. But expect progress in the moun-tainous areas to be slowed down by herds of cattle, ice in winter, or snowmelt floods in spring. The principal railroad lines operate from Zaragoza to Madrid, Barcelona, and Valencia. Buses tend to be infrequent, except between the main population centers. In Zaragoza there is a small international airport.

KEY

▬▬▬	Freeway
▬▬▬	Major road
▬▬▬	Minor road
▬▬▬	Scenic route
◗	River
✺	Viewpoint

0 kilometers   20

0 miles   20

Mudéjar tower of Tarazona cathedral

The town hall, Sos del Rey Católico

Sos del Rey Católico ❶

Zaragoza. 🏠 1,000. 🚌 ℹ️ Plaza de la Villa 1, (948) 88 80 65. 🛒 Fri.
🎉 San Esteban (third week of Aug).

F ERNANDO OF ARAGON – the so-called "Catholic King" who married Isabel of Castile, thereby uniting Spain (see pp52–3) – was born in this small town in 1452, hence its distinguished royal name.

The **Palacio de Sada**, the king's reputed birthplace, with a beautiful inner courtyard, is among the town's grandest stone mansions. It stands in a small square amid a maze of narrow cobbled streets.

At the top of the town are the stumpy remnants of a castle and the **Iglesia de San Esteban**. The church's ancient font and carved capitals are noteworthy, as are the 13th-century frescoes in two of the crypt's apses. From both the castle and the church there are magnificent views of the surrounding hills.

The Gothic-arched **Lonja** (commodities exchange) and the 16th-century **town hall** (ayuntamiento) are located on the adjacent main square.

ENVIRONS: The "Cinco Villas" are five towns recognized by Felipe V for their loyalty during the War of the Spanish Succession (see p58). Sos del Rey Católico is the most appealing of these. The others are Ejea de los Caballeros, Tauste, Sábada, and **Uncastillo**. This last town, 20 km (12 miles) to the southeast, has a fortress and a Romanesque church, the Iglesia de Santa María.

Los Valles ❷

Huesca. 🚆 Jaca. 🚌 from Jaca to Hecho. ℹ️ Plaza Condes Xiquena, Hecho, (974) 37 53 29.

T HE DELIGHTFUL VALLEYS of Ansó and Hecho, formed by the Veral and Aragón Subordán rivers respectively, were isolated until recently due to poor road links. Their villages have retained traditional customs and a local dialect called cheso, which is passed down from parents to children. Now the area's crafts and costumes have made it popular with tourists, especially in summer. The Pyrenean foothills and pine forests above the valleys are particularly good for walking, fishing, and cross-country skiing.

Ansó lies in the prettiest valley, which becomes a shadowy gorge where the Río Veral and the road next to it squeeze between vertical crags and through rock tunnels. Many of its buildings have stone façades and steep, tiled roofs. In the Gothic church (16th century) there is a museum dedicated to local costume.

Hecho is host to an open-air festival of modern sculpture. Previous years' exhibits lie scattered around the village. The bucolic village of **Siresa**, which contains the 11th-century church of San Pedro, lies to the north of Hecho.

Puerto de Somport ❸

Huesca. 🚌 Somport. ℹ️ Canfranc, (974) 37 30 29.

J UST INSIDE THE BORDER with France, the Somport Pass was for centuries a strategic crossing point for the Romans and Moors, and for medieval pilgrims en route to Santiago de Compostela (see pp78–9). Today the austere scenery is specked with vacation apartments built for skiers. **Astún** is modern and well organized, while **El Formigal**, to the east, is a stylish, custom-built resort with long, gentle runs for beginners. Non-skiers can enjoy the scenery around the Panticosa gorge. **Sallent de Gállego** is popular for rock-climbing and fishing.

Steep, tiled roofs of Hecho, with a typical pepperpot chimney

Rough and craggy landscape around Benasque

Parque Nacional de Ordesa ④

See pp222–3.

Benasque ⑤

Huesca. 🏠 1,100. 🛈 Calle de San Pedro, (974) 55 12 89. 🚌 Tue. 🎪 San Marcial (Jun 30 Jun–Jul 6).

TUCKED AWAY IN THE northeast corner of Aragón, at the head of the Esera valley, the village of Benasque presides over a ruggedly beautiful stretch of Pyrenean scenery. Although the village has expanded greatly to meet the tourist trade, a sympathetic use of wood and stone has resulted in buildings that complement the existing older houses. A stroll through the old center filled with aristocratic mansions is a delight.

The most striking buildings in Benasque are the 13th-century **Iglesia de Santa María Mayor** and the **Palacio de los Condes de Ribagorza**. The latter has a Renaissance façade.

Above the village rises the Maladeta massif. There are magnificent views from its ski slopes and hiking trails. Several local mountain peaks, including **Posets** and **Aneto**, exceed 3,000 m (9,800 ft).

ENVIRONS: For walkers, skiers, and climbers, the area around Benasque has a great deal to offer, for all levels of ability.

The neighboring resort of **Cerler** was developed with care from a rustic village into a popular base for skiing and other winter sports.

At Castejón de Sos, 15 km (9 miles) south of Benasque, the road passes through the **Congosto de Ventamillo**, a scenic rocky gorge.

Ainsa ⑥

Huesca. 🏠 1,000. 🚌 🛈 Cruce de Carreteras, (974) 51 00 03. 🚌 Tue. 🎪 San Sebastián (Jan 20).

THE CAPITAL of the kingdom of Sobrarbe in medieval times, Ainsa has retained its charm. The Plaza Mayor, a broad cobbled square, is surrounded by neat terraced arcades of brown stone. On one side stands the shapely belfry of the **Iglesia de Santa María** – consecrated in 1181 – and beyond, old streets lead up to the restored castle.

Jaca ⑦

Huesca. 🏠 14,000. 🚌 🚌 🛈 Avda Regimento de Galicia 2, (974) 36 00 98. 🚌 Fri. 🎪 La Victoria (first Fri of May), Santa Orosia (late Jun).

JACA DATES BACK as far as the 2nd century AD. In the 8th century the town bravely repulsed the Moors – an act that is commemorated in the festival of La Victoria – and in 1035 it became the first capital of the kingdom of Aragón. Jaca's 11th-century **cathedral**, one of Spain's oldest, is much altered inside. Traces of its original splendor can be seen on the restored south porch and doorway, where carvings depict biblical scenes involving Isaac and David. The dim nave and chapels are decorated with ornate vaulting and sculpture. A museum of sacred art, in the cloisters, contains a collection of Romanesque and Gothic frescoes and sculptures from local churches. The streets that surround the cathedral form an attractive quarter.

Sculpture in Jaca cathedral

Jaca's only other significant tourist sight is its 16th-century **citadel**, a fort decorated with corner turrets, on the edge of town. Today the town serves as a principal base for the Aragonese Pyrenees.

The arcaded main square of Ainsa with the Iglesia de Santa María

Parque Nacional de Ordesa ❹

Signpost in Ordesa National Park

WITHIN ITS BORDERS the Parque Nacional de Ordesa y Monte Perdido combines all the most dramatic elements of Spain's Pyrenean scenery. At the heart of the park are four glacial canyons – the Ordesa, Añisclo, Pineta, and Escuain valleys – that carve the great upland limestone massifs into spectacular cliffs and chasms. Most of the park is accessible only on foot: even then, snow during autumn and winter makes it inaccessible to all except those with special climbing equipment. In summer, however, the crowds testify to the park's well-earned reputation as a paradise for walkers and nature lovers alike.

Valle de Ordesa
The Río Arazas cuts through foreste... limestone escarpments, providing some of Ordesa's most popular walk...

El Taillón

Brecha ... Roland...

3,144 m (10,315 ft)

Gruta de Casteret

Mondarruego
2,848 m (9,344 ft)

VALLE DE ORD...

Cascada Torrombotera

SIERRA DE LAS CU...

Torla

BIESCAS

Broto

Oto

Ara

Sarvisé

Jalle

AINSA

Torla
This village, at the gateway to the park, huddles beneath the forbidding slopes of Mondarruego. With its core of cobbled streets and slate-roofed houses around the church, Torla is a popular base for visitors to Ordesa.

PYRENEAN WILDLIFE

Spanish Ibex

Ordesa is a spectacle of flora and fauna, with many of its species unique to the region. Trout streams rush along the valley floor, where slopes provide a mantle of various woodland harboring all kinds of creatures, including otters, marmots, and capercaillies (large grouse). On the slopes, flowers burst out before the snow melts, with gentians and orchids sheltering in crevices and edelweiss braving the most hostile crags. Higher up, the Pyrenean chamois is still fairly common; but the unique Ordesa ibex, or mountain goat, is now becoming scarce and is a protected species. The rocky pinnacles above are the domain of birds of prey.

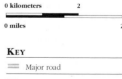

Spring gentian (*Gentiana verna*)

0 kilometers   2

0 miles   2

KEY

▭	Major road
—	Minor road
- -	Footpath
—	Spanish/French border
—	National park boundary
🛈	Tourist information
⚜	Viewpoint

View from Parador de Bielsa
The parador (see p548), at the foot of Monte Perdido, looks out at stunning sheer rock faces streaked with waterfalls.

VISITORS' CHECKLIST

🛈 Visitors' center, 9 km (5.5 miles) north of Torla on road to Valle de Ordesa, (974) 24 33 61.
🚌 Change at Sabiñánigo for Torla. 🚊 Sabiñánigo.

Parador de Bielsa

Perdido

VALLE DE PINETA

Cinca

BIELSA

55 m
(08 ft)

Refugio de Góriz

SIERRA DE LAS TUCAS

Cascada
Cola de Caballo

de Soaso

Vellos

CAÑON DE AÑISCLO

GARGANTA DE ESCUAIN

Revilla

Escuaín

BIELSA

Tella

Nerín

Bestué

Puértolas

Vellos

Cola de Caballo
The 70-m (230-ft) "Horse's Tail" waterfall makes a scenic stopping point near the northern end of the long trail around the Circo Soaso. It provides a taste of the spectacular scenery found along the route.

Hikers in Ordesa National Park

TIPS FOR WALKERS

Several well-marked trails follow the valleys and can be easily tackled by anyone reasonably fit, though walking boots are a must. The mountain routes may require climbing gear, so check first with the visitors' center and get a detailed map. Pyrenean weather changes rapidly – beware of ice and snow early and late in the season – but in case of need there are several *refugios* that provide basic overnight shelter.

Cañon or Garganta de Añiscló
A wide path leads along this beautiful, steep-sided gorge, following the wooded course of the turbulent Río Vellos through dramatic limestone scenery.

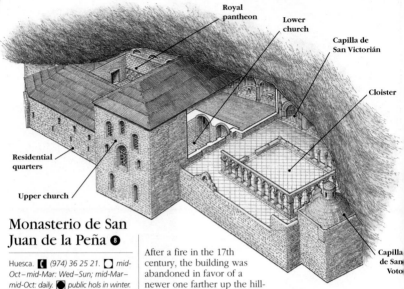

Royal pantheon

Lower church

Capilla de San Victorián

Cloister

Residential quarters

Upper church

Capilla de San Voto

Monasterio de San Juan de la Peña ❽

Huesca. 📞 (974) 36 25 21. ⏰ mid-Oct–mid-Mar: Wed–Sun; mid-Mar–mid-Oct: daily. ● public hols in winter.

SET UNDER a bulging rock, this monastery, founded in the 9th century, was an early guardian of the legendary Holy Grail (see p240). In the 11th century it underwent reformation in Cluniac style and was the first monastery to introduce the Latin Mass in Spain.

After a fire in the 17th century, the building was abandoned in favor of a newer one farther up the hill-side. This was later sacked by Napoleon's troops, although the Baroque façade survives.

The church of the old monastery is on two storys. The lower one is a primitive rock-hewn crypt built in the early 10th century. The upper story contains an 11th-century church with a simple triple apse hollowed out of the side of the cliff. The well-preserved Romanesque pantheon contains the neatly stacked tombs of the early Aragonese kings. The exterior cloister is San Juan de la Peña's pièce de résistance, the capitals of its columns splendidly carved with biblical scenes.

Agüero ❾

Huesca. 🏘 169. ℹ Plaza Mayor 1, (974) 38 04 98. 🎎 San Roque (Aug 15–19).

THE PICTURESQUE setting of this attractive village, clustered against a dramatic crag of eroded pudding stone, amply rewards a brief detour from the main road. The most important reason for visiting Agüero, however, is to see the 12th-century Iglesia de Santiago. This Romanesque church is reached by a long stony track leading uphill just before the village.

The capitals of the columns in this unusual triple-naved building are carved with fantastical beasts as well as scenes from the life of Jesus and the Virgin Mary. The beautiful carvings on the doorway display biblical events, including scenes from the Epiphany

and Salome dancing ecstatically. The lively, large-eyed figures are attributed to the mason responsible for the superb carvings in the monastery at San Juan de la Peña.

Castillo de Loarre ❿

Loarre (Huesca). 📞 (974) 38 26 27. 🚉 Ayerbe. 🚌 from Huesca. ⏰ Tue–Sun. ● Dec.

THE RAMPARTS of this sturdy, imposing fortress stand out majestically above the road approaching from Ayerbe. It is so closely molded around the contours of a rock that at night or in poor visibility it could be mistaken for a natural outcrop. On a clear day, the hilltop setting is awesome, with magnificent views of the surrounding orchards and reservoirs of the Ebro plain. Inside the stout curtain walls

Village of Agüero, situated under a rocky crag

ies a complex founded in the 11th century on the site of a Roman castle. It was later remodeled under Sancho I (Sancho Ramírez) of Aragón, who established a religious community here, placing the complex under the rule of the Order of St. Augustine.

Within the castle walls is a Romanesque church that is decorated with alabaster windows, a checkered frieze, and interesting carved column capitals. Its crypt contains the remains of St. Demetrius.

Sentry paths, iron ladders, and flights of steps ramble precariously around the castle's towers, dungeons, and keep.

The formidable Castillo de Loarre looming above the surrounding area

Huesca ⓫

Huesca. 🏘 45,000. 🚊 🚌 🛈 Calle Coso Alto 23, (974) 22 57 78. 🚘 Mon, Tue & Thu. 🎉 San Vicente (Jan 22), San Lorenzo (Aug 9–15).

Altarpiece by Damià Forment, in Huesca cathedral

FOUNDED IN THE 1st century BC, the independent state of Osca (present-day Huesca) had a senate and an advanced education system. From the 8th century, the area grew into a Moorish stronghold. In 1096 it was captured by Peter of Aragón and was the region's capital until 1118, when the title passed to Zaragoza.

Huesca is now the provincial capital. The pleasant old town has a Gothic **cathedral**. The eroded west front is surmounted by an unusual wooden gallery in Mudéjar style. Above the nave is slender-ribbed star vaulting studded with golden bosses. The cathedral's best feature is an alabaster altarpiece by the master sculptor,

Damià Forment. On the altarpiece, a series of energetic Crucifixion scenes in relief is highlighted by illumination.

Opposite the cathedral is the Renaissance **town hall** (*ayuntamiento*). Inside hangs *La Campana de Huesca*, a gory 19th-century painting depicting the town's most memorable event: the beheading of a group of troublesome nobles in the 12th century by order of King Ramiro II.

The massacre occurred in the Sala de la Campana of the 17th-century university. This now houses the superb **Museo Arqueológico Provincial**, containing archaeological finds and a collection of art, including Gothic frescoes and early Aragonese works.

🏛 Museo Arqueológico Provincial

Plaza de la Universidad. 📞 (974) 22 05 86. 🕑 Tue–Sun. 🔴 public hols. 🎟

Alquézar ⓬

Huesca. 🏘 300. 🛈 Calle Baja, (974) 31 80 67. 🎉 San Sebastián (Jan 21).

THIS MOORISH VILLAGE attracts much attention because of its spectacular setting. Its main monument, the stately 16th-century **collegiate church**, dominates a hill jutting above the strange rock formations of the canyon of the Río Vero. Inside, the church's cloisters have capitals carved with biblical scenes. Next to it is the chapel built after Sancho I recaptured Alquézar from the Moors. Nearby are the ruined walls of the original alcazar, which gives the village its name.

Santuario de Torreciudad ⓭

Huesca. 📞 (974) 30 40 25. 🚌 to El Grado from Barbastro. 🕑 daily. 🔥

THIS SHRINE was built in memory of the founder of the Catholic lay order of Opus Dei – José María Escrivá de Belaguer – who died in 1975. It occupies a high promontory, with picturesque views over the turquoise waters of the **Embalse de El Grado** at Torreciudad. The huge church is made of angular red brick in a stark, modern design.

Inside, the elaborate modern altarpiece of white marble, sheltering a glittering Romanesque Virgin, is in contrast to the bleak, functional nave.

ENVIRONS: The small town of **Barbastro**, 20 km (12 miles) to the south, has an arcaded *plaza mayor* and a 16th-century cathedral with an altar by Damià Forment.

The ruins of Alquézar castle, rising above the village

Houses with frescoed façades on the Plaza de España, Graus

Graus ⑭

Huesca. 🏠 *3,300.* 🚌 🛈 *Plaza de España 15, (974) 54 00 02.* 🚍 *Mon.* 🎭 *Santo Cristo and San Vicente (Sep 13–14).*

CONCEALED IN THE HEART of Graus's old town lies the unusual **Plaza de España**, surrounded by brick arcades and brightly frescoed half-timbered houses. One of these was the home of the infamous Tomás de Torquemada, the Inquisitor General *(see p52).* The old quarter, with its narrow streets, is best explored on foot. At fiesta time, this small town is a good place to see typical Aragonese dancing.

ENVIRONS: About 20 km (12 miles) northeast, the hill village of **Roda de Isábena** has the smallest cathedral in Spain. Dating from 1067, this striking building has a 12th-century cloister off which is a chapel with 13th-century frescoes. North of the village is the picturesque Isábena valley.

Tarazona ⑮

Zaragoza. 🏠 *11,000.* 🚌 🛈 *Calle Iglesia 5, (976) 64 00 74.* 🚍 *every other Thu.* 🎭 *San Agustín (Aug 28), San Atilano (Oct 5).*

MUDEJAR TOWERS stand high above the earth-colored, mottled tiles of this ancient bishopric. On the outskirts of the old town is the **cathedral**, all turreted finials and pierced brickwork with Moorish cloister tracery and Gothic tombs. In the upper town on the

other side of the river, more churches, in typical Mudéjar style, can be found amid the maze of narrow, hilly streets. More unusual perhaps are the former bullring, now a circular plaza enclosed by houses, and the splendid Renaissance **town hall** *(ayuntamiento).* The town hall, built of golden stone, has a façade carved with mythical giants and a frieze showing the fall of Granada in 1492 *(see pp52–3).*

Monasterio de Veruela ⑯

Vera de Moncayo (Zaragoza). 📞 *(976) 64 90 25.* 🚌 *Vera de Moncayo.* 🕐 *Tue–Sun.* 🎫 ♿

THIS ISOLATED CISTERCIAN retreat, set in the green Huecha valley near the Sierra de Moncayo, is one of the greatest monasteries in Aragón. Founded in the 12th century by French monks, the huge abbey church has a mixture of Romanesque and Gothic

features. Worn green and blue Aragonese tiles line the floor of its handsomely vaulted triple nave. The well-preserved cloisters sprout exuberantly decorated beasts, heads of human beings, and foliage in the Plateresque style *(see p21).* The plain, dignified chambers make a suitable venue for art exhibitions in the summer.

ENVIRONS: In the hills to the west the small **Parque Natural de Moncayo** rises to a height of 2,315 m (7,600 ft). Streams race through the woodland of this nature preserve that throngs with bird life. A tortuous, potholed road leads to a chapel at the highest point.

Zaragoza ⑰

Zaragoza. 🏠 *600,000.* ✈ 🚌 🚍 🛈 *Glorieta de Pío XII, (976) 39 35 37.* 🚍 *Wed, Sun.* 🎭 *San Valero (Jan 29), Cincomarzada (Mar 5), San Jorge (Apr 23), Virgen del Pilar (Oct 12).*

A CELTIBERIAN settlement called Salduba existed on the site of the present city; but it is from the Roman settlement of Cesaraugusta that Zaragoza takes its name. Its fortuitous location on the fertile banks of the Río Ebro ensured the ascendancy of Zaragoza, now Spain's fifth largest city and the capital of Aragón.

Badly damaged during the War of Independence *(see p58),* the city was largely rebuilt, but the old center retains a number of interesting buildings. Most of the city's main sights are grouped around the vast Plaza del Pilar. The most

Entrance and tower of the Monasterio de Veruela

impresssive of them is the **Basílica de Nuestra Señora del Pilar**, with its huge church sporting 11 brightly tiled cupolas. Inside, the Santa Capilla (Lady Chapel) by Ventura Rodríguez contains a small statue of the Virgin on a pillar amid a blaze of silver and flowers. Her long, skirtlike *manta* is changed every day, and devout pilgrims pass behind the chapel to kiss an exposed section of the pillar.

Nearby, on the square, stand the **town hall** *(ayuntamiento)*, the Gothic-Plateresque **Lonja** (commodities exchange) and the **Palacio Episcopal**.

Occupying the east end of the square is Zaragoza's cathedral, **La Seo**, displaying a great mix of styles. Part of the exterior is faced with typical Mudéjar brick and ceramic decoration, and inside are a fine Gothic reredos and splendid Flemish tapestries.

Close by are the flamboyant Mudéjar bell tower of the **Iglesia de la Magdalena** and remains of the Roman forum. Parts of the **Roman walls** can also be seen at the opposite side of the Plaza del Pilar, near the **Mercado de Lanuza**, a market with sinuous ironwork in Art Nouveau style.

Some of the cupolas of the Basílica de Nuestra Señora del Pilar

The **Museo Camón Aznar** exhibits the eclectic collection of a wealthy local art historian whose special interest was Goya. The top floor contains a collection of his etchings. Many minor works by artists of other periods can be seen, as well as good contemporary art. The **Museo de Zaragoza** contains many paintings, as well as archaeological artifacts.

The **Museo Pablo Gargallo** is a showroom for the Aragonese sculptor after whom it is named, who was active at the beginning of the 20th century.

One of the most important monuments in Zaragoza lies on the busy road to Bilbao. The **Alfajería** is an enormous Moorish palace built in the 11th century. A courtyard of lacy arches surrounds a sunken garden and a small mosque.

🏛 **Museo Camón Aznar**
Calle Espoz y Mina 23. ((976) 39 73 28. ◯ Tue–Sun.
🏛 **Museo de Zaragoza**
Plaza de los Sitios 5. ((976) 22 21 81. ◯ Tue–Sun. 🖾
🏛 **Museo Pablo Gargallo**
Plaza de San Felipe 3. ((976) 39 20 58. ◯ Tue–Sun & public hols. 🖾

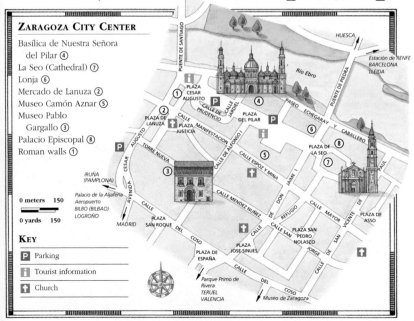

ZARAGOZA CITY CENTER

0 meters   150

0 yards   150

KEY

🅿 Parking

ℹ Tourist information

✝ Church

Gateway through the medieval walls of Daroca

Calatayud ⓲

Zaragoza. 🏚 20,000. 🚊 🚌
ⅰ Plaza el Fuerte, (976) 88 63 22.
🚌 Tue. 🎪 San Roque (Aug 14–17).

THE HUGE MOORISH FORTRESS and minaret-like church towers of Calatayud are visible far across the surrounding clay hills and fertile red plains. Only ruins are left of the 8th-century Arab castle of the ruler, Ayub, which gave the town its name (*Kalat Ayub* means castle of Ayub). The church of **Santa María la Mayor** has a Mudéjar tower and an elaborate façade in the Plateresque style.

The ruins of the Roman settlement of Bilbilis, birthplace of the poet Martial, are east of Calatayud, near Huérmeda.

Monasterio de Piedra ⓳

3 km (2 miles) south of Nuévalos.
🆑 (976) 84 90 11. 🚊 Calatayud.
🚌 from Zaragoza. 🕐 daily. 🈂 🎫

FOUNDED BY Alfonso II of Aragón in 1195, this Cistercian monastery suffered damage in the 19th century and was subsequently rebuilt.

Some of the original buildings survive, however, including the chapterhouse, refectory, and hostel – all of which date back to the 13th century.

In the damp, blackened cellars, the monks once distilled strong potions of herbal liqueur in a large alembic. The kitchen was allegedly the first place in Europe where drinking chocolate, from Mexico, was prepared *(see p55).*

The park in which the monastery stands is a picturesque nature preserve full of grottoes and waterfalls. A hotel is now located in the old monastery buildings *(see p548).*

Daroca ⓴

Zaragoza. 🏚 2,400. ⅰ Plaza de España 4, (976) 80 01 29. 🚌 Thu.
🎪 Santo Tomás (Mar 7).

AN IMPRESSIVE ARRAY of battlemented medieval walls stretches approximately 4 km (2 miles) around this old Moorish stronghold. Although parts of the walls have decayed, the 114 towers and fortified gateways are still a remarkable sight, particularly from the main road to Zaragoza.

The **Colegial de Santa María**, a church in the central square, houses the Holy Cloths from the Reconquest *(see pp50–51).* After a surprise attack by the Moors in 1239, priests celebrating Mass in the countryside hastily bundled the consecrated bread into the linen sheets used to cover the altar. When the cloths were unwrapped they were miraculously stained with blood.

ENVIRONS: The agricultural town of **Monreal del Campo**, 42 km (26 miles) south of Daroca, has a saffron museum. The backbreaking labor of harvesting the autumn crocus, formerly an important crop, is no longer profitable.

Fuendetodos ㉑

Zaragoza. 🏚 180. ⅰ Calle Zuloaga, (976) 14 38 01. 🎪 San Roque (last Sat of May), San Bartolomé (Aug 24).

THIS SMALL VILLAGE was the birthplace of one of Spain's best-known artists of the late 18th and early 19th centuries,

Interior of Goya's cottage in Fuendetodos

Castle-parador above Alcañiz

Francisco de Goya. The **Casa-Museo de Goya** is a cottage said to have been the painter's home. It has been restored and furnished in appropriate period style. On display are some of the artist's personal effects as well as engravings.

ENVIRONS: Lying 20 km (12 miles) east of Fuendetodos is **Belchite**, the site of one of the most horrific battles of the Spanish Civil War *(see pp62–3)*, fought for control of the strategic Ebro valley. Remains of the old, shell-torn town have been left as a monument to the horrors of war.

In **Cariñena**, 25 km (16 miles) west of Fuendetodos, wine shops offer the opportunity to sample and buy the excellent, full-bodied red wine for which the region is justly renowned *(see pp192–3)*.

🏛 **Casa-Museo de Goya**
Calle Alfóndiga 3. 📞 *(976) 14 38 30.* ⭕ *Tue–Sun.* 📷

Alcañiz ㉒

Teruel. 🏔 *12,800.* 🚌 ℹ *Calle Mayor 1, (978) 83 12 13.* 🚌 *Tue.* 🎉 *Fiestas Patronales (Sep 8–14).*

FROM A DISTANCE, two buildings rise above the town of Alcañiz. One is the **castle**, which was the headquarters of the Order of Calatrava in the 12th century. This historic building has been converted into a parador *(see p548)*. The keep, the Torre del Homenaje, has a collection of 14th-century frescoes depicting the conquest of Valencia by Jaime I.

The other building is the **Colegiata de Santa María**. This church, on the sloping Plaza de España, has a Gothic tower and a Baroque façade.

On the same square are the elegantly galleried **Lonja** (commodities exchange), with its lacy Gothic arches, and the **town hall** *(ayuntamiento)*, with one Mudéjar and one Renaissance façade.

FRANCISCO DE GOYA

Self-portrait by Goya

Born in Fuendetodos in 1746, Francisco de Goya specialized in drawing designs for the tapestry industry *(see p296)* in his early life, and in decorating churches such as Zaragoza's Basílica del Pilar with vivacious frescoes. In 1799 he became painter to Carlos IV and depicted the king and his wife María Luisa with unflattering accuracy *(see p29)*. The invasion of Madrid by Napoleon's troops in 1808 *(see pp58–9)* and its attendant horrors had a profound and lasting effect on Goya's temperament, and his later works are imbued with cynical despair and isolation. He died in Bordeaux in 1828.

ARAGÓN'S FIESTAS

Las Tamboradas
(Maundy Thursday and Good Friday), Teruel province. During Easter Week, brotherhoods of men wearing long black robes beat drums in mourning for Christ. Las Tamboradas begins with "the breaking of the hour" at midnight on Thursday in Híjar. The Tamborada in Calanda begins the following day at midday. The solemn drum rolls continue for several hours. Aching arms and bleeding hands are considered to be signs of religious devotion.

Young drummer in Las Tamboradas, Alcorija

Carnival *(Feb/Mar)*, Bielsa (Huesca). The protagonists of this fiesta, known as *Trangas*, have rams' horns on their heads, blackened faces, and teeth made of potatoes. They are said to represent fertility.

Romería de Santa Orosia *(Jun 25)*, Yebra de Basa (Huesca). Pilgrims in folk costume carry St. Orosia's skull to her shrine.

Día del Pilar *(Oct 12)*, Zaragoza. Aragón's distinctive folk dance, the *jota*, is performed everywhere during the city's festivities in honor of its patroness, the Virgin of the Pillar *(see p227)*. On the Día del Pilar there is a procession with cardboard giants, and a spectacular display of flowers dedicated to the Virgin.

Alcalá de la Selva castle, overlooking the town

Valderrobres ㉓

Teruel. 🏛 *1,980.* 🅸 *Plaza de
España 1, (978) 85 00 01.* 🚌 *Sat.*
🎇 *San Roque (Aug 15–19).*

J UST INSIDE Aragón's border
with Catalonia, the delightful
town of Valderrobres overlooks
the shallow, trout-filled Río
Matarrana. Dominating the
town is the restored **castle**,
which was formerly a palace
for Aragonese royalty. Below
it stands the imposing Gothic
**Iglesia de Santa María la
Mayor**, with an enorous rose
window in Catalan Gothic
style. The unusual arcaded
plaza has a pleasing town hall
(ayuntamiento) completed in
the end of the 16th century.

ENVIRONS: To the south lies
tiny **Mirambel**, a carefully
restored medieval village surrounded by sturdy ramparts.

♟ **Castillo de Valderrobres**
🔲 *Jul–Sep: Mon, Oct–Jun: Sat.* 🎫

Sierra de Gúdar ㉔

Teruel. 🚌 *Mora de Rubielos.* 🚌 *Alcalá
de la Selva.* 🅸 *Plaza de la Iglesia 4,
(978) 80 10 00.*

T HIS RANGE OF HILLS, northeast of Teruel, is a region
of pine woods and jagged
limestone outcrops erupting
from scrub-covered slopes. At
2,019 m (6,624 ft), **Peñarroya**
is the highest point. Nearby
Valdelinares, Aragón's third-
highest village, is a ski center.
From the access roads there
are panoramic views of the
hills. Especially noteworthy are
the views from the towns of
Linares de Mora and **Alcalá**

de la Selva, which has a castle
set against a backdrop of rock
faces. Its Baroque church, with
shell motifs and twisted columns, shelters the shrine of
the Virgen de la Vega.

Mora de Rubielos ㉕

Teruel. 🏛 *1,400.* 🅸 *Plaza de la
Villa 1, (978) 80 00 00.* 🚌 *Mon & Fri.*
🎇 *San Miguel (Sep 28–Oct 1).*

D OMINATED BY one of the
best-preserved castles in
Aragón, Mora de Rubielos has
a medieval old town.
Its fortified Gothic
collegiate church
has chapels deco-
rated with *azulejos*
from Manises, near
Valencia. There is
an elegant black
fountain nearby
that depicts
dolphins
playing.

ENVIRONS: Rubielos de Mora,
lying 10 km (6 miles) to the
southeast, is worth exploring
simply for its well-preserved
stone and timber buildings.
Among the balconied houses
is an Augustinian convent with
a Gothic reredos.

Teruel ㉖

Teruel. 🏛 *31,000.* 🚉 🚌 🅸 *Calle
Tomás Nougués 1, (978) 60 22 79.*
🚌 *Thu.* 🎇 *Día del Mesón de las
Tortillas (Tue of Easter week), La
Vaquilla del Ángel (mid-Jul), Feria del
Jamón (mid-Sep).*

T HIS INDUSTRIAL TOWN has
been the scene of much
desperate fighting throughout
the centuries. It began with
the Romans, the first to capture
and civilize Celtiberian Turba.
During the Reconquest the
town became a strategic frontier prize. In 1171 Alfonso II
recaptured Teruel for Christian
Spain, but many Muslims continued to live peacefully in
the city, which they embellished with beautiful Mudéjar
towers. The last mosque was
closed only at the height of
the Inquisition *(see p264)*, in
1502. More recently, during
the terrible, freezing winter of
1937, the bitterest battle of
the Civil War *(see pp62–3)*
was fought here. There were
many thousands of casualties.
The old quarter is home to
the wedge-shaped Plaza del
Torico, with a monument of a

Tiled towers and rooftops of Teruel cathedral

Balconied café above Albarracín's main square

small bull, the city's emblem. Within walking distance lie the five remaining Mudéjar towers. Most striking are those of **San Salvador** and **San Martín**, both dating back to the 12th century. The latter has multi-patterned brickwork studded with blue and green ceramics.

Inside the **Iglesia de San Pedro** are the tombs of the famous Lovers of Teruel. The **cathedral** has more colorful Mudéjar work, including a lantern dome of glazed tiles, and a tower completed in the 17th century. The dazzling coffered ceiling is painted with lively scenes of medieval life.

The **Museo Provincial**, one of Aragón's best museums, is housed in an elegant mansion. It has a large collection of ceramics, testifying to an industry for which Teruel has long been known. North of the center is the **Acueducto de los Arcos**, a 16th-century aqueduct.

🏛 **Museo Provincial**
Pl Fray Anselmo Polanco 3. 📞 (978) 60
01 50. ⭕ Tue–Sun. ⚫ public hols.

Albarracín ㉗

Teruel. 🏘 1,200. 🚌 🛈 Plaza Mayor,
(978) 71 02 51. 🎉 Los Mayos (Apr
30–May 1), Patronales (Sep 13–15).

I T IS EASY TO SEE WHY this pic-turesque town earned the honor of an international award for historical preserva-tion. A dramatic cliff above the Río Guadalaviar is the perfect setting for this attractive cluster of mellow, pink buildings. Standing on a ridge behind

the town are the defensive walls, interspersed with towers dating from Muslim times.

There is a good view of the town from below the **Palacio Episcopal** (Bishop's Palace). Inside the neighboring 16th-century **cathedral**, which is topped by a belfry, there is a carved wooden Renaissance altarpiece depicting scenes from the life of St. Peter. The treasury museum contains 16th-century Brussels tapestries and enameled chalices.

Some of Albarracín's sturdy beamed and galleried houses are built with an unusual two-tier structure. The ground floor is made of limestone, and the overhanging upper story is covered in rough, coral-pink plasterwork. Many have been

restored to their original, medieval form. Just outside the town are the caves of Navazo and Callejón, with their prehistoric rock paintings. Reproductions can be seen in Teruel's Museo Provincial.

ENVIRONS: In the surrounding **Montes Universales**, which rise to 1,170 m (3,840 ft), is the source of the Tagus, one of Spain's longest rivers. From fertile fields of grain to crum-bling rocks, this area is a colorful mixture of poplars, junipers, and pine woods, with poppies in spring. At **Cella**, northeast of Albarracín, the Río Jiloca has its source.

Rincón de Ademuz ㉘

Valencia. 🚌 Ademuz. 🛈 Valencia,
(96) 352 54 78.

T HIS REMOTE ENCLAVE south of Teruel officially belongs to the Comunidad Valenciana (see p233); but is effectively an island of territory, stranded between the borders of Aragón and Castilla-La Mancha. The area has not prospered in re-cent years – because of its isolated location – and many houses are abandoned. But it has its own austere charm and some peaceful tracts of country scattered with red rocks.

THE LOVERS OF TERUEL

According to legend, in 13th-century Teruel two young people, Diego de Marcilla and Isabel de Segura, fell in love and wished to marry. She came from a wealthy family, but he was poor, and her parents forbade the match. Diego was given five years in which to make his fortune and establish a name for himself. At the end of this time he returned to Teruel, laden with wealth, only to find his bride-to-be already married to a local nobleman. Diego died of a broken heart and Isabel, full of despair at his death, died the following day.

Isabel de Segura   Diego de Marcilla

VALENCIA AND MURCIA

CASTELLÓN · VALENCIA · ALICANTE · MURCIA

ODAY, THE CENTRAL REGION *of Spain's eastern Mediterranean coast is an important vacation destination – the beaches of the Costa Blanca, the Costa del Azahar, and the Costa Cálida draw millions of tourists annually. Centuries ago, Muslim settlers made these regions bloom, and the fertile fields and citrus groves of the coastal plains are still Spain's citrus orchard and market garden.*

These productive lands have been occupied for more than 50,000 years. The Greeks, Phoenicians, Carthaginians, and Romans all settled here before the Moors arrived, trading the products of land and sea.

The provinces of Castellón, Valencia, and Alicante (which make up the Comunidad Valenciana) were reconquered from the Moors by a Catalan army. The language these troops left behind them developed into a dialect, *valenciano*, which is widely spoken and increasingly seen on signposts. Murcia, to the south, is one of Spain's smallest autonomous regions.

The population is concentrated on the coast where the historic towns and cities of Valencia, Alicante, and Cartagena have been joined by modern package vacation resorts, such as Benidorm and La Manga del Mar Menor. Inland, where tourism has barely reached, the landscape rises into the chains of mountains that stand between the coast and the plateau of central Spain. The scenery inland ranges from picturesque valleys and hills in the Maestrat, in the north of Castellón, to the semi desert terrain around Lorca in southern Murcia.

The warm climate encourages outdoor life and exuberant fiestas. Most famous of these are Las Fallas of Valencia; the mock battles between Moors and Christians staged in Alcoi; and the lavish, costumed Easter processions in Murcia and Lorca.

Hill terraces of olive and almond trees ascending the hillsides near Alcoi

◁ The Penyal d'Ifach, rising directly out of the sea to tower above the Costa Blanca near Calp

Exploring Valencia and Murcia

THE COASTS OF VALENCIA AND MURCIA are popular for seaside
vacations and ideal for water sports almost all year round.
Principal resorts include Benidorm, Benicassim, and La Manga
del Mar Menor. Some coastal towns such as Peñíscola, Gandia,
Dénia, Alicante, and Cartagena have charming old quarters,
castles, and other monuments well worth visiting. Close to the
sea are several scenic nature preserves: the freshwater lagoon
of L'Albufera, and, on the Costa Blanca, the salt pans of Santa
Pola and the striking limestone crag of the Penyal d'Ifach.

Inland, the region offers excursions to such undiscovered
beauty spots as El Maestrat and the mountains around Alcoi,
as well as the undervisited historic towns of Xàtiva and Lorca.
The two regional capitals, Valencia and Murcia, are both lively
university cities with fine cathedrals and numerous museums.

Fishing nets strung out in the lagoon of L'Albufera

GETTING AROUND

The region's principal roads are the A7 expressway
(toll-paying from Alicante northward except for the
Valencia bypass) and the N332 along the coast. Other
major roads, most of which are divided highways,
connect Valencia with Madrid (NIII), Murcia with
Madrid (N301), and Valencia with Teruel and the
north of Spain (N234). There are main rail lines
from Alicante, Valencia, and Murcia to
Madrid, but the rest of the rail network
is rather fragmented and buses are
often quicker than trains. A scenic
narrow-gauge railroad line along
the Costa Blanca connects Dénia
to Alicante via Benidorm. The
region's international airports
are at Alicante and Valencia.

0 kilometers   25

0 miles   20

SEE ALSO

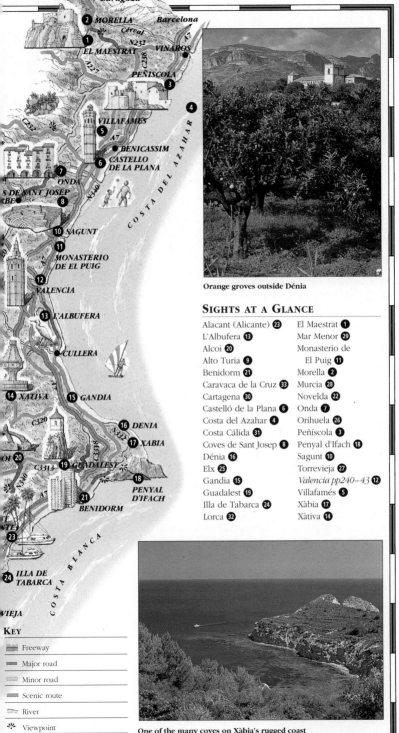

Orange groves outside Dénia

SIGHTS AT A GLANCE

One of the many coves on Xàbia's rugged coast

The unbroken medieval wall surrounding the historic hilltop town of Morella in El Maestrat

El Maestrat ❶

Castellón & Teruel. 🚌 Morella.
ℹ️ Morella, (964) 17 30 32.

CRUSADING WARLORDS of the Knights Templar and the Knights of Montesa – known as *maestres* (masters) – gave their name to this lonely upland region. To rule over this frontier land, which straddles the border between Valencia and Aragón, they built fortified settlements in dramatic defensive positions, often on rocky crags. The best preserved of them is **Morella**, the principal town. **Forcall**, not far from Morella, has two 16th-century mansions on its porticoed

The Torre de la Sacristía, in the restored village of Mirambel

square. To the south, the village of **Ares del Maestre** is spectacularly sited beneath a 1,318-m (4,300-ft) high rock.

Cantavieja is the most important town in the Aragonese part of El Maestrat (where it is known as El Maestrazgo). It has a handsome, arcaded square. The walled village of **Mirambel**, nearby, has been meticulously restored to its medieval condition.

There are several spooky but fascinating shrines to the Virgin in El Maestrat, notably the cave at **La Balma**, which is reached via a rocky ledge.

The scenery in most parts is striking: fertile valleys alternate with breathtaking cliffs and bare, flat-topped mountains overflown by eagles and vultures. Tourism is developing very slowly here: there are few places to stay, and the roads can be winding and slow.

Morella ❷

Castellón. 🏛 2,900. 🚌 ℹ️ Plaza de San Miguel 3, (964) 17 30 32. 🚪 Sun. 🎭 Sexeni (Aug, every six years).

BUILT ON a high, isolated outcrop and crowned by a ruined castle, Morella cuts a dramatic profile. Its unbroken medieval walls retain six gateways, which lead into a fan-shaped maze of streets and

steep, tapering alleys, many of which are shaded by the eaves of ancient houses. The main street is lined with shady porticoes. In the upper part of town is the **Basílica de Santa María la Mayor**. Its unique raised choir loft is reached by a finely carved spiral staircase.

EN ESTA CASA OBRÓ SAN VICENTE FERRER EL PEDIGIOSO MILAGRO DE LA RESURRECCION DE UN NIÑO QUE SU MADRE NAJENADA HABIA DESCUARTIZADO Y GUISADO EN OBSEQUIO AL SANTO (1414)

MORELLA'S MIRACLE

A plaque on the wall of Morella's Calle de la Virgen marks the house in which St. Vincent Ferrer is said to have performed a bizarre miracle in the early 15th century. A housewife, distraught at having no meat to offer the saint, cut up her son and put him in the cooking pot. When St. Vincent discovered this, he reconstituted the boy – except for one of his little fingers, which his mother had eaten to see if the dish was sufficiently salted.

Peñíscola ❸

Castellón. 👥 4,100. 🚌 ℹ️ Paseo Marítimo, (964) 48 02 08. 🚆 Mon. 🎉 Patronales (mid-Sep).

THE FORTIFIED OLD TOWN of Peñíscola clusters around the base of a castle built on a rocky promontory, surrounded on three sides by the sea. This labyrinth of narrow winding streets and white houses is enclosed by massive ramparts. These are entered by either the Fosch Gate – reached by a ramp from the Plaza del Caudillo – or through the San Pedro Gate, from the harbor.

The **Castell del Papa Luna** was built on the foundations of an Arab fortress in the late 13th century by the Knights Templar. Their cross is carved above the door. It later became the residence of the papal pretender Pedro de Luna, cardinal of Aragón. He was elected Pope Benedict XIII during the Great Schism that split the Catholic Church at the end of the 14th century. Although he was deposed by the Council of Constance in 1414, he continued to proclaim his right to the papacy until his death as a nonagenarian in 1423.

The uppermost battlements of the castle are false: they were built for a scene from the 1961 film *El Cid*. Modern Peñíscola has expanded beyond the old walls and is now a thriving vacation resort.

♜ Castell del Papa Luna
Calle Castillo. 📞 (964) 48 00 21.
🕐 daily. ● Sep 9, Dec 6 & 25. 🎫

Sunset view of the beach and old town of Peñíscola

Costa del Azahar ❹

Castellón. 🚆 Castelló de la Plana. 🚌 Castelló de la Plana. ℹ️ Castelló de la Plana, (964) 22 10 00.

THE "ORANGE BLOSSOM COAST" of Castellón province is named after the dense citrus groves of the coastal plain. The two principal resorts are Benicassim, where handsome old villas have been supplemented by modern hotels and other tourist amenities, and Peñíscola. Alcossebre and Oropesa also have popular beaches. Vinaròs – the most northerly point – and Benicarló are key fishing ports supplying shrimp and mussels to local restaurants.

Sculpture in the Casa del Batle

Villafamés ❺

Castellón. 👥 1,400. 🚌 ℹ️ Plaza del Ayuntamiento 1, (964) 32 90 01.
🚆 Fri. 🎉 Patronales (mid-Aug).

THIS MEDIEVAL TOWN climbs from a flat plain along a rocky ridge to the restored round keep of its castle. The older, upper part of the town is a warren of sloping streets filled with sturdy houses.

A 15th-century mansion houses the **Casa del Batle**, a museum of contemporary art. The works on display, some of which are for sale, date from 1959 to the present.

🏛 Casa del Batle
Calle Diputación. 📞 (964) 32 91 52.
🕐 daily. 🎫

Castelló de la Plana's planetarium, close to the beach

Castelló de la Plana ❻

Castellón. 👥 140,000. 🚆 🚌 ℹ️ Plaza María Agustina 5, (964) 22 10 00. 🚆 Mon. 🎉 Fiesta de la Magdalena (second week of Mar).

ORIGINALLY FOUNDED on high ground inland, the capital of Castellón province was relocated nearer to the coast in the 13th century.

The city center, the Plaza Mayor, is bordered by the market, the town hall, the cathedral, and **El Fadri**, a 58-m (190-ft) high octagonal bell tower erected in the 1590s.

The **Museo Provincial de Bellas Artes**, in an 18th-century house, contains a collection of artifacts dating from the middle paleolithic era, paintings from the 15th to the 20th centuries and modern ceramics from the region. Among the artworks is José de Ribera's *Saint Jerome*.

The **Convento de las Madres Capuchinas** has an important collection of paintings which are attributed to Francisco de Zurbarán.

In **El Planetario** there are demonstrations of the night sky, the solar system, and the nearest stars. It also has exhibits on perception, holography, and minerals.

🏛 Museo Provincial de Bellas Artes
Calle Cavelleres 25. 📞 (964) 35 97 11.
🕐 Mon–Sat.
⛪ Convento de las Madres Capuchinas
Calle Núñez de Arce 11. 📞 (964) 22 06 41. 🕐 daily. ♿
🔭 El Planetario
Paseo Marítimo 1, El Grao. 📞 (964) 28 25 84. 🕐 Jul–Aug: Tue–Sat, Oct–Jun: Tue–Sun. 🎫 ♿

Onda 7

Castellón. 16,800. *Calle Cervantes 10,* (964) 77 18 40. Thu. Feria (last week of Oct).

ONDA, HOME to a thriving ceramics industry, is overlooked by a ruined **castle**, which was known to its Moorish founders as the "Castle of the Three Hundred Towers." The old quarter of the town has some character, especially the charming square of **Plaza del Almudín**, with its medieval porticoes.

But the main reason to visit Onda is to take a look at the **Museo El Carmen**, a natural history museum belonging to a Carmelite monastery just outside the town.

The collection was begun in 1952 by the monks for their own private scientific study. It was only opened to the public a decade later. The clever use of subdued lighting lends dramatic effect to the 10,000 plant and animal specimens which are exhibited over three floors. Objects include large stuffed animals placed in naturalistic settings, butterflies and other insects, shells, fossils, minerals, and grisly, preserved anatomical specimens.

Museo El Carmen

Carretera de Tales. (964) 60 07 30. Tue–Sun.

Two butterfly exhibits in the Museo El Carmen

Boat ride through the winding Coves de Sant Josep

Coves de Sant Josep 8

Vall d'Uixó (Castellón). (964) 69 05 76. Vall d'Uixó.

THE CAVES OF St. Joseph were first explored in 1902. The subterranean river that formed them, and which still flows through them, has been charted for almost 2.5 km (1.5 miles). However, its source has not yet been discovered and only part of this distance can be explored on a visit.

Boats take visitors along the serpentine course of the river. You may have to duck to avoid projections of rock on the way. Here and there the narrow caves open out into large chambers such as the *Sala de los Murciélagos* (Hall of the Bats – the bats left when the floodlights were installed). The water reaches its deepest point of 12 m (39 ft) in the *Lago Azul* (Blue Lake). You can explore a further 255 m (837 ft) along the *Galería Seca* (Dry Gallery) on foot. The caves are often closed to visitors after heavy rain.

Alto Turia 9

Valencia. Chelva. C234, northwest of Tuéjar, (96) 163 50 84.

THE ATTRACTIVE WOODED HILLS of the upper reaches of the Río Turia in Valencia (Alto Turia) are popular with hikers and day-trippers. **Chelva**, the main town, has an unusual clock on its church that shows not only the hour but the day and month as well. The town is overlooked by the **Pico del Remedio** (1,054 m/ 3,458 ft), from the summit of which there is a fine panoramic view of the region. In a valley near Chelva, at the end of an unpaved but drivable track, are the remains of a Roman aqueduct, **Peña Cortada**.

The most attractive and interesting village in Alto Turia is **Alpuente**, situated above a dry gorge. Between 1031 to 1089, when it was captured by El Cid *(see p352)*, Alpuente was the capital of a small *taifa*, a Moorish kingdom. In the 14th century it was still important enough for the kingdom of Valencia's parliament to meet here. The town hall is confined to a small tower over a 14th-century gateway, which was later extended in the 16th century by the addition of a rectangular council chamber.

Requena, to the south is Valencia's main wine town. Further south, Valencia's other principal river, the Xúquer (Júcar), carves tremendous gorges near Cortes de Pallas on its way past the **Muela de Cortes**. This massive, wild plateau and nature preserve is crossed by one small road and a lonely dirt track.

LA TOMATINA

The highpoint of the annual fiesta in Buñol (Valencia) is a sticky food fight on the last Wednesday of August that attracts thousands of visitors dressed in their worst clothes. Truckloads of ripe tomatoes are provided by the town council for participants to hurl at each other. No one in range of the combatants is spared: foreigners and photographers are prized targets.

The battle originated in 1944. Some say it began with a fight between friends. Others say irreverent locals pelted civic dignitaries with tomatoes during a procession. Increasing national and international press coverage means that more people attend, and more tomatoes are thrown, every year.

Sagunt's ruined fortifications, added to by successive rulers of the town

Sagunt ⑩

Valencia. 🏘 60,000. 🚊 🚌 🅸 Pl Cronista Chabret, (96) 266 22 13. 🗓 Wed. 🎏 Fiestas (mid-Jul–mid-Aug).

SITED NEAR THE JUNCTION of two Roman roads, Sagunt (Sagunto) played a crucial role in Spain's ancient history.

The general Hannibal had been the Carthaginian commander in southern Spain since 221 BC. In 219 BC he stormed and sacked Rome's ally Saguntum. All the inhabitants of the town were said to have died in the assault, the last throwing themselves on to bonfires rather than fall into the hands of Hannibal's troops. The incident sparked off the Second Punic War, which ended with Rome's occupation of the peninsula (see pp46–7).

The town still contains several reminders of the Roman occupation, including the 1st-century AD **Roman theater**. Built out of limestone on the hillside above the town, it has been controversially restored by the regional government using modern materials. The theater is now used as a venue for music, plays, and Sagunt's annual theater festival.

The ruins of the **castle**, sprawling along the crest of the hill above the modern-day town, mark the original site of Saguntum. Superimposed on each other are the excavated remains of various civilizations, including the Iberians, the Carthaginians, the Romans, and the Moors. The ruins of the castle are divided into seven divisions, or plazas, the highest of them being La Ciudadella.

⚜ **Castillo de Sagunt**
◻ Tue–Sat. 📷

Monasterio de El Puig ⑪

El Puig (Valencia). 📞 (96) 147 02 00. 🚊 El Puig. 🚌 El Puig. ◻ daily. ⚫ Mon pm. 📷 ♿

THIS MERCEDARIAN monastery was founded by King Jaime I of Aragón, who conquered Valencia from the Moors in the 13th century.

The monastery is now home to a collection of 240 paintings from between the 16th and 18th centuries and the Museo de la Imprenta y de la Obra Gráfica (Museum of Printing and Graphic Art). The museum commemorates the printing of the first book in Spain – thought to have been in Valencia in 1474 – and illustrates the development of the printing press. Exhibits include printers' blocks and a replica of the smallest book in the world.

Messy participants throwing tomatoes at each other in the annual fiesta of La Tomatina

Valencia ⑫

S PAIN'S THIRD LARGEST CITY is located in the middle of the *huerta*: a fertile plain of orange groves and market gardens that is one of Europe's most intensively farmed regions. With its warm coastal climate, Valencia is known for its exuberant outdoor living and nightlife. In March the city stages one of Spain's most spectacular fiestas, Las Fallas *(see p245)*, in which giant papier-mâché sculptures are burned in the streets. Modern Valencia is a center for trade and manufacturing, notably ceramics. A ferry service connects the city with the Balearic Islands.

Flowers in honor of Valencia's patroness, Virgen de los Desamparados

Exploring Valencia

Valencia stands on the course of the Río Turia. The city center and the crumbling old quarter of El Carmen are on the right bank. Most of the monuments are within walking distance of the Plaza del Ayuntamiento, the triangular main square that is presided over by the town hall.

The city was founded by the Romans in 138 BC and later conquered by the Moors. It was captured by El Cid *(see p352)* in 1096, retaken by the Moors, and finally recaptured by Jaime I, the Conqueror, in 1238, to become absorbed into the kingdom of Aragón.

The three finest buildings in Valencia were built during its economic and cultural heyday in the 14th and 15th centuries: the Torres de Serranos, a gateway that survived the demolition of the medieval walls in the 19th century, La Lonja, and the cathedral.

🏛 Palau de la Generalitat

Plaza de la Virgen. 【 (96) 386 61 00. ◯ *by prior appointment only.*
This palace, which is now used by the Valencian regional government, was built in Gothic style between 1482 and 1579 but added to in the 17th and 20th centuries. It surrounds an enclosed stone patio from which two staircases ascend to splendidly decorated rooms.

The larger of the two Salas Doradas (Golden Chambers), on the mezzanine level, has a multicolored coffered ceiling and tiled floor. The walls of the parliament chamber are decorated with frescoes.

🔒 Basílica de la Virgen de los Desamparados

The ornately dressed statue of Valencia's patroness, the Virgin of the Helpless, stands above an altar in this 17th-century church, lavishly adorned with flowers and candles. She is honored during Las Fallas by La Ofrenda ("the Offering"), a display of flowers in the square outside the church.

🔒 Cathedral

Built originally in 1262, the cathedral has been added to over the ages, and its three doorways are all in different styles. The oldest is the Romanesque Puerta del Palau but the main entrance is the 18th-century Baroque portal, the Puerta de los Hierros.

A unique court meets on Thursdays at midday in front of the other doorway, the Gothic Puerta de los Apóstoles. For an estimated 1,000 years, the Water Tribunal has settled disputes between farmers over the distribution of irrigation water in the *huerta*.

Inside the cathedral, a chapel holds an agate cup claimed to be the Holy Grail. According to legend it arrived in Valencia from Jerusalem, by way of San Juan de la Peña monastery in Aragón *(see p224)*.

The Miguelete, the cathedral's bell tower on Plaza de Zaragoza

The cathedral's 68-m (223-ft) high octagonal belltower, the Miguelete, built between 1380 and 1420, is Valencia's main landmark. From its top there are fine views of the city.

♔ La Lonja
Plaza del Mercado. ☎ (96) 391 36 08. ○ Tue–Sun.
An exquisite Late Gothic hall, built between 1482 and 1498 as a commodities exchange, La Lonja is now used for hosting cultural events such as concerts and exhibitions. The outside walls are decorated with gargoyles and a variety of other grotesque figures. The high ceiling of the transactions hall is formed by star-patterned vaulting that is supported on graceful spiral columns.

▣ Mercado Central
Plaza del Mercado. ☎ (96) 391 03 31. ○ Mon–Sat.
This huge iron, glass, and tile Art Nouveau building, with its parrot and swordfish weathervanes, opened in 1928 and is one of the largest and most attractive markets in Europe.

Ornate toilet sign outside Valencia's Mercado Central

Every morning its thousand or so stalls are filled with a bewildering variety of seafood, vegetables, fruit, spices, and herbs.

▥ Museo Nacional de Cerámica
Calle González Martí 2. ☎ (96) 351 63 92. ○ Tue–Sat. ● Jan 1, Mar 19, May 1, Dec 6 & 25. ▨
Spain's National Ceramics Museum is housed in the Baroque mansion of the Marqués de Dos Aguas, an 18th-century fantasy of colored plasterwork. The doorway is surrounded by an elaborate carving by

Ignacio Vergara. The exhibits include prehistoric, Greek, and Roman ceramics, pieces by Picasso, and a traditional tiled Valencian kitchen.

♙ Colegio del Patriarca
This seminary was built in the mid-16th century around a two-story Renaissance courtyard. The walls and ceiling of the church are entirely covered with richly colored frescoes by Bartolomé Matarana. During the Friday morning mass, the painting above the altar, The Last Supper by Francisco Ribalta, is theatrically lowered to reveal a painting of the crucifixion by an anonymous 15th-century German artist.

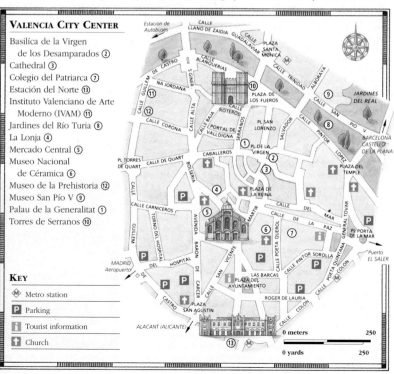

VALENCIA CITY CENTER

Basilíca de la Virgen de los Desamparados ②
Cathedral ③
Colegio del Patriarca ⑦
Estación del Norte ⑬
Instituto Valenciano de Arte Moderno (IVAM) ⑪
Jardines del Río Turia ⑧
La Lonja ④
Mercado Central ⑤
Museo Nacional de Céramica ⑥
Museo de la Prehistoria ⑫
Museo San Pío V ⑨
Palau de la Generalitat ①
Torres de Serranos ⑩

KEY

◈ Metro station
P Parking
ⓘ Tourist information
✝ Church

0 meters 250
0 yards 250

The Palau de la Música, Valencia's prestigious concert hall

Beyond the Center

The center of the city is bordered by two wide avenues, the Gran Vía Marqués del Turia and the Gran Vía Ramón y Cajal. Beyond these lie the 19th-century suburbs laid out symmetrically on a grid plan.

The left bank of the river is dominated by the Avenida Blasco Ibáñez (named after a local novelist), running from the Jardines Reales towards the sea, 4 km (2.5 miles) from the center. The best way to get around beyond the city center is by the metro system, one line of which is a trolley to the beaches of El Cabañal and La Malvarrosa.

♣ Jardines del Río Turia

Where once there was a river there is now a 5-km (3-mile) long strip of gardens, athletic fields, and playgrounds crossed by a dozen bridges. Standing in a prominent position above the riverbed is the Palau de la Música, a world-class concert hall built in the 1980s. The centerpiece of the nearby children's playground is the enormous figure of Gulliver pinned to the ground and covered with steps and slides. Inside the figure there is a scale model of Valencia.

The best of Valencia's other public gardens stand near the banks of the river. The largest of them, the Jardines Reales – known locally as Los Viveros – contain a small zoo. The intimate Italian-style Monforte Gardens are dotted with marble statues and filled with hibiscus and magnolia. The Jardín Botánico was created in 1802 by the botanist Antonio José Cavanilles. It is planted with 7,000 species of shrubs and trees, including many subtropical varieties.

⏛ Museo San Pío V

Calle San Pío 9. **(** (96) 360 57 93. **◯** Tue –Sun. **●** Jan 1, Good Fri, Dec 25 & 31.

An important collection of 2,000 paintings and statues dating from antiquity to the last century is housed in this former seminary, which was built between 1683 and 1744.

Valencian art dating from the 14th and 15th centuries is represented by a series of huge golden altarpieces. They are the work of Alcanyis, Pere Nicolau, and Maestro de Bonastre. *The Passion* – a triptych by the Flemish painter Hieronymus Bosch hangs on the first floor, together with Velázquez's self-portrait, and several works by El Greco, Murillo, Ribalta, Van Dyck, and the local Renaissance painter Juan de Juanes.

On the top floor there are six paintings by Goya and pictures by three important Valencian artists from the 19th and 20th centuries: Ignacio Pinazo, Joaquín Sorolla, and Antonio Muñoz Degrain. A large collection of the latter's hallucinatory colored paintings are gathered together in one room, among them the disturbing *Amor de Madre.*

♠ Torres de Serranos

Plaza de los Fueros.

Erected in 1238 as a triumphal arch in the city's walls, this gateway combines defensive and decorative features. Its two imposing towers are crowned with battlements and at the same time lightened by delicate Gothic tracery. Valencia's other surviving gateway is the 15th-century Torres de Quart,

Ecce Homo **(16th century) by Juan de Juanes in the Museo San Pío V**

The towering gateway of the Torres de Serranos

providing access to the city from the west. It is more functional in appearance than the Torres de Serranos and, although restored, it still bears the pockmarks of cannon fire – reminders of the War of Independence *(see p59)*.

🏛 Instituto Valenciano de Arte Moderno (IVAM)
Calle Guillem de Castro 118. 🄲 *(96) 386 30 00.* ⬤ *Tue–Sun.* 📷 ♿
The Valencian Institute of Modern Art is housed in two buildings. The Centro Julio González, built in the 1980s, has nine galleries including ones devoted to two artists from Valencia, Julio González, considered to be the father of 20th-century Spanish sculpture, and the painter Ignacio Pinazo. A well-preserved 13th-century Carmelite convent in the nearby Calle Museo has been converted into the Centro del Carmen, which is devoted to temporary exhibitions of contemporary works. The interior has been left bare, allowing the visitor to appreciate the mixture of architectural styles, including Gothic and Renaissance.

🏛 Museo de la Prehistoria
Calle Corona 36. 🄲 *(96) 388 35 88.* ⬤ *Tue –Sun.*
Valencia's prehistory museum displays part of a unique collection of 5,000 Stone Age engravings of deer and horses made on limestone plaques that were found in the Cueva de Parpalló, in the hills above the coast near Gandia *(see*

p244). The neighboring Museo de Etnología (Folk Museum), which shares the same opening hours, contains displays illustrating traditional rural village life.

🚉 Estación del Norte
Calle Játiva. 🄲 *(96) 352 02 02.* ⬤ *daily.*
Valencia's mainline railroad station was built between 1907 and 1917 in a style inspired by Austrian Art Nouveau. Its twin white towers are adorned with bunches of sculpted oranges. Inside the building, the lobby and cafeteria are decorated with ceramic murals and stained glass depicting the life and crops of the *huerta* and L'Albufera *(see p244).*

Art Nouveau-style column in the Estación del Norte

🏛 Museo del Gremio Artistas Falleros
Calle del Ninot 24. 🄲 *(96) 347 65 85.* ⬤ *daily.* ♿
Up to 170 artists and craftsmen labor all year in the *barrio* of Ciudad Fallera to build the elaborate papier-mâché

sculptures that are burned during Las Fallas *(see p245).* They sometimes show visitors around their workshops – except during their busiest period in the months leading up to March. Each year the best *ninots* (papier-mâché cartoonlike figures) are saved from the flames and put on display in this craft guild museum, along with posters, photographs, and other memorabilia dating from 1902.

El Cabañal and La Malvarrosa Beaches
To the east of the city, the beaches of El Cabañal and La Malvarrosa are bordered by a broad and lively esplanade about 2 km (1.5 miles) long. Although these two former fishermen's districts were carelessly developed in the 1960s and 1970s, they retain some quaint, traditional houses tiled on the outside to keep them cool in summer. The light of La Malvarrosa inspired the Impressionist painter Joaquín Sorolla *(see p295).* The Paseo de Neptuno, near the port, is lined with restaurants, many of which specialize in paella.

ENVIRONS: The fertile and intensively farmed plain of the *huerta* is a maze of fields planted with artichokes and *chufas*, the raw ingredient of *horchata.* Here you can find a few surviving examples of Valencia's traditional farmhouse, the *barraca*, with its steeply pitched, thatched roof.
  Manises, near the airport, is renowned for its ceramics, which are sold in shops and factories. There is also a ceramics museum.

VALENCIA'S SUMMER SPECIALTY

In summer, the bars and cafés of Valencia offer a thirst-quenching drink unique to the area. *Horchata*, a sweet, milky drink produced mainly in the nearby town of Alboraia, is made from *chufas* (earth almonds). It is served semi-frozen and usually eaten with *fartons* – soft, sweet bread sticks – or *rosquilletas* – crunchy wafer sticks. The oldest *horchatería* in the city center is Santa Catalina, off the Plaza de la Virgen.

Painted tiles showing woman serving *horchata*

Fishing boats on the shore of the freshwater lake, L'Albufera

L'Albufera ⓫

Valencia. 🚍 🛈 *Raco de l'Olla,*
(96) 162 73 45.

A FRESHWATER LAKE situated on
the coast just south of
Valencia, L'Albufera is one of
the prime wetland habitats for
birds in Eastern Spain.

It is cut off from the sea by
a wooded sandbar, the Dehesa,
and fringed by a network of
paddies that produce a third
of Spain's rice.

L'Albufera is fed by the Río
Turia and connected to the sea
by three channels fitted with
sluice gates to control the
water level. The lake reaches
a maximum depth of 2.5 m
(8 ft), and is gradually
shrinking because of natural
silting and the reclamation of
land. In the Middle Ages the
lake encompassed an area
over ten times its present size.

Over 250 species of birds –
including large numbers of
egrets and herons – have been
recorded in the lake's reed
beds and marshy islands, the
matas. L'Albufera was declared
a nature preserve in 1986 to
protect its birdlife. Many birds
can be seen with binoculars
from the shores of the lake.

A visitors' center at Raco de
l'Olla provides information on
the ecology of lake, the paddy
fields and the Dehesa.

Xàtiva ⓬

Valencia. 🚶 *25,000.* 🚍 🚍
🛈 *Calle Alameda de Jaime 50, (96)*
227 33 46. 🕙 *Tue & Fri.* 🎉 *Las Fallas*
(third week of Mar).

A LONG THE NARROW RIDGE of
Mount Vernissa, above
Xàtiva, run the ruins of a once-
grand **castle** of 30 towers. It
was largely destroyed by Felipe
V in the War of the Spanish
Succession *(see p58).* Felipe
also set fire to the town, which
continues to wreak its revenge
in an extraordinary way – by
hanging Felipe's full-length
portrait upside down in the
Museo Municipal.

Until the attack, Xàtiva was
the second town of the kingdom of Valencia. It may have

been founded by the Phoenicians. It became prosperous
under the Moors, and in the
12th century it was the first
European city to make paper.

Among the sights in the
narrow streets and squares of
the old town are a former
hospital with a Plateresque
façade and a medieval fountain in the Plaça de la Trinidad.

The oldest church in Xàtiva
is the **Ermita de San Feliú**
(Chapel of St. Felix) on the
road to the fortress. It dates
from around 1269 and is
hung with 14th- to 16th-
century icons.

♦ **Castillo de Xàtiva**
Subida del Castillo. 🎟 *(96) 227 42*
74. 🕙 *Tue –Sun.*
🏛 **Museo Municipal**
Carrer de la Corretgeria 46. 🎟 *(96)*
227 65 97. 🕙 *Tue–Sun.*

Gandia ⓭

Valencia. 🚶 *53,000.* 🚍 🛈 *Calle*
Marqués de Campo, (96) 287 77 88.
🚍 *Sat.* 🎉 *Las Fallas (19 Mar).*

I N 1485, Rodrigo Borja (who
became Pope Alexander VI)
was granted the title of Duke
of Gandia. He founded the
Borgia clan and, together with
his son Cesare and daughter
Lucretia, was later implicated
in murder and debauchery.

Felipe V's full-length portrait
hanging upside down in Xàtiva

Rodrigo's great-grandson later redeemed the family name by joining the Jesuit order. He was canonized as St. Francis Borja by Pope Clement X in 1671.

The house in which he was born and lived, the **Palacio Ducal** (Duke's Palace), is now owned by the Jesuits. Its simple Gothic courtyard belies the richly decorated chambers within, especially the Baroque Golden Gallery. The small patio has a tiled floor depicting the four elements of earth, air, fire, and water.

Palacio Ducal
Calle Santo Duque 1. ((96) 287 12 93. ☐ Mon–Sat. ✎

The ornate and gilded interior of the Palacio Ducal, Gandia

Dénia ⑯

Alicante. 27,000. ☐ ☐ ☒
☐ Pl Oculista Buigues 9, (96) 642 23 57. ☐ Mon. ☒ Patronales (early Jul).

THIS TOWN was founded as a Greek colony. It takes its name from the Roman goddess Diana – a temple in her honor was excavated here. It was the capital of an 11th-century Muslim kingdom that extended from Andalusia to the Balearic Islands.

It is now a fishing port and vacation resort. The town center spreads around the base of a low hill. A large **castle**, originally an Arab fortress, stands on its summit, overlooking the small harbor. The entrance gateway, the Portal de la Vila, survives, though it was altered in the 17th century. The Palacio del Gobernador (Governor's House), within the castle, contains an archaeological museum with exhibits that show the development of Dénia from 200 BC to the 18th century.

North of the harbor is the sandy beach of Las Marinas. To the south is the rocky and less developed Las Rotas beach, which is good for snorkeling.

Castillo de Dénia
Calle San Francisco. ((96) 642 06 56. ☐ daily. ☒

Xàbia ⑰

Alicante. 17,000. ☐ ☐ Plaza de la Iglesia 4, (96) 579 43 56. ☐ Thu. ☒ Aduanas de Mar (first week of Sep).

PIRATES AND SMUGGLERS once took advantage of the hiding places afforded by the cliffs, caves, inlets, and two rocky islands that make up Xàbia's attractive coastline.

The town center is perched on a hill a short way inland, on the site of an Iberian walled settlement. Many of the buildings lining its streets are made from the local Tosca sandstone. The 16th-century **Iglesia de San Bartolomé** was fortified to serve its congregation as a refuge in times of invasion. It has openings over the door through which missiles could be dropped on to attackers.

The seafront is overlooked by ruined 17th- and 18th-century windmills. Because of council policy, Xàbia's beaches have been kept mercifully free of the high-rise apartment houses that dominate many other Spanish resorts.

Entrance to the Gothic Iglesia de San Bartolomé in Xàbia

The ceremonial burning of Las Fallas on St. Joseph's Day

VALENCIA AND MURCIA'S FIESTAS

Las Fallas *(Mar 19)*. Huge papier-mâché monuments *(fallas)* are erected in the crossroads and squares of Valencia around March 15 and ceremonially set alight on the night of the 19th, St. Joseph's Day. Costing millions of pesetas each, the *fallas* depict satirical scenes and can take up to a year to build. During the fiesta, the city echoes with the sound of fire crackers.

Good Friday, Lorca (Murcia). The "blue" and "white" brotherhoods compete to outdo each other in pomp and finery during a grand procession of biblical characters.

Moors and Christians. *(Apr 22–4)*, Alcoi (Alicante). Two costumed armies march into the city, where they perform ceremonies and fight mock battles in commemoration of the Reconquest.

Bous en la Mar *(early Jul)*, Dénia (Alicante). People dodge bulls on the dock until one or the other falls into the sea *(see p35)*.

Misteri d'Elx *(Aug 14–15)*, Elx (Alicante). This choral play, in the Iglesia de Santa María, has spectacular special effects.

La Tomatina *(last Wed of Aug)*, Buñol (Valencia). Thousands of participants pelt each other with ripe tomatoes *(see pp238–9)*.

The Costa Blanca

L ESS HECTIC than the Costa del Sol *(see pp448–9)* and with warmer winters than the Costa Brava *(see p207),* the Costa Blanca occupies a prime stretch of Spain's Mediterranean coastline. Alicante, with its airport and mainline railroad station, is the arrival and departure point for most tourists. Between Alicante and Altea there are long stretches of sandy beach that have been heavily built up with apartment houses and hotels. North of Altea there are more fine beaches, but they are broken by cliffs and coves. South from Alicante, as far as the resort of Torrevieja, the scenery is drier and more barren, relieved only by the wooded sand dunes of Guardamar del Segura.

Gandia marks the southern end of the Costa de Valencia, whose extensive beaches of fine sand and shallow water are popular with the Spanish.

Dénia's Las Marinas beach is a flat, sandy strip lined by hotels. The rocky Les Rotes beach is good for snorkeling.

Xàbia's busiest beach is El Arenal. Most of the resort's coastline is punctuated by cliffs and coves.

Altea is a resort with an unspoiled, whitewashed old town on a hilltop. Beneath it is a long, stoney beach.

***Santa Pola** is still a working fishing port, but its long, sandy beaches are very popular.*

Benidorm's liveliest beach, Levante, is considered to be one of the ten best beaches in the world. Poniente is farther from the town center.

Platja de Sant Joan has a long strip of seamless sand bordered by a road and a narrow-gauge railroad that gives easy access to the beach.

The Illa de Tabarca attracts day-'trippers with its natural beauty and clear waters, good for snorkeling.

Guardamar del Segura has one of the coast's least busy beaches. It is bordered by windswept sand dunes covered with aromatic pine woods.

Torrevieja is a very popular package vacation resort with sweeping, sandy beaches to the south. It has been highly developed in recent years.

***Alicante's** city center is served by the popular Postiguet beach. Nearby are vast, sandy beaches such as La Albufereta and Sant Joan.*

Gandia

Oliva

Dénia

Xàbia

Moraira

Calp

Altea

Benidorm

La Vila Joiosa

El Campello

Platja de Sant Joan

Alacant (Alicante)

Santa Pola

Illa de Tabarca

Guardamar del Segura

Torrevieja

0 kilometers   25

0 miles   25

◁ **Entrance of the Moorish army, part of a festival to commemorate the Reconquest, Ontinyent, Valencia**

Penyal d'Ifach ⑱

Alicante. 🚉 *Calp.* 🚌 *Calp.* ℹ️ *Calp, (96) 583 69 20.*

WHEN VIEWED from afar, the rocky outcrop of the Penyal d'Ifach seems to rise vertically out of the sea. One of the Costa Blanca's most dramatic sights, this 332-m (1,089-ft) tall block of limestone looks virtually unclimbable. However, a short tunnel, built in 1918, allows walkers access to the much gentler slopes on its seaward side.

Allow about two hours for the round trip, which starts at the visitors' center above Calp harbor. It takes you up gentle slopes covered with juniper and fan palm, with the waves crashing below. As you climb, and at the exposed summit, there are spectacular views of a large stretch of the Costa Blanca. On a clear day you can see the hills of Ibiza *(see p486)*.

The Penyal d'Ifach is also home to 300 types of wild plant, including several rare species. Migrating birds use it as a landmark, and the salt flats below them are an important habitat for them. The rock was privately owned until 1987, when the regional government acquired it and turned it into a nature preserve.

Situated below the rock is the Iberian town of Calp, renowned for its beaches, such as Levante and Les Bassetes.

The magnificent limestone rock Penyal d'Ifach

Guadalest ⑲

Alicante. 🐎 *170.* ℹ️ *Plaza de San Gregorio 1, (96) 588 52 19.* 🎉 *Fiestas de los Jóvenes (Jun 6), Virgen de la Asunción (mid-Aug).*

DESPITE DRAWING busloads of day-trippers from Benidorm, the pretty mountain village of Castell de Guadalest remains relatively unspoiled. This is largely because its older part is accessible only on foot by a single entrance: a sloping tunnel cut into the rock on which the castle ruins and the church's distinctive belfry are precariously perched.

Guadalest was founded by the Moors, who carved the surrounding hillsides into terraces and planted them with crops. These are still irrigated by the original ditches constructed by the Moors. The village was badly damaged by earthquakes in 1644 and 1748.

From the main square, a flight of steps ascends to the **castle**, from which there are magnificent views of the surrounding mountains.

At the **Museo de Miniaturas** you can see a microscopic version of Leonardo da Vinci's *Last Supper*, painted on a grain of rice, Goya's *The Naked Maja* *(see p283)*, painted on the wing of a fly, and a sculpture of a camel passing through the eye of a needle.

🏛 Museo de Miniaturas
Calle de la Iglesia 5. 📞 *(96) 588 50 62.* 🗓 *daily.* 🚫

The belfry of Guadalest, perched on top of a rock

Alcoi ⑳

Alicante. 🐎 *65,000.* 🚉 🚌 ℹ️ *Plaza de España 1, (96) 554 52 11.* 🎉 *Moors and Christians (Apr 22–4).*

SITED AT THE confluence of three rivers and surrounded by high mountains, Alcoi is an industrial city. But it is best known for its mock battles between Moors and Christians *(see p245)* and its *peladillas* – almonds coated in sugar.

On the slopes above it is **Font Roja** (the red spring), a nature preserve and shrine marked by a towering statue of the Virgin Mary.

ENVIRONS: To the north of Alcoi is the **Sierra de Mariola**, a mountain range famed for its medicinal and culinary herbs. The best point of access is the village of **Agres**. A scenic route runs from the north of Agres to the summit of Mont Cabrer at 1,390 m (4,560 ft). It passes two ruined *neveras* – pits once used to store ice for preserving fish and meat.

The bullring of **Bocairent**, 10 km (6 miles) west of Agres, was carved out of rock in 1813. A nearby cliff is pockmarked with **Les Covetes dels Moros** ("the Moors' Caves"). Despite their name, the origin of these man-made caves is a mystery.

Benidorm ㉑

Alicante. 🏠 47,000. 🚌 🚍 ℹ Calle
Martínez Alejos 16, (96) 585 13 11.
🛋 Wed, Sun. 🎊 Virgen del Carmen
(Mar 16), Las Fallas (Mar 19).

WITH FORESTS of skyscrapers
overshadowing its two
long beaches, this famous
vacation resort is more reminiscent of Manhattan than the
obscure fishing village it still
was in the early 1950s.

Benidorm boasts more ac-
commodations than any other
resort on the Mediterranean,
but its clientele has changed
since the 1980s when it attracted a beer-swilling crowd. An
enormous public park and
open air auditorium used for
cultural events, the **Parque
de l'Aigüera**, is emblematic of
the facelift Benidorm has gone
through in recent years. The
town now attracts more elderly
vacationers from the north of
Spain than young people from
England. Even so, the top
attractions of this resort are
still said to be sex, sun, nightclubs, and "English" pubs.

A small park on a promon-
tory between the Levante and
Poniente beaches, called the
Balcón del Mediterráneo,
ends in a giant waterspout –
a single-jet fountain. From
here there is a panoramic view
of most of Benidorm. A short
way out to sea is the Illa de
Benidorm, a wedge-shaped

**Main staircase with floral lamp in
the Casa Modernista, Novelda**

island served by ferries from
the harbor. The island is being
converted into a nature preserve to protect its sea birds.

ENVIRONS: La Vila Joiosa
(Villajoyosa), to the south, is
much older than Benidorm.
Its principal sight is a line of
brightly painted houses that
overhang the riverbed. They
were painted in such vivid
colors, it is said, so that their
fishermen owners would be
able to identify their homes
when they were out at sea.

The older part of **Altea**, to
the north of Benidorm, stands
on a hill above modern beachfront developments. It is a
delightful jumble of white
houses, narrow streets, and
alleys, and long flights of steps
arranged round a promi-
nent, blue-domed church.

The old town of Altea, dominated by its domed church

Novelda ㉒

Alicante. 🏠 23,000. 🚌 🚍
ℹ Plaza de España 1, (96) 560 03 77.
🛋 Wed, Sat. 🎊 Santa María
Magdalena (third week of Jul).

THE INDUSTRIAL TOWN of
Novelda is dominated by
its many marble factories, but
it is the exquisitely preserved
Art Nouveau house, the **Casa
Modernista**, that is of special
interest. It was built in 1903
and rescued from demolition
in 1975 by a local bank. The
three-story building is furnished in period style. There
are few straight lines or functional shapes and almost every
inch of wall space has some
floral or playful motif.

ENVIRONS: Villena town hall
has a collection of Bronze
Age gold objects, the **Tesoro
de Villena** (see pp44–5).

🏛 **Casa Modernista**
Calle Mayor 24. 📞 (96) 560 02 37.
⬤ Sat & Sun.
🏛 **Tesoro de Villena**
Ayuntamiento. 📞 (96) 580 11 50.
◯ by prior arrangement.

Alicante ㉓

Alicante. 🏠 270,000. ✈ 🚌 🚍 ⛴
ℹ Explanada de España 2, (96) 520
00 00. 🛋 Thu, Sat. 🎊 Hogueras
(third week of Jun).

A PORT AND SEASIDE resort built
around a natural harbor,
Alicante (Alacant) is the principal city of the Costa Blanca.
Both the Greeks and Romans
established settlements here.
In the 8th century the Moors
refounded the city under the
shadow of Mount Benacantil.
The summit of this hill is now
occupied by the **Castillo de
Santa Bárbara**, which dates
mainly from the 16th century.
From its top battlements there
is a view over the whole city.

The focus of the city is the
Explanada de España, a
palm-lined promenade along
the waterfront. The 18th-
century Baroque **town hall**
(ayuntamiento), is worth seeing for the Salón Azul (Blue
Room) with its mirrored gallery. A metal disk on the pink
marble staircase is used as a

Yachts moored in Alicante harbor, beside the Explanada de España

reference point in measuring the sea level all around Spain. A local painter, Eusebio Sempere (1924–85), put together the eclectic range of 20th-century art on display in the 17th-century **Casa de la Asegurada**. It includes paintings by Dalí, Miró, Picasso *(see pp28–9)*, and Sempere himself.

♦ **Castillo de Santa Bárbara**
Playa de Postiguet. 〖 *(96) 516 21 28.* ☐ *daily.* 🎦 ♿
🏛 **Ayuntamiento**
Plaza del Ayuntamiento. 〖 *(96) 514 91 00.* ☐ *Mon–Sat by arrangement.*
🏛 **Casa de la Asegurada**
Plaza de Santa María 3. 〖 *(96) 514 94 69.* ☐ *Tue–Sun.*

Illa de Tabarca ㉔

Alicante. 🚢 *from Santa Pola/Alicante.*
🛈 *Santa Pola, (96) 669 22 76.*

T HE BEST POINT of departure for the Illa de Tabarca is Santa Pola. Small and flat, this island is divided into two parts: a stony, treeless area of level ground known as *el campo* (the countryside), and a walled settlement, which is entered through three monumental gateways. The settlement was laid out on a grid plan in the 18th century, on the orders of Carlos III, to prevent the island being used by pirates.
   Tabarca is a popular place to swim or snorkel, and it can get crowded in the summer.
   Fish and salt have long been important to the economy of Santa Pola. A Roman fish salting works has been excavated here, and outside the town are some modern salt pans.

Elx ㉕

Alicante. 🚶 *200,000.* 🚇 🚆
🛈 *Parque Municipal, (96) 545 38 31.*
☐ *Mon, Sat.* 🎦 *Virgen de la Asunción (second week of Aug).*

T HE FOREST of over 300,000 palm trees that surrounds Elx (Elche) on three sides is said to have been planted by the Phoenicians around 300 BC. Part of it has been enclosed as a private garden called the **Huerto del Cura**. Some of the palms – one with a trunk which has divided into eight branches – are dedicated to various notable people, such as the Empress Elizabeth of Austria, who visited here in 1894.
   The first settlement in the area, around 5000 BC, was at La Alcudia, where a 5th-century BC Iberian stone bust of a priestess, *La Dama de Elche (see p44)*, was discovered in 1897. The original is in Madrid, but there are several replicas scattered around Elx.
   The blue-domed Baroque church, the **Basílica de Santa María**, was built in the 17th century to house the **Misteri d'Elx** *(see p37)*. Next to it is **La Calahorra**, a Gothic tower, which is a surviving part of the city's defenses.
   A clock on the roof next to the town hall has two 16th-century mechanical figures that strike the hours on bells.

🌿 **Huerto del Cura**
Porta de la Morera 49. 〖 *(96) 545 19 36.* ☐ *daily.* 🎦 ♿
🏛 **La Calahorra**
Calle Uberna. 〖 *(96) 545 28 19.*
☐ *Tue–Sun.* 🎦

Orihuela ㉖

Alicante. 🚶 *51,000.* 🚇 🚆 🛈 *Calle Francisco Día 25, (96) 530 27 47.*
☐ *Tue.* 🎦 *La Reconquista (Jul 17).*

I N THE 15TH CENTURY Orihuela was prosperous enough for Fernando and Isabel to stop and collect men and money on their way to do battle against the Moors at Granada. The Gothic **cathedral**, with its Romanesque cloister, contains Velázquez's *The Temptation of St. Thomas Aquinas.* Among the 18th-century processional floats displayed in the **Museo de Semana Santa** (Easter Week Museum) is one bearing a statue of a she-devil, *La Diablesa.*

🏛 **Museo de Semana Santa**
Plaza de la Merced 1. 〖 *(96) 530 27 47.* ☐ *Mon–Sat.* 🎦 ♿

La Diablesa, Orihuela

Torrevieja ㉗

Alicante. 🚶 *30,000.* 🛈 *Carretera de Cartagena, (96) 571 59 36.* ☐ *Fri.*
🎦 *Habaneras (Aug).*

D URING THE 1980s, Torrevieja grew at a prodigious rate as thousands of Europeans purchased homes here. Before tourism, the town's source of income was sea salt. The salt works are the most productive in Europe and the second most important in the world.
   Torrevieja stages a festival of *habaneras*, melodic songs originating in Cuba, brought back to Spain by salt exporters.

Capilla del Junterón, Murcia

Murcia ㉘

Murcia. 🏠 *140,000.* 🚊 🚌
ℹ️ *Alejandro Seiquer 4, (968) 21
37 16.* 🛒 *Thu.* 🎭 *Semana Santa
(Easter Week).*

A REGIONAL CAPITAL and university city on the Segura
River, Murcia was founded in
825 by the Moors, following
successful irrigation of the
surrounding fertile plain.

The center of the modern
city is the 18th-century square,
La Glorieta. The pedestrianized Calle de la Trapería, linking the cathedral and the former marketplace (now the
Plaza Santo Domingo), is the
city's main street.

On it stands a gentlemen's
club founded in 1847, the
Casino (ask the doorman for
permission to look around). It is
entered through an Arab-style
patio, fashioned on the royal
chambers of the Alhambra. The
huge romantic ballroom has a
highly polished parquet floor
and is illuminated by five large
crystal chandeliers. A painting
covering the ceiling of the
ladies' cloakroom depicts the
goddess Selene.

Work on the **cathedral**
began in 1394 over the foundations of Murcia's central
mosque, and it was finally
consecrated in 1467. The large
tower was added much later
and constructed in stages from
the 16th to the 18th centuries.
The architect Jaime Bort built
the main, Baroque façade
between 1739 and 1754.

The cathedral's finest features
are two exquisitely ornate side
chapels. The first, the Capilla
de los Vélez, is in Late Gothic

style and was built between
1490 and 1507. The second,
the Renaissance Capilla del
Junterón, dates from the early
16th century.

The **cathedral museum**
displays grand Gothic altarpieces, a frieze from a Roman
sarcophagus, and the third
largest monstrance in Spain.

Francisco Salzillo (1707–83),
one of Spain's greatest sculptors, was born in Murcia, and
a museum in the **Iglesia de
Jesús** (Church of Jesus)
exhibits nine of his *pasos* –
sculptures on platforms. These
are carried through the streets

Arab-style patio, Murcia Casino

of the city on Good Friday
morning. The figures are so
lifelike that a fellow sculptor
is said to have told the men
carrying a *paso*: "Put it down,
it will walk by itself."

ENVIRONS: The folk museum,
the **Museo de Tradiciones y
Artes Populares**, stands beside
a large water wheel – a 1955
copy in iron of the original

15th-century wooden wheel.
The three galleries display
agricultural and domestic
items, some of them 300 years
old. A traditional, thatched
Murcian farmhouse *(barraca)*
forms part of the museum.

♟️ **Casino**
Calle Trapería 18. 📞 *(968) 21 22 55.*
🔓 *daily, by permission.* 📷
🏛️ **Museo Etnológico de la
Huerta de Alcantarilla**
Carretera de Granada. 📞 *(968)
80 03 40.* 🔓 *Tue–Sun.* ♿

Mar Menor ㉙

Murcia. ✈️ *San Javier.* 🚌 *from
Cartagena.* 🚌 *La Manga.* ℹ️ *La
Manga, (968) 14 18 12.*

THE ELONGATED, high-rise
vacation resort of La Manga,
built on a long, thin, sandy
strip, separates the Mediterranean and the Mar Menor,
literally "the Smaller Sea."

Really a large lagoon, the
sheltered Mar Menor can be
5°C (10°F) warmer than the
Mediterranean in summer. Its
high mineral concentrations
first drew spa tourists in the
early 20th century. They
stayed at the older resorts of
Santiago de la Ribera and Los
Alcázares, which still have
pretty wooden jetties protruding from their beaches.

From Santiago de la Ribera
you can take a ferry to two of
the five islands in the Mar
Menor, the biggest of which is
called the Isla Mayor.

The old saltpans at Lo Pagán,
near San Pedro del Pinatar, are
now a nature preserve.

The resort of Los Alcázares on the edge of the Mar Menor

View of the domes and spires of Cartagena's town hall from the seafront

Cartagena ③⓪

Murcia. ⚐ 170,000. ✈ San Javier.
⬛ ⬛ ⬛ ⬛ Plaza Ayuntamiento,
(968) 50 64 83. ⬛ Wed. ⚑ Semana
Santa (Easter Week), Carthaginians
and Romans (Sep 23).

THE FIRST SETTLEMENT founded in the natural harbor
of Cartagena was constructed
in 223 BC by the Carthaginians,
who called it *Quart Hadas*
(New City). After conquering
the city in 209 BC, the Romans
renamed it *Carthago Nova*
(New Carthage).

Although the city declined
in importance in the Middle
Ages, its prestige increased
in the 18th century when it
became a major naval base.

You can get an overview of
the city from the park which
surrounds the ruins of the
Castillo de la Concepción,
Cartagena's castle. On the
dock below is a prototype
submarine designed by Isaac
Peral in 1888. The city hall,
opposite, marks the end of
the Calle Mayor, a street overlooked by balconies and lined
with handsome buildings. Excavations in the city include a
Roman street and the **Muralla
Bizantina** (Byzantine Wall),
built between 589 and 590.

The **National Underwater
Archaeology Museum** has
an interesting collection of
ancient Roman and Greek jars.

🏛 **Muralla Bizantina**
Calle Nueva. ⬛ (968) 50 79 66.
◯ Tue–Sat.
🏛 **Museo Nacional de
Arqueología Submarino**
Carretera Faro de Navidad. ⬛ (968)
50 84 15. ◯ Tue–Sun. ⬛

Costa Cálida ③①

Murcia. ⬛ Cartagena. ⬛ Murcia.
⬛ Águilas, (968) 41 33 03.

THE MOST POPULAR RESORTS of
Murcia's "Warm Coast" are
around the Mar Menor. Between Cabo de Palos and Cabo
Tinoso the few small beaches
are dwarfed by cliffs and headlands. The resorts of the
southern part of the coast are
relatively quiet for Spain.
There are several fine beaches
at Puerto de Mazarrón; and at
nearby Bolnuevo the wind has
eroded soft rocks into strange
shapes. The growing resort of
Águilas marks the southern
limit of the coast, at the border
with Andalusia.

Lorca ③②

Murcia. ⚐ 70,000. ⬛ ⬛
⬛ Palacio de Guevara, (968) 46 61 57.
⬛ Thu. ⚑ Semana Santa (Easter
Week), Feria (3rd week Sep), Día de
San Clemente (Nov 23).

THE FERTILE FARMLAND
around Lorca, Murcia's
third most important town,
is an oasis in one of the
most arid areas of Europe.
Lorca was an important
staging post on the Vía
Heraclea, as witnessed
by the Roman milepost
standing in a corner
of the Plaza San
Vicente. During the
wars between Moors
and Christians in the 13th
to 15th centuries, Lorca
became a frontier town
between Al Andalus and
the Castilian territory of

Murcia. Its castle dates from
this era, although only two of
its original 35 towers remain.
After Granada fell the town
lost its importance and, except
for one surviving gateway, its
walls were demolished.

The center of the town, the
Plaza de España, is lined with
handsome stone buildings.
One side is occupied by the
Colegiata de San Patricio
(Church of St. Patrick), built
between 1533 and 1704, the
only church in Spain dedicated
to the Irish saint. At the head
of the square is the town hall.
A former prison, it was built in
two blocks between 1677 and
1739, and later connected by
an arch that spans the street.

Caravaca de
la Cruz ③③

Murcia. ⚐ 21,500. ⬛ Plaza del
Arco 1, (968) 70 20 00. ⬛ Mon.
⚑ Vera Cruz (May).

A TOWN OF ancient churches,
Caravaca de la Cruz's
fame lies in its castle, which
houses the **Santuario de la
Vera Cruz** (Sanctuary of the
True Cross). This is where a
double-armed cross is said to
have appeared miraculously
in 1231 – 12 years before the
town was seized by Christians.
The highlight of the Vera Cruz
fiesta is the Race of the Wine
Horses, which commemorates
the lifting of a Moorish siege
of the castle. The Cross of
Caravaca was dipped in wine
that the thirsty defenders
then drank and recovered
their fighting strength.

ENVIRONS: Just to the
north is the pretty
village of **Moratalla**,
an attractive jumble of
steep streets and brightly painted houses lying
beneath a 15th-
century castle. The
village is among the
foothills of the range
of mountains marking
Murcia's western border. **Cehegín**, east of
Caravaca, is a partially
preserved medieval town.

**Roman milepost topped by a
statue of St. Vincent, Lorca**

MADRID

Introducing Madrid

SPAIN'S CAPITAL, a city of over three million people, is situated close to the geographical center of the country, at the hub of both road and rail networks. Because of its distance from the sea and its altitude – 660 m (2,165 ft) – the city endures cold winters and hot summers, making spring and autumn the best times to visit. Madrid's attractions include three internationally famous art galleries, a royal palace, grand public squares, and many museums filled with the treasures of Spain's history. The city is surrounded by its own small province, the Comunidad de Madrid, which takes in the Sierra de Guadarrama and one of Spain's most famous monuments, the palace of El Escorial.

The Palacio Real (see pp266–7) *the royal palace built by Spain's first Bourbon kings, dominates the western part of Old Madrid. Its lavishly decorated chambers include the throne room.*

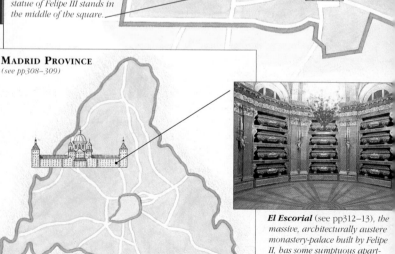

The Plaza Mayor (see p263), *Old Madrid's great 17th-century square, has been a focal point of the city since the days when it was used as a public arena for bullfights, trials by the Inquisition, and executions (see p264). An equestrian statue of Felipe III stands in the middle of the square.*

OLD MADRID
(see pp258–71)

MADRID PROVINCE
(see pp308–309)

0 kilometers   25

0 miles   20

El Escorial (see pp312–13), *the massive, architecturally austere monastery-palace built by Felipe II, has some sumptuous apartments decorated with great works of art. Marble sarcophagi in the octagonal Royal Pantheon contain the mortal remains of most Spanish monarchs.*

The Museo Thyssen-Bornemisza (see pp278–9), *one of the most important privately assembled art collections in the world, was given to Spain in 1993. The 18th-century palace houses major works by Titian, Rubens, Goya, Van Gogh, and Picasso.*

The Plaza de Cibeles *(see p276), one of the city's most impressive squares, is ringed by distinctive buildings, including the 19th-century Banco de España and Madrid's main post office, with sculptures on its white façade.*

BOURBON MADRID
(see pp272–89)

The Parque del Retiro *(see p287) has leafy paths and avenues, and a boating lake overlooked by a majestic colonnade. It is an ideal place in which to relax between visits to the great art galleries and museums of Bourbon Madrid.*

The Museo del Prado (see pp282–5) *is one of the world's greatest art galleries. It has important collections of paintings by Velázquez and Goya, whose statue stands outside the main entrance.*

| 0 meters | 500 |
| 0 yards | 500 |

The Centro de Arte Reina Sofía *(see pp288–9), an outstanding museum of 20th-century art, is entered by exterior glass elevators. Inside, the star exhibit is Guernica, Picasso's famous painting of the horrors of the Civil War.*

OLD MADRID

W HEN FELIPE II chose Madrid as his capital in 1561, it was a small Castilian town of little real significance. In the following years, it was to grow into the nerve center of a mighty empire.

According to tradition, it was the Moorish chieftain Muhammad ben Abd al Rahman who established a fortress above the Río Manzanares. Magerit, as it was called in Arabic, fell to Alfonso VI of Castile between 1083 and 1086. Narrow streets with houses

Drawer designed for storing herbs, Palacio Real

and medieval churches began to grow up on the higher ground behind the old Arab alcazar, which was replaced by a Gothic palace in the 15th century.

When this burned down in 1734, it was replaced in turn by the present Bourbon palace, the Palacio Real.

The population had scarcely reached 20,000 when Madrid was chosen as capital, but by the end of the century it had more than tripled. The 16th-century city is known as the "Madrid de los Austrias," after the reigning Hapsburg dynasty. During this period royal monasteries were endowed and churches and private palaces were built. In the 17th century, the Plaza Mayor was added, and the Puerta del Sol, the "Gate of the Sun," became the spiritual and geographical heart of not only Madrid but of all Spain.

SIGHTS AT A GLANCE

Historic Buildings
Palacio Real pp266–7 **9**

Museums and Galleries
Real Academia de
  Bellas Artes **14**

Churches and Convents
Catedral de San Isidro **2**
Iglesia de San Nicolás **5**
Monasterio de las
  Descalzas Reales **13**

Monasterio de la
  Encarnación **10**
Nuestra Señora de la
  Almudena **7**

Streets, Squares and Parks
Campo del Moro **8**
Gran Vía **12**
Plaza de España **11**
Plaza Mayor **4**
Plaza de Oriente **6**

Plaza de la Villa **3**
Puerta del Sol **1**

GETTING THERE
The metro is the fastest and easiest way to get to Old Madrid. Take line 1 to Gran Vía or Sol; alternatively, lines 2, 3, 5, and 10 are also good for getting to the main sights. Useful buses include the 51, 52, and 150 to Puerta del Sol.

KEY

Street-by-Street map *pp260–61*	
M	Metro station
	Main bus stop
i	Tourist information
P	Parking

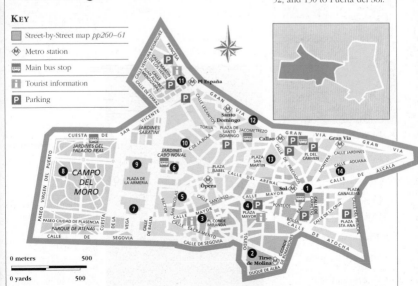

0 meters	500
0 yards	500

◁ **Statue of Cervantes by Lorenzo Coullaut-Valera in the Plaza de España**

Street-by-Street: Old Madrid

STRETCHING FROM THE MEDIEVAL Plaza de la Villa to the busy Puerta del Sol, the compact heart of Old Madrid is steeped in history and full of interesting sights. Trials by the Inquisition *(see p264)* and executions were once held in the Plaza Mayor. This porticoed square is Old Madrid's finest piece of architecture, a legacy of the Hapsburgs *(see pp54–7)*. Other buildings of note are the Catedral de San Isidro and the Palacio de Santa Cruz. For a more relaxing way of enjoying Old Madrid, sit in one of the area's numerous cafés or browse among the stalls of the Mercado de San Miguel.

★ **Plaza Mayor**
This beautiful 1[7]th-century square competes with the Puerta del Sol as the focus of Old Madrid. The arcades at the base of the three-storey buildings are filled with cafés and craft shops ❹

The Mercado de San Miguel is housed in a 19th-century building with wrought-iron columns. The market sells a variety of food and household goods.

To Palacio Real

Town Hall (ayuntamiento)

Casa de Cisneros

Arco de Cuchilleros

★ **Plaza de la Villa**
The 15th-century Torre de los Lujanes is the oldest of several historic buildings standing on this square ❸

0 meters	100
0 yards	100

STAR SIGHTS

★ Plaza Mayor

★ Plaza de la Villa

★ Puerta del Sol

The Basílica Pontificia de San Miguel is an imposing 18th-century church with a beautiful façade and a graceful interior. It is one of very few churches in Spain inspired by the Italian Baroque style.

★ Puerta del Sol
With its shops and cafés, the Puerta del Sol is one of the city's liveliest areas. This sign for Tío Pepe, a brand of sherry, has become synonymous with the square ❶

LOCATOR MAP
See Street Finder map 2

Iglesia de San Ginés

Sol Metro

To Bourbon Madrid

Tirso de Molina Metro

KEY

--- --- Suggested route

The Palacio de Santa Cruz was built as the court prison in the 17th century. This Baroque *(see p21)* palace is now occupied by the Foreign Ministry.

Catedral de San Isidro
This was Madrid's provisional cathedral until La Almudena was completed (see p265). It is named after the city's patron, St. Isidore, a local 12th-century farmer ❷

Kilometer Zero, the center of Spain's road network, Puerta del Sol

Puerta del Sol ❶

Map 2 F3. Sol.

NOISY WITH TRAFFIC, chatter, and policemen's whistles, the Puerta del Sol ("Gateway of the Sun") makes a fitting center for Madrid. This is one of the city's most popular meeting places, and huge crowds converge on this famous square on their way to the shops and sights in the old part of the city.

The square marks the site of the original eastern entrance to the city, once occupied by a gatehouse and castle. These disappeared long ago, and in their place came a succession of churches. In the late 19th century the area was turned into a square and became the center of café society.

Today the square is shaped like a half moon. Its straight southern side is occupied by an austere redbrick building, originally the city's post office, built in the 1760s under Carlos III. In 1847 it became the headquarters of the

The bronze bear and strawberry tree of Madrid, Puerta del Sol

Ministry of the Interior. In 1866 the clocktower that gives the building much of its identity was added. During the Franco regime (see pp62–3), the police cells beneath the building were the site of many human rights abuses. In 1963, Julián Grimau, a member of the underground Communist party, allegedly fell from an upstairs window and miraculously survived, only to be executed shortly afterward.

The building is now home to the regional government, the Comunidad de Madrid, and is the focus of many festive events. At midnight on New Year's Eve dense crowds fill the square and people swallow a grape on each stroke of the clock, a tradition supposed to bring good luck for the rest of the year. Outside the building, a symbol on the ground marks Kilometer Zero, considered the center of Spain's huge road network.

The buildings opposite are arranged in a semicircle and contain modern shops and cafés. On the corner of Calle del Carmen is a bronze statue of the symbol of Madrid – a bear reaching for the fruit of a madroño (strawberry tree).

The Puerta del Sol has witnessed many important historical events. On May 2, 1808, the uprising against the occupying French forces began here, but the crowd, pitted against the well-armed French troops, was crushed (see p59). In 1912 the liberal prime minister José Canalejas was assassinated in the square, and, in 1931, the Second Republic (see p61) was proclaimed from the balcony of the Ministry of the Interior.

Catedral de San Isidro ❷

Calle de Toledo 37. **Map** 2 E4.
 (91) 369 20 37. La Latina.
 8am–12:30pm, 6–8:45pm Mon–Sat, 8am–2:30pm, 5:45–8:45pm Sun.

BUILT IN THE Baroque style (see p21) for the Jesuits in the mid-17th century, this twin-towered church served as Madrid's cathedral until La Almudena (see p265) was completed in 1993.

After Carlos III expelled the Jesuits from Spain in 1767 (see p58), Ventura Rodríguez was commissioned to redesign the interior of the church. It was then rededicated to Madrid's patron saint, St. Isidore, and two years later the saint's remains were moved here from the Iglesia de San Andrés. San Isidro was returned to the Jesuits during the reign of Fernando VII (1814–33).

Altar in the Catedral de San Isidro

Plaza de la Villa ❸

Map 2 D4. Ópera, Sol.

THE MUCH RESTORED and frequently remodeled Plaza de la Villa is one of the most atmospheric spots in Madrid. Some of the city's most historic secular buildings are situated around this square.

The oldest building is the early 15th-century Torre de los Lujanes, with its Gothic portal and Mudéjar-style horseshoe arches. François I of France was allegedly imprisoned in it following his defeat at the Battle of Pavia in 1525. The Casa de Cisneros was built in 1537 for the nephew

Portal of the Torre de los Lujanes

of Cardinal Cisneros, founder of the historic University of Alcalá *(see pp314–15)*. The main façade, on the Calle de Sacramento, is an excellent example of the Plateresque style *(see p21)*.

Linked to this building, by an enclosed bridge, is the town hall *(ayuntamiento)*. Designed in the 1640s by Juan Gómez de la Mora, architect of the Plaza Mayor, it exhibits the same combination of steep roofs with dormer windows, steeplelike towers at the corners, and an austere façade of brick and stone. Before construction was finished – more than 50 years later – the building had acquired handsome Baroque doorways. A balcony was later added by Juan de Villanueva, the architect of the Prado *(see pp282–5)*, so that the Royal Family could watch Corpus Christi processions passing by.

Plaza Mayor ➍

Map 2 E4. ✦ *Sol.*

T HE PLAZA MAYOR forms a splendid rectangular square, all balconies and pinnacles, dormer windows and steep slate roofs. The square, with its theatrical atmosphere, is very Castilian in character. Much was expected to happen here and a great deal did – bullfights, executions, pageants, and trials by the Inquisition *(see p264)* – all watched by crowds, often in the presence of the reigning king and queen.

The first great public scene was the beatification of Madrid's patron, St. Isidore, in 1621. In the same year, the execution of Rodrigo Calderón, secretary to Felipe III, was held here. Although hated by the Madrid populace, Calderón bore himself with such dignity on the day of his death that the phrase "proud as Rodrigo on the scaffold" survives to this day. Perhaps the greatest occasion of all, however, was the arrival here – from Italy – of Carlos III in 1760.

The square was started in 1617 and built in just two years, replacing slum houses. Its architect, Juan Gómez de la Mora, was successor to Juan de Herrera, designer of Felipe II's austere monastery palace, El Escorial *(see pp312–13)*. Mora echoed the style of his master, softening it slightly. The fanciest part of the arcaded construction is the

Casa de la Panadería (bakery). Its façade, recently and crudely reinvented, is decorated with allegorical paintings.

The equestrian statue in the center is of Felipe III, who ordered the square's construction. Started by the Italian Giovanni de Bologna and finished by his pupil Pietro Tacca in 1616, the statue was moved here in 1848 from the Casa de Campo *(see p292)*. Nowadays the square is lined with outdoor cafés and is the site of a collectors' market on Sundays *(see p305)*. The southern exit of the square leads into the Calle de Toledo toward the streets where the Rastro, Madrid's famous flea market *(see p292)*, is held. A flight of steps in the southwest corner takes you under the Arco de Cuchilleros to the Calle de Cuchilleros, where there are a number of *mesones*, traditional restaurants.

Allegorical paintings on the Casa de la Panadería, Plaza Mayor

The Spanish Inquisition

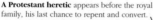

THE SPANISH INQUISITION was set up by Fernando and Isabel in 1480 to create a single, monolithic Catholic ideology in Spain. Protestant heretics and alleged "false converts" to Catholicism from the Jewish and Muslim faiths were tried, to ensure the religious unity of the country. Beginning with a papal bull, the Inquisition was run like a court, presided over by the Inquisitor-General. However, the

Inquisition banner

defendants were denied counsel, not told the charges facing them, and tortured to obtain confessions. Punishment ranged from imprisonment to beheading, hanging, or burning at the stake. A formidable system of control, it gave Spain's Protestant enemies a major propaganda weapon by contributing to the *Leyenda Negra* (Black Legend) that lasted, along with the Inquisition, into the 18th century.

A Protestant heretic appears before the royal family, his last chance to repent and convert.

A convicted defendant, forced to wear a red *sanbenito* robe, is led away to prison.

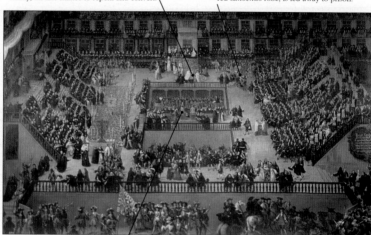

Those who have refused to confess are sentenced in public by day, and then executed before nightfall.

AUTO-DA-FÉ IN THE PLAZA MAYOR
This painting by Francisco Rizi (1683) depicts a trial, or *auto-da-fé* – literally, act of faith – held in Madrid's main square on June 30, 1680. Unlike papal inquisitions elsewhere in Europe, it was presided over by the reigning monarch, Carlos II, accompanied by his queen.

Torture *was widely used by the Inquisitors and their assistants to extract confessions from their victims. This early 19th-century German engraving shows a man being roasted on a wheel.*

The Procession of the Flagellants *(c.1812) by Goya shows the abiding influence of the Inquisition on the popular imagination. The penitents in the picture are wearing the tall conical hats of heretics tried by the Inquisition. These hats can still be seen in Easter Week processions (see p34) throughout Spain.*

Iglesia de San Nicolás ❺

Calle San Nicolás 1. **Map** 1 C3. ☎
(91) 559 40 64. ⓜ Ópera. ⏰ 9am–
1:30pm, 5:30–8pm Mon, 9am–noon,
5:30–8pm Tue, 9–10am, 6:30–8pm
Wed–Sat; 10am–2pm, 6:30–8pm Sun.

THE FIRST MENTION of the
church of San Nicolás is in
a document of 1202. Its brick
tower, with horseshoe arches,
is the oldest surviving ecclesiastical structure in Madrid. It
is thought to be 12th-century
Mudéjar in style, and may have
originally been the minaret of
a Moorish mosque.

Plaza de Oriente ❻

Map 1 C3. ⓜ Ópera.

DURING HIS DAYS as king of
Spain, Joseph Bonaparte
(see p59) carved out this
stirrup-shaped space from the
jumble of buildings to the
east of the Palacio Real (see
pp266–7), providing the view
of the palace enjoyed today.

The square was once an
important meeting place for
state occasions; kings, queens,
and dictators all made public
appearances on the palace
balcony facing the plaza. The
many statues of early kings
which stand here were originally intended for the palace
roofline, but proved too heavy.
The equestrian statue of Felipe
IV in the center of the square
is by Italian sculptor Pietro

Equestrian statue of Felipe IV, by
Pietro Tacca, Plaza de Oriente

View of Nuestra Señora de la Almudena and the Royal Palace

Tacca and is based on drawings by Velázquez. Facing the
palace, across the square, is
the imposing Teatro Real, or
Teatro de la Ópera, inaugurated in 1850 by Isabel II.

Nuestra Señora de la Almudena ❼

Calle de Bailén. 8–10. **Map** 1 B3.
☎ (91) 542 22 00. ⓜ Ópera. ⏰
10am–1:30pm, 6–7:30pm Mon–Sat,
10am–2:30 pm, 6–7:30pm Sun. ♿

DEDICATED TO the city's
patron, the cathedral of
La Almudena was begun in
1879 and completed over a
century later. Construction
was slow – ceasing completely
during the Civil War – and
involved several architects. The
cathedral's Neo-Gothic gray
and white façade is similar to
that of the Palacio Real, which
stands opposite. The crypt
houses a 16th-century image
of the Virgen de la Almudena.

Farther along the Calle
Mayor is the site of excavations, which have unearthed
the remains of Moorish and
medieval city walls.

Campo del Moro ❽

Map 1 A3. ⓜ Norte. ⏰ 10:30am–
8pm daily.

THE CAMPO DEL MORO (the
"Field of the Moor") is a
pleasing park, rising steeply
from the Río Manzanares to
offer one of the finest views of
the Palacio Real (see pp266–7).

The park has a varied
history. In 1109 a Moorish
army, led by Ali ben Yusuf
bivouacked here, hence the
name. The park went on to
become a jousting ground for
Christian knights. In the late
19th century it was used as a
lavish playground for royal
children. Around the same
time it was landscaped in what
is described as English style,
with winding paths, grass and
woodland, fountains, and
statues. It was reopened to
the public in 1931 under the
Second Republic (see p61),
closed again under Franco, and
not reopened until 1983. The
Museo de Carruajes is situated
in the lower part of the park,
but is closed indefinitely. It
houses official royal carriages
and sedan chairs.

Palacio Real ❾

M ADRID'S VAST AND LAVISH ROYAL PALACE was built to impress. The site, on a high bluff over the Rió Manzanares, had been occupied for centuries by a royal fortress, but after a fire in 1734, Felipe V commissioned a truly palatial replacement. Construction lasted 26 years, spanning the reign of two Bourbon monarchs, and much of the exuberant decor reflects the tastes of Carlos III and Carlos IV *(see p67)*. The palace was used by the royal family until the abdication of Alfonso XIII in 1931. The present king, Juan Carlos I, lives in the more modest Zarzuela Palace outside Madrid, but the Royal Palace is still used for state occasions.

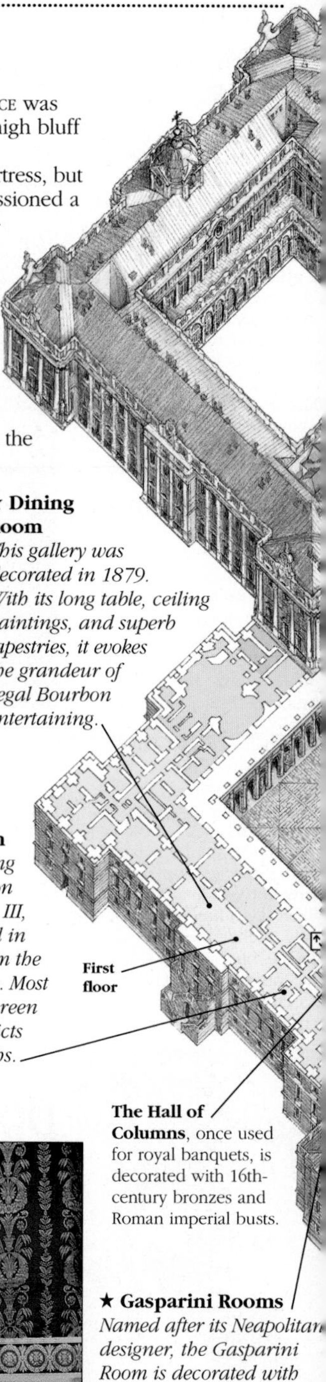

Statue of Carlos III

★ Dining Room
This gallery was decorated in 1879. With its long table, ceiling paintings, and superb tapestries, it evokes the grandeur of regal Bourbon entertaining.

★ Porcelain Room
The walls and ceiling of this room, built on the orders of Carlos III, are entirely covered in royal porcelain from the Buen Retiro factory. Most of the porcelain is green and white and depicts cherubs and wreaths.

First floor

The Hall of Columns, once used for royal banquets, is decorated with 16th-century bronzes and Roman imperial busts.

★ Gasparini Rooms
Named after its Neapolitan designer, the Gasparini Room is decorated with lavish rococo chinoiserie. The adjacent antechamber, with painted ceiling and ornate chandelier, houses Goya's portrait of Carlos IV.

STAR FEATURES

★ Dining Room

★ Porcelain Room

★ Gasparini Rooms

★ Throne Room

Plaza de la Armería
The square in front of the main entrance is named after the palace's Royal Armory. The outstanding collection of weaponry includes the suits of armor belonging to Charles V and Felipe II.

Entrance Hall
A marble staircase by ...batini, next to the statue of ...los III as a Roman emperor, ...eads to the main floor. The painted rococo ceiling by Giaquinto vividly depicts allegorical scenes.

Billiards room

Hall of the Halberdiers

Entrance

Plaza de la Armería

Ticket office

oyal rmory

★ **Throne Room**
The two gold and scarlet thrones here are exact reproductions of those of Charles V. The enormous mirrors were made in the royal glass factory of La Granja.

Pharmacy
This unique collection includes decorated Talavera pottery storage jars and herb drawers. The Pharmacy Museum has recipe books detailing medications prescribed for the royal family.

KEY TO FLOOR PLAN

☐	Exhibition rooms
☐	Entrance rooms
☐	Carlos III rooms
☐	Chapel rooms
☐	Carlos IV rooms

Entrance to the Monasterio de la Encarnación

Monasterio de la Encarnación ⑩

Plaza de la Encarnación 1. **Map** 1 C2.
C *(91) 547 05 10.* **M** *Ópera, Santo Domingo.* ☐ *10:30am–12:30pm, 4–5:30pm Wed & Sat, 11am–2pm Sun.* 🎫 🚹

STANDING in a delightful tree-shaded square, this tranquil Augustinian convent was founded in 1611 for Margaret of Austria, wife of Felipe III. The architect, Juan Gómez de la Mora, also built the Plaza Mayor *(see p263)*, and the façade clearly reveals his work.

The interior of the convent, which is still inhabited by nuns, has the atmosphere of old Castile, with its blue and white Talavera tiles, wooden doors, exposed beams, and portraits of royal benefactors.

Inside is a collection of 17th-century art, with paintings by José de Ribera and Vincente Carducho lining the walls. Polychrome wooden statues include *Christ at the Column*, by Gregorio Fernández.

The convent's main attraction is the reliquary chamber with a ceiling painted by Carducho. It is used to store the skulls and bones of saints. There is also a phial containing the dried blood of St. Pantaleon. According to a popular myth, the blood liquefies each year on July 27, the anniversary of the saint's death. Should the blood fail to lique-fy, it is said that disaster will befall Madrid. The church,

rebuilt by Ventura Rodríguez after a fire in 1767, has paintings by Francisco Bayeu (Goya's brother-in-law) and frescoes by Luca Giordano.

Plaza de España ⑪

Map 1 C1. **M** *Plaza de España.*

ONE OF MADRID's busiest traffic intersections and most popular meeting places is the Plaza de España, which slopes down toward the Palacio Real *(see pp266–7)* and the Sabatini Gardens. In the 18th and 19th centuries the square was occupied by military barracks, built here because of the square's close proximity to the palace. How-ever, further expansion of Madrid resulted in the square being left as a public space.

The square acquired its present appearance during the Franco period *(see pp62–3)*, with the construction, on the northern side, of the massive Edificio de España in 1948. Across the square is the Torre de Madrid (1957), known as

La Jirafa (the Giraffe), which, for a while, was the tallest concrete structure in the world. The most attractive part of the square is its center, occupied by a massive stone obelisk built in 1928. In front of it is a statue of the author Cervantes *(see p315)*. Below him, Don Quixote *(see pp376–7)* rides his horse Rocinante while the plump Sancho Panza trots alongside on his donkey. On the left-hand side is Dulcinea, Don Quixote's sweetheart.

Gran Vía ⑫

Map 2 D1. **M** *Plaza de España, Santo Domingo, Callao, Gran Vía.*

A MAIN TRAFFIC ARTERY of the modern city, the Gran Vía, was inaugurated in 1910. Its construction spanned several decades and required the demolition of large numbers of run-down buildings and small lanes between the Calle de Alcalá and the Plaza de España. This somewhat hap-hazard road-building plan soon became the subject of a

Stone obelisk with statue of Miguel de Cervantes, Plaza de España

◁ **Nighttime traffic on the Gran Vía, seen from the Plaza de España**

One of the many 1930s buildings lining the Gran Vía

zarzuela – a comic opera – that most *Madrileño* of art forms *(see p306)*. Nowadays, the Gran Vía is at the center of city life and, following a much needed restoration program, it has become an architectural showpiece.

The most interesting buildings are clustered at the Alcalá end, starting with the Corinthian columns, high level statuary, and tiled dome of the Edificio Metrópolis *(see p274)*.

A temple with Art Nouveau mosaics on its upper levels crowns Number 1 Gran Vía. One feature of buildings at this end of the street is colonnaded galleries on the upper floors, imitating medieval Aragonese and Catalan architecture. Another is the fine wrought-iron balconies and carved stone details, such as the gargoyle-like caryatids at Number 12. This part of the Gran Vía has a number of old-world Spanish shops.

On the Red de San Luis, an intersection of four major roads, is the Telefónica building. As the capital's first skyscraper (1929) the building caused a sensation. Beyond here, the Gran Vía becomes much more American in character, with movie theaters, tourist shops and many cafés.

Opposite Callao metro station, on the corner of the Calle Jacometrezo, is another of Madrid's well-known buildings, the Art Deco Capitol cinema and bingo hall, which was built in the 1930s.

Monasterio de las Descalzas Reales **❸**

Plaza de las Descalzas 3. **Map** 2 E3.
 (91) 542 00 59. Sol, Callao.
 10:30am–12:30pm, 4–5:30pm Tue–Thu & Sat, 10:30am–12:30pm Fri, 11am–1:30pm Sun.

MADRID'S MOST notable religious building has a soothing, handsome exterior in red brick and granite. This is one of the rare surviving examples of 16th-century architecture in the city.

Around 1560 Felipe II's sister, Doña Juana, decided to convert the original medieval palace which stood here into a convent for nuns and women of the royal household. Her high rank, and that of her fellow nuns, accounts for the massive store of art and wealth of the Descalzas Reales (Royal Barefoot Sisters).

The richly painted stairway has a fresco of Felipe IV and his family looking downwards, as if from a balcony, and a fine ceiling by Claudio Coello and his pupils. It leads up to a small first-floor cloister, which is ringed with chapels containing works of art and precious objects relating to the lives of the former nuns. The main chapel contains the tomb of Doña Juana. The Gran Sala de Tapices contains several series

Decorated chapel, Monasterio de las Descalzas Reales

of tapestries, one woven in Brussels in 1627 for Felipe II's daughter, Isabel Clara Eugenia. Another, *The Triumph of the Eucharist*, is based on drawings by Rubens. Major paintings on show include works by Brueghel the Elder, Titian, Zurbarán, Murillo, and Ribera.

Fray Pedro Machado by Zurbarán

Real Academia de Bellas Artes **❹**

Calle de Alcalá 13. **Map** 3 A5.
 (91) 532 15 46. Sevilla, Sol.
 9am–7pm Tue–Fri, 9am–2:30pm Sat–Mon & public hols.

FAMOUS FORMER STUDENTS of this art academy, housed in an 18th-century building by Churriguera *(see p21)*, include Dalí and Picasso. Its art gallery displays a large selection of works, including excellent drawings by Raphael and Titian. A superb collection of old masters includes paintings by Rubens and Van Dyck. Spanish artists from the 16th to the 19th centuries are particularly well represented, with several magnificent works by Ribera, Murillo, El Greco, and Velázquez. One of the highlights is Zurbarán's *Fray Pedro Machado*, typical of the artist's paintings of monks.

An entire room is devoted to Goya, a former director of the academy. On display here are his painting of a relaxed Manuel Godoy *(see p58)*, the *Burial of the Sardine (see p35)*, the grim *Madhouse*, and a self-portrait painted in 1815.

BOURBON MADRID

To the east of Old Madrid there once lay an idyllic district of market gardens known as the Prado, the "Meadow." In the 16th century a monastery was built on this rising ground. The Hapsburgs extended it to form a palace *(see p287)*, of which only fragments now remain; the palace gardens are now the popular Parque del Retiro. The Bourbon monarchs, especially Carlos III, chose this area to expand and embellish the city in the 18th century. Around the Paseo del Prado they built grand squares with fountains, a triumphal gateway, and what was to become the Museo del Prado, one of the world's greatest art galleries. A more recent addition to the area is the Centro de Arte Reina Sofía, a collection of modern Spanish art.

SIGHTS AT A GLANCE

Historic Buildings
Ateneo de Madrid ⑬
Café Gijón ⑮
Casa de Lope de Vega ⑩
Congreso de los Diputados ⑭
Estación de Atocha ㉑
Hotel Ritz ①
Real Academia de la
  Historia ⑪
Teatro Español ⑫

Museums and Galleries
*Centro de Arte Reina
  Sofía pp288–9* ㉒
Museo Arqueológico
  Nacional ⑱
Museo del Ejército ⑦
Museo Nacional de
  Artes Decorativas ⑥
Museo del Prado pp282–5 ⑨
*Museo Thyssen-
  Bornemisza pp278–9* ③

Churches
Iglesia de San Jerónimo
  el Real ⑧

Monuments
Puerta de
  Alcalá ⑤

Streets, Squares, and Parks
Calle de Serrano ⑰
Parque del Retiro ⑲
Plaza Cánovas del Castillo ②
Plaza de Cibeles ④
Plaza de Colón ⑯
Real Jardín Botánico ⑳

GETTING THERE
The subway is the fastest and easiest way to get to and around Bourbon Madrid. Lines 1, 2, and 4 serve all of the main sights. Useful buses include routes 14, 15, and 27 to the Plaza de Cibeles.

KEY

   Street-by-Street map *pp272–3*

◈ Metro station

🚉 Railroad station

🚌 Bus station

ℹ Tourist information

🅿 Parking

| 0 meters | 200 |
| 0 yards | 200 |

◁ **The expansive Parque del Retiro, which once formed the gardens of a Hapsburg palace**

Street-by-Street: Paseo del Prado

Façade of Banco de España

I N THE LATE 18TH CENTURY, before the museums and lavish hotels of Bourbon Madrid took shape, the Paseo del Prado was laid out and soon became a fashionable spot for strolling. Today the Paseo's main attraction lies in its museums and art galleries. Most notable are the Museo del Prado (just south of the Plaza Cánovas del Castillo) and the Museo Thyssen-Bornemisza, both displaying world famous collections of paintings. Among the grand monuments built under Carlos III are the Puerta de Alcalá and the Fuente de Cibeles, which stand in the middle of busy traffic circles.

The Paseo del Prado, based on the Piazza Navona in Rome, was built by Carlos III as a center for the arts and sciences in Madrid.

Banco de Espana Metro

The Edificio Metrópolis
(see p271), on the corner of Gran Vía and Calle de Alcalá, was built in 1905. Its façade is distinctively Parisian.

Banco de España

★ **Museo Thyssen-Bornemisza**
This excellent art collection occupies the Neo-Classical Villahermosa Palace, completed in 1806 ❸

STAR SIGHTS

★ **Museo Thyssen-Bornemisza**

★ **Puerta de Alcalá**

★ **Plaza de Cibeles**

Congreso de los Diputados
Spain's parliament has been witness to the transition from dictatorship to democracy (see pp64–5) ⓴

Plaza de Canovas del Castillo
In the middle of this large square stands a sculpted fountain of the god Neptune in his chariot ❷

PLAZA DE LAS CORTES

PLAZA CANOVAS

DEL CASTILLO

To Museo del Prado

Hotel Palace

0 meters	100
0 yards	100

★ Puerta de Alcalá
Sculpted from granite, this former gateway into the city is especially beautiful when floodlit at night 5

LOCATOR MAP
See Street Finder maps 3–6

Palacio de Comunicaciones

Palacio de Linares

★ Plaza de Cibeles
A fountain with a statue of the Roman goddess Cybele stands in this square 4

The Museo Nacional de Artes Decorativas
This museum, near the Retiro, was founded in 1912 as a showcase for Spanish ceramics and interior design 6

Museo del Ejército
This huge collection of military memorabilia is housed in part of the former Retiro Palace 7

Casón del Buen Retiro
(see p285)

Hotel Ritz
With its belle époque *interior, the Ritz is one of the most elegant hotels in Spain* 1

The Monumento del Dos de Mayo commemorates the War of Independence against the French *(see p59)*.

KEY

– – – Suggested route

Hotel Ritz ❶

Plaza de la Lealtad 5. **Map** 5 C1.
█ *(91) 521 28 57.* ⓜ *Banco de España.* ⓧ ♿

A FEW MINUTES' walk from the
Prado, this hotel is said to
be Spain's most extravagant.
It was commissioned in 1906
by Alfonso XIII because he
was embarrassed at the lack
of luxury accommodation in
the city for his wedding guests.

The opulence of the Ritz
(see p553) is reflected in its
prices. Each of the 158 rooms
is beautifully decorated in a
different style, with carpets
made by hand at the Real
Fábrica de Tapices *(see p296).*

At the start of the Civil War
(see pp62–3) the hotel was
converted into a hospital, and
it was here that the Anarchist
leader Buenaventura Durruti
died of his wounds in 1936.

The Fuente de Neptuno

Plaza Cánovas del Castillo ❷

Map 5 C1. ⓜ *Banco de España.*

T HIS BUSY TRAFFIC CIRCLE is
named after Antonio
Cánovas del Castillo, one of
the leading statesmen of 19th-
century Spain *(see p60),* who
was assassinated in 1897.

Dominating the plaza is the
Fuente de Neptuno – a fountain with a statue depicting
Neptune in his chariot, being
pulled by two horses. The
statue was designed in 1780
by Ventura Rodríguez as part
of Carlos III's plan to beautify
the eastern part of Madrid.

**Visitors admiring the works of art
in the Museo Thyssen-Bornemisza**

Museo Thyssen-Bornemisza ❸

See pp278–9.

Plaza de Cibeles ❹

Map 3 C5. ⓜ *Banco de España.* **Casa
de América** █ *(91) 595 48 00.* ⬜
11am–7pm Tue–Sat, 11am–2pm Sun.

I N ADDITION TO BEING one of
Madrid's best-known land-
marks, the Plaza de Cibeles is
also one of the most beautiful.

The Fuente de Cibeles stands
in the middle of the busy traffic island at the junction of the
Paseo del Prado and the Calle
de Alcalá. This fine sculpted
fountain is named after Cybele,
the Greco-Roman goddess of
nature, and shows her sitting in
her chariot, drawn by a pair of
lions. Designed in the late 18th
century by José Hermosilla and
Ventura Rodríguez, it is considered a symbol of Madrid.

Around the square rise four
important buildings, the most
impressive of which is the
main post office, the Palacio
de Comunicaciones, mock-
ingly known as "Our Lady of
Communications." Its unique
appearance – white, with high
pinnacles – is often compared
to a wedding cake. It was
built between 1905 and 1917
on the site of former gardens.

On the northeast side of the
square is the stone façade of
the Palacio de Linares, built by
the Marquis of Linares at the
time of the second Bourbon
restoration of 1875 *(see p60).*
At one time threatened with
demolition, the palace was
reprieved and converted into
the Casa de América, and
now displays a collection of
paintings by Latin American
artists. It is also used as a
venue for theatrical performances and lectures.

In the northwest corner of
the Plaza de Cibeles, surrounded by attractive gardens, is the
heavily guarded Army Headquarters, which is housed in
the buildings of the former
Palacio de Buenavista. The
palace was commissioned by
the Duchess of Alba in 1777
as a family residence, though
its construction was twice
delayed by fires.

Occupying a whole block
on the opposite corner is the
Banco de España, constructed
between 1884 and 1891. Its
design was inspired by the
Venetian Renaissance style,
with delicate ironwork adorning the roof and windows.
Much-needed renovation work
has returned the bank to its
late 19th-century magnificence.

The Fuente de Cibeles, with the Banco de España in the background

View through the central arch of the Puerta de Alcalá

Museo del Ejército **7**

Calle Méndez Núñez 1. **Map** 6 D1.
 (91) 522 89 77. Retiro.
 10am–2pm Tue–Sun.

SPAIN'S ARMY MUSEUM occupies one of the remaining parts of the 17th-century Palacio del Buen Retiro. Individual rooms are dedicated to the military history of different periods and house a vast array of weapons, from Moorish times up to the present day. The museum's grandest room, the Salón de Reinos, is named after the kingdoms which once made up Spain. These are depicted on the ceiling.

One of the highlights of the museum is the sword of El Cid – *La Tizona* – on display in the Sala de Armas. The tunic and sword of Boabdil, the final Moorish ruler of Granada *(see pp52–3)*, are exhibited in the Sala Árabe.

In the Sala Colonial there is a fragment of the cross which was planted in the ground by Columbus upon reaching the New World. In the same room is a piece of the tree under which Hernán Cortés took shelter during a rebellion by the Aztecs in Mexico *(see p54)*.

More recent events are illustrated by busts and flags from Spain's War of Independence *(see p59)*, in the Sala del Dos de Mayo. There are also several rooms devoted to the Spanish Civil War *(see pp62–3)*, as well as an entire room of tin soldiers.

Puerta de Alcalá **5**

Map 4 D5. Retiro.

THIS CEREMONIAL GATEWAY is the grandest of the monuments erected by Carlos III in his attempt to improve the looks of eastern Madrid. It was designed by Francesco Sabatini to replace a smaller Baroque gateway that had been built by Felipe III for the entry into Madrid of his wife, Margaret of Austria.

Construction of the gate began in 1769 and lasted nine years. It was built from granite in Neo-Classical style, with a lofty pediment and sculpted angels. It has five arches – three central and two outer rectangular ones.

Until the mid-19th century the gateway marked the city's easternmost boundary. It now stands in the busy Plaza de la Independencia, and is best seen when floodlit at night.

Museo Nacional de Artes Decorativas **6**

Calle de Montalbán 12. **Map** 4 D5.
 (91) 532 64 99. Retiro.
 9am–3pm Tue–Fri, 10am–2pm Sat, Sun & public hols.

HOUSED IN A 19th-century palace overlooking the Parque del Retiro, the National Museum of Decorative Arts contains an interesting collection of furniture and *objets d'art*. The exhibits are mainly from Spain and date back as far as Phoenician times.

One of the finest exhibits on the museum's five floors is a kitchen, moved here from an 18th-century Valencian mansion. Its 1,500 tiles depict a domestic scene from the era. There are also some excellent ceramic pieces from Talavera de la Reina *(see p368)*, and a collection of jewelry and ornaments from the Far East.

The sword of El Cid, *La Tizona*, in the Museo del Ejército

Museo Thyssen-Bornemisza ❸

THIS MAGNIFICENT MUSEUM is based on the collection assembled by Baron Heinrich Thyssen-Bornemisza and his son, Hans Heinrich, the present baron. It was installed in Madrid's 18th-century Villahermosa Palace in 1992, and was given to the nation the following year. From its beginnings in the 1920s, the collection was intended to illustrate the history of Western art, from Italian and Flemish primitives, through to 20th century Expressionism and Pop Art. The museum's outstanding collection, consisting of some 800 paintings, includes masterpieces by Titian, Goya, Van Gogh, and Picasso, as well as works by lesser known artists. It is regarded by many critics as the most important privately assembled art collection in the world.

★ Our Lady of the Dry Tree (c.1450)
This tiny painted panel is by Bruges master Petrus Christus. The letter A hanging from the tree stands for "Ave Maria."

★ Harlequin with a Mirror
The figure of the harlequin was a frequent subject of Picasso's. The careful composition in this 1923 canvas, which is thought by some to represent the artist himself, is typical of Picasso's "Classical" period.

STAR PAINTINGS

★ **Our Lady of the Dry Tree** by Christus

★ **Harlequin with a Mirror** by Picasso

★ **The Toilet of Venus** by Rubens

GALLERY GUIDE
The galleries are arranged around a covered central courtyard, which rises the full height of the building. The top floor starts with early Italian art and goes through to the 17th-century. The middle floor continues the story with 17th-century Dutch works and ends with German Express-ionism. The ground floor is dedicated to 20th-century paintings.

24
25
26
27
28
41
42
43
44
45
46
47
48

Hotel Room (1931)
Edward Hopper's painting is a study of urban isolation. The solitude is made less static by the suitcases and the train timetable on the woman's knee.

Portrait of Baron Thyssen-Bornemisz:
This informal portrait the present baron, aga the background of a Watteau painting, wa painted by Lucian Fre between 1981 and 19

★ **The Toilet of Venus**
This reflection of ideal beauty was painted by the Flemish master Rubens after 1629, showing his typically luscious use of color and form.

VISITORS' CHECKLIST

Paseo del Prado 8. **Map** 5 C1.
📞 *(91) 369 01 51.* Ⓜ *Banco de España, Sevilla.* 🚌 *1, 2, 5, 9, 14, 15, 20.* ◻ *10am–7pm Tue–Sun.* 🎫 ♿ 📷 🍴

St. Jerome in the Wilderness *(c.1575)*
Titian's work, painted when he was over 80, shows St. Jerome as a penitent, meditating on Christ's Passion. In his later career, the artist strove for poetic rather than simply narrative effects.

St. Casilda *(c.1630)*
Francisco de Zurbarán, best known for his depiction of monks in white habits, also painted saints. Here, the brilliant colors of St. Casilda's robe stand out against the plain background.

Main entrance

KEY TO FLOOR PLAN

- ◻ Ground floor
- ◻ First floor
- ◻ Second floor
- ◻ Nonexhibition space

Autumn Landscape in Oldenburg
Karl Schmidt-Rottluff was a member of the Brücke Expressionist group, founded in Dresden in 1905. He painted this North German landscape two years later.

Iglesia de San Jerónimo el Real ⑧

Calle del Moreto 4. **Map** 6 D1. ☎ *(91) 420 35 78.* Ⓜ *Banco de España.* ☐ *Oct–Jun: 8am–1:30pm, 5–8:30pm daily, (6–8:30pm Jul–Sep).* ⬤ *Easter Sat.* ♿

BUILT IN THE 16TH century for Queen Isabel, but since remodeled, San Jerónimo is Madrid's royal church. From the 17th century it became virtually a part of the Retiro palace which once stood here *(see p287)*. The church was

Castizos **during San Isidro**

MADRID'S FIESTAS

San Isidro *(May 15).* Madrid's great party around May 15 is in honor of St. Isidore, the humble 12th-century farmworker who became the city's patron. With a *corrida* every day, this is Spain's biggest bullfighting event. Throughout the city there are also art exhibitions, open-air concerts and fireworks. Many people dress in Madrid's *castizo* folk costume for the occasion.
The Passion *(Easter Saturday),* Chinchón. A passion play is performed in the town's atmospheric arcaded Plaza Mayor.
Dos de Mayo *(May 2).* This four-day holiday marks the city's uprising against Napoleon's troops in 1808 *(see p59).*
New Year's Eve. The nation focuses on the Puerta del Sol *(see p262)* at midnight as crowds gather to swallow a grape on each chime of the clock.

originally attached to the Hieronymite monastery that today stands beside it in ruins.

The church was the setting for the marriage of Alfonso XIII and Victoria Eugenia of Battenberg in 1906, and today it is a popular venue for high society weddings. King Juan Carlos I's coronation was held here in 1975.

Museo del Prado ⑨

See pp282–5

Casa de Lope de Vega ⑩

Calle de Cervantes 11. **Map** 5 B1. ☎ *(91) 429 92 16.* Ⓜ *Antón Martín.* ☐ *9:30am–2pm Tue–Fri, 10am–1:30pm Sat.* ⬤ *public hols.* 📷 ⦸

FÉLIX LOPE DE VEGA, a leading Golden Age writer *(see p30),* moved into this somber house in 1610. Here he wrote over two-thirds of his plays, thought to total almost 2,000.

Félix Lope de Vega

Meticulously restored in 1935 using some of Lope de Vega's own furniture, the house gives a great feeling of Castilian life in the early 17th century. A dark chapel with no external windows occupies the center, separated from the writer's bedroom by only a barred window. The small garden at the rear, complete with the original well, is planted with the flowers and fruit trees mentioned by the writer in his works. He died here in 1635.

Statue of Goya in front of the Prado

Sunlit balcony of the magnificent Teatro Español

Real Academia de la Historia ⓫

Calle León 21. **Map** 5 A2. *(91) 429 06 11.* ⓜ *Antón Martin.* ◯ *4–7pm Mon–Fri with letter of introduction from your embassy.* ⓘ

THE ROYAL ACADEMY of History is an austere brick building with stone trimmings, built by Juan de Villanueva in 1788. Its location, in the so-called Barrio de los Literatos (Writers' Quarter), is apt.

In 1898, the great intellectual and bibliophile, Marcelino Menéndez Pelayo, became director of the academy, living here until his death in 1912. The library, with more than 200,000 books and several important manuscripts, can be seen by arrangement.

Teatro Español ⓬

Calle del Príncipe 25. **Map** 5 A1. *(91) 429 62 97.* ⓜ *Sol.* ◯ *for performances from 7pm Tue–Sun.* ⓘ ⓘ

DOMINATING the Plaza Santa Ana is the Teatro Español, one of Madrid's oldest and most beautiful theaters. From 1583 on, many of Spain's finest plays, by leading dramatists of the time such as Lope de Rueda, were first performed in the Corral del Príncipe, which originally stood on this site. In 1802 this was replaced by the Teatro Español. The Neo-Classical façade, with pilasters and medallions, is by Juan de

Villanueva. Engraved on it are the names of great Spanish dramatists, including that of celebrated writer Federico García Lorca (see p31).

Ateneo de Madrid ⓭

Calle del Prado 21. **Map** 5 B1. *(91) 429 17 50.* ⓜ *Antón Martin, Sevilla.* ◯ *9am–1am Mon–Sat, 9am–10pm Sun & public hols.* ⓘ

FORMALLY FOUNDED IN 1835, this learned association has strongly liberal political leanings. It is similar to a gentlemen's club in atmosphere, with a grand stairway and paneled hall hung with the portraits of famous fellows. Closed down during past periods of repression and dictatorship, it is still a mainstay of liberal thought in Spain. Many leading Socialists are members of the Ateneo, along with writers and other intellectuals.

Carving on the façade of the Ateneo de Madrid

Congreso de los Diputados ⓮

Plaza de las Cortes. **Map** 5 B1. *(91) 390 60 00.* ⓜ *Sevilla.* ◯ *10am–12:30pm Sat and Mon–Fri by appointment.* ⓘ ⓘ

THIS IMPOSING YET attractive building is home to the Spanish parliament, the Cortes. Built in the mid-19th century on the site of a former convent, it is characterized by Classical columns, heavy pediments, and guardian bronze lions. It was here, in 1981, that Colonel Tejero of the Civil Guard held the deputies at gunpoint on national television, as he tried to spark off a military coup (see p64). His failure was seen as an indication that democracy was now firmly established in Spain.

Bronze lion guarding the Cortes

Café Gijón ⓯

Paseo de Recoletos 21. **Map** 3 C4. *(91) 521 54 25.* ⓜ *Banco de España.* ◯ *9am–1:30am Sun–Fri, 9am–2am Sat & public hols.* ⓘ

MADRID'S CAFE LIFE (see pp306–7) was one of the most attractive features of the city from the turn of the 20th century right up to outbreak of the Civil War. Of the many intellectuals' cafés which once thrived, only the Gijón survives. Today the café continues to attract a lively crowd of literati. With its cream-painted wrought-iron columns and black and white table tops, it is perhaps better known for its atmosphere than for its appearance.

Museo del Prado ❾

THE PRADO MUSEUM contains the world's greatest assembly of Spanish painting – especially works by Velázquez and Goya – ranging from the 12th to 19th centuries. It also houses impressive foreign collections, particularly of Italian and Flemish works. The Neo-Classical building was designed in 1785 by Juan de Villanueva on the orders of Carlos III. It opened as a museum in 1819 to display the royal collection of paintings, sculpture, and decorative arts. The Casón del Buen Retiro, the Prado's annex, has 19th- and 20th-century paintings and sculptures.

★ Velázquez Collection
The Triumph of Bacchus *(1628),*
Velázquez's first portrayal of a
mythological subject,
shows the god of wine
(Bacchus) with a group
of Bacchantes.

The Adoration of the Shepherds *(1612–14)*
This dramatic work shows the elongated figures and swirling garments typical of El Greco's style. It was painted during his late Mannerist period for his own funerary chapel.

STAR EXHIBITS

★ **Velázquez Collection**

★ **Goya Collection**

The Annunciation
Fra Angelico's work of c.1430 is a high point of Italy's Early Renaissance, as illustrated by the detailed architectural setting and deep perspective of the interior.

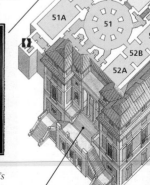

The Garden of Delights *(c.1516)*
Hieronymus Bosch (El Bosco in Spanish), one of Felipe II's favorite artists, is especially well represented in the Prado. This enigmatic painting depicts paradise and hell.

Main entrance

GALLERY GUIDE

The best way to enter the Prado is through the Puerta de Goya, on Calle Felipe IV, which leads on to the first floor. The works are arranged in schools. The first floor is largely dedicated to the Spanish School, the ground floor to the Flemish.

First floor

Ground floor

VISITORS' CHECKLIST

Paseo del Prado. **Map** 5 C2.
(91) 420 28 36. Atocha, Banco de España. 6, 10, 14, 19, 27, 34, 37, 45. 9am–7pm Tue–Sat, 9am–2pm Sun & public hols. Jan 1, Good Fri, May 1, Dec 25.
Cason del Buen Retiro: Calle de Alfonso XII 28. (91) 420 26 28. as above. one ticket covers both parts of museum.

★ **Goya Collection**
In The Clothed Maja *and* The Naked Maja *(both c.1800), Goya tackled the taboo subject of nudity, for which he was later accused of obscenity.*

The Three Graces *(c.1639)*
This was one of the last paintings by the Flemish master Rubens, and was part of the artist's personal collection. The three figures dancing in a ring – the Graces – are the daughters of Zeus, and represent Love, Joy, and Revelry.

The Martyrdom of St. Philip *(c.1630)*
José de Ribera moved from his native Valencia to Naples as a young man. There he was influenced by Caravaggio's dramatic use of light and shadow, known as chiaroscuro, as seen in this work.

KEY TO FLOOR PLAN

- Spanish painting
- Flemish and Dutch painting
- Italian painting
- French painting
- German painting
- Sculpture
- Temporary exhibitions
- Nonexhibition space

Exploring the Prado's Collection

THE IMPORTANCE OF THE PRADO is founded on its royal collections. The wealth of foreign art, including many of Europe's finest works, reflects the historical power of the Spanish crown (see pp54–9). The Low Countries and parts of Italy were under Spanish domination for centuries. The 18th century was an era of French influence, following the Bourbon accession to the Spanish throne. The Prado is worthy of repeated visits, but if you go only once, see the Spanish works of the 17th century.

Saturn Devouring One of His Sons (1820–23) by Francisco de Goya

St. Dominic of Silos Enthroned as Abbot (1474–7) by Bermejo

SPANISH PAINTING

RIGHT UP TO THE 19th century, Spanish painting focused on religious and royal themes. Although the limited subject matter was in some ways a restriction, it also offered a sharp focus that seems to have suited Spanish painters.

Spain's early medieval art is represented somewhat sketchily in the Prado, but there are some examples such as the anonymous mural paintings from the Holy Cross hermitage in Maderuelo, which show a Romanesque heaviness of line and forceful characterization.

Spanish Gothic art can be seen in the Prado in the works of Bartolomé Bermejo and Fernando Gallego. The sense of realism in their paintings was borrowed from Flemish masters of the time.

Renaissance features began to emerge in the works of painters such as Pedro de Berruguete, whose Auto-da-fé is both chilling and lively. St. Catherine, by Fernando Yáñez de la Almedina, shows the influence of Leonardo da Vinci, for whom Yáñez probably worked while training in Italy.

What is often considered as a truly Spanish style – with its highly-wrought emotion and deepening somberness – first started to emerge in the 16th century in the paintings of the Mannerists. This is evident both in Pedro Machuca's fierce Descent from the Cross and in the Madonnas of Luis de Morales, "the Divine." The elongation of the human figure in Morales' work is carried to a greater extreme by Domenikos Theotocopoulos, better known as El Greco (see p28). Although many of his masterpieces remain in his adopted town

of Toledo (see p373), the Prado has an impressive collection, including The Nobleman with His Hand on His Chest.

The Golden Age (see pp56–7) was a particularly productive time for Spanish art. José de Ribera, who lived in (Spanish) Naples, followed Caravaggio in combining realism of character with the techniques of chiaroscuro and tenebrism. Another master who employed this method was Francisco Ribalta, whose Christ Embracing St. Bernard is here. Zurbarán, known for his still lifes and portraits of saints and monks, is also a notable presence in the Prado.

This period, however, is best represented by the work of Diego Velázquez. As the country's leading court painter from his late twenties until his death, he produced scenes of heightened realism, royal portraits, and religious as well as mythological paintings. Some examples of all of these are displayed in the Prado. Perhaps his greatest work is Las Meninas (see pp28–9).

Another great Spanish painter, Goya, revived Spanish art in the 18th century. He initially specialized in designs for tapestries, then became a court painter. His work went on to embrace the horrors of war, as seen here in The Third of May (see pp58–9), and culminated in a somber series known as The Black Paintings.

Still Life with Four Vessels (c.1658–64) by Francisco de Zurbarán

CASÓN DEL BUEN RETIRO

On the hill behind the Prado is its annex, the Casón del Buen Retiro, once part of the Palacio del Buen Retiro *(see p287)*. Its exhibits include late 19th-century and early 20th-century works, as well as Neo-Classical and Romantic art, and paintings on historical themes. Some of the best paintings are by artists such as Mariano Fortuny, Santiago Rusiñol, and the Impressionist Joaquín Sorolla *(see p295)*.

Children at the Beach (1910) by Joaquín Sorolla

FLEMISH AND DUTCH PAINTING

SPAIN'S LONG CONNECTION with the Low Countries *(see pp56–7)* led naturally to an intense admiration for the so-called Flemish primitives. Many exceptional works now hang in the Prado. *St. Barbara*, by Robert Campin, has a quirky intimacy, and Rogier van der Weyden's *The Deposition* is an unquestioned masterpiece. Most notable of all, however, are Hieronymus Bosch's weird and eloquent inventions, which were collected by Felipe II. The Prado has some of his major paintings, including the *Temptation of St. Anthony* and *The Haywain*. Works from the 16th century include the magnificent *Triumph of Death* by Brueghel the Elder. There are nearly 100 canvases by the 17th-century Flemish painter Peter Paul Rubens, of which the greatest is *The Adoration of the Magi*. The two most notable Dutch paintings on display are by Rembrandt: *Artemisia*, and a fine self-portrait.

David Victorious over Goliath (c.1600) by Caravaggio

ITALIAN PAINTING

THE PRADO IS THE ENVY of many museums, not least for its vast collection of Italian paintings. Botticelli's dramatic wooden panels telling *The Story of Nastagio degli Onesti*, a vision of a knight forever condemned to hunt down and kill his own beloved, are a sinister high point. Raphael contributes the superb *Christ Falls on the Way to Calvary* and the sentimental *The Holy Family of the Lamb*.

Christ Washing the Disciples' Feet, by Tintoretto, is a profound masterpiece. Venetian masters Veronese and Titian are also very well represented. Titian served as court painter to Charles V, and few works express the drama of Hapsburg rule so deeply as his somber painting *The Emperor Charles V at Mühlberg*. Also on display are works by Giordano, Caravaggio and Tiepolo, master of Italian rococo.

FRENCH PAINTING

MARRIAGES BETWEEN French and Spanish royalty in the 17th century, culminating in the Bourbon accession to the throne in the 18th century, brought French art to Spain. The Prado has eight works attributed to Poussin, among them his serene *Parnassus* and *Landscape with St. Jerome*. The magnificent *Landscape with the Embarkation of St. Paula Romana at Ostia* is the best work here by Claude Lorrain. Among the 18th-century artists featured are Antoine Watteau and Jean Ranc. *Felipe V* is the work of the royal portraitist Louis-Michel van Loo.

GERMAN PAINTING

ALTHOUGH GERMAN ART is not especially well represented in the Prado, there are several paintings by Albrecht Dürer, such as his lively *Self-Portrait*, painted at the age of 26. Lucas Cranach also figures. Works by the late 18th-century painter Anton Raffael Mengs include portraits of Carlos III.

The Deposition (c.1430) by Rogier van der Weyden

Floor mosaic in the Museo Arqueológico Nacional

Plaza de Colón ⑯

Map 4 D3. 🚇 *Serrano, Colón.*

THIS LARGE SQUARE, one of Madrid's focal points, is dedicated to Christopher Columbus (Colón in Spanish). It is overlooked by huge highrises, built in the 1970s to replace the 19th-century mansions that stood here.

On the south side is a palace housing the National Library and Archaeological Museum. The Post-Modernist skyscraper the Heron Corporation towers over the square from the far side of the Paseo de la Castellana.

The real feature of the square, however, is the pair of monuments dedicated to the discoverer of the Americas. The prettiest, and oldest, is a Neo-Gothic spire made in 1885, with Columbus at its top, pointing west. Carved reliefs on the plinth give highlights of his discoveries. Across the square is the second, more modern monument – a cluster of four large concrete shapes inscribed with quotations about Columbus's journey to America *(see p53)*.

Constantly busy with traffic, the plaza may seem an unlikely venue for cultural events. Beneath it, however, is an extensive complex, the Centro Cultural de la Villa de Madrid, which includes the city's municipal art center,

Statue of Columbus, Plaza de Colón

exhibition halls, lecture rooms, a theater, and a café. The terminal for the bus that runs to and from the airport *(see p626)* is also located underground.

Calle de Serrano ⑰

Map 4 D4. 🚇 *Serrano.*

NAMED AFTER a 19th-century politician, Madrid's most stylish shopping street runs from the Plaza de la Independencia to the Plaza de la República Argentina, in the district of Salamanca. The street is lined with shops *(p304)* – many with luxury items – housed in old mansions. Several of the country's top designers, including Adolfo Domínguez and Alfredo Villalba, have boutiques toward the north, near the Museo Lázaro Galdiano *(see p295)*. Branches of both Versace and Armani can be found on the Calle de José Ortega y Gasset. Lower down the Calle de Serrano, toward Serrano metro station, is a branch of the British chain store Marks & Spencer, which has become popular among Spaniards and tourists alike. On the Calle de Claudio Coello, which runs parallel with Serrano, there are several lavish antique shops, in keeping with the upscale atmosphere of this area.

Museo Arqueológico Nacional ⑱

Calle de Serrano 13. **Map** 4 D3.
📞 (91) 577 79 12. 🚇 *Serrano.*
🕐 9:30am – 8:30pm Tue – Sat,
9:30am – 2:30pm Sun. 📷 ♿

WITH HUNDREDS of exhibits, ranging from prehistoric times to the 19th century, this museum is one of Madrid's best. Founded by Isabel II in 1867, it consists mainly of material uncovered during excavations all over Spain, as well as pieces from Egypt, Ancient Greece, and the Etruscan civilization.

The earliest finds – from the prehistoric era – are arranged in chronological order in the basement. Highlights include an exhibition on the ancient civilization of El Argar in Andalusia *(see p44)*, and a display of jewelry uncovered at the Roman settlement of Numantia, near Soria *(see p359)*.

The museum's ground floor is largely devoted to the period between Roman and Mudéjar Spain. Iberian culture is also represented on this floor, with two notable sculptures – *La Dama de Elche (see p44)* and *La Dama de Baza.*

The Roman period is illustrated with some impressive mosaics, including *Monks and Seasons*, from Hellín (Albacete), and *Bacchus and his Train*, from Zaragoza.

Outstanding pieces from the Visigothic period include a collection of 7th-century gold votive crowns from Toledo province, known as the Treasure of Guarrazar.

The Islamic era is represented by pottery uncovered from Medina Azahara in Andalusia *(see p453)*, as well as bronze and metal objects.

Romanesque exhibits include an ivory crucifix carved in 1063 for Fernando I of Castilla-León and his Queen, Doña Sancha, and the *Madonna and Child* from Sahagún, considered a masterpiece of Spanish art.

Steps outside the museum's entrance lead underground to an exact replica of the Altamira caves in Cantabria *(see p108)* – complete with their paintings of the early Paleolithic era.

Parque del Retiro ⑲

Map 6 E1. 📞 *(91) 573 60 82.*
Ⓜ *Retiro, Ibiza, Atocha.* ♿

T HE RETIRO PARK, in Madrid's stylish Jerónimos district, takes its name from Felipe IV's royal palace complex, which once stood here. Nowadays, all that remains of the palace is the Casón del Buen Retiro *(see p285)* and the Museo del Ejército *(see p277)*.

Used privately by the royal family from 1632, the park became the scene of elaborate pageants, bullfights, and mock naval battles. In the 18th century it was partially opened to the public, provided visitors were formally dressed, and in 1869 it was fully opened. Today, the Retiro remains one of the most popular places for relaxing in Madrid.

A short stroll from the park's northern entrance down the tree-lined avenue leads to the pleasure lake, where row boats can be rented. On one side of the lake is a half-moon colonnade in front of which an equestrian statue of Alfonso XII rides high on a column. Opposite, portrait painters and fortune-tellers ply their trade.

To the south of the lake are two attractive palaces. The Neo-Classical, red brick Palacio de Velázquez and the Palacio de Cristal (Crystal Palace) were built by Velázquez Bosco in 1887 as venues for exhibitions held during the same year.

Statue of Bourbon king Carlos III in the Real Jardín Botánico

Real Jardín Botánico ⑳

Plaza de Murillo 2. **Map** 6 D2.
📞 *(91) 420 30 17.* Ⓜ *Atocha.*
🕙 *10am–8pm daily.* ♿

S OUTH OF the Prado *(see pp282–5)*, the Royal Gardens are a suitable place for resting after visiting the gallery. Inspired by Carlos III, they were designed in 1781 by botanist Gómez Ortega and Juan de Villanueva, the architect of the Prado.

Interest in the plants of South America and the Philippines took hold during the Spanish Enlightenment *(see p58)*, and the neatly laid out beds offer a huge variety of flora, ranging from trees and shrubs to medicinal plants and herbs.

Estación de Atocha ㉑

Plaza del Emperador Carlos V. **Map** 6 D4. 📞 *(91) 506 68 46.* Ⓜ *Atocha RENFE.* 🕙 *7am –11:30pm daily.* ♿

M ADRID'S FIRST railroad service, from Atocha to Aranjuez, was inaugurated in 1851. Forty years later Atocha station was replaced by a new building that was given a modern extension in the 1980s. The older part of the station, built of glass and wrought iron, now houses a pleasant indoor palm garden. Adjoining it is the modern terminal for the high-speed AVE trains to Córdoba and Seville *(see p630)*.

The Ministerio de Agricultura, across the road, is a splendid late 19th-century building adorned with tiled corner domes and rooftop statuary.

Entrance of Madrid's Estación de Atocha, busy with travelers

Monument of Alfonso XII (1901), facing the Retiro's boating lake

Centro de Arte Reina Sofía ㉒

THE HIGHLIGHT of this museum of 20th-century art is without doubt Picasso's *Guernica*. There are other major works not to be missed, by influential artists including Miró and Picasso. The collection is housed in Madrid's former General Hospital, built in the late 18th century. Two exterior glass elevators were added in 1992 when the building was converted into the Art Center. The interior is now a computer-controlled environment, but it retains much of the atmosphere of the original building.

Portrait II *(19...*
*Joan Miró's hu...
enigmatic wor...
shows element...
Surrealism, de...
being painted ...
than ten years ...
after the end o...
his true
Surrealist
period.*

★ **Woman in Blue** *(1901)*
Picasso disowned this work after it won only an honorable mention in a national competition. Decades later it was located and acquired by the Spanish state.

Guernica

Landscape at Cadaqués
Salvador Dalí was born in Figueres in Catalonia. He became a frequent visitor to the town of Cadaqués, on the Costa Brava (see p207), where he painted this landscape in the summer of 1923.

Second floor

Accident
Alfonso Ponce de León's disturbing work, painted in 1936, prefigured his death in a car crash later that same year.

STAR EXHIBITS

★ **Woman in Blue**
by Picasso

★ **La Tertulia del Café
de Pombo** by Solana

★ **Guernica** by Picasso

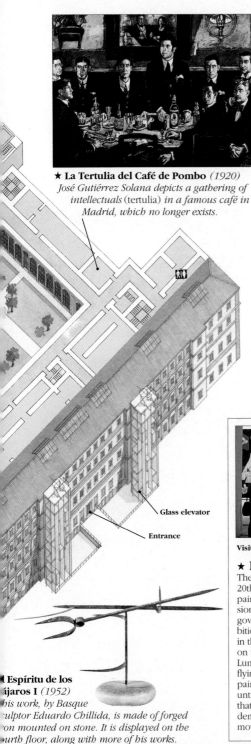

★ **La Tertulia del Café de Pombo** *(1920)*
*José Gutiérrez Solana depicts a gathering of
intellectuals* (tertulia) *in a famous café in
Madrid, which no longer exists.*

Glass elevator

Entrance

◄ **Espíritu de los
 ájaros I** *(1952)*
*his work, by Basque
 :ulptor Eduardo Chillida, is made of forged
 on mounted on stone. It is displayed on the
 ourth floor, along with more of his works.*

VISITORS' CHECKLIST

Calle Santa Isabel 52. **Map** 5 C3.
[*(91) 467 50 62.* **⊕** *Atocha.*
⊞ *6, 14, 18, 19, 27, 45, 55, 68.*
◯ *10am–9pm Mon & Wed–Sat,
10am–2:30pm Sun.* **●** *Jan 1,
Dec 24, 25, 31 & some public
hols.* **☒** *(free of charge on Sun).*
⊘ ⅙ ⅋ ¶

GALLERY GUIDE
*The permanent collection is on
the second and fourth floors,
arranged around an open
courtyard. It traces art through
the 20th century, from its
beginnings to the present day.
The second floor is dedicated to
paintings from the earlier part
of the century, with individual
rooms allocated to significant
artists such as Dalí, Miró, and
Picasso. The fourth floor continues with post-World War II
to contemporary works, via
movements such as Abstract,
Pop, and Minimalist Art.*

KEY TO FLOOR PLAN

☐ Exhibition space

☐ Nonexhibition space

Visitors admiring *Guernica*

★ PICASSO'S GUERNICA
The most famous single work of the
20th century, this Civil War protest
painting *(see pp62–3)* was commissioned by the Spanish Republican
government in 1937 for a Paris exhibition. The artist found his inspiration
in the mass air attack of the same year
on the Basque town of Guernika-
Lumo *(see p114)*, by German pilots
flying for the Nationalist air force. The
painting hung in a New York gallery
until 1981, reflecting the artist's wish
that it should not return to Spain until
democracy was reestablished. It was
moved here from the Prado in 1992.

FARTHER AFIELD

SEVERAL OF MADRID'S best sights, including some interesting but little-known museums, lie outside the city center. The axis of modern Madrid is the Paseo de la Castellana, a long, wide avenue lined by skyscraper offices, and busy with traffic. A journey along it gives a glimpse of Madrid as Spain's commercial and administrative capital. La Castellana skirts the Barrio de Salamanca, an up-scale district of stylish boutiques, named after the 19th-century aristocrat who built it, the Marquis de Salamanca.

Statue in Plaza de Cascorro

The districts around Old Madrid, especially Malasaña and La Latina, offer a more typically authentic *Madrileño* atmosphere. On Sundays, some of the old streets are crowded with bargain-hunters at the sprawling second-hand market, El Rastro. If you need to escape from the bustle of the city for a while, west of Old Madrid, across the Río Manzanares, is Madrid's vast, green recreation ground, the Casa de Campo, with its pleasant pine woods, boating lake, amusement park, and zoo.

SIGHTS AT A GLANCE

Historic Buildings
Palacio de Liria **9**
Real Fábrica de Tapices **16**
Templo de Debod **6**

Churches and Convents
Ermita de San Antonio de la Florida **5**

Museums and Galleries
Museo de América **7**
Museo Cerralbo **8**
Museo Lázaro Galdiano **13**

Museo Municipal **11**
Museo Sorolla **12**

Streets, Squares, and Parks
Casa de Campo **4**
La Latina **2**
Malasaña **10**
Paseo de la Castellana **14**
Plaza de la Paja **3**
Plaza de Toros de Las Ventas **15**
El Rastro **1**

```
0 kilometers          2
0 miles          1
```

KEY

	Main sightseeing area
	Parks and open spaces
🚉	Railroad station
▬	Freeway
▬	Major road
▬	Minor road

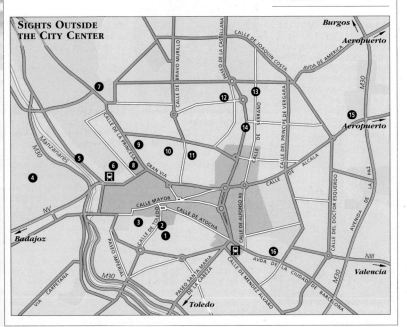

SIGHTS OUTSIDE THE CITY CENTER

El Rastro ❶

Calle Ribera de Curtidores. **Map** 2 E5.
Ⓜ *La Latina, Embajadores.* ⏰ *10am – 2pm Sun & public hols.*

Madrid's celebrated flea market *(see p305),* established in the Middle Ages, has its hub in the Plaza de Cascorro and sprawls downhill toward the Río Manzanares. The main street is the Calle Ribera de Curtidores, or "Tanners' Riverbank," once the center of the slaughterhouse and tanning industry.

Although some people claim that the Rastro has changed a great deal since its heyday during the 19th century, there are still plenty of *Madrileños,* as well as tourists, who shop here. They come in search of a bargain from the stalls that sell a huge range of wares – anything from new furniture to second-hand clothes. The wide range of goods and the lively crowds in the Rastro make it an ideal way to spend a Sunday morning.

The Calle de Embajadores is the market's other main street. It runs down past the dusty Baroque façade of the Iglesia de San Cayetano, designed by José Churriguera and Pedro de Ribera. Its interior has been restored since fire destroyed it during the Civil War.

Farther along the street is the Real Fábrica de Tabacos (the Royal Tobacco Factory), begun as a state enterprise in 1809. Its female labor force has long had a reputation for taking an uncompromising, hard-line stance in labor disputes.

Shoppers browsing around the Rastro flea market

La Latina ❷

Map 2 D5. Ⓜ *La Latina, Lavapiés.*

The district of La Latina, together with the adjacent Lavapiés, is considered to be the heart of *castizo* Madrid. This term is used to describe the culture of the traditional working classes of Madrid – that of the true *Madrileño.*

La Latina runs along the city's southern hillside from the Plaza Puerta de Moros, southwards through the streets where the Rastro is held. To the east it merges with Lavapiés.

La Latina's steep streets are lined with tall, narrow houses, renovated to form an attractive neighborhood. There are a number of old-fashioned bars around the Plaza de Tirso de Molina, although this square and the streets to the north of La Latina, around the Puerta del Sol, have sadly become notorious for petty crime.

Bottles of wine for sale in an old-style bar in Lavapiés

Plaza de la Paja ❸

Map 1 C4. Ⓜ *La Latina.*

Once the focus of medieval Madrid, the area around the Plaza de la Paja – literally Straw Square – is still atmospheric. Despite its location, in a less than affluent district, many interesting buildings are located on the square.

Climbing upward from the Calle de Segovia, a glimpse left along the Calle Príncipe Anglona yields a view of the Mudéjar-style brick tower of the Iglesia de San Pedro, dating

Interior of San Francisco el Grande

from the 14th century. Up past the fountain, the Plaza de la Paja ends with the harsh stone walls of the Capilla del Obispo, or Bishop's Chapel, belonging originally to the adjoining Palacio Vargas. The superb Plateresque altarpiece is by Francisco Giralte. Up to the left, the Baroque, cherub-covered dome of the Iglesia de San Andrés stands out.

Nearby is a small cluster of interlinked squares, ending in the Plaza Puerta de Moros, a reminder of the Muslim community that once occupied the area. From here, a right turn leads to the domed bulk of San Francisco el Grande, an impressive landmark. Inside the church is a collection of paintings by Goya and his brother-in-law Francisco Bayeu. The choir stalls were moved here from the monastery of El Paular *(see pp310 – 11).*

Casa de Campo ❹

Avenida de Portugal. 📞 *(91) 463 63 34.* Ⓜ *Batán, Lago, Norte.*

This former royal hunting ground, with pines and scrubland stretching over 4,300 acres, lies in western Madrid. Its wide range of amenities make it a popular recreation area for *Madrileños.*

Attractions include a boating lake, a zoo, and an amusement park – the Parque de Atracciones *(see p307)* – with over 50 rides. Sports enthusiasts can make use of the swimming pool and jogging track. In the summer the park is also used as a venue for rock concerts.

Egyptian temple of Debod, with two of its original gateways

The temple is carved with shallow reliefs and stands in a line with two of its original three gateways. They are situated on high ground above the Río Manzanares, in the gardens of the Parque del Oeste. From the park there are sweeping views over the Casa de Campo stretching to the Guadarrama mountains.

The park is the site of the former Montaña barracks, which were stormed by the populace at the start of the Civil War in 1936.

Farther to the west, below the brow of the hill, there is an attractive rose garden.

Museo de América ❼

Avenida de los Reyes Católicos 6.
☎ (91) 549 26 41. 🚇 *Moncloa.*
🕐 *10am–3pm Tue–Sat, 10am–
2:30pm Sun & public hols.* 🈺 ♿

T HIS HANDSOME MUSEUM houses a unique collection of artifacts related to Spain's colonization of parts of the Americas. Many of the exhibits, which range from prehistoric times to the present, were brought back to Europe by early explorers of the New World *(see pp54–5).*

The collection is arranged on the first and second floors, and individual rooms are given a cultural theme such as society, communication, or religion. There is documentation of the Atlantic voyages by the first explorers, and examples of the objects that they found. The highlight of the museum is perhaps the rare Mayan *Códice Trocortesiano* (AD 1250–1500) from Mexico, a type of parchment illustrated with hieroglyphics of scenes from everyday life. Also worth seeing are the solid gold funereal ornaments from Colombia, the Treasure of the Quimbayas (AD 500–1000), and the collection of contemporary folk art from some of Spain's former American colonies.

Ermita de San Antonio de la Florida ❺

Glorieta San Antonio de la Florida 5.
☎ (91) 542 07 22. 🚇 *Norte
(Príncipe Pío).* 🕐 *10am –2pm, 4 – 8pm
Tue – Fri, 10am – 2pm Sat & Sun.*
● *public hols.* 🈺 📷 ♿

G OYA ENTHUSIASTS should not miss a visit to the Neo-Classical Ermita de San Antonio de la Florida, built during the reign of Carlos IV. The present church stands on the site of two previous ones and is dedicated to St. Anthony. It is named after the pasture-land of la Florida, on which the original church was built.

Goya took just four months, in 1798, to paint the cupola with an immense fresco. It depicts the resurrection of a murdered man who rises in order to prove the innocence of the falsely accused father of St. Anthony. The characters in it are everyday people of the late 18th century: lurking, low-life types and lively *majas (see p283)* – shrewd but elegant women. The fresco is considered by many art critics to be among Goya's finest works.

The tomb of the artist is housed in the chapel. His remains were brought here from Bordeaux, where he died in exile in 1828 *(see p229).*

Templo de Debod ❻

Paseo de Pintor Rosales. **Map** 1 B1.
☎ (91) 409 61 65. 🚇 *Ventura
Rodríguez.* 🕐 *10am–1pm
Sat & Sun; Jul–Sep: 10am–3pm
Tue–Fri; Oct–Jun: 10am–1pm,
4–7pm Tue – Fri.* ● *public hols.*

T HE EGYPTIAN temple of Debod, built in the 4th century BC, was rescued from the area flooded by the Aswan Dam and given to Spain as a tribute to Spanish engineers involved in the project.

**Piece of the Treasure
of the Quimbayas**

Museo Cerralbo ⑧

Calle Ventura Rodríguez 17. **Map** 1 C1. 🅒 *(91) 547 36 46.* ◈ *Plaza de España, Ventura Rodríguez.* ⭘ *9:30am–2:30pm Tue–Sat, 10am–2pm Sun.* 🖻 🚫

T HIS 19TH-CENTURY mansion near the Plaza de España is a monument to Enrique de Aguilera y Gamboa, the 17th Marquis of Cerralbo. A compulsive collector of art and artifacts, he bequeathed his collection of a lifetime to the nation in 1922, stipulating that the exhibits remain in the same arrangement as he left them. They range from Iberian pottery to 18th-century marble busts.

One of the star exhibits is El Greco's *The Ecstasy of Saint Francis of Assisi.* There are also lesser-known paintings by Ribera, Zurbarán, Alonso Cano, and Goya, which hang in the Picture Gallery.

The focal point of the main floor is the ballroom, lavishly decorated with mirrors. A large collection of European and Japanese weaponry is on display on this floor.

Palacio de Liria ⑨

Calle de la Princesa 20. 🅒 *(91) 547 53 02.* ◈ *Ventura Rodríguez.* ⭘ *write in advance for permission.* 🚫

T HE LAVISH though much restored Palacio de Liria was completed by Ventura Rodríguez in 1780. Once the residence of the Alba family, and still belonging to the Duchess, it can be visited by appointment only.

The palace houses the Albas' outstanding collection of art, and Flemish tapestries. There are paintings by Titian, Rubens, and Rembrandt. Spanish art is particularly well represented, with major works by Goya, such as his 1795 portrait of the Duchess of Alba, as well as examples of work by El Greco, Zurbarán, and Velázquez.

Behind the palace is the **Cuartel del Conde-Duque**, the former barracks of the Count-Duke Olivares, Felipe IV's minister. They were built in 1720 by Pedro de Ribera, who adorned them with a Baroque façade. The barracks now house a cultural center.

Rooftops in the Malasaña district

Malasaña ⑩

Map 2 F1. ◈ *Tribunal, Bilbao.*

A FEELING OF the authentic old Madrid pervades this district of narrow, sloping streets and tall houses. For some years it was the center of the *movida*, the frenzied nightlife which began after the death of Franco.

A walk along the Calle San Andrés leads to the Plaza del Dos de Mayo. In the center is a monument to artillery officers Daoiz and Velarde, who defended the barracks which stood here at the time of the uprising against the French in 1808 *(see p59)*.

On Calle de la Puebla is the Iglesia de San Antonio de los Alemanes. The church was founded by Felipe III in the 17th century as a hospital for Portuguese immigrants, and was later given over for use by German émigrés. Inside, the walls are decorated with 18th-century frescoes by Giordano.

Museo Municipal ⑪

Calle de Fuencarral 78. **Map** 3 A3. 🅒 *(91) 588 86 72.* ◈ *Tribunal.* ⭘ *9:30am–8pm Tue–Fri, 10am–2pm Sat & Sun.* ⬤ *public hols.* 🖻

T HE MUNICIPAL MUSEUM is worth visiting just for its majestic Baroque doorway *(see p21)* by Pedro de Ribera, arguably the finest in Madrid. Housed in the former hospice of St. Ferdinand, the museum was inaugurated in 1929. The

Main staircase of the exuberant Museo Cerralbo

basement is devoted to the city's archaeology, while upstairs is a series of bird's-eye views and maps showing how radically Madrid has been transformed over the years. Among them is Pedro Texeiro's map of 1656, thought to be the oldest of the city. There is also a meticulous model of Madrid, made in 1830 by León Gil de Palacio.

Modern exhibits include a reconstruction of the collage-filled study of Ramón Gómez de la Serna, a key figure of the famous literary gatherings in the Café de Pombo (see p289). In the garden is the Baroque *Fuente de la Fama* (Fountain of Fame), also by Ribera.

Baroque façade of the Museo Municipal, by Pedro de Ribera

Museo Sorolla ⑫

Paseo del General Martínez Campos 37. (91) 310 15 84. Rubén Darío, Iglesia. ◻ 10am–3pm Tue–Sat, 10am–2pm Sun. 🖼

THE FORMER studio mansion of Valencian Impressionist painter Joaquín Sorolla, now a museum housing his paintings, has been left virtually as it was when he died in 1923.

Although Sorolla is perhaps best known for his brilliantly lit Mediterranean beach scenes, the changing styles of his paintings are well represented in the museum, with examples of his gentle portraiture and a series of works representing people from different parts of Spain. Also on display are various objects amassed during the artist's lifetime, including Spanish tiles and ceramics. The

Sorolla's former studio in the Museo Sorolla

house, which was constructed in 1910, is surrounded by an Andalusian-style garden, designed by Sorolla himself.

Museo Lázaro Galdiano ⑬

Calle de Serrano 122. (91) 561 60 84. Núñez de Balboa. ◻ 10am–2pm Tue–Sun. 🖼 Ø

THIS IS ONE of the best art museums in the city. It is housed in the former mansion home of the writer José Lázaro Galdiano, and consists of his private collection of fine and applied art, bequeathed to the nation in 1947. A colossal central hall, which rises through two floors,

Charles V's fob watch

dominates the mansion. The collection contains items of exceptional quality, ranging from a group of less familiar Goya portraits to a mass of fob watches, including a cross-shaped pocket-watch worn by Charles V when hunting. Among the most beautiful objects are a series of Limoges enamels, miniature sculptures, and *The Saviour*, a portrait attributed to Leonardo da Vinci.

The outstanding collection of art features paintings by English artists Constable, Turner, Gainsborough, and Reynolds, as well as 17th-century works by Velázquez, Zurbarán, Ribera, Murillo, and El Greco. The *Ecce Homo* is by Dutch painter Hieronymus Bosch.

LA MOVIDA

With Franco's death in 1975 came a new period of personal and artistic liberty. For the young, this was translated into the freedom to stay out late, drinking and sometimes sampling drugs. The phenomenon was known as *la movida*, "the action," and it was at its most intense in Madrid. Although analysts at the time saw it as having serious intellectual content, *la movida* has had few lasting cultural results, except for the emergence of satirical film director Pedro Almodóvar.

Poster for Almodóvar's *Women on the Verge of a Nervous Breakdown*

Torre de Picasso towering over the Paseo de la Castellana

Paseo de la Castellana ⑭

🚇 *Lima, Cuzco, Plaza de Castilla.*

THE BUSY TRAFFIC artery that cuts through eastern Madrid consists of several parts. Its southernmost portion, the Paseo del Prado *(see pp274–5)*, starts just north of the Estación de Atocha *(see p287)*. The oldest section of the road, it dates from the reign of Carlos III, who built it as part of his embellishment of eastern Madrid *(see p287)*. At the Plaza de Cibeles, the avenue becomes the handsome Paseo de Recoletos, which boasts fashionable cafés, including the Café Gijón *(see p281)*.

The Plaza de Colón marks the start of the Paseo de la Castellana, whose sidewalk cafés have become a focal point for young Madrid's social life. This northernmost section has several notable examples of modern architecture, including the huge gray Nuevos Ministerios building, completed under Franco. Farther on, before the Plaza de Lima, is the Torre de Picasso *(see p21)*, one of Spain's tallest buildings. East of the square is the Estadio Bernabéu, home of Real Madrid soccer team *(see p173)*. The building that dominates the Paseo, however, is the Puerta de Europa, locally known as "Torres Kio": twin glass blocks on either side of the road built at an angle as if leaning toward each other.

Plaza de Toros de Las Ventas ⑮

Calle de Alcalá 237. 🕿 *(91) 356 22 00.* 🚇 *Ventas.* ⭕ *for bullfights and concerts only.* **Museo Taurino** 🕿 *(91) 725 18 57.* ⭕ *10am–1pm Tue–Fri & Sun.* ♿

WHATEVER your opinion of bullfighting, Las Ventas is undoubtedly one of the most beautiful bullrings in Spain. Built in 1929 in Neo-Mudéjar style, it replaced the city's original bullring, which stood near the Puerta de Alcalá. With its horseshoe arches around the outer galleries and the elaborate tilework decoration, it makes an attractive venue for the *corridas* held during the bullfighting season, from May to October. The statues outside the bullring are monuments to two renowned Spanish bullfighters: Antonio Bienvenida and José Cubero.

Adjoining the bullring is the Museo Taurino. The museum contains an interesting and varied collection of bullfighting memorabilia, including portraits and sculptures of famous matadors, as well as the heads of several bulls killed during fights at Las Ventas. Visitors can examine close up the tools of the bullfighter's trade: capes and *banderillas* – sharp darts used to wound the bull *(see pp32–3)*. For some people, the gory highlight of the exhibition is the blood-drenched *traje de luces* worn by the legendary Manolete during his fateful bullfight at Linares

in Andalusia in 1947. Also on display is a costume which belonged to Juanita Cruz, a female bullfighter of the 1930s who was forced, in the face of prejudice, to leave Spain. In September and October, the bullring is used as a venue for a season of rock concerts.

Real Fábrica de Tapices ⑯

Calle Fuenterrabia 2. 🕿 *(91) 551 34 00.* 🚇 *Menéndez Pelayo.* ⭕ *9am–12:30pm Mon–Fri.* 🎧

FOUNDED BY Felipe V in 1721, the Royal Tapestry Factory is the sole survivor of several factories that were opened by the Bourbons *(see pp58–9)* during the 18th century. In 1889 the factory was relocated to this building just south of the Parque del Retiro.

Visitors can see the making of the carpets and tapestries by hand, a process that has changed little since the factory was established. Goya and his brother-in-law Francisco Bayeu created drawings, or cartoons, that were the inspiration for tapestries made for the royal family. Some of the cartoons are on display here; others can be seen in the Museo del Prado *(see pp282–5)*. Some of the tapestries can be seen at El Pardo *(see p314)* and at El Escorial *(see pp312–13)*. Nowadays one of the factory's main tasks is making and repairing the beautiful carpets decorating the Hotel Ritz *(see p276)*.

Plaza de Toros de Las Ventas, Madrid's beautiful bullring

MADRID STREET FINDER

THE MAP REFERENCES given with the sights, shops, and entertainment venues described in the Madrid section of the guide refer to the street maps on the following pages. Map references are also given for Madrid hotels

(see pp552–4) and for bars and restaurants *(pp592–4)*. The schematic map below shows the area of Madrid covered by the *Street Finder.* The symbols used for the sights and other features are listed in the key at the foot of the page.

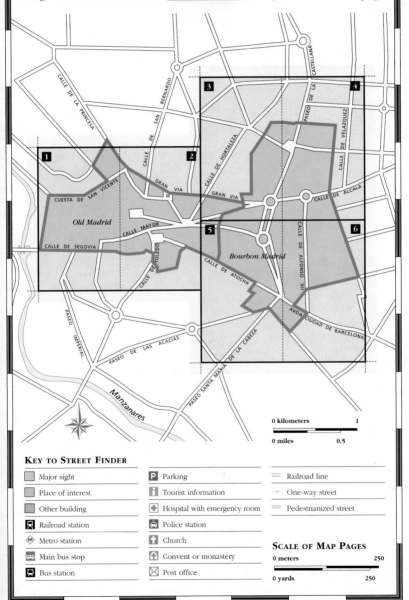

KEY TO STREET FINDER

▢ Major sight	ⓟ Parking	═ Railroad line
▢ Place of interest	ⓘ Tourist information	→ One-way street
▢ Other building	✚ Hospital with emergency room	▬ Pedestrianized street
▥ Railroad station	▦ Police station	
◈ Metro station	⛪ Church	**SCALE OF MAP PAGES**
▭ Main bus stop	⛪ Convent or monastery	0 meters 250
▣ Bus station	⊠ Post office	0 yards 250

Map scale:
0 kilometers   1
0 miles   0.5

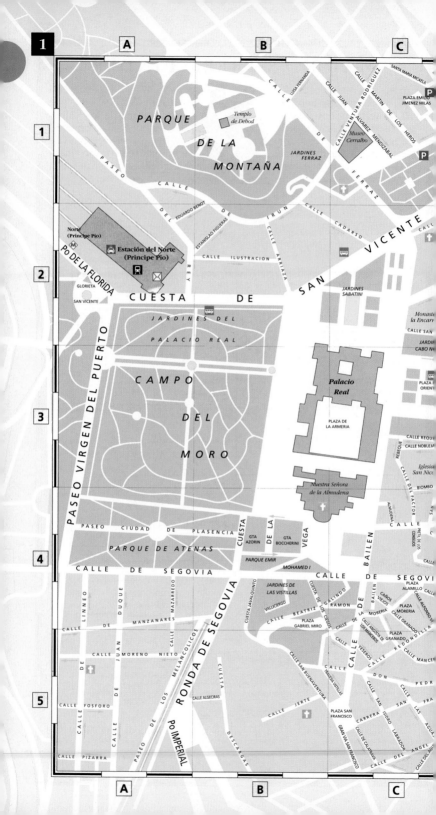

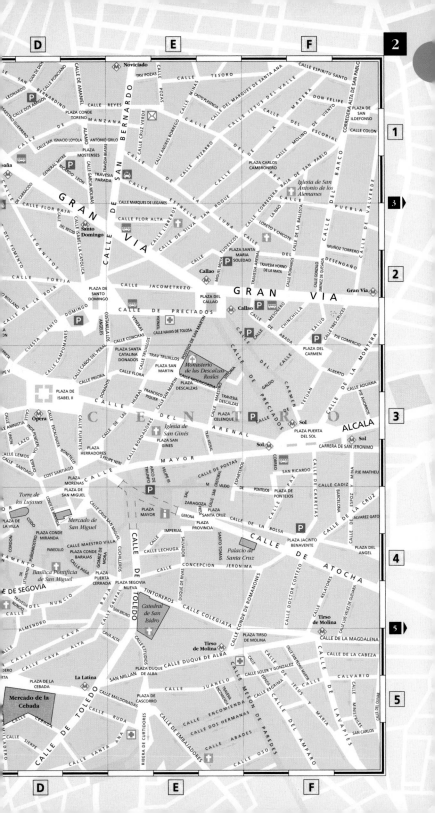

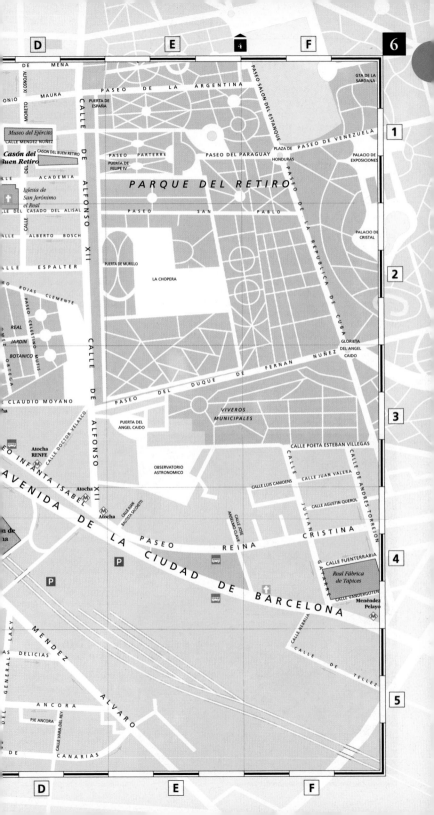

DE MENA

IX ONOLITO

ANTONIO

MORETO

MAURA

CALLE

PASEO DE LA ARGENTINA

PASEO SALON DEL ESTANQUE

GTA DE LA SARDANA

PUERTA DE ESPAÑA

1

Museo del Ejército
CALLE MENDEZ NUÑEZ

Casón del
Buen Retiro
CASON DEL BUEN RETIRO

PASEO DE VENEZUELA

PLAZA DE

PASEO PARTERRE

PASEO DEL PARAGUAY

HONDURAS

PALACIO DE EXPOSICIONES

PUERTA DE FELIPE IV

DE

CALLE

ACADEMIA

Iglesia de
San Jerónimo
el Real
CALLE CASADO DEL ALISAL

PARQUE DEL RETIRO

PALACIO DE CRISTAL

CALLE

ALBERTO BOSCH

PASEO

SAN

PABLO

ALFONSO XII

CALLE

ESPALTER

PUERTA DE MURILLO

ROJAS CLEMENTE

LA CHOPERA

PASEO CELESTINO MUTIS

REAL

JARDIN

GOMEZ ORTEGA

BOTANICO

CALLE

DE

PASEO DE LA REPUBLICA DE CUBA

CLAUDIO MOYANO

cha

PASEO DEL DUQUE DE FERNAN NUÑEZ

GLORIETA DEL ANGEL CAIDO

ALFONSO

VIVEROS MUNICIPALES

Atocha
RENFE

CALLE DOCTOR VELASCO

PUERTA DEL ANGEL CAIDO

CALLE POETA ESTEBAN VILLEGAS

AVENIDA

INFANTA ISABEL

Atocha
XII

Atocha

DE

OBSERVATORIO ASTRONOMICO

CALLE LUIS CAMOENS

CALLE JUAN VALERA

CALLE DE ANDRES TORREJON

CALLE JUAN BAUTISTA SACCHETTI

CALLE JOSE ANSELMO CLAVE

JULIANA

CALLE AGUSTIN QUEROL

PASEO

REINA

CRISTINA

CALLE FUENTERRABIA

P

DE

LA

CIUDAD

Real Fábrica
de Tapices

P

CALLE VANDERGOTEN

Menéndez
Pelayo

DE

BARCELONA

LACY

MENDEZ

DELICIAS

CALLE NEBRIJA

CALLE

DE

TELLEZ

GENERAL

ANCORA

ALVARO

PJE ANCORA

CALLE VARA DEL REY

DE

CANARIAS

SHOPPING IN MADRID

MADRID IS A CITY that offers the best of everything, from its handmade Spanish guitars to the latest designer clothes. That the city's shopping areas are quite well defined is an additional bonus. The elegant, up-scale fashion stores are mostly concentrated in the Salamanca district, and the latest in street fashion is available in

Selection of Madrid's cakes

the Chueca district, while most of the general clothing stores are situated in the city center. There are food markets throughout the city, though the best specialty food and wine stores are to be found within Old Madrid. Not to be missed is the centuries-old Rastro *(see p292)* every Sunday, one of the greatest flea markets in the world.

FOOD AND DRINK

EVERY DISTRICT in Madrid has a food market with fresh meat, fish, fruit, and vegetables. For gourmet specialties, take a walk around Old Madrid, where branches of the **Museo del Jamón** have enormous selections of the many different types of Spanish hams, cured sausages, and cheeses. They also have bars and restaurants inside. A comprehensive stock of Spanish wines is sold in the beautiful **Mariano Madrueño**, which was established in 1895. North of Old Madrid is the

Horno San Onofre with its mouthwatering displays of cakes, breads, and savories, especially at Christmas.

DEPARTMENT STORES AND SHOPPING MALLS

THE DEPARTMENT STORE CHAIN, **El Corte Inglés**, has branches all over the city, selling clothes, foods, and virtually everything else. They also offer services like photo-developing and shoe repairing.

Shopping malls have grown rapidly in Madrid in recent years, and among the best are

the **Galería del Prado**, the **Jardín de Serrano**, and **ABC Serrano**. For everything under one roof, go to the huge **La Vaguada** mall on the north side of the city. There are also several hypermarkets, mostly around the M30 ring road.

FASHION

A VARIED MIX of clothing stores is located around the Calle de Preciados in the center of town, but the best-known Spanish and international fashion names are on the Calle de Serrano *(see p286)* and Calle Ortega y Gasset in the Salamanca district. **Ekseption** has a wide range of top designer labels, while the young, eccentric **Agatha Ruíz de la Prada** displays

On the catwa in Madrid

her unique creations in a shop on a street off the west side of the Paseo de la Castellana.

The best place for clothes by young designers is the Chueca district, in and around the Calle del Almirante, with shops such as **Ararat**.

CRAFTS, DESIGN, AND GIFTS

MADRID's specialty craft shops are concentrated around the Plaza Mayor. They sell traditional craftwork like lace, embroidery, and, at **Almoraima**, fans. **Arco de Cuchilleros** sells ceramics, leather, and jewelry.

Two other districts, Huertas and Lavapiés, have many unusual old shops such as

The enticing frontage of the Museo del Jamón

Inside one of the many antique shops in the streets around the Rastro

Cerámica El Alfar for modern and traditional ceramics, and **Guitarrería F Manzanero** for handmade guitars.

Among the best modern design shops is **La Oca** at the Puerta de Toledo, which has striking contemporary kitchen and household goods.

ART AND ANTIQUES

THE COMMERCIAL galleries and antique shops of Madrid are conveniently grouped together. In the Salamanca district, especially along Calle de Claudio Coello, are some of the most exclusive antique shops. Cheaper and more unusual antiques can be found in the Huertas and La Latina districts, particularly around the streets where the Rastro is held. Here, there are several arcades of small shops which open on weekdays, as well as during the Sunday market.

BOOKS AND NEWSPAPERS

THE GIANT French-owned **FNAC** book and video store has a good selection of books and magazines in English and other languages, and also a very efficient theater and concert ticket desk. **Booksellers** is a good English-language bookshop.

The second hand bookstalls on the Calle Claudio Moyano, near the Parque del Retiro, are a permanent fixture. Here, rare volumes as well as cheap paperbacks can be acquired.

MARKETS

EACH SUNDAY thousands pack the long, narrow hill of Calle Ribera de Curtidores, center of **El Rastro** market (*see p292*) which spreads over into the surrounding streets. At the top of the hill, in the Plaza de Cascorro, the stalls sell mostly clothes and jewelry, but elsewhere you can find just about anything.

The coin and stamp market, which is held every Sunday morning in the Plaza Mayor, is a little less hectic and also fascinating. There are also stalls selling second hand books and magazines, badges, and other collectibles.

Sunday morning in the busy Rastro flea market

ENTERTAINMENT IN MADRID

MADRID'S NIGHTLIFE is not for the faint-hearted. On a typical Saturday night the first stirrings of activity start in the cafés in the early evening, with the accent gradually shifting to tapas bars, restaurants and clubs; like the city's clamoring traffic, the reveling goes on through the night. Those with a slightly less frenetic evening

Flamenco guitarist in Parque del Retiro

in mind will find the best in all the Spanish arts – particularly flamenco and Madrid's own comic opera style, *zarzuela*. There is a good choice of classical music, and thriving jazz and rock circuits. Theater lovers can choose between Spanish Golden Age classics, or modern mainstream and experimental drama.

Madrid's Teatro Real

ENTERTAINMENT GUIDES

THE BEST GUIDE to what's on currently in Madrid is the *Guía del Ocio*, which includes complete movie listings and is on sale every Friday. Two daily newspapers have weekly entertainment supplements: *El Mundo*, on Thursday, and *El País*, on Friday.

SEASONS AND TICKETS

THE MAIN CONCERT and theater seasons run from September to June. May's San Isidro fiesta *(see p280)* and the Festival de Otoño – from September to November – attract many top Spanish and international names in music, theater and other arts – ask at tourist offices for details.

The FNAC bookstore *(see p305)* sells concert and theater tickets with little or no commission. State-funded theaters, like the **Auditorio Nacional** and **Teatro de la Zarzuela**, sell their own and each other's tickets. Bullfight and soccer tickets can be bought in advance at the **TEYCI** agency.

CLASSICAL MUSIC, DANCE, AND ZARZUELA

THE TWO CONCERT HALLS of the **Auditorio Nacional** host a range of programs each year by the Orquesta Nacional de España and international orchestras. Madrid's opera company is due to move into the **Teatro Real**, currently being restored.

The main dance company is the contemporary Compañía Nacional de Danza. **Teatro Albéniz** hosts dance performance as well as Madrid's own musical form, *zarzuela*, comic opera similar to operetta. There are productions at the **Teatro de la Zarzuela** and other theaters in summer.

THEATER

MADRID'S MOST prestigious theaters are the **Teatro de la Comedia**, home to the Compañía Nacional de Teatro Clásico and its productions of Spanish Golden Age classics, and the **Teatro María Guerrero**, which presents modern drama in Spanish and

also hosts foreign productions. In addition, there is a thriving network of avantgarde spots, among the best of which is the frequently provocative **Teatro Alfil**. An enormous range of Spanish and international theater talent, from established companies to radical new fringe groups, takes part in the annual Festival de Otoño.

FLAMENCO

ANDALUSIA MAY BE the home of flamenco *(see pp406–7)*, but Madrid is now where the best exponents are based. A club like **Casa Patas**, totally without amplification, perfectly catches the raw power of genuine flamenco guitar and *cante* singing at its finest. The **Café de Chinitas** is a good place to see spontaneous flamenco dancing.

CAFÉS, BARS, AND CLUBS

MADRID'S BARS have a style of their own. The city has conserved many of its old grand cafés, which are wonderful places to sit and

Dancing the night away at the Joy Eslava dance club

Exterior of the historic Café Gijón

people-watch or chat. Of the literary cafés, the most famous is **Café Gijón** *(see p281)*.

A plush, popular club that attracts a lively young crowd is **Joy Eslava**, which doesn't heat up until well after midnight.

Wherever the night has been spent, an excellent way to finish is with a breakfast of *chocolate con churros (see p576)* at the **Chocolatería San Ginés**, just as the people of Madrid have been doing since it opened in 1894.

ROCK, JAZZ, AND WORLD MUSIC

MAJOR INTERNATIONAL acts play regularly in Madrid's stadiums and sports arenas, but **Sala Riviera** is a small, lively venue that has hosted acts such as Bob Dylan and The Cranberries. In summer there are open-air rock con-

certs in the Casa de Campo's **Parque de Atracciones**. The **Café Central**, one of Europe's best jazz clubs, is near the Plaza Santa Ana, site of several jazz and Latin music clubs, where you can see a live act, then dance the night away to the sinuous rhythms of salsa.

AMUSEMENT PARKS

THE **Parque de Atracciones** funfair, in the Casa de Campo *(see p292)*, is popular with young and old. Modern water parks are also popular, and **Aqualung** is the most central of several in Madrid.

BULLFIGHTING AND SOCCER

BULLFIGHTING remains hugely popular in Madrid, and **Las Ventas** bullring *(see p296)*, the most important in Spain, holds *corridas* every Sunday from March to October. During the fiesta of San Isidro, in May, there are fights every day.

Real Madrid *(see p173)* are the local aristocrats of soccer and their Bernabéu stadium is one of the great theaters of the game. The field of their rivals **Atlético de Madrid** is smaller and cheaper, and often has a better atmosphere.

Las Ventas bullring on the day of a bullfight

DIRECTORY

TICKETS

TEYCI
Calle de Goya 7. **Map** 4 D3.
(91) 576 45 32.

CLASSICAL MUSIC, DANCE, AND ZARZUELA

Auditorio Nacional de Música
C/ Príncipe de Vergara 146.
(91) 337 01 00.

Teatro Albéniz
C/ Paz 11. **Map** 2 F4.
(91) 531 83 11.

Teatro Real
Plaza de Isabel II.
Map 2 D3.

Teatro de la Zarzuela
C/ Jovellanos 4. **Map** 3 B5.
(91) 524 54 00.

THEATER

Teatro Alfil
Calle del Pez 10.
Map 2 E1.
(91) 521 42 96.

Teatro de la Comedia
Calle del Príncipe 14.
Map 5 A1.
(91) 521 49 31.

Teatro María Guerrero
Calle Tamayo y Baus 4.
Map 3 C4.
(91) 319 47 69.

FLAMENCO

Café de Chinitas
Calle Torija 7.
Map 2 D2.
(91) 547 15 02.

Casa Patas
Calle de Cañizares 10.
Map 5 A2.
(91) 369 04 96.

CAFÉS, BARS, AND CLUBS

Café Gijón
Paseo de Recoletos 21.
Map 3 C4.
(91) 521 54 25.

Chocolatería San Ginés
Pasadizo de San Ginés 5.
Map 2 E3.
(91) 365 65 46.

Joy Eslava
Calle del Arenal.
Map 2 E3.
(91) 366 32 84.

ROCK, JAZZ, AND WORLD MUSIC

Café Central
Pl del Ángel 10. **Map** 5 A1.
(91) 369 41 43.

Sala Riviera
Paseo de la Virgen del
Puerto. **Map** 1 A4.
(91) 365 24 15.

AMUSEMENT PARKS

Aqualung
Paseo de la Ermita del
Santo 40–48.
(91) 526 43 92.

Parque de Atracciones
Casa de Campo.
(91) 463 29 00.

BULLFIGHTING AND SOCCER

Atlético de Madrid
Estadio Vicente Calderón,
Paseo de la Virgen del
Puerto 67.
(91) 366 47 07.

Plaza Toros de Las Ventas
Calle de Alcalá 237.
(91) 726 48 00.

Real Madrid
Estadio Santiago Bernabéu,
Avenida de Concha Espina.
(91) 344 00 52.

MADRID PROVINCE

MADRID PROVINCE (the Comunidad de Madrid) sits high on Spain's central plateau. There is plenty of superb scenery and good walking country in the sierras to the north, which are a refuge for city dwellers who go there to ski in winter or cool down during the torrid summers. In the western foothills of these mountains stands El Escorial, the royal palace-monastery built by Felipe II, from which he ruled his empire. Close by is the Valle de los Caídos, the war monument erected by Franco. The smaller royal palace of El Pardo is on the outskirts of Madrid, and south of the city is the 18th-century summer palace of Aranjuez, set in lush parkland. Historic towns include Alcalá de Henares, which has a Renaissance university building, and Chinchón, where taverns cluster around a picturesque arcaded market square.

SIGHTS AT A GLANCE

Towns and Cities
Alcalá de Henares ❾
Buitrago del Lozoya ❷
Chinchón ❿
Manzanares el Real ❼

Historic Buildings
El Escorial pp312–13 ❻
Monasterio de Santa María de
   El Paular ❸
Palacio de El Pardo ❽

Palacio Real de Aranjuez ⓫
Santa Cruz del Valle de los
   Caídos ❺

Mountain Ranges
Sierra Centro de Guadarrama ❹
Sierra Norte ❶

0 kilometers   25

0 miles   20

KEY

	Madrid city
	Madrid province
✈	Barajas Airport
	Freeway
	Major road
	Minor road
- -	Province boundary

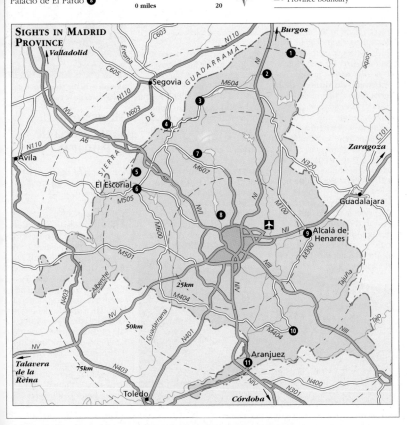

SIGHTS IN MADRID PROVINCE

◁ **Celebration of Mass in the church of the Monasterio de Santa María de El Paular**

The village of Montejo de la Sierra in the Sierra Norte

Sierra Norte ❶

Madrid. 🚌 *Montejo.* 🛈 *Calle Real 1, Montejo, (91) 869 70 58.*

THE BLACK SLATE HAMLETS of the Sierra Norte, which were once known as the Sierra Pobre (Poor Sierra), are located in the most attractively rural part of Madrid province.

At **Montejo de la Sierra**, the largest village in the area, an information center organizes riding, the rental of traditional houses (*see p531*), and visits to the nearby nature preserve of the **Hayedo de Montejo de la Sierra**. This is one of the most southern beech woods (*see p76*) in Europe and a relic of a previous era when climatic conditions here were more suitable for the beech. From Montejo, you can drive on to picturesque hamlets such as **La Hiruela** or **Puebla de la Sierra**, both of which are set in lovely walking country.

The drier southern hills slope down to the **Embalse de Puentes Viejas**, a reservoir where summer chalets cluster around artificial beaches. On the eastern edge

of the sierra is the village of **Patones**, which is thought to have escaped invasion by the Moors and Napoleon's troops because of its isolated location.

Buitrago del Lozoya ❷

Madrid. 🏘 *1,300.* 🚌 🛈 *Plaza de Picasso 1, (91) 868 00 56.* 🛒 *Sat.* 🎉 *La Asunción and San Roque (Aug 15).*

PICTURESQUELY SITED above a bend in the Río Lozoya is the walled town of Buitrago del Lozoya. Founded by the Romans, it was fortified by the Arabs and became an important market town in medieval times. The 14th-century Gothic-Mudéjar castle is in ruins, although the gatehouse, arches, and stretches of the original Arab wall have survived. Today, the castle is used only as a venue for bullfights.

The old quarter, located within the walled enclosure, retains its charming atmosphere. The church of **Santa María del Castillo**, dating

back to the 15th century, has a beautiful Mudéjar tower and ceilings moved here from the old hospital. The **town hall** *(ayuntamiento)*, in the newer part of Buitrago, preserves a 16th-century processional cross. In the town hall's basement is the small **Museo Picasso**. The prints, drawings and ceramics on display were collected by the artist's friend and barber, Eugenio Arias, a native of Buitrago.

🏛 **Museo Picasso**
Plaza de Picasso 1. 【 *(91) 868 00 56.* ⬤ *Tue.*

Altarpiece in the Monasterio de Santa María de El Paular

Monasterio de Santa María de El Paular ❸

Southwest of Rascafría on M604.
【 *(91) 869 14 25.* 🚌 *Rascafría.* ⬤ *daily from noon.* 🎗

FOUNDED IN 1390 as Castile's first Carthusian monastery, Santa María de El Paular stands on the site of a medieval royal hunting lodge. Although it is mainly Gothic in style, Plateresque and Renaissance features were added later. The monastery was abandoned in 1836 when government minister Mendizábal ordered the sale of church goods (*see p59*). It fell into disrepair until the state restored it in the 1950s. Today the complex consists of a working Benedictine monastery, a church, and a private hotel (*see p554*).

The church's delicate alabaster altarpiece, attributed to

Buitrago del Lozoya, standing next to the river

lemish craftsmen, dates from
he 15th century. Its panels
epict scenes from the life of
esus. The lavish Baroque
amarín (chamber), behind
he altar, was designed by
rancisco de Hurtado in 1718.

Every Sunday, the monks
ing an hour-long Gregorian
hant in the church. If they
re not busy, they will show
ou the cloister's Mudéjar brick
aulting and double sun clock.

The monastery is a good
tarting point for exploring the
ountry towns of **Rascafría**
nd **Lozoya** in the surrounding
ozoya valley. To the south-
vest is the nature preserve of
agunas de Peñalara.

Sierra Centro de Guadarrama ❹

Madrid. 🚃 *Puerto de Navacerrada,
Cercedilla.* 🚌 *Navacerrada, Cercedilla.*
🛈 *Navacerrada, (91) 856 00 06.*

THE CENTRAL SECTION of the
Sierra de Guadarrama was
ittle visited until the 1920s,
when the area was first linked
by train to Madrid. Today, the
granite slopes are planted with
pines and specked by holiday
chalets. Villages such as
Navacerrada and **Cercedilla**
have grown into popular
resorts for skiing, mountain
biking, rock climbing, and
riding. Walkers wanting to
enjoy the pure mountain air
can follow marked routes
from Navacerrada.

The **Valle de Fuenfría**, a
nature preserve of wild forests,
is best reached via Cercedilla.
It has a well-preserved stretch
of the original Roman road,
as well as several picnic spots
and marked walking routes.

The gigantic cross at Valle de los Caídos

Santa Cruz del Valle de los Caídos ❺

North of El Escorial on M600. 📞
(91) 890 56 11. 🚌 *from El Escorial.*
⏰ *Tue – Sun.* ⬤ *some public hols.* 🏛

GENERAL FRANCO had the
Holy Cross of the Valley
of the Fallen built as a memorial to those who died in the
Civil War *(see pp62–3)*. The

vast cross is located some
13 km (8 miles) north of El
Escorial *(see pp312–13)* and
dominates the surrounding
countryside. Some Spaniards
find it too chilling a symbol of
the dictatorship to be enjoyable, while for others its sheer
size is rewarding.

The cross is 150 m (490 ft)
high and rises above a basilica
carved 250 m (820 ft) deep
into the rock by Republican
prisoners of war. A number
of them are said to have died
in the 16-year project.

Next to the basilica's high
altar is the plain white tombstone of Franco, and, opposite,
that of José Antonio Primo de
Rivera, founder of the Falange
Española party. Another 40,000
coffins of soldiers from both
sides in the Civil War lie here
out of sight, including those
of two unidentified victims.

Visitors can take an elevator
up to the arms of the cross,
from which there are fine
views over the pine forests.

Navacerrada pass in the Sierra de Guadarrama

El Escorial ❻

Fresco by Luca Giordano

FELIPE II'S IMPOSING GRAY PALACE of San Lorenzo de El Escorial stands out against the foothills of the Sierra de Guadarrama to the northwest of Madrid. It was built between 1563 and 1584 in honor of St. Lawrence, and its unornamented severity set a new architectural style, which became one of the most influential in Spain. The interior was conceived as a mausoleum and contemplative retreat rather than a splendid residence. Its artistic wealth, which includes some of the most important works of art of the royal Hapsburg collections, is concentrated in the museums, chapterhouses, church, royal pantheon, and library. In contrast, the royal apartments are remarkably humble.

★ Royal Pantheon
The funerary urns of Spanish monarchs line the marble mausoleum.

Basilica
The highlight of this huge church, which is decorated only in parts, is the lavish altarpiece. The main chapel houses the cenotaphs of Felipe II and Charles V.

The Alfonso XII College
was founded by monks in 1875 as a boarding school.

Main entrance

Bourbon Palace

Architectural Museum

Sala de Batallas

Patio de los Reyes

Entrance to Basilica only

★ Library
This impressive array of 40,000 books incorporates Felipe II's personal collection. On display are precious manuscripts, including a poem by Alfonso X the Learned. The 16th-century ceiling frescoes are by Tibaldi.

STAR FEATURES
★ Royal Pantheon
★ Library
★ Museum of Art

The royal apartments, on the second floor of the palace, consist of Felipe II's modestly decorated living quarters. His bedroom opens directly on to the high altar of the basilica.

★ Museum of Art
Flemish, Italian, and Spanish paintings hang in the museum, located on the first floor. One of the highlights is The Calvary, *by 15th-century Flemish artist Roger van der Weyden.*

VISITORS' CHECKLIST

Paseo de José Antonio. (91) 890 59 02. from Atocha or Chamartin. 661, 664 from Moncloa. Apr–Sep: 10am– 6pm Tue –Sun; Oct–Mar: 10am– 5pm Tue –Sun. public hols. 9:30am daily; 7pm, 8pm Sat & Sun.

In the Patio de los Evangelistas
is a temple by Herrera, adorned with statues of the Evangelists.

Chapterhouses
On display here is Charles V's portable altar. The ceiling frescoes depict monarchs and angels.

The monastery was founded in 1567, and has been run by Augustinian monks since 1885. It is closed to the public.

The Glory of the Spanish Monarchy by Luca Giordano
This beautiful fresco, above the main staircase, depicts Charles V and Felipe II, and scenes of the building of the monastery.

The Building of El Escorial
When chief architect Juan Bautista de Toledo died in 1567 he was replaced by Juan de Herrera, royal inspector of monuments. The plain architectural style of El Escorial is called desornamentado, *literally, "unadorned."*

Climber resting on a rock face of La Pedriza, near Manzanares el Real

Manzanares el Real ⑦

Madrid. 🏠 3,000. 🚌 🛈 Plaza del Pueblo 1, (91) 853 00 09. 🚍 Tue & Fri. 🎉 Fiesta de Verano (early Aug), Cristo de la Nave (Sep 14).

FROM A DISTANCE, the skyline of Manzanares el Real is dominated by its restored 15th-century castle. Although the castle is equipped with some traditionally military features, such as double machicolations and turrets, it was used mainly as a residential palace by the Dukes of Infantado. Below the castle is a 16th-century church,

a Renaissance portico and fine capitals. Behind the town, bordering the foothills of the Sierra de Guadarrama, is **La Pedriza**, a mass of granite screes and ravines, very popular with climbers. It now forms part of an attractive nature preserve.

ENVIRONS: **Colmenar Viejo**, 12 km (7.5 miles) to the south-east of Manzanares, has a superb Gothic-Mudéjar church.

Palacio de El Pardo ⑧

El Pardo, northwest of Madrid on N605. 📞 (91) 376 15 00. 🚌 from Moncloa. ◯ daily. 🎟

THIS ROYAL HUNTING lodge and palace, set in parkland just outside Madrid's city limits, boasts King Juan Carlos I and General Franco among its former residents. A guided tour takes visitors round the moated palace's original Hapsburg wing and the identical 18th-century extension, designed by Francesco Sabatini.

The ornamental Bourbon interior is heavy with frescoes, gilt moldings, and tapestries, many of which were woven to designs by Goya (see p296). Today the palace is primarily used for accommodating visiting heads-of-state and for

entertaining royal guests. Surrounding the palace and the elegant 18th-century village of El Pardo is an enormous forest of holm oak. The area is popular for picnicking, and some game animals still run free.

Façade of Colegio de San Ildefonso in Alcalá de Henares

Alcalá de Henares ⑨

Madrid. 🏠 170,000. 🚌 🚍 🛈 Callejón Santa María, (91) 889 26 94. 🚍 Mon. 🎉 Feria de Alcalá (late Aug).

AT THE HEART of a modern industrial town is one of Spain's most renowned university quarters. Founded in 1508 by Cardinal Cisneros, Alcalá's **university** became one of the

Lavish 18th-century tapestry inside the Palacio de El Pardo

foremost places of learning in 16th-century Europe. It was transferred to Madrid in the 19th century. Most of the original 40 colleges have since been destroyed, but the most historic one, **San Ildefonso**, survives. Former students include Golden Age playwright Lope de Vega *(see p280)*. In 1517 the university produced Europe's first polyglot bible, which had text in Latin, Greek, Hebrew, and Chaldean.

Alcalá's other sights are the cathedral and the **Casa-Museo de Cervantes**, birthplace of the Golden Age author. It is now an interesting museum.

🏛 Casa-Museo de Cervantes
Calle Imagen 2. 📞 *(91) 889 96 54.*
🕐 *Tue–Sun.* ⬤ *public hols.*

Chinchón ⑩

Madrid. 🏘 *4,200.* 🚌 ℹ️ *Plaza Mayor 3, (91) 894 00 84.* 🚃 *Sat.* 🎉 *Semana Santa (Easter Week), San Roque (Aug 12–18).*

CHINCHÓN IS arguably Madrid province's most picturesque town. The 16th-century, typically Castilian, porticoed **Plaza Mayor** has a splendidly theatrical air. It comes alive for the Easter passion play, acted out by the townspeople *(see p280)*, and during the August bullfights. The 16th-century church, perched above the square, has an altar painting by Goya, whose brother was a priest here. Just off the square is the 18th-century Augustinian monastery, which has been converted into a **parador**

Chinchón's unique porticoed Plaza Mayor

with a peaceful patio garden *(see p554)*. A ruined 15th-century castle is on a hill to the west of town. Although it is closed to the public, there are views of Chinchón and the countryside from outside it.

Chinchón is a popular weekend destination for *Madrileños*, who come here to sample the excellent chorizo and locally produced *anís (see p577)* in the town's many taverns.

Palacio Real de Aranjuez ⑪

Plaza de Parejas, Aranjuez. 📞 *(91) 891 07 40.* 🚌 🚃 🕐 *Tue–Sun.* ⬤ *some public hols.* 🎫 ♿

THE ROYAL SUMMER PALACE and gardens of Aranjuez grew up around a medieval hunting lodge standing beside a natural weir, the meeting point of the Tagus and Jarama rivers.

Today's palace of brick and white stone was built in the 18th century to replace the earlier Hapsburg palace that burned down. A guided tour takes you through numerous Baroque rooms, among them the Chinese Porcelain Room,

the Hall of Mirrors, and the Smoking Room, modeled on the Alhambra in Granada. It is worth visiting Aranjuez for the simple pleasure of walking in the 740 acres of shady royal gardens that inspired Joaquín Rodrigo's *Concierto de Aranjuez*. The small Parterre Garden and the Island Garden, between the rivers, survive from the original 16th-century palace.

Between the palace and the River Tagus is the 18th-century Prince's Garden, decorated with sculptures, fountains, and lofty trees from the Americas. In the garden is the Casa de Marinos (Sailors' House), a museum housing the launches once used by the royal family for trips along the river. At the far end of the garden is the Casa del Labrador (Laborer's Cottage), a decorative royal pavilion built by Carlos IV.

The town's restaurants are deservedly popular because of the exceptional quality of local produce, especially asparagus and strawberries. In summer, a 19th-century steam train, built to carry strawberries to the market in Madrid, runs between here and the capital.

MIGUEL DE CERVANTES

Miguel de Cervantes Saavedra, Spain's greatest literary figure *(see p30)*, was born in Alcalá de Henares in 1547. After fighting in the naval Battle of Lepanto (1571), he was held captive by the Turks for more than five years. In 1605, when he was almost 60 years old, the first of two parts of his comic masterpiece *Don Quixote (see p377)* were published to popular acclaim. He continued writing novels and plays until his death in Madrid on April 23, 1616, the same day that Shakespeare died.

Gardens surrounding the Royal Palace at Aranjuez

CENTRAL SPAIN

Introducing Central Spain

MUCH OF SPAIN'S VAST CENTRAL PLATEAU, the *meseta*, is covered with wheat fields or dry, dusty plains, but there are many attractive places to explore. Central Spain's mountains, gorges, forests, and lakes are filled with wildlife. A deep sense of history permeates the towns and cities of the tableland, reflected in some stunning architecture: the Roman ruins of Mérida, the medieval mansions of Cáceres, the Gothic cathedrals of Burgos, León, and Toledo, the Renaissance grandeur of Salamanca, and castles almost everywhere.

León Cathedral (see p336–7), *an outstanding Gothic building, was completed during the 13th century. As well as many glorious windows of medieval glass, it has superb carved choir stalls depicting biblical scenes and everyday life.*

León

CASTILLA Y LEÓN
(see pp328–59)

Zamora

Vall

Salamanca (see pp340–43) *is the site of some of the finest Renaissance and Plateresque architecture in Spain. Among the city's most notable buildings are the university, its façade a mass of carved detail; the old and new cathedrals (built side by side); and the handsome Plaza Mayor, built of warm golden sandstone.*

Salamanca

Ávila

Cáceres

EXTREMADURA
(see pp382–95)

The Museo Nacional de Arte Romano *in Mérida (see p392) houses Roman treasures. The city has a well-preserved Roman theater.*

Badajoz

| 0 kilometers | 50 |
| 0 miles | 50 |

◁ **Roofs and walls in the old part of Toledo**

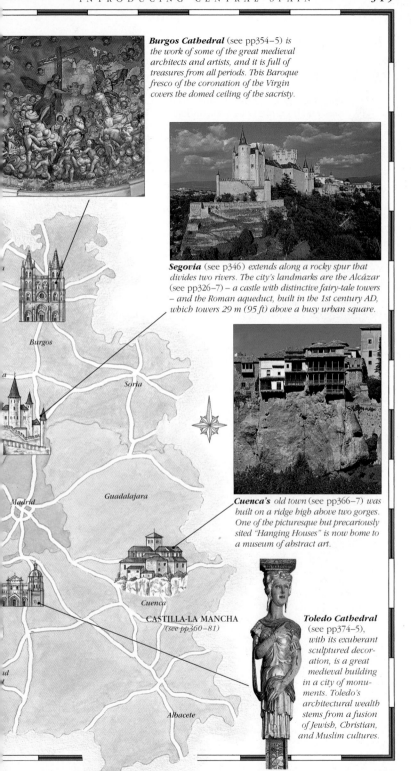

Burgos Cathedral (see pp354–5) *is the work of some of the great medieval architects and artists, and it is full of treasures from all periods. This Baroque fresco of the coronation of the Virgin covers the domed ceiling of the sacristy.*

Segovia (see p346) *extends along a rocky spur that divides two rivers. The city's landmarks are the Alcázar (see pp326–7) – a castle with distinctive fairy-tale towers – and the Roman aqueduct, built in the 1st century AD, which towers 29 m (95 ft) above a busy urban square.*

Cuenca's old town (see pp366–7) *was built on a ridge high above two gorges. One of the picturesque but precariously sited "Hanging Houses" is now home to a museum of abstract art.*

CASTILLA-LA MANCHA
(see pp360–81)

Toledo Cathedral (see pp374–5), *with its exuberant sculptured decoration, is a great medieval building in a city of monuments. Toledo's architectural wealth stems from a fusion of Jewish, Christian, and Muslim cultures.*

Burgos

Soria

Madrid

Guadalajara

Cuenca

Albacete

Regional Food: Central Spain

THE RESTAURANTS OF MADRID are a rich source of specialties from every Spanish region, along with superb fresh fish that is often on the table within a few hours of being caught. Game, such as wild boar, pheasant, and partridge, is plentiful throughout Central Spain, but especially in Extremadura, where wild frog and tench are also eaten. Castilla y León and Castilla-La Mancha maintain a tradition of homey, robust cooking with a variety of warming one-pot pea and bean stews. The north also produces excellent bread, which is eaten with everything. Sausages and simple **Garlic** rabbit or pork dishes, spiced with cumin and garlic, are typical of Castilla-La Mancha; while Castilla y León is known for its suckling pig and milk-fed lamb, roasted whole in enormous bread ovens. Little cakes, such as Toledo's famous marzipans, are popular, and many convents continue to make and sell their own.

Patatas a la importancia *are egg-coated potatoes fried and then simmered in wine seasoned with onions and saffron.*

Saffron (azafrán) *comes from the purple autumn crocus, which has three deep red stigmas. Introduced by the Moors centuries ago, it is the world's most expensive spice because it must be picked by hand. The plains of La Mancha (see p376) yield Spain's highest quality saffron, which is sold in strands and date stamped. Saffron is soaked, crushed, or toasted to add its taste and golden color to a variety of dishes.*

Pollo al padre Pero, *a dish of Extremadura, is half a young chicken simmered in a spicy pepper and tomato sauce.*

Sopa de ajo *is a warming garlic soup thickened with bread. Poached eggs and paprika are often added to it.*

Chickpeas — Chicken

Beef — Cabbage

Salt pork belly — Sausage

Cocido madrileño *is a widely available meat dish and every region has its own variation. It is essentially a slow-simmered stew of beef, chicken, ham, and pork belly with chickpeas. Cabbage, chorizo, and* morcilla *(black sausage) are also included. The broth is drunk first, as soup, and the rest often served as two additional courses.*

Migas, *originally a shepherd's dish, is fried breadcrumbs. It is often served with fried peppers or, in Extremadura, with bacon*

Perdiz con chocolate *is braised partridge with carrots and onions, served with a rich, dark, chocolate-tasting gravy.*

Pisto, *La Mancha's best dish, is Spain's version of ratatouille. It combines peppers, tomatoes, onions, and zucchini.*

El frite, *from Extremadura, is a dish of fried lamb with garlic, onion, and lemon, flavored with the local paprika.*

Sausages are made in most of the villages of Extremadura and vary in their taste and appearance. Those made in Guijelo (including chorizo) and Montanchez are particularly good, as are the hams, cured loins, and shoulders produced in Extremadura.

Menestra de ternera *is a stew in which veal is simmered gently with young vegetables, such as carrots and peas.*

Cabrito al ajillo *is kid fried with onions and herbs. This savory dish can also include pounded goat's liver.*

Manchego, *made from sheep's milk on the plains of La Mancha, is widely regarded as Spain's greatest cheese. When fully mature it becomes very hard, similar to Parmesan. The texture and the taste vary depending on whether it is* fresco *(young),* curado *(over 13 weeks old), or* añejo *(at least 7 months old).*

Yemas *means yolks, which these sugary cakes resemble in their shape, color, and content. The best come from Ávila (see p344).*

Chickpeas

Lentils

Pinto beans

LEGUMES

An enormous variety of legumes, in all colors, shapes, and sizes is grown on the plains of Castilla y León. The best legumes are expensive, and their names are legally protected. The best-known white beans are the *alubias blancas* of Barco de Ávila; the best chickpeas are grown in Fuentesauco; and the finest lentils come from La Armuña.

Wines of Central Spain

THE WINES OF CENTRAL SPAIN originate in either the small, high-quality regions of northwest Castilla y León or in the vast wine-producing plains of La Mancha and Valdepeñas. Ribera del Duero has become Spain's most fashionable red wine region, with its aromatic, rich, yet fine reds made from Tinto Fino grapes (the local name for Tempranillo) and, more recently, lighter, fruity wines. Rueda makes a good white wine, made from the Verdejo grape. La Mancha and Valdepeñas both produce lots of simple white wine, and reds that can be mellow and fruity.

Harvesting Viura grapes at Rueda

Artesian well for irrigating vines in La Mancha

Toro *makes the most powerful and fiery of all red wines from the ubiquitous Tempranillo grape.*

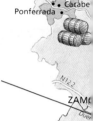

Villafranca
del Bierzo
Cacabe
Ponferrada

N122

ZAM(

Duer

SALAMANC

N630

N620

KEY FACTS ABOUT WINES OF CENTRAL SPAIN

 Location and Climate
Ribera del Duero, Rueda, and Toro are all high-lying areas with extreme climates – very hot summer days combined with cool nights, and cold winters. The marked difference of temperature between day and night helps to preserve the acidity in the grapes. Both La Mancha and Valdepeñas are extremely hot and dry areas. In recent years, droughts have caused a severe shortage of grapes.

Grape Varieties
The Tempranillo grape – also known as Tinto Fino, Tinto del Toro, and Cencibel – produces nearly all the best red wines of Central Spain. Cabernet Sauvignon is permitted in some regions; it is used in some Ribera del Duero wines

and occasionally surfaces as a single varietal, as at the estate of the Marquis of Griñón in Méntrida. Verdejo, Viura, and Sauvignon Blanc are used for white Rueda. The white Airén grape predominates in the vineyards of Valdepeñas and La Mancha.

Good Producers
Toro: Fariña (Gran Colegiata). ***Rueda:*** Álvarez y Diez, Los Curros, Marqués de Riscal, Sanz. ***Ribera del Duero:*** Alejandro Fernández (Pesquera), Boada, Hermanos Pérez Pascuas (Viña Pedrosa), Ismael Arroyo (Valsotillo), Vega Sicilia, Victor Balbás. ***Méntrida:*** Marqués de Griñón. ***La Mancha:*** Fermín Ayuso Roig (Estola), Vinícola de Castilla (Castillo de Alhambra). ***Valdepeñas:*** Casa de la Viña, Félix Solís, Luis Megía (Marqués de Gastañaga), Los Llanos.

Traditional earthenware *tinaj* still used for fermenting wine

0 kilometers	100
0 miles	50

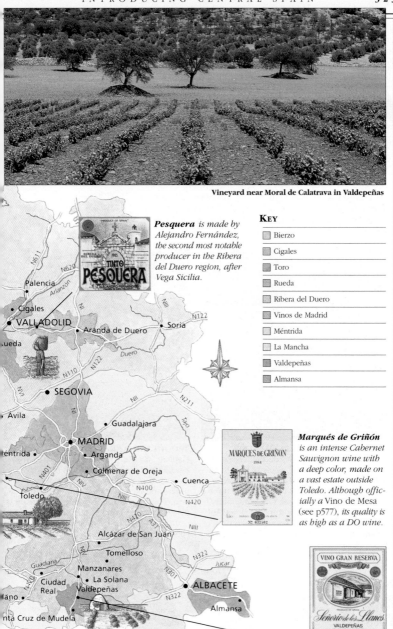

Vineyard near Moral de Calatrava in Valdepeñas

Pesquera *is made by Alejandro Fernández, the second most notable producer in the Ribera del Duero region, after Vega Sicilia.*

Marqués de Griñón *is an intense Cabernet Sauvignon wine with a deep color, made on a vast estate outside Toledo. Although officially a* Vino de Mesa *(see p577), its quality is as high as a DO wine.*

Señorío de los Llanos *is produced in Valdepeñas. Its fine reds – made from Cencibel (Tempranillo) and aged in oak – are an excellent value.*

WINE REGIONS

The wine regions of Ribera del Duero, Toro, and Rueda are situated on remote, high plateaus, straddling the Río Duero. To the northwest lies the isolated region of Bierzo, whose wines have more in common with neighboring Valdeorras in Galicia. Some wine is produced around Madrid, and southwest of the capital is the largely undistinguished region of Méntrida. Most of central Spain's wine is produced in La Mancha – the world's largest single wine region – and in the smaller enclave of Valdepeñas, which produces wines of a higher quality.

Birds of Central Spain

Bee-eater

THE VAST AND VARIED wild habitats of central Spain are home to the richest avifauna in the peninsula. White storks' nests are a common sight on the church towers and chimneys of towns. Grebes, herons, and shovelers can be seen in the marshlands; the distinctive hoopoe is often spotted in woods; and grasslands are the nesting grounds of bustards and cranes. The mountains and high plains are the domain of birds of prey such as the imperial eagle, peregrine falcon, and vulture. Deforestation, changing agricultural practices, and hunting have all taken their toll in recent decades. Today, almost 160 bird species are the subject of conservation initiatives.

MIGRATION ROUTES

— Cranes

— Storks

— Raptors

— Wildfowl

MARSHLAND AND WET MEADOW

Wetlands such as Lagunas de Ruidera *(see p379)* on the edge of the plains of La Mancha, are vital feeding grounds for a wide range of waterfowl, some of which may remain in Spain throughout the year. Other migratory species use such sites as stopover points to feed, rest, and build up enough energy to enable them to complete their journeys.

WOODLAND AND SCRUB

Habitats in areas of woodland, such as the Parque Nacional de Cabañeros *(see p369)*, and scrub support many species, such as rollers and woodpeckers, throughout the year. Food is plentiful, and there are many places to roost and nest. Early in the morning is the best time for spotting some of the rarer species, such as the bluethroat.

Little egrets are recognized by their snow white plumage and graceful slow flight. They feed largely on frogs, snails, and small fish.

Rollers are commonly found in woodland, often nesting in tree stumps or holes left by woodpeckers. Their food includes grasshoppers, crickets, and beetles.

Shovelers feed on the water surface with a characteristic shoveling motion. The male has brightly colored plumage, but the female is a dull brown.

Hoopoes can be easily identified by their striking plumage and by the crest that can be raised if the bird is alarmed. They feed on ground insects.

STORKS

Both the white and the much rarer black stork breed in Spain. They can be recognized in flight by their slow, steady wingbeats and may occasionally be seen soaring on thermals, usually during migration.
During the breeding season they put on elaborate courtship displays, which involve "dancing," wing-beating, and bill-clapping. Their large nests, made of branches and twigs and lined with grasses, are constructed on roofs, towers, spires, and chimneys, where they are easy to watch.
They feed on insects, fish, and amphibians. Stork populations are threatened by wetland reclamation and the use of pesticides.

The endangered black stork

Nesting on a monastery roof

GRASSLAND AND FIELD

Many of Spain's natural grasslands have been plowed over to plant grain and other crops. Remaining vestiges are rich in wild grasses and flowers and are vital habitats for species such as bustards and larks.

Cranes perform elegant courtship dances and are also stately birds in flight, their long necks extended to the limit. They are omnivores, feeding on amphibians, crustaceans, plants, and insects.

Great bustards nest in shallow depressions formed in open areas and cultivated fields. Spain is home to half the world's bustard population.

MOUNTAIN AND HIGH PLAIN

Some of Spain's most spectacular birds of prey live in mountain ranges, such as the Sierra de Gredos *(see p344)*, and the high plains of Central Spain. The broad wingspans of eagles and vultures allow them to soar on currents of warm air as they scan the ground below for prey and carrion.

Imperial eagles, with their vast wingspan of 2.25 m (7 ft), are extremely rare – only around 100 pairs are left in all Spain.

Griffon vultures, a gregarious species, nest in trees and on rocky crags, often using the same place from year to year. Their broad wingspans can exceed 2 m (6 ft).

The Castles of Castile

13th-century fresco of the siege of a castle

THE GREATEST CONCENTRATION of Spain's 2,000 castles is in Castile (now part of Castilla y León), which derived its name from the word *castillo*, or castle. In the 10th and 11th centuries this region was the battleground between Moors and Christians. Villages and towns were fortified as protection against one side or the other. Most of the surviving castles in Castile, however, were built as noble residences after the area had been reconquered and there was no longer a military purpose for them. Fernando and Isabel *(see pp52–3)* banned the building of new castles at the end of the 15th century; many existing ones were converted to domestic use.

Coca Castle *(see p347)*, a classic Mudéjar design in brick

La Mota Castle (see p348), *at Medina del Campo, near Valladolid, was originally a Moorish castle but was rebuilt after 1440 and later became the property of Fernando and Isabel. The square-shaped Torre del Homenaje has twin bartizan turrets at its corners and machiolations beneath its battlements. Great curtain walls surround the castle.*

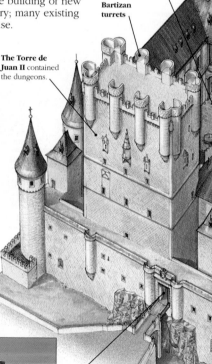

Patio de armas (courtyard)

Bartizan turrets

The Torre de Juan II contained the dungeons.

The barbican, with the coat of arms of the Catholic Monarchs carved over the gate, contains the portcullis and guards' watchrooms.

Belmonte Castle (see p376) *was built in the 15th century as the stronghold of the quarrelsome Marquis of Villena, Juan Pacheco. Late-Gothic in style, it has a sophisticated, hexagonal ground plan, with a triangular bailey.*

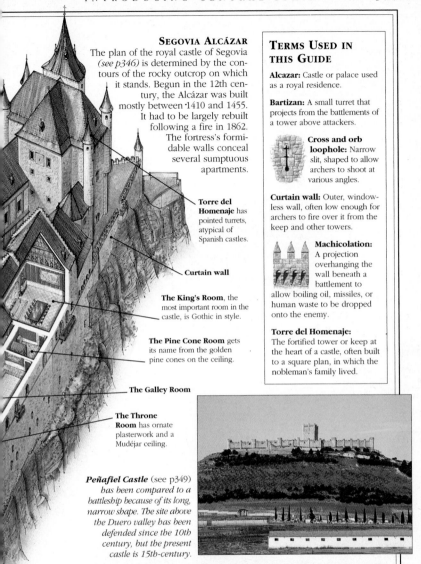

Segovia Alcázar

The plan of the royal castle of Segovia *(see p346)* is determined by the contours of the rocky outcrop on which it stands. Begun in the 12th century, the Alcázar was built mostly between ·1410 and 1455. It had to be largely rebuilt following a fire in 1862. The fortress's formidable walls conceal several sumptuous apartments.

Torre del Homenaje has pointed turrets, atypical of Spanish castles.

Curtain wall

The King's Room, the most important room in the castle, is Gothic in style.

The Pine Cone Room gets its name from the golden pine cones on the ceiling.

The Galley Room

The Throne Room has ornate plasterwork and a Mudéjar ceiling.

Peñafiel Castle (see p349) has been compared to a battleship because of its long, narrow shape. The site above the Duero valley has been defended since the 10th century, but the present castle is 15th-century.

Terms Used in this Guide

Alcazar: Castle or palace used as a royal residence.

Bartizan: A small turret that projects from the battlements of a tower above attackers.

Cross and orb loophole: Narrow slit, shaped to allow archers to shoot at various angles.

Curtain wall: Outer, windowless wall, often low enough for archers to fire over it from the keep and other towers.

Machicolation: A projection overhanging the wall beneath a battlement to allow boiling oil, missiles, or human waste to be dropped onto the enemy.

Torre del Homenaje: The fortified tower or keep at the heart of a castle, often built to a square plan, in which the nobleman's family lived.

The Castles of Castilla y León

Some of Central Spain's finest surviving castles can be visited today. A few, such as Ciudad Rodrigo *(see p339)*, have been turned into luxurious paradors *(see pp534–5).*

CASTILLA Y LEÓN

LEÓN · ZAMORA · SALAMANCA · ÁVILA · SEGOVIA
VALLADOLID · PALENCIA · BURGOS · SORIA

*A*WESOME EXPANSES OF OCHER PLAINS *stretch to hills crowned with the castles that cover this vast region. Through Spain's history, these central provinces have had a major influence on its language, religion, and culture. Their many historic cities preserve some of the country's most magnificent architectural sights.*

The territories of the two rival medieval kingdoms of Castile and León, occupying the northern half of the great plateau in the center of Spain, now form the country's largest region, or *comunidad autónoma*.

Castile and León were first brought together under one crown in 1037 by Fernando I, but the union was not consolidated until the early 13th century. The kingdom of Castile and León was one of the driving forces of the Reconquest. El Cid, the legendary hero, was born near Burgos.

Wealth pouring in from the wool trade and the New World, reaching a peak in the 16th century, financed the many great artistic and architectural treasures that can be seen today in the cities of Castilla y León. Burgos has an exuberantly decorated Gothic cathedral. León cathedral is famous for its medieval stained glass. At the heart of the monumental city of Salamanca is the oldest university in the peninsula. Segovia's aqueduct is the largest Roman structure in Spain, and its Alcázar is the country's most photographed castle. Ávila is surrounded by an unbroken wall, built by Christian forces against the Moors. In Valladolid, the regional capital, a superb collection of multicolored sculpture is displayed in a magnificent 15th-century building.

Beyond the cities, in Castilla y León's varied countryside, there are many attractive small towns that preserve outstanding examples of the region's vernacular architecture.

Grain fields and vineyards covering the fertile Tierra de Campos in Palencia province

◁ **The battle-scarred castle of Calatañazor (Soria), site of a Christian victory against the Moors in 1002**

Exploring Castilla y León

COVERING THE NORTHERN PART of central Spain's vast tableland, Castilla y León has a huge variety of sights. Many – the university of Salamanca, the Alcázar and aqueduct of Segovia, the medieval walls of Ávila, the monastery at Santo Domingo de Silos, and the great cathedrals of Burgos and León – are well known. Other historic towns and villages worthy of a detour include Ciudad Rodrigo, Covarrubias, Pedraza de la Sierra, and Zamora. This region also has great tracts of beautiful countryside, especially in the mountains of the Sierra de la Peña de Francia and the Sierra de Gredos.

SIGHTS AT A GLANCE

Tour

SEE ALSO

• ***Where to Stay*** pp555–7

• ***Restaurants and Bars*** pp595–6

Oviedo
N630
Lugo
1 EL BIERZO
C63
CUEVAS DE VALPORQUERO 6
VILLAFRANCA DEL BIERZO
2
A66
LEÓN
7
3 PONFERRADA
N536
ASTORGA 5
N62
N601
VALENC
DE DON
C622
NVI
Esla
4 PUEBLA DE SANABRIA
Bragança
Embalse de Cernadilla
N525
BENAVENTE
Tera
N610
N631
MEDINA DE RIOSE
N122
NVI
N122
ZAMORA 8
TORO
Duero
TORDESILL
C527
N630
N620
Embalse de Almendra
MEDINA
CA
Duero
Agueda
N620
11 SALAMANCA
ALBA DE TORMES
N501
Guarda
9 CIUDAD RODRIGO
N620
10
Embalse de Santa Teresa
SIERRA DE LA PEÑA DE FRANCIA
Tormes
N110
C526
BÉJAR
Cáceres
12
SIERRA DE GREDOS
0 kilometers 50
0 miles 30
Tiétar

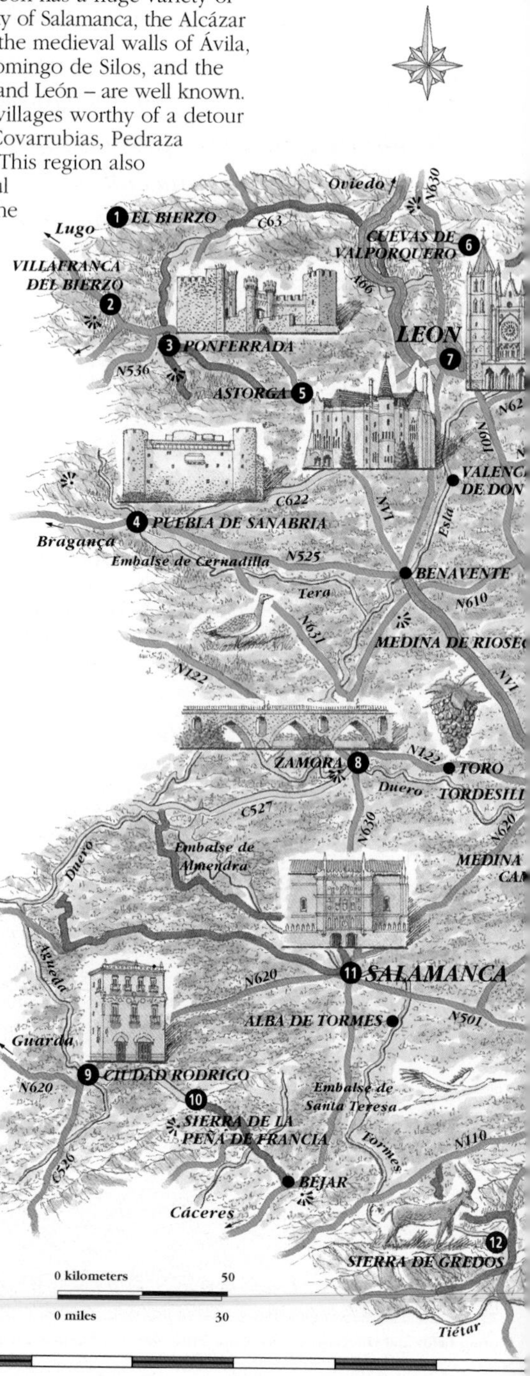

GETTING AROUND

Madrid makes a convenient springboard for touring in Castilla y León. The major cities of the region are connected by rail, but the bus is often a quicker alternative. If you intend to explore rural areas or to visit small towns, it is advisable to hire a car. There are few major highways and as a result main roads tend to be dominated by trucks. Minor roads, generally in good condition, are a more enjoyable way of seeing the countryside.

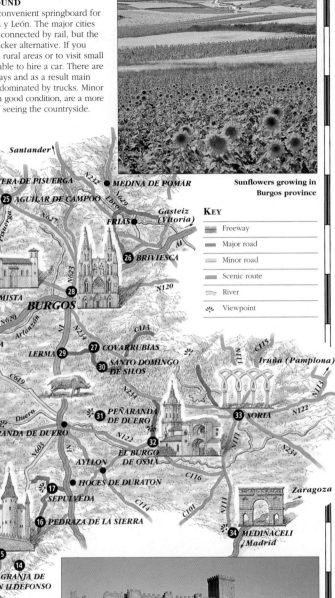

Sunflowers growing in
Burgos province

KEY

▬▬	Freeway
▬▬	Major road
▭▭	Minor road
▬▬	Scenic route
⟿	River
☇	Viewpoint

Santander

● CERVERA DE PISUERGA   ● MEDINA DE POMAR

25 AGUILAR DE CAMPOO

N621

N611

Pisuerga

N627

N232

N629

Ebro

Gasteiz
(Vitoria)

FRIAS ●

A1

N623

26 BRIVIESCA

N120

C615

24 FROMISTA

28

BURGOS

Arlanzón

N620

N1

N234

CL13

CL13

Iruña (Pamplona)

N111

N113

510 **23** PALENCIA

LERMA **29**

27 COVARRUBIAS

☇

30 SANTO DOMINGO
DE SILOS

N234

C619

VALLADOLID

Duero

N122

ARANDA DE DUERO

N603

N1

31 PEÑARANDA
DE DUERO

☇

N122

32

EL BURGO
DE OSMA

33 SORIA

N122

N111

N234

AYLLON

● HOCES DE DURATON

CL116

C116

CASTILLO
DE COCA **18**

17 SEPULVEDA

☇

CL114

C101

Zaragoza

N111

34 MEDINACELI
/Madrid

☇

VALO

16 PEDRAZA DE LA SIERRA

SEGOVIA **15**

14 LA GRANJA DE
SAN ILDEFONSO

A

N1

Madrid

N403

Toledo

Peñaranda de Duero castle

El Bierzo ❶

León. 🚉 Ponferrada. 🚌 Ponferrada.
ℹ️ Ponferrada, (987) 42 42 36.

THIS NORTHWESTERN region of
León province was at one
time the bed of an ancient
lake. Sheltered by hills from
the worst extremes of central
Spain's climate, its sun-soaked,
alluvial soils make for fertile
orchards and vineyards. Over
the centuries, the area has also
yielded rich mineral treasure
including coal, iron, and gold.
Many hiking routes and picnic spots are within reach of
the main towns of Ponferrada
and Villafranca del Bierzo.
   In the eastern section, you
can trace the course of the old
Road to Santiago *(see pp78–9)*
through the **Montes de León**,
past the pilgrim church and
medieval bridge of Molinaseca.
Turning off the road at the remote village of Acebo you pass
through a deep valley where
there are signs pointing to the
Herrería de Compludo, a
fascinating water-powered
ironworks which dates from
the 7th century. The machinery is still in working order and
is demonstrated regularly.
   The **Lago de Carucedo**, to
the southwest of Ponferrada,
is an ancient artificial lake. It
acted as a reservoir in Roman
times, a by-product of a vast
gold mining operation. Millions
of tons of alluvium were
washed from the hills of Las

A *palloza* in the Sierra de Ancares

Médulas by a complex system
of canals and sluice gates.
The ore was then panned,
and the gold dust collected on
sheep's wool. It has been
estimated that more than 500
tons of precious metal were
extracted from the hills between the 1st and 4th centuries
AD. These ancient workings
lie within a memorable
landscape of wind-eroded
crags, and hills pierced by tunnels and colonized by gnarled
chestnut trees. You can best
appreciate the area from a
viewpoint at Orellán, which is
reached via a rough, steep
track. **Las Médulas**, a village
south of Carucedo, is another
place to go for a fine view.
   To the north of the NVI highway lies the Sierra de Ancares,
a wild region of rounded, slate
mountains marking the borders

of Galicia and Asturias. Part
of it now forms the **Reserva
Nacional de los Ancares
Leoneses**, an attractive nature
preserve. The heathland dotted
with oak and birch groves is
home to deer, wolves, brown
bears, and capercaillies.
   Several isolated villages high
in the hills contain *pallozas* –
primitive, pre-Roman stone
dwellings thatched with rye.
One of the most striking collections of these huts can be
found in the isolated village of
Campo del Agua, in the west.

🏛 **Herrería de Compludo**
Compludo. ☎ (987) 45 91 66.
◻ Tue–Sat.

Villafranca del Bierzo ❷

León. 🏘 2,700. 🚌 ℹ️ Plaza Mayor 1,
(987) 54 02 91. 🚌 Tue. 🎉 Winter
Fiesta (Jan 28), Fiesta del Cristo (Sep 14).

EMBLAZONED MANSIONS line the
ancient streets of this delightful town on the Road to
Santiago. The solid, early 16th-
century, drum-towered castle
is still inhabited. Near the Plaza
Mayor a number of imposing
churches and convents compete for attention. Particularly
worth seeing are the fine sculptures adorning the north portal
of the simple, Romanesque
Iglesia de Santiago. At the
church's Puerta del Perdón
(Door of Mercy), pilgrims who

Craggy, tree-clad hills around the ancient gold workings near the village of Las Médulas

were too weak to make the final grueling hike across the hills of Galicia could obtain dispensation. Visitors to the town can also sample the local specialty, cherries marinated in *aguardiente*, a liqueur.

ENVIRONS: One of the finest views of El Bierzo is from **Corullón**, to the south. This pretty village with gray, stone houses is set in a sunny location above the broad, fertile basin of the Río Sil where the vines of the Bierzo wine region flourish (*see pp74–5*). Two churches, the late 11th-century San Miguel and the restored Romanesque San Esteban, are worth a visit. Down in the valley, the Benedictine monastery at **Carracedo del Monasterio** stands in ruined splendor. Founded in 990, it was at one time the most powerful religious community in El Bierzo.

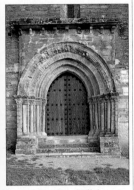

Puerta del Perdón of Villafranca's Iglesia de Santiago

Ponferrada ❸

León. 🏘 60,000. 🚆 🚌 🛈 C/ Gil y Carrasco 4, (987) 42 42 36. 🚌 Wed & Sat. 🎉 Virgen de la Encina (Sep 7).

A MEDIEVAL BRIDGE reinforced with iron (*pons ferrata*), erected for the benefit of pilgrims on their way to Santiago de Compostela, gave this town its name. Today, prosperous from both iron and coal deposits, Ponferrada has expanded into a sizable town.

Most of its attractions are confined to the small old quarter. Ponferrada's majestic **castle** was constructed between the

The imposing Templar castle of Ponferrada

12th and 14th centuries by the Knights Templar to protect pilgrims. During the Middle Ages it was one of the largest fortresses in northwest Spain.

Standing on the main square is the Baroque **town hall** *(ayuntamiento).* One entrance to the square is straddled by a tall clock tower, which sits above one of the gateways of the medieval wall. Nearby is the Renaissance **Basílica de la Virgen de la Encina**. The older **Iglesia de Santo Tomás de las Ollas** is hidden away in the town's villagelike northern suburbs. Mozarabic, Romanesque, and Baroque elements combine in the architecture of this simple church. The 10th-century apse has beautiful horseshoe arches. Ask at the nearest house for the key.

ENVIRONS: A pleasant drive through the idyllic **Valle de Silencio** (Valley of Silence) south of Ponferrada follows a poplar-fringed stream past several bucolic villages. The last and most beautiful of these is **Peñalba de Santiago**, sheltering beneath an attractive ring of mountains. The 10th-century Mozarabic church of Santiago de Peñalba has horseshoe arches above its double portal.

Puebla de Sanabria ❹

Zamora. 🏘 1,800. 🚆 🛈 Plaza Mayor 1, (980) 62 00 02. 🚌 Fri. 🎉 Las Victorias (Sep 9).

THIS ATTRACTIVE OLD village lies beyond the undulating broom and oak scrub of the Sierra de la Culebra. A steep cobbled street leads past stone and slate houses with huge, overhanging eaves and walls bearing coats of arms, to a hilltop church and castle.

The village has become the center of a popular inland resort based around the largest glacial lake in Spain, the **Lago de Sanabria**, now a nature preserve. Among the many activities available are fishing, walking, and water sports.

Local touring routes beckon visitors to Ribadelago on the lakeshore, but the road to the quaint hill village of **San Martín de Castañeda** has better views. There's a small visitors' center for the nature preserve in San Martín's restored monastery. The village is so traditional that you may still see cattle yoked to wooden carts and women dressed in black from head to toe.

The 12th-century church and 15th-century castle of Puebla de Sanabria

The nave of Astorga cathedral

Astorga ❺

León. 👥 13,500. 🚉 🚌 ℹ️ *Plaza de España.* 📞 *(987) 61 68 38.* 🗓️ *Tue.* 🎉 *Santa Marta (late Aug).*

THE ROMAN TOWN of Asturica Augusta was a strategic halt on the Vía de la Plata (Silver Road), a Roman road linking Andalusia and northwest Spain. Later it came to form a stage on the pilgrimage route to Santiago *(see pp78–9).*

Soaring above the ramparts in the upper town are Astorga's two principal monuments, the cathedral and the Palacio Episcopal. The **cathedral** was built between the 15th and the 18th centuries and displays a variety of architectural styles ranging from its Gothic apse to the effusive Baroque of its two towers, which are carved with various biblical scenes. The gilt altarpiece by Gaspar Becerra is a masterpiece of the Spanish Renaissance. Among the many fine exhibits found in the cathedral's museum are the 10th-century carved casket of Alfonso III the Great, the jeweled Reliquary of the True Cross, and a lavish silver monstrance which is studded with enormous emeralds.

Opposite the cathedral is a fairy-tale building of multiple turrets and quasi-Gothic windows. The unconventional **Palacio Episcopal** (Bishop's Palace) was designed at the end of the 19th century by Antoni Gaudí, the highly original Modernista architect *(see p160),* for the incumbent bishop, a fellow Catalan, after a fire in 1887 had destroyed the previous building. Its bizarre appearance as well as its phenomenal cost so horrified the diocese that no subsequent bishops ever lived in it. Today it houses an assembly of medieval religious art devoted to the history of Astorga and the pilgrimage to Santiago. Roman relics, including coins and fragments of mosaics unearthed in the Plaza del Parque, are evidence of Astorga's importance as a Roman settlement. The palace's interior is decorated with Gaudí's splendid ceramic tiles and stained glass.

Reliquary of the True Cross

🏛️ **Palacio Episcopal**
Pl Eduardo de Castro. 📞 *(987) 61 68 82.* ⏰ *Mon–Sat.* 🔴 *Jan 1 & 6.* ♿

Cuevas de Valporquero ❻

Valporquero. 📞 *(987) 29 21 89.* 🚌 *from León.* ⏰ *Apr–May: Sat & Sun; Jun–Sep: daily; Oct–Nov: Fri–Sun.* ♿

THIS COMPLEX OF limestone caves – technically a single cave with three separate entrances – is directly beneath the village of Valporquero de Torío in the northern part of León province. The caves were formed in the Miocene period between 5 and 25 million years ago. Severe weather conditions in the surrounding mountains make the water-sculpted caverns inaccessible between December and Easter. Less than half of the huge system, which stretches 3,100 m (10,170 ft) under the ground, is open to the public. Guided tours take parties through an impressive series of galleries in which lighting picks out the beautiful limestone concretions. Iron and sulphur oxides have tinted the rocks many subtle shades of red, gray, and black. The massive Gran Rotonda, covering an area of 5,600 sq m (60,280 sq ft) and reaching a height of 20 m (65 ft), is the most stunning cave in the complex.

As the interior is cold, and the surface often slippery to walk on, it is advisable to wear warm clothes and sturdy shoes.

Illuminated stalactites hanging from the roof of one of the chambers in the Cuevas de Valporquero

León ❼

León. 🏛 150,000. 🚉 ✈ ℹ Plaza
de la Regla 4, (987) 23 70 82.
🛒 Wed & Sat. 🎉 San Juan and San
Pedro (Jun 24–9), San Froilán (Oct 5).

F OUNDED AS a camp for the
Romans' Seventh Legion,
León became the capital of a
kingdom in the Middle Ages.
As such it played a central
role in the early years of the
Reconquest (see pp48–9).

The city's most important
building – apart from its great
cathedral (see pp336–7) – is
the **Basílica de San Isidoro**,
built into the Roman walls
which encircle the city. A separate entrance leads through
to the Romanesque **Panteón
Real** (Royal Pantheon), the
last resting place of more than
20 monarchs. It is superbly
decorated with carved capitals and 12th-century frescoes
illustrating a variety of biblical
and mythical subjects as well
as scenes of medieval life.

The alleyways in the picturesque old quarter around the
Plaza Mayor are interspersed
with bars and cafés, decrepit
mansions, and churches. Two
well-preserved palaces stand
near to the Plaza de Santo
Domingo: the **Casa de los
Guzmanes**, with its elegantly
arcaded Renaissance patio,
and Antoni Gaudí's unusually
restrained **Casa de Botines**
(which is now a bank).

The **Hostal de San Marcos**,
down beside the river, is a
prime example of Spanish

Frescoes in Basílica de San Isidoro showing medieval seasonal tasks

Renaissance architecture (see
p21). It was founded during
the 12th century as a monastery to lodge travelers en route
to Santiago. The present building was begun in 1513 as the
headquarters of the Knights of
Santiago. The incredibly elaborate project continued into the
18th century, when a Baroque
pediment added a final flourish
to the beautiful Plateresque
façade studded with scallop

shells. The main hall has a fine
16th-century coffered ceiling.
A parador (see p534) now occupies the main part of the
Hostal de San Marcos. In the
vaulted galleries off the church
and cloister is the **Museo de
León**, whose many treasures
include a haunting little ivory
crucifix, the Cristo de Carrizo.

ENVIRONS: Around 30 km
(20 miles) east of León is the
**Iglesia de San Miguel de
Escalada**. Dating from the 10th
century, it is one of the finest
surviving churches built by the
Mozarabs – Christians influenced by the Moors. Notice
the Visigothic panels and the
exterior gallery of stately horseshoe arches resting on carved
capitals. At **Sahagún**, 70 km
(40 miles) southeast of León,
are the Mudéjar churches of
San Tirso and San Lorenzo,
with triple apses and belfries.
A colossal ruined castle overlooks the Río Esla beside
Valencia de Don Juan, 40 km
(25 miles) south of León.

🏛 **Museo de León**
Plaza de San Marcos. 📞 (987) 24 50
61. 🗓 Tue–Sun. 🚫

THE MARAGATOS

Astorga is the principal town of
the Maragatos, an ethnic
group of unknown origin,
thought to be descended
from 8th-century Berber
invaders. By marrying
only among themselves,
they managed to preserve
their customs through the
centuries and keep them-
selves apart from the rest
of society. Although the
demise of their traditional
trade of mule-driving has
changed their way of life, the
Maragatos still keep to their
communities. Their costumes
can be seen during fiestas.

**Maragatos dressed in
traditional costume**

León Cathedral

Carved detail from the choir

T HE MASTER BUILDERS of this Spanish Gothic cathedral *par excellence* (*see p20*) were inspired by French techniques of vaulting and buttressing. The present structure of golden sandstone, built on the site of three previous cathedrals, was begun in the mid-13th century and completed less than 100 years later. It combines a slender but very high nave with the huge panels of stained glass – on a variety of themes – which are the cathedral's most magnificent feature. Although it has survived for 700 years, today there is concern about air pollution, which in places is attacking the soft stone.

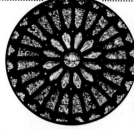

West Rose Window
This window, measuring 8 m (26 ft) in diameter, dates from the 13th century, making it one of the cathedral's oldest.

The 13th- to 14th-century cloister galleries are decorated with Gothic frescoes by Nicolás Francés.

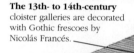

Cathedral Museum
Pedro de Campaña's panel, The Adoration of the Magi, *is one of the many magnificent treasures displayed in the museum.*

Entrance

★ **West Front**
The three portals are decorated with 13th-century carvings. Those above the Portada del Juicio *depict a scene from the Last Judgment, where the Blessed pass into Paradise.*

Inside the Cathedral

The plan of the building is a Latin cross. The tall nave is slender and long, measuring 90 m (295 ft) by 40 m (130 ft) at its widest. To appreciate the dazzling colors of the stained glass it is best to visit on a sunny day.

The altarpiece includes five original panels by Gothic master Nicolás Francés.

Silver reliquary
Made in the 16th century by Enrique de Arfe, this ornate chest holds the mortals remains of the patron of León, St. Froilan.

The Capilla de la Virgen Blanca contains an original Gothic sculpture of the Virgin smiling. A copy stands by the west door.

The choir has two tiers of 15th-century stalls. Behind it is the carved and gilded retrochoir, in the shape of a triumphal arch.

★ Stained Glass
The windows, covering an area of 1,800 sq meters (19,375 sq ft), are the highlight of the cathedral.

STAR FEATURES

★ West Front

★ Stained Glass

LEÓN'S STAINED GLASS

León cathedral's great glory is its magnificent glasswork. The 125 large windows and 57 smaller, round ones date from every century from the 13th to the 20th. They cover an enormous range of subjects, from mythical beasts to plants. Many depict saints and characters from biblical stories.

Window with plant motif

Some of the windows reveal fascinating details about medieval life: *La Cacería*, in the north wall, depicts a hunting scene, and the rose window in the Capilla del Nacimiento shows pilgrims worshipping at the tomb of St. James in Santiago de Compostela in Galicia (*see pp88–9*).

A large window in the south wall

Zamora ❽

Zamora. 🏛 65,000. 🚉 🚌 ℹ️ *Calle de Santa Clara 20, (980) 53 18 45.* 🗓 *Tue.* 🎭 *Semana Santa (Easter Week), San Pedro (Jun 29).*

LITTLE REMAINS of Zamora's past as an important strategic border town. In Roman times, it was on the Vía de la Plata *(see p334)*, and during the Reconquest was fought over fiercely. The city has now expanded far beyond its original boundaries, but the old quarter contains a wealth of Romanesque churches.

The ruins of the **city walls**, built by Alfonso III in 893, are pierced by the Postigo de la Traición (Traitor's Gate), where Sancho II was betrayed and stabbed to death in 1072. The **parador** *(see p557)* is housed in a former palace with a Renaissance courtyard adorned with coats of arms.

Two other palaces, the **Casa de los Momos** and the **Casa del Cordón**, have ornately carved façades and windows.

Zamora's most important monument is its unique **cathedral**, a 12th-century structure built in Romanesque style but with a number of later Gothic additions. The building's most eye-catching feature is its striking, scaly, hemispherical dome. Inside, there are superb iron grilles and Mudéjar pulpits surround Rodrigo Alemán's 15th-century choir stalls. The

allegorical carvings of nuns and monks on the misericord and armrests were once considered risqué. The museum, off the sober cloisters, displays an important collection of 15th-century Flemish tapestries known as the *Black Tapestries*. These illustrate classical and military scenes.

Nearby, several churches exhibit features characteristic of Zamora's architectural style, notably multilobed arches and heavily carved portals. The best are the 12th-century **Iglesia de San Ildefonso** and the **Iglesia de la Magdalena**.

Another reason for visiting Zamora is for its lively Easter Week celebrations, when elaborate *pasos* (sculpted floats) are paraded through the streets. During the rest of the year the *pasos* can be admired in the **Museo de Semana Santa**.

Peaceful gardens of the Colegiata de Santa María in Toro

ENVIRONS: The 7th-century Visigothic church of **San Pedro de la Nave**, 12 km (7.5 miles) northwest of Zamora, has charming carvings adorning its

Sierra de la Peña de Francia ❿

THESE ATTRACTIVE schist hills buttress the western edges of the Sierra de Gredos *(see p344)*. Narrow roads wind their way through picturesque chestnut, olive, and almond groves, and quaint rural villages of wood and stone. The highest point of the range is La Peña de Francia, which, at 1,732 m (5,700 ft), is easily recognizable from miles around. The views from the peak, and from the roads leading up to it, offer a breathtaking panorama of the surrounding empty plains and rolling hills.

La Peña de Francia ①
Crowning the peak is a windswept Dominican monastery sheltering a blackened, Byzantine-style statue of the Virgin and Child.

La Alberca ②
This pretty and much-visited village sells local honey, hams, and handicrafts. On August 15 each year it celebrates the Assumption with a traditional mystery play performed in costume.

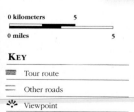

Las Batuecas ③
The road from La Alberca careers down into a green valley, the monastery whe Luis Buñuel made film *Tierra sin Par (Land without Bre*

| 0 kilometers | 5 |
| 0 miles | 5 |

KEY

    Tour route

    Other roads

🔆 Viewpoint

The unmistakable peak of La Peña de Francia

Fish-scale tiling on dome of Zamora cathedral

capitals and friezes. **Toro**, 33 km (21 miles) east of Zamora, is at the heart of a wine region *(see pp322–3)*. The highlights of its **Colegiata de Santa María** are the west portal, and, inside, a fine Hispano-Flemish painting, *La Virgen de la Mosca* (The Virgin and the Fly). In 1476, the forces of Isabel I *(see pp52–3)* secured a crucial victory over the Portuguese at Toro, confirming her succession to the throne of Castile.

Ciudad Rodrigo ❾

Salamanca. 🏠 *16,000.* 🚌 🚗 🛈
Plaza de Amayuelas 5, (923) 46 05 61. 🛍 *Tue.* 🎉 *San Sebastián (Jan 20), Romería de San Blas (Feb 3), La Charrada (Sat before Easter).*

DESPITE ITS LONELY setting – stranded on the country's western frontier miles from anywhere – this lovely old town is well worth a detour. Its frontier location inevitably gave rise to fortification, and its robust 14th-century castle is now an atmospheric **parador** *(see p555)* with good views of the Río Agueda. The prosperous 15th and 16th centuries were Ciudad Rodrigo's heyday. In 1812, during the War of Independence *(see pp58–9)*, the city, then occupied by the French, was besieged for 11 days before falling to the Duke of Wellington's forces.

The golden stone buildings within the ramparts are delightful. The main monument is the **cathedral**, whose belfry still bears the marks of shellfire from the siege. The exterior has a shapely curved balustrade and accomplished portal carvings. Inside, it is worth seeing the cloisters (in a variety of architectural styles) and the choir stalls, carved with lively scenes by Rodrigo Alemán. The main attraction of the adjacent **Capilla de Cerralbo** (Cerralbo Chapel) is a Ribera altarpiece. Off the chapel's south side is the quiet, arcaded Plaza del Buen Alcalde.

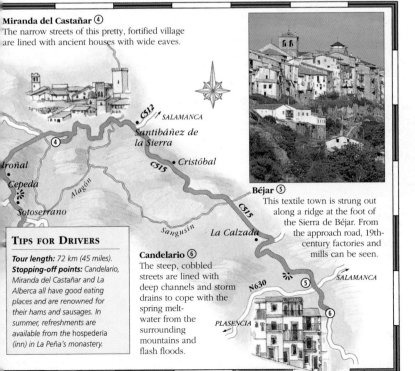

Miranda del Castañar ④
The narrow streets of this pretty, fortified village are lined with ancient houses with wide eaves.

C512 *SALAMANCA*

Santibáñez de la Sierra

④

C515 • *Cristóbal*

ironal

• *Cepeda*

Alagón

• *Sotoserrano*

C515

Sangusín   *La Calzada*

Béjar ⑤
This textile town is strung out along a ridge at the foot of the Sierra de Béjar. From the approach road, 19th-century factories and mills can be seen.

TIPS FOR DRIVERS

Tour length: *72 km (45 miles).*
Stopping-off points: *Candelario, Miranda del Castañar and La Alberca all have good eating places and are renowned for their hams and sausages. In summer, refreshments are available from the hospedería (inn) in La Peña's monastery.*

Candelario ⑥
The steep, cobbled streets are lined with deep channels and storm drains to cope with the spring melt-water from the surrounding mountains and flash floods.

PLASENCIA

N630

⑤   *SALAMANCA*

⑥

Street-by-Street: Salamanca ⓫

**Shell detail,
façade of the Casa
de las Conchas**

THE GREAT UNIVERSITY CITY of Salamanca is
Spain's finest showcase of Renaissance
and Plateresque architecture. Founded as
an Iberian settlement in pre-Roman times,
the city fell to Hannibal in 217 BC. Pre-
eminent among its artists and master craftsmen of later years were the Churriguera
brothers *(see p21)*. Their work can be seen
in many of Salamanca's golden stone buildings, notably in the Plaza Mayor. Other major sights are
the two cathedrals and the 13th-century university, one of
Europe's oldest and most distinguished.

The Casa de las Conchas
is easily identifiable from the
stone scallop shells that stud
its walls. It is now a library.

**The Palacio de
Monterrey** is a
Renaissance mansion.

★ Universidad
*In the center of the university's
elaborate façade is this medal-
lion, carved in relief, which
depicts the Catholic Monarchs.*

★ Catedral Vieja and
Catedral Nueva
*Despite being in different
architectural styles, the
adjoining old and new
cathedrals blend well
together. This richly
colored altarpiece
painted in 1445 is in
the old cathedral.*

CALLE DE LA COMPAÑIA

CALLE DE SERRANOS

CALLE DE LOS LIBREROS

CALLE VERACRUZ

PASEO

Puente Romano
*The Roman bridge across the Río
Tormes, built in the 1st century AD,
retains 15 of its original 26 arches. It
provides an excellent view of the city.*

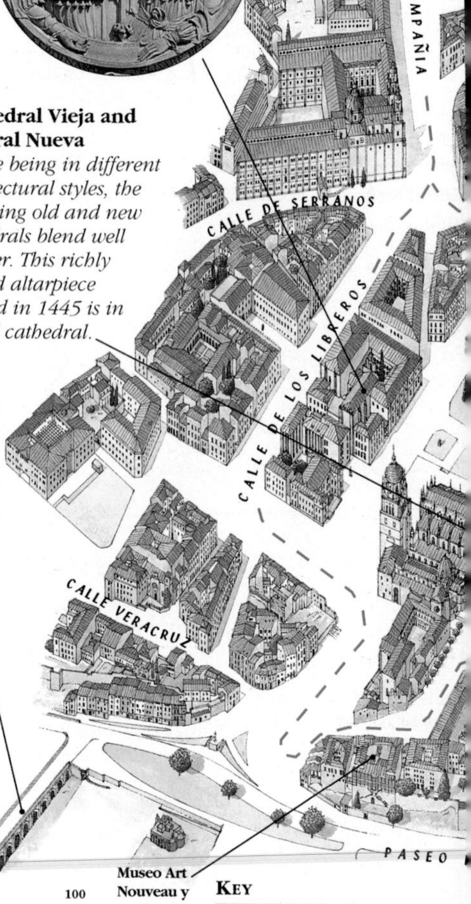

STAR SIGHTS

★ Universidad

★ Catedral Vieja and
  Catedral Nueva

★ Plaza Mayor

---

0 meters   100

0 yards   100

**Museo Art
Nouveau y
Art Deco**

KEY

– – – Suggested route

★ Plaza Mayor
This 18th-century square is one of Spain's largest and grandest. On the east side is the Royal Pavilion, decorated with a bust of Felipe V, who built the square.

VISITORS' CHECKLIST

Salamanca. 180,000. ✈ 6 km (3.5 miles) east. 🚆 Paseo de la Estación, (923) 12 02 02. 🚌 Avda de Filiberto Villalobos 71, (923) 23 67 17. 🛈 Plaza Mayor 14, (923) 21 83 42. 🎉 Sun. 🎊 San Juan de Sahagún (Jun 12), Virgen de la Vega (Sep 8).

Iglesia de San Martín

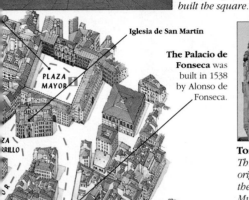

PLAZA MAYOR

ZA RRILLO

CALLE DE SAN PABLO

CALLE DEL CONSUELO

PLAZA DEL CONCILIO DE TRENTO

ARROYO SANTO DOMINGO

R ESPERABE

The Palacio de Fonseca was built in 1538 by Alonso de Fonseca.

Torre del Clavero
This 15th-century tower still has its original turrets. They are adorned with the coats of arms of its founders and Mudéjar trelliswork.

Iglesia-Convento de San Esteban
The Plateresque façade of the church is carved with delicate relief. Above the door is a frieze decorated with medallions and coats of arms.

Convento de las Dueñas
Sculptures on the capitals of the beautiful two-story cloister show demons, skulls, and tormented faces, in contrast with serene carvings of the Virgin.

Exploring Salamanca
The majority of Salamanca's monuments are located in the city center, which is compact enough to explore on foot. The university, the Plaza Mayor, and the old and new cathedrals are all must-sees.

⌂ Catedral Vieja and Catedral Nueva
Unusually, the 16th-century new cathedral did not replace the old, but was constructed beside it. It is in a mix of architectural styles, being mainly Gothic, with Renaissance and Baroque additions. The west front has elaborate Late Gothic stonework and a central panel carved with religious scenes.

The 12th- to 13th-century Romanesque old cathedral is entered through the new one. The highlight is a wonderful altarpiece of 53 panels, painted in lustrous colors by Nicolás Florentino. It frames a statue of Salamanca's patron saint, the 12th-century Virgen de la Vega, which was crafted in Limoges enamel. In the vault above it is a fresco depicting scenes from the Last Judgment, which is also by Florentino.

The 13th-century Capilla de Anaya (Anaya Chapel) contains the superb 15th-century alabaster tomb of Diego de Anaya, an archbishop of Salamanca.

Façade of Salamanca University, on the Patio de las Escuelas

🏛 Universidad
Patio de las Escuelas 1. **C** *(923) 29 44 00.* ○ *daily.* ● *Dec 25.* 🈸
Salamanca's historic university was founded by Alfonso IX of León in 1218. The extravagant 16th-century façade of the Patio de las Escuelas (Schools Square) is a perfect example of the Plateresque style *(see p21).* Opposite is a statue of Fray Luis de León, who taught theology at the university. Inside, his former lecture room is preserved in its original style. Off the Patio de las Escuelas is the Escuelas Menores building, which houses a huge zodiac fresco, *The Salamanca Sky.*

🏛 Plaza Mayor
This magnificent square was built by Felipe V to thank the city for its support during the War of the Spanish Succession *(see p58).* Designed by the Churriguera brothers *(see p21)* in 1729 and completed in 1755, it was once used for bullfights, but nowadays is a delightful place to stroll or shop. Within the harmonious blend of arcaded buildings and cafés are the Baroque town hall and, opposite, the Royal Pavilion, from where the royal family used to watch events in the square. The Plaza Mayor is built of warm golden sandstone and is especially resplendent at dusk.

Royal Pavilion in Salamanca's beautiful Plaza Mayor

⌂ Iglesia-Convento de San Esteban
The 16th-century church of this Dominican monastery is particularly interesting for its superb ornamented façade. The relief on the central panel, completed by Juan Antonio Ceroni in 1610, depicts the stoning of St. Stephen, to whom the monastery is dedicated. Above this is a frieze, delicately carved with figures of children and horses.

The interior of the large single-nave church is equally stunning. The ornate altarpiece, of twisted gilt columns decorated with vines, is the work of José Churriguera and dates from 1693. Below it is one of Claudio Coello's last paintings, another representation of the martyrdom of St. Stephen.

The double-galleried Claustro de los Reyes, completed in Plateresque style in 1591, has capitals carved with the heads of the prophets.

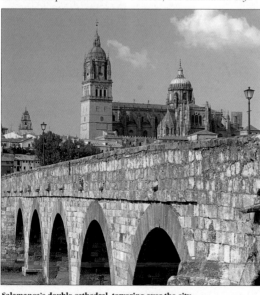

Salamanca's double cathedral, towering over the city

Sculpted shells on the walls of the Casa de las Conchas

Casa de las Conchas
Calle de la Compañía. *(923) 26 93 17.* ☐ *Mon–Sat.*
The name of this mansion – House of the Shells – derives from the golden stone scallop shells that cover most of its walls. The shells are a symbol of the Order of Santiago, one of whose knights, Rodrigo Maldonado, built the mansion at the beginning of the 16th century. He also adorned the building with his family's coat of arms. It is now a library.

Convento de las Dueñas
Plaza del Concilio de Trento.
(923) 21 54 42. ☐ *daily.*
The main feature of this Dominican convent, which stands opposite San Esteban, is its Renaissance double cloister, whose tranquil gardens seem strangely at odds with the grotesques carved on the capitals. The cloister also preserves a tiled Moorish arch.

Museo Art Nouveau y Art Deco
Calle Gibraltar 14. *(923) 12 14 25.* ☐ *daily.*
This important art collection, housed in a 19th-century building, includes paintings, jewelry, and furniture from all over Europe. Individual rooms are devoted to porcelain and Limoges enamel, and stained-glass work by Lalique.

Palacio de Fonseca
Calle Fonseca. *(923) 29 45 70.* ☐ *daily.*
The patio of this Renaissance palace has a first-floor arcade on huge pedestals. Today it houses the council offices.

Convento de las Úrsulas
Calle de las Úrsulas 2. *(923) 21 98 77.* ☐ *Mon–Sat.*
In the church of this convent is the superbly carved tomb of its founder, Alonso de Fonseca, the powerful 16th-century Archbishop of Santiago. The museum includes fine paintings by Luis de Morales.

Casa de las Muertes
Calle Bordadores. ● *to public.*
The House of the Dead takes its name from the small skulls that embellish its façade. Grotesques and other figures are also featured, and there is a cornice decorated with cherubim. The façade, designed by Diego de Siloé in 1513, is an accomplished example of the early Plateresque style.

The adjacent house is where author and philosopher Miguel de Unamuno died in 1936. The Casa-Museo de Unamuno, next door to the university, contains information about his life.

Skull carving on the façade of the Casa de las Muertes

Colegio de los Irlandeses
Calle de Fonseca 2. *(923) 29 45 70.* ☐ *daily.*
Also known as the Colegio del Arzobispo, this college was founded by the Archbishop of Toledo in 1521 as a seminary for Irish priests. It has an Italianate courtyard and a chapel with a Plateresque doorway.

Torre del Clavero
Plaza de Colón.
The tower is the last vestige of a palace that once stood here. It was built around 1480 and is named after a former resident, the key warden *(clavero)* of the Order of Alcántara.

The octagonal Torre del Clavero

ENVIRONS: To the northwest of the city, the course of the Río Tormes leads through the fortified old town of **Ledesma**, across lonely countryside to the Arribas del Duero, a series of massive reservoirs near to the Portuguese border.

Dominating the town of **Alba de Tormes**, 20 km (12 miles) east of Salamanca, is the Torre de la Armería, the only remaining part of the castle of the Dukes of Alba. St. Teresa of Ávila *(see p345)* is buried in the town. Pilgrims flock to the Iglesia-Convento de las Madres Carmelitas, which she founded in 1571, and where her remains are now kept.

The castle of **Buen Amor**, 26 km (16 miles) to the north of Salamanca, was founded in 1227. Later, it was converted into a palace and used as a residence by the Catholic Monarchs while fighting against Juana la Beltraneja *(see p52).*

Sierra de Gredos 12

Ávila. ☐ Hoyos del Espino.
ℹ️ Hoyos del Espino, (920) 34 90 35.

THIS GREAT mountain range,
west of Madrid, has abun-
dant wildlife, especially ibex
and birds of prey. Some parts
have been developed to cater
to weekenders who come skiing, fishing, hunting, or hiking. Tourism here isn't a recent phenomenon – Spain's
first parador opened in Gredos
in 1928 (see p556). Despite
this, there are many traditional
villages off the beaten track.

The slopes on the south side
of the range, extending into
Extremadura, are fertile and
sheltered, with pinewoods and
apple and olive trees. The austere northern slopes, in contrast, have a covering of thin
scrub and are scattered with
granite boulders.

A single main road, the
N502, crosses the center of the
range via the Puerto del Pico, a
pass at 1,352 m (4,435 ft), leading to Arenas de San Pedro,
the largest town of the Sierra
de Gredos. On this road is the
castle of **Mombeltrán**, built
at the end of the 14th century.

Near Ramacastañas, south of
the town of Arenas de San
Pedro, are the limestone caverns of the **Cuevas del Águila**.

The sierra's highest summit,
the Pico Almanzor (2,592 m,
8,500 ft) dominates the west.
Around it lies the **Reserva
Nacional de Gredos**, protecting the mountain's wildlife.

The Toros de Guisando near El Tiemblo in the Sierra de Gredos

Near El Tiemblo, in the east,
stand the **Toros de Guisando**,
four stone statues resembling
bulls, believed to be of Celt-
iberian origin (see pp44–5).

Ávila 13

Ávila. 🏠 50,000. ☐ ☐ ℹ️ Plaza
de la Catedral 4, (920) 21 13 87.
☐ Fri. 🎭 Summer Fiesta (mid-Jul),
Santa Teresa (Oct 15).

AT 1,131 M (3,710 FT)
above sea level,
Ávila de los Caballeros
("of the Knights") is the
highest provincial capital
in Spain. In winter, access
roads can be blocked
with snow, and at night
the temperature plummets.
The center of the city is
encircled by the finest-
preserved **medieval
walls** in Europe. One
of the best views of the
walls is from Los Cuatro
Postes (Four Posts) on the road
to Salamanca. This is the place
where the young St. Teresa,

Tuna in Ávila

who had run away from home,
was caught by her uncle. Built
in the 11th century, the walls
are over 2 km (1 mile) long.
They are punctuated by 88
sturdy turrets, on which storks
can be seen nesting in season.
The ground falls away very
steeply from the walls on three
sides, making the city practically impregnable. The east
side, however,
is relatively
flat, and there-
fore had to be for-
tified more heavily.
The oldest sections
of the wall are here.
They are guarded by
the most impressive of
the city's nine gate-
ways, the **Puerta de
San Vicente**. The apse
of the **cathedral** also
forms part of the walls.
The cathedral's warlike
(and unfinished) ex-
terior, decorated with
beasts and scaly wild
men, is an unusual design.
The interior is a mixture of
Romanesque and Gothic styles

The superbly preserved 11th-century walls, punctuated with 88 cylindrical towers, which encircle Ávila

using an unusual mottled red and white stone. Finer points to note are the carvings on the retrochoir and, in the apse, the tomb of a 15th-century bishop known as El Tostado, "the Tanned One," because of his dark complexion.

Many churches and convents in Ávila are linked to St. Teresa, who was born here. The **Convento de Santa Teresa** was built on the site of her home within the walls and she lived for more than 20 years in the **Monasterio de la Encarnación** outside the walls. There is even a local confection, *yemas de Santa Teresa*, named after her.

The **Iglesia de San Vicente**, also located just outside the eastern walls, is Ávila's most important Romanesque church, distinguished by its ornamented belfry. It was begun in the 12th century but has some Gothic features that were added later. The west door-

Beautiful gardens and palace of San Ildefonso

way is often compared to the Pórtico da Gloria of Santiago cathedral *(see p88)*. Inside, the carved tomb of St. Vincent and his sisters depicts their hideous martyrdom in graphic detail. Another Romanesque-Gothic church worth seeing is the **Iglesia de San Pedro.**

Some way from the center is the **Real Monasterio de Santo Tomás**, with three cloisters. The middle one, carved with the yoke and arrow emblem of the Catholic Monarchs, is the most beautiful. The last cloister leads to a museum displaying chalices and processional crosses. The church contains the tomb of Prince Juan, the only son of Fernando and Isabel. In the sacristy lies another historic figure: Tomás de Torquemada, head of the Inquisition *(see p52)*.

In Ávila, you may see groups of *tunas* – students dressed in traditional costume walking the town's streets while singing songs and playing guitars.

Cloisters of the Real Monasterio de Santo Tomás in Ávila

La Granja de San Ildefonso ⑭

Segovia. [📞] *(921) 47 00 19.*
[🚌] *from Madrid or Segovia.*
[◯] *Tue–Sun.* [🏛] [♿]

THIS SUMPTUOUS royal pleasure palace is set against the backdrop of the Sierra de Guadarrama mountains. It stands on the site of a hunting lodge built by Enrique IV during the 15th century.

In 1720, Felipe V embarked on a project to recreate fond childhood memories of his grandfather Louis XIV's glorious court at Versailles. A succession of different artists and architects contributed to the rich furnishings inside and the splendid gardens without.

Many rooms were damaged in a fire in 1918. Although they were sumptuously restored, the interior never quite regained its original splendor.

A guided tour meanders through countless impressive salons decorated with ornate *objets d'art* and Classical frescoes against settings of marble, gilt, and velvet. Huge glittering chandeliers, produced in the local crystal factory, hang from the ceiling. In the private apartments there are superb court tapestries. The church is fittingly adorned in lavish high Baroque style, and the Royal Mausoleum contains the tomb of Felipe V and his queen.

In the gardens, stately chestnut trees, clipped hedges, and statues frame a complex series of pools. On some summer afternoons spectacular fountains are set in motion.

ST. TERESA OF JESUS

Teresa de Cepeda y Ahumada (1515–82) was one of the Catholic Church's greatest mystics and reformers. When just seven, she ran away from home in the hope of achieving martyrdom at the hands of the Moors, only to be recaptured by her uncle on the outskirts of the city. She became a nun at 19 but rebelled against her order. From 1562, when she founded her first convent, she traveled around Spain with her disciple, St. John of the Cross, founding more convents for the followers of her order, the Barefoot Carmelites. Her remains are in Alba de Tormes near Salamanca *(see p343).*

Statue of St. Teresa in the cathedral museum

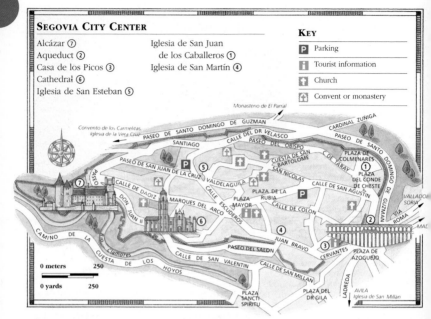

SEGOVIA CITY CENTER

Alcázar ⑦
Aqueduct ②
Casa de los Picos ③
Cathedral ⑥
Iglesia de San Esteban ⑤

Iglesia de San Juan
  de los Caballeros ①
Iglesia de San Martín ④

KEY

P   Parking

i   Tourist information

🏠   Church

🏠   Convent or monastery

Segovia ⑮

Segovia. 🏠 56,000. 🚊 🚌 ℹ Plaza
Mayor 10, (921) 46 03 34. 🛒 Thu.
🎉 San Juan (Jun 24), San Pedro
(Jun 29), San Frutos (Oct 25).

SEGOVIA IS THE MOST spectacularly sited city in Spain. The
old town is set high on a rocky
spur and surrounded by the
Río Eresma and Río Clamores.
It is often compared to a ship
– the Alcázar on its sharp crag
forming the prow, the pinnacles of the cathedral rising
like masts, and the aqueduct
trailing behind like a rudder.
The view of it from the valley
below at sunset is magical.

The **aqueduct**, in use until
the late 19th century, was
built at the end of the 1st century AD by the Romans, who
turned ancient Segobriga into
an important military base.

The **cathedral**, dating from
1525 and consecrated in 1678,
is the last great Gothic church
in Spain. It was built to replace
the old cathedral, which was
destroyed in 1520 during the
revolt of the Castilian towns
(see p54). The cloister, however, survived and was rebuilt
on the new site. The pinnacles,
flying buttresses, tower, and
dome form an impressive sil-
houette, while the interior is

light and elegantly vaulted.
Graceful ironwork grilles enclose the side chapels. The
chapterhouse museum, with a
coffered ceiling, houses 17th-
century Brussels tapestries.

At the city's western end is
the **Alcázar** *(see pp326–7)*.
Rising sheer above crags with
a multitude of gabled roofs,
turrets, and crenellations, it
appears like the archetypal
fairy-tale castle. Although there
has been a fortress here since
the Middle Ages, the present
building is mostly a fanciful
reconstruction following a fire
in 1862. It contains a museum

of weaponry and a series of
elaborately decorated rooms.

Notable churches in Segovia
include the Romanesque **San
Juan de los Caballeros**, which
has an outstanding sculptured
portico, **San Esteban** with a
striking five-story tower, and
San Martín with its beautiful
arcades and capitals. Just inside
the city walls is the **Casa de
los Picos**, a mansion whose
unique façade is adorned with
diamond-shaped stones.

ENVIRONS: The vast palace of
Riofrío, 11 km (7 miles) to the
southwest, is set in a deer park.

The imposing Gothic cathedral of Segovia

SEGOVIA'S AQUEDUCT

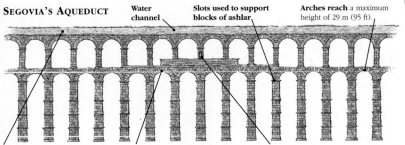

Water channel

Slots used to support blocks of ashlar

Arches reach a maximum height of 29 m (95 ft).

Water from the Río Frío flowed into the city, filtered through a series of tanks along the way.

Two tiers of arches – a total of 728 m (2,400 ft) in length – were needed to cope with the ground's gradient.

In this niche a statue of the Virgin Mary replaces an earlier inscription relating to the founding of the aqueduct.

Zuloaga (1870–1945). The castle museum shows some of his works. On weekends, *Madrileños* flock to Pedraza's restaurants for roast lunches.

ENVIRONS: The main sight at **Turégano**, 30 km (19 miles) north, is a large hilltop castle that incorporates the 15th-century Iglesia de San Miguel.

Sepúlveda ⓱

Segovia. 🏘 *1,050.* 🚻 *Plaza del Trigo 3, (921) 54 00 95.* 🚌 *Wed.* 🎉 *Patronales (last week of Aug).*

SPECTACULARLY SITED on a slope above the Río Duratón, this picturesque town offers views of the Sierra de Guadarrama. Parts of its medieval walls and castle survive. Of its several Romanesque churches, the **Iglesia del Salvador**, behind the main square, is purely 11th century and is notable for possessing one of the oldest side doors in Spain (1093).

ENVIRONS: Winding through a canyon haunted by griffon vultures is the Río Duratón, 7 km (4 miles) west of Sepúlveda. This area of striking beauty has been designated a natural park, the **Parque Natural de las Hoces del Duratón**.

Ayllón, 45 km (28 miles) northeast of Sepúlveda, has an arcaded main square and the Plateresque *(see p21)* Palacio de Juan de Contreras of 1497.

The Iberian and Roman ruins at **Tiermes**, 28 km (17 miles) farther southeast, have been partially excavated, and finds can be seen in Soria's Museo Numantino *(see p359).*

Segovia's distinctive Alcázar, towering over the city

It was built as a hunting lodge by Felipe V's widow, Isabel Farnese, in 1752, and has richly decorated rooms. It also houses a hunting museum.

♟ **Alcázar de Segovia**
Plaza del Alcázar. 🇨 *(921) 46 07 59.* ◯ *daily.* ◯ *Jan 1, Dec 25.* 🎫 🔥
🏛 **Palacio de Riofrío**
🇨 *(921) 47 00 19.* ◯ *Tue–Sun.* 🎫

Pedraza de la Sierra ⓰

Segovia. 🏘 *400.* 🚻 *Plaza Mayor 1, (921) 50 98 17.* 🎉 *Nuestra Señora la Virgen del Carrascal (Sep 8).*

THE ARISTOCRATIC little town of Pedraza de la Sierra is perched high over rolling countryside. Within its medieval walls, old streets lead past mansions, emblazoned with coats of arms, to the porticoed **Plaza Mayor** *(see p23).* The huge, austere **castle**, standing on a rocky outcrop, was the home of local artist Ignacio

Castillo de Coca ⓲

Coca (Segovia). 🇨 *(921) 58 60 62.* 🚌 *from Segovia.* ◯ *Wed–Mon.* 🎫

BUILT IN THE late 15th century for the influential Fonseca family, Coca castle *(see p326)* is one of Castilla y León's most memorable fortresses. It was used more as a residential palace than a defensive castle, although its multiplicity of turrets and battlements are a fine example of Mudéjar military architecture. Built of thin, rose-tinted bricks, it is a complex, moated structure comprising three concentric walls which surround a massive keep. The castle is now a forestry school, which has a display of Romanesque woodcarvings.

ENVIRONS: The 14th-century castle of **Arévalo**, 26 km (16 miles) southwest, is where Isabel I spent her childhood. The porticoed Plaza de la Villa is surrounded by a number of attractive half-timbered houses.

Massive keep of the 15th-century Castillo de Coca

Medina del Campo ⑲

Valladolid. 👥 20,000. 🚌 🚆
🛈 *Plaza Mayor 27, (983) 81 13 57.*
🗓 *Sun.* 🎉 *San Antolín (Sep 2–8).*

MEDINA BECAME wealthy in medieval times on the proceeds of huge sheep fairs and is still an important agricultural center today. The vast brick Gothic-Mudéjar **Castillo de la Mota** (*see p326*), on its outskirts, was built in 1440 by the powerful Fonseca family. However, the town transferred the castle's ownership to the Crown in 1475. Isabel I and her daughter Juana "la Loca" ("the Mad") both stayed here. Later, it served as a prison – Cesare Borgia, one of its more celebrated inmates, was incarcerated here from 1506–08. In a corner of the Plaza Mayor stands the modest house (built over an arch) where Isabel died in 1504; her statue presides over the square.

ENVIRONS: Towering over the plains, some 25 km (16 miles) to the south of Medina del Campo, are the walls of **Madrigal de las Altas Torres**. In 1451 Isabel was born here in a palace that became the Monasterio de las Agustinas in 1527.

Statue of Isabel, Medina del Campo

🏰 **Castillo de la Mota**
Avda Castillo de la Mota. 📞 (983) 80 10 24. 🗓 *daily.* ⬤ *public hols.*

Tordesillas ⑳

Valladolid. 👥 10,000. 🚆 🛈 *Plaza Mayor, (983) 77 06 54.* 🗓 *Tue.*
🎉 *Semana de la Peña (Sep 16–22).*

THIS PLEASANT TOWN is where the historic treaty between Spain and Portugal was signed in 1494, dividing the lands of the New World (*see p53*). A fateful oversight by the Spanish map makers left the immense prize of Brazil to Portugal.

The town's main sight is the **Convento de Santa Clara**. It was constructed by Alfonso XI in 1350 and converted by his

Castillo de la Mota at Medina del Campo

son Pedro the Cruel into a residence for his mistress, María de Padilla. Pining for her native Andalusia, she had the convent decorated with fine Moorish arches, baths, and tiles. Most impressive are the patio and the main chapel. There is a display of royal musical instruments, including the portable organ of Juana "la Loca." After the death of her husband, Juana spent 46 years in semi-confinement here until her own death in 1555.

In the old quarter, the **Iglesia de San Antolín** is a sculpture museum.

🏛 **Convento de Santa Clara**
📞 (983) 77 00 71. 🗓 *Tue–Sun.* 🎟
🏛 **Iglesia de San Antolín**
Calle Postigo. 📞 (983) 77 05 25.
🗓 *Apr–Oct: Tue–Sun; Nov–Mar: phone for opening times.*

Moorish patio in the Convento de Santa Clara, Tordesillas

Valladolid ㉑

Valladolid. 👥 350,000. 🚌 🚆
🛈 *Plaza de Zorrilla 3, (983) 35 18 01.*
🗓 *Sun.* 🎉 *San Pedro Regalado (May 13), San Mateo (Sep 21–9).*

THE ARABIC CITY of Belad-Walid (meaning "Land of the Governor") is located at the confluence of the Río Esgueva and Río Pisuerga. Although it has become sprawling and industrialized, Valladolid has some of Spain's best Renaissance art and architecture.

Fernando and Isabel (*see pp52–3*) were married in the Palacio Vivero in 1469 and, following the completion of the Reconquest in 1492, they made Valladolid their capital. Less spectacularly, Columbus died here, alone and forgotten, in 1506. In 1527 Felipe II was born in the Palacio de los Pimentel. José Zorrilla, who popularized the legendary Don Juan in his 1844 play (*see p31*), was also born in the city.

The city's university dates from the 15th century. The Baroque façade (*see p21*) was begun in 1715 by Narciso Tomé, who later created the remarkable Transparente of Toledo cathedral (*see p375*).

The **Iglesia de San Pablo** has a spectacular façade embellished with angels and coats of arms in Plateresque style. Among the other noteworthy churches are **Santa María la Antigua**, with its slim Romanesque belfry, and the **Iglesia**

le Las Angustias, where Juan
de Juni's fine sculpture of the
Virgen de los Cuchillos (Virgin
of the Knives) is on display.

🎫 Casa de Cervantes
Calle Rastro 7. 🎫 *(983) 30 88 10.*
🕐 *Tue–Sun.* ⬤ *public hols.*
The Golden Age author of
Don Quixote (see p30) lived in
this simple house with whitewashed walls for the last years
of his life. The rooms have
been thoroughly restored and
contain some of Cervantes'
original furnishings and fittings.

⛪ Cathedral
Calle Arribas 1. 🎫 *(983) 30 43 62.*
Work started on the unfinished
cathedral in 1580 by Felipe II's
favorite architect, Juan de
Herrera, but gradually lost mo-
mentum over the centuries.
Churrigueresque *(see p21)*
flourishes on the façade are in
contrast to the somber, square-
pillared interior, whose only
redeeming flamboyance is a
Juan de Juni altarpiece. The
Museo Diocesano inside, however, contains some fine pieces
of religious art and sculpture.

🏛 Museo Nacional de
Escultura
Cadenas de S Gregorio 1. 🎫 *(983) 25
03 75.* 🕐 *Tue–Sat.* ⬤ *public hols.* 📷
The art collection of the Museo
Nacional de Escultura is located in the beautiful Colegio de
San Gregorio. The display consists mainly of multicolored
wooden religious sculptures
from the 13th–18th centuries. It
is Europe's most distinguished
collection of such works. They
include examples by many of

**Façade of Colegio de San
Gregorio, Valladolid**

**Berruguete's *Natividad*, in Museo
Nacional de Escultura, Valladolid**

the masters of the Spanish Renaissance, including Juan de
Juni's emotive depiction of the
burial of Christ and *Recumbent
Christ* by Gregorio Fernández.
An Alonso Berruguete altarpiece, and walnut choir stalls
by Diego de Siloé and other
artists, are among the other
fine works to be found here.
    The building itself is worthy
of attention, particularly the
Plateresque *(see p21)* staircase,
the chapel by Juan Güas, and
the superb patio of twisted
columns and delicate basket
arches. The façade is an astonishing example of Isabelline
(see p20) sculpture, portraying
a bewildering mêlée of naked
children scrambling about in
thorn trees, hairy wild men,
and strange birds and beasts.
It is attributed mainly to Gil de
Siloé and Simon of Cologne.

🏛 Museo Oriental
Paseo de los Filipinos 7. 🎫 *(983)
30 69 00.* 🕐 *daily.* 📷
Beyond the Parque de Campo
Grande is this small but in-
teresting museum. The Museo
Oriental is housed in the Real
Colegio de los Agustinos
Filipinos, a grandiose Neo-
Classical Augustinian college,
and contains an important
collection of curios and art
brought from China and the
Philippines by missionaries.

ENVIRONS: The moated gray
castle that dominates the village of **Simancas**, 11 km (7
miles) southwest of Valladolid,
was converted by Charles V
into Spain's national archive.

The Visigothic church in the
village of **Wamba**, 15 km (9
miles) to the west, contains
the tomb of King Recceswinth.
    An unusual long, narrow
14th-century castle on a ridge
overlooks the wine town of
Peñafiel, 60 km (40 miles)
east of Valladolid *(see p327).*

Medina de
Rioseco ㉒

Valladolid. 🏠 *4,900.* 🚌 ℹ *Plaza
Mayor, (983) 70 08 25.* 🚌 *Wed.*
🎉 *San Juan (Jun 24–9).*

DURING THE MIDDLE AGES this
town, like Medina del
Campo, grew wealthy from the
profitable wool trade. These
riches enabled it to commission leading artists, mainly of
the Valladolid school, to decorate its churches. The dazzling star vaulting and superb
woodwork of the **Iglesia de
Santa María de Mediavilla**,
near the center of town, are
evidence of this. Inside, the
Benavente Chapel is a **tour de
force**, with a colorful stucco
ceiling by Jerónimo del Corral
(1554), and an altarpiece by
Juan de Juni. The enormous
monstrance (1585) in the treasury is by Antonio de Arfe.
    The interior of the **Iglesia
de Santiago** is equally stunning, with a triple altarpiece
by the Churriguera brothers
of Salamanca *(see p21).*
    The ancient buildings on
Medina de Rioseco's main
street, the Calle de la Rúa, are
supported on wooden pillars,
forming shady porticoes.

**Altarpiece by Juan de Juni, Iglesia
de Santa María de Mediavilla**

CASTILLA Y LEÓN'S FIESTAS

El Colacho *(Sun after Corpus Christi, May/Jun)*, Castrillo de Murcia (Burgos). Babies born during the previous 12 months are dressed in their best Sunday clothes and laid on mattresses in the streets. Crowds of people, including the anxious parents, watch as *El Colacho* – a man dressed in a bright red and yellow costume – jumps over the babies in order to free them from illnesses, especially hernias. He is said to represent the devil fleeing from the sight of the Eucharist. This ritual is thought to have originated in 1621.

El Colacho **jumping over babies in Castrillo de Murcia**

St. Agatha's Day *(Sun closest to Feb 5)*, Zamarramala (Segovia). Every year two women are elected as mayoresses to run the village on the day of St. Agatha, patron saint of married women. They ceremonially burn a stuffed figure representing a man. **Good Friday**, Valladolid. The procession of 28 multicolored sculptures that depict various scenes of the Passion is one of the most spectacular in Spain. **Fire-walking** *(Jun 23)*, San Pedro Manrique (Soria). Men, some carrying people on their backs, walk barefoot over burning embers. It is said that only local people can do this without being burned.

The beautiful carved retrochoir of Palencia cathedral

Palencia ㉓

Palencia. 🏛 79,000. 🚌 🚉
🛈 Calle Mayor 105, (979) 74 00 68.
🚌 Tue, Wed & Thu. 🎨 Virgen de la Calle (Feb 2), San Antolín (Sep 2).

IN MEDIEVAL TIMES, Palencia was a royal residence and the site of Spain's first university, founded in 1208. The city gradually diminished in importance following its involvement in the failed revolt of the Castilian towns of 1520 *(see p54)*.

Although Palencia has since expanded considerably on profits from coal and wheat, its center, by the old stone bridge over the Río Carrión, remains almost villagelike.

The city's main sight is the **cathedral**, known as *La Bella Desconocida* (the Unknown Beauty). It is especially worth a visit for its superb works of art, many the result of Bishop Fonseca's generous patronage. The retrochoir, exquisitely sculpted by Gil de Siloé and Simon of Cologne, and the two altarpieces are also noteworthy. The altarpiece above the high altar was carved by Philippe de Bigarny early in the 16th century. The inset panels are by Juan de Flandes, Isabel I's court painter. Behind the high altar is the Chapel of the Holy Sacrament, with an altarpiece dating from 1529 by Valmaseda. In this chapel, high on a ledge to the left, is the colorful tomb of Doña Urraca of Navarra. Below the retrochoir, a Plateresque *(see p21)* staircase leads down to the fine Visigothic crypt.

ENVIRONS: Baños de Cerrato, 12 km (7 miles) to the south, contains the tiny Visigothic Iglesia de San Juan Bautista. Founded in 661, it is alleged to be the oldest intact church in Spain. Typical Visigothic carved capitals and horseshoe arches decorate the interior.

Frómista ㉔

Palencia. 🏛 1,000. 🛈 Plaza de Tui, (979) 81 00 01. 🚌 Fri. 🎨 Patrón de Frómista (week after Easter), Virgen del Otero (Sep 8).

THIS TOWN on the Road to Santiago de Compostela *(see pp78–9)* is the site of one of Spain's purest Romanesque churches. The **Iglesia de San Martín** is the highlight of the town, partly due to an energetic restoration in 1904. Decadent additions were swept away, leaving the church, dating from 1066, entirely Romanesque in style. The presence of Pagan and Roman motifs suggest it may have pre-Christian origins.

ENVIRONS: Carrión de los Condes, 20 km (12 miles) to the northwest, is also on the Road to Santiago. The frieze on the door of the Iglesia de Santiago depicts not religious figures but local artisans. There are carvings of bulls on the façade of the 12th-century Iglesia de Santa María del Camino. The Convento de San Zoilo has a Gothic cloister, and offers simple accommodations.

Located at **Gañinas**, 20 km (12 miles) to the northwest (just south of Saldaña), is the well-preserved Roman villa,

Interior of the Iglesia de San Juan Bautista at Baños de Cerrato

Posada of the Monasterio de Santa María la Real, Aguilar de Campoo

La Olmeda. It has a number of impressive mosaics, including a hunting scene with lions and tigers. Finds from the villa are displayed in the archaeological museum located in the Iglesia de San Pedro in Saldaña.

⋔ Villa Romana La Olmeda
Pedrosa de la Vega. ⬤ *Tue–Sun.*
⬤ *Dec 22–Jan 31.* 🎟 *ticket also covers archaeological museum.*

Aguilar de Campoo ㉕

Palencia. 🏘 *7,000.* 🚌 🛈 *Calle Modesto la Fuente 1, (979) 12 20 05.* 🚍 *Tue.* 🎪 *San Pedro (Jun 29).*

SITUATED BETWEEN the parched plains of central Spain and the lush green foothills of the Cantabrian Mountains is the old fortified town of Aguilar de Campoo. At one end of its ancient porticoed main square

is the impressive bell tower of the **Colegiata de San Miguel**. In this church is a mausoleum containing the tomb of the Marquises of Aguilar.

Among the other places of interest include the **Ermita de Santa Cecilia**, near the castle, and the restored Romanesque-Gothic **Monasterio de Santa María la Real**, on the outskirts of town, which has a small, friendly *posada* (inn), ideal for a night's stay *(see p555)*.

ENVIRONS: Six km (4 miles) south, at **Olleros de Pisuerga**, is a church built in a cave. From the parador at **Cervera de Pisuerga**, 25 km (15 miles) northwest of Aguilar, there are stunning views, and tours of the **Reserva Nacional de Fuentes Carrionas**. This is a rugged region of mountain lakes overlooked by Fuentes Carrionas, a 2,487-m (8,159-ft) summit, and other peaks.

Briviesca ㉖

Burgos. 🏘 *6,100.* 🚌 🚍 🛈 *Calle Marqués de Torre Soto 8, (947) 59 18 18.* 🚍 *Sat.* 🎪 *Feria de San José (Mar 19), Santa Casilda (May 9).*

THIS LITTLE WALLED TOWN, in the northeast of Burgos province, has an arcaded main square and several dignified mansions. The best known of its churches is the **Convento de Santa Clara**, with its 16th-century walnut reredos carved with religious scenes. In 1388 Juan I of Aragón created the title Príncipe de Asturias for his son, Enrique, in the town. The Santuario de Santa Casilda, situated outside Briviesca, has a collection of votive objects.

ENVIRONS: Oña, 25 km (15 miles) north, is an attractive town. Its former Benedictine monastery of San Salvador was founded in 1011.

Overlooking a fertile valley, 20 km (12 miles) farther northeast, is the little hilltop town of **Frías**. Its craggy castle overlooks cobbled streets lined with many pretty old houses. Crossing the Río Ebro is a fortified medieval bridge, which still has its central gate tower.

At **Medina de Pomar**, 30 km (20 miles) north of Oña, is a 15th-century castle, once the seat of the Velasco family. Inside are the ruins of a palace with Mudéjar stucco decoration and Arabic inscriptions.

The medieval bridge over the Río Ebro at Frías, with its central gate tower

Flemish triptych inside the collegiate church in Covarrubias

Covarrubias ㉗

Burgos. 🏠 600. 🚆 🚌 ℹ️ *Plaza Mayor, (947) 40 30 51.* 🚌 *Tue.* 🎉 *San Cosme and San Damián (Sep 26–7).*

NAMED AFTER the reddish caves on its outskirts, the delightful town of Covarrubias stands on the banks of the Río Arlanza. Medieval walls surround the charming old center with its arcaded half-timbered houses *(see p22)*. The distinguished **collegiate church** gives an inkling of the historical importance of Covarrubias, for here is the tomb of Fernán González, first independent Count of Castile, and one of great figures in Castilian history. By uniting several fiefs in battles against the Moors in the 10th century, he set in motion the rise in Castilian power that ensured the resulting kingdom of Castile would play a leading role in the unification of Spain. The church museum in the sacristy contains treasures, notably a Flemish triptych of the Adoration of the Magi, attributed to Gil de Siloé, and a 17th-century organ.

ENVIRONS: A short distance east along the Río Arlanza lies the ruins of the 11th-century Romanesque monastery of **San Pedro de Arlanza**. At **Quintanilla de las Viñas**, 24 km (15 miles) north of Covarrubias, is a ruined 7th-century Visigothic church. The reliefs on the columns of the triumphal arch are remarkable, depicting sun and moon symbols that may be pagan.

Burgos ㉘

Burgos. 🏠 106,000. 🚆 🚌 ℹ️ *Plaza de Alonso Martínez 7, (947) 20 31 25.* 🚌 *daily.* 🎉 *San Lesmes (Jan 30), San Pedro and San Pablo (Jun 30).*

FOUNDED IN 884, Burgos has played a significant political and military role in Spanish history. It was the capital of the united kingdoms of Castile and León from 1073 until losing that honor to Valladolid after the fall of Granada in 1492 *(see pp52–3)*. During the 15th and 16th centuries, like many Castilian towns, Burgos grew wealthy from the wool trade and used its riches to finance most of the great art and architecture that can be seen in the city today. Less auspiciously, Franco chose Burgos as his headquarters during the Civil War *(see pp62–3)*.

The city's strategic location on the main Madrid–France highway and on the route to Santiago *(see pp78–9)* ensure many visitors; but even without this Burgos would justify a long detour. Despite its size and extremes of climate, it is one of most agreeable provincial capitals in Castilla y León.

Approach via the bridge of Santa María, which leads into the old quarter through the **Arco de Santa María**, a gateway carved with statues of various local worthies. The main bridge into the city, however, is the Puente de San Pablo, where a statue commemorates the city's hero, El Cid. Not far

from the bridge stands the **Casa del Cordón**, a 15th-century palace (now a bank) that has a Franciscan cord motif carved over the portal. A plaque declares that this is the spot where the Catholic Monarchs welcomed Columbus on his return, in 1497, from the second of his famous voyages to the Americas.

The lacy, steel-gray spires of the **cathedral** *(see pp354–5)* are a prominent landmark from almost anywhere in the city. On the rising ground behind it stands the **Iglesia de San Nicolás**, whose main feature is a superb altarpiece by Simon of Cologne (1505). The crowded carvings vividly depict a number of scenes from the life of St. Nicholas. Other churches worth visiting are the **Iglesia de San Lorenzo**, with its superb Baroque ceiling, and the **Iglesia de San Esteban**, which has a museum of altarpieces. The **Iglesia de Santa Águeda**, is the place where El Cid made King Alfonso VI swear that he

The Arco de Santa María in Burgos, adorned with statues and turrets

EL CID (1043–99)

Rodrigo Díaz de Vivar was born into a noble family in Vivar del Cid, north of Burgos, in 1043. He served Fernando I, but was banished from Castile after becoming embroiled in the fratricidal squabbles of the king's sons, Sancho II and Alfonso VI. He switched allegiance to fight for the Moors, then changed side again, capturing Valencia for the Christians in 1094, ruling the city until his death. For his heroism he was named El Cid, from the Arabic *Sidi* (Lord). He was a charismatic man of great courage, but it was an anonymous poem, *El Cantar del Mío Cid*, in 1180, that immortalized him as a romantic hero of the Reconquest *(see pp50–51)*. The tombs of El Cid and his wife, Jimena, are in Burgos cathedral.

Statue of El Cid in Vivar del Cid

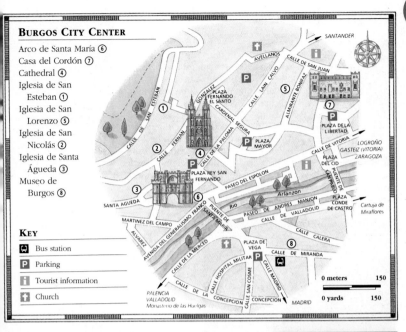

Burgos City Center

Arco de Santa María ⑥
Casa del Cordón ⑦
Cathedral ④
Iglesia de San
    Esteban ①
Iglesia de San
    Lorenzo ⑤
Iglesia de San
    Nicolás ②
Iglesia de Santa
    Águeda ③
Museo de
    Burgos ⑧

Key

🚌 Bus station

🅿 Parking

ℹ Tourist information

✝ Church

| 0 meters | 150 |
| 0 yards | 150 |

---

played no part in the murder of his elder brother, King Sancho II *(see p338)*.

Across the river, the palace of the Casa de Miranda houses the archaeological section of the **Museo de Burgos,** with finds from the Roman city of Clunia. Nearby, the Casa de Angulo contains the Fine Arts section, whose prize exhibits are Juan de Padilla's tomb by Gil de Siloé and a Moorish casket in enameled ivory.

Two religious houses on the outskirts of Burgos are worth visiting. Just west of the city is the **Real Monasterio de las**

Sculpted tomb of Juan de Padilla by Gil de Siloé, in Casa de Angulo

Huelgas, a Cistercian convent founded in 1187 by Alfonso VIII. It was lavishly endowed and soon achieved great prestige, accepting only the most distinguished nuns. One of the most interesting parts is the Museo de Ricas Telas, a textile museum containing ancient fabrics from the convent's many royal tombs. Another highlight is the Gothic cloister of San Fernando, decorated with Moorish designs of peacocks and stars. In the Capilla de Santiago is a curious articulated wooden figure of St. James holding a sword, with which, according to tradition, royal princes were dubbed Knights of Santiago.

To the east of Burgos is the **Cartuja de Miraflores,** a Carthusian monastery founded during the 15th century. The church includes two of Spain's most notable tombs, attributed to Gil de Siloé. One holds the bodies of Juan II and Isabel of Portugal (the parents of Isabel the Catholic); the other contains that of her brother, Prince Alfonso. Equally spectacular is the multicolored altarpiece by Gil de Siloé, allegedly gilded with the first consignment of gold brought back to Spain from the New World.

Polychrome altarpiece by Gil de Siloé, in Cartuja de Miraflores

🏛 **Museo de Burgos**
Calle Calera 23. 📞 *(947) 26 58 75.*
◻ *Tue–Sun.* 🎫 ♿
🔒 **Real Monasterio de las Huelgas**
Calle de las Huelgas. 📞 *(947) 20 16 30.* ◻ *Tue–Sun.* ♿
🔒 **Cartuja de Miraflores**
Ctra de San Pedro Cardeña. ◻ *daily.*

Environs: Ten km (6 miles) southeast of Burgos is the **Monasterio de San Pedro de Cardeña.** El Cid led his family to safety here while he rode into exile after King Alfonso VI had banished him from the territory of Castile.

Burgos Cathedral

SPAIN'S THIRD-LARGEST CATHEDRAL was founded in 1221 by Bishop Mauricio under Fernando III. The ground plan – a Latin cross – measures 84 m (92 yds) by 59 m (65 yds). Its construction was carried out in several stages over three centuries and involved many of the greatest artists and architects in Europe. The style is almost entirely Gothic and shows influences from Germany, France, and the Low Countries. First to be built were the nave and cloisters, while the intricate, crocketed spires and the richly decorated side chapels are mostly later work. The architects cleverly adapted the cathedral to its sloping site, incorporating stairways inside and out.

Christ at the Column, by Diego de Siloé

West Front
The lacy, steel-gray spires soar above a sculpted balustrade depicting Castile's early kings.

Lantern

Tomb of El Cid

★ Golden Staircase
This elegant Renaissance staircase by Diego de Siloé (1523) links the nave with the Puerta Alta (kept locked) at street level.

STAR FEATURES

- ★ **Golden Staircase**
- ★ **Constable's Chapel**
- ★ **The Crossing**

Capilla de Santa Tecla

Puerta de Santa María (main entrance)

Capilla de Santa Ana
The altarpiece (1492) in this chapel is by the sculptor Gil de Siloé. The central panel shows the Virgin with St. Joachim.

Capilla de la Presentación (1519–24) is a funerary chapel with a star-shaped, traceried vault.

Retrochoir

Several of the reliefs around the chancel were carved by Philippe de Bigarny. This expressive scene, which was completed in 1498, depicts the road to Calvary.

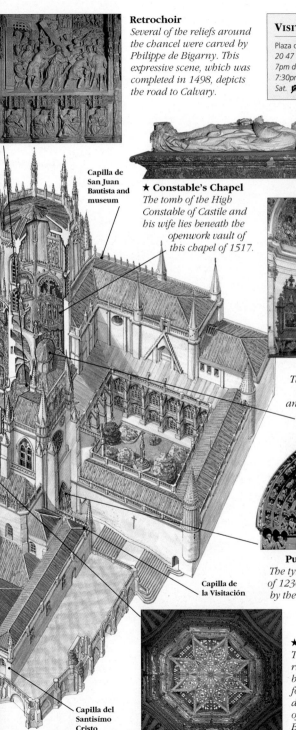

Capilla de San Juan Bautista and museum

★ Constable's Chapel

The tomb of the High Constable of Castile and his wife lies beneath the openwork vault of this chapel of 1517.

Sacristy (1765)
The sacristy was rebuilt in Baroque style, with an exuberant plasterwork vault and rococo altars

Puerta de la Coronería
The tympanum of this portal of 1230 shows Christ flanked by the Evangelists. Statues of the apostles sit below.

Capilla de la Visitación

★ The Crossing

The magnificent star-ribbed central dome, begun in 1539, rises on four huge pillars. It is decorated with effigies of prophets and saints. Beneath it is the tomb of El Cid and his wife.

Capilla del Santisímo Cristo

Lerma ㉙

Burgos. 🏘 2,600. 🚆 🚌 🛈 Calle Audiencia 6, (947) 17 01 43. 🛒 Wed. 🎉 Nuestra Señora (8–9 Sep).

THE GRANDIOSE APPEARANCE of this town is largely due to the ambition of the notorious first Duke of Lerma (see p56), Felipe III's corrupt favorite and minister from 1598–1618. He misused vast quantities of Spain's new-found wealth on new buildings in his home town – all strictly Classical in style, in accordance with prevailing fashion. At the top of the town, the haughty **Palacio Ducal**, built in 1605 as his residence, contrasts strikingly with the agreeable jumble of earlier houses leading down to the medieval gateway.

There are good views of the Río Arlanza from the archways near to the **Convento de Santa Clara** and also from the **Colegiata de San Pedro** church, which has a bronze statue of the Duke's uncle.

The narrow, sloping streets of the old town of Lerma

Cloisters of the Monasterio de Santo Domingo de Silos

Monasterio de Santo Domingo de Silos ㉚

Santo Domingo de Silos (Burgos). 📞 (947) 39 00 68. 🚌 from Burgos. 🕐 daily. 🕑 9am, 7pm & 9:30pm.

ST. DOMINIC gave his name to the monastery that he rebuilt in 1042 over the ruins of a Visigothic abbey destroyed by the Moors. It is a place of spiritual and artistic pilgrimage, and its tranquil setting has inspired countless poets.

Others come to admire the beautiful Romanesque cloisters, whose capitals are sculpted in a great variety of designs, both symbolistic and realistic, many showing fantastic beasts. The carvings on the corner piers depict various scenes from the Bible and the ceilings are coffered in Moorish style. The body of St. Dominic rests in a sarcophagus supported by

three Romanesque lions in the north gallery. The old pharmacy, just off the cloister, has a display of jars from Talavera de la Reina (see p368).

The Benedictine community holds regular services in Gregorian chant in the Neo-Classical church by Ventura Rodríguez. The monastery offers accommodations for male guests.

ENVIRONS: Just to the southwest lies the **Garganta de la Yecla** (Yecla Gorge), where a path leads down to a narrow fissure cut by the river. To the northeast are the peaks and wildlife preserve of the **Sierra de la Demanda**, extending over the border into La Rioja.

The 15th-century castle of Peñaranda de Duero

Peñaranda de Duero ㉛

Burgos. 🏘 600. 🚌 🛈 Calle Real 1, (947) 55 20 68. 🛒 Wed. 🎉 Santiago (Jul 25), Virgen de la Asunción (Aug 15).

THE CASTLE OF Peñaranda was built during the Reconquest (see pp50–51) by the Castilians, who had driven the Moors back south of the Río Duero. From its hilltop site there are views down to one of the most charming villages in old Castile, where tiled-roof houses cluster around a huge church. The main square is lined with porticoed, timber-framed buildings and the superb Renaissance **Palacio de los Condes de Miranda**. Framing its main doorway are various heraldic devices, and inside is a patio that has double galleries and

GREGORIAN PLAINCHANT

At regular intervals throughout the day, the monks of Santo Domingo de Silos sing services in plainchant, an unaccompanied singing of Latin texts in unison. The origins of chant date back to the beginnings of Christianity, but it was Pope Gregory I (590–604) who codified this manner of worship. It is an ancient and austere form of music that has found a new appeal with modern audiences. In 1994 a recording of the monks became a surprise hit all over the world.

Manuscript for an 11th-century Gregorian chant

Curtain walls and drum towers of Berlanga de Duero castle

fine decorated ceilings.
On Calle de la Botica, off the square, is a 17th-century pharmacy displaying antique blue and white apothecary jars.

ENVIRONS: In the old quarter of **Aranda de Duero**, 20 km (12 miles) to the west, is a notable church, the **Iglesia de Santa María**, with an elaborate Isabelline façade (*see p20*).

🏛 **Palacio de Avellaneda**
Plaza de Peñaranda.
((947) 55 20 13. ☐ *Tue–Sun.*

El Burgo de Osma ❷

Soria. 🏠 *5,000.* **ℹ** *Plaza Mayor 7, (975) 34 01 07.* 🔄 *Sat.* 🎎 *Virgen del Espino and San Roque (Aug 14–19).*

THE MOST INTERESTING sight in this attractive village is the **cathedral**. Although it is mostly Gothic (dating from 1232), with Renaissance additions, the tall tower is Baroque (1739). Its treasures include a Juan de Juni altarpiece, a white marble pulpit, and the tomb of the founder, San Pedro de Osma. The museum contains a valuable collection of illuminated manuscripts and codices.

Porticoed buildings line the streets and the Plaza Mayor, and storks nest on the Baroque Hospital de San Agustín.

ENVIRONS: Overlooking the Río Duero at **Gormaz**, 15 km (9.5 miles) south, is a massive castle with 28 towers. There are also mighty medieval fortresses at **Berlanga de Duero**, 12 km (7.5 miles) farther to the

southeast, and at **Calatañazor**, 25 km (15.5 miles) northeast of El Burgo de Osma, near the place where the Moorish leader al Mansur was killed in battle in 1002 (*see p49*).

Soria ❸

Soria. 🏠 *33,000.* **ℹ** *Plaza Ramón y Cajal, (975) 21 20 52.* 🔄 *Thu.* 🎎 *San Juan (late Jun), San Saturio (Oct 2).*

CASTILLA Y LEON'S smallest provincial capital stands on the banks of the Río Duero. Soria's stylish, modern parador (*see p557*) is named after the poet Antonio Machado (1875–1939, *see p31*), who wrote in praise of the town and the surrounding plains. Many of the older buildings are gone, but notable among those remaining are the imposing russet **Palacio de los Condes de Gómara** and the handsome **Concatedral de San Pedro**, both built in the 16th-century.

The **Museo Numantino**, opposite the municipal gardens, displays a variety of finds from the nearby Roman ruins

of Numantia and Tiermes (*see p347*). Across the Duero is the ruined monastery of **San Juan de Duero**, with a 13th-century cloister of interlacing arches.

ENVIRONS: North of Soria are the ruins of **Numantia**. The Celtiberian inhabitants endured a year-long Roman siege in 133 BC before defiantly burning the town and themselves (*see p46*). To the northwest is the Sierra de Urbión, a range of pine-clad hills with a lake, the **Laguna Negra de Urbión**.

🏛 **Museo Numantino**
Paseo de Espolón 6. **(** (975) 22 13 97. ☐ *Tue–Sun.*

Medinaceli ❹

Soria. 🏠 *1,500.* 🚌 **ℹ** *C/ Campo de San Nicolás 1, (975) 32 60 12.* 🎎 *Julián de San Agustín (Aug 28), Cuerpos Santos (Nov 13).*

ONLY A triumphal arch remains of Roman Ocilis, perched on a high ridge over the Río Jalón. Built in the 2nd or 3rd century AD, it is the only one in Spain with three arches. It has been adopted as the symbol for ancient monuments on Spanish road signs.

ENVIRONS: Lying just to the east are the red cliffs of the Jalón gorges. On the Madrid–Burgos road is the Cistercian monastery of **Santa María de Huerta**, founded in 1179. Its glories include a 13th-century Gothic cloister and the superb, cryptlike Monks' Refectory.

⛪ **Monasterio de Santa María de Huerta**
((975) 32 70 02. ☐ *daily.*

Decorative arches in the cloister of the monastery of San Juan de Duero

CASTILLA–LA MANCHA

GUADALAJARA · CUENCA · TOLEDO · ALBACETE · CIUDAD REAL

*L*A MANCHA'S EMPTY BEAUTY, *its windmills and medieval castles, silhouetted above the sienna plains, was immortalized by Cervantes in Don Quixote's epic adventures. Its brilliantly sunlit, wide horizons are one of the classic images of Spain. This scarcely visited region has great, scenic mountain ranges, dramatic gorges, and the two monument-filled cities of Toledo and Cuenca.*

You will always find a castle nearby in this region – as the name Castilla suggests. Most were built in the 9th–12th centuries, when the region was a battle-ground between Christians and Moors. Others mark the 14th- and 15th-century frontiers between the kingdoms of Aragón and Castile. Sigüenza, Belmonte, Alarcón, Molina de Aragón, and Calatrava La Nueva are among the most impressive.

Toledo, which was the capital of Visigothic Spain, is an outstanding museum city. Its rich architectural and artistic heritage derives from a coalescence of Muslim, Christian, and Jewish cultures with medieval and Renaissance ideas and influences.

Cuenca is another attractive city. Its old town is perched above converging gorges; on two sides it spills down steep hillsides. Villanueva de los Infantes, Chinchilla, Alcaraz, and Almagro are towns of character built between the 16th and 18th centuries. Ocaña and Tembleque each has a splendid *plaza mayor* (main square).

La Mancha's plains are brightened by natural features of great beauty in its two national parks – the Tablas de Daimiel, and Cabañeros, within the Montes de Toledo. Rimming the plains are beautiful upland areas: the olive groves of the Alcarria; Cuenca's limestone mountains; and the peaks of the Sierra de Alcaraz. The wine region of La Mancha is the world's largest expanse of vineyards. Around Consuegra and Albacete fields turn mauve in autumn as the valuable saffron crocus blooms.

Windmills above Campo de Criptana on the plains of La Mancha

◁ Old houses in Cuenca, a city dramatically located over two gorges

Exploring Castilla-La Mancha

THE HISTORIC CITY OF TOLEDO is Castilla-La Mancha's major tourist destination. Less crowded towns with historical charm include Almagro, Oropesa, Alcaraz, and Guadalajara. At Sigüenza, Calatrava, Belmonte, and Alarcón there are medieval castles, reminders of the region's eventful past. Some towns on the plains of La Mancha, such as El Toboso and Campo de Criptana, are associated with the adventures of Don Quixote *(see p377)*. The wooded uplands of the Serranía de Cuenca, the Alcarria, and the Sierra de Alcaraz provide picturesque scenic routes. A haven for bird lovers is the wetland nature preserve of the Tablas de Daimiel.

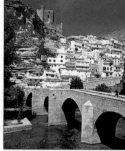

The village of Alcalá del Júcar

SIGHTS AT A GLANCE

Alarcón ⑳
Albacete ㉒
Alcalá del Júcar ㉑
Alcaraz ㉔
La Alcarria ④
Almagro ㉚
Atienza ①
Belmonte ⑲
Calatrava la Nueva ㉙
Campo de Criptana ⑰
Consuegra ⑯
Cuenca pp366–7 ⑦
Guadalajara ⑤
Illescas ⑩
Lagunas de Ruidera ㉕
Molina de Aragón ③
Montes de Toledo ⑬
Oropesa ⑫
Segóbriga ⑧
Serranía de Cuenca ⑥
Sigüenza ②
Tablas de Daimiel ㉛
Talavera de la Reina ⑪
Tembleque ⑮
El Toboso ⑱
Toledo pp370–75 ⑭
Uclés ⑨
Valdepeñas ㉗
Valle de Alcudia ㉜
Villanueva de los Infantes ㉖
Viso del Marqués ㉘

Tours

Sierra de Alcaraz ㉓

SEE ALSO

• *Where to Stay* pp558–60

• *Restaurants and Bars* pp597–8

Cattle grazing on the isolated
plains of La Mancha

GETTING AROUND

Castilla-La Mancha is best explored by car since it is has a good network of highways radiating outward from Madrid. These are the N401 to Toledo, the NII to Sigüenza, the NIII to Albacete, the NIV to Valdepeñas, and the NV to Oropesa. The region is also served by the high-speed AVE train that runs between Madrid and Seville, stopping at Ciudad Real. Otherwise, public transportation is infrequent and slow. Albacete and Toledo have domestic airports.

KEY

▬▬	Freeway
▬▬	Major road
▬▬	Minor road
▬▬	Scenic route
◿	River
☀	Viewpoint

C114
ATIENZA ❶
G101
SIGÜENZA ❷
Zaragoza
N11
C202
MOLINA DE ARAGÓN ❸
N211
BRIHUEGA
GUADALAJARA ❺
LA ALCARRIA ❹
id
C200
Embalse de Buendía
N320
C202
SERRANIA DE CUENCA ❻
Teruel
N420
N400
CUENCA ❼
N330
Turia
UCLÉS ❾
OBRIGA ❽
C320
N111
N320
Cabriel
Embalse de Alarcón
CU501
OSO
N420
ALARCON ❿... **ALARCON** ⓴
BELMONTE ⓳
Júcar
N111
→ *Valencia*
NA
Zancara
N310
N301
N322
VAS DE IDERA ㉕
ALCALA DEL JUCAR ㉑
N301
N430
ALBACETE ㉒
C415
Azuer
N322
N430
ALMANSA
N430
ILLANUEVA DE NFANTES
C503
N301
ALCARAZ ㉔
SIERRA DE ALCARAZ ㉓
HELLIN
CR212
Alacant (Alicante)
N322
ELCHE DE LA SIERRA
C415
R621
Segura
NERPIO

0 kilometers   50
0 miles   30

The tranquil Montes de Toledo

Atienza ①

Guadalajara. ![icon] 500. ![icon] *Plaza de España 11, (949) 39 90 01.* ![icon] *Thu.* ![icon] *La Caballada (May/Jun).*

RISING HIGH above the valley it once protected, Atienza contains vestiges of its medieval past. Crowning the hill are a ruined 12th-century castle. The arcaded Plaza Mayor and the Plaza del Trigo are joined by an original gateway. The **Museo de San Gil**, a religious art museum, is in the church of the same name. The **Iglesia de Santa María del Rey**, at the foot of the hill, displays a Baroque altarpiece.

ENVIRONS: Campisábalos, to the west, has an outstanding 12th-century Romanesque church. The **Hayedo de Tejera Negra**, farther west, is a nature preserve of beech woods.

🏛 Museo de San Gil
Calle Juela de San Gil. ![icon] *(949) 39 90 14.* ![icon] *Sep–Jun: Sat & Sun; Jul–Aug: daily.* ![icon] ![icon]

Sigüenza ②

Guadalajara. ![icon] 5,000. ![icon] ![icon] *Plaza Mayor 1, (949) 39 32 51.* ![icon] *Sat.* ![icon] *San Juan (Jun 24), San Roque (Aug 15).*

DOMINATING the hillside town of Sigüenza is its impressive castle-parador *(see p559)*. The **cathedral**, in the old town, is Romanesque, with later additions, such as the Gothic-Plateresque cloisters. In one of the chapels is the Tomb of El Doncel, built for Martín Vázquez de Arce, Isabel

Semirecumbent figure of El Doncel on his tomb in Sigüenza cathedral

of Castile's page *(see p52)*. He was killed in battle against the Moors in 1486. The sacristy has a beautiful ceiling carved with flowers and cherubs, by Alonso de Covarrubias.

Molina de Aragón ③

Guadalajara. ![icon] 3,000. ![icon] *Calle del Carmen 1, (949) 83 24 53.* ![icon] *Thu.* ![icon] *Día del Carmen (Jul 16), Ferias (Aug 30–Sep 5).*

MOLINA'S ATTRACTIVE medieval quarter is at the foot of a hill next to the Río Gallo. The town was disputed during the Reconquest and then captured from the Moors by Alfonso I of Aragón in 1129. Many monuments were destroyed during the War of Independence *(see p59)*, but the 11th-century hilltop castle preserves six original towers. It is possible to visit the newly restored Romanesque **Iglesia de Santa Clara**.

ENVIRONS: West of Molina is the chapel of the **Virgen de la Hoz**, set in a beautiful rust-red ravine. Farther southwest is a nature preserve, the **Parque Natural del Alto Tajo**.

Arab ramparts above Molina de Aragón's old town

La Alcarria ④

Guadalajara. ![icon] *Guadalajara.* ![icon] *Guadalajara, (949) 22 06 98.*

THIS VAST STRETCH of undulating olive groves and fields east of Guadalajara is still evocative of Camilo José Cela's *(see p31)* classic book *Journey to the Alcarria*. Driving through the rolling hills dotted with small villages, it seems that little has changed since this account of the hardship of Spanish rural life was written in the 1940s.
 Toward the center of the Alcarria are three immense adjoining reservoirs called the **Mar de Castilla** (Sea of

Olive groves in La Alcarria in the province of Guadalajara

Castile). The first reservoir was built in 1946, and vacation cottages have subsequently sprung up close to the shores and on the outskirts of villages.

Historic **Pastrana**, which is situated 40 km (25 miles) southeast of Guadalajara, is one of the most attractive towns in the Alcarria. It grew up around a mansion, the **Palacio Mendoza**, and by the 17th century had become larger and more affluent than Guadalajara. The **Iglesia de la Asunción** contains four 15th-century Flemish tapestries and a painting by El Greco.

Brihuega, 30 km (19 miles) northeast of Guadalajara, has a pleasant old center.

Guadalajara ⑤

Guadalajara. 🕮 60,000. 🚆 🚍 🚪
Plaza Mayor 7, (949) 22 06 98. 🛒 Tue,
Sat. 🎪 Virgen de la Antigua (Sep).

GUADALAJARA'S HISTORY is largely lost within the modern city, although traces of its Renaissance splendor survive. The **Palacio de los Duques del Infantado**, built between the 14th and 17th centuries by the powerful Mendoza dynasty, is an outstanding example of Gothic-Mudéjar architecture *(see p20)*. The main façade and the two-story patio are adorned with delicate carving. Following Civil War bombing, the palace was restored and now houses the Museo Provincial. Among the churches in the town is the **Iglesia de Santiago**, with a

Detail of the façade of the Palacio de los Duques del Infantado

Sculpted rock figures in Ciudad Encantada

Gothic-Plateresque chapel by Alonso de Covarrubias. The 15th-century **Iglesia de San Francisco** is home to the mausoleum of the Mendoza family. The cathedral is built on the site of a mosque.

ENVIRONS: At **Lupiana**, 11 km (7 miles) east of Guadalajara**,** is the two-story Monasterio de San Bartolomé, which was founded in the 14th century.

🏛 Palacio de los Duques del Infantado
Avenida del Infantado del Ejército.
🎫 (949) 21 33 01. 🔲 daily. 🎫

Serranía de Cuenca ⑥

Cuenca. 🚍 Cuenca. 🚪 Cuenca,
(969) 23 21 19.

TO THE NORTH AND EAST of Cuenca stretches the vast *serranía*, a mountainous area of forests and pastures dissected by deep gorges. Its two most popular scenic areas are the **Ciudad Encantada**

(Enchanted City), where the limestone has been eroded into spectacular shapes, and the moss-clad waterfalls and rock pools of the **Nacimiento del Río Cuervo** (Source of the River Cuervo).

The main river flowing through the area, the Júcar, carves a gorge near Villalba de la Sierra. The viewpoint of the **Ventana del Diablo** gives the best view of the gorge.

Between Beteta and Priego (known for its pottery and canework), to the north, is another spectacular river canyon, the **Hoz de Beteta**, where the Río Guadiela has cut its way through the surrounding cliffs. There are good views from the convent of **San Miguel de las Victorias**. A small road leads to the 18th-century royal spa of **Solán de Cabras**.

In the emptier eastern and southern tracts is **Cañete**, a fortified old town with a parish church displaying 16th-century paintings. To the southeast of Cañete are the eerie ridgetop ruins of the abandoned town of **Moya**.

Street-by-Street: Cuenca ❼

CUENCA'S PICTURESQUE OLD TOWN sits astride a steep-
sided spur that drops precipitously on either side to
the deep gorges of the Júcar and Huécar rivers. Around
the Moorish town's narrow, winding streets grew the
Gothic and Renaissance city, its monuments built with
with the profits of the wool and textile trade. The main
sight is the cathedral, one of the most original works
of Spanish Gothic, with Anglo-Norman influences.
One of the picturesque Hanging Houses,
which jut out over the Huécar ravine, has
been converted into the excellent
Museum of Abstract Art.

The Plaza de la Merced
buildings contrast with the
modern Museo de Ciencia
(Science Museum) nearby.

**Museo de
Ciencia**

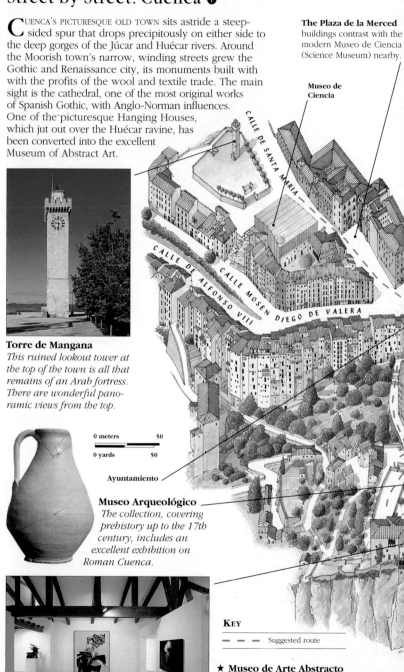

Torre de Mangana
*This ruined lookout tower at
the top of the town is all that
remains of an Arab fortress.
There are wonderful pano-
ramic views from the top.*

| 0 meters | 50 |
| 0 yards | 50 |

Ayuntamiento

Museo Arqueológico
*The collection, covering
prehistory up to the 17th
century, includes an
excellent exhibition on
Roman Cuenca.*

CALLE DE SANTA MARIA

CALLE DE ALFONSO VIII

CALLE MOSEN DIEGO DE VALERA

KEY

‒ ‒ ‒ Suggested route

★ **Museo de Arte Abstracto**
*Spain's abstract art museum is inside one
of the Hanging Houses. It contains works by
the movement's leading artists, including
Antoni Tàpies and Eduardo Chillida.*

Plaza Mayor
This café-lined, arcaded square is in the heart of the old town. The 18th-century Baroque town hall (ayun-tamiento), built over arches, stands at the south end.

VISITORS' CHECKLIST

Cuenca. 🚹 40,000. 🚍 Calle Mariano Catalina, (969) 22 07 20. 🚍 Calle Fermín Caballero 20, (969) 22 70 87. 🛈 Plaza Mayor 1, (969) 23 21 19. 🚌 Tue. 📅 Semana Santa (Easter Week). **Museo Diocesano** ◯ Tue–Sun. 📷 **Museo de Arte Abstracto** ◯ Tue–Sun. 📷 **Museo Arqueológico** ◯ Tue–Sun. 📷

The Iglesia de San Miguel, perched over the Júcar gorge, was built in the Gothic style. It has a beautiful Mudéjar ceiling.

SEVERO CATALINA

PLAZA MAYOR

CALLE DE SAN PEDRO

O VALERO

CALLE DE JULIAN ROMERO

→ To Parador de Cuenca

Museo Diocesano
The cathedral's treasures, which are housed in the Palacio Episcopal, include paintings by El Greco.

★ Cathedral
Highlights of the 12th–16th-century building are the decorated altar, chapter-house, and the side chapels.

STAR SIGHTS

★ **Museo de Arte Abstracto**

★ **Hanging Houses**

★ **Cathedral**

★ Hanging Houses
The 14th-century beamed Casas Colgadas were once used as a summer residence for the royal family.

Remains of a Roman building in Segóbriga

Segóbriga **8**

Saelices (Cuenca). **[** (969) 13 20 64. ☐ Tue –Sun. **Museum** ☐ public hols, Dec 24, 25 & 31.

THE SMALL RUINED Roman city of Segóbriga, near the town of Saelices, is located in open, unspoiled countryside close to the Madrid–Valencia highway. The Romans who lived here exploited the surrounding area, growing grain, felling timber, and mining minerals.

Many parts of the city can be explored. The 3rd-century theater – which has a capacity of 2,000 people – is sometimes used for dramatic performances today. Segóbriga also had a necropolis, an amphitheater, a temple to Diana, and public baths. The quarries that supplied the stone to build the city can also be seen.

Nearby, there is a small museum containing some of the site's finds, although the best statues are in Cuenca's Museo Arqueológico *(see p366)*.

Monasterio de Uclés **9**

Uclés (Cuenca). **[** (969) 13 50 58. ☐ 9am – dusk daily.

THE SMALL VILLAGE OF Uclés, to the south of the Alcarria, is dominated by its impressive castle-monastery, nicknamed "El Escorial de La Mancha" for the similarity of its church's profile to that of El Escorial *(see pp312–13)*. Originally an impregnable medieval fortress, Uclés became the monastery seat of the Order of Santiago from 1174, because of its cen-

tral geographical location. The austere building you see today, used as a seminary school, is mainly Renaissance, but overlaid with ornamental Baroque detail. Among its attractive features are a magnificent carved wooden ceiling and staircase.

Illescas **10**

Toledo. 7,500. ☐ **i** Plaza Mayor 1, (925) 51 10 51. ☐ Thu. Fiesta de Milagro (Mar 11), Fiesta Patronal (Aug 31).

JUST OFF THE Madrid–Toledo highway, Illescas was the summer location for Felipe II's court. While there is little to see of its old town, the 16th-century **Hospital de la Caridad**, next to the Iglesia de la Asunción (which is easily identified by its Mudéjar tower), is important for its art collection. The hospital has five outstanding late El Grecos

Ceramics in Talavera workshop

(see p373) hanging in its 16th-century interior. The subjects of three of these are the Nativity, the Annunciation, and the Coronation of the Virgin.

♙ Hospital de la Caridad
Plaza de los Leones. **[** (925) 51 12 23. ☐ daily.

Talavera de la Reina **11**

Toledo. 80,000. ☐ ☐ **i** Plaza del Pan 13, (925) 82 53 22. ☐ Wed. Virgen del Prado (May 24), San Mateo (Sep 27).

A RUINED 15TH-CENTURY bridge across the Tagus marks the entrance to the old part of this busy market town, famous for its ceramics. From the bridge you can walk past the surviving section of the Roman and medieval wall to the **collegiate church**. This is the largest of the town's four Gothic-Mudéjar churches and is notable for its fine rose window.

Talavera's ceramic workshops are on the western edge of town. They still produce the blue and yellow *azulejos* (tiles) that have been a trademark of the town since the 16th century, but nowadays they also make domestic and decorative objects.

A good selection of the town's *azulejos* can be seen in the large **Ermita del Virgen del Prado** by the river. Many of the interior walls have superb 16th- to 20th-century tile friezes of religious scenes.

Part of a frieze of tiles in Talavera's Ermita del Virgen del Prado

Traditional embroidery work in Lagartera, near Oropesa

Oropesa **⑫**

Toledo. 🏠 2,900. 🚌 📋 *Plaza del Navarro 9, (925) 43 00 02.* 🎉 *Virgen de Peñitas (Sep 8–9), Beato Alonso de Orozco (Sep 19).*

O ROPESA'S MEDIEVAL and Renaissance splendor as one of Toledo's satellite communities has left a charming old quarter at the center of today's small farming town. A circular Ruta Monumental starts from the massive, mainly 15th-century **castle** on the top of the hill. A Renaissance extension – thought to be the work of Juan de Herrera, co-architect of El Escorial (see pp312–13) – was added to the castle in the 16th-century by the wealthy and influential Álvarez family. A large part of the castle has been converted into a parador (see p559).

The Ruta Monumental continues around the town, taking in several churches, convents, a small ceramics museum, and the town hall, which presides over the main square.

ENVIRONS: The area around Oropesa is excellent for buying handicrafts. **Lagartera**, just to the west of the town, is famous for the embroidery and lacework by the women in the village, and **El Puente del Arzobispo**, 12 km (7 miles) south of Oropesa, is a good source of painted ceramics and *esparto* (grass-weaving) work. **Ciudad de Vascos**, farther southeast, is a ruined 10th-century Arab city in splendid countryside around Azután.

Montes de Toledo **⑬**

Toledo. 🚌 *San Martín de Montalbán.* 📋 *Toledo, (925) 22 08 43.*

T O THE SOUTHWEST of Toledo a range of low mountains sweeps toward Extremadura. In medieval times the Montes de Toledo were owned by bishops and the kings. They cover an area of approximately 1,000 sq km (386 sq miles).

The new nature preserve of the **Parque Nacional de Cabañeros** (see pp26–7) encloses a sizable area of woodland and pastures used for grazing sheep. The easiest access to the park is from **Pueblo Nuevo del Bullaque**. From here it is possible to make four-hour guided trips in Landrovers, during which you may spot wild boar, deer, and imperial eagles. In the pasturelands stand *chozos*, conical shelters for shepherds and their families.

In the eastern foothills of the Montes de Toledo is **Orgaz**, with a parish church which contains works by El Greco. Nearby villages, such as **Los Yébenes** and **Ventas con Peña Aguilera**, are known for their leather goods and restaurants serving game.

On the plains stands the small church of **Santa María de Melque**, believed to date back to the 8th century. Close by is the Templar castle of **Montalbán**, a vast but ruined 12th-century fortress. Nearer to Toledo, at **Guadamur**, there is another handsome castle.

A *chozo* (shepherd's cabin) in the Parque Nacional de Cabañeros

CASTILLA-LA MANCHA'S FIESTAS

La Endiablada *(Feb 2–3)* Almonacid del Marquesado (Cuenca). At the start of the two-day-long "Fiesta of the Bewitched," men and boys, gaudily dressed as "devils," with cowbells strapped to their backs, gather in the house of their leader, the *Diablo Mayor*. They accompany the images of the Virgen de la Candelaria (Virgin of Candlemas) and St. Blaise in procession. As the devils dance alongside the floats bearing the saints' images, they ring their bells loudly and incessantly.

One of the so-called "devils" in La Endiablada fiesta

Romería del Cristo del Sahúco *(Pentecost, May/ Jun)*, Peñas de San Pedro (Albacete). A cross-shaped coffin bearing a figure of Christ is carried 15 km (9 miles) here from its shrine by men dressed in white.
La Caballada *(Pentecost)*, Atienza (Guadalajara). Horsemen follow the route across country taken by the 12th-century muleteers of Atienza, who are said to have saved the boy King Alfonso VIII of Castile from his uncle, Fernando II.
Corpus Christi *(May/ Jun)*, Toledo. One of Spain's most dramatic Corpus Christi (see p34) processions. The cathedral monstrance (see p374) is paraded in the streets.

Street-by-Street: Toledo ⓮

Damascene work, typical of Toledo

PICTURESQUELY SITED on a hill above the River Tagus is the historic center of Toledo. Behind the old walls lies much evidence of the city's rich history. The Romans built a fortress on the site of the present-day Alcázar. The Visigoths made Toledo their capital in the 6th century AD and left behind several churches. In the Middle Ages, Toledo was a melting pot of Christian, Muslim, and Jewish cultures, and it was during this period that the city's most outstanding monument – its cathedral – was built. In the 16th century the painter El Greco came to live in Toledo, and today the city is home to many of his works.

The Iglesia de San Román, of Visigothic origin, now contains a museum relating the city's past under the Visigoths.

Puerta de Valmardón

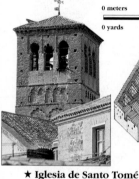

★ Iglesia de Santo Tomé
This church, with a beautiful Mudéjar tower, houses El Greco's masterpiece, The Burial of the Count of Orgaz *(see p28).*

To Sinagoga de Santa María la Blanca and Monasterio de San Juan de los Reyes

To Sinagoga del Tránsito and Casa-Museo de El Greco

0 meters 100
0 yards 100

CARDENAL LORENZANA

CALLE DE SAN ROMAN

CALLE DE ALFONSO X

CALLE DE ALFONSO XII

CALLE DE LA TRINIDAD

Archbishop's Palace

Taller del Moro
Once used as a workshop by craftsmen building the cathedral, this Mudéjar palace now houses a museum of Mudéjar ceramics and tiles.

STAR SIGHTS
★ Iglesia de Santo Tomé
★ Museo de Santa Cruz
★ Cathedral

Puerta del
as a double
ish arch and
two towers.

Ermita del Cristo de la Luz
This small mosque, the city's only remaining Muslim building, dates from around AD 1000.

To tourist information, Estación de Autobuses, and Estación de RENFE

The Plaza de Zocodover is named after the market held here in Moorish times. It is still the city's main square, with many cafés and shops.

PLAZA DE ZOCODOVER
FILERITOS
CALLE DEL COMERCIO
CUESTA DE CARLOS V
SIXTO RAMON PARRO
AL CISNEROS

★ Museo de Santa Cruz
The city's main fine arts collection includes several tapestries from Flanders. Among them is this 15th-century zodiac tapestry, with well-preserved, rich colors.

KEY
 Suggested route

★ Cathedral
Built on the site of a Visigothic cathedral and a mosque, this impressive structure is one of the largest cathedrals in Christendom (see pp374–5). The Flamboyant Gothic high altar reredos (1504) is the work of several artists.

Alcázar
Outside the fortress is this monument, in memory of the Nationalists who died here in a 70-day siege during the Civil War.

Toledo cathedral rising above the rooftops of the medieval part of the city

Exploring Toledo

Toledo is easily reached from Madrid by rail, bus, or car, and is then best explored on foot. To visit all the main sights you need at least two days, but it is possible to walk around the medieval and Jewish quarters in a long morning. To avoid the heavy crowds, go midweek and stay for a night, when the city is at its most atmospheric.

♠ Alcázar

Cuesta del Alcázar. 【 (925) 22 30 38. ◯ Tue – Sun. 🖉

Charles V's fortified palace stands on the site of former Roman, Visigothic, and Muslim fortresses. Its severe square profile suffered damage by fire three times before being almost completely destroyed in 1936 when the Nationalists survived a 70-day siege by the Republicans. Restoration followed the original plans, and the building now houses an army museum. The siege headquarters have been preserved as a monument to Nationalist heroism. Much is made of an alleged telephone conversation between the besieged Colonel Moscardó and his son, held by the Republicans and threatened with death unless his father surrendered. The Colonel refused, and his son was later killed, though not necessarily as a direct result of his father's refusal to capitulate.

🏛 Museo de Santa Cruz

Calle Cervantes 3. 【 (925) 22 10 36. ◯ daily. 🖉

This museum is housed in a 16th-century hospital founded by Cardinal Mendoza. The building has some outstanding Renaissance architectural features, including the main doorway, staircase, and cloister. The four main wings, laid out in the shape of a Greek cross, are dedicated to the fine arts. The collection is especially strong in medieval and Renaissance tapestries, paintings and sculptures. There are also works by El Greco, including one of his last paintings, *The Assumption* (1613), still in its original altarpiece. Decorative

The Assumption by El Greco (1613) in the Museo de Santa Cruz

arts on display include two typically Toledan crafts: armor and damascened swords, made by inlaying blackened steel with gold wire. Damascene work such as plates and jewelery (as well as swords) is still produced in the city.

⛪ Iglesia de Santo Tomé

Plaza del Conde 1. 【 (925) 21 02 09. ◯ daily. 🖉

Visitors come to Santo Tomé mainly to admire El Greco's masterpiece, *The Burial of the Count of Orgaz (see p28)*. An important patron of the church, the Count paid for much of the 14th-century building that stands today. The painting, commissioned in his memory by a parish priest, depicts the miraculous appearance of St. Augustine and St. Stephen at his burial, to raise his body to heaven. It has never been moved from the setting for which it was painted, nor restored. Nevertheless, it is remarkable for its contrast of glowing and somber colors. In the foreground, allegedly, are the artist himself and his son (both looking out) as well as Cervantes. The church itself is thought to date back to the 12th century, and its tower is one of the best examples of Mudéjar architecture in the city.

Nearby is the **Pastelería Santo Tomé**, a good place to buy locally made marzipan.

♛ Sinagoga de Santa María la Blanca

Calle de los Reyes Católicos 4.
◖ (925) 22 72 57. ☐ daily. 📷
The oldest and largest of the city's eight original synagogues, this monument dates back to the 12th century. In 1405 it was taken over as a church by the military-religious Order of Calatrava. Restoration has returned it as far as possible to its original beauty – finely carved stone capitals and wall panels stand out against plain white horseshoe arches and plasterwork. In the main chapel is a Plateresque altarpiece. In 1391 a massacre of Jews took place on this site, a turning point after years of religious tolerance in the city.

Mudéjar arches in the Sinagoga de Santa María la Blanca

♛ Sinagoga del Tránsito

Calle Samuel Leví. ◖ (925) 22 36 65.
☐ Tue–Sun. 📷
The most elaborate Mudéjar interior in the city is hidden behind the deceptively humble façade of this former synagogue, built in the 14th century by Samuel Ha-Leví, the Jewish treasurer to Pedro the Cruel. The interlaced frieze of the lofty prayer hall harmoniously fuses Islamic, Gothic, and Hebrew geometric motifs below a wonderful coffered ceiling.

Adjoining the synagogue is an interesting museum dedicated to Sephardic (Spanish Jewish) culture. The manuscripts, tombstones, wedding costumes, and sacred objects of worship date from both before and after the Jews' expulsion from Spain at the end of the 15th century (see p53).

Ornate ceiling in the Monasterio de San Juan de los Reyes

♙ Monasterio de San Juan de los Reyes

Calle de los Reyes Católicos 17.
◖ (925) 22 38 02. ☐ daily. 📷 ♿
A wonderful mixture of architectural styles, this monastery was commissioned by the Catholic Monarchs in honor of their victory over the Portuguese at the battle of Toro in 1476 (see p339). Originally, it was intended to be their burial place, but they were actually laid to rest in Granada (see p462). Largely the work of Juan Güas, the church's main Isabelline structure was completed in 1492. Although it was badly damaged by Napoleon's troops in 1808 (see p59), it has been restored to its original splendor. It retains superb features such as a Gothic cloister (1510) – unique in the city – which has a beautiful multicolored Mudéjar ceiling. Near to the church is a stretch of the Jewish quarter's original wall.

🏛 Casa-Museo de El Greco

Calle Samuel Leví. ◖ (925) 22 40 46. ☐ Tue–Sun. 📷
It is not clear whether El Greco actually lived in or simply near to this house in the heart of the Jewish quarter, which has been turned into a museum containing an important collection of his works. Canvases on display include View of Toledo, a detailed depiction of the city at the time, and the superb series Christ and the Apostles. Underneath the museum, on the ground floor, is a domestic chapel with a fine Mudéjar ceiling and a collection of art by painters of the Toledan School, such as Luis Tristán, a student of El Greco.

♙ Iglesia de Santiago del Arrabal

This is one of Toledo's most beautiful Mudéjar monuments. It can be easily identified by its tower, reminiscent of a minaret, which is said to date back to the 12th-century Reconquest (see pp50–51). The church, which was built slightly later, has a beautiful woodwork ceiling. The ornate Mudéjar pulpit and Plateresque altarpiece stand out against the otherwise plain Mudéjar interior.

♛ Puerta Antigua de Bisagra

When Alfonso VI conquered Toledo in 1085, he entered it through this gateway, alongside El Cid. It is the only gateway in the city to have kept its original 10th-century military architecture. The huge towers are topped by a 12th-century Arab gatehouse.

EL GRECO

Born in Crete in 1541, El Greco ("the Greek") came to Toledo in 1577 to paint the altarpiece in the convent of Santo Domingo el Antiguo. Enchanted by the city, he stayed here, painting religious portraits and altarpieces for other churches. Although El Greco was trained in Italy and influenced by masters such as Tintoretto, his works are closely identified with the city where he settled. He died in Toledo in 1614.

Domenikos Theotocopoulos, better known as El Greco

Toledo Cathedral

THE SPLENDOR OF TOLEDO'S massive cathedral reflects its history as the spiritual heart of the Spanish church and the seat of the Primate of all Spain. Still today, the Mozarabic Mass, which dates back to Visigothic times, is said here by papal permission. The present cathedral was built on the site of a 7th-century church. Work began in 1226 and spanned three centuries, until the completion of the last vaults in 1493. This long period of construction explains the cathedral's mixture of styles: pure French Gothic – complete with flying buttresses – on the exterior; with Spanish decorative styles, such as Mudéjar and Plateresque work, used in the interior.

Sacristy
El Greco's The Denuding of Christ, *above the marble altar, was painted especially for the cathedral. Also here are works by Titian, Van Dyck, and Goya.*

The Cloister, on two floors, was built in the 14th century on the site of the old Jewish market.

View of Toledo Cathedral
Dominating the city skyline is the Gothic tower at the west end of the nave. The best view of the cathedral, and the city, is from the parador (see p560).

The belfry in the tower contains a heavy bell known as *La Gorda* ("the Fat One").

The Puerta de Mollete, on the west façade, is the main entrance to the cathedral. From this door, *mollete*, or soft bread, was distributed to the poor.

★ Monstrance
In the Treasury is the 16th-century Gothic silver monstrance, over 3 m (10 ft) high. It is carried through the streets of Toledo during the Corpus Christi celebrations (see p369).

STAR FEATURES
★ Monstrance
★ Transparente
★ High Altar Reredos
★ Choir

★ Transparente
This Baroque altarpiece of marble, jasper, and bronze, by Narciso Tomé, is illuminated by an ornate sky-light. It stands out from the mainly Gothic interior.

Capilla de Santiago

The Capilla de San Ildefonso contains the superb Plateresque tomb of bishop Alonso Carrillo de Albornoz.

Chapterhouse
Above 16th-century frescoes by Juan de Borgoña is this multicolored Mudéjar ceiling, unique in the city.

Puerta de los Leones

★ High Altar Reredos
The polychrome reredos, one of the most beautiful in Spain, depicts scenes from Christ's life.

The Puerta del Pardón, or Door of Mercy, has a tympa-num decorated with religious characters.

The Capilla Mozárabe has a beautiful Renaissance ironwork grille, carved by Juan Francés in 1524.

★ Choir
The carvings on the wooden lower stalls depict scenes of the fall of Granada. The alabaster upper ones show figures from the Old Testament.

Windmills on the ridge above Consuegra, overlooking the plains of La Mancha

Tembleque ⓮

Toledo. 🏘 2,500. ℹ Plaza Mayor 1, (925) 14 55 25. 🚌 Wed. 🎭 Jesús de Nazareno (late Aug).

THE WELL-PRESERVED, timbered Plaza Mayor (see p23) at Tembleque dates from the 17th century. It is decorated with the red cross of the Knights Hospitallers, the military order that once ruled the town.

ENVIRONS: Ocaña, 30 km (20 miles) north of Tembleque, centers on the enormous yet elegant, late 18th-century brick *plaza mayor*. It is one of the largest squares in Spain, after those in Madrid and Salamanca.

Consuegra ⓰

Toledo. 🏘 9,600. 🚌 ℹ Molino de Viento Volero, (925) 47 57 31. 🚌 Sat. 🎭 La Rosa de Azafrán (late Oct).

CONSUEGRA'S ELEVEN windmills (see p23) and ruined castle stand on a ridge above the town, overlooking the plains of La Mancha. One windmill has working machinery that is set in motion every year during the town's festival to celebrate the autumn harvest of a colorful local crop: saffron (see p320). During the fiesta, pickers compete to see who can strip petals from the saffron crocus the fastest.

ENVIRONS: About 4 km (2.5 miles) along the road to **Urda** is a ruined Roman dam. An old restaurant (see p598) at **Puerto Lápice**, off the NIV 20 km (13 miles) south of Consuegra, claims to be the inn in which Don Quixote was "knighted" by the indulgent landlord.

Campo de Criptana ⓱

Ciudad Real. 🏘 14,500. 🚌 ℹ Los Molinos, (926) 56 22 31. 🚌 Tue. 🎭 Virgen de Criptana (Apr 17).

THE REMAINING TEN windmills of what was originally La Mancha's largest collection – 32 – stand on a hillcrest above wheat plains. Three date back to the 16th century and have their original machinery intact. One windmill is the tourist information office. Another four contain museums of local life.

ENVIRONS: More windmills stand above nearby **Alcázar de San Juan** and **Mota del Cuervo**, a good place to buy *queso Manchego*, La Mancha sheep's cheese (see p321).

El Toboso ⓲

Toledo. 🏘 2,200. ℹ Plaza de Juan Carlos I, (925) 19 73 75. 🚌 Wed. 🎭 San Agustín (Aug 27–30).

OF ALL THE villages of La Mancha claiming links to Don Quixote, El Toboso has the clearest ties. It was chosen by Cervantes as the birthplace of Dulcinea, Don Quixote's sweetheart. The **Casa de Dulcinea**, the home of Doña Ana Martínez Zarco, on whom the character of Dulcinea was allegedly based, has been refurbished for visitors in its original 16th-century style.

The village was considered to be of such cultural importance that the French army is said to have refused to attack it during the War of Independence (see pp58–9).

🏛 **Casa de Dulcinea**
📞 (925) 19 72 88. 🕐 Tue–Sun. 📷

Belmonte ⓳

Cuenca. 🏘 2,600. 🚌 ℹ Plaza del Caudillo 1, (967) 17 00 68. 🚌 Mon. 🎭 San Bartolomé (late Aug), Virgen de Gracia (second week of Sep).

BELMONTE'S MAGNIFICENT 15th-century **castle** (see p326) is one of the best preserved in the region. It was built by Juan Pacheco, Marquis of Villena, after Enrique IV gave him the town in 1456. Inside it has decorative carved coffered ceilings and Mudéjar plasterwork. The **collegiate church** is especially

Belmonte's splendid 15th-century castle

remarkable for its richly decorated chapels and Gothic choir
stalls, which were brought
here from Cuenca cathedral
(see p367). There is also outstanding ironwork, a Renaissance reredos and the font at
which the Golden Age poet
Fray Luis de León (1527–91),
was baptized.

ENVIRONS: Two villages near
Belmonte also flourished
under the Marquis of Villena.
The church at **Villaescusa de
Haro**, 6 km (4 miles) to the
northeast, has an outstanding
16th-century reredos. **San
Clemente**, some 40 km (25
miles) further southeast, clus-
ters around two near-perfect
Renaissance squares. There is a
Gothic alabaster cross in the
Iglesia de Santiago Apóstol.

🏰 **Castillo de Belmonte**
◻ *daily.* 🖼

The chalk cliffs of Alcalá del Júcar, honeycombed with tunnels

**The castle of Alarcón, which has
been converted into a parador**

Alarcón ⓴

Cuenca. 👥 230. 🚏 *Plaza Infante Don
Juan Manuel 1, (969) 33 03 54.*
🎉 *Cristo de la Fé (Sep 14).*

PERFECTLY PRESERVED, the
fortified village of Alarcón
guards a narrow loop of the
Río Júcar from on top of a
rock. As you drive through its
defenses, you may have the
impression of entering a
movie-set for a medieval epic.
   The village dates back to the
8th century. It became a key
military base for the Reconquest *(see pp50–51)* and was
recaptured from the Moors by
Alfonso VIII in 1184 following
a nine-month siege. It was
later acquired by the Marquis

of Villena. Alarcón has dramatic walls and three defensive
precincts. The small, triangular
castle, high above the river,
has been turned into a parador
(see p558), preserving much
of its medieval atmosphere.
   Two churches in the village
are worth visiting. The **Iglesia
de Santa María** is a lovely
Renaissance church with a
fine portico and an altarpiece
attributed to the Berruguete
school. The nearby **Iglesia de
Santísima Trinidad** is in
Plateresque style *(see p21)*.

Alcalá del Júcar ㉑

Albacete. 👥 200. 🚏 *Calle Pósito 1,
(967) 47 30 01.* 🚌 *Sun (Apr–Oct).*
🎉 *San Lorenzo (Aug 7–15).*

WHERE THE RÍO JÚCAR runs
through the chalk hills
to the northeast of Albacete
it cuts a deep, winding gorge,

the Hoz de Júcar, along which
you can drive for a stretch of
40 km (25 miles). Alcalá del
Júcar is dramatically situated
on the side of a spur of rock
jutting out into the gorge. The
town is a warren of steep alleys and flights of steps. At
the top of the town, below
the castle, houses have been
extended by digging caves
into the soft rock. Some of
these have been transformed
into tunnels cut from one side
of the spur to the other.

ENVIRONS: To the west, the
gorge runs past fertile orchards
to the Baroque **Ermita de San
Lorenzo**. Farther on is the picturesque village of **Jorquera**,
which was an independent
state for a brief period during
the Middle Ages, refusing to
be ruled by the crown. It retains its Arab walls. A collection of shields is on display in
the Casa del Corregidor.

DON QUIXOTE'S
LA MANCHA

Cervantes *(see p315)* doesn't
specify where his hero was
born, but several places are
mentioned in the novel. Don
Quixote is knighted in an inn
in Puerto Lápice, believing it
to be a castle. His sweetheart,
Dulcinea, lives in El Toboso.
The windmills he tilts at, im-
agining them to be giants, are
thought to be those at Campo
de Criptana. Another adven-
ture takes place in the Cueva
de Montesinos *(see p379)*.

**Illustration from a 19th-century
edition of *Don Quixote***

Albacete ②

Albacete. 🕍 160,000. ✕ 🚌 🚇 ℹ️
Calle del Tinte 2, (967) 58 05 22. 🚢
Tue. 🎪 Virgen de los Llanos (Sep 8).

DESPITE BEING LABELED one of
Spain's least interesting
cities, this provincial capital is
not without its attractions.
The main one is the excellent
Museo Provincial, which has
exhibits ranging from Iberian
sculptures and unique Roman
amber and ivory dolls to 20th-
century paintings. The city's
cathedral, begun in 1515, has
a Renaissance altarpiece.
Albacete is also renowned
for its daggers and jackknives,
which have been crafted here
since Muslim times, and the
agricultural and trade fair, held
each September.

🏛 Museo Provincial
Parque Abelardo Sánchez. 📞 (967) 22
83 07. 🕐 daily. 🚫 ♿

Restored castle of Almansa, overlooking the town

**ENVIRONS: Chinchilla de
Monte Aragón**, 12 km (7
miles) to the southeast, has a
well-preserved old quarter
around a main square. Above
the town is the picturesque
shell of its 15th-century castle.
Almansa, 70 km (43 miles)
farther east, is dominated by
another imposing castle, which
is of Moorish origin.

Alcaraz ②

Albacete. 🕍 1,900. ℹ️ Plaza Mayor 1,
(967) 38 00 02. 🚢 Wed. 🎪 Rosario
de Cortes (May 1), Feria (Sep 4–9).

AN IMPORTANT ARAB and Christian stronghold, Alcaraz's
military power waned after the
Reconquest, but its economy
flourished around its (now de-
funct) carpet-making industry.
Standing in the attractive
Renaissance Plaza Mayor are
the "twin towers" of **Tardón**
and **Trinidad**, and an 18th-
century commodity exchange,

Sierra de Alcaraz ②

WHERE THE SIERRAS of Segura and Alcaraz
push northwards into the southeastern
plains of La Mancha, they form spectacular
mountains, broken up by dramatic gorges and
fertile valleys. The source of the Río Mundo is
a favorite scenic spot. Nearby Riópar, perched
on the side of the mountain, has a 15th-century
parish church. Among the less-explored villages,
Letur, Ayna, Yeste, and Liétor
are especially picturesque.
Their narrow, winding streets
and craft traditions clearly
reflect their Muslim origins.

Source of the Río Mundo ⑤
The river begins as a waterfall,
inside the Cueva de Los
Chorros, and tumbles down a
dramatic cliff face into a
bubbling pool at the bottom.

0 kilometers   5

0 miles   5

KEY
🚞 Tour route

═ Other roads

🔭 Viewpoint

Yeste ④
The village of Yeste, which stands at the
foot of the Sierra de Ardal, is crowned by
a hilltop Arab castle. It was reconquered
under Fernando III and was later ruled
by the Order of Santiago.

↑ ALBACETE

Peñascosa

Alcaraz

JAÉN

Cortes

C415

C415

C415

SIERRA DE ALCARAZ

Mundo

El

⑤

CALAR DEL MUN

④

he **Lonja del Corregidor,**
vith Plateresque decoration.
he square is surrounded by
vely, narrow streets with
raditional houses. On the outskirts of the town are the castle
uins and the one surviving
rch of a Gothic aqueduct.
Alcaraz also makes a good
base for touring the sierras of
Alcaraz and Segura.

**The twin towers of Tardón and
Trinidad on Alcaraz's main square**

Lagunas de Ruidera 25

Cuidad Real. 🚌 *Ossa de Montiel.*
ℹ️ *Ruidera, (926) 52 81 16.*

ONCE NICKNAMED "The Mir-
rors of La Mancha," the
16 interconnected lakes which
make up the Parque Natural de
las Lagunas de Ruidera stretch
for 20 km (12 miles) through
a valley. They allegedly take
their name from a story in *Don
Quixote (see p377)* in which a
certain Mistress Ruidera, her
daughters and her nieces, are
said to have been turned into
lakes by a magician.

Although La Mancha's falling
water table has led to a decline
in the amount of water in the
lakes, they are still worth visiting for their wealth of wildlife,
which includes great and little
bustards, herons, and many
types of ducks. The wildlife
has recently come under threat
due to the number of tourists,
and the development of

**One of the lakes in the Parque
Natural de las Lagunas de Ruidera**

vacation cottages on the lakes'
shores. In Ruidera village there
is an information center for the
park. Near one of the lakes,
the Laguna de San Pedro, is
the **Cueva de Montesinos**, a
deep, explorable cave which
is the setting for an episode
in *Don Quixote.*

To the northwest, the lakes
link up with the Embalse de
Peñarroya reservoir, which is
overlooked by a castle.

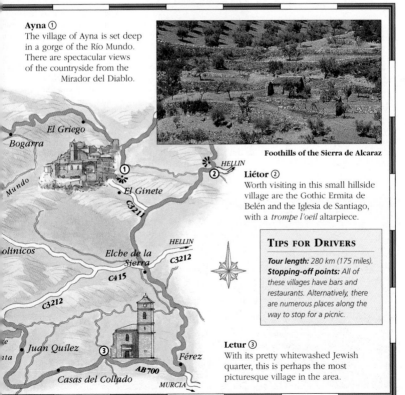

Ayna ①
The village of Ayna is set deep
in a gorge of the Río Mundo.
There are spectacular views
of the countryside from the
Mirador del Diablo.

El Griego

Bogarra

Mundo

El Ginete

C3211

olinicos   Elche de la
Sierra

C415

C3212

Juan Quílez

AB700

Casas del Collado

Férez

MURCIA

HELLIN

HELLIN

C3212

Foothills of the Sierra de Alcaraz

Liétor ②
Worth visiting in this small hillside
village are the Gothic Ermita de
Belén and the Iglesia de Santiago,
with a *trompe l'oeil* altarpiece.

TIPS FOR DRIVERS

Tour length: 280 km (175 miles).
Stopping-off points: All of
these villages have bars and
restaurants. Alternatively, there
are numerous places along the
way to stop for a picnic.

Letur ③
With its pretty whitewashed Jewish
quarter, this is perhaps the most
picturesque village in the area.

Villanueva de los Infantes ⓦ

Ciudad Real. 🏘 *6,000.* 🚌
ℹ *Plaza Mayor 3, (926) 36 00 24.*
🗓 *Fri.* 🎪 *Ferias (late Aug), Virgen de Antigua (Sep 8), Santo Tomás (Sep 18).*

VILLANUEVA'S OLD TOWN, which centers on the graceful Neo-Classical Plaza Mayor, is one of the most attractive in La Mancha. Many buildings on the square have wooden balconies and arcades. Also on the square is the **Iglesia de San Andrés**, which has a Renaissance façade. Inside are a Baroque altarpiece and organ, as well as the now empty tomb of the Golden Age author Francisco de Quevedo. He lived and died in the **Convento de los Domínicos**.

ENVIRONS: The village of **San Carlos del Valle**, 16 km (10 miles) to the northwest, has a perfectly preserved 18th-century square and galleried houses built of rust-red stone.

Valdepeñas ⓦ

Ciudad Real. 🏘 *26,000.* 🚉 🚌 ℹ
Pl de España, (926) 31 25 52. 🗓 *Thu.*
🎪 *Grape Harvest (first week of Sep).*

VALDEPEÑAS is the capital of La Mancha's vast wine region, the world's largest expanse of vineyards, producing vast quantities of red wine *(see pp192–3)*. This largely modern town comes alive for its September wine festival. In the network of older streets around the café-lined Plaza de España are the **Iglesia de la Asunción** and the municipal museum.

Valdepeñas has over 30 bodegas which can be visited. One of them, **Bodega Museo**, has some of the few remaining traditional cellars, with huge earthenware jars, *tinajas*.

🍷 **Bodega Museo**
Calle Mártires 6. 📞 *(926) 31 17 21.*
🔓 *daily.*

Courtyard of the Palacio del Viso in Viso del Marqués

Viso del Marqués ⓦ

Ciudad Real. 🏘 *3,300.* 🚌 ℹ *Plaza del Teatro Fortuny 8, (926) 33 60 01.*
🗓 *Tue.* 🎪 *San Andrés (second Sun of May), Feria (Jul 24–8).*

THE SMALL VILLAGE of Viso del Marqués in La Mancha is the unlikely setting of the **Palacio del Viso**, a grand Renaissance building. This mansion was commissioned in 1564 by the Marquis of Santa Cruz, the admiral of the fleet that defeated the Turks at Lepanto in 1571 *(see p55)*. One of the main features of the house is a Classical patio. Inside, the principal rooms have been decorated with Italian frescoes.

ENVIRONS: About 25 km (16 miles) to the northeast of Viso del Marqués is Spain's oldest bullring at **Las Virtudes**. Square and galleried, it was built in 1641 next to a 14th-century church, which has a Churrigueresque altarpiece.

🏛 **Palacio del Viso**
Plaza del Pradillo 12. 📞 *(926) 33 60 08.* 🔓 *Tue–Sun.*

Calatrava la Nueva ⓦ

Carretera de Calzada de Calatrava.
📞 *(926) 69 31 19.* 🔓 *Tue–Sun.*

MAGNIFICENT in its isolated hilltop setting, the ruined castle-monastery of Calatrava la Nueva is reached by a stretch of original medieval road. The castle was founded in 1217 by the Knights of Calatrava, Spain's first military-religious order *(see p50)*, to be used as their headquarters. The complex is of huge proportions, with a double patio and a church with a triple nave. The church has been restored and is illuminated by a beautiful rose window above the entrance.

Expanse of vineyards near Valdepeñas

Calatrava la Nueva castle, dominating the plains of La Mancha

After the Reconquest, the building continued to be used as a monastery until it was abandoned in 1802 following earthquake damage.

Opposite the castle are the ruins of a Muslim border fortress, **Salvatierra**, that was captured from the Moors by the Order of Calatrava in the 12th century.

Almagro ㉚

Ciudad Real. 🏠 *10,000.* 🚊 🚌
🛈 *Plaza Mayor 1, (926) 86 07 17.*
🗓 *Wed.* 🎪 *Virgen de las Nieves (Aug 5), San Bartolomé (Aug 25).*

ALMAGRO was disputed during the Reconquest, until the Order of Calatrava captured it and built the castle of Calatrava la Nueva to the southwest of the town. The rich architectural heritage of the atmospheric old town is partly the legacy of the Fugger brothers, the Hapsburgs' bankers who settled in nearby Almadén during the 16th century.

The town's main attraction is its colonnaded stone plaza, with characteristic enclosed, green balconies. On one side is a unique 17th-century courtyard-theater – the **Corral de Comedias** – the site of a drama festival held every August in honor of St. Bartholomew.

Other monuments worth seeing include the Fuggers' Renaissance warehouse and former university, and also the parador *(see p558).*

ENVIRONS: To the northwest is **Ciudad Real**, founded by Alfonso X the Learned in 1255. Among its sights are the cathedral, the Iglesia de San Pedro, and the Mudéjar gateway, the Puerta de Toledo.

Raised walkway in the Parque Nacional de Las Tablas de Daimiel

Tablas de Daimiel ㉛

Ciudad Real. 🚊 *Daimiel.* 🛈 *Daimiel, (926) 69 31 18.*

THE MARSHY WETLANDS of the Tablas de Daimiel, northeast of Ciudad Real, are the feeding and nesting grounds of a huge range of aquatic and migratory birds. Despite being national parkland since 1973, they have become an ecological *cause célèbre* due to the growing threat from the area's lowering water table. This has affected the area's wildlife in recent years.

One corner of the park is open to the public, with walking routes to islets and observation towers. Breeding birds here include great crested grebes and mallards. Otters and red foxes are among the mammals that have traditionally inhabited the park.

Valle de Alcudia ㉜

Ciudad Real. 🚊 *Fuencaliente.*
🛈 *Ciudad Real, (926) 47 00 01.*

ALCUDIA'S LUSH lowlands, which border the Sierra Morena foothills to the south, are among central Spain's most unspoiled countryside. The area is used largely as pasture land. In late autumn it starts to fill up with sheep, whose milk is used to make the excellent farmers' cheese for which the valley is known.

The mountain village of **Fuencaliente** has thermal baths that open in the summer. Farther north, **Almadén** is the site of a large mercury mine. **Chillón**, to the northwest, has a late Gothic church.

Small isolated farmhouse in the fertile Valle de Alcudia

EXTREMADURA

CÁCERES · BADAJOZ

O F ALL THE SPANISH REGIONS, *far-flung Extremadura – "the land beyond the River Douro" – is the most remote from the modern world. Green sierras run southward through rolling hills strewn with boulders. Forests and reservoirs shelter rare wildlife. The towns, with their atmospheric old quarters, have a romantic, slow-paced charm. In winter, storks nest on their spires and chimneys.*

The finest monuments in Extremadura are the ruins of ancient settlements scattered across the region. Many are exceptionally well preserved. Some of Spain's finest Roman architecture is to be seen in Mérida, capital of the Roman province of Lusitania, which has an aqueduct and a magnificent theater. Other Classical remains dot the countryside – notably a Tartessan temple at Cancho Ruano and a Roman bridge at Alcántara. Smaller finds are displayed in Badajoz museum.

Modern development has bypassed the old town of Cáceres, whose ancient walls, winding streets, and nobles' mansions are still marvelously intact. Trujillo, Zafra, and Jerez de los Caballeros have medieval and Renaissance quarters; and there are small, splendidly decorated cathedrals in Plasencia, Coria, and Badajoz. The castles and stout walls of Alburquerque and Olivenza mark frontiers embattled through history. Many cathedrals and monasteries were built in the troubled times during and after the Reconquest by the large military-religious orders, which then governed the region for the crown.

Extremadura was the birthplace of many conquistadors and emigrants to the New World; the riches they found there financed a surge of building. Guadalupe monastery, in the eastern hills, is the most splendid monument to the region's New World ties.

View over the rooftops of the historic town of Cáceres

◁ An old stone cross in the woods near Yuste, a Hieronymite monastery founded in 1404

Exploring Extremadura

EXTREMADURA IS IDEAL for nature lovers and those who want to get off the beaten track to discover the old Spain. It offers beautiful driving and walking country in its northern sierras and valleys, and exceptional wildlife in Monfragüe Natural Park. Some of the best Roman ruins in Spain can be found in Extremadura, especially in the regional capital, Mérida. The walled old town of Cáceres, with its well-preserved Jewish quarter, and the monasteries of Guadalupe and Yuste, are other historic sights not to be missed. To the south, the Templar towns in the Sierra Morena, such as Jerez de los Caballeros, have fine old buildings, while the small, historic towns of Coria, Zafra, and Llerena all make charming bases for excursions.

SIGHTS AT A GLANCE

Alcántara 12
Arroyo de la Luz 11
Badajoz 15
Cáceres pp390–91 10
Cancho Ruano 17
Coria 4
Guadalupe 8
Hervás 3
Las Hurdes 1
Jerez de los Caballeros 19
Llerena 20
Mérida 14
Monasterio de Yuste 6
Olivenza 16
Parque Natural de Monfragüe 7
Plasencia 5
Sierra de Gata 2
Tentudía 21
Trujillo 9
Valencia de Alcántara 13
Zafra 18

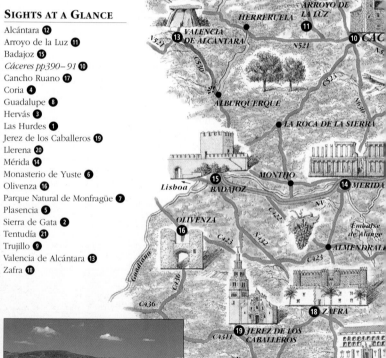

Orchards near Hervás in the
Valle del Ambroz

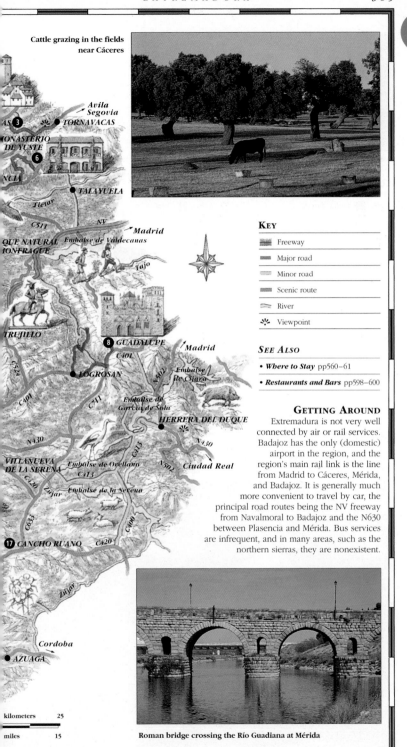

Cattle grazing in the fields
near Cáceres

Avila
Segovia
AS ③ ✵ ● TORNAVACAS
IONASTERIO
DE YUSTE ⑥
NCIA
● *TALAYUELA*
Tiétar
C511
NV ● *Madrid*
QUE NATURAL *Embalse de Valdecanas*
IONFRAGUE
Tajo
TRUJILLO
C524
C401 ⑧ *GUADALUPE* / *Madrid*
C401
● *LOGROSÁN* *N502* *Embalse*
C711 *de Cíjara*
Embalse de
García de Sola
HERRERA DEL DUQUE ✵
N430 *C413* *N430*
VILLANUEVA *C403* *N502* *Ciudad Real*
DE LA SERENA *Embalse de Orellana*
C420 *Zújar* *C413*
Zújar *Embalse de la Serena*
C633
⑰ *CANCHO RUANO* *C420* *C401*
Zújar
Cordoba
● *AZUAGA*

kilometers   25
miles   15

KEY

▬▬ Freeway

▬▬ Major road

▬▬ Minor road

▬▬ Scenic route

∿ River

✵ Viewpoint

SEE ALSO

• **Where to Stay** pp560–61

• **Restaurants and Bars** pp598–600

GETTING AROUND

Extremadura is not very well
connected by air or rail services.
Badajoz has the only (domestic)
airport in the region, and the
region's main rail link is the line
from Madrid to Cáceres, Mérida,
and Badajoz. It is generally much
more convenient to travel by car, the
principal road routes being the NV freeway
from Navalmoral to Badajoz and the N630
between Plasencia and Mérida. Bus services
are infrequent, and in many areas, such as the
northern sierras, they are nonexistent.

Roman bridge crossing the Río Guadiana at Mérida

Beehives, a common sight in Las Hurdes

Las Hurdes ❶

Cáceres. 🚌 *Pinofranqueado, Caminomorisco, Nuñomoral.* **i** *Pinofranqueado, (927) 67 41 81.*

L AS HURDES' slate mountains, goats, and beehives were memorably caught in the 1932 Luis Buñuel film, *Tierra sin Pan (Land without Bread)*. The area's legendary poverty disappeared with the arrival of roads in the 1950s, but the black slopes, riverbeds, and hill terraces remain.

From Pinofranqueado or Vegas de Coria, roads climb past picturesque "black" villages like Batequilla, Fragosa, and El Gasco, which sits under an extinct volcano. The more developed **Lower Hurdes** area, crossed by the Río Hurdano and the main access route (C512), is dotted with camp sites and restaurants serving traditional cuisine.

Sierra de Gata ❷

Cáceres. 🚌 *Cáceres.* **i** *Moraleja, (927) 51 50 75.*

T HERE ARE 40 hamlets in the Sierra de Gata, scattered between olive groves, orchards, and fields. The area has retained its old-fashioned rural charm by conserving hunters' paths for woodland walking, and its local crafts, most notably lace-making. In the lowland towns of Valverde de Fresno and Acebo, the local dialect, *chapurriau*, is still spoken. On the higher slopes, **Eljas**, **Gata**, and **Villamiel** have ruins

Coat of arms on a house front in Acebo

of medieval fortresses. The old granite houses have carved family crests on the front and distinctive outside staircases.

Hervás ❸

Cáceres. 🚶 *4,000.* **i** *Plaza de González Fiori 6, (927) 48 10 45.* 🚌 *Sat.* 🎡 *Nuestra Señora de la Asunción (Aug 14–17).*

S ITTING AT THE TOP of the wide Valle del Ambroz, Hervás is known for its medieval Jewish quarter, with its whitewashed houses. The tiny streets, dotted with taverns and craft workshops, slope down toward the Río Ambroz. Just off the main plaza is the **Museo Pérez Comendador-Leroux**, named after the town's noted 20th-century sculptor, whose work is exhibited here.

The next town up toward the Béjar pass is **Baños de Montemayor**, whose name comes from its sulfurous baths, which date back to Roman times. These were revived in the early 1900s and are open to the public in summer. At **Caparra**, southwest of Hervás, a triumphal arch stands on the Roman road, the Vía de la Plata *(see p334).*

🏛 Museo Pérez Comendador-Leroux
Calle Asensio Nelia 5. **(** *(927) 48 16 55.* ⬜ *Tue–Sun.* ⬤ *public hols.*

Traditional lace-making in one of the villages of the Sierra de Gata

Ancient wall and olive groves in the Valle del Ambroz

Coria ❹

Cáceres. 🏠 11,600. 🚉 🛈 Avenida de Extremadura 39, (927) 50 13 51. 🚌 Thu. 🎉 Día de la Virgen (week after Easter), San Juan (Jun 24).

CORIA'S WALLED old town, perched above the Río Alagón, boasts a Gothic-Renaissance **cathedral** with rich Plateresque carving, and the 16th-century **Convento de la Madre de Dios**, which has a fine Renaissance cloister.

Forming part of the town walls, which are a Muslim and medieval patchwork, are an impressive castle tower and four gates, two of which date back to Roman times. The gates are closed during the fiesta of San Juan in June for nighttime bull-running. Situated below the old town is the **Puente Seco**, a Roman bridge over the river.

Plasencia ❺

Cáceres. 🏠 40,000. 🚉 🚌 🛈 Calle del Rey 8, (927) 42 21 59. 🚌 Tue. 🎉 Ferias (Jun 8–11).

PLASENCIA'S golden-gray walls, rising above a curve in the banks of the Río Jerte, tell of the town's past as a military bastion. Nowadays Plasencia is best known for its Tuesday market, dating back to the 12th century, which is held in the main square.

A short walk away are the town's two cathedrals, which are built back-to-back. The 16th-century **Catedral Nueva**

has a Baroque organ and carved wooden choirstalls. The Romanesque **Catedral Vieja**, next to it, has a museum with works by Ribera, and a late 14th-century Bible.

The nearby **Museo Etnográfico y Textil**, housed in a 14th-century hospital, has displays of crafts and costumes.

The rest of the Jerte valley has pockets of outstanding beauty, such as the **Garganta de los Infiernos**, a nature preserve with dramatic, rushing waterfalls.

🏛 **Museo Etnográfico y Textil**
Plazuela del Marqués de la Puebla. 📞 (927) 42 18 43. ⬜ Wed–Sun.

Monasterio de Yuste ❻

Cuacos de Yuste (Cáceres). 📞 (927) 17 21 30. ⬜ daily. 🎟

THE HIERONYMITE monastery of Yuste, where Charles V *(see p55)* retired from public life in 1556 and died two years later, is remarkable for its simplicity and its lovely setting in the wooded valley of La Vera.

The church's Gothic and Plateresque cloisters and the austere palace are open to visitors. Just below it is **Cuacos de Yuste**, the most unspoiled of La Vera's old villages, where peppers, for making paprika, hang outside the houses.

Paprika peppers hanging up around a door in Cuacos de Yuste

A *Carantoña*, during the fiesta of St. Sebastian, Acehuche

EXTREMADURA'S FIESTAS

Encamisá *(Jan 16),* Navalvillar de Pela (Badajoz). Riders on horseback parade around town, where bonfires are set alight for the occasion.
Carantoñas *(Jan 20),* Acehuche (Cáceres). During the fiesta of St. Sebastian, the *Carantoñas* take to the streets of the town dressed up in animal skins, with their faces covered by grotesque masks designed to make them look terrifying. They represent the wild beasts that are said to have left the saint unharmed.
Pero Palo *(Carnival Feb/Mar),* Villanueva de la Vera (Cáceres). In this ancient ritual a wooden figure dressed in a suit and representing the devil is paraded around the streets and then destroyed – except for the head, which is reused the year after.
Los Empalaos *(Maundy Thursday),* Valverde de la Vera (Cáceres). Men do penance by walking in procession through the town with their arms outstretched and bound to small tree trunks.
Los Escobazos *(Dec 7),* Jarandilla de la Vera (Cáceres). At night, the town is illuminated by bonfires in the streets and torches are made from burning brooms.

Parque Natural de Monfragüe ❼

Cáceres. ⊞ *Villareal de San Carlos.* ⓘ *Villareal de San Carlos, (927) 45 51 04.*

To THE SOUTH of Plasencia rolling hills drop from scrubby peaks through wild olive, cork, and holm oak woods to the dammed Tagus and Tiétar river valleys. In 1979, some 500 sq km (200 sq miles) of these hills were granted natural park status in order to safeguard the area's outstandingly varied wildlife species, which include a large proportion of Spain's protected bird species *(see pp324–5)*.

The many species of birds that breed here include the black-winged kite, black vulture and, most notably, the black stork, as well as more

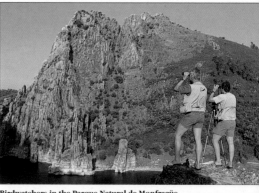

Birdwatchers in the Parque Natural de Monfragüe

common aquatic species on and near the water. Mammals living here include the lynx, red deer, and wild boar. At **Villareal de San Carlos**, a hamlet founded in the 18th

century, there is parking and an information center that gives out maps of walks. An ideal time to visit the park is September, when many migrating birds stop off here.

Guadalupe ❽

Cáceres. ⚄ *2,500.* ⊞ ⓘ *Plaza de Santa María de Guadalupe 1, (927) 15 41 28.* ⊟ *Wed.* ⚘ *San Blas (Feb 3), Cruz de Mayo (first Sun of May).*

This VILLAGE grew around the magnificent Hieronymite **Monasterio de Guadalupe**, founded in 1340. In the main square there are shops that sell handmade ceramics and beaten copper cauldrons, both traditional monastic crafts, now made as souvenirs.

The turreted towers of the monastery, which is set in a deep, wooded valley, help give it a fairy-tale air. According to legend, a shepherd found a charred wooden image of the Virgin Mary here in the early 14th century. The monastery grew to splendor under royal patronage, acquiring schools of

grammar and medicine, three hospitals, an important pharmacy, and one of the largest libraries in Spain.

Adjoining the monastery is a 16th-century *hospedería* (guest house) where royalty once stayed. This is now a hotel run by the monks *(see p560)*. The old hospital has been converted into a parador. In the parking lot is a plaque commemorating Spain's first human dissection, which took place here in 1402.

By the time the New World was discovered, the monastery was very important and in 1496 was the site of the baptism of some of the first native Caribbeans brought to Europe by Columbus *(see pp52–3)*.

The monastery was sacked by Napoleon in 1808 but was refounded by Franciscans a century later. Today it is still a

major center of Catholicism, visited every year by thousands of pilgrims from around the Spanish-speaking world.

Guided tours (in Spanish only) begin in the museums of illuminated manuscripts, embroidered vestments, and fine art. They continue to the choir and the magnificent Baroque sacristy, nicknamed "the Spanish Sistine Chapel," because of Zurbarán's portraits of monks hanging on the highly decorated walls. For many, the chance to touch or kiss the tiny Virgin's dress in the *camarín* (chamber) behind the altar is the highlight of the tour. Finally, you can linger in the 16th-century Gothic cloister that has two tiers of horseshoe arches around an ornate central pavilion. The church, with a magnificent 16th-century iron grille partly forged from the chains of freed slaves, may be visited separately.

ENVIRONS: The surrounding **Villuercas** and **Los Ibores** sierras, where herbs were once picked for the monastery pharmacy, have good woodland walks. The road south also gives access to the pasture lands of **La Serena**, a vital breeding ground for birds of the steppe *(see pp324–5)*, and the huge reservoir of **Cíjara**, enclosed by a game preserve.

Monasterio de Guadalupe, overlooking the town

Trujillo 9

Cáceres. 👥 9,000. 🚌 ℹ Plaza Mayor, (927) 32 26 77. 🛒 Thu. 🧀 Feria del Queso (Apr/May), San Miguel (Sep 29).

WHEN THE PLAZA MAYOR of the medieval hilltop town of Trujillo is floodlit at night, it is one of the most beautiful squares in Spain. By day, there is much to visit, including the **Iglesia de Santa María la Mayor**, on one of the town's winding streets, which contains various sarcophagi.

At the top of the hill is an Islamic fortress that defended the town against the Christian advance during the Re-conquest *(see pp50–51)*; but in 1232 was retaken by the forces of Fernando III. Trujillo was the birthplace of several

Statue of Francisco Pizarro in Trujillo's main square

conquistadors, most notably Francisco Pizarro, the con-queror of Peru *(see p54)*, of whom there is a statue in the main square. His half brother, Hernando Pizarro, founded

the **Palacio del Marqués de la Conquista**, one of several palaces and convents built with New World wealth. It has an elaborate corner window with carved stone heads of the Pizarro brothers and their Inca wives. The beautiful 16th-century **Palacio de Orellana-Pizarro** was built by Francisco de Orellana, the explorer of Ecuador and the Amazon. It has a fine Plateresque patio.

Once a year, in late April or early May, gourmets descend on the town for its renowned week-long cheese fair.

🏛 **Palacio del Marqués de la Conquista**
Plaza Mayor. ⬚ daily.
🏛 **Palacio de Orellana-Pizarro**
Plaza de Don Juan Tena. 📞 (927) 32 11 62. ⬚ daily.

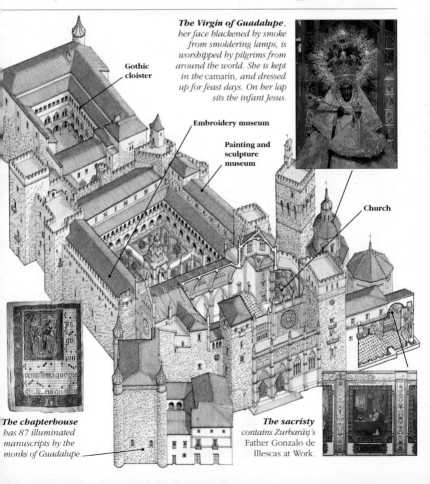

The Virgin of Guadalupe, her face blackened by smoke from smoldering lamps, is worshipped by pilgrims from around the world. She is kept in the camarín, and dressed up for feast days. On her lap sits the infant Jesus.

Gothic cloister

Embroidery museum

Painting and sculpture museum

Church

The chapterhouse has 87 illuminated manuscripts by the monks of Guadalupe.

The sacristy contains Zurbarán's Father Gonzalo de Illescas at Work.

Street-by-Street: Cáceres ❿

A FTER ALFONSO IX OF LEON conquered Cáceres in 1227, its growing prosperity as a free trade town attracted merchants, and later aristocracy, to settle here. They rivaled each other with stately homes and palaces fortified by watchtowers, most of which Isabel and Fernando, the reigning monarchs *(see pp52–3)*, ordered to be demolished in 1476 to halt the continual jostling for power. Today's serene Renaissance town dates from the late 15th and 16th centuries, after which economic decline set in. Untouched by the wars of the 19th and 20th centuries, Cáceres became Spain's first listed heritage city in 1949.

★ Casa de los Golfines de Abajo
The ornamental façade of this 15th-century mansion displays the shield of one of the town's leading families, the Golfines.

Casa y Torre de Carvajal
This typical Renaissance mansion has a 13th-century round Arab tower and a peaceful garden with a patio.

★ Iglesia de Santa María
Facing the Palacio Episcopal, this Gothic-Renaissance church has a beautiful cedarwood reredos and a 15th-century crucifix – the Cristo Negro *(Black Christ).*

PLAZA DE SANTA MARÍA

To tourist information

Arco de la Estrella
This low-arched gateway was built by Manuel Churriguera in 1726. It leads through the city walls from the Plaza Mayor into the old town and is flanked by a 15th-century watchtower.

| 0 meters | | 50 |
| 0 yards | | 50 |

KEY

– – – Suggested route

Barrio de San Antonio

This quaint old Jewish quarter, with narrow streets of whitewashed houses restored to their original condition, takes its name from the nearby hermitage of St. Anthony.

★ Museo Provincial

Housed in the Casa de las Veletas, this museum has contemporary art and archaeology from the region.

The Convento de San Pablo
sells delicious *yemas* (candied egg yolks) made by the nuns.

Casa y Torre de la Cigüeña

The slender, battlemented tower of the House of the Stork was allowed to remain after 1476 because of the owner's loyalty to Isabel. It is now owned by the army.

The Iglesia de San Mateo, built between the 14th and 17th centuries, is one of Cáceres' earliest churches.

Casa del Sol (Casa de los Solis)

The façade of this elegant Renaissance building, once home of the Solis family, is emblazoned with a sun (sol) motif.

STAR SIGHTS

★ Casa de los Golfines de Abajo

★ Iglesia de Santa María

★ Museo Provincial

Arroyo de la Luz ⓫

Cáceres. 🚶 6,900. 🚌 🚆 🛈 Plaza de
la Constitución 16, (927) 27 00 02.
🗓 Thu. 🎭 Día de la Patrona
(Easter Mon).

THE SMALL TOWN of Arroyo
de la Luz is home to one
of the artistic masterpieces of
Extremadura. Its **Iglesia de la
Asunción**, completed in 1565,
contains a spectacular altarpiece that incorporates 20
paintings by the mystical religious painter Luis de Morales.

ENVIRONS: The area has a
large population of white
storks (see p325). Nearby
Malpartida is home to the
largest colony, whose nests
adorn the church roof. There
are some good picnic spots in
the surrounding countryside.

**Altarpiece in the Iglesia de la
Asunción, Arroyo de la Luz**

Alcántara ⓬

Cáceres. 🚶 1,900. 🚌 🛈 Plaza de
España 1, (927) 39 01 27. 🗓 Tue. 🎭
Feria (Apr 15–17), San Pedro (Oct 19).

ALCANTARA has two important
sights. One is the drystone
Roman bridge, 71 m (233 ft)
above the Tagus river that
has an honorary arch and a
temple. The other is the ruined
Convento de San Benito.
This was built as the headquarters of the Knights of the
Order of Alcántara, during the
16th century, and was sacked
by Napoleon. Its surviving
treasures are in the **Iglesia de
Santa María de Almocóvar**.

**Walls of the 16th-century Convento
de San Benito, Alcántara**

Valencia de
Alcántara ⓭

Cáceres. 🚶 6,000. 🚌 🚆 🛈 Calle
de Hernan Cortes, (927) 58 03 44.
🗓 Mon. 🎭 Día de los Mayos (May 1).

THE GOTHIC QUARTER of this
hilltop border town is
given an elegant air by its
fountains and shady orange
trees. The **Castillo de Buena
Piedra**, which was built by
the Knights of the Order of
Alcántara, now houses a youth
hostel. On the outskirts of the
town are more than 40 dolmens, or megalithic burial sites.

ENVIRONS: Alburquerque, to
the southeast, is sited on a
rocky outcrop with a magnificent panoramic view from the
ramparts and keep of its castle.
Below are the walled old town
and the 15th-century Iglesia
de Santa María del Mercado.

Mérida ⓮

Badajoz. 🚶 60,000. 🚌 🚆
🛈 Avenida José Álvarez y Saenz de
Buruaga, (924) 31 53 53. 🗓 Tue.
🎭 Fiestas Patronales (Dec 10).

FOUNDED BY AUGUSTUS in 25
BC, Augusta Emerita grew
into the cultural and economic
capital of Rome's westernmost
province, Lusitania, but lost its
eminence under the Moors.
Though a small city, Mérida,
the capital of Extremadura, has
many fine Roman monuments.
The best approach is from
the west of town, via the modern suspension bridge over the
Río Guadiana, bringing you to
the original entrance of the
Roman city and Arab fortress.
The city's centerpiece is the
Roman theater (see pp46–7).
One of the best preserved
Roman theaters anywhere, it
is still used in summer for the
city's drama festival and is
part of a larger site with an
amphitheater (anfiteatro)
and gardens. Nearby are the
remains of a Roman house,
the **Casa del Anfiteatro**,
where there are underground
galleries and large areas of
well-preserved mosaics.
Opposite stands Rafael
Moneo's stunning red-brick
**Museo Nacional de Arte
Romano**. The semicircular
arches of its main hall are built
to the same height as the city's
Los Milagros aqueduct. Off this
hall, which features sculptures
from the Roman theater, there
are three galleries exhibiting
ceramics, mosaics, coins, and
statuary. There is also an excavated Roman street. Near

Megalithic tomb on the outskirts of Valencia de Alcántara

Mérida's well-preserved Roman theater, still used as a venue for classical drama

the museum are several other monuments, namely two villas with fine mosaics, and a racecourse (closed for excavation).

A chapel in front of the 3rd century **Iglesia de Santa Eulalia** is dedicated to the child saint who was martyred on this site in Roman times. Towards the center of the town are the **Templo de Diana** (1st century AD), with tall, fluted columns,

Sculpture of Emperor Augustus

and the **Arco de Trajano**. The **Museo de Arte Visigodo** (Museum of Visigothic Art) is in the Convento de Santa Clara, which is situated off the main square. From the huge **Puente de Guadiana** there is a good view of the massive walls of the **Alcazaba**, one of Spain's oldest Moorish buildings (AD 835), whose precinct includes towers, a cistern, and more Roman ruins. To the

east of the town stands the **Casa del Mithraeo**, also known as the Casa Romana, with its Pompeiian-style frescoes and superb mosaics.

The grand, ruined Los Milagros aqueduct, made of granite and brick, is off the N630 towards Cáceres.

🏛 **Museo de Arte Visigodo**
Calle Santa Julia. 【 (924) 30 01 06. ☐ Tue–Sun. ● public hols.
🏛 **Museo Nacional de Arte Romano**
Calle José Ramón Mélida. 【 (924) 31 93 85. ☐ Tue–Sun. 🈁 &

MÉRIDA TOWN CENTER

Alcazaba ⑦
Amphitheater ④
Arco de Trajano ⑩
Casa del Anfiteatro ③
Casa del Mithraeo ⑥
Iglesia de Santa Eulalia ①
Museo de Arte Visigodo ⑨
Museo Nacional de Arte
 Romano ②
Puente de Guadiana ⑧
Roman theater ⑤
Templo de
 Diana ⑪

KEY

🚉 Railroad station

ℹ Tourist information

✝ Church

0 meters   250

0 yards   250

Badajoz ⑮

Badajoz. 🏠 100,000. ✈ 🚉 🚌
🛈 Plaza de la Libertad 3, (924) 22 27
63. 🛒 Tue & Sun. 🎉 Feria (Jun 24).

B ADOJOZ is a plain, modern
city, though it retains traces
of its former importance. It was
a major city under the Moors,
but the plundering resulting
from centuries of conflicts with
Portugal, and most recently
the Civil War, robbed Badajoz
of its former splendor.

The Alcazaba is now the
Museo Arqueológico with
its more than 15,000 artifacts,
some dating from Paleolithic
times. Nearby is the medieval
cathedral, with a stunning
tiled cloister and rich interior.

🏛 Museo Arqueológico
Plaza José Álvarez y Saenz de Buruaga.
📞 (924) 22 23 14. ⬜ Tue–Sun.
📷 &

Olivenza ⑯

Badajoz. 🏠 8,000. 🚌 🛈 Plaza de
España, (924) 49 01 51. 🛒 Sat.
🎉 Muñecas de San Juan (Jun 23).

A PORTUGUESE ENCLAVE until
1801, Olivenza has a
colorful, hybrid character.
Within the walled town are
the medieval castle, housing
the **Museo Municipal**, a
museum of rural life, and
three churches. **Santa María
del Castillo** has a wonder-
fully naive family tree of the
Virgin Mary. **Santa María
Magdalena**, with its glorious
spiraling columns, is a fine
example of the 16th-century
Portuguese Manueline style.

**Interior of Santa María Magdalena
church, Olivenza**

Don't miss the 16th-century
Santa Casa de Misericordia
with its blue and white tiled
friezes. In one, God is shown
offering a coat to Adam and
Eve as he banishes them from
the Garden of Eden.

Off the main square is the
Pastelería Fuentes, which
sells *técula mécula*, a custard
cake it has patented.

🏛 Museo Municipal
Plaza de Santamaría. 📞 (924) 49
02 22. ⬜ Tue–Sun. 📷 &

Cancho Ruano ⑰

Zalamea de la Serena. 📞 (924) 78
00 32. ⬜ daily.

T HIS SANCTUARY-PALACE, which
is thought to have been
built under the civilization of
Tartessus *(see p45)*, was discovered in 1978. Excavations
on this small but unique site
have revealed a moated temple
that was rebuilt three times –

many of the walls and slate
floors are still intact. Each
temple was constructed on a
grander scale than the previous one and then burned in
the face of invasion during
the 6th century BC.

Most of the artifacts unearthed, including jewelery, ceramics, and furniture, are on
display in the archaeological
museum at Badajoz.

ENVIRONS: A Roman funereal
monument stands next to the
church in nearby **Zalamea de
la Serena**. The town comes
alive during the September
fiestas, when the townsfolk
act out the classic 17th-century
play, *The Mayor of Zalamea*,
by Calderón de la Barca *(see
p30)*, which was supposedly
based on a local character.
Shops in the town also sell
torta de la Serena, a cheese
made of sheep's milk.

**Remains of the Tartessan
sanctuary at Cancho Ruano**

Zafra ⑱

Badajoz. 🏠 15,000. 🚉 🚌
🛈 Plaza de España, (924) 55 10 36.
🛒 Fri. 🎉 San Miguel (Oct 2–8).

A T THE HEART of this graceful
town, nicknamed "little
Seville" because of its similarity
to the capital of Andalusia,
are two arcaded squares. The
Plaza Grande, the larger of the
two, is the site of the **Iglesia
de la Candelaria**, which has a
Zurbarán altarpiece. Converging on it is the older, 15th-
century **Plaza Chica**, which
used to be the marketplace.
Situated on the nearby Calle

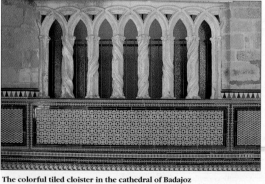
The colorful tiled cloister in the cathedral of Badajoz

Altarpiece by Zurbarán in the Iglesia de la Candelaria at Zafra

Sevilla is the 15th-century Convento de Santa Clara and the **Alcázar de los Duques de Feria**, which is now a parador *(see p561)* with a marble court-yard by Juan de Herrera.

ENVIRONS: Some 25 km (16 miles) to the south, in **Fuente de Cantos**, is the house in which the painter Francisco de Zurbarán was born in 1598.

Jerez de los Caballeros ⑲

Badajoz. 🏠 10,500. 🚌 🚹 *Plaza de la Alcazaba, (924) 73 00 11.* 🗓 *Wed.* 🎫 *Feria del Jamón (May 3–5), San Bartolomé (Aug 24).*

T HE HILLSIDE PROFILE of Jerez, which is broken by three Baroque church towers, is one of the most picturesque in Extremadura. This small town is also historically important – Vasco Núñez de Balboa, who claimed the Pacific for Spain, was born here. In the **castle**,

now a garden, knights of the Order of Knights Templar were beheaded in the Torre Sangrienta (Bloody Tower) in 1312. The old quarters of the town grew up around three churches: **San Bartolomé**, its façade studded with glazed ceramics; **San Miguel**, whose brick tower dominates the Plaza de España; and **Santa María de la Encarnación**.

ENVIRONS: Fregenal de la Sierra, 25 km (16 miles) to the south, is an attractive old town with a bullring.

Llerena ⑳

Badajoz. 🏠 6,000. 🚌 🚌 🚹 *Plaza de España 1, (924) 87 00 68.* 🗓 *Thu.* 🎫 *Nuestra Señora de la Granada (Aug 1–15), San Miguel (late Sep).*

E XTREMADURA'S southeastern gateway to Andalusia, the town of Llerena, is a mixture of Mudéjar and Baroque build-ings. In the pretty main square,

which is lined with palm trees, stands the arcaded, whitewash-and-brick church of **Nuestra Señora de la Granada**, its sumptuous interior reflecting its former importance as a seat of the Inquisition *(see p264)*. At one end of the square is a fountain designed by Zurbarán, who lived in the town for 13 years. Also worth seeing is the 16th-century **Convento de Santa Clara**, on a street leading out of the main square.

ENVIRONS: At **Azuaga**, 30 km (20 miles) east of Llerena, is the Iglesia de la Consolación, which contains Renaissance and Mudéjar tiles.

Tentudía ㉑

Badajoz. 🚌 *Calera de León.* 🚹 *Calera de León, (924) 584 101.*

W HERE THE SIERRA MORENA runs into Andalusia, fortified towns and churches founded by the medieval military orders stand among the wooded hills of Tentudía. Here, on a hilltop, stands the tiny **Monasterio de Tentudía**. Founded in the 13th century by the Order of Santiago, the monastery contains a superb Mudéjar cloister and a reredos with Seville *azulejos* (tiles).

At **Calera de León**, just 6 km (4 miles) north of Tentudía, there is a magnificent, partly ruined, Renaissance convent, also founded by the Order of Santiago. The convent has a Gothic church and a two-story cloister.

Bullring at Fregenal de la Sierra

SOUTHERN SPAIN

Southern Spain at a Glance

O NE LARGE REGION – Andalusia – extends across the south of Spain. Its landscape varies from the deserts of Almería in the east to the wetlands of Doñana National Park in the west, and from the snow-capped peaks of the Sierra Nevada to the beaches of the Costa del Sol. Three inland cities between them share the greatest of Spain's Moorish monuments: Granada, Córdoba, and Seville, the capital, which stands on the banks of the Río Guadalquivir. Andalusia has many other historic towns as well as attractive, whitewashed villages, important nature preserves, and sherry producing vineyards around Jerez de la Frontera.

Córdoba's Mezquita *(see pp456–70) has a remarkable forest of arches in its interior and an exquisitely decorated* mihrab *(prayer niche) facing Mecca.*

SEVILLE

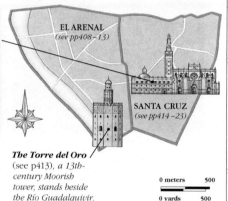

EL ARENAL
(see pp408–13)

SANTA CRUZ
(see pp414–23)

Córdoba

La Giralda *(see pp418–19), the Moorish bell tower of Seville cathedral, was built as a minaret in 1198, but extended to include a belfry in the 16th century.*

The Torre del Oro *(see p413), a 13th-century Moorish tower, stands beside the Río Guadalquivir.*

| 0 meters | 500 |
| 0 yards | 500 |

ANDALUS
(see pp434–

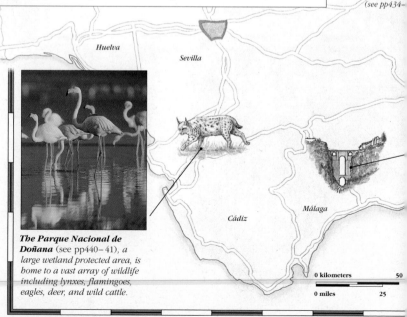

Huelva

Sevilla

Cádiz

Málaga

The Parque Nacional de Doñana *(see pp440–41), a large wetland protected area, is home to a vast array of wildlife including lynxes, flamingoes, eagles, deer, and wild cattle.*

| 0 kilometers | 50 |
| 0 miles | 25 |

◁ **Whitewashed houses with red-tiled roofs in Montefrío, near Granada**

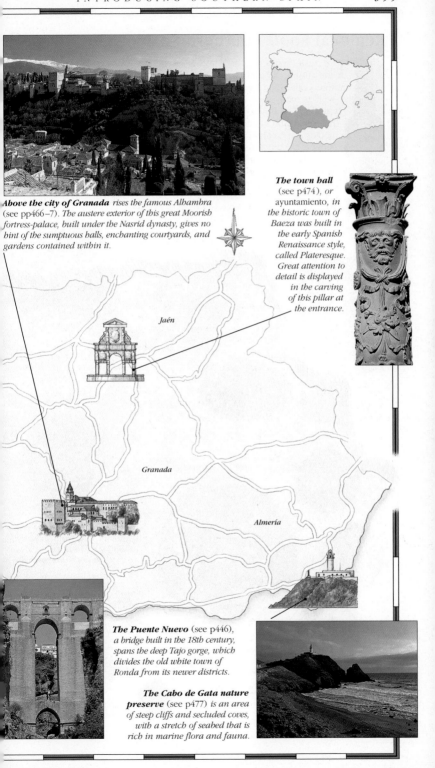

Above the city of Granada *rises the famous Alhambra (see pp466–7). The austere exterior of this great Moorish fortress-palace, built under the Nasrid dynasty, gives no hint of the sumptuous halls, enchanting courtyards, and gardens contained within it.*

Jaén

Granada

Almería

The town hall *(see p474), or* ayuntamiento, *in the historic town of Baeza was built in the early Spanish Renaissance style, called Plateresque. Great attention to detail is displayed in the carving of this pillar at the entrance.*

The Puente Nuevo *(see p446), a bridge built in the 18th century, spans the deep Tajo gorge, which divides the old white town of Ronda from its newer districts.*

The Cabo de Gata nature preserve *(see p477) is an area of steep cliffs and secluded coves, with a stretch of seabed that is rich in marine flora and fauna.*

Regional Food: Southern Spain

Cachorreñas *is a fish soup from Cádiz. It is made with bread, and often clams, and flavored with bitter orange peel.*

T HE ARAB PRESENCE made a lasting impact on the cuisine of Southern Spain. Rice, lemons, oranges, olives, and grapes were introduced, as well as many new vegetables and spices. Typical today are barbecued meats, sauces flavored with cumin or saffron, and candies made from crushed almonds. Tomatoes and peppers are much used. Local sherry vinegars are used for dressing salads. The region is famous for its grilled fish, especially sardines, and deep-fried *calamares* (squid). Quality ham and pork are used widely in sausages; and in the mountains, stews of tripe or chickpeas are common fare. Tapas *(see pp574–5)* were invented in Andalusia and a wide variety of them is still served throughout the region.

Old sherry vinegar

Olives and olive oil *have been an important product of Andalusia since Roman times. Today, a third of Europe's olive oil is made here. Fruity green extra virgin oil comes from the olive mills of Baena and the Sierra de Segura. The many types of table olives include fat* gordales, *small green* manzanillas *and stuffed olives.*

Aceitunas aliñadas *are marinated, cracked olives.*

Olive oil and olives

Fritura de pescado *is a typical dish from Málaga and Cádiz, where squid and fish are served with wedges of fresh lemon.*

Red pepper

Cold gazpacho soup

Fideos a la malagueña *is a variation on paella made with the local spaghetti (instead of rice), shellfish, and peppers.*

Croutons

Cucumber

Gazpacho *is a chilled raw soup that is made by pounding bread and garlic with tomatoes, cucumber, and peppers. Olive oil makes it creamy and vinegar gives it a refreshing tang. It is usually garnished with diced vegetables and croutons.*

Pescado a la sal *is fish baked whole in a crust of salt. It is often eaten accompanied by garlic mayonnaise or parsley sauce.*

Habas a la rondeña, *lima beans with cured ham, are so well known they are often called "Spanish-style" beans.*

Rabo de toro *is bull's tail braised with vegetables and red wine – one of the best dishes to employ bull's meat.*

Ternera con alcachofas, *a traditional Cordoban dish, combines veal and artichoke hearts in a Montilla wine sauce.*

Huevos a la flamenca *is a simple gypsy meal of eggs baked in small dishes with vegetables. Chorizo is often included.*

Tocino de cielo *is the most luscious of the custard and caramel desserts; the name means "heavenly bacon."*

Cookies *include roscones or rings, round cinnamon- and almond-flavored mantecados, and soft, fried empanadillas.*

FRUITS

Everything grows in the south, the market garden of Europe. Crops include strawberries, apples, and pears as well as oranges and lemons. Tropical fruit is grown too, and Spain is also known for its melons. Figs grow wild, while the city of Granada owes its name to the locally grown pomegranate.

Oranges

Figs

Melon

Pomegranates

Persimmons

Strawberries

HAMS AND SAUSAGES

Some of the best *jamón serrano* (cured ham) comes from the mountains of Andalusia, in particular from Jabugo *(see p438)* and Trevélez *(see p460)*. Cooking sausages include paprika-flavored chorizos and black *morcillas*, made using blood and spices. Cured sausages like chorizo and *salchichones* are often sliced and served as tapas.

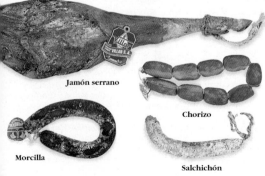

Jamón serrano

Chorizo

Morcilla

Salchichón

Wines of Southern Spain

Andalusia is a land of fortified wines, and the best of these is *Jerez* (sherry). Andalusians drink the light, dry fino and manzanilla styles of sherry as wines (they only have 15.5 percent alcohol) – always chilled, and often as an accompaniment to tapas *(see pp576–7).* The longer-aged, richer, yet still dry styles of amontillado and oloroso sherry go well with the cured *jamón serrano (see p574).* Other wines include fino, which may or may not be fortified, and Madeira-like Málaga.

González Byass logo

Working the soil in Jerez

Tío Pepe is one of the finos of Jerez, which are noted for their bouquet of flor (yeast), pale color, and appetizing finish.

Wine Regions

The Jerez wine region covers the chalky downs between the towns of Jerez, Sanlúcar, and El Puerto de Santa María. South of the Montilla-Moriles region are Málaga's vineyards, which have been reduced by urban development.

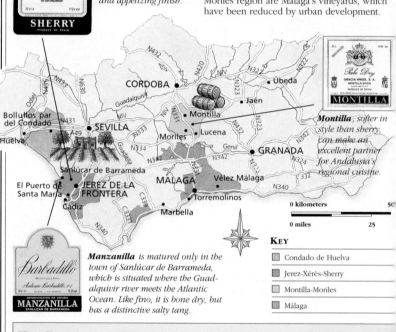

Montilla, softer in style than sherry, can make an excellent partner for Andalusia's regional cuisine.

Manzanilla is matured only in the town of Sanlúcar de Barrameda, which is situated where the Guadalquivir river meets the Atlantic Ocean. Like fino, it is bone dry, but has a distinctive salty tang.

0 kilometers   50

0 miles   25

Key

- Condado de Huelva
- Jerez-Xérès-Sherry
- Montilla-Moriles
- Málaga

Key Facts about Wines of Southern Spain

Location and Climate
The Jerez region has one of the sunniest climates in Europe – summer heat tempered by ocean breezes. The best type of soil is white, chalky *albariza*. In Montilla it is more clayey.

Grape Varieties
The best dry sherry is produced from the Palomino grape. Pedro Ximénez is used for the sweeter styles and is the main grape in Montilla and Málaga. Muscatel is also grown in Málaga.

Good Producers
Condado de Huelva: Manuel Sauci Salas (Riodiel), A.Villarán (Pedro Ximénez Villarán). **Jerez:** Barbadillo (Solear), Blázquez (Carta Blanca), Caballero (Puerto), Garvey (San Patricio), González Byass (Alfonso, Tío Pepe), Hidalgo (La Gitana, Napoleón), Lustau, Osborne (Quinta), Pedro Domecq (La Ina), Sandeman. **Montilla-Moriles:** Alvear (C.B., Festival), Gracia Hermanos, Pérez Barquero, Tomás García. **Málaga:** Scholtz Hermanos, López Hermanos.

HOW SHERRY IS MADE

Sherry is mixed from two principal grape varieties: Palomino, which makes a drier, more delicate sherry; and Pedro Ximénez, which is made into a fuller, sweeter type of sherry.

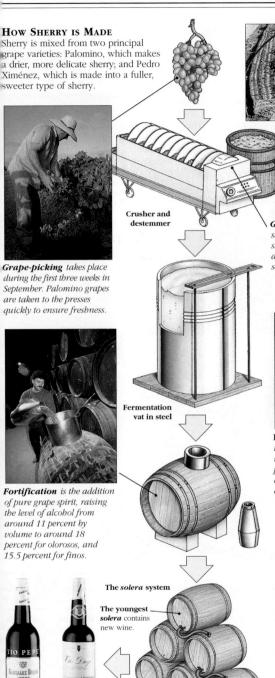

Grape-drying is only required for Pedro Ximénez grapes. They are laid on esparto mats to shrivel in the sun, concentrating the sugar.

Crusher and destemmer

Grape-pressing and de-stalking, in cylindrical stainless steel vats, is usually done at night to avoid the searing Andalusian heat.

Grape-picking takes place during the first three weeks in September. Palomino grapes are taken to the presses quickly to ensure freshness.

Fermentation vat in steel

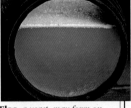

Flor, a yeast, may form on the exposed surface of young wine in the fermentation vat, preventing oxidization and adding a delicate taste. If flor develops, the wine is a fino.

Fortification is the addition of pure grape spirit, raising the level of alcohol from around 11 percent by volume to around 18 percent for olorosos, and 15.5 percent for finos.

The *solera* system

The youngest *solera* contains new wine.

Sherry for bottling is taken from the oldest *solera* on the bottom row.

The finished product

The solera system assures that the qualities of a sherry remain constant. The wine from the youngest solera is mixed with the older in the barrels below and as a result takes on its character.

Moorish Architecture

The first significant period of Moorish architecture arrived with the Cordoban Caliphate. The Mezquita was extended lavishly during this period and possesses all the enduring features of the Moorish style: arches, stuccowork, and ornamental use of calligraphy. Later, the Almohads imported a purer Islamic style, as can be seen in La Giralda *(see pp418–19)*. The Nasrids built the superbly crafted Alhambra *(see pp466–7)*, while the Mudéjares *(see p51)* used their skill to create beautiful Moorish-style buildings such as the Palacio Pedro I in Seville's Reales Alcázares *(see pp422–3)*.

Reflections *in water, combined with an overall play of light, were central to Moorish architecture.*

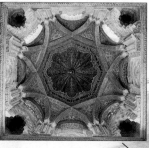

Moorish domes *were frequently unadorned on the outside. Inside, an intricate lattice of stone ribs supported the dome's weight. Like this one in the Mezquita* (see pp456–7)*, they were inlaid with multicolored mosaics featuring stylized flowers.*

Defensive walls

Moorish gardens were often arranged around gently rippling pools and channels.

Azulejos (see p420), *gla[zed] tiles, often adorned wall[s in] geometric patterns, as her[e in] the Reales Alcázares* (p4[...]

DEVELOPMENT OF MOORISH ARCHITECTURE

Pre-Caliphal era 710–929	Caliphal era 929–1031	Almoravid and Almohad era 1091–1248	Nasrid era 1238–1492
	1031–91 *Taifa period (see p50)*		**c.1350** Alhambra palace

700	800	900	1000	1100	1200	1300	1400
	785 Mezquita in Córdoba begun			**1184** La Giralda in Seville begun		**c.1350** Palacio Pedro I	
		936 Medina Azahara near Córdoba begun			**Mudéjar era, after c.1215**		

MOORISH ARCHES

The Moorish arch was developed from the horseshoe arch that the Visigoths used in the construction of churches. The Moors modified it and used it as the basis of great architectural endeavors, such as the Mezquita. Subsequent arches show more sophisticated ornamentation and the slow demise of the basic horseshoe shape.

Caliphal arch, Medina Azahara *(see p453)*

Almohad arch, Reales Alcázares *(see p422)*

Mudéjar arch, Reales Alcázares *(see p422)*

Nasrid arch, the Alhambra *(see p466)*

MOORISH PALACE

The palaces of the Moors were designed with gracious living, culture, and learning in mind. The imaginary palace here shows how space, light, water, and ornamentation were combined to harmonious effect.

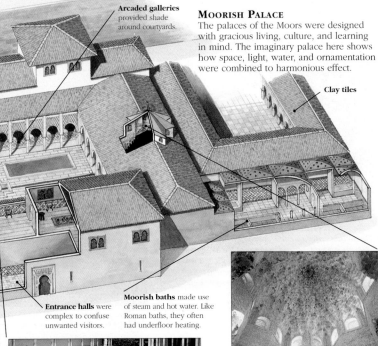

Arcaded galleries provided shade around courtyards.

Clay tiles

Entrance halls were complex to confuse unwanted visitors.

Moorish baths made use of steam and hot water. Like Roman baths, they often had underfloor heating.

Elaborate stuccowork typifies the Nasrid style of architecture. The Sala de los Abencerrajes in the Alhambra (see p467) was built using only the simplest materials, but it is nevertheless widely regarded as one of the most outstanding monuments of the period of the Moorish occupation.

Water cooled the Moors' elegant courtyards and served a contemplative purpose, as here in the Patio de los Leones in the Alhambra (see p467).

Flamenco, the Soul of Andalusia

Seville feria poster 1953

MORE THAN JUST A DANCE, flamenco is a forceful artistic expression of the sorrows and joys of life. Although it has interpreters all over Spain and even the world, it is a uniquely Andalusian art form, traditionally performed by gypsies. There are many styles of *cante* (song) from different parts of Andalusia, but no strict choreography – dancers improvise from basic movements, following the rhythm of the guitar and their feelings. Flamenco was neglected in the 1960s and 1970s, but recent years have seen a revival of serious interest in traditional styles and the development of exciting new forms.

Sevillanas*, *a folk dance that strongly influenced flamenco, is danced by Andalusians in their bars and homes.

At a ***tablao*** (flamenco club) there will be at least four people on stage, including the hand clapper.

The origins of flamenco *are hard to trace. Gypsies may have been the main creators of the art, mixing their own Indian-influenced culture with existing Moorish and Andalusian folklore, and with Jewish and Christian music. There were gypsies in Andalusia by the early Middle Ages, but only in the 18th century did flamenco begin to develop into its present form.*

THE SPANISH GUITAR

The guitar has a major role in flamenco, traditionally accompanying the singer. The flamenco guitar developed from the modern classical guitar, which evolved in Spain in the 19th century. Flamenco guitars have a lighter, shallower construction and a thickened plate below the soundhole, used to tap rhythms. Today, flamenco guitarists often perform solo. One of the greatest, Paco de Lucía, began by accompanying singers and dancers, before making his debut as a soloist in 1968. His inventive style, which combines traditional playing with Latin, jazz, and rock elements, has influenced many musicians outside the realm of flamenco, such as the group Ketama, who play flamenco-blues.

Classical guitar

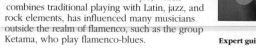

Expert guitarist Paco de Lucía

Singing is an integral part of flamenco and the singer often performs solo. Camarón de la Isla (1952–92), a gypsy born near Cádiz, was among the most famous contemporary cantaores (flamenco singers). He began as a singer of expressive cante jondo (literally, "deep song"), from which he developed his own, rock-influenced style. He has inspired many singers.

WHERE TO ENJOY FLAMENCO

Most of the leading performers are based in Madrid (see p306). In Granada, Sacromonte's caves (p465) are an exciting venue. In Seville, the Barrio de Santa Cruz (pp414–23) has good tablaos.

La Chanca is a bailaora (female dancer) who is renowned for her fiery and forceful movements. Cristina Hoyos, another dancer famous for her highly polished personal style, leads her own flamenco dance company, which received worldwide acclaim in the 1980s.

The proud yet graceful posture of the *bailaora* is suggestive of a restrained passion.

A harsh, vibrating voice is typical of the singer.

Traditional polka-dot dress

The bailaor (male dancer) plays a less important role than the bailaora. However, many have achieved fame, including Antonio Canales. He has introduced a new beat through his original foot movements.

THE FLAMENCO TABLAO

These days it is rare to come across spontaneous dancing at a *tablao*, but if dancers and singers are inspired, an impressive show usually results. Artists performing with *duende* ("magic spirit") will hear appreciative *olés* from the audience.

FLAMENCO RHYTHM

The unmistakable rhythm of flamenco is created by the guitar. Just as important, however, is the beat created by hand-clapping and by the dancer's feet in high-heeled shoes. The *bailaoras* may also beat a rhythm with castanets; Lucero Tena (born in 1939) became famous for her solos on castanets. Graceful hand movements are used to express the dancer's feelings of the moment – whether pain, sorrow, or happiness. Like the movements of the rest of the body, they are not choreographed, and the styles used vary from person to person.

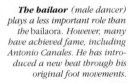

Castanets made of wood

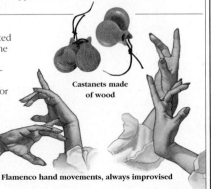

Flamenco hand movements, always improvised

EL ARENAL

BOUNDED BY the Río Guadalquivir and guarded by the 13th-century Torre del Oro, El Arenal used to be a district of munitions warehouses and shipyards. Today it is dominated by the dazzling white bullring, the Plaza de Toros de la Maestranza, where the Sevillians have been staging *corridas* for more than two centuries. The many bars and wine shops in the neighboring streets are especially busy during the summer bullfighting season.

Once central to the city's life, the influence of the Guadalquivir declined as it silted up during the 17th century. By then El Arenal had become a notorious underworld

Torre del Oro shown on 20th-century tiles

haunt clinging to the city walls. The river was converted into a canal in the early 20th century but restored to its former navigable glory in time for Expo '92. The east bank was transformed into a tree-lined promenade with excellent views of Triana and La Isla de la Cartuja across the water *(see p428)*.

The Hospital de la Caridad testifies to the city's continuing love affair with the Baroque. Its church is filled with famous paintings by Murillo, and the story of the Seville School is told in the immaculately restored Museo de Bellas Artes farther north. The city's stunning collection of art includes great works by Zurbarán, Murillo, and Valdés Leal.

SIGHTS AT A GLANCE

Historic Buildings
Hospital de la Caridad ④
Plaza de Toros de la
  Maestranza ③
Torre del Oro ⑤

Museums
Museo de Bellas Artes ①

Churches
Iglesia de la Magdalena ②

GETTING THERE

This area is well served by the orange Tussam buses. Take the C4, which runs along the Paseo de Colón. Alternatively, use one of the numerous routes to Plaza Nueva.

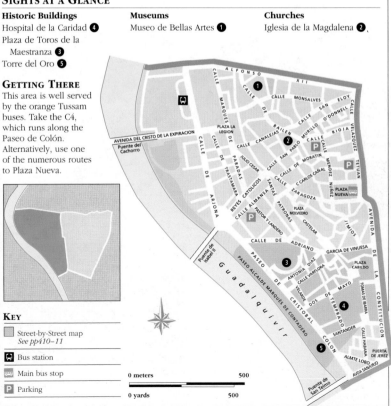

KEY

	Street-by-Street map *See pp410–11*
🚌	Bus station
	Main bus stop
🅿	Parking

0 meters   500
0 yards   500

◁ **Pasting up an advertisement for a bullfight on the walls of the Plaza de Toros de la Maestranza**

Street-by-Street: El Arenal

ONCE HOME TO THE PORT of Seville, El Arenal also housed the ammunition works and the artillery headquarters. Now its atmosphere is set by the city's bullring, the majestic Plaza de Toros de la Maestranza. During the bullfighting season *(see p412)* the area's bars and restaurants are packed, but for the rest of the year El Arenal's backstreets remain quiet. The riverfront is dominated by one of Seville's best-known monuments, the Moorish Torre del Oro, and the long, tree-lined promenade beside the Paseo de Cristóbal Colón is perfect for a slow, romantic walk along the Guadalquivir.

Statue of Carmen

★ **Plaza de Toros de la Maestra**
Seville's 18th-century bullring, on Spain's oldest, has a Baroque façe in white and ocher ❸

Carmen
(see p427), sculpted in bronze, stands opposite the bullring.

CALLE DE ADRIANO

CALLE ANTONIA DIAZ

PASEO DE CRISTOBAL COLON

The Teatro de la Maestranza, a showpiece theater and opera house, was opened in 1991. Home of the Orquesta Sinfónica de Sevilla, the theater also features international opera and dance companies.

Paseo Alcalde Marqués de Contadero

STAR SIGHTS

★ Plaza de Toros de la Maestranza

★ Hospital de la Caridad

★ Torre del Oro

The Guadalquivir used to cause catastrophic inundations. Following floods in 1947 a barrage was constructed. Today, tourists enjoy peaceful boat trips, starting from the Torre del Oro.

El Buzo ("The Diver") is one of many traditional tapas bars and *freidurías* on or just off Calle Arfe. Nearby is Mesón Sevilla Jabugo I, a bar where jamón ibérico (*see p438*) is served.

LOCATOR MAP
See Street Finder map 3

El Postigo is an arts and crafts market.

GARCIA VINUESA

To the Cathedral

El Torno, in the secluded Plaza de Cabildo, sells candies made in a convent.

ARFE

AVENIDA DE LA CONSTITUCION

DE MAYO

TOMAS DE IBARRA

TEMPRADO

★ Hospital de la Caridad
The walls of this Baroque hospital church are hung with fine paintings by Bartolomé Esteban Murillo and Juan de Valdés Leal ❹

To Reales Alcázares

Maestranza de Artillería

CALLE SANTANDER

Bodegón Torre del Oro
(see p600)

0 meters	75
0 yards	75

KEY

- - - Suggested route

★ Torre del Oro
Built in the 13th century to protect the port, this crenelated Moorish tower now houses a small maritime museum ❺

Madonna and Child in the Baroque Iglesia de la Magdalena

Museo de Bellas Artes ❶

Plaza del Museo 9. **Map** 1 B5. ❰ (95) 422 07 90. ▥ 43, C3. ◯ 9am–3pm Tue–Sun (also 4–7pm during temporary exhibitions; phone to check). ▦ ⌀ ♿

T HE CONVENTO de la Merced Calzada has been restored to create one of the best art museums in Spain. Completed in 1612 by Juan de Oviedo, the building is designed around three patios, which today are adorned with trees, flowers, and some fine *azulejos (see p420)*. The Patio Mayor is the largest of these, remodeled by the architect Leonardo de Figueroa in 1724. The convent church is notable for its Baroque domed ceiling, painted by Domingo Martínez.

The museum's collection of Spanish art and sculpture, from the medieval to the modern, focuses on the work of Seville School artists. Among the star attractions is *La Servilleta*, a Virgin and Child (1665–8), which is said to be painted on a napkin *(servilleta)*. One of Murillo's most popular works, it may be seen in the restored convent church. The boisterous *La Inmaculada* (1672) by Juan de Valdés Leal is on display in a gallery devoted to the artist's forceful religious

San Jerónimo Penitente in the Museo de Bellas Artes

paintings. The museum also contains several fine works by Zurbarán including *San Hugo en el Refectorio* (1655), which was painted for the monastery at La Cartuja *(see p428)*.

Iglesia de la Magdalena ❷

Calle San Pablo 10. **Map** 3 B1. ❰ (95) 422 96 03. ▥ 43. ◯ 7:30–11am, 6:30–9pm Mon–Fri, 7:30am–1pm Sat & Sun. ▦

T HIS IMMENSE BAROQUE church by Leonardo de Figueroa, completed in 1709, is gradually being restored to its former glory. In its southwest corner stands the Capilla de la Quinta Angustia, a Mudéjar chapel with three cupolas. This chapel survived from an earlier church where the great Seville School painter Batolomé Murillo was baptized in 1618. The font that was used for his baptism is now in the baptistry of the present building. The church's west front is topped by a belfry, which is painted in vivid colors.

Among the religious works inside are a painting by Francisco de Zurbarán, *St. Dominic in Soria*, housed in the Capilla Sacramental (to the right of the south door) and frescoes by Lucas Valdés over the sanctuary. On the wall of the north transept there is a cautionary fresco of a medieval *auto-da-fé (see p264)*.

Plaza de Toros de la Maestranza ❸

Paseo de Cristóbal Colón. **Map** 3 B2. ❰ (95) 422 45 77. ▥ C4. ◯ 10am–1:30pm Mon–Sat. ▦ ▦

S EVILLE'S FAMOUS bullring, built between 1761–1881, is arguably the most magnificent in Spain and well worth a visit.

The arcaded arena holds up to 14,000 spectators. Guided tours of this immense building start from the main entrance on Paseo de Cristóbal Colón. On the west side is the Puerta del Príncipe (Prince's Gate), through which the triumphant matadors are carried aloft by admirers from the crowd.

Just beyond the *enfermería* (emergency hospital) is a museum of portraits, posters, and costumes, including a purple cape painted by Pablo Picasso. The tour continues on to the chapel where matadors pray for success, and then to the stables where the horses of the *picadores* (lance-carrying horsemen) are kept.

The bullfighting season starts with the April fair and continues intermittently until October. Most *corridas* take place on Sunday evenings. Tickets can be bought from the *taquilla* (booking office) at the bullring.

Next to the Plaza de Toros, and echoing its circular bulk, is the Teatro de la Maestranza. Seville's austere opera house and theater, designed by Luis Marín de Terán and Aurelio de Pozo, opened in 1991. Fragments of ironwork from the 19th-century ammunition works that first occupied the site adorn the river façade.

Arcaded arena of the Plaza de Toros de la Maestranza, begun in 1761

Finis Gloriae Mundi by Juan de Valdés Leal in the Hospital de la Caridad

Hospital de la Caridad ❹

Calle Temprado 3. **Map** 3 B2. 【 (95) 422 32 32. ▥ C4. ◯ 10am–1pm, 4:30–6:30pm Mon–Sat. ◐ public hols. 🎫 🚫

THIS CHARITY HOSPITAL was founded in 1674, and it is still used today as a sanctuary for elderly and infirm people. In the gardens stands a statue of its benefactor, Miguel de Mañara, whose dissolute life before he joined a brotherhood is said to have inspired the story of Don Juan. The façade of the hospital church, with its whitewashed walls, reddish stonework, and framed *azulejos*, provides a glorious example of Sevillian Baroque.

Inside are two square patios decorated with plants, 18th-century Dutch tiles, and fine fountains with Italian statues depicting Charity and Mercy. At their northern end a passage to the right leads to another patio, containing a 13th-century arch, which survives from the city's shipyards. Here, too, a bust of Mañara stands amid pretty rose bushes.

Inside the church there are a number of original canvases by some of the leading painters of the 17th century, despite the fact that some of its greatest artworks were looted by Marshal Soult during the Napoleonic occupation of 1808–14 *(see p58)*.

Directly above the entrance is the ghoulish *Finis Gloriae Mundi* (The End of the World's Glory) by Juan de Valdés Leal, and opposite hangs his morbid *In Ictu Oculi* (In the Blink of an Eye). Many of the other works that can be seen are by Murillo, including *St. John of God Carrying a Sick Man* and portraits of the Child Jesus and *St. John the Baptist as a Boy*.

Torre del Oro ❺

Paseo de Cristóbal Colón. **Map** 3 B2. 【 (95) 422 24 19. ▥ C4. ◯ 10am–2pm Tue–Fri, 11am–2pm Sat & Sun. ◐ Aug & public hols. 🎫 🚫

IN MOORISH SEVILLE the Tower of Gold formed part of the walled defenses, linking up with the Reales Alcázares *(see pp422–3)*. It was built as a defensive lookout in 1220, with a companion tower on the opposite riverbank. A mighty metal chain was stretched between the two to prevent hostile ships from sailing upriver. The turret was not added until 1760. The gold referred to in its name may be the gilded *azulejos* that once clad its walls, or treasures from the Americas unloaded here. The tower has had many uses: a gunpowder store, a chapel, a prison, and port offices. Now, as the Museo Marítimo, it exhibits maritime maps and antiques.

The Torre del Oro, built by the Almohads

SANTA CRUZ

S EVILLE'S OLD JEWISH QUARTER, the Barrio de Santa Cruz, is a warren of white alleyways and patios that has long been the most picturesque corner of the city. Many of the best-known sights are located here: the cavernous Gothic cathedral with its landmark tower, La Giralda; the splendid Reales Alcázares, with the royal palaces and lush gardens of Pedro I and Carlos V; and the Archivo de Indias, whose documents tell of Spain's exploration and conquest of the Americas.

Spreading northeast from these great monuments is an enchanting maze of whitewashed streets. The Golden Age artist Bartolomé Esteban

Ornate streetlamp, Plaza del Triunfo

Murillo lived here in the 17th century, while his contemporary, Juan de Valdés Leal, decorated the Hospital de los Venerables with superb Baroque frescoes. Farther north is one of Seville's favorite shopping streets, the Calle de las Sierpes. The market squares around it, such as the charming Plaza del Salvador, provided backdrops for some of the stories of Cervantes. Nearby, the ornate façades and interiors of the Ayuntamiento (town hall) and the Casa de Pilatos, a gem of Andalusian architecture, testify to the great wealth that flowed into the city from the New World during the 16th century, much of it spent on art.

SIGHTS AT A GLANCE

Historic Buildings
Archivo de Indias **6**
Ayuntamiento **2**
Casa de Pilatos **4**
Hospital de los Venerables **5**
Reales Alcázares pp422–3 **7**

Churches
Cathedral and La Giralda pp418–19 **1**

Streets and Plazas
Calle de las Sierpes **3**

GETTING THERE
This area is well served by orange Tussam buses. Take any of routes 21, 22, 23, 25, 26, 30, 31, 33, 34, 40, 41 or 42 to reach the Avenida de la Constitución, convenient for most of the sights. *Circular* C3 or C4 will take you instead to the Puerta de Jerez.

KEY

Street-by-Street map *(pp416–17)*

Tourist information

0 meters   400

0 yards   400

◁ **La Giralda seen from the gardens of the Reales Alcázares**

Street-by-Street: Santa Cruz

Window grille, Santa Cruz

THE MAZE of narrow streets to the east of Seville cathedral and the Reales Alcázares represents Seville at its most romantic and compact. As well as the expected souvenir shops, tapas bars, and strolling guitarists, there are plenty of picturesque alleys, hidden plazas, and flower-decked patios to reward the casual wanderer. Once a Jewish ghetto, its re-stored buildings, with characteristic window grilles, are now a harmonious mix of up-scale residences and tourist accommodations. Good bars and restaurants make the area well worth an evening visit.

Plaza Virgen de los Reyes is ofter lined by horse-drawn carriages. In the center of the square is an early 20th-century fountain by José Lafita.

Palacio Arzobispal, the 18th-century Archbishop's Palace, is still used by Seville's clergy.

★ Cathedral and La Giralda
This huge Gothic cathe-dral and its Moorish bell tower are Seville's most popular sights ❶

Convento de la Encarnación

AVENIDA DE LA CONSTITUCION

ROMERO

SANTO TOMAS

MIGUEL MAÑARA

Museo de Arte Contemporáneo

Archivo de Indias
Built in the 16th century as a merchants' exchange, the Archive of the Indies now houses documents relating to the Spanish colonization of the Americas ❻

Plaza del Triunfo has a Baroque colum celebrating the city's survival of the great earthquake of 1755. the center is a mod statue of the Virgi Mary of the Imma Conception.

Calle Mateos Gago is shaded by orange trees and filled with souvenir shops, cafés, and tapas bars. Bar Giralda at No. 2, whose vaults are the remains of a Moorish bath house, is popular for its wide variety of tapas.

LOCATOR MAP
See Street Finder maps 3–4

Plaza Santa Cruz is adorned by an ornate iron cross from 1692.

MESON DEL MORO

XIMENEZ ENCISO

SANTA TERESA

ODRIGO CARO

JAMERDANA

REINOSO

LOPE DE RUEDA

PLAZA STA CRUZ

GLORIA

JUSTINO DE NEVE

PL DOÑA ELVIRA

PIMIENTA

CALLEJON DEL AGUA

SUSONA

VIDA

★ **Hospital de los Venerables**
The 17th-century home for elderly priests has a splendidly restored Baroque church **5**

Callejón del Agua is a whitewashed alleyway offering glimpses into enchanting plant-filled patios. It is called "Water Street" because it was once a water conduit to the Reales Alcázares.

0 meters	50
0 yards	50

★ **Reales Alcázares**
Seville's Royal Palaces are a rewarding combination of exquisite Mudéjar (see pp422–3) craftsmanship, regal grandeur, and landscaped gardens **7**

STAR SIGHTS

★ **Cathedral and La Giralda**

★ **Hospital de los Venerables**

★ **Reales Alcázares**

KEY

– – – Suggested route

Seville Cathedral and La Giralda ❶

16th-century stained glass

Ｓeville's cathedral occupies the site of a great mosque built by the Almohads (*see p50*) in the late 12th century. La Giralda, its bell tower, and the Patio de los Naranjos are a legacy of this Moorish structure. Work on the Christian cathedral, the largest in Europe, began in 1401 and took just over a century to complete. As well as enjoying its Gothic immensity and the works of art in its chapels and sacristy, visitors can climb La Giralda for stunning views over the city.

★ La Giralda
The Moorish bell tower is crowned with a 16th-century bronze portraying Faith. This weather vane (giraldillo) *has given La Giralda its name.*

Entrance

★ Patio de los Naranjos
In Moorish times worshippers would wash their hands and feet in the fountain under the orange trees before praying.

THE RISE OF LA GIRALDA

The tower was built as a minaret in 1198. In the 14th century the bronze spheres at its top were replaced by Christian symbols. A new belfry was planned in 1557, but built to a more ornate design by Hernán Ruiz in 1568.

| 1198 | 1400 | 1557 | 1568 |

Puerta del Perdón

Roman pillars
brought from Itálica (*see p452*) surround the cathedral steps.

Retablo Mayor
Santa María de la Sede, the cathedral's patron saint, sits at the high altar below a waterfall of gold. The 44 gilded relief panels of the reredos were carved by Spanish and Flemish sculptors between 1482 and 1564.

VISITORS' CHECKLIST

Plaza Virgen de los Reyes.
Map 3 C2. **[** (95) 456 33 21.
[=] 21, 22, 23, 31, 33, 40.
Cathedral **[]** 11am–5pm
Mon–Sat, 2–4pm Sun. **[] [†]**
9am, 10am, noon, 5pm Mon–
Sat, 11am, noon, 1pm Sun. **[&]**
La Giralda **[]** 11am–5pm
Mon–Sat, 10am–4pm Sun.

The Sacristía Mayor houses many works of art, including paintings by Murillo.

★ Capilla Mayor
Monumental iron grilles forged in 1518–32 enclose the main chapel, which is dominated by the overwhelming Retablo Mayor.

The Tomb of Columbus dates from the 1890s. His coffin is carried by bearers representing the kingdoms of Castile, León, Aragón, and Navarra *(see p50).*

Puerta del Bautismo

Iglesia del Sagrario, a large 17th-century chapel, is now used as a parish church.

STAR FEATURES

★ La Giralda

★ Patio de los Naranjos

★ Capilla Mayor

Puerta de la Asunción
Though Gothic in style, this portal was not completed until 1833. A stone relief of the Assumption of the Virgin decorates the tympanum.

Genoese fountain in the Mudéjar Patio Principal of the Casa de Pilatos

Ayuntamiento ❷

Plaza Nueva 1. **Map** 3 C1. [☎] *(95) 459 01 01.* [🚌] *21, 30.* [◯] *5:30–7:30pm Tue & Wed (entry with passport).* [📷]

Seville's city hall stands between the Real Plaza de San Francisco, where *autos-da-fé* (public trials of heretics) were held, and the Plaza Nueva.

The building was completed between 1527 and 1534. The side bordering the Plaza de San Francisco is a fine example of the ornate Plateresque style *(see p21)* favored by the architect Diego de Riaño. The west front, meanwhile, is part of a Neo-Classical extension built in 1891. Richly sculpted ceilings survive in the vestibule and in the lower Casa Consistorial (Council Meeting Room). This contains Velázquez's *Imposition of the Chasuble on St. Ildefonso.* The upper Casa Consistorial has a dazzling coffered ceiling and paintings by Zurbarán and Valdés Leal.

Calle de las Sierpes ❸

Map 3 C1. [🚌] *21, 30.* **Casa de la Condesa Lebrija** [☎] *(95) 421 81 83.* [◯] *5–7pm Mon & Fri.*

Seville's main pedestrianized shopping promenade, the "Street of the Snakes," runs north from the Plaza de San Francisco. Long-established stores selling hats, fans, and traditional *mantillas* (lace headdresses) stand alongside clothes and souvenir shops. The parallel streets of Cuna and Tetuán also offer some enjoyable window-shopping.

About half way up the street walking north, Calle Jovellanos on the left leads to the 17th-century Capillita de San José. Farther on, at the junction with Calle Pedro Caravaca, is the anachronistic, upholstered world of the Real Círculo de Labradores, a private men's club founded in 1856.

Opposite – with its entrance in Calle Cuna – is a 15th-century private mansion, the Casa de la Condesa Lebrija. Among the Lebrija family's countless Roman treasures on display on the ground floor is a mosaic from the ruins of nearby Itálica *(see p452).*

Right at the end of the street, take the opportunity to buy a cake in La Campana, Seville's best-known *pastelería.*

Casa de Pilatos ❹

Plaza de Pilatos 1. **Map** 4 D1. [☎] *(95) 422 52 98.* [🚌] *C3, C4.* [◯] **Ground floor** *9am–8pm.* **First floor** *10am–2pm, 4–6pm.* [📷] [📷] [♿] *ground floor.*

Enraptured by by the architectural and decorative wonders of High Renaissance Italy and the Holy Land, the first Marquis of Tarifa built the Casa de Pilatos. It was so called because it was thought to resemble Pontius Pilate's home in Jerusalem. Today it is the residence of the Dukes of Medinaceli and is still one of the finest palaces in Seville.

Visitors enter it through a marble portal, commissioned by the Marquis in 1529 from Genoese craftsmen. Across the arcaded Apeadero (carriage yard) is the Patio Principal. This courtyard is essentially Mudéjar *(see p51)* in style and decorated with *azulejos* and intricate plasterwork. In its corners are three Roman statues depicting Minerva, a dancing muse, and Ceres, and a Greek statue of Athena that dates from the 5th century BC. In its center is a fountain that was imported from Genoa. To the right, through the Salón del Pretorio with its coffered ceiling and marquetry, is the Corredor de Zaquizamí.

AZULEJOS

Colorful *azulejos*, glazed ceramic tiles, are a striking feature of Seville. The craft was introduced to Spain by the Moors, who created fantastic mosaics in sophisticated geometric patterns for palace walls – the word *azulejo* derives from the Arabic for "little stone." New techniques were introduced in the 16th century and later mass production extended their use to decorative signs, shop façades, and billboards.

***Azulejo* billboard for Studebaker Motor Cars (1924), Calle Tetuán**

Fresco by Juan de Valdés Leal in the Hospital de los Venerables

The antiquities on display in adjacent rooms include a bas-relief of *Leda and the Swan* and two Roman reliefs commemorating the Battle of Actium of 31 BC.

Coming back to the Patio Principal, you turn right into the Salón de Descanso de los Jueces. Beyond is a rib-vaulted Gothic chapel with Mudéjar plasterwork walls and ceiling. On the altar is a copy of a 4th-century sculpture in the Vatican, *The Good Shepherd*. Left through the Gabinete de Pilatos, with its small central fountain, is the Jardín Grande.

As you return to the main patio, a tiled staircase behind the statue of Ceres leads to the upper floor. It is roofed with a *media naranja* (half orange) cupola built in 1537. There are Mudéjar ceilings in some of the rooms, which are filled with family portraits, antiques, and furniture.

Hospital de los Venerables **⑤**

Plaza de los Venerables 8. **Map** 3 C2.
📞 (95) 456 26 96. 🚌 C3, C4.
🕐 10am–2pm, 4–8pm daily. 📷 🎫

SET IN THE HEART of the Barrio de Santa Cruz, this home for elderly priests was begun in 1675 and completed around 20 years later by Leonardo de Figueroa. It has recently been restored as a cultural center by FOCUS (Fundación Fondo de Cultura de Sevilla).

Stairs from the central, rose-colored, sunken patio lead to the upper floors, which, along with the infirmary and cellar, are used as exhibition galleries.

A separate guided tour visits the Hospital church, a show-case of Baroque splendors, with frescoes by both Juan de Valdés Leal and his son Lucas Valdés. Other highlights of the church include sculptures of St. Peter and St. Ferdinand by Pedro Roldán, flanking the east door and *The Apotheosis of St. Ferdinand* by Lucas Valdés, top center in the reredos of the main altar. Its frieze (in-scribed in Greek) recommends that visitors should "Fear God and Honor the Priest."

In the sacristy, the ceiling has an effective *trompe l'oeil* depicting *The Triumph of the Cross* by Juan de Valdés Leal.

Archivo de Indias **⑥**

Avda de la Constitución. **Map** 3 C2.
📞 (95) 421 12 34. 🚌 C3, C4, 21, 26, 31, 33, 34, 40. 🕐 10am–1pm Mon–Fri (research 8am–3pm). 📷

THE ARCHIVE of the Indies illustrates Seville's pre-eminent role in the coloniza-tion and exploitation of the New World. Built between 1584–98 to designs by Juan de Herrera, co-architect of El Escorial *(see pp312–13)*, it was originally a *lonja* (exchange), where merchants traded. In 1785, Carlos III had all Spanish documents relating to the "Indies" collected under one roof. Among the archive's 86 million handwritten pages and 8,000 maps and drawings are letters from Columbus, Cortés, and Cervantes, and the extensive correspondence of Felipe II. Some documents are now stored on CD-ROM.

Upstairs, the library rooms contain regularly changing displays of drawings, maps, and facsimile documents.

Façade of the Archivo de Indias by Juan de Herrera

Reales Alcázares ❼

Mudéjar stucco

IN 1364 PEDRO I ordered the construction of a royal residence within the palaces that had been built by the city's Almohad *(see p50)* rulers. Within two years, craftsmen from Granada and Toledo had created a jewel box of Mudéjar patios and halls, the Palacio Pedro I, now at the heart of Seville's Reales Alcázares. Later monarchs added their own distinguishing marks: Isabel I *(see p52)* dispatched navigators to explore the New World from her Casa de la Contratación, while Carlos I (the Holy Roman Emperor Charles V – *see p54*) had grandiose, richly decorated apartments built.

Jardín de Troya

Gardens of the Alcázares
Laid out with terraces, fountains, and pavilions, these gardens provide a delightful refuge from the heat and bustle of Seville.

★ Charles V Rooms
Vast tapestries and lively 16th-century azulejos *decorate the vaulted halls of the apartments and chapel of Charles V.*

Patio del Crucero lies above the old baths.

PLAN OF THE REALES ALCÁZARES

The complex has been the home of Spanish kings for almost seven centuries. The palace's upper floor is used by the royal family today.

KEY

☐ Area illustrated above

☐ Gardens

★ Patio de las Doncellas
The Patio of the Maidens boasts plasterwork by the top craftsmen of Granada.

★ Salón de Embajadores
Built in 1427, the dazzling dome of the Ambassadors' Hall is of carved and gilded, interlaced wood.

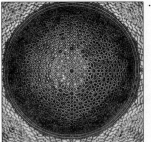

Horseshoe Arches
Azulejos *and complex plasterwork decorate the Ambassadors' Hall, which has three symmetrically arranged, ornate archways, each with three horseshoe arches.*

Casa de la Contratación

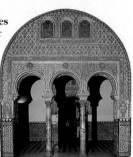

The Patio de la Montería was where the court met before hunting expeditions.

Patio de las Muñecas
The Patio of the Dolls and its surrounding bedrooms formed the domestic heart of the palace. It derives its name from two tiny faces on one of its arches.

The façade of the Palacio Pedro I is a prime example of Mudéjar style.

Puerta del León (entrance)

STAR FEATURES

- ★ **Charles V Rooms**
- ★ **Patio de las Doncellas**
- ★ **Salón de Embajadores**

Patio del Yeso
The Patio of Plaster, a garden with flower beds and a water channel, retains features of the earlier, 12th-century Almohad Alcázar.

FARTHER AFIELD

THE NORTH OF Seville, La Macarena, is a character-ful mix of decaying Baroque and Mudéjar churches and old-style tapas bars. The place to visit here is the Basílica de la Macarena, a shrine to Seville's much-venerated Virgen de la Esperanza Macarena. Among the many convents and churches in the area, the Convento de Santa Paula offers a rare opportunity to peep behind the walls of an enclosed community.

The area south of the city is dominated by the extensive, leafy Parque María Luisa. A large part of the park originally formed the grounds of the Baroque Palacio de San Telmo. Many of the historic buildings in the park were erected for the Ibero-American Exposition of 1929. The grand, five-star Hotel Alfonso XIII

Roman column, Alameda de Hércules

and the crescent-shaped Plaza de España are the most striking legacies of this upsurge of Andalusian pride. Nearby is the Royal Tobacco Factory, forever associated with the fictional gypsy heroine Carmen, who toiled in its sultry halls. Today, it is part of the Universidad, Seville's university.

There is more to see across the river from the city center. With its cobbled streets and shops selling ceramics, the Triana quarter retains the feel of old Seville. In the 15th century a Carthusian monastery, the Monasterio de Santa María de las Cuevas, was built north of Triana. Columbus resided there and, largely due to this connection, the area around it, the Isla de la Cartuja, was chosen as the site for Expo '92. Today the site is being developed as cultural and educational theme parks.

SIGHTS AT A GLANCE

Historic Buildings
Palacio de San Telmo **4**
Universidad **5**

Churches and Convents
Basílica de la Macarena **1**
Convento de Santa Paula **2**
Iglesia de San Pedro **3**

Historic Areas
Isla de la Cartuja **8**
Parque María Luisa **6**
Triana **7**

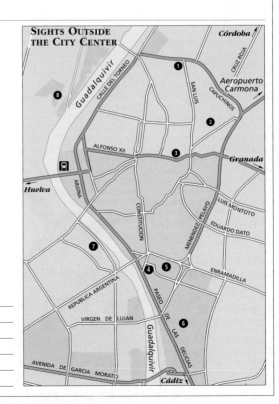

0 kilometers 1
0 miles 0.5

KEY

City center

Parks and open spaces

Railroad station

Major road

Minor road

◁ **Pabellón de Andalucía, built on the Isla de la Cartuja for Expo '92**

St. John the Baptist by Montañés in the Convento de Santa Paula

Basílica de la Macarena ❶

Calle Macarena. **Map** 2 D3.
📞 *(95) 437 01 95.* 🚌 *C1, C2, 2, 10.*
🕐 *9:30am–12:30pm, 5–7pm daily.*
Treasury 🕐 *9am–1pm, 5–9pm daily.*

THE BASILICA de la Macarena was built in 1949 in the Neo-Baroque style by Gómez Millán as a new home for the much-loved Virgen de la Esperanza Macarena. It abuts the 13th-century Iglesia de San Gil, where the image was housed until a fire in 1936.

The image of the Virgin, standing above the main altar amid waterfalls of gold and silver, has been attributed to Luisa Roldán (1656–1703), the most talented female artist of the Seville School. The wall-paintings, by Rafael Rodríguez Hernández, date from 1982.

The Virgin's magnificent pro-cessional gowns and jewels are among the exhibits displayed in the museum in the Treasury.

Convento de Santa Paula ❷

Calle Santa Paula 11. **Map** 2 E5.
📞 *(95) 442 13 07.* 🚌 *10, 11.* 🕐
9:30am–1pm, 4:30–6:30pm daily. 📷

FOUNDED IN 1475, Santa Paula is still a working convent and home to 40 nuns. You can visit the museum, which con-sists of two galleries filled with religious artifacts and paintings,

and buy jams and marmalades, made by the nuns, from a room near the exit. The nave of the convent church has an elaborately carved wooden roof, dating from 1623. Among the statues in the church are St. John the Evangelist and St. John the Baptist, both the work of Juan Martínez Montañés.

Iglesia de San Pedro ❸

Calle Doña María Coronel 1. **Map** 2 D5. 📞 *(95) 421 68 58.* 🚌 *10, 11, 24.* 🕐 *7–10pm Mon–Sat, 9am–noon, 7–8pm Sun.*

DIEGO VELAZQUEZ, the Golden Age painter *(see p28)*, was baptized in this church in 1599. It is built in a typically Sevil-lian mix of architectural styles. Mudéjar elements survive in the lobed brickwork of its tower, which is surmounted by a Baroque *(see p21)* belfry. The principal portal – facing the Plaza de San Pedro – is also Baroque, and was added by Diego de Quesada in 1613.

The poorly lit interior has a Mudéjar wooden ceiling and west door. The vault of one of its chapels is decorated with exquisite geometric patterns of interlacing bricks.

Behind the church, in Calle Doña María Coronel, cakes and cookies are sold from a revolving drum in the wall of the 14th-century Convento de Santa Inés. Fronting its re-stored church is an arcaded patio, which is decorated with 17th-century frescoes by Francisco de Herrera.

Modern tilework adorning the front of the Iglesia de San Pedro

Palacio de San Telmo ❹

Avenida de Roma. **Map** 3 C3. 📞 *(95) 459 75 05.* 🚌 *C3, C4, 5, 34.* 🕐 *by appointment only.* 📷

THIS IMPOSING PALACE, named after the patron saint of navigators, was built in 1682 as a university to train ships' pilots, navigators, and high-ranking officers. In 1849 the palace became the residence of the Dukes of Monpensier, and until 1893 its vast grounds included what is now the Parque María Luisa. Today it is the presidential headquarters of the Junta de Andalucía (the regional government).

The most striking feature of the Palacio de San Telmo is the

Parque María Luisa ❻

Map 4 D4. 🚌 *C1, C2, 30, 31, 33, 34, 70, 72.* 🏛 **Museo Arqueológico** 📞 *(95) 423 24 01.* 🕐 *9am–2pm Tue–Sun.* 📷 📷 🏛 **Museo de Artes y Costumbres Populares** 📞 *(95) 423 25 76.* 🕐 *9am–2:30pm Tue–Sun.* 📷 📷 🏛

PRINCESS MARIA LUISA donated part of the grounds of the Palacio de San Telmo to the city for this park in 1893. It was landscaped by

Plaza de España
was built in a theatrical style by Aníbal González.

The Glorieta de Bécquer
is an arbor with sculpted figures depicting the phases of love – a tribute to poet Gustavo Adolfo Bécquer.

exuberant Churrigueresque portal designed by Leonardo de Figueroa, and completed in 1734. Surrounding the Ionic columns are allegorical figures representing the Sciences and Arts. St. Telmo, holding a ship and charts, is flanked by the sword-bearing St. Ferdinand and St. Hermenegildo, with a cross. On the north façade is ranged a row of sculptures of Sevillian celebrities, added by Susillo in 1895. Among them are artists such as Montañés, Murillo, and Velázquez.

Opposite is Seville's most famous hotel, the Alfonso XIII, dating from the 1920s. Its centerpiece is a grand patio with a fountain and orange trees. Nonresidents are welcome to visit the bar and the restaurant.

Universidad ❺

Calle San Fernando 4. **Map** 3 C3.
📞 (95) 455 10 00. 🚌 C3, C4, 5, 25, 26, 34. ⏰ 8am–8:30pm Mon–Fri.
⬤ public hols.

THE FORMER Real Fábrica de Tabacos (Royal Tobacco Factory) is now part of Seville University. In the 19th century, three-quarters of Europe's cigars were manufactured here, rolled by 10,000 *cigarreras* (female cigar-makers). It was these hot-blooded *cigarreras* who inspired French author Mérimée to create his famous gypsy heroine, *Carmen*.

Built in 1728–71, the factory complex is the largest building in Spain after El Escorial (*see pp312–13*) near Madrid.

Baroque fountain in one of the patios in the Universidad

The moat and watchtowers are evidence of the importance given to protecting the king's lucrative tobacco monopoly.

Jean Forestier, director of the Bois de Boulogne in Paris, who created a leafy setting for the 1929 Ibero-American Exposition. The most dazzling legacies of this extravaganza are the Plaza de España, decorated with regional scenes painted on ceramic tiles, and the Plaza de América, both the work of Aníbal González.

On the latter, in the Pabellón Mudéjar, the Museo de Artes y Costumbres Populares displays traditional Andalusian folk arts. Nearby, the Neo-Renaissance Pabellón de las Bellas Artes houses the provincial Museo Arqueológico. Among the exhibits devoted to the Roman era are statues and fragments found at Itálica (*see p452*).

Fuente de los Leones

Plaza de América

Museo Arqueológico

Pabellón Real

The Isleta de los Patos sits in a lake graced by ducks and swans.

Museo de Artes y Costumbres Populares

Isla de la Cartuja ❽

Map 1 B2. 📞 (95) 448 06 11.
🚌 C1, C2, C3, C4, E5. **Monasterio
de Santa María de las Cuevas**
🕐 Oct–Mar: 11am–7pm Tue–Sun;
Apr–Sep: 11am–9pm Tue–Sun. 📷
♿ **Pabellón de la Navegación**
📞 (95) 446 00 89. 🕐 10am–1pm,
5–8pm Tue–Sun. 📷 ♿

T HE ISLA DE LA CARTUJA was
the site of Expo '92 (see
pp64–5). Since then, large-scale
redevelopment has been gradually transforming it into a
complex of exhibition halls,
museums, and recreation areas.

The 15th-century Carthusian
**Monasterio de Santa María
de las Cuevas**, inhabited by
monks until 1836, is at the
heart of the area. Columbus
stayed and worked here, and
his body lay buried in the crypt
of its church, the Capilla Santa
Ana, between 1507 and 1542.
The monastery was restored
as an exhibit for Expo '92.

By the river, south of the
monastery, is the **Pabellón
de la Navegación**, a maritime
museum, and a replica of the
Nao Victoria, a 16th-century
ship. Nearby is the high-tech
Omnimax Cinema, whose
specially created films about
the earth, explorers, and space
travel were among the most
popular of the exhibits of Expo
'92. Films are projected on an
immense, semicircular screen,
24 m (80 ft) in diameter.

The centerpiece of Expo,
the Lago de España, is to be
turned into a mock ocean with
islands and galleon battles, as
part of a new theme park.

Tours around La Cartuja can
be arranged. Contact the tourist
office for further information.

Decorative tiles at Cerámica Santa Ana, a popular ceramics shop in Triana

Triana ❼

Map 3 A2. 🚌 C3, 40, 43.

T HIS CLOSE-KNIT AREA, named
after the Roman Emperor
Trajan, was once Seville's
gypsy quarter. Triana remains
a traditional working-class
district, with compact, flower-
filled streets and a tangibly
independent atmosphere. For
centuries it has been famous
for its potteries. The best-
known of its ceramics shops
today is **Cerámica Santa Ana**
at No. 31 Calle San Jorge.

A good way to approach
Triana is across the Puente de
Isabel II, leading to the Plaza
del Altozano. This square has
glass-fronted, wrought-iron
balconies called miradores.
Nearby is one of the characteristic streets of the area, the
Calle Rodrigo de Triana, with
its houses painted in white and
ocher. It is named after the
Andalusian sailor who was the
first to sight the shores of the
New World on Columbus's
momentous voyage of 1492.

The Iglesia de Santa Ana,
founded in the 13th century
and splendidly renovated, is
Triana's most popular church.
In the baptistry is the Gypsy
Font, which is believed to pass
on the gift of flamenco song
to the children of the faithful.

Main entrance of the Carthusian Monasterio de Santa María de las Cuevas, founded in 1400

SEVILLE STREET FINDER

THE MAP REFERENCES given with the sights described in the Seville section of the guide refer to the maps on the following pages. Map references are also given for Seville hotels (see pp561–2) and restaurants (pp600–601). The schematic map below shows the area of Seville covered by the *Street Finder*. The symbols used for the sights and other features are listed in the key at the foot of the page.

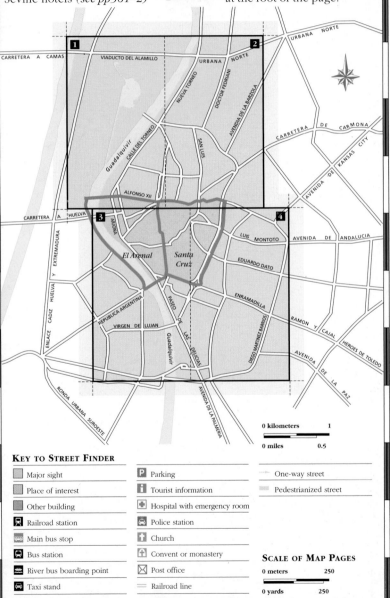

KEY TO STREET FINDER

Major sight

Place of interest

Other building

🚆 Railroad station

🚏 Main bus stop

🚌 Bus station

⛴ River bus boarding point

🚕 Taxi stand

🅿 Parking

ℹ Tourist information

✚ Hospital with emergency room

🚓 Police station

✝ Church

✝ Convent or monastery

✉ Post office

═ Railroad line

→ One-way street

▬ Pedestrianized street

0 kilometers 1

0 miles 0.5

SCALE OF MAP PAGES

0 meters 250

0 yards 250

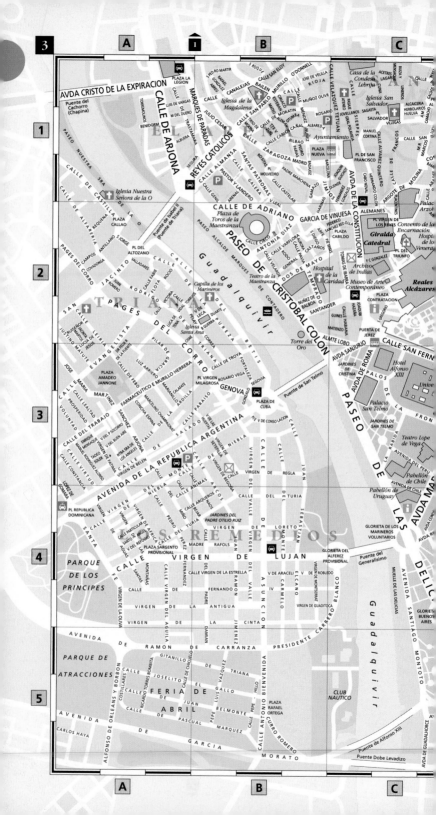

ANDALUSIA

HUELVA · CÁDIZ · MÁLAGA · GIBRALTAR · SEVILLA
CÓRDOBA · GRANADA · JAÉN · ALMERÍA

ANDALUSIA IS WHERE *all Spain's stereotypes meet. Bullfighters, beaches, flamenco, white villages, cave houses, gaudy fiestas, religious processions, tapas, and sherry are all here in abundance. But each is part of a larger whole, which includes great art and architecture, nature preserves, and an easy-going way of life.*

The eight provinces of Andalusia stretch across southern Spain from the deserts of Almería to the Portuguese border. One of Spain's longest rivers, the Guadalquivir, bisects the region. Andalusia is linked to the central tableland by a pass, the Desfiladero de Despeñaperros. The highest peaks on the Spanish mainland are in Andalusia's Sierra Nevada.

Successive invaders left their mark on Andalusia. The Romans built cities in this southern province, which they called Baetica, among them Córdoba, its capital, and the well-preserved Itálica near Seville. It was in Andalusia that the Moors lingered longest and left their greatest buildings – Córdoba's Mezquita and the splendid palace of the Alhambra in Granada.

Inevitably, perhaps, the most visited places are the great cities and the busy Costa del Sol, with Gibraltar, a geographical and historical oddity, at its western end. But there are many attractions tucked into other corners of the region. Many of the sights of Huelva province, bordering Portugal, are associated with Christopher Columbus, who set sail from here in 1492. Film directors have put to good use the atmospheric landscapes of Almería's arid interior, which are reminiscent of the Wild West or Arabia. Discreetly concealed among the countless olive groves that cover Jaén province, but not to be missed, are Andalusia's two lovely Renaissance towns, Úbeda and Baeza.

The city of Jaén surrounded by olive groves, seen from the Castillo de Santa Catalina

◁ Doorway into the *mihrab* (prayer niche) in the Mezquita at Córdoba

Exploring Andalusia

ANDALUSIA IS SPAIN'S MOST VARIED region. It offers dramatic desert scenery at Tabernas, water sports on the Costa del Sol, skiing in the Sierra Nevada, and sherry tasting in Jerez. Of the many nature preserves, the vast, watery Doñana teems with birdlife, while Cazorla is a rugged limestone massif. Granada and Córdoba are unmissable for their Moorish heritage; Úbeda and Baeza are Renaissance gems; and Ronda is one of dozens of superb white towns.

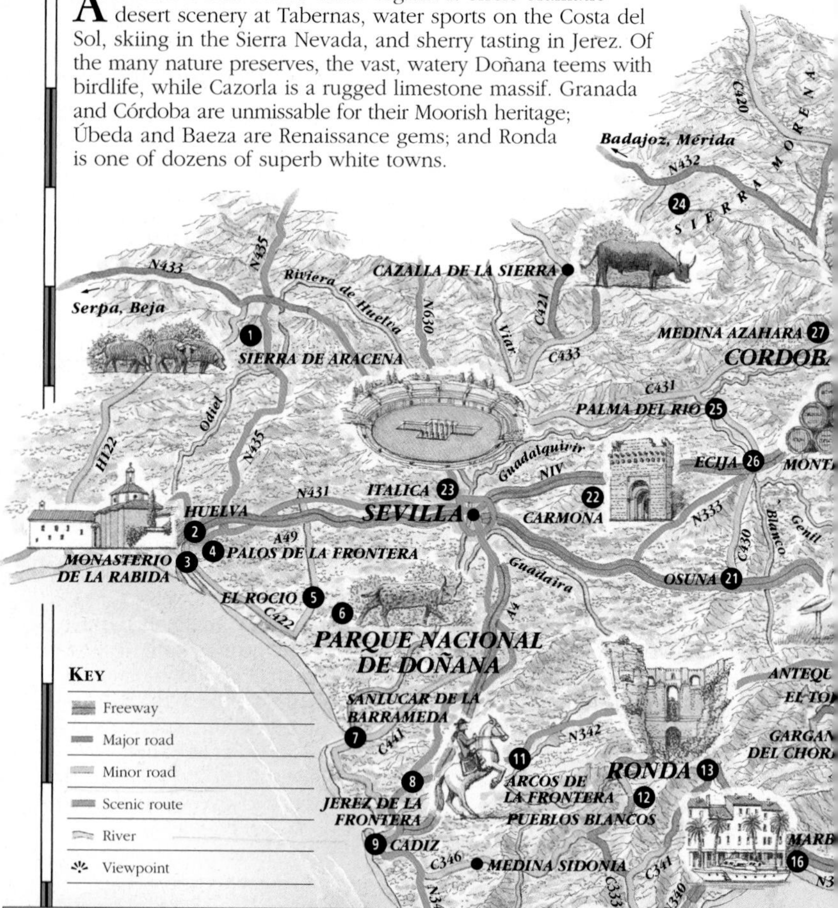

Badajoz, Mérida
C420
N432
SIERRA MORENA
24
N433
N435
Riviera de Huelva
CAZALLA DE LA SIERRA
Serpa, Beja
N630
Viar
C421
MEDINA AZAHARA 27
CORDOB
1
SIERRA DE ARACENA
C433
Odiel
C431
PALMA DEL RIO 25
H122
N435
Guadalquivir
NIV
ECIJA 26
MONT
N431
ITALICA 23
22
HUELVA
SEVILLA
CARMONA
N333
Blanco
Genil
2
A49
4 PALOS DE LA FRONTERA
C430
MONASTERIO DE LA RABIDA 3
Guadaira
OSUNA 21
EL ROCIO 5
C422
6
A4
PARQUE NACIONAL DE DOÑANA
KEY
Freeway
Major road
Minor road
Scenic route
River
Viewpoint
ANTEQU
EL TO
SANLUCAR DE LA BARRAMEDA
7
C441
N342
GARGAN
DEL CHOR
11
RONDA 13
8
ARCOS DE LA FRONTERA 12
JEREZ DE LA FRONTERA
PUEBLOS BLANCOS
MARB
9 CADIZ
C346
MEDINA SIDONIA
C341
16
N340
C3331
N340
COSTA DEL
COSTA DE LA LUZ
10
ALGECIRAS 14
15 GIBRALTAR
TARIFA
0 kilometers 25
0 miles 25

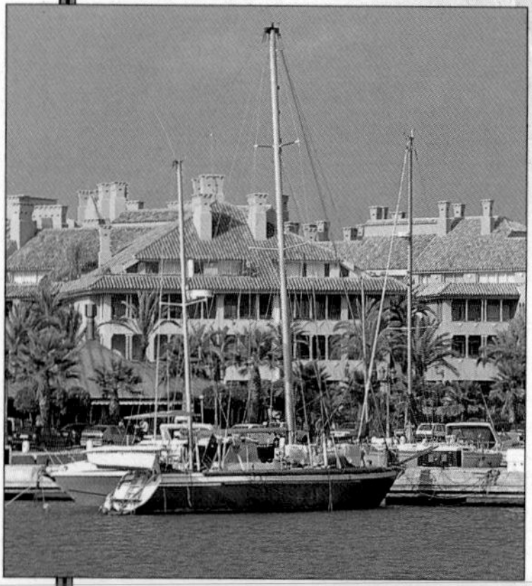

The stylish marina at Sotogrande

GETTING AROUND

Andalusia has a modern network of freeways, with the principal NIV from Madrid following the Guadalquivir valley to Córdoba, Seville and Cádiz. The fast AVE train links Seville and Córdoba with Madrid. Although most other large towns are on the rail network, services may be infrequent. Buses – sometimes slow – cover most of the regions; a car is needed to explore remoter areas. The main airports are Málaga, Seville, Jerez, and Gibraltar.

Singers in festive spirit at a village christening

SIGHTS AT A GLANCE

The famed *jamón ibérico* hanging in a bar in Jabugo, Sierra de Aracena

Sierra de Aracena **1**

Huelva. 🚌 *El Repilado*. 🚌 *Aracena*.
i *Aracena, (959) 12 83 55.*

THIS WILD MOUNTAIN RANGE is
one of the most remote
and least visited corners of
Andalusia. On the hill-
side above its main
town, Aracena, are
the ruins of a Moorish
fort. The hill is pitted
with caverns, and in
one of these, the **Gruta
de las Maravillas**, is a
lake in a chamber hung
with many stalactites.
The village of **Jabugo**
is famed for the tastiest
cured ham in Spain,
jamón ibérico, or *pata
negra (see p401).*
Off the N435, going
south, are the giant pit mines at
Minas de Riotinto, where iron,
copper, and silver have been
exploited since Phoenician
times. The **Museo Minero** in
the village traces the history
of the Rio Tinto Company.

**Bronze jug, Museo
Provincial, Huelva**

🏕 Gruta de las Maravillas
Calle San José. **(** *(959) 12 83 55.*
🕐 *daily.* 🎟

🏛 Museo Minero
Plaza del Museo. **(** *(959) 59 00 25.*
🕐 *Tue–Sun.* 🎟

Huelva **2**

Huelva. 🏔 *142,000.* 🚊 🚌 **i**
Avda Alemania 12, (959) 25 74 03.
📅 *Fri.* 🎎 *Las Colombinas (Aug 3).*

FOUNDED AS ONUBA by the
Phoenicians, Huelva had
its grandest days as a Roman
port. It was almost wiped out
in the great Lisbon earthquake
of 1755. It is an industrial city
today, sprawling around the
waterfront on the Río Odiel.
Columbus's departure for the
New World *(see p52)* from
Palos de la Frontera, across the
Río Odiel estuary, is celebrated
in the exhibits of the excellent **Museo Provincial**,
which also charts the history of the Riotinto mines.
To the east of the center,
the Barrio Reina Victoria
is a bizarre example of
English mock-Tudor
suburban bungalows
built by the Rio Tinto
Company for its workers
in the early 20th century.
South of the town, at
Punta del Sebo, the
Monumento a Colón,
a rather bleak statue of
Columbus created by Gertrude
Vanderbilt Whitney in 1929,
dominates the Odiel estuary.

ENVIRONS: There are three resorts with sandy beaches near
Huelva: **Punta Umbria**, on a
promontory next to the bird-
rich wetlands of the Marismas
del Odiel; **Isla Cristina**, which
is also an important fishing
port and has excellent seafood
restaurants; and **Mazagón** with
miles of windswept dunes.
The hilly region east of
Huelva known as **El Condado**
produces several of Andalusia's
finest wines, and Bollullos del
Condado has the largest wine
cooperative in the region.
Niebla, nearby, has a Roman
bridge. The town walls and
12th-century **Castillo de los
Guzmanes** are both Moorish.

🏛 Museo Provincial
Alameda Sundheim 13. **(** *(959) 25
93 00.* 🕐 *Tue –Sat.* 🚹

♣ Castillo de los Guzmanes
C/ Castillo, Niebla. **(** *(959) 36 22 70.*
🕐 *Mon–Sat. Phone to arrange visit.*

Monasterio de la Rábida **3**

Huelva. 🚌 *from Palos de la Frontera.*
(*(959) 35 04 11.* 🕐 *Tue–Sun.* 🚹

FOUR KILOMETERS (2.5 miles)
to the north of Palos de la
Frontera is the Franciscan
Monasterio de la Rábida,
founded in the 15th century.
In 1491, a dejected Columbus
sought refuge here after his
plans to sail west to find the
East Indies had been rejected
by the Catholic Monarchs. Its
prior, Juan Pérez, fatefully used
his considerable influence as
Queen Isabella's confessor to
reverse the royal decision.
Inside, frescoes painted by
Daniel Vásquez Díaz in 1930
glorify the explorer's life and
discoveries. Also worth seeing
are the Mudéjar cloisters, the
flower-filled gardens, and the
beamed chapterhouse.

Frescoes depicting the life of Columbus at the Monasterio de la Rábida

Palos de la Frontera ❹

Huelva. 👥 7,000. 🏢 ℹ️ C/ Rábida 3, (959) 35 08 51. 🔄 Sat. 🎉 Virgen de Santa María de la Rábida (Aug 3 & 16).

COLUMBUS PUT TO SEA on August 3, 1492, from Palos, the home town of his two captains, the brothers Martín and Vicente Pinzón. Martín's former home, the **Casa Museo de Martín Alonso Pinzón**, is now a small museum of exploration, and his statue stands in the main square.

The 15th-century **Iglesia de San Jorge** has a fine portal, through which Columbus left after hearing Mass before leaving to board his caravel, the *Santa María*. The pier is now forlornly silted up.

ENVIRONS: In the beautiful white town of **Moguer** are treasures such as the 16th-century hermitage of Nuestra Señora de Montemayor and the Neo-Classical town hall *(ayuntamiento)*. The **Convento de Santa Clara** and the Monasterio de San Francisco have pretty cloisters.

🏛️ **Casa Museo de Martín Alonso Pinzón**
Calle Colón 28. 📞 (959) 35 01 99. 🔄 Tue –Sun.
🔒 **Convento de Santa Clara**
Plaza de las Monjas. 📞 (959) 37 01 07. 🔄 Tue –Sat. ⚫ public hols. 🎫

El Rocío ❺

Huelva. 👥 1,200. 🏢 ℹ️ Avda de la Canaliega, (959) 44 26 84. 🔄 Tue. 🎉 Romería (May/Jun).

BORDERING the wetlands of the Parque Nacional de Doñana *(see pp 440–41)*, El Rocío is famous for its annual *romería*, which sees almost a million people converge on the village. Many of the pilgrims travel from distant parts of Spain, some on gaudily decorated ox-carts, to visit the **Iglesia de Nuestra Señora del Rocío**. A statue of the Virgin in the church is believed to have performed miraculous healings since 1280. Early on the Monday morning, men from Almonte fight to carry the statue in procession, and the crowd clambers onto the float to touch the image.

Iglesia de Nuestra Señora del Rocío, El Rocío

Parque Nacional de Doñana ❻

DOÑANA NATIONAL PARK is ranked among Europe's greatest wetlands. Together with its adjoining protected areas, the park covers in excess of 185,000 acres of marshes and sand dunes. The area used to be a hunting ground *(coto)* belonging

Bird-spotting from boat on the Guadalquivir

to the Dukes of Medina Sidonia. Because the land was never suitable for humans, wildlife was

able to flourish. In 1969, this large area became officially protected. In addition to a wealth of endemic species, thousands of migratory birds stop over in winter when the marshes become flooded again, after months of drought.

Shrub Vegetation
Backing the sand dunes is a thick carpet of lavender, rock rose, and other low shrubs.

Umbrella Pine
This species of pine tree (Pinus pinea) *thrives in the wide dune belt, putting roots deep into the sand. The trees may get buried beneath the dunes.*

Coastal Dunes
Softly rounded, white dunes, up to 30 m (100 ft) high, fringe the park's coastal edge. The dunes, ribbed by prevailing winds off the Atlantic, shift constantly.

Monte de Doñana, the wooded area behind the sand dunes, provides shelter for lynx, deer, and boar.

The Interior
The number of visitors to the park's interior is strictly controlled to ensure minimal environmental impact. The only way to view the wildlife here is on officially guided day tours.

KEY

▢	Marshes
▢	Dunes
•••	National park boundary
•••	Protected area
▬	Road
☀	Viewpoint
ℹ	Tourist information
P	Parking
🚌	Bus stop

Deer
Fallow deer (Dama dama) *and larger red deer* (Cervus elaphus) *roam the park. Stags engage in fierce contests in late summer as they prepare for breeding.*

Wild cattle use the marshes as watering holes

Imperial Eagle
The imperial eagle (Aquila heliaca adalberti) *is one of Doñana's rarest birds.*

Greater Flamingo
During the winter months, the salty lakes and marshes provide the beautiful, pink greater flamingo (Phoenicopterus ruber) *with crustaceans, its main diet.*

THE LYNX'S LAST REFUGE

The lynx is one of Europe's rarest mammals. In Doñana about 60 pairs of Spanish lynx *(Lynx pardellus)* have found a refuge. They have yellow-brown fur with dark brown spots and pointed ears with black tufts. Research is under way into this shy, nocturnal animal, which tends to stay hidden in scrub. It feeds mainly on rabbits and ducks, but might catch an unguarded fawn.

The elusive lynx, seen only with patience

Río Guadiamar

Marisma de Iznaícazar

Marisma Gallega

Río Guadalquivir

Sanlúcar de Barrameda

0 kilometers   5

0 miles   5

Sanlúcar de Barrameda ❼

Cádiz. 🏠 55,000. 🚉 ❶ *Calzada del Ejército, (956) 36 61 10.* 🚍 *Wed.* 🎏 *Exaltación al Río Guadalquivir and horse races (mid-Aug).*

A FISHING PORT at the mouth of the Río Guadalquivir, Sanlúcar is overlooked by a Moorish **castle**. This was the departure point for Columbus's third voyage in 1498 and also for Magellan's 1519 expedition to circumnavigate the globe.

Sanlúcar is best known for its light, dry manzanilla sherry made by, among other producers, **Bodegas Barbadillo**. Boats from the dock take visitors across the river to the Parque Nacional de Doñana *(see pp440–41).*

ENVIRONS: Chipiona, along the coast, is a lively little resort town with an excellent beach. The walled town of **Lebrija**, inland, enjoys views over vineyards. Its Iglesia de Santa María de la Oliva is a reconsecrated 12th-century Almohad mosque.

🍷 **Bodegas Barbadillo**
C/ Luis de Eguilaz 11. ☎ *(956) 36 08 94.* 🕐 *Thu (by appointment).* ♿

Entrance to the Barbadillo bodega in Sanlúcar de Barrameda

Jerez de la Frontera ❽

Cádiz. 🏠 190,000. ✈ 🚉 🚍 ❶ *Alameda Cristina 7, (956) 33 11 50.* 🚍 *Mon.* 🎏 *Grape Harvest (Sep).*

J EREZ IS THE CAPITAL of sherry production *(see pp402–403)*, and many bodegas can be visited. Among the well-known names are **González Byass** and **Pedro Domecq**.

The city is also famous for its **Real Escuela Andaluza de Arte Ecuestre**, a school of equestrian skills. There are public dressage displays on Thursdays. If you visit on another day you may be able to watch the horses being trained.

The **Museo de Relojes**, nearby, has one of the largest clock collections in Europe. On the Plaza de San Juan, the 18th-century **Palacio de Penmartín** houses the Centro Andaluz de Flamenco, where exhibitions give a good introduction to this music and dance tradition *(see pp406–407)*. The partially restored 11th-century **Alcázar** encompasses a well-preserved mosque, now a church. Just to the north is the **cathedral**, whose most interesting exhibit, *The Sleeping Girl* by Zurbarán, is in the sacristy.

ENVIRONS: The port of **El Puerto de Santa María** exports great quantities of sherry. Here, too, several bodegas can be visited including **Osborne** and **Terry**. The town also has a 13th-century castle and one of the largest and most famous bullrings in Spain.

🏟 **Real Escuela Andaluza de Arte Ecuestre**
Avda de Abrantes. ☎ *(956) 31 11 11.* 🕐 *Mon–Fri.* ● *public hols.* 🎦 ♿
🏛 **Museo de Relojes**
Calle Cervantes. ☎ *(956) 18 21 00.* 🕐 *Mon–Sat.* ● *public hols.* 🎦 ♿
🏟 **Palacio de Penmartín**
Plaza de San Juan 1. ☎ *(956) 34 92 65.* 🕐 *Mon–Fri.* ● *public hols.*
♣ **Alcázar**
Alameda Vieja. 🕐 *Mon–Sat.* ● *public hols.* ♿
🍷 **Sherry Bodegas**
🕐 *phone in advance for tour times.*
González Byass, C/ Manuel María González 12, Jerez. ☎ *(956) 34 00 00.*
Pedro Domecq, C/ San Ildefonso 3, Jerez. ☎ *(956) 15 15 00.* **Sandeman**, C/ Pizarro 10, Jerez. ☎ *(956) 30 11 04.* **Osborne**, C/ de los Moros, Puerto de Santa María. ☎ *(956) 85 52 11.* **Terry**, C/ Santísima Trinidad, Puerto de Santa María. ☎ *(956) 48 30 00.*

Real Escuela Andaluza de Arte Ecuestre, Jerez de la Frontera

Cádiz ⑨

Egyptian mask, Museo de Cádiz

JUTTING OUT OF the Bay of Cádiz, and almost entirely surrounded by water, Cádiz lays claim to being Europe's oldest city. Legend names Hercules as its founder, although history credits the Phoenicians with establishing the town of Gadir in 1100 BC. Occupied by the Carthaginians, Romans, and Moors in turn, the city also prospered after the Reconquest *(see pp50–51)* on wealth taken from the New World. In 1587 Sir Francis Drake sacked the city in the first of many British attacks in the war for world trade. In 1812 Cádiz briefly became Spain's capital when the nation's first constitution was declared here *(see p59)*.

VISITORS' CHECKLIST

Cádiz. 🚗 155,000. 🚉 Plaza de Sevilla, (956) 25 43 01. 🚌 Plaza de la Hispanidad, (956) 21 17 63. ℹ️ Calle Calderón de la Barca 1, (956) 21 13 13. 🏛 Mon. 🎭 Carnival (Feb/Mar), Día de la Patrona (Oct 7).

Exploring Cádiz

The joy of visiting Cádiz is to wander along the waterfront with its well-tended gardens and open squares before exploring the old town, which is full of narrow alleys full of market and street life.

The pride of the city is its Carnival *(see p439)* – a riotous explosion of festivities, fancy dress, singing and drinking.

🔒 Catedral

Known as the Catedral Nueva (New Cathedral) because it was built over the site of an older one, this Baroque and Neo-Classical church, with its dome of golden yellow tiles, is one of Spain's largest. Its carved stalls came from a Carthusian monastery. In the crypt is the tomb of the composer Manuel de Falla (1876–1946), a native of Cádiz. The cathedral's treasures are stored in the adjacent museum.

🏛 Museo de Cádiz

Plaza de Mina. 📞 (956) 21 22 81. 🕐 Tue–Sun. 🔴 public hols. ♿
On the ground floor of this spacious museum there are archaeological exhibits charting the history of Cádiz, including Phoenician stone sarcophagi and statues of Roman emperors. Upstairs is one of the largest art galleries in Andalusia, displaying works by Rubens, Zurbarán, and Murillo, as well as paintings by contemporary Spanish artists. On the third floor is a collection of puppets made for village fiestas. Some more recent ones satirize current political figures.

🔒 Oratorio de San Felipe Neri

This 18th-century church has been a shrine to liberalism since 1812. In that year, as Napoleon tightened his grip on Spain during the War of Independence *(see pp58–9)*, a provisional government assembled here to try to lay the foundations of Spain's first constitutional monarchy. The liberal constitution it declared was bold but ineffectual.

Zurbarán's *Saint Bruno in Ecstasy*, in the Museo de Cádiz

CÁDIZ CATHEDRAL

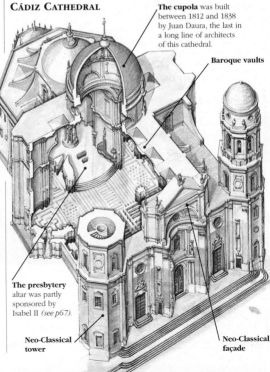

The cupola was built between 1812 and 1838 by Juan Daura, the last in a long line of architects of this cathedral.

Baroque vaults

The presbytery altar was partly sponsored by Isabel II *(see p67)*.

Neo-Classical tower

Neo-Classical façade

Fishing boats at the resort of Zahara de los Atunes on the Costa de la Luz

Costa de la Luz ⑩

Málaga. 🚉 Cádiz. 🚌 Cádiz, Tarifa.
ℹ️ Cádiz, (956) 24 01 61.

THE COSTA DE LA LUZ (Coast of Light) between Cádiz and Tarifa, at Spain's southernmost tip, is an unspoiled, windswept stretch of coast characterized by strong, pure light – the source of its name. From the Sierra del Cabrito, to the west of Algeciras, it is often possible to see the outline of Tangier and the parched Moroccan landscape below the purple-tinged Rif mountains across the narrow Strait of Gibraltar.

Tarifa is named after an 8th-century Moorish commander, Tarif ben Maluk, who landed there with his forces during the Moorish conquest *(see pp48–9)*. Later, Tarifa and its 10th-century castle were defended by the legendary hero Guzmán, during a siege by the Moors in 1292.

Tarifa has since become the windsurfing capital of Europe. The breezes that blow onto this coast also drive the numerous wind turbines visible in the hills above Tarifa.

Off the N340, at the end of a long, narrow road that strikes out across a wilderness of cacti, sunflowers, and lone cork trees, is **Zahara de los Atunes**, a modest tourist resort with a few hotels. **Conil de la Frontera**, to the west, is busier and more built up.

The English admiral, Nelson, defeated a Spanish and French fleet off **Cabo de Trafalgar** in 1805, but died in the battle.

A Tour Around the Pueblos Blancos ⑫

INSTEAD OF SETTLING on Andalusia's plains, where they would have fallen prey to bandits, some Andalusians chose to live in fortified hilltop towns and villages. These are known as *pueblos blancos* (white towns) because they are whitewashed in the Moorish tradition *(see p22)*. They are working agricultural towns today, but touring them will reveal a host of references to the past.

Ubrique ②
Nestling at the foot of the Sierra de Ubrique, this *pueblo* is known for its flourishing leather industry.

Jimena de la Frontera ⑨
Set amid hills, where wild bulls graze among cork and olive trees, this town has a ruined Moorish castle.

↑ SEVILLA

Arcos de la Frontera ①

CADIZ, JEREZ

C344

Embalse los Huron

Charco de los Hurones

CA521

Majacette

CA503

La Sauceda

KEY

▬ Tour route

= Other roads

TIPS FOR DRIVERS

Tour length: 205 km (127 miles).
Stopping-off points: There are places to stay and eat at all of these pueblos, but Ronda has the widest range of hotels (see p566) and restaurants (see p605). Arcos has a parador (see p563).

Gaucín ⑧
From here there are unsurpassed vistas over the Mediterranean, the Atlantic, the Rock of Gibraltar and across the strait to the Rif mountains of North Africa.

0 kilometers   10

0 miles   5

Arcos de la Frontera ⑪

Cádiz. 👥 *30,000.* 🚍 ℹ️ *Calle Cuesta de Belén, (956) 70 22 64.* 🅿️ *Fri.* 🎭 *Velada de Nuestra Señora de las Nieves (Aug 4–6).*

ALTHOUGH LEGEND has it that a son of Noah founded Arcos, it is more probable that it was the Iberians. It gained the name Arcobriga in the Roman era and, under the Caliphate of Córdoba *(see p48)*, became the Moorish stronghold of Medina Arkosh. It is an archetypal white town, with a labyrinthine old quarter twisting up to a ruined castle.

On the Plaza de España, at the top of the town, are the **parador** *(see p563)* and the **Iglesia de Santa María de la Asunción**, a Late Gothic-Mudéjar building noted for its choir stalls and altarpiece. The huge, Gothic **Iglesia de San Pedro**, perched on the edge of a cliff formed by the Río Guadalete, is a striking building. Nearby is the **Palacio del Mayorazgo**, which has an ornate Renaissance façade. The **town hall** *(ayuntamiento)* has a fine Mudéjar ceiling.

ENVIRONS: In the 15th-century the Guzmán family was granted the dukedom of **Medina Sidonia**, a white town atop a conical hill, southwest of Arcos de la Frontera. The family grew wealthy from its investments in the Americas and, as a result, Medina Sidonia became one of the most important ducal seats in Spain. The Gothic Iglesia de Santa María la Coronada is the town's finest building. It contains a notable collection of Renaissance religious art.

Iglesia de Santa María de la Asunción in Arcos de la Frontera

🏛️ **Palacio del Mayorazgo**
C/ San Pedro 2. ☎ *(956) 70 30 13.*
⭕ *Mon–Fri.* ⬤ *public hols.* ♿

🏛️ **Ayuntamiento**
Plaza Cavildo. ☎ *(956) 70 00 02.*
⭕ *by permission.* ⬤ *public hols.*

Zahara de la Sierra ③
Fanning out below a castle ruin, this fine *pueblo blanco* has been declared a national monument.

Grazalema ④
This village in the Sierra de Grazalema has the highest rainfall in Spain.

Ronda la Vieja ⑤
Significant remains of the Roman town of Acinipo, including a theater, can be visited.

Setenil ⑥
Some of the streets of this unusual white town, which climbs up the sides of a gorge, are covered by rock overhangs. The gorge was carved out of volcanic tufa rock by the Río Trejo.

Ronda ⑦
(see pp446–7)

Street-by-Street: Ronda ⑬

Plate hand-painted in Ronda

O NE OF THE MOST spectacularly located cities in Spain, Ronda sits on a massive rocky outcrop, straddling a precipitous limestone cleft. Because of its impregnable position, this town was one of the last Moorish bastions, finally falling to the Christians in 1485. On the south side perches a classic Moorish *pueblo blanco (see pp444–5)* of cobbled alleys, window grilles, and dazzling whitewash – most historic sights are in this part of the town. Located in El Mercadillo, the newer town, is one of the oldest bullrings in Spain.

★ Puente Nuevo
An impressive feat of 18th-century civil engineering, the "New Bridge" over the 100-m (330-ft) deep Tajo gorge joins old and new Ronda.

Convento de Santo Domingo was the local headquarters of the Inquisition *(see p264).*

To El Mercadillo, Plaza de Toros, parador (see p566), and tourist information

Casa del Rey Moro
From this 18th-century mansion, built on the foundations of a Moorish palace, 365 steps lead down to the river.

Mirador El Campillo (viewpoint)

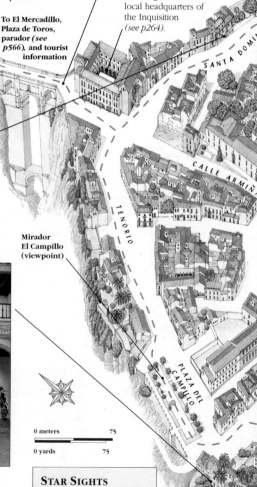

SANTA DOMIN

CALLE ARMIÑA

TENORIO

PLAZA DEL CAMPILLO

0 meters   75
0 yards   75

★ Palacio Mondragón
Much of this palace was rebuilt following the Reconquest (see pp50–51), but its arcaded patio is adorned with original Moorish mosaics and plasterwork.

STAR SIGHTS

★ **Puente Nuevo**

★ **Palacio Mondragón**

Palacio del Marqués de Salvatierra
*Bizarre images of biblical scenes and
South American Indians embellish
the façade of this palace, built in
Renaissance style in the 18th century.*

To Puente Viejo,
Baños Árabes

Santa María la Mayor
*A minaret and a Muslim
prayer niche survive from
the 13th-century mosque
that once stood on the site
of this church.*

**Minarete San
Sebastián** is a
remnant of a
14th-century
mosque.

MARQUES DE SALVATIERRA

CARMEN

ESCALERA

ARMIÑAN

PLAZA
DUQUESA
DE PARCENT

Ayuntamiento
*The town hall was remodeled in the
20th century and incorporates parts
of older buildings. It has a two-tier
arcaded façade and Mudéjar ceiling.*

KEY

– – – Suggested route

BULLFIGHTING AT RONDA

Ronda's Plaza de Toros is the spiritual home
of bullfighting. Inaugurated in 1785, it is one
of the oldest, most important bullrings in Spain.
In September, aficionados travel from all over
the country for the singular atmosphere of
the Corrida Goyesca, and millions watch it on
television. It is the dream of
every aspiring matador to fight
at Ronda. The classic Ronda
style (more severe than
the exuberant School of
Seville) was de-
veloped by Pedro
Romero. Born in
1754, he is widely
considered to be the
father of modern
bullfighting.

**Romero, who killed
over 6,000 bulls**

Algeciras ⑭

Cádiz. 🏘 *150,000.* 🚉 ℹ️ *Calle Juan de la Cierva, (956) 57 26 36.* 🛳 *Tue.* 🎊 *Feria Real (Jun 24–Jul 2).*

FROM THE INDUSTRIAL city of Algeciras, there are spectacular views of Gibraltar, 14 km (9 miles) away across its bay. The city is a major fishing port and Europe's main gateway for ferries between Europe and North Africa, especially Tangier and Spain's overseas territories of Ceuta and Melilla.

Gibraltar ⑮

British Crown Colony. 🏘 *30,000.* 🚉 ℹ️ *32B Rosia Rd, (9567) 749 50.* 🛳 *Mon.* 🎊 *Nat Day (Sep 10).*

THE HIGH, ROCKY headland of Gibraltar was signed over to Britain "in perpetuity" at the Treaty of Utrecht in 1713 *(see p58)*. Today, about 4 million people, mostly intent on duty-free shopping, stream across the the border every year from La Línea de la Concepción in Spain.

Among the chief sights of Gibraltar are those testifying to its strategic military importance

St. Michael's Cave. During World War II it served as a hospital.

over the centuries. Halfway up the famous Rock are an 8th-century Moorish castle, whose **keep** is still used as a prison, and 80 km (50 miles) of **siege tunnels** housing storerooms and barracks. **St. Michael's Cave**, which served as a hospital during World War II, is now used for classical concerts.

The **Apes' Den**, near Europa Point, Gibraltar's southernmost tip, is home to the tailless apes. Legend says that the British will keep the Rock only as long as the apes remain there. A cable car takes visitors to the **Top of the Rock** at 450 m (1,475 ft). **Gibraltar Museum** charts the colony's history.

🏰 **The Keep, Siege Tunnels, St. Michael's Cave, Apes' Den**
Upper Rock Area. 🎫 *(9567) 424 00.* ⭕ *daily.* ⬤ *Jan 1, Dec 25.* 🎟
🏛 **Gibraltar Museum**
18 Bombhouse Lane. 🎫 *(9567) 742 89.* ⭕ *Mon–Sat.* ⬤ *public hols.* 🎟

The Costa del Sol

THANKS TO ITS AVERAGE of 300 days' sunshine a year and its varied coastline, the Costa del Sol, between Gibraltar and Málaga, offers a full range of beach-based vacations and water sports. Complementing the sophistication and luxury of Marbella are many other popular resorts aimed at the mass market. More than 30 of Europe's finest golf courses lie just inland.

Puerto Banús is Marbella's ostentatious marina. The expensive shops, restaurant and glittering nightlife refle the wealth of its clientele.

Estepona's quiet evenings make it popular with families with young children. Behind the big hotels are old squares shaded by orange trees.

Marina at Sotogrande *is an exclusive resort of luxury villas. The marina is fronted by good seafood restaurants.*

San Pedro de Alcántar
Puerto
Estepona
Sotogrande
San Roque
Algeciras
Gibraltar
Tarifa

San Pedro de Alcántara *is a quiet resort with a modern marina and stylish tourist developments.*

Yachts and motorboats in the exclusive marina of Marbella – the summer home of the international jet set

Marbella ⑯

Málaga. 🏠 *80,000.* 🚉 🅸 *Glorieta de la Fontanilla, (95) 277 14 42.* 🚌 *Mon.* 🎉 *San Bernabé (Jun 11).*

MARBELLA IS ONE of Europe's most exclusive resorts, frequented by royalty and film stars. In winter, the major attraction is the golf. Among the delights of the old town, with its spotlessly clean alleys, squares, and fashionable shops and restaurants, is the **Iglesia de Nuestra Señora de la Encarnación**. Some of Picasso's least-known work can be seen in the **Museo de Grabado Contemporáneo**.

Taking part in the nightlife means bringing a full wallet; luckily the beaches – Babaloo, Victor's, Don Carlos, Cabopino, and Las Dunas – are free.

🏛 **Museo de Grabado Contemporáneo**
C/ Hospital Bazan. 📞 *(95) 282 50 35.* 🕐 *Mon – Fri.* ⬤ *public hols.* 📷

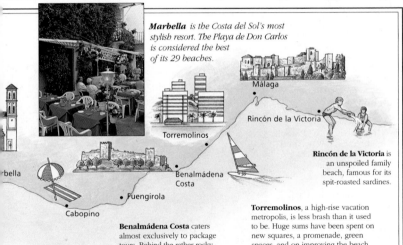

Marbella is the Costa del Sol's most stylish resort. The Playa de Don Carlos is considered the best of its 29 beaches.

Málaga

Rincón de la Victoria

Torremolinos

Rincón de la Victoria is an unspoiled family beach, famous for its spit-roasted sardines.

Benalmádena Costa

Fuengirola

Cabopino

Benalmádena Costa caters almost exclusively to package tours. Behind the rather rocky beaches and very large marina is a plethora of tourist attractions.

Torremolinos, a high-rise vacation metropolis, is less brash than it used to be. Huge sums have been spent on new squares, a promenade, green spaces, and on improving the beach with millions of tons of golden sand.

Cabopino, on a not-too-crowded stretch of coast, is a wide, sandy, nudist beach beside a modern marina.

0 kilometers   10

0 miles   10

PESCADO FRESCO DE FUENGIROLA

Fuengirola still has an active fishing port – as these boxes of fresh fish suggest – although it is better known today as a package-tour resort with a chiefly British clientele. It has a spectacular backdrop of steep, ocher mountains.

The main façade of Málaga's cathedral, consecrated in 1588

Málaga ⑰

Málaga. 🏛 *600,000.* ✈ 🚉 🚌
ℹ️ *Pasaje de Chinitas 4, (95) 221 34 45.* 🚌 *Sun.* 🎭 *Carnival (Feb/Mar), Feria (second Sat–third Sun of Aug).*

MÁLAGA, the second largest city in Andalusia, is today a thriving port, just as it was in Phoenician times (when it was known as Malaca), and again under the Romans and then the Moors. It also flourished during the 19th century, when sweet Málaga wine *(see p402)* was one of Europe's most popular drinks – until phylloxera ravaged the area's vineyards in 1876.

The **cathedral** was begun in 1528 by Diego de Siloé, but it is a bizarre mix of styles. The half-built second tower, abandoned in 1765 when funds ran out, gave the cathedral its nickname: La Manquita ("the one-armed one").

Málaga's **Museo de Bellas Artes** has paintings by Ribera, Murillo, Zurbarán, and Morales, and some childhood sketches by Pablo Picasso. The **Casa Natal de Picasso**, where the painter spent his early years, is now the headquarters of the Picasso Foundation.

Málaga's vast **Alcazaba** *(see p49)* was built between the 8th–11th centuries. There is a partially excavated Roman amphitheater by its entrance, but the real attraction is the display of Phoenician, Roman, and Moorish artifacts in the **Museo Arqueológico**.

On the hill directly behind the Alcazaba are the ruins of the **Castillo de Gibralfaro**, a 14th-century Moorish castle.

ENVIRONS: In the beautiful hills to the north and east of Málaga is the **Parque Natural de los Montes de Málaga**. Wildlife, such as eagles and wild boars, thrive here amid the scent of lavender and wild herbs. Walkers can follow a number of scenic marked trails. Going north on the C345 you can also visit a small preserved winery of the 1840s.

🏛 **Museo de Bellas Artes**
Calle San Agustín 8. 📞 *(95) 221 83 82.* ⏰ *Tue–Sun.* 🎭
♦ **Alcazaba and Museo Arqueológico**
Calle Alcazabilla. 📞 *(95) 221 60 05.* ⏰ *Tue–Sun.* 🎭

Garganta del Chorro ⑱

Málaga. 🚉 *El Chorro.* 🚌 *Parque Ardeles.* ℹ️ *Avenida de la Constitución, Álora, (95) 249 83 80.*

UP THE FERTILE Guadalhorce valley, just beyond the village of El Chorro, is one of the geographical wonders of Andalusia. The Garganta del Chorro is an immense chasm, 180 m (590 ft) deep and in places only 10 m (33 ft) wide, cut by the river through a limestone mountain. Downstream, a hydroelectric plant detracts from the wildness of the gorge.

From the village, for a true sense of the gorge's dizzying dimensions, take the **Camino del Rey**, a catwalk clinging to the rock face and leading to a bridge across the gorge.

ENVIRONS: Álora, a classic white town *(see pp444–5)* with a ruined Moorish hilltop castle and an 18th-century church, lies 12 km (7 miles) down the valley.

Along the twisting MA441 from Álora is the village of **Carratraca**. In the 19th and early 20th centuries, Europe's highest society traveled here for the healing powers of the sulfurous springs. These days, Carratraca has a faded glory – water still gushes out at 700 liters (185 gal) a minute, and the outdoor baths remain open, but they are little used.

The Garganta del Chorro, rising high above the Guadalhorce river

Weathered limestone formations in El Torcal

El Torcal ⑲

Málaga. 🚌 *Antequera.* 🚌 *Antequera.* ℹ️ *Antequera, (95) 270 25 05.*

A MASSIVE EXPOSED HUMP of limestone upland that has been slowly weathered into bizarre rock formations and caves, the Parque Natural del Torcal is very popular with hikers. Trails lead from a visitors' center in the middle. Walks of up to two hours are marked by yellow arrows; longer walks by red.

The park is also a pleasure for natural historians, with fox and weasel populations, and colonies of eagles, hawks, and vultures. It also protects rare plants and flowers, among them species of wild orchid.

Antequera ⑳

Málaga. 🏛 *40,000.* 🚌 🚌 ℹ️ *Pl San Sebastián 7, (95) 270 25 05.* 🚌 *Sun.* 🎊 *Ferias (end May & mid-Aug).*

THIS BUSY MARKET TOWN was strategically important first as Roman Anticaria and later as a Moorish border fortress defending Granada.

Of its many churches, the **Iglesia de Nuestra Señora del Carmen**, with its vast Baroque altarpiece, is not to be missed. At the opposite end of the town is the 19th-century **Plaza de Toros**, with a museum of bullfighting.

The hilltop **castle** was built in the 13th century on the site of a Roman fort. Visitors can walk round the castle walls by approaching through the 16th-century Arco de los Gigantes.

There are excellent views of Antequera from the Torre del Papabellotas on the best-preserved part of the wall.

In the town below, the 18th-century **Palacio de Nájera** is the setting for the Municipal Museum, the star exhibit of which is a splendid Roman bronze statue of a boy.

The massive **dolmens**, just outside the town, are thought to be the burial chambers of tribal leaders and date from around 2500–2000 BC.

ENVIRONS: Laguna de la Fuente de Piedra, north of Antequera, teems with bird life, including huge flocks of flamingoes, which arrive to breed after wintering in West Africa. A road off the N334 leads to a lakeside viewing point. There is a visitors' center in Fuente de Piedra village. To the east, also off the N334, is **Archidona**, worth a stop to admire its extraordinary, 18th-century, octagonal Plaza

The triumphal, 16th-century Arco de los Gigantes, Antequera

Ochavada built in French style, but which also incorporates traditional Andalusian features.

🎪 **Plaza de Toros**
Carretera de Sevilla. 📞 *(95) 270 26 76.* 🕐 *Tue–Sun.* **Museo Taurino** 🕐 *Sat, Sun, public hols.*
🏛 **Palacio de Nájera**
Coso Viejo. 📞 *(95) 270 40 51.*
🕐 *Tue–Sun.* ● *public hols.* 📷 ♿

Osuna ㉑

Sevilla. 🏛 *17,500.* 🚌 🚌 ℹ️ *Casa de Cultura, Calle Sevilla 22, (95) 481 22 58.* 🚌 *Mon.* 🎊 *San Alcadio (Jan 12), Virgen de la Consolación (Sep 8).*

Palacio del Marqués de la Gomera, in Osuna, completed in 1770

O SUNA was once a key Roman garrison town. It rose again to prominence in the 16th century under the Dukes of Osuna, who wielded immense power. In the 1530s they founded the **Colegiata de Santa María**, a grand church with a Baroque reredos and paintings by José de Ribera. This was followed in 1548 by the **University**, a rather severe building with a beautiful patio. Some fine mansions, among them the **Palacio del Marqués de la Gomera**, also reflect the town's former glory.

ENVIRONS: To the east lies **Estepa**, whose modern-day fame rests on its biscuits – *polvorones* and *mantecados* *(see p401)*. The Iglesia del Carmen has a black and white, Baroque façade.

Tomb of Servilia in the Roman necropolis in Carmona

Carmona ㉒

Sevilla. 🏛 *25,000.* 🚉 🚌 ℹ️ *Plaza de San Fernando 14, (95) 419 09 55.* 🛒 *Mon & Thu.* 🎭 *Feria (May), Fiestas Patronales (Sep 8–16).*

C ARMONA IS THE FIRST major town east of Seville on the NIV, its old quarter built on a hill above the sprawling suburbs on the plain. Beyond the **Puerta de Sevilla**, a gateway in the Moorish city walls, is a dense cluster of mansions, Mudéjar churches, squares, and winding, cobbled streets.

The Plaza de San Fernando has a feeling of grandeur that is characterized by the Renaissance façade of the old **Ayuntamiento**. The present town hall, set just off the square, dates from the 18th century; in its courtyard are some Roman mosaics. Close by is the **Iglesia de Santa María la Mayor**. Built in the 15th century over a mosque, whose patio still survives, this is the finest of Carmona's churches.

Dominating the town are the ruins of the **Alcázar del Rey Pedro**, once a palace of Pedro I, known as Pedro the Cruel. Parts of it now form a parador *(see p563)*.

Just outside Carmona is the **Necrópolis Romana**, the extensive remains of a Roman burial ground. A museum on the site displays items found in the graves, including statues, glass, and jewelry.

Roman mosaic from Itálica

🏛 **Ayuntamiento**
Calle Salvador 2. 📞 *(95) 414 00 11.* 🕐 *Mon–Sat.* 🔴 *public hols.*
⛪ **Necrópolis Romana**
Avenida Jorge Bonsor 9. 📞 *(95) 414 08 11.* 🕐 *Tue–Sun.* 🔴 *public hols.*

Itálica ㉓

Sevilla. 📞 *(95) 599 73 76.* 🚌 *from Seville.* 🕐 *Tue–Sun* 📷

I TALICA WAS FOUNDED in 206 BC by Scipio Africanus. One of the earliest Roman cities in Hispania *(see pp46–7)*, it grew to be one of the most important during the 2nd and 3rd centuries AD. Emperors Trajan and Hadrian were both born in the city, and the latter, who reigned from AD 117–138, added marble temples and other grand buildings. Archaeologists have speculated that the changing course of the Río Guadalquivir may have led to Itálica's subsequent demise during Moorish times.

Next to the vast but crumbling **amphitheater**, which once seated 25,000 people, is a display of finds from the site. More treasures are displayed in the Museo Arqueológico in Seville *(see p427)*.

Visitors are free to wander among the traces of Itálica's streets and admire the mosaic floors of villas. However, little remains of the city's temples or baths, as most of the stone and marble has been plundered over the centuries. Some better-preserved Roman

remains, including baths and a theater, can be seen in the village of **Santiponce**, just outside of the site.

Sierra Morena ㉔

Sevilla and Córdoba. 🚉 *Estación de Cazalla y Constantina.* 🚌 *Constantina, Cazalla.* ℹ️ *El Robledo, (95) 588 15 97.*

T HE SIERRA MORENA, clad in oak and pine woods, runs across the north of the provinces of Sevilla and Córdoba. It forms a natural border between Andalusia and the plains of neighboring Extremadura and La Mancha. Smaller sierras (ranges of hills) within the Sierra Morena chain are also named individually.

Fuente Obejuna, north of Córdoba, was immortalized by Lope de Vega *(see p280)* in his play about an uprising in 1476 against a local overlord. The Iglesia de San Juan Bautista in **Hinojosa del Duque** is a vast church in both Gothic and Renaissance styles. **Belalcázar** is dominated by the huge tower of a ruined 15th-century castle dominates. Storks nest on the church towers of the plateau of **Valle de los Pedroches**, east of Belalcázar.

Cazalla de la Sierra, the main town of the sierra north of Seville, is cosmopolitan, and popular with young *Sevillanos* on weekends. A unique, pungent concoction of cherry liqueur and anise, Liquor de Guindas, is produced here.

Constantina, to the east, is more peaceful and has superb views across the countryside.

A cow grazing in the pastures of the Sierra Morena north of Seville

Palma del Río 25

Córdoba. 🏠 19,000. 🚂 🚌
ℹ Casa de Cultura, Calle Gracia 15,
(957) 71 02 45. 🚌 Tue. 🎎 Ferias
(May 19–21 & Aug 18–20).

THE ROMANS sited a strategic
settlement here, on the
road between Córdoba and
Itálica, almost 2,000 years ago.
The remains of the 12th-
century city walls are a
reminder of the town's
frontier days under the
Almohads (see p50).
The **Iglesia de la
Asunción**, a Baroque
church, dates from
the 18th century.
The **Monasterio
de San Francisco**
is now a hotel (see
p566), and guests
can eat dinner in
the 15th-century
refectory of the
Franciscan monks.
Palma del Río is
the home town of
El Cordobés, one
of Spain's most
famous matadors.
His biography, *Or I'll Dress
You in Mourning*, paints a vivid picture of life in the town
and of the days of desperate
hardship that followed the
end of the Civil War.

**Bell tower,
Asunción**

ENVIRONS: One of the most
dramatic silhouettes in Southern Spain breaks the skyline
of **Almodóvar del Río**. The
Moorish castle – parts of it
dating from the 8th century –
stands on a hilltop over-
looking the whitewashed
town and fields of cotton.

♣ **Castillo de Almodóvar
del Río**
📞 (957) 63 51 16. ⬜ daily for
guided tours only.

Écija 26

Sevilla. 🏠 38,000. 🚌 ℹ Plaza de
España 1, (95) 590 02 40. 🚌 Thu.
🎎 Feria (Sep 21–4).

ÉCIJA IS NICKNAMED "the frying
pan of Andalusia" because
of its famously torrid climate.
In the searing heat, the palm
trees on the Plaza de España
provide some blissful shade.

This is an ideal place to sit and
observe daily life passing by,
and is also where people come
to stroll in the evening.
Écija has eleven Baroque
church steeples. Many of them
are adorned with gleaming
azulejos (see p420), and when
seen together they make a very
impressive sight. The most
florid of these is the **Iglesia
de Santa María**, which overlooks the Plaza de España. The
Iglesia de San Juan, with its
exquisite, brightly colored
bell tower, is a very close rival.
The façade of the **Palacio
de Peñaflor** is also in the
Baroque style. Its pink marble
doorway is topped by twisted
columns, and an attractive
wrought-iron balcony runs
along the whole front façade.

🏛 **Palacio de Peñaflor**
Calle Caballeros. 📞 (95) 483 02 73.
⬜ daily (courtyard only).

Medina Azahara 27

Córdoba. 📞 (957) 32 91 30. 🚌
Córdoba. ⬜ Tue–Sun. 🎫 ♿

THIS ONCE-GLORIOUS palace
was built in the 10th century for Caliph Abd al Rahman
III, who named it after his
favorite wife, Azahara. He
spared no expense in its construction, employing more than
15,000 mules, 4,000 camels, and
10,000 workers to bring build-

Detail of wood carving in the
main hall of Medina Azahara

ing materials from North Africa
and other parts of Andalusia.
The palace is built on three
levels and includes a mosque,
the caliph's residence, and
fine gardens (see pp404–405).
Marble, ebony, jasper, and
alabaster once adorned its
many halls, and it is believed
that shimmering pools of
quicksilver added lustre.
Unfortunately, the glory was
short-lived. The palace was
sacked by Berber invaders in
1010, and over subsequent
centuries it was ransacked for
its building materials. Now, the
ruins give only glimpses of its
former splendor – a Moorish
main hall, for instance, decorated with marble carvings,
still with its fine ceiling of
carved wood. The palace is
currently being restored, but so
far progress has been slow.

Trompe l'oeil on the ornate Baroque façade of the Palacio de Peñaflor, Écija

Street-by-Street: Córdoba ㉘

Statue of Maimónides

THE HEART OF CORDOBA is the old Jewish quarter, situated to the west of the Mezquita's towering walls. A walk around this area gives the sensation that little has changed since the 10th century when this was one of the greatest cities in the Western world. Wrought ironwork decorates cobbled streets too narrow for cars, where silversmiths create fine jewelry in their workshops. Most of the chief sights are here, while modern city life takes place some blocks north, around the Plaza de Tendillas. To the east of this square is the Plaza de la Corredera, a 17th-century arcaded square with a daily market.

Sinagoga
Hebrew script covers the walls of this 14th-century synagogue. Spain's only other synagogues are in Toledo (see p373).

Museo Taurino
A replica of the tomb of the famous torero, Manolete, and the hide of the bull that killed him (see p33) are the star exhibits in this museum of bullfighting.

The Capilla de San Bartolomé, in Mudéjar style, is decorated with elaborate plasterwork.

★ **Alcázar de los Reyes Cristianos**
Water terraces and fountains add to the tranquil atmosphere of the gardens belonging to the palace-fortress of the Catholic Monarchs (see pp52–3), built in the 14th century.

KEY

– – – Suggested route

STAR SIGHTS

★ **Alcázar de los Reyes Cristianos**

★ **Mezquita**

The Callejón de las Flores brims with colorful geraniums, that contrast with the whitewashed walls of this alley, leading to a tiny square.

VISITORS' CHECKLIST

Córdoba. 305,000. Avda de América, (957) 49 02 02. Avda Medina Azahara 29, (957) 23 64 74. Palacio de Congresos, Calle Torrijos 10, (957) 47 12 35. daily. Semana Santa (Easter Week), Cruces de Mayo (May 1–4), Festival de los Patios (May 5–11), Feria (late May). **Sinagoga** Tue–Sun. **Museo Taurino** Tue–Sun. **Alcázar de los Reyes Cristianos** Tue–Sun.

The Palacio Episcopal now houses the tourist office.

Moorish bronze stag from Medina Azahara, Museo Arqueológico

Exploring Córdoba

Córdoba lies on a sharp bend in the Río Guadalquivir, which is spanned by a Roman bridge linking the 14th-century Torre de la Calahorra and the old town. One of the most atmospheric squares in Andalusia is the Plaza de los Capuchinos. With its haunting stone calvary surrounded by wrought-iron lamps, it is particularly evocative when seen by moonlight.

⛫ Museo de Bellas Artes

Plaza del Potro 1. (957) 47 33 45. Tue–Sun.
Exhibits in a former charity hospital include sculptures by local artist Mateo Inurria (1867–1924) and works by Valdés Leal, Zurbarán, and Murillo of the Seville School.

⛫ Museo Arqueológico

Plaza Jerónimo Páez 7. (957) 47 40 11. Tue–Sun.
Located in a Renaissance mansion, displays include Roman mosaics, pottery, and relief carvings, and impressive finds from the Moorish era.

⛩ Palacio de Viana

Plaza Don Gome 2. (957) 48 01 34. Thu–Tue. June 1–15.
Furniture, tapestries, paintings, and porcelain are displayed in the 17th-century former home of the Viana family. There are twelve beautiful patios.

⛫ Museo Romero de Torres

Plaza del Potro 1. (957) 49 19 09. Tue–Sun.
Julio Romero de Torres (1874–1930), who was born in this house, captured the soul of Córdoba in his paintings.

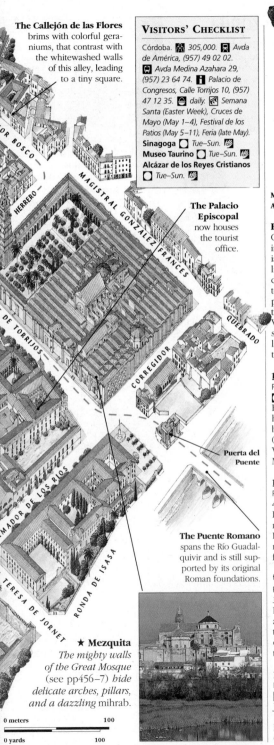

Puerta del Puente

The Puente Romano spans the Río Guadalquivir and is still supported by its original Roman foundations.

★ **Mezquita**
The mighty walls of the Great Mosque (see pp456–7) hide delicate arches, pillars, and a dazzling mihrab.

0 meters   100

0 yards   100

Córdoba: the Mezquita

ÓRDOBA'S GREAT MOSQUE, dating back
12 centuries, embodied the power of
Islam on the Iberian Peninsula. Abd al
Rahman I *(see p48)* built the original
mosque between 785 and 787. The
building evolved over the centuries,
blending many architectural forms.
In the 10th century al Hakam II
made some of the most lavish
additions, including the elaborate
mihrab (prayer niche) and the
maqsura (caliph's enclosure).
During the 16th century a
cathedral was built in the heart
of the reconsecrated mosque,
part of which was destroyed.

Patio de los Naranjos
*Orange trees grow in the courtyard
where the faithful washed
before prayer.*

Torre del Alminar
*This bell tower, 93 m (305 ft)
high, is built on the site of
the original minaret. Steep
steps lead to the top for a
fine view of the city.*

**The Puerta del
Perdón** is a Mudéjar-
style entrance gate, built
during Christian rule in
1377. Penitents were
pardoned here.

**Puerta de
San Esteban** is
set in a section of
wall from an earlier
Visigothic church.

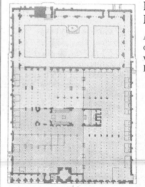

EXPANSION OF THE MEZQUITA

Abd al Rahman I built the
original mosque. Extensions
were added by Abd al Rahman
II, al Hakam II, and al Mansur.

KEY TO ADDITIONS

☐ Mosque of Abd al Rahman I

☐ Extension by Abd al Rahman II

☐ Extension by al Hakam II

☐ Extension by al Mansur

☐ Patio de los Naranjos

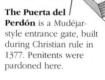

STAR FEATURES

★ **Mihrab**

★ **Capilla de
Villaviciosa**

★ **Arches and Pillars**

Cathedral
Part of the mosque was destroyed to accommodate the cathedral, started in 1523. Featuring an Italianate dome, it was designed chiefly by members of the Hernán Ruiz family.

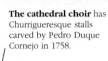

The cathedral choir has Churrigueresque stalls carved by Pedro Duque Cornejo in 1758.

Capilla Mayor

Capilla Real

★ **Arches and Pillars**
More than 850 columns of granite, jasper, and marble support the roof, creating a dazzling visual effect. Many were taken from Roman and Visigothic buildings.

★ **Mihrab**
This prayer niche, richly ornamented, held a gilt copy of the Koran. The worn flagstones indicate where pilgrims circled it seven times on their knees.

★ **Capilla de Villaviciosa**
The first Christian chapel was built in the mosque in 1371 by Mudéjar (see p51) craftsmen. Its multilobed arches are stunning.

Baroque statuary in the Fuente del Rey at Priego de Córdoba

Montilla 🕗

Córdoba. 🔗 24,000. 🚻 🚉 🛈 C/ Padre Miguel Molina, (957) 65 41 94. 🗓 Fri. 🎪 Grape Harvest (late Aug).

MONTILLA IS THE CENTER of an important wine region that produces an excellent smooth white fino (see p402). Unlike sherry, it is not fortified with alcohol. Several bodegas, including **Alvear** and **Pérez Barquero**, will show visitors around by prior arrangement.

The Mudéjar **Convento de Santa Clara** dates from 1512. The town library is in the **Casa del Inca**, so named because Garcilaso de la Vega, who wrote about the Incas, lived there in the 16th century.

ENVIRONS: Aguilar, 13 km (8 miles) to the south, has the unusual, eight-sided Plaza de San José (built in 1810) and several seigneurial houses.

Baena, 40 km (25 miles) to the west of Montilla, has been famous for its olive oil since Roman times. On the Plaza de la Constitución stands the Casa del Monte, an arcaded mansion dating from the 18th century. During Easter Week thousands of costumed drummers take to the streets.

🍷 **Bodega Alvear**
Avda María Auxiliadora 1. 📞 (957) 65 28 00. 🕐 Mon–Fri. 🔴 public hols.
🍷 **Bodega Pérez Barquero**
Avda de Andalucía. 📞 (957) 65 05 00. 🕐 Mon–Fri. 🔴 public hols.

Priego de Córdoba 🕗

Córdoba. 🔗 22,000. 🚉 🛈 Calle del Río 33, (957) 70 06 25. 🗓 Sat. 🎪 Feria Real (Sep 1–6).

PRIEGO DE CORDOBA's claim to be the capital of Cordoban Baroque is borne out by the dazzling work of carvers, ironworkers, and gilders in the many houses, and especially churches, built with wealth generated by a prosperous 18th-century silk industry.

A restored Moorish fortress stands in the whitewashed medieval quarter, the **Barrio de la Villa**. Close by is the outstanding **Iglesia de la Asunción**, converted from Gothic to Baroque style by Jerónimo Sánchez de Rueda. Its pièce de résistance is the sacristy, created in 1784 by local artist Francisco Javier Pedrajas. The main altar is Plateresque (see p21).

At midnight every Saturday the brotherhood of another Baroque church, the **Iglesia de la Aurora**, parades the streets singing songs in praise of the Virgin.

Silk merchants built many of the imposing mansions that follow the curve around the Calle del Río. At the end of the street is the Baroque **Fuente del Rey** (The King's Fountain). Some 139 spouts splash water into three basins that are adorned with exuberant statuary.

La Asunción, Priego de Córdoba

ENVIRONS: Zuheros, perched on a crag in the limestone hills northwest of Priego, is one of Andalusia's prettiest villages. **Rute**, to the southwest, is known for its anís (see p577).

Alcalá la Real, in the lowlands east of Priego, is overlooked by the hilltop ruins of a castle and a church. There are two handsome Renaissance buildings on its central square: the Fuente de Carlos V and the Palacio Abacia.

Montefrío 🕗

Granada. 🔗 8,500. 🚉 🛈 Plaza España 7, (958) 33 61 36. 🗓 Mon. 🎪 Fiesta patronal (Aug 14–18).

THE APPROACH to Montefrío from the south offers wonderful views of its tiled rooftops and pretty, whitewashed houses running up to a steep crag. This archetypal Andalusian town is topped by the remains of its Moorish fortifications and the 16th-century Gothic **Iglesia de la Villa**, attributed to Diego de Siloé. In the center of town is the Neo-Classical **Iglesia de la Encarnación**, identifiable by its large dome. The architect Ventura Rodríguez (1717–85) is credited with its design. The town is known for its chorizo.

ENVIRONS: Santa Fé was built by the Catholic Monarchs at the end of the 15th century. Their army camped here while

Barrels of Montilla, the sherrylike wine from the town of the same name

The castle overlooking the resort of Almuñécar on the Costa Tropical

laying siege to Granada, and this was the site of the formal surrender of the Moors in 1492 *(see pp52–3).* A Moor's severed head, carved in stone, adorns the spire of the parish church.

Sited above a gorge, **Alhama de Granada** was named Al hamma (hot springs) by the Moors. Their baths, close to the spot where the hot water gushes from the ground just outside town, can be seen in the Hotel Balneario.

Loja, on the Río Genil, near Los Infiernos gorge, is known as "the city of water" because of its spring-fed fountains.

Nerja ⬛

Málaga. 🏚 *15,000.* 🚌 🛈 *Calle Puerta del Mar 2, (95) 252 15 31.* 🗓 *Tue.* 🎪 *Feria (Oct 8–12).*

T HIS WELL-ESTABLISHED resort, built on a cliff above sandy coves, lies at the foot of the beautiful Sierra de Almijara. There are sweeping views up and down the coast from the rocky promontory known as **El Balcón de Europa** (the Balcony of Europe). Along it runs a promenade lined with cafés and restaurants.

East of the town are the **Cuevas de Nerja,** a series of vast caverns that were discovered in 1959. Wall paintings found here are believed to be about 20,000 years old. Only a few of the many cathedral-sized chambers are open to public view. One of these has been converted into an impressive auditorium that has a capacity of several hundred people. Concerts are held here in the summer.

ENVIRONS: In **Vélez-Málaga,** the ruins of the Fortaleza de Belén, a Moorish fortress set dramatically on a rocky outcrop, dominates the medieval Barrio de San Sebastián.

🦟 Cuevas de Nerja
Carretera de las Cuevas de Nerja. 📞 *(95) 252 95 20.* ⭕ *daily.* 🅰

Almuñécar ⬛

Granada. 🏚 *20,500.* 🚌 🛈 *Avda Europa, (958) 63 11 25.* 🗓 *Fri.* 🎪 *Virgen de la Antigua (Aug 15).*

A LMUÑÉCAR LIES on the Costa Tropical, so named because its climate allows the cultivation of exotic fruit. Just inland, mountains rise to more than 2,000 m (6,560 ft). The Phoenicians founded the first settlement here, called Sexi, and the Romans constructed an aqueduct, the remains of which can be seen today. Almuñécar is now a vacation resort, and apartment buildings fringe its beaches.

Above the old town is the **castle,** which was built by the Moors and altered in the 16th century. Below it is the **Parque Ornitológico** (comprising an aviary and botanic gardens) and the ruins of a Roman fish-salting factory. The **Museo Arqueológico** displays a variety of Phoenician artifacts.

ENVIRONS: The ancient white town of **Salobreña** is set amid fields of sugar cane. Narrow streets lead up a hill, first fortified by the Phoenicians, to the restored Arab castle. There are fine views of the Sierra Nevada *(see p461)* from here. Modern developments now line part of Salobreña's beach.

🦅 Parque Ornitológico
Plaza de Abderraman. 📞 *(958) 63 54 75.* ⭕ *daily.* 🅰
🏛 Museo Arqueológico
Cueva 7 Palacios. ⭕ *Mon–Sat.* 🅰
♟ Castillo de Salobreña
Calle Castillo. ⭕ *daily.* 🅰

One of the succession of sandy coves that make up the resort of Nerja

The majestic peaks of the Sierra Nevada towering, in places, to over 3,000 m (9,800 ft) above sea level

Lanjarón ㉞

Granada. 24,000. Plaza de la Constitución, (958) 77 00 02. Tue & Fri. San Juan (Jun 24).

SCORES OF CLEAR, SNOW-FED springs bubble from the slopes of the Sierra Nevada; their abundance at Lanjarón, on the southern side of this great range of mountains, has given the town a long history as a health spa. From June to October, visitors flock to take the waters for arthritic, dietary, and nervous ailments. Bottled water from Lanjarón is sold all over the country.

A major festival begins on the night of June 23 and ends in an uproarious water battle in the early hours of June 24, the Día de San Juan. Everyone in the streets gets doused.

The town is on the threshold of Las Alpujarras, a scenic upland area of dramatic landscapes, where steep, terraced hillsides and deep-cut valleys conceal remote, whitewashed villages. Roads to and from Lanjarón wind slowly and dizzily around the slopes.

A Tour of Las Alpujarras ㉟

THE FERTILE, UPLAND VALLEYS of Las Alpujarras, clothed with chestnut, walnut, and poplar trees, lie on the southern slopes of the Sierra Nevada. The architecture of the quaint white villages that cling to the hillsides – compact clusters of irregularly shaped houses with tall chimneys sprouting from flat, gray roofs – is unique in Spain. Local specialties are ham cured in the cold, dry air of Trevélez and brightly colored, handwoven rugs.

Trevélez ④
Trevélez, in the shadow of Mulhacén Spain's highest mountain, is famous for its cured ham.

Orgiva ①
This is the largest town of the region, with a Baroque church in the main street and a lively Thursday market.

Poqueira Valley ②
Capileira, Bubión, and Pampaneira are three villages typical of Las Alpujarras in this pretty river valley.

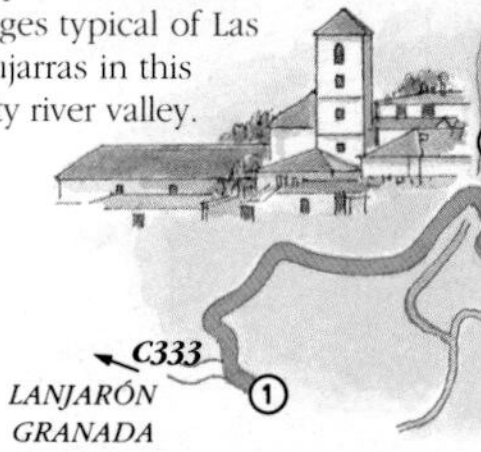

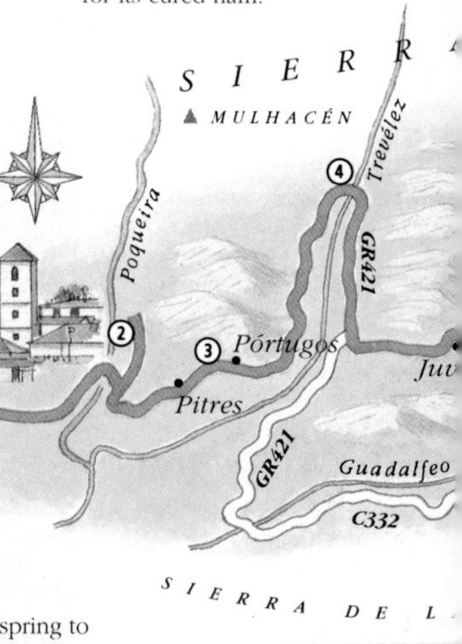

SIERRA
MULHACÉN
Trevélez
Poqueira
GR421
Pórtugos
Pitres
Guadalfeo
C332
SIERRA DE L

Fuente Agria ③
People come to this spring to drink the iron-rich, naturally carbonated waters.

Laujar de Andarax ㊱

Almeria. 🏘 *1,900.* 🚉 ℹ️ *Almeria, (950) 25 11 35.* 🗓 *3 & 17 of each month.* 🎉 *San Vicente (Jan 22), Virgen de la Salud (Sep 19).*

Laujar, IN THE ARID foothills of the Sierra Nevada looks southward across the Andarax valley toward the Sierra de Gádor.

According to legend, Laujar de Andarax was founded by one of the grandsons of Noah. In the 16th century, Abén Humeya, leader of the greatest Morisco rebellion *(see p55),* made his base here. The revolt was cruelly crushed by Christian troops, and Abén Humeya was murdered by his own treacherous followers.

Painting, Iglesia de la Encarnación

Inside Laujar's 17th-century church, **La Encarnación**, is a statue of the Virgin by Alonso Cano. Next to the Baroque **town hall** *(ayuntamiento)* is a fountain inscribed with some lines written by Francisco Villespesa, a dramatist and poet who was born in Laujar in 1877: *"Six fountains has my pueblo/He who drinks their waters/ will never forget them/so heavenly is their taste."*

El Nacimiento, a park to the east of Laujar, is a suitable place to have a picnic. You can accompany it with one of the area's hearty red wines. **Ohanes**, above the Andarax valley farther to the east, is an attractive hill town of steep streets and whitewashed houses known for its crops of table grapes.

Sierra Nevada ㊲

Granada. 🚉 *from Granada.* ℹ️ *Plaza de Andalucia, Monachil, (958) 24 91 95.*

Fourteen peaks more than 3,000 m (9,800 ft) high crown the heights of the Sierra Nevada. The snow lingers until July and begins falling again in late autumn. One of Europe's highest roads, the GR411, runs past **Solynieve**, an expanding ski resort at 2,100 m (6,890 ft), and skirts the two highest peaks, **Pico Veleta** at 3,398 m (11,149 ft) and **Mulhacén** at 3,482 m (11,420 ft).

The Sierra's closeness to the Mediterranean and its altitude account for the great diversity of the indigenous flora and fauna found on its slopes – the latter including golden eagles and some rare butterflies.

There are several mountain shelters for the use of serious hikers and climbers.

Yegen ⑥
A plaque marks the house where Gerald Brenan, the author of *South from Granada*, lived in the 1920s.

Puerto de la Ragua ⑧
This pass, which leads across the mountains to Guadix, is nearly 2,000 m (6,560 ft) high and is often snowbound in winter.

Válor ⑦
Abén Humeya, leader of a rebellion by Moriscos in the 16th century, was born here. A commemorative battle between Moors and Christians is staged each year in mid-September.

Cádiar ⑤
Free wine is traditionally on tap during the village's October fiesta.

KEY

▬▬ Tour route

═══ Other roads

▲ Mountain peak

0 kilometers   5

0 miles   5

TIPS FOR DRIVERS

Tour length: 85 km (53 miles).
Stopping-off points: There are bars and restaurants in Orgiva, Capileira, Bubión (see p602), and Trevélez. Orgiva, Bubión, and Trevélez have good hotels (see pp563–7). Orgiva is the last fuel stop before Cádiar.

Granada

Stone relief,
Museo
Arqueológico

THE GUITARIST ANDRES SEGOVIA (1893–1987) described Granada as a "place of dreams, where the Lord put the seed of music in my soul." It was first occupied by the Moors in the 8th century, and its golden period came during the rule of the Nasrid dynasty *(see p51)* from 1238 to 1492, when artisans, merchants, scholars, and scientists all contributed to the city's international reputation as a center for culture. Under Christian rule, following its fall to the Catholic Monarchs in 1492 and the expulsion of the Moors *(see pp52–3)*, the city blossomed in Renaissance splendor. There was a period of decline in the 19th century, but Granada has recently been the subject of renewed interest, and efforts are being made to restore parts of it to their past glory.

Entrance to the Moorish *mihrab* in the Palacio de la Madraza

Façade of Granada cathedral

Exploring Granada

The old city center around the cathedral is a maze of narrow one-way streets. It contains the Alcaicería – a reconstruction of a Moorish bazaar that burned down in 1843. Granada's two main squares are the Plaza Bib-Rambla, near the cathedral, and the Plaza Nueva. From the latter, Cuesta de Gomérez leads up to the city's two principal monuments: the Alhambra and the Generalife. On a hill opposite is the Albaicín district.

Churches well worth a visit are the Iglesia de San Juan de Dios, almost overwhelming in its wealth of Baroque decoration, and the Renaissance Iglesia de San Jerónimo.

🔒 Cathedral

On the orders of the Catholic Monarchs, work on the cathedral began in 1523 on plans in a Gothic style by Enrique de Egas. It continued under the Renaissance maestro, Diego

de Siloé, who also designed the façade and the magnificent, circular Capilla Mayor. Under its dome, windows of 16th-century glass depict Juan del Campo's *The Passion*. The west front was designed by the Baroque artist Alonso Cano, who was born in the city. His grave and many of his works can be seen in the cathedral.

🔒 Capilla Real

The Royal Chapel was built for the Catholic Monarchs between 1506 and 1521 by Enrique de Egas. A magnificent *reja* (grille) by Maestro Bartolomé de Jaén encloses the high altar and the Carrara marble figures of Fernando and Isabel, their daughter Juana la Loca (the Mad), and her husband Felipe el Hermoso (the Fair). Their coffins are in the crypt. In the sacristy there are art treasures, including paintings by Botticelli and Van der Weyden, as well as Isabel's crown, Fernando's sword, and their army banners.

🏛 Palacio de la Madraza

Calle Oficios 14. ☎ *(958) 22 34 47.* ◯ *Sep–Jul: Mon–Fri.* ♿
Originally an Arab university, this building later became the city hall. The façade dates from the 18th century. Inside is a Moorish hall with a finely decorated *mihrab* (prayer niche).

🏛 Corral del Carbón

Calle Mariana Pineda. ☎ *(958) 22 59 90.* ◯ *Mon–Sat.* ♿
This galleried courtyard, formerly a storehouse and inn for merchants, is a unique relic of the Moorish era. In Christian times it was a venue for theatrical performances; it later became a coal exchange. Today it houses craft shops and the main tourist office.

🏛 Casa de los Tiros

Calle Cementerio Santa Escolástica 19. ☎ *(958) 22 10 72.* ◯ *to the public.*
This fortresslike palace was built in Mudéjar style in the 16th century. It originally belonged to the family that was awarded the Generalife after the fall of Granada. Among

Grille by Maestro Bartolomé de Jaén enclosing the altar of the Capilla Real

Cupola in the sanctuary of the Monasterio de la Cartuja

their possessions was a sword
that had belonged to Boabdil.
This is carved on the façade,
along with statues of Mercury,
Hector, Hercules, Theseus, and
Jason. The building owes its
name to the muskets that project from its battlements: *tiro,*
in Spanish, meaning shot.

🔫 Alhambra and Generalife
See pp466–7.

🔫 El Bañuelo
Carrera del Darro 41. 📞 (958) 22 23
39. ☐ Tue–Sat. ⬤ public hols.
These brick-vaulted Arab baths
were built in the 11th century.
The columns are topped by
reused Visigothic and Roman
capitals as well as Arab ones.

🏛 Museo Arqueológico
Carrera del Darro 41. 📞 (958) 22 56
40. ☐ Tue–Sun. ⬤ public hols.

This museum occupies the
Casa de Castril, a Renaissance
mansion with a Plateresque
(see p21) portal. It displays
Iberian, Phoenician, and Roman
finds from Granada province.

🏠 Monasterio de la Cartuja
A Christian warrior called El
Gran Capitán founded this
monastery outside Granada
in 1516. There is a dazzling
cupola by Antonio Palomino,
and an extravagant Churrigueresque *(see p21)* sacristy by Luis
de Arévalo and Luis Caballo.

GRANADA CITY CENTER

Alhambra ⑥
El Bañuelo ⑦
Capilla Real ②
Casa de los Tiros ⑤
Cathedral ①
Corral del Carbón ④
Museo Arqueológico ⑧
Palacio de la Madraza ③

0 meters   250
0 yards   250

KEY

	See pp464–5
P	Parking
🛈	Tourist information
✝	Church
🏠	Convent or monastery

Street-by-Street: the Albaicín

Ornate plaque on a house in the Albaicín

THIS CORNER OF THE CITY, clinging to the hillside opposite the Alhambra, is where one feels closest to Granada's Moorish ancestry. A fortress was first built here in the 13th century and there were once over 30 mosques. Most of the city's churches were built over their sites. Along the cobbled alleys stand *cármenes*, villas with Moorish decoration and gardens, secluded from the world by their high walls. In the jasmine-scented air of evening, take a walk up to the Mirador de San Nicolás. The view over the maze of rooftops of the Alhambra glowing in the sunset is magical.

Street in the Albaicín
Steep and sinuous, the Albaicín's streets are truly labyrinthine. Many street names start with Cuesta, *meaning slope.*

Real Chancillería
Built in 1530 by the Catholic Monarchs, the Royal Chancery has a beautiful Renaissance façade.

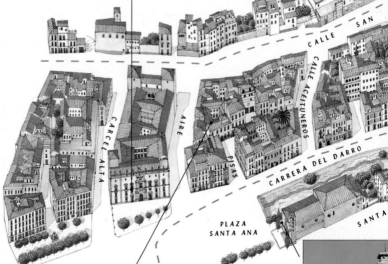

0 meters　　　50

0 yards　　　50

Casa de los Pisa, belonging to the Knights Hospitalers, displays works of art – some depicting St. John of God, who died here in 1550.

STAR SIGHTS

★ Iglesia de Santa Ana

★ Museo Arqueológico

★ El Bañuelo

★ Iglesia de Santa Ana
At the end of the Plaza Nueva stands this 16th-century brick church in Mudéjar style. It has an elegant Plateresque portal and, inside, a coffered ceiling.

★ **Museo Arqueológico**
The ornate Plateresque carvings on the museum's façade include this relief of two shields. They show heraldic devices of the Nasrid kings of Granada, who were defeated by the Catholic Monarchs in 1492 (see pp52–3).

Carrera del Darro
The road along the Río Darro leads past crumbling bridges and the fine façades of ancient buildings, now all restored.

To Mirador de San Nicolás

KEY

--- Suggested route

To Sacromonte

The Convento de Santa Catalina was founded in 1521.

CALLE DE LOS REYES
PLAZA CONCEPCIÓN
CARNERO
BAÑUELO
CONCEPCIÓN
CALLE ZAFRA
CALLE GLORIA
CARRETERA DEL SANTÍSIMO
CARRERA DEL DARRO
RÍO DARRO

★ **El Bañuelo**
Star-shaped openings in the vaults let light into these well-preserved Moorish baths, which were built in the 11th century.

SACROMONTE

Granada's gypsies formerly lived in the caves honey-combing this hillside. In the past, travelers would go there to enjoy spontaneous outbursts of flamenco. Today, virtually all the gypsies have moved away, but touristy flamenco shows of variable quality are still performed here in the evenings *(see pp406–407).* Sitting at the very top of the hill is the Abadía del Sacromonte, a Benedictine monastery. The ashes of St Cecilio, Granada's patron saint, are kept inside.

Gypsies dancing flamenco, 19th century

The Alhambra

A MAGICAL USE of space, light, water, and decoration characterizes this most sensual piece of architecture. It was built under Ismail I, Yusuf I, and Muhammad V, caliphs when the Nasrid dynasty (see pp50–51) ruled Granada. Seeking to belie an image of waning power, they created their idea of paradise on Earth. Modest materials were used (plaster, timber, and tiles), but they were superbly worked. Although the Alhambra suffered pillage and decay, including an attempt by Napoleon's troops to blow it up, in recent times it has undergone extensive restoration and its delicate craftsmanship still dazzles the eye.

Sala de la Barca

★ **Salón de Embajadores**
The ceiling of this sumptuous throne room, built from 1334 to 1354, represents the seven heavens of the Muslim cosmos.

★ **Patio de Arrayanes**
This pool, set amid myrtle hedges and graceful arcades, reflects light into the surrounding halls.

Patio de Machuca

Entrance

Patio del Mexuar
This council chamber, completed in 1365, was where the reigning sultan listened to the petitions of his subjects and held meetings with his ministers.

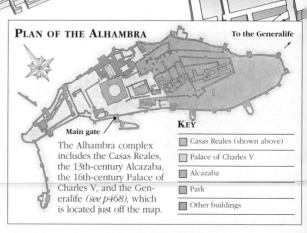

PLAN OF THE ALHAMBRA

To the Generalife

Main gate

The Alhambra complex includes the Casas Reales, the 13th-century Alcazaba, the 16th-century Palace of Charles V, and the Generalife (see p468), which is located just off the map.

KEY

☐ Casas Reales (shown above)
☐ Palace of Charles V
☐ Alcazaba
☐ Park
☐ Other buildings

Palacio del Partal
A pavilion with an arched portico and a tower is all that remains of this palace, the oldest building in the Alhambra.

Washington Irving's apartments

Baños Reales

Jardín de Lindaraja

VISITORS' CHECKLIST

For the Alhambra and Generalife.
☎ (958) 22 04 45. **Group reservations** ☎ (958) 22 09 12.
🚌 2. ☐ summer: 9am–8pm Mon–Sat, 9am–6pm Sun; winter: 9am–6pm daily. **Last adm:** 15 minutes before closing time.
Night visits: summer: 10pm–midnight Tue, Thu & Sat; winter: 8–10pm Sat. 🖼 ✔ 🍴

Sala de las Dos Hermanas, with its honeycomb dome, is regarded as the ultimate example of Spanish Islamic architecture.

Sala de los Reyes
This great banqueting hall was used to hold extravagant parties and feasts. Beautiful ceiling paintings on leather, from the 14th century, depict tales of hunting and chivalry.

Puerta de la Rawda

★ Sala de los Abencerrajes
This hall takes its name from a noble family, who were rivals of Boabdil (see pp52–3). According to legend, he had them massacred while they attended a banquet here. The geometrical ceiling pattern was inspired by Pythagoras' theorem.

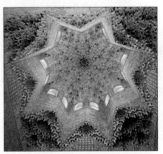

The Palace of Charles V (1526) houses a collection of Spanish-Islamic art, whose highlight is the Alhambra vase *(see p48).*

★ Patio de los Leones
Built by Muhammad V, this patio is lined with arcades supported by 124 slender marble columns. At its center, a fountain rests on 12 stocky marble lions.

STAR FEATURES

★ **Salón de Embajadores**

★ **Patio de Arrayanes**

★ **Sala de los Abencerrajes**

★ **Patio de los Leones**

Granada: Generalife

F ROM THE ALHAMBRA'S northern side, a footpath leads
to the Generalife, the country estate of the Nasrid
kings. Here, they could escape from palace intrigues
and enjoy tranquility high above the city, a little closer
to heaven. The name Generalife, or Yannat al Arif, has
various interpretations, perhaps the most pleasing
being "the garden of lofty paradise." The gardens,
begun in the 13th century, have been modified over
the years. They originally contained orchards and
pastures. The Generalife provides a magical setting for
Granada's annual music and dance festival *(see p37).*

The Patio de la Acequia *is an
enclosed oriental garden built
around a long central pool. Rows
of water jets on either side make
graceful arches above it.*

Sala Regia

**Jardines Altos
(Upper Gardens)**

**The Escalera del
Agua** is a staircase with
water flowing gently down it.

The Patio de los Cipreses,
otherwise known as the Patio de
la Sultana, was the secret meeting
place for Zoraya, wife of the
Sultan Abu-l-Hasan, and her lover,
the chief of the Abencerrajes.

Entrance

The Patio de Polo
was the courtyard
where palace visitors,
arriving on horse-
back, would tether
their steeds.

The Patio del Generalife *lies just
before the entrance to the Generalife.
The walk from the Alhambra to the
Generalife gardens passes first through
the Jardines Bajos (lower gardens),
before crossing this Moorish patio with
its characteristically geometric pool.*

The forbidding exterior of the castle above Lacalahorra

Castillo de Lacalahorra ③⑨

Lacalahorra (Granada). [C] (958) 67 70 98. [R] Guadix. [O] Wed.

GRIM, IMMENSELY THICK walls and stout, cylindrical corner towers protect the castle on a hill above the village of Lacalahorra. It was Rodrigo de Mendoza, son of Cardinal Mendoza, who ordered the castle to be built for his bride. The work was carried out between 1509 and 1512 by Italian architects and craftsmen. Inside is an ornate, two-storied, arcaded Renaissance courtyard with pillars and a staircase carved from Carrara marble.

Guadix ④⓪

Granada. [🏃] 20,000. [R] [R] [i] Ctra de Granada, (958) 66 26 65. [A] Sat. [📷] Fiesta & Feria (Aug 31–Sep 5).

THE TROGLODYTE QUARTER, with 2,000 caves that have been inhabited for centuries, is the town's most remarkable sight. The **Cueva-Museo** (cave museum) shows how people live underground.

The **cathedral** was begun in 1594 by Diego de Siloé and finished, by Gaspar Cayón and Vicente de Acero, between 1701 and 1796. Relics of San Torcuato, who founded Spain's first Christian bishopric, are kept in the cathedral museum.

Near the Moorish **Alcazaba**, dating from the 10th and 11th centuries, is the Mudéjar-style **Iglesia de Santiago**, a church with a fine, coffered ceiling. The 16th-century **Palacio de Penaflor** is being restored.

🏛 Cueva-Museo
Plaza de la Ermita Nueva. [O] daily. [📷]

Jaén ④①

[🏃] 100,000. [R] [R] [i] Calle Arquitecto Berges 1, (953) 22 27 37. [A] Thu. [📷] Nuestra Señora de la Capilla (Jun 11), San Lucas (Oct), Romería de Santa Catalina (Nov 25).

THE MOORS called Jaen *Geen* – meaning "way station of caravans" – because of its strategic site on the road beween Andalusia and Castile. Their hilltop fortress was rebuilt as the **Castillo de Santa Catalina** after it was captured by King Fernando III in 1246. Part of it is now a parador *(see p565)*.

Andrés de Vandelvira, who was responsible for many of Úbeda's fine buildings *(see pp472–3)*, designed Jaén's **cathedral** in the 16th century. Later additions include the two 17th-century towers that now flank the west front.

An old mansion, the **Palacio Villardompardo**, houses a museum of arts and crafts, and also gives access to the **Baños Árabes**, the 11th-century baths of Ali, a Moorish chieftain. These have horseshoe arches, ceilings with small, star-shaped windows, and two ceramic vats in which bathers once immersed themselves. Tucked away in an alley is the **Capilla**

de San Andrés, a Mudéjar chapel founded in the 16th century by Gutiérrez González who, as treasurer to Pope Leo X, was given extensive privileges. A gilded iron screen by Maestro Bartolomé de Jaen is the highlight of the chapel.

The **Real Monasterio de Santa Clara** was founded in the 13th century and has a lovely cloister dating from the late 16th century. Its church, which has a coffered ceiling, contains a bamboo image of Christ made in Ecuador.

The **Museo Provincial** displays Roman mosaics and sculptures, and Iberian, Greek, and Roman ceramics.

Horseshoe arches supporting the dome at the Baños Árabes, Jaén

♠ Castillo de Santa Catalina
Carretera al Castillo.
[C] (953) 23 00 00. [O] Wed.
🏯 Palacio Villardompardo
Plaza Santa Luisa de Marillac.
[C] (953) 23 62 92. [O] Tue–Sun.
[O] public hols. [📷]
🏛 Museo Provincial
Po de la Estación 27. [C] (953) 25 03 20. [O] Tue–Sun. [O] public hols. [📷]

Whitewashed cave dwellings in the troglodyte quarter of Guadix

Roman bridge spanning the Guadalquivir at Andújar

Andújar 🔼

Jaén. 🏠 35,000. 🚌 🚆 ℹ️ *Plaza de España 1, (953) 50 12 50.* 🗓️ *Tue.* 🎉 *Romería (last Sun of April).*

Aᴺᴅᴜᴊᴀʀ ɪꜱ ᴋɴᴏᴡɴ ꜰᴏʀ its olive oil and its pottery. It stands on the site of an Iberian town, Iliturgi, which was destroyed in the Punic Wars *(see p46)* by Scipio. The Roman conquerors built the 15-arched bridge spanning the Río Guadalquivir.

In the central square is the Gothic **Iglesia de San Miguel**, with paintings by Alonso Cano. The **Iglesia de Santa María la Mayor** has a Renaissance façade and a Mudéjar tower. Inside it is El Greco's *Christ in the Garden of Olives* (c.1605). A pilgrimage takes place to the nearby **Santuario de la Virgen de la Cabeza** in April.

Eɴᴠɪʀᴏɴꜱ: The mighty fortress of **Baños de la Encina** has 15 towers and ramparts built by Caliph Al Hakam II in AD 967. Farther north, the road and railroad between Madrid and Andalusia squeeze through a spectacular gorge in the eastern reaches of the Sierra Morena, the **Desfiladero de Despeñaperros**.

Baeza 🔼

See pp474–5.

Úbeda 🔼

Jaén. 🏠 34,000. 🚌 🚆 ℹ️ *Plaza del Ayuntamiento, (953) 75 08 97.* 🗓️ *Fri.* 🎉 *San Miguel (Sep 28– Oct 4).*

Uᴮᴇᴅᴀ ɪꜱ ᴀ ꜱʜᴏᴡᴄᴀꜱᴇ of Renaissance magnificence, thanks to the patronage of some of Spain's most influential men of the 16th century. These included such dignitaries as Francisco de los Cobos, secretary of state, and his greatnephew, Juan Vázquez de Molina, who gave his name to Úbeda's most historic square. Surrounded by elegant palaces and churches, it is undoubtedly the jewel in Úbeda's crown. The old town is contained within city walls that were first raised by the Moors in 852.

Created on the orders of the Bishop of Jaén around 1562, the colossal former **Hospital de Santiago** was designed by Andrés de Vandelvira, who was credited with refining the Spanish Renaissance style to give it its more austere characteristics. The façade is flanked by square towers, one topped with a distinctive blue-and-white tiled spire. Today the building is a conference center.

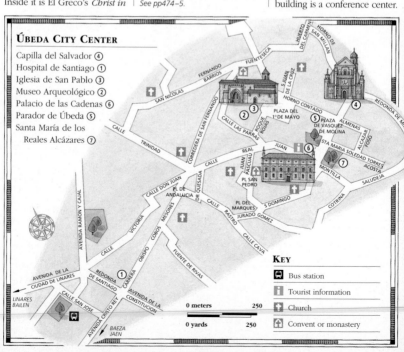

ÚBEDA CITY CENTER

Capilla del Salvador ④
Hospital de Santiago ①
Iglesia de San Pablo ③
Museo Arqueológico ②
Palacio de las Cadenas ⑥
Parador de Úbeda ⑤
Santa María de los
   Reales Alcázares ⑦

Kᴇʏ

🚌 Bus station

ℹ️ Tourist information

✝️ Church

✝️ Convent or monastery

0 meters   250
0 yards   250

◁ **Fields of poppies and olive groves south of Andújar in the province of Jáen**

Laguna de Valdeazores in the Parque Nacional de Cazorla

Parque Natural de Cazorla ⑮

Jaén. 🚍 Cazorla. ℹ️ Carretera del Tranco km 17, (953) 72 01 15.

FIRST-TIME VISITORS are amazed by the spectacular scenery of this 529,409-acre nature preserve with thickly wooded mountains rising to peaks of 2,000 m (6,560 ft) and varied, abundant wildlife.

Access to the Parque Natural de Cazorla, Segura y Las Villas is via the town of Cazorla. Its imposing Moorish **Castillo de la Yedra** houses a folklore museum. From Cazorla, the road winds upwards beneath the much-photographed remains of the clifftop castle at **La Iruela**. After crossing a pass it drops down to a crossroads (El Empalme del Valle) in the thickly wooded valley of the Río Gudalquivir. Roads from here lead to the source of the river and to the peaceful modern parador *(see p564)*.

The main road through the park follows the river. The information center at Torre del Vinagre is 17 km (10.5 miles) from the crossroads.

ENVIRONS: There is a well-restored Moorish castle at **Segura de la Sierra**, 30 km (19 miles) from the preserve's northern edge. Below it is an unusual rock-hewn bullring.

♠ Castillo de la Yedra
📞 (953) 71 00 39. ⬜ Tue–Sat.
⬤ public hols. 📷

Located in the 15th-century Casa Mudéjar, the **Museo Arqueológico** exhibits artifacts from Neolithic to Moorish times.

The **Iglesia de San Pablo** has a 13th-century apse and a beautiful 16th-century chapel by Vandelvira. It is surmounted by a Plateresque tower completed in 1537.

A monument to the poet and mystic St. John of the Cross (1549–91) stands in the **Plaza de Vázquez de Molina**. The **Capilla del Salvador**, on the square, was designed by three 16th-century architects – Diego de Siloé, Andrés de Vandelvira, and Esteban Jamete – as the personal chapel of Francisco de los Cobos. Behind it stand Cobos' palace, with a Renaissance façade, and the Hospital de los Honrados Viejos (Hospital of the Honored Elders), looking onto the Plaza de Santa Lucía. From here, the Redonda de Miradores follows the line of the city walls and offers views of the countryside.

The Plaza Vazquez de Molina also holds Úbeda's **parador** *(see p567)*. Built in the 16th century, but much altered in the 17th, it was the residence of Fernando Ortega Salido, dean of Málaga and chaplain of the Capilla del Salvador.

Úbeda's town hall and tourist office occupy the **Palacio de las Cadenas**, a mansion built for Vázquez de Molina by Vandelvira. It gets its name from the iron chains *(cadenas)* once attached to the columns supporting the main doorway.

Also on the square is the church of **Santa María de los Reales Alcázares**, which

dates mainly from the 13th-century, and the **Cárcel del Obispo** (Bishop's Jail), where nuns who had been punished by the bishop were confined.

🏛 Museo Arqueológico
Casa Mudéjar, Calle Cervantes.
📞 (953) 75 37 02. ⬜ Tue–Sun. ♿
🏥 Hospital de Santiago
Calle Obispo Cobos. 📞 (953) 75 08 42. ⬜ daily.

Capilla del Salvador, Úbeda, one of Spain's finest Renaissance churches

---

CAZORLA'S WILDLIFE

More than 100 bird species live in this nature preserve, some very rare, such as the golden eagle and the griffon vulture. Cazorla is the only habitat in Spain, apart from the Pyrenees, where the lammergeier lives. Mammals in the park include the otter – active at dawn and dusk – mouflon, and wild boar, and a small remaining population of Spanish ibex. The red deer was reintroduced in 1952. Among the flora supported by the limestone geology is the indigenous *Viola cazorlensis*.

Wild boar foraging for roots, insects, and small mammals

Street-by-Street: Baeza ㊸

Coat of arms, Casa del Pópulo

Nestling amid the olive groves that characterize much of Jaén province, beautiful Baeza is a small town, unusually rich in Renaissance architecture. Called Beatia by the Romans and later the capital of a Moorish fiefdom, Baeza is portrayed as a "royal nest of hawks" on its coat of arms. It was conquered by Fernando III in 1226 – the first town in Andalusia to be definitively won back from the Moors – and was then settled by Castilian knights. An era of medieval splendor followed, reaching a climax in the 16th century, when Andrés de Vandelvira's splendid buildings were erected. In the early 20th century, Antonio Machado, one of his generation's greatest poets, lived here.

★ Palacio de Jabalquinto
An Isabelline-style (see p20) façade, flanked by elaborate, rounded buttresses, fronts this splendid Gothic palace.

Antigua Universidad
From 1542 until 1825, this Renaissance and Baroque building was one of Spain's first universities.

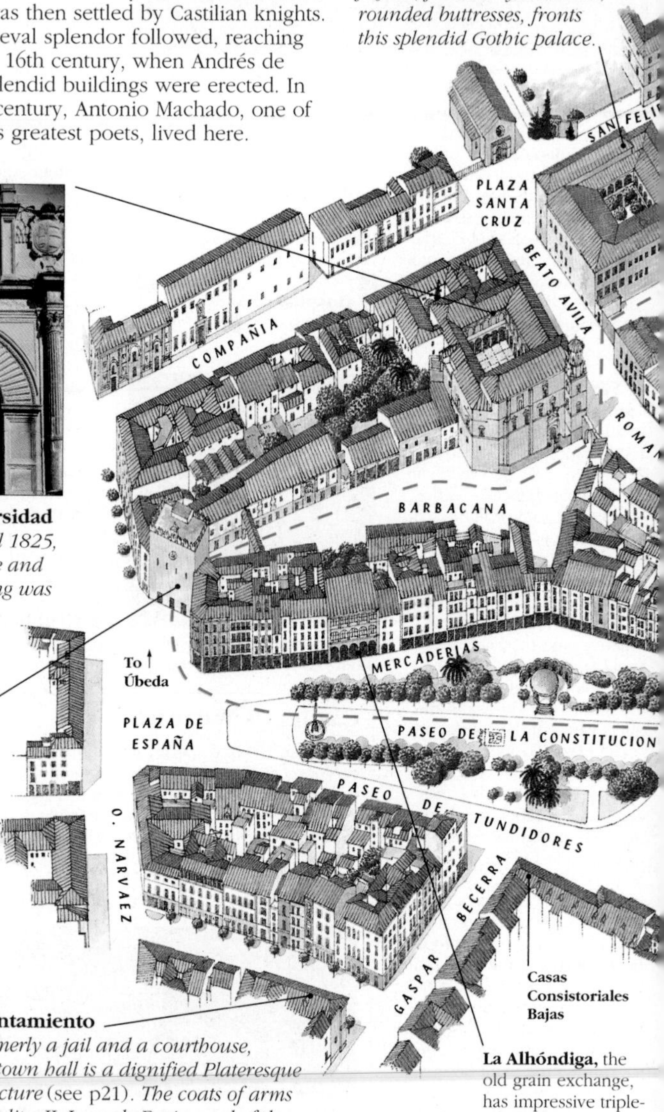

Torre de los Aliatares is a 1,000-year-old tower built by the Moors.

Ayuntamiento
Formerly a jail and a courthouse, the town hall is a dignified Plateresque structure (see p21). The coats of arms of Felipe II, Juan de Borja, and of the town of Baeza adorn its upper façade.

La Alhóndiga, the old grain exchange, has impressive triple-tier arches running along its front.

Casas Consistoriales Bajas

To ↑ Úbeda

PLAZA DE ESPAÑA

O. NARVAEZ

PASEO DE TUNDIDORES

PASEO DE LA CONSTITUCION

MERCADERIAS

BARBACANA

COMPAÑIA

PLAZA SANTA CRUZ

BEATO AVILA

SAN FELI

ROMA

GASPAR BECERRA

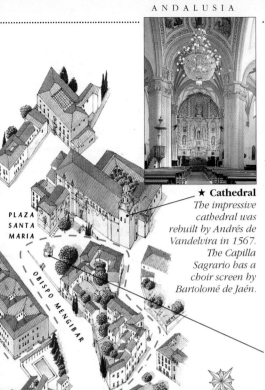

★ **Cathedral**
The impressive cathedral was rebuilt by Andrés de Vandelvira in 1567. The Capilla Sagrario has a choir screen by Bartolomé de Jaén.

Fuente de Santa María
Architect-sculptor Ginés Martínez of Baeza designed this fountain in the form of a triumphal arch. It was completed in 1564.

Antigua Carnicería is the 16th-century former slaughterhouse.

Puerta de Jaén y Arco de Villalar
This gateway in the city ramparts is adjoined by an arch erected in 1521 to appease Carlos I (see p54) after a rebellion.

| 0 meters | 75 |
| 0 yards | 75 |

KEY

⚏ Tourist information

– – – Suggested route

★ **Plaza del Pópulo**
The Casa del Pópulo, a fine Plateresque palace, now the tourist office, overlooks this square. In its center is the Fuente de los Leones, a fountain with an Ibero-Roman statue flanked by lions.

STAR SIGHTS

★ **Palacio de Jabalquinto**

★ **Cathedral**

★ **Plaza del Pópulo**

Renaissance castle overlooking
the village of Vélez Blanco

Vélez Blanco ⑥

Almería. ⚇ *2,400.* 🚉 *Vélez Rubio.*
🛈 *Ayuntamiento, Calle Corredera 38,
(950) 41 50 01.* 🚌 *Wed.* 🎉 *Cristo
de la Yedra (second Sun of Aug).*

DOMINATING THIS pleasant
village is the mighty
Castillo de Vélez Blanco. It
was built between 1506 and
1513 by the first Marquis de
Los Vélez. The castle's rich
Renaissance interiors are now
displayed in the Metropolitan
Museum in New York, but
there is a reconstruction of one
of the original patios.

Just outside Vélez Blanco,
the **Cueva de los Letreros**
contains paintings from c.4000
BC. One depicts the Indalo, a
figure holding a rainbow and
believed to be a deity with
magical powers, now adopted
as the symbol of Almería.

⚘ **Cueva de los Letreros**
◻ *Sat & Sun.* 📷

Mojácar ㊼

Almería. ⚇ *3,800.* 🚉 🛈 *Plaza del
Castillo, (950) 47 51 62.* 🚌 *Wed,
Sun.* 🎉 *Moors and Christians (second
weekend of Jul), San Agustin (Aug 28).*

FROM A DISTANCE, Mojácar
shimmers like the mirage
of a Moorish citadel, its white
houses cascading over a lofty
ridge, 2 km (1.2 miles) inland
from long, sandy beaches.

Following the Civil War *(see
pp62–3)*, the village fell into
ruin as most of its inhabitants
emigrated, but in the 1960s it
was discovered by tourists,
giving rise to a new era of
prosperity. The old gateway
in the walls still remains, but
other than that the village has
been completely rebuilt and
vacation complexes have
grown up along the beaches.
The coast south of Mojácar is
among the least built up in
Spain, with only small resorts
and villages along its length.

Tabernas ㊽

Almería. ⚇ *3,100.* 🚉 🛈 *Ayuntamiento, Plaza del Pueblo 1, (950) 36
50 02.* 🚌 *Wed.* 🎉 *Virgen de las
Angustias (Aug 11–15).*

TABERNAS IS SET in Europe's
only desert. The town's
Moorish fortress dominates the
harsh surrounding scenery of
cactus-dotted, rugged, eroded
hills, and dried-out riverbeds
that have provided the setting
for many classic spaghetti
westerns, such as *A Fistful of
Dollars.* Two movie sets can
be visited: **Mini-Hollywood**

and **Texas Hollywood**, 1.5 km
(1 mile) and 4 km (2.5 miles)
from Tabernas respectively.

Not far from town is a solar
energy research center, where
hundreds of heliostats follow
the course of southern Andalusia's powerful sun.

ENVIRONS: Sorbas sits on the
edge of the deep chasm of
the Río de Aguas. It has two
notable buildings: the 16th-
century Iglesia de Santa María
and a 17th-century mansion
said to have been a summer
retreat for the Duke of Alba.

Nearby is the karst scenery,
honeycombed with hundreds
of cave systems, of the **Yesos
de Sorbas** nature preserve.
Permission to explore them is
required from Andalusia's
environmental department.

🎬 **Mini-Hollywood**
Carretera N340. 📞 *(950) 36 52 36.*
◻ *daily.* ⬤ *Mon in winter.* 📷
🎬 **Texas Hollywood**
Carretera N340, Tabernas. 📞 *(950)
16 54 58.* ◻ *daily.* 📷

Desert landscape around Tabernas,
reminiscent of the Wild West

Still from *For a Few Dollars More* by Sergio Leone

SPAGHETTI WESTERNS

Two Wild West towns lie off the N340 highway west of Tabernas. Here, visitors can
re-enact classic movie scenes or watch stunt
men performing bank holdups and saloon
brawls. The *poblados del oeste* were built
during the 1960s and early 1970s when low
costs and eternal sunshine made Almería
the ideal location for spaghetti westerns.
Sergio Leone, director of *The Good, the Bad,
and the Ugly*, built a ranch here, and
movie sets sprang up in the desert. Local
gypsies played Indians and Mexicans. The
deserts and Arizona-style badlands are still
used for television commercials and series,
and by directors such as Steven Spielberg.

The 10th-century Alcazaba, which dominates Almería's old town

Almería ㊾

Almería. 🏛 *170,000.* 🚉 🚌 🛈
*Parque Nicolás Salmerón, (950) 27 43
55.* 🛒 *Fri & Sat.* 🎭 *Feria (last week
of Aug), Winter Fiesta (Dec–early Jan).*

ALMERÍA's colossal **Alcazaba**,
dating from 995 AD, is
the largest fortress built by
the Moors in Spain. The huge
structure bears witness to the
city's golden age, when it was
an important port under the
Caliphate of Córdoba *(see
pp48–9)*. The Moorish city,
known as Al Mariyat (Mirror
of the Sea), exported mainly
brocade, silk, and cotton.

During the Reconquest, the
Alcazaba withstood two major
sieges before eventually falling
to the armies of the Catholic
Monarchs *(see pp52–3)* in
1489. The royal coat of arms
can be seen on the Torre del
Homenaje, built during their
reign. The Alcazaba also has a
Mudéjar chapel and gardens.

Adjacent to the Alcazaba is
the old fishermen's and gypsy
quarter of **La Chanca**, where
some families live in caves
with brightly painted façades
and modern interiors. On
Mondays a lively street market
is held. Although this district
is picturesque, it is also des-
perately poor, and it is unwise
to walk around here alone or
at night with valuables.

Berber pirates from North
Africa often raided Almería.
Consequently, the **cathedral**
looks almost more like a castle
than a place of worship, with
its four towers, thick walls,
and small windows. The site
was originally occupied by a
mosque. This was converted
into a church, but in 1522 the

building was destroyed in an
earthquake. Work on the present building began in 1524
under the direction of Diego
de Siloé, who designed the
nave and high altar in Gothic
style. The Renaissance façade
and the carved walnut choir
stalls are by Juan de Orea.

Brightly colored entrance to a
gypsy cave in La Chanca district

Traces of Moorish Almería's
most important mosque can be
seen in the **Templo San Juan**.
The **Plaza Vieja** is an attractive
17th-century arcaded square.
On one side is the **town hall**
(ayuntamiento), a flamboyant
building with a cream and
pink façade dating from 1899.

ENVIRONS: One of Europe's
most important examples of a
Bronze Age settlement lies at
Los Millares, near Gádor, 17
km (10.5 miles) to the north
of Almería. As many as 2,000
people may have occupied the
site around 2500 BC.

🏰 **Alcazaba**
Calle Almanzor. 📞 *(950) 27 16 17.*
◻ *daily.* ● *Jan 1, Dec 25.* 🎦
🏛 **Los Millares**
Carretera Santa Fé de Mondújar.
📞 *(950) 23 50 10.* ◻ *Tue–Sun.*

Parque Natural de
Cabo de Gata ㊿

Almería. 🚌 *San José.* 🛈 *Almería–
Cabo de Gata road, (950) 16 04 35.*

TOWERING CLIFFS of volcanic
rock, sand dunes, salt flats,
and secluded coves characterize the 71,700-acre Parque
Natural de Cabo de Gata.
Within its confines are a few
fishing villages and the small
resort of San José, on a fine,
sandy bay. A lighthouse
stands at the dramatic end of
the *cabo* (cape), which can be
reached by road from the
village of Cabo de Gata. The
park includes a stretch of seabed 2 km (1.2 miles) wide,
and the marine flora and fauna
protected within it attract scuba
divers and snorkelers.

The dunes and saltpans between the cape and the Playa
de San Miguel are a habitat
for thorny jujube trees. Thousands of migrating birds stop
here en route to and from
Africa and among the 170 or
so bird species recorded are
flamingoes, avocets, griffon
vultures, and Dupont's larks.

ENVIRONS: Set amid an oasis
of citrus trees on the edge of
the harsh Sierra de Alhamilla,
Níjar's fame stems from the
colorful pottery and the handwoven *jarapas* – blankets and
rugs – that are made here. The
barren plain between Níjar
and the sea has been brought
under intensive cultivation using vast plastic greenhouses
to conserve the scarce water.

The dramatic, dark volcanic rocks
at Cabo de Gata, east of Almería

SPAIN'S ISLANDS

Introducing Spain's Islands

SPAIN'S TWO GROUPS OF ISLANDS lie in separate seas –
the Balearics in the Mediterranean and the Canaries
in the Atlantic, off the African coast. Both are popular
package-tour destinations blessed with warm climates,
good beaches, and clear waters. But each has more to
offer than high-rise hotels, fast-food restaurants, and
discos. The Balearics have white villages, wooded
hills, caves, and prehistoric monuments, while the
extraordinary volcanic landscapes of the Canaries are
unlike any other part of Spain. Four of Spain's national
parks *(see pp26–7)* are in the Canary Islands.

Ibiza *(see pp486–8) is the liveliest
of the Balearic Islands. Ibiza town
and Sant Antoni are the main tourist
centers, offering good nightlife and
excellent beaches.*

*Eivissa
(Ibiza)*

Formentera

CANARY ISLANDS
(See pp504–27)

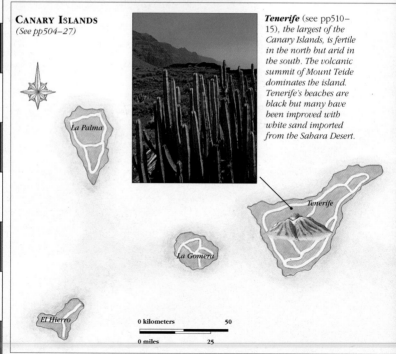

La Palma

Tenerife

La Gomera

El Hierro

Tenerife *(see pp510–
15), the largest of the
Canary Islands, is fertile
in the north but arid in
the south. The volcanic
summit of Mount Teide
dominates the island.
Tenerife's beaches are
black but many have
been improved with
white sand imported
from the Sahara Desert.*

0 kilometers   50

0 miles   25

◁ **Vines growing in the volcanic soil of Lanzarote, protected by stone walls**

In Menorca (see pp498–503) *tourism has developed more slowly than in Mallorca and Ibiza, and the island has largely avoided being over-commercialized. Scattered across the countryside are the ruins of unique Bronze Age buildings.*

BALEARIC ISLANDS
(See pp482–503)

Menorca

Mallorca

Mallorca (see pp490–97), *best known for its beaches, has caves and other natural features to explore. The most spectacular of the island's historic sights is the great Gothic cathedral in Palma, which rises above the boats moored in the old harbor.*

0 kilometers   50
0 miles   25

Lanzarote (see pp524–6) *is the most attractive of the Canary Islands, even though the landscape is strikingly bare. White houses contrast starkly with black volcanic fields. The most dramatic attraction is Timanfaya National Park, including the Montañas del Fuego.*

Lanzarote

n Canaria

Fuerteventura

Gran Canaria (see p518–21) *centers on a symmetrical volcanic cone. The capital city of Las Palmas has some interesting museums and monuments. In contrast, the sprawling Maspalomas, on the south coast, is the biggest vacation resort in Spain.*

THE BALEARIC ISLANDS

IBIZA · FORMENTERA · MALLORCA · MENORCA

C HIC RESORTS *and attractive coves and beaches, combined with a climate that is hot but never uncomfortably so, have made tourism the mainstay of life along the coasts of the Balearic Islands. Inland, there is peace and quiet in abundance, and a great variety of sights to seek out: wooded hills, pretty white villages, monasteries, country churches, caves, and prehistoric monuments.*

Standing at a crossroads in the Mediterranean, the Balearic Islands have been plundered or colonized in turn by Phoenicians, Greeks, Carthaginians, Romans, Moors, and Turks. In the 13th century Catalan settlers brought their language, a dialect of which is widely spoken today.

The islands can justifiably claim to cater to all tastes: from sun-seekers on tour-package vacations, for whom the larger resorts serve as brash fun factories, to jet-setters and movie stars, who head for luxurious but discreet hideaways in the hills. The largest island, where tourism has been established the longest, is Mallorca. A massive Gothic cathedral stands near the waterfront of Palma, the capital. The countryside of Menorca is dotted with prehistoric monuments and its towns full of historic mansions. The coast of Ibiza is notched by innumerable rocky coves. The island's hilly interior is characterized by brilliant white farmhouses and robust churches. On Formentera, small and relatively undeveloped, the pace of life is slow. The islets surrounding the four principal islands are mainly uninhabited; one of them, Cabrera (off Mallorca), is a national park.

View through the window of one of Ibiza's traditional whitewashed farmhouses

◁ The massive, heavily buttressed cathedral overlooking Palma de Mallorca's harbor

Exploring the Balearics

THOUGH THE BALEARIC ISLANDS are often associated with crowded, inexpensive package tourism, they offer enough variety to satisfy everyone's tastes. For those unattracted by the bustle of the coastal resorts and their beautiful beaches, the countryside and the old towns of Palma, Ibiza, Maó, and Ciutadella are relatively undisturbed. Mallorca is by far the most culturally rich of the Balearics, with its distinguished collection of modern and traditional galleries and interesting museums. Menorca is strong on Neolithic remains and Neo-Colonial architecture, while Ibiza is for lovers of clear, painterly light and rustic peasant houses; it also has some of the wildest nightclubs in Europe. Formentera – for many, the most alluring island – has crystal water, white sand, a pure, parched landscape, and total tranquillity.

Poblat des Pescadors in the tourist village of Binibeca

Early-morning mist on the waters of Port de Pollença in Menorca

```
0 kilometers        25
0 miles            15
```

MALLORCA

SOLLÉ

VALLDEMOSSA 9 10 ALI

LA GRANJA 8

ANDRATX 7 C719

PMI 14 PAL

CAPOCOR.

IBIZA

ELS AMUNTS

SANT MIQUEL 4

SANT ANTONI 1 C731

SANT JOSEP 2 5 SANTA EULARIA

3 EIVISSA (IBIZA)

FORMENTERA 6

GETTING AROUND

Nearly all foreign visitors to the Balearics arrive by plane: Mallorca, Menorca, and Ibiza have connections to major European cities as well as Madrid, Barcelona, and Valencia. Aviaco airline flies to most other Spanish cities out of Son Sant Joan airport in Palma. Another way of arriving is by boat from Barcelona, Valencia, Alicante, or Dénia. Between the islands there are regular ferry services, run by Transmediterránea and Flebasa. Mallorca is the only island with rail services, which run between Palma and Inca, and between Palma and Sóller. Roads vary from excellent to poor, depending on how far you stray from the tourist trail. The best way to get around the islands is by car, except on Formentera, where the ideal mode of transport is the bicycle.

Sights at a Glance

A peaceful stroll on the sands of
Ibiza's Sant Miquel beach

See Also

• *Where to Stay* pp568–9

• *Restaurants and Bars* pp605–607

The rocky coast around the Coves d'Artá in Mallorca

Key

 Freeway

 Major road

Minor road

Scenic route

River

Viewpoint

Ibiza

THIS SMALL ISLAND, the nearest of the Balearics to the coast of Spain, was unknown and untouched by tourism until the 1960s, when it suddenly appeared in Europe's vacation brochures along with Benidorm and Torremolinos. There is still a curious, indefinable magic about Ibiza (Eivissa), and the island has not entirely lost its character. The countryside, particularly in the north, is a rural patchwork of groves of almonds, figs, and olives, and wooded hills. Ibiza town retains the air of a 1950s Spanish provincial borough. At once package-tour paradise, hippie hideout, and glamor hot spot, this is one of the Mediterranean's mythical destinations.

An Ibizan shepherdess

The bustling harbor of the resort of Sant Antoni

Sant Antoni ➊

Baleares. 🏠 14,500. 🚌 🚢
ℹ️ *Passeig de Ses Fonts, (971) 34 33 63.* 🎉 *Sant Antoni (Jan 17), Sant Bartolomé (Aug 24).*

IBIZA'S SECOND TOWN, Sant Antoni was known by the Romans as Portus Magnus because of its large natural harbor. Formerly a tiny fishing village situated on an immaculate bay, it has turned into a sprawling and exuberant resort. Although it was once notoriously over-commercialized, the town has recently undergone a dramatic facelift. Nevertheless, the 14th-century parish church of Sant Antoni is practically marooned in a sea of modern high-rise hotels.

To the north of Sant Antoni, on the road to Cala Salada, is the chapel of **Santa Agnès**, an unusual early Christian temple (not to be confused with the village of the same name). When this catacomb-like chapel was discovered, in 1907, it contained Moorish weapons and fragments of pottery.

Sant Josep ➋

Baleares. 🏠 12,000. ℹ️ *Carrer Pedro Escanellas 33–9, (971) 80 01 25.* 🎉 *Sant Josep (Mar 19).*

THE VILLAGE of Sant Josep, the administrative center of southwest Ibiza, lies in the shadow of Ibiza's highest mountain. At 475 m (1,560 ft), Sa Talaiassa offers a panorama of all Ibiza, including the islet of **Es Vedrá**, rising from the

The salt lakes of Ses Salines, a haven for many bird species

sea like a rough-cut pyramid. For the most accessible view of this enormous rock, take the coastal road to the sandy cove of Cala d'Hort, where there are a number of good restaurants and a quiet beach.

ENVIRONS: Before tourism, salt was Ibiza's main industry, most of it coming from the salt flats at **Ses Salines** in the southeast corner of the island. Mainland Spain is the chief consumer of this salt, but much goes to the Faroe Islands and Scandinavia for salting fish. It is loaded onto ships at Ibiza's southernmost port, La Canal. Ses Salines is also an important refuge for birds, including the flamingo. **Es Cavallet**, 3 km (2 miles) east, is an unspoiled stretch of soft, white sand.

Ibiza ➌

Baleares. 🏠 75,000. ✈️ 🚌 🚢
ℹ️ *Carrer Historiador José Clapés 4, (971) 30 24 90.* 🕐 *Wed–Sat (summer only).* 🎉 *Sant Antoni Abat (Jan 17), San Juan Bautista (Jun 24).*

THE OLD QUARTER of Ibiza (Eivissa), known also as Dalt Vila, or upper town, is a miniature citadel guarding the mouth of the almost circular bay. The **Portal de ses Taules**, a magnificent gateway in the north wall of the 16th-century fortifications, carries the finely carved coat of arms of the kingdom of Aragón, to which the Balearic Islands belonged in the Middle Ages *(see p217).* Outside the walls is the 16th-century **Església de Santo Domingo** with its three red-tiled domes. The Baroque interior, with its barrel-vaulted ceiling and frescoed walls, has been restored to its former glory. Works of art by Erwin Bechtold, Barry Flanagan, and other artists connected with Ibiza are on display in the **Museu d'Art Contemporani**, just inside the Portal de ses Taules. Crowning the whole Dalt Vila, and visible for miles around, is the **cathedral**, a 13th-century Catalan Gothic building with 18th-century additions. The cathedral's Museo de la Sacristia houses assorted works of art.

Under the Carthaginians, the soil of Ibiza was considered holy. The citizens of Carthage deemed it an honor to be buried in the **Necropolis of Puig d'es Molins**, thought to contain over 4,000 graves.

The crossroads village of **Jesús**, 3 km (2 miles) north, is well worth a visit for its pretty 16th-century church.

A view across the port toward Ibiza's upper town

A backstreet in the Sa Penya district of Ibiza town

Originally built as part of a Franciscan monastery, it has arguably the finest work of art in the Balearics, a 16th-century altarpiece by Rodrigo de Osona the Younger.

🏛 Museu d'Art Contemporani
C/ Ronda Narces Puget. **[** (971) 30 27 23. **☐** Mon–Sat. **●** public hols. **🗭**
⋔ Necropolis of Puig d'es Molins
Via Romana. **[** (971) 30 17 71.
● Mon–Sat. **🗭**

Els Amunts ❹

Baleares. **☐** Sant Miquel. **❗** Santa Eulària d'es Riu, (971) 33 07 28.

Els Amunts is the local name for the uplands of northern Ibiza, which stretch from Sant Antoni on the west coast to Sant Vicenç in the northeast. Though hardly a mountain range – Es Fornás is the highest point, at a mere 450 m

(1,480 ft) – the area's inaccessibility has kept it unspoiled. There are few special sights here, apart from the landscape: pine-clad hills sheltering fertile valleys whose rich red soil is planted with olive, almond, and fig trees, and the occasional vineyard. Tourist enclaves are also scarce – except for a handful of small resorts, such as Port de Sant Miquel, Portinatx, and Sant Vicenç. Inland, villages like Sant Joan and Santa Agnès offer an insight into Ibiza's quiet, rural past.

The architectural highpoints of northern Ibiza are several beautiful white churches, like the one in **Sant Miquel** that, in summer, is host to a weekly display of Ibizan folk dancing. Outside Sant Llorenç is the tranquil, fortified hamlet of **Balàfia**, which has flat-roofed houses, tiny whitewashed alleys, and a watchtower that was used as a fortress during raids by the Turks.

IBIZA'S HOTTEST SPOTS

Ibiza's reputation for extraordinary nightlife is largely justified. The main action takes place in two areas: the Calle de la Virgen in the old harbor district, with its bars, fashion boutiques, and restaurants; and the mega-discos out of town – Ku, Pachá, Amnesia, and Es Paradis. When the last of these is closing, at about 7am, the wildest club of them all, Space, is only just opening its doors. Ibiza has long been a magnet for the rich and famous. Celebrities seem to have become more elusive of late, but a few well-known faces can often be glimpsed dining in the restaurant Las Dos Lunas, and sunning the next day on the beach at Ses Salines.

Nightclubbers enjoying a bubble bath at Amnesia

One of the many beautiful beaches along the unspoiled shores of the island of Formentera

Santa Eulària ❺

Baleares. 🏠 *5,000.* ▣ ▲ ℹ *Carrer Mariano Riquer Wallis 4, (971) 33 07 28.* ▣ *Wed.* 🎭 *Es Cana (Aug 15).*

DESPITE CATERING to tourism, the town of Santa Eulària d'es Riu (Santa Eulalia del Río), situated on the island's only river, has managed to hold on to its character far more than many other Spanish resorts.

The 16th-century church, with its pretty covered court-yard, and the surrounding old town, were built on the top of a little hill, the **Puig de Missa**, because this site was more easily defended in times of war than the shore below.

Ajdacent to the church is the **Museu Etnològic**, a folk mu-seum, which is housed in an ancient but tastefully adapted Ibizan farmhouse. Included in the exhibits (labeled in Catalan only) are traditional costumes, farming implements, an olive

The domed roof of Santa Eulària's 16th-century church

press, and toys. A fascinating collection of old photographs reveals the drastic and irrever-sible changes Ibiza has suffered over the last 50 years.

🏛 Museu Etnològic
Puig de Missa. ☎ *(971) 33 28 45.* ◯ *daily.*

Formentera ❻

Baleares. ⛴ *from Ibiza.* ℹ *La Savina, (971) 32 20 57.*

AN HOUR'S BOAT RIDE from Ibiza harbor will bring you to this largely unspoiled island where the waters are blue and the way of life slow.

From the small port of La Savina, where the boat docks, there are buses to other parts of the island. As the service is limited, it is more advisable to rent a car, moped or bicycle from one of the shops nearby. **Sant Francesc**, Formentera's tiny capital, is situated 3 km (2 miles) from La Savina. Most of the island's amenities are in this town, plus a pretty church (built in 1729), in the main square, and a folk museum.

From Sant Francesc, a bumpy minor road leads for 9 km (6 miles) southward, ending at Cap de Barbaria, the site of an 18th-century defensive tower and a lighthouse.

Formentera is entirely flat, apart from the small plateau of **La Mola**, which takes up the whole eastern end of the is-land. From the fishing port of Es Caló the road winds up-

ward past the Restaurante Es Mirador, with its panoramic view of western Formentera, to the village of Nostra Senyora del Pilar on top of the plateau. About 3 km (2 miles) to the east is a lighthouse, Far de la Mola, sited on the highest point of the island. Nearby stands a monument to Jules Verne (1828–1905), who used For-mentera for the setting of one of his novels, *Hector Servadac.*

Although there are many purple road signs indicating places of cultural interest on Formentera, most lead only to disappointment. But one sight well worth seeking out is the megalithic sepulcher of **Ca Na Costa** (1800–1600 BC) near Sant Francesc, the only one of its kind in the Balearics. This monument, a circle of upright stone slabs, pre-dates the Carthaginians *(see pp45–6).*

However, the island's great strength is not its history and culture, but its landscape, which has a spare and delicate beauty and some of the Mediterranean's last unspoiled shorelines. The finest beaches are, arguably, Migjorn, Tramuntana, and Cala Saona, all southwest of Sant Francesc. Illetes and Llevant are two beautiful beaches on either side of a long sandy spit in the far north of the island. If the water is calm you can wade through it from the Pas d'es Trocadors (where Illetes and Llevant meet) to the island of **Espalmador** – with its natural springs, superb beaches, and lighthouse – which lies be-tween Formentera and Ibiza.

Regional Food: The Balearic Islands

TRADITIONAL FOOD is being rediscovered in the Balearics. It varies from island to island but reflects the cuisine of Catalonia, with its combinations of sweet and savory, and nuts and dried fruit. Pork is a main ingredient, and vegetable dishes and soups are also typical

Mayonnaise

fare. Menorca's capital, Maó, lays claim to the invention of mayonnaise, which is often served with succulent fish and shellfish. Mallorca is the home of the savory *sobrassada (see p493)*, a delicious spicy sausage, and the sweet pastry known as *ensaimada*.

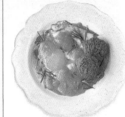

Huevos a la sollerica *are fried eggs served on top of smooth, red* sobrassada *sausage, served with a pea sauce.*

Langosta a la parrilla *partners spiny lobster with the local mayonnaise, which is made with eggs and olive oil.*

Berenjenas rellenas *are eggplant stuffed with onions, herbs, and bread. Tomatoes and pork are also often added.*

Tumbet, *made in a brown earthenware* greixera *or casserole, combines layers of peppers and tomato with potato.*

Coca de trampó *is a pizza-style dish, topped with a selection of fresh vegetables, especially onions and peppers.*

Ensaimada *is a spiral-shaped yeast bun from Mallorca and can be eaten either for breakfast or as a teatime snack.*

DRINKS

While in Menorca 200 years ago, sailors from the English navy introduced the islanders to the potent drink of gin with lemon. A highly perfumed gin is still made on the island. A large selection of herb and other liqueurs is made in the Balearics, including *palo*, flavored with crushed almond shells. The Balearics produce few wines. The main wine region, a *denominación de origen (see p576)*, is around Binissalem in Mallorca, and produces mainly light whites and rosés. There are several red Mallorcan wines, which are best drunk young. The most popular Spanish drinks from the mainland, such as *anís*, brandy, beer, and sangria *(see p577)*, are available everywhere in the Balearics.

Herb liqueur

Almond liqueur

Gin

Mallorca

MALLORCA IS OFTEN LIKENED TO A CONTINENT rather than simply an island. Its varied nature never fails to astonish, whether you are looking for landscape, culture, or just entertainment. No other European island has a wider range of scenery, from the fertile plains of central Mallorca to the almost alpine peaks of the Tramuntana. The island's mild climate and lovely beaches have made it one of Spain's foremost package tour destinations but there is a wealth of culture, too, evident in sights like Palma Cathedral (*see pp496–7*). Mallorca's appeal lies also in its charm as a living, working island: the grain and fruit crops of the central plains, and the vineyards around Binissalem are vital to the island's economy.

Terraced orange grove in the Sierra Tramuntana

Andratx **7**

Baleares. **7,000.** Plaça Miguel Moner 1, (971) 67 10 01. Wed. San Pedro (Jun 29), La Virgen de Carmen (Jul 16).

THIS SMALL TOWN lies amid a valley of almond groves in the shadow of Puig de Galatzó, which rises to 1,026 m (3,366 ft). With its ocher and white shuttered houses and the old watchtowers perched high on a hill above the town, Andratx is a very pretty place.

The road southwest leads down to **Port d'Andratx** 5 km (3 miles) away. Here, in an almost totally enclosed bay, expensive yachts are moored in rows along the harbor and luxury vacation homes pepper the surrounding hillsides. In the past, Port d'Andratx's main role was as the fishing port and harbor for Andratx, but since the early 1960s it has gradually been transformed into an exclusive vacation resort for the rich and famous. When visiting Port d'Andratx, it is a good idea to leave all thoughts of the real Mallorca behind and simply enjoy it for what it is – a chic and affluent resort.

La Granja **8**

Esportes. (971) 61 00 32. daily.

LA GRANJA is a pivate estate, or *possessió*, near the little country town of Esportes. Formerly a Cistercian convent, it is now the property of the Seguí family, who have opened their largely unspoiled 18th-century house to the public as a kind of living museum of traditional Mallorca. Peacocks roam the gardens, salt cod and hams hang in the kitchen, *The Marriage of Figaro* plays in the ballroom, and the slight air of chaos just adds to the charm of the place.

Valldemossa **9**

Baleares. **1,500.** Jardin de la Cartuja, (971) 61 20 02. Sun. Santa Catalina Tomas (Jul 28), San Bartolomé (Aug 24).

THIS PLEASANT mountain town will forever be linked with the name of George Sand, the French novelist who stayed here during the winter of 1838–9 and later wrote unflatteringly of the island and its people in *Un Hiver à Majorque*. Dearer to Mallorcans is the Polish composer and pianist Frédéric Chopin (1810–49) who stayed with Sand at the **Real Cartuja de Jesús de Nazaret**. "Chopin's cell," off the monastery's main courtyard, is where a few of his works were written, and it still houses the piano on which he composed.

Bust of Frédéric Chopin at Valldemossa

A few doors away is a 17th-century pharmacy displaying outlandish medicinal preparations such as "powdered nails of the beast." In the cloisters is a contemporary art museum with works by Tàpies, Hartung, and Miró, and the Mallorcan artist Juli Ramis (1909–90). There is also a series of Picasso illustrations titled *The Burial of the Count of Orgaz*, inspired by the El Greco painting of the same name (*see p28*).

🏛 **Real Cartuja de Jesús de Nazaret**
Plaça de la Cartuja de Valldemossa.
(971) 61 21 06. Sun.

A view across the harbor of Port d'Andratx

Alfàbia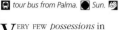

Off C711. [(971) 61 31 23.
🚌 tour bus from Palma. ● Sun. 📷

VERY FEW *possessions* in
Mallorca are open to the
public, which makes Alfàbia
all the more worth visiting. The
house and garden are an excellent example of a typical
Mallorcan aristocratic estate
and exude an unmistakably
Moorish atmosphere. Very little
remains of the original 14th-
century architecture, so it is
well worth looking for the
Mudéjar inscription on the ceiling of the entrance hall and the
Hispano-Arabic fountains and
pergola. The garden is a sumptuous 19th-century creation,
making imaginative use of
shade and the play of water.

Sóller ⓫

Baleares. 🏠 11,000. 🚉 🚌 ℹ️
Plaça Constitució 1, (971) 63 02 00.
🗓 Mon–Sat. 🎉 second Sun of May.

SOLLER IS A LITTLE TOWN grown
fat on the produce of its
olive groves and orchards,
which climb up the slopes of
the Sierra Tramuntana. In the
19th century Sóller traded its
oranges and wine for French
goods, and the town retains a
faintly Gallic, bourgeois feel.

One of Sóller's best-known
features is its delightfully old-
fashioned narrow-gauge railway, complete with quaint
wooden cars. The town,
whose station is in the Plaça
d'Espanya, lies on a scenic
route between Palma and the
fishing village of Port de Sóller
5 km (3 miles) to the west.

ENVIRONS: From Sóller a road
winds southward along the
spectacular west coast to **Deià**
(Deyá). This village was once
the home of Robert Graves
(1895–1985), the English poet
and novelist, who came to
live here in 1929. His simple
tombstone can be seen in the
small cemetery. The **Museu
Arqueològic**, curated by the
archaeologist William Waldren,
offers a glimpse into prehistoric
Mallorca. Outside the village
is **Son Marroig**, the estate of
Austrian Archduke Ludwig

Houses and trees crowded together on the hillside of Deià

Salvator (1847–1915), who
documented the Balearics in a
series of books included in a
display of his possessions on
the first floor.

🏛 Museu Arqueològic
Es Clot Deià. [(971) 63 90 01.
🗓 Apr–Oct: Tue–Sun. 📷 ♿

Statue of La Moreneta at the
Monasteri de Lluc

Monasteri de
Lluc ⓬

Lluc. 🚌 from Palma. [(971) 51
70 25. 🗓 daily. 📷 museum only. ♿

HIGH IN THE MOUNTAINS of
the Sierra Tramuntana, in
the remote village of Lluc, is
an institution regarded by
many as the spiritual heart of
Mallorca. The Monasteri de
Lluc was built mainly in the
17th and 18th centuries on the
site of an ancient shrine. The
monastery's Baroque church
with its imposing façade

contains the stone image of
La Moreneta, the Black Virgin
of Lluc, supposedly found by
a young shepherd boy on a
nearby hilltop in the 13th
century. Along the Camí dels
Misteris, the paved walkway
up to this hilltop, there are
some bronze bas-reliefs by the
Catalan architect and designer
Antoni Gaudí *(see pp136–7)*.
Just off the main Plaça dels
Pelegrins are a café and bar, a
pharmacy, and a shop selling
local handicrafts, wines, and
foods. The museum, situated
on the first floor, includes
Mallorcan paintings and
medieval manuscripts. The
monastery incorporates a guest
house *(see p568)*.

From Lluc, 13 km (8 miles)
of tortuous road wind through
the hills and descends toward
the coast, ending at the beautiful rocky bay of **Sa Calobra**.
From here, it is just 5 minutes'
walk farther up the coast to the
Torrent de Pareis, a deep gorge
opening into the sea.

Sheer cliff face rising out of the
sea at Sa Calobra

The cloisters of the Convent de Santo Domingo in Pollença

Pollença ⑬

Baleares. 🏛 *12,000.* 🚌 ℹ *Ctra de Formentor, Port de Pollença, (971) 86 54 67.* 🏛 *Sun.* 🎭 *Sant Antoni (Jan 17).*

Aʟᴛʜᴏᴜɢʜ ᴘᴏʟʟᴇɴçᴀ has become one of Mallorca's most popular tourist spots, it still appears unspoiled. The town, with its ocher-colored stone houses and winding lanes, is picturesquely sited on the edge of fertile farmland. The Plaça Major, with its bars frequented mainly by locals, has an old-world atmosphere.

Pollença has several fine churches, including the elegant 18th-century **Parròquia de Nostra Senyora dels Angels** and the Convent de Santo Domingo, which contains the **Museu Municipal**, with its displays on local archaeology. This convent is also the venue for Pollença's Music Festival, held every August. A chapel perched on the top of a hill, **El Calvari**, is reached either by road or a torturous climb of 365 steps. On the altar there is a charming Gothic Christ, carved in wood.

Eɴᴠɪʀᴏɴs: Alcúdia, 10 km (6 miles) to the east, is surrounded by 14th-century walls pierced by two majestic gateways. Near the town center is the **Museu Monogràfic de Pollença**, which exhibits statues, jewelry, and other remains found in the Roman settlement of Pollentia, 1.5 km (1 mile) south of Alcúdia.

🏛 **Museu Municipal**
Carrer Santo Domingo. 📞 *(971) 53 00 15.* ⏰ *Tue, Thu & Sun.*
🏛 **Museu Monogràfic de Pollença**
Carrer Sant Jaume 30. 📞 *(971) 53 00 15.* ⏰ *Tue, Thu & Sun.* 🎟 ♿

Palma de Mallorca ⑭

See pp494–7.

Puig de Randa ⑮

8 km (5 miles) northeast of Llucmajor. 🚌 *to Llucmajor, then taxi.* ℹ *El Arenal, (971) 44 04 14.*

Iɴ ᴛʜᴇ ᴍɪᴅᴅʟᴇ of a fertile plain called the *pla* rises a mini-mountain 543 m (1,781 ft) high, the Puig de Randa. It is said that Mallorca's greatest son, the 14th-century theologian and mystic Ramon Llull, came to a hermitage on this mountain to meditate and write his religious treatise, *Ars Magna*. On the way up Puig de Randa there are two small monasteries, the 14th-century Santuari de Sant Honorat and the Santuari de Nostra Senyora de Gràcia. The latter, built on a ledge under an overhanging cliff, contains a 15th-century chapel with fine Valencian tiles inside, and offers an open view of the *pla*.

On the mountain top is the **Santuari de Cura**, built to commemorate Llull's time on the *puig*, and largely devoted to the study of his work. Its central courtyard is built in the typical beige stone of Mallorca. A small museum, housed in a 16th-century former school off the courtyard, contains some of Llull's manuscripts.

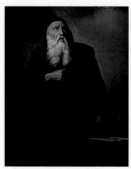

The philosopher Ramon Llull

Capocorb Vell ⑯

14 km (9 miles) south of Llucmajor. 📞 *(971) 66 16 26.* 🚌 *from El Arenal.* ⏰ *Fri–Wed.* 🎟

Mᴀʟʟᴏʀᴄᴀ is not as rich in megalithic remains as Menorca, but this *talaiotic* village *(see p503)* in the stony flatlands of the southern coast is worth seeing – particularly on a quiet day when you can wander among the stones in peace. The settlement, which dates back to around 1000 BC, originally consisted of five *talaiots* (stone towerlike structures with timbered roofs) and 28 smaller dwellings. Little is known about its inhabitants and the uses for some of the rooms inside the buildings, such as the tiny underground gallery. Too small for living in, this room may have been used to perform magic rituals.

Part of the charm of this place lies in its surroundings among fields of fruit trees and dry stone walls, a setting that somehow complements the ruins. Apart from a snack bar nearby, the site remains mercifully undeveloped.

One of the *talaiots* of Capocorb Vell

Cabrera ⑰

Baleares. 🚢 *from Colònia Sant Jordi.*
ℹ️ *Carrer Doctor Barraquer 5,*
Colònia Sant Jordi, (971) 65 60 73.

F ROM THE BEACHES of Es Trenc and Sa Ràpita, on the south coast of Mallorca, Cabrera looms on the horizon. The largest island in an archipelago of the same name, it lies 18 km (11 miles) from the most southerly point of Mallorca. Cabrera is home to several rare plants, reptiles, and seabirds, such as Eleonora's falcon. The waters around it are important for their marine life. All this has resulted in the archipelago being declared a national park *(see pp26–7).* For centuries Cabrera was used as a military base and it was never colonized. On it stands a 14th-century castle.

A street in Felanitx

Felanitx ⑱

Baleares. 🏠 *9,000.* 🚌 ℹ️ *Plaça Constitució 1, (971) 58 00 51.* 🛒 *Sun.* 🎉 *Sant Joan Pelós (Jun 24).*

T HIS BUSTLING agricultural town is the birthplace of Renaissance architect Guillem Sagrera (1380–1456) and the 20th-century painter Miquel Barceló. Felanitx is visited mainly for three reasons: the imposing façade of the 13th-century church, the **Esglesia de Sant Miquel**; its *sobrassada de porc negre* (a spiced raw sausage made from the meat of the local black pig); and its lively religious fiestas including Sant Joan Pelós *(see p499).*

About 5 km (3 miles) southeast is the **Castell de Santueri**, founded by the Moors but rebuilt in the 14th century by the kings of Aragón, who ruled Mallorca. Though a ruin, it is worth the detour for the views to the east and south from its vantage point, 400 m (1,300 ft) above the plain.

Coves del Drac ⑲

1.5 km (1 mile) south of Porto Cristo.
🚌 *from Porto Cristo.* 📞 *(971) 82 07 53.* ⏰ *daily.* ⏹ *Jan 1, Dec 25.* 📷

M ALLORCA has innumerable caves, ranging from mere holes in the ground to cathedral-like halls. The four vast chambers of the **Coves del Drac** are reached by a steep flight of steps, at the bottom of which is the beautifully lit cave known as "Diana's Bath." Another chamber holds the large underground lake, Martel, which is 39 m (128 ft) below ground level and is 177 m (580 ft) long. A boat trip on this lake is an unforgettable experience. Equally dramatic are the two remaining caves, imaginatively named "The Theater of the Fairies" and "The Enchanted City."

ENVIRONS: The **Coves dels Hams** is so called because some of its stalactites are shaped like hooks – *hams* in Mallorcan. The caves are 500 m (1,640 ft) long and contain the "Sea of Venice," an underground lake on which musicians sail in a small boat.

The entrance to the **Coves d'Artá**, near Capdepera, is 40 m (130 ft) above sea level and affords a wonderful view. The caves' main attraction is a stalagmite 22 m (72 ft) high.

🏛 **Coves dels Hams**
11 km (7 miles) from Manacor towards Porto Cristo. 📞 *(971) 82 09 88.*
⏰ *daily.* ⏹ *Jan 1, Dec 25.* 📷
🏛 **Coves d'Artá**
Canyamel, nr Capdepera. 📞 *(971) 56 32 93.* ⏰ *daily.* ⏹ *Jan 1, Dec 25.* 📷

The dramatically lit stalactites of the Coves d'Artá

Street-by-Street: Palma ⑭

Forn des Teatre pastry shop

O N AN ISLAND whose name has become synonymous with mass tourism, Palma surprises by its cultural richness. Under the Moors it was already a prosperous town of fountains and cool courtyards. After he had conquered it in 1229, Jaime I wrote, "It seemed to me . . . the most beautiful city we had ever seen." Signs of Palma's past wealth are still evident in the sumptuous churches, grand public buildings, and fine private mansions that crowd the old town. The hub of the city is the old-fashioned Passeig des Born, whose cafés invite you to try one of Mallorca's specialties, the *ensaimada*, a spiral of pastry dusted with powdered sugar.

The Forn des Teatre is an old pastry shop noted for its *ensaimadas* and *gató* (almond cake).

The Fundació la Caixa, once the Gran Hotel, is now a cultural center.

Palau de l'Almudaina
This once-royal Moorish palace now houses a museum, whose highlights include the chapel of Santa Ana, with its Romanesque portal, and the Gothic tinell *or salon.*

STAR SIGHTS

★ **Cathedral**

★ **Basílica de Sant Francesc**

La Llotja is a beautiful 14th-century stock exchange with tall windows and delicate tracery.

PLAÇA REI JOAN CARLES

PASSEIG DES BORN

CARRER UNIO

CARRER DE PALAU REIAL

AVINGUDA D'ANTONI MAURA

CARRER DE SAN

CARRER MIR

To Castell de Bellver and Fundació Pilar i Joan Miró

★ **Cathedral**
Built of golden limestone quarried from Santanyi, Palma's huge Gothic cathedral stands in a dramatic location near the waterfront.

Parc de la Mar

KEY

 — — — Suggested route

Estació de RENFE and
ció de Autobuses

Plaça del Marqués
de Palmer

0 meters 100

0 yards 100

A view along the circular walls of
the Castell de Bellver

★ **Basílica de Sant Francesc**
*The church and cloister
of St. Francis are in a
refined Gothic style with
a Baroque altarpiece
and rose window.*

The Museu Diocesà,
housed in the
Bishop's Palace,
has a collection of
religious artifacts.

Museu de Mallorca
*The museum has displays on
local history, art, and
architecture, including this
statue of an ancient warrior.*

Banys Àrabs
*The 10th-century baths,
with their well-preserved
arches, are a remnant of
the Balearic Islands'
Moorish culture.*

♟ Castell de Bellver
West side of Palma Bay. (971) 73
06 57. daily.
About 2.5 km (1.5 miles) from
the city center, standing 113 m
(370 ft) above sea level, is
Palma's Gothic castle. It was
commissioned by Jaime II
during the short-lived Kingdom of Mallorca (1276–1349)
as a summer residence, but
soon after became a prison
and remained as such until
1915. The castle, situated on
a wooded hill overlooking
the bay of Palma, is of an
unusual circular design.
Three of its towers are set
into the main castle wall; the
other is set apart from it, but
linked by a high walkway.
From some angles the castle
looks more decorative than
defensive: witness the cloister
of delicate arches that rings
the central courtyard.

⛟ Fundació Pilar
i Joan Miró
Carrer Joan de Saridakis 29. (971)
70 14 20. Mon.
When Joan Miró died in 1982,
his wife took on the task of
converting his former studio
and home into an art center.
The building – christened
"the Alabaster Fortress" by
the Spanish press – is a
stunning example of modern
architecture designed by
Navarrese architect Rafael
Moneo. It incorporates Miró's
original studio (complete with
unfinished paintings), a
permanent collection of the
painter's work, a shop, a
library, and an auditorium.

Palma Cathedral

ACCORDING TO LEGEND, when Jaime I of Aragón was caught in a storm on his way to conquer Mallorca in 1229, he vowed that if God led him to safety he would build a great church in His honor. In the following years the old mosque of Medina Mayurqa was torn down and architect Guillem Sagrera (1380–1456) drew up plans for a new cathedral. In 1587 the last stone was added to the soaring vaults. Over subsequent years the cathedral has been rebuilt, notably early this century when the interior was remodeled by Antoni Gaudí *(see pp136–7)*. Today Palma Cathedral, or Sa Seu, as Mallorcans call it, is one of the most breathtaking buildings in Spain, combining vast scale with typically Gothic elegance *(see p20)*.

Bell Tower
This robust tower was built in 1389 and houses nine bells, the largest of which is known as Aloi, meaning "praise."

Palma Cathedral
One of the best-sited cathedrals anywhere, it is spectacularly poised high on the sea wall, above what was once Palma's harbor.

STAR FEATURES

★ **Great Rose Window**

★ **Baldachino**

19th-century tower

Entrance to cathedral museum

Portal Major

Flying buttresses

Cathedral Museum
One of the highlights of the beautifully displayed collection in the Old Chapterhouse is a 15th-century reliquary of the True Cross which is encrusted with jewels and precious metals.

★ **Great Rose Window**
The largest of seven rose windows looks down from above the High Altar like a gigantic eye. Built in 1370 with stained glass added in the 16th century, the window has a diameter of over 11 m (36 ft).

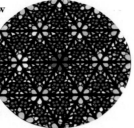

VISITORS' CHECKLIST

Carrer Palau Reial 29. ▮ (971) 72 31 30. ◯ Apr–Oct: 10am–6pm Mon–Fri; Nov–Mar: 10am–3pm Mon–Fri, 10am–2pm Sat. ◉ public hols. ▨ ✝ 9am, 7pm daily (Oct–Mar: 9am, 5:30pm Mon–Fri; 9am, 7pm Sat, Sun). ♿

The Great Organ was built with a Neo-Gothic case in 1795 and restored in 1993 by Gabriel Blancafort.

Capella de la Trinitat
This tiny chapel was built in 1329 as the mausoleum of Jaime II and III of Aragón. It contains their alabaster tombs.

The Capella Reial, or Royal Chapel, was redesigned by Antoni Gaudí between 1904 and 1914.

Bishop's Throne
Built in 1269 and made of Carrara marble, the chair is embedded in a Gothic vaulted niche.

Choir stalls

Portal del Mirador

Nave
The magnificent ceiling, 44 m (144 ft) high, is held up by 14 slender pillars. At over 19 m (62 ft) wide, it is one of the broadest naves in the world.

★ **Baldachino**
Gaudí's bizarre wrought-iron canopy above the altar incorporates lamps, tapestries and a multicolored crucifix.

Menorca

MENORCA IS THE BALEARIC ISLAND farthest from the mainland, and it is set apart from the rest of the country in many other ways. The coastline of Menorca is, arguably, more unspoiled than in any other part of Spain. Its countryside remains largely green and pleasant, with cows roaming the meadows. The old towns of Maó – the island's capital – and Ciutadella are filled with noble, historic buildings and beautiful squares. Menorca also has abundant reminders of its more distant history: the island boasts a spectacular hoard of Bronze Age stone structures, which provide an invaluable insight into its prehistoric past. The Menorcans are often more inclined to drink the locally brewed gin *(ginebra)* than the wine which is favored elsewhere in Spain.

Fishermen mending their nets in Ciutadella's harbor

The peaceful seafront of Ciutadella at twilight

Ciutadella ⑳

Baleares. 22,000. Plaça de la Catedral, (971) 38 26 93. Fri & Sat. Sant Joan (Jun 24).

THE KEY DATE in the history of Ciutadella is 1558. In that year the Turks, under Barbarossa, entered and decimated the city, consigning 3,495 of its citizens to the slave markets of Constantinople. Of Ciutadella's main public buildings, only the fine Catalan Gothic **Església Catedral de Menorca** managed to survive this fearsome onslaught in more or less its original condition, only later to be stripped of all its paintings, ornaments, and other treasures by Republican extremists during the Civil War.

The nearby **Plaça des Born** was built as a parade ground for Moorish troops and from 1558 was gradually rebuilt in Renaissance style. Today it is one of Spain's most impressive squares, containing pleasant cafés and bordered by shady palm trees. At the center of the Plaça des Born is an obelisk that commemorates the "Any de sa Desgràcia" (Year of Misfortune), when the Turks invaded the city. Around the square are the Gothic-style **town hall** *(ajuntament)*, the late 19th-century **Teatre Municipal des Born**, and a series of aristocratic mansions with Italianesque façades, the grandest of which is the early 19th-century **Palau de Torre-Saura**. From the northern end of the Plaça des Born there is a fine view over Ciutadella's small sheltered harbor.

The historic Plaça des Born in the center of Ciutadella

If you walk up the Carrer Major des Born past the cathedral, you come to **Ses Voltes**, an alley lined on both sides by whitewashed arches. Turn right along the Carrer des Seminari for the Baroque **Església dels Socors** and the **Museu Diocesà** with its displays of ecclesiastical paraphernalia. In the narrow streets of the old town there are many impressive palaces, but only the early 19th-century **Palau Salort**, on the Carrer Major des Born, is open to the public. The delightful Art Nouveau **market** (1895), its ironwork painted in neat municipal dark green, stands nearby.

The peace of Ciutadella is disturbed every June by the Festa de Sant Joan, an entertaining and spectacular ritual of horsemanship. During the festival the local gin *(ginebra)* is drunk copiously and the city grinds to a halt for a week.

Museu Diocesà
Carrer Mirador 5. (971) 71 40 63. daily.

Palau Salort
Carrer Major del Born 9. (971) 38 00 56. May–Oct: daily.

Ferreries ㉑

Baleares. **3,800.** **Carrer Sant Bartomeu 55, (971) 37 30 03.** Tue, Fri, Sat. Sant Bartomeu (Aug 23–5).

FERRERIES LIES in between Maó and Ciutadella and sprang up when a road was built to connect the two towns. Today Ferreries is an attractive village of white houses, built against the slope of a hill. The simple church, Sant Bartomeu, dates from the late 16th century.

The bay of **Santa Galdana**, 10 km (6 miles) to the south, is even prettier. You can take a pleasant walk from beach inland through the fertile riverbed of Barranc d'Algendar.

Courtyard in the Santuari del Toro

Es Mercadal ㉒

Baleares. **2,500.** **Carrer Major 16, (971) 37 50 02.** Sun. Sant Marti (third Sun of Jul).

ES MERCADAL is a small country town – one of the three, with Alaior and Ferreries, that are strung out along the main road from Maó to Ciutadella.

The town is unremarkable in itself, but within reach of it are three places of interest.

El Toro, 3 km (2 miles) to the east, is Menorca's highest mountain, at 350 m (1,150 ft). It is also the spiritual heart of the island, and at its summit is the Santuari del Toro, built in 1670, which is run by nuns.

About 10 km (6 miles) north of Es Mercadal, the fishing village of **Fornells** transforms itself every summer into an outpost of St. Tropez. In the harbor, smart yachts jostle with fishing boats, and jet-set Spaniards crowd into the Bar Palma. Fornells' main culinary specialty is the *caldereta de llagosta* (lobster casserole), but the quality varies and the prices can be high.

The dirt road to the **Cap de Cavalleria**, 13 km (8 miles) north of Es Mercadal, passes through one of the Balearics' finest landscapes. Cavalleria is a rocky promontory, whipped by the cold, dry tramontana wind from the north. It juts out into a choppy sea that, in winter, looks more like the North Atlantic than the Mediterranean. At the western edge of the peninsula are the remains of Sanitja, a Phoenician village mentioned by Pliny in the 1st century AD. The road leads to a headland, with a lighthouse and cliffs 90 m (295 ft) high, where peregrine falcons, sea eagles, and kites ride the wind.

Farther west along the coast is a string of fine, unspoiled beaches, though with difficult access: Cala Pregonda, Cala del Pilar, and La Vall d'Algaiarens are three of the most beautiful.

Horse rearing in the fiesta of Sant Lluís

THE BALEARIC ISLANDS' FIESTAS

Sant Antoni Abat *(Jan 17)*, Mallorca. This fiesta is celebrated with parades and the blessing of animals all over Mallorca and in Sant Antoni in Ibiza.

Sant Joan *(Jun 24)*, Ciutadella (Menorca). The horse plays a major part in Menorca's festivals. In the streets and squares of Ciutadella on June 24, the Day of St. John the Baptist, elegantly dressed riders put their horses through ritualized medieval maneuvers. The fiesta reaches a climax when the horses rear up on their hind legs and the jubilant crowds swarm around them trying to hold them up with their hands. Similarly, the annual fiesta in Sant Lluís, which takes place at the end of August, sees many of the locals taking to the streets on horseback.

Sant Joan Pelós *(Jun 24)*, Felanitx (Mallorca). As part of this fiesta, a man is dressed in sheepskins to represent John the Baptist.

Romeria de Sant Marçal *(Jun 30)*, Sa Cabeneta (Mallorca). A feature of this fiesta is a market selling *siurells*, primitive Mallorcan whistles.

Our Lady of the Sea *(Jul 16)*, Formentera. The island's main fiesta honors the Virgen del Carmen, patroness of fishermen, with a flotilla of fishing boats.

A quiet stretch of beach at Santa Galdana

The steep hillside of Maó running up from the harbor

Maó ❷❸

Baleares. 🕍 23,000. ✈ 🚢 🚌 🛈
Plaça de S'Esplanada, (971) 36 37 90.
🚍 Tue, Sat. 🎊 Fiestas de Gracia (Sep
7–8), Fiesta de Sant Antoni (Jan 17).

THE QUIETLY ELEGANT town of
Maó has lent its Spanish
name, Mahón, to mayonnaise
(see p489). It was occupied
by the British three times during the 18th century. The legacy of past colonial rule can be
seen in sober Georgian town-
houses, with their dark green
shutters and sash windows.

Maó's harbor is one of the
finest in the Mediterranean.
Taking the street leading from
the port to the upper town,
the S-shaped Costa de Ses
Voltes, you come to the 18th-
century **Església del Carme**,
a former Carmelite church
whose cool white cloister now
houses an attractive fruit and
vegetable market. Behind the
market is Maó's only museum,
the **Col·lecció Hernández**

Mora, which houses Menorcan
art and antiques. The nearby
Plaça Constitució is overlooked
by the church of Santa Maria,
which has a huge and well-
preserved organ, built in 1810.
Next door is the **town hall**
(ajuntament) with its Neo-
Classical façade, into which is
mounted the famous clock
donated by Sir Richard Kane
(1660–1736), the first British
governor of Menorca.

Located at the end of the
Carrer Isabel II is the **Església
de Sant Francesc**, with an
intriguing Romanesque doorway and Baroque façade. The
church houses the Museu de
Menorca (currently undergoing
refurbishment). Two minutes'
walk south of here will take
you to Maó's main square, the
Plaça de S'Esplanada, behind
which is the **Ateneu Científic
Lliterat Artistic**, a center of
Menorca-related culture and
learning. Inside are collections
of local ceramics and maps,
and a library. It is advisable

to obtain permission before
looking around. On the north
side of the harbor is a mansion known as **Sant Antoni**
or the Golden Farm. As Maó's
finest example of Palladian
architecture, it has an arched
façade, painted plum red, with
white arches, in the traditional
Menorcan style. The British
admiral, Nelson, is thought to
have stayed here. The house
has a collection of Nelson
memorabilia and a fine library,
but is closed to the public.

🏛 **Col·lecció Hernández
Mora**
C/ Claustre del Carme 5. 📞 (971) 35
05 97. 🕐 Mon–Sat. 🎦
🏛 **Ateneu Cientìfic Lliterat
Artistic**
C/ Conde de Cifuentes 25. 📞 (971)
36 05 53. 🌑 Sun, public hols.

Cales Coves ❷❹

Baleares. 🚍 Sant Climent. 📞 Maó,
(971) 36 37 90.

ON EITHER SIDE of a pretty
bay can be found Cales
Coves – the site of Neolithic
dwellings of up to 9 m (30 ft)
in length, hollowed out of the
rock face. The caves, thought
to have been inhabited since
prehistoric times, are today
occupied by a community of
people seeking an alternative
lifestyle. Some of the caves
have front doors, chimneys,
and even butane stoves.

About 8 km (5 miles) west,
along the coast, lies Binibeca,
a tourist village built in a style
sympathetic to old Menorca.
The jumble of white houses
and tiny streets of the Poblat
de Pescadors, an imitation
fishing village, have the look
of the genuine article.

**Modern sculpture outside one of
the dwellings at Cales Coves**

◁ **The clear blue waters of Cala Turqueta in Menorca**

Ancient Menorca

Menorca is exceptionally rich in pre-historic remains – the island has been described as an immense open-air museum. The majority of the sites are the work of the "talaiotic" people who lived between 2000–1000 BC and are named after the *talaiots* or huge stone towers that characterize the Menorcan landscape. There are hundreds of these Bronze Age villages and structures dotted around the island. Usually open to the public and free of charge, these sites provide an invaluable insight into the ancient inhabitants of the Balearics.

Huge *talaiot* amid the settlement of Trepucó

DIFFERENT STRUCTURES

The ancient stone structures scattered around the countryside of Menorca and, to a lesser extent, Mallorca can be placed into three main categories: *taulas, talaiots,* and *navetas.*

Taulas *are two slabs of rock, one placed on top of the other, in a "T" formation. Suggestions as to their possible function range from a sacrificial altar to a roof support.*

Talaiots *are circular or square buildings that may have been used as meeting places and dwellings.*

Navetas *are shaped like upturned boats and apparently had a dual role as dwellings and burial quarters. At least ten of these remain in Menorca.*

Spectacular *taula* at Talatí de Dalt, standing 3 m (10 ft) high

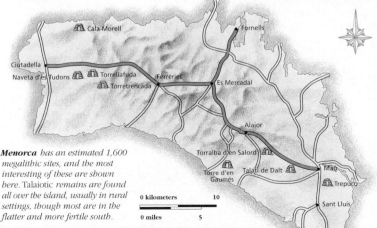

Menorca has an estimated 1,600 megalithic sites, and the most interesting of these are shown here. Talaiotic remains are found all over the island, usually in rural settings, though most are in the flatter and more fertile south.

0 kilometers   10

0 miles   5

THE CANARY ISLANDS

LA PALMA · EL HIERRO · LA GOMERA · TENERIFE
GRAN CANARIA · FUERTEVENTURA · LANZAROTE

P OISED ON THE EDGE OF THE TROPICS *west of Morocco, the Canaries enjoy a generous supply of sunshine, pleasantly tempered by the trade winds. Their scenery ranges from lava desert to primeval forest and from sand dunes to volcanic peaks. The old towns on the main islands have colonial centers, full of character.*

Seven islands and half a dozen islets make up the Canary archipelago. They are the tips of hundreds of volcanoes that first erupted from the sea bed 14 million years ago. Teneguía on La Palma last erupted in 1971.

In the 14th and 15th centuries, when navigators discovered the islands and claimed them for Spain, they were inhabited by the Guanches, who practiced a stone culture. Sadly, little evidence of them remains.

Today the islands are divided into two provinces. The four western isles, making up the province of Santa Cruz de Tenerife, are all mountainous; Tenerife's colossal dormant volcano, Mount Teide, casts the world's biggest sea-shadow. La Palma, El Hierro, and La Gomera, where Columbus stayed on his voyages, are all small, unspoiled islands, not yet developed for mass tourism.

The eastern islands belong to the province of Las Palmas. Rocky, forested Gran Canaria is the biggest island, and its capital, Las Palmas, is a charming colonial town. Lanzarote, by contrast, is flat, with lunar landscapes, while Fuerteventura has long, virgin beaches.

Protected area of sand dunes at Maspalomas, next to the busy Playa del Inglés, Gran Canaria

◁ **La Rambla banana plantation on the north coast of the island of Tenerife**

Exploring the Western Islands

TENERIFE HAS THE WIDEST RANGE of tourist attractions of any of the Canary Islands. The province of Santa Cruz de Tenerife also includes the three tiny westerly islands of La Palma, La Gomera, and El Hierro, which are scarcely developed for tourism and have no large resorts. Gradually, more visitors are discovering these peaceful, green havens. If you enjoy walking, wildlife, and mountain scenery, visit one of these hideaways. All three islands have comfortable hotels, including paradors. But compared with Gran Canaria and the eastern islands, there are fewer sandy beaches here, and little organized entertainment or sightseeing.

Las Teresitas artificial beach, Santa Cruz de Tenerife

SIGHTS AT A GLANCE

Candelaria **8**
Los Cristianos **4**
La Gomera **3**
El Hierro **2**
La Laguna **9**
Montes de Anaga **10**
La Orotava **7**
La Palma **1**
Parque Nacional del Teide
pp514–15 **5**
Puerto de la Cruz **6**
Santa Cruz de Tenerife **11**

Roque Bonanza on the rocky east coast of El Hierro

KEY

 Freeway

Major road

Minor road

Scenic route

River

Viewpoint

Terraced hillside, maximizing cultivation in the lush green Valle Gran Rey, in western La Gomera

GETTING AROUND

From mainland Spain there are flights *(see p628)* and ferries *(see p629)* to the Canary Islands. Transportation to the small islands is mainly from Tenerife. La Gomera is easily reached by ferry (90 mins) or hydrofoil (40 mins) from Los Cristianos. Small airports on La Palma and El Hierro are served by regular flights from Tenerife's northern airport of Los Rodeos. Unless you take an organized bus trip, a car is essential to see the island scenery. Roads are improving, but great care is needed for mountain driving.

MONTES DE-ANAGA

TENERIFE

LA LAGUNA ⑨
SANTA CRUZ DE TENERIFE ⑪
⑩

BUENAVISTA DEL NORTE

PUERTO DE LA CRUZ ⑥
LA OROTAVA ⑦
TF5
C820
C821
CANDELARIA
⑧
C824

PARQUE NACIONAL DEL TEIDE ⑤
C822
VILAFLOR
C821
C822
GRANADILLA DE ABONA
TF1
④
LOS CRISTIANOS

0 kilometers	25
0 miles	10

SEE ALSO

- *Where to Stay* pp570–71

- *Restaurants and Bars* pp608–609

The wild landscape of Punta de Teno in western Tenerife

La Palma ❶

Santa Cruz de Tenerife. ✈ ⛴ Santa Cruz de la Palma. ℹ Calle O'Daly 22, Santa Cruz de la Palma, (922) 41 21 06.

REACHING AN ALTITUDE of 2,426 m (7,959 ft) on a land base of less than 728 sq km (280 sq miles), La Palma is the world's steepest island. It lies on the northwestern tip of the archipelago and has a cool, moist climate and lush vegetation. The mountainous interior of the island is covered with forests of indigenous pine, laurel, and giant fern.

The center of the island is dominated by **La Caldera de Taburiente**, a volcano's massive crater, more than 8 km (5 miles) wide. National park status (see pp26–7) is an indication of its botanical and geological importance. The International Astrophysics Observatory crowns the summit. A couple of adventurously engineered roads traverse La

The Parque Nacional de la Caldera de Taburiente, La Palma

Palma's dizzy heights, offering spectacular views of the craters of La Cumbrecita and Roque de los Muchachos.

Santa Cruz de la Palma, the island's main town and port, is an elegant place of old houses with balconies, some fine churches, and several 16th-century buildings. In the cobbled street behind the seafront, Calle O'Daly (named after an Irish banana trader), are the Iglesia de San Salvador, boasting a Mudéjar coffered ceiling, and the town hall (ayuntamiento), which is housed in a cardinal's palace. A full-sized cement replica of the Santa María, Columbus' flagship, stands at the end of the Plaza Alameda.

The tortuous mountain road southwest of Santa Cruz winds over Las Cumbres mountains via Breña Alta to **El Paso** in the center of the island. A relatively sizable community, the village is known for its silk production and hand-rolled cigars.

Pastel façades and delicate wooden balconies in Santa Cruz, La Palma

Among the almond terraces and vineyards of southern La Palma, solidified lava from the Teneguía volcano is a reminder of its recent activity (see p527).

Craters on El Hierro, Spain's most western territory

El Hierro ❷

Santa Cruz de Tenerife. ✈ ⛴ Puerto de Estaca. ℹ Calle Licenciado Bueno 5, Valverde, (922) 55 03 02.

DUE TO A DEARTH of sandy beaches, El Hierro has escaped the tourist invasions experienced by other islands. Instead it has caught the attentions of naturalists. Its hilly landscape and unusual fauna and flora are part of its appeal. El Hierro is the smallest of the Canaries, and the territory farthest west of the mainland; consequently it is the last place in Spain where the sun sets.

Valverde, the island's capital, stands inland at 600 m (1,969 ft) above sea level. Canary pines and peculiarly twisted

LA GOMERA'S WHISTLE LANGUAGE

The problems of communication posed by La Gomera's rugged terrain produced an unusual language, known as El Silbo. This system of piercing whistles probably developed because its sounds carry across the great distances from one valley to the next. Its origins are mysterious, but it was allegedly invented by the Guanches (see p523). Few young Gomerans have any use for El Silbo today, and the language would probably be dead if it were not for the demonstrations of it still held for interested visitors at the parador, and in the restaurant at Las Rosas.

El Silbo practiced on La Gomera

juniper trees cover El Hierro's mountainous interior, best seen from the many footpaths and scenic viewpoints along the roads. A ridge of woodland, curving east-west across the island, marks the edge of a volcano. The crater forms a fertile depression known as El Golfo.

In the far west is the **Ermita de los Reyes**, a place of pilgrimage and the starting point of the island's biggest fiesta, held in July every four years.

The turquoise seas off the south coast are popular with skin divers, who base themselves in the small fishing village of **La Restinga**.

La Gomera ❸

Santa Cruz de Tenerife. 🚢 🛈 *Calle Real 4, San Sebastián de la Gomera, (922) 14 01 47.*

Terraced hillsides in the fertile Valle Gran Rey, La Gomera

A S YET LA GOMERA has no airport, but it is the most accessible and visited of the smaller western islands, only 40 minutes by hydrofoil from Los Cristianos on Tenerife (90 minutes by ferry). Many people come to La Gomera for a day only, taking a bus trip to get around about half of it. Others rent a car and explore independently: a scenic but exhausting drive for a single day because the terrain is intensely buckled, and the central plateau is deeply scored by dramatic ravines. Driving across these gorges involves negotiating countless dizzying hairpin turns.

The best way to enjoy the island is to stay awhile and explore it at leisure, preferably doing some walking. On a fine day, La Gomera's scenery is glorious. Rock pinnacles jut above steep slopes studded with ferns, while terraced hillsides glow with palms and flowering vines. The best section, the **Parque Nacional de Garajonay**, is a UNESCO World Heritage Site.

San Sebastián, La Gomera's main town and ferry terminal, is situated on the east coast, a scattering of white buildings around a small beach. Among its sights are some places associated with Columbus *(see pp54–5)*, who filled up his water supplies here before setting out on his adventurous voyages. A well in the customs house bears the grand words "With this water America was baptized." According to legend, Columbus also prayed in the Iglesia de la Asunción and stayed at a local house.

Beyond the arid hills to the south lies **Playa de Santiago**, the island's only real resort, which has a gray pebble beach. **Valle Gran Rey**, in the far west, is a fertile valley of palms and terraces. These days it is colonized by foreigners attempting alternative lifestyles. In the north, tiny roads weave a tortuous course around several pretty villages, plunging here and there to small, stony beaches. **Las Rosas** is a popular stop-over for bus tours, which can enjoy the visitors' center and a restaurant with a panoramic view.

The road toward the coast from Las Rosas leads through the town of **Vallehermoso**, dwarfed by the huge **Roque de Cano**, an impressive mass of solidified lava. Just off La Gomera's north coast stands **Los Órganos**, a fascinating rock formation of crystallized basalt columns resembling the pipes of an organ.

Juniper trees on El Hierro, twisted and bent by the wind

Tenerife

IN THE LANGUAGE of its aboriginal Guanche inhabitants, Tenerife means "Snowy Mountain," a tribute to its most striking geographical feature, the dormant volcano of Mount Teide, Spain's highest peak. The largest of the Canary Islands, Tenerife is a roughly triangular landmass rising steeply on all sides toward the cloud-capped summit that divides it into two distinct climatic zones: damp and lushly vegetated in the north, sunny and arid in the south. Tenerife offers a more varied range of attractions than any of the other Canary Islands, including its spectacular volcanic scenery, water sports, and a vibrant atmosphere after dark. Its beaches, however, have unenticing black sand and are rather poor for swimming. The main resorts are crowded with high-rise hotels and apartments, offering nightlife but little peace and quiet.

Bananas in northern Tenerife

Los Cristianos ❹

Santa Cruz de Tenerife. 🏘 20,000. 🚇 🚌 🚲 Calle General Franco, (922) 75 24 92. 🚢 Sun. 🎉 Fiesta del Carmen (first Sun of Sep).

THE OLD FISHING VILLAGE of Los Cristianos, on Tenerife's south coast, has grown into a town spreading out along the foot of barren hills. Ferries and hydrofoils make regular trips from its little port to La Gomera (see p509).

To the north lies the modern expanse of **Playa de las Américas**, Tenerife's largest development. It offers visitors a cheerful, relaxed, undemanding cocktail of sun and fun.

A brief sortie inland leads to the much older town of **Adeje** and to the **Barranco del Infierno**, a wild gorge with an attractive waterfall (two hours' walk from Adeje).

Along the coast to the east, the **Costa del Silencio** is a pleasant contrast to most of the other large resorts, with

its less imposing bungalow developments surrounding fishing villages. El Abrigo has lively, bustling fish restaurants lining its small harbor.

Farther east, **El Médano** shelters below an ancient volcanic cone. Its two beaches are popular with windsurfers.

Parque Nacional del Teide ❺

See pp514–15.

Puerto de la Cruz ❻

Santa Cruz de Tenerife. 🏘 30,000. 🚇 🏢 Plaza de la Iglesia, (922) 38 60 00. 🚢 Tue, Thu & Sat. 🎉 Fiesta del Carmen (second Sun of Jul).

PUERTO DE LA CRUZ, the oldest resort in the Canaries, first sprang to prominence in 1706, when a volcanic eruption obliterated Tenerife's principal port of Garachico. Puerto de

la Cruz took its place, later becoming popular with genteel English convalescents. The older buildings, concentrated around the Plaza del Charco de los Camerones and the Puerto Pesquero, give the town much of its present character.

The beautiful Lago Martiánez lido, designed by the Lanzarote architect César Manrique (see p524), compensates for a lack of good beaches with its sea-water pools, palms, and fountains. Other local attractions include the Botanical Gardens, founded in 1788, which display over 1,000 different species.

Outside town, the **Bananera El Guanche** plantation has an exhibition on bananas and other tropical crops. **Icod de los Vinos**, a short drive west, attracts crowds for its spectacular ancient dragon tree.

🌿 **Bananera El Guanche**
Carretera Botánico, La Dehesa. 📞 (922) 33 18 53. 🚪 daily. 🎦 ♿

THE DRAGON TREE

The Canary Islands have many unusual plants, but the dragon tree (Dracaena draco) is one of the strangest. This primitive creature looks a little like a giant cactus, with swollen branches that sprout multiple tufts of spiky leaves. When cut, the trunk exudes a reddish sap once believed to have magical and medicinal properties. Dragon trees form no annual rings, so their age is a mystery. Some are thought to be thousands of years old. The most venerable surviving specimen can be seen at Icod de los Vinos.

The landscaped Lago Martiánez lido, Puerto de la Cruz

La Orotava ❼

Santa Cruz de Tenerife. 🏛 *40,000.*
🚍 ℹ *Santa Cruz de Tenerife, (922)
60 55 92.* 🎭 *Carnival (Feb/Mar),
Corpus Christi (May/Jun).*

A SHORT distance from Puerto de la Cruz, in the fertile hills above the Orotava valley, La Orotava makes a popular excursion. The old part of this historic town clusters around the large **Iglesia de Nuestra Señora de la Concepción**. This domed Baroque building with twin towers was built in the late 18th century to replace an earlier church that was destroyed in earthquakes at the beginning of that century.

In the surrounding streets and squares are numerous old churches, convents, and grand houses with elaborately carved wooden balconies. The **Casas de los Balcones** and **Casa del Turista** both have pretty interior courtyards that are open to the public.

Statue of a Guanche chief on the seafront of Candelaria

Nuestra Señora de la Candelaria, patron saint of the Canary Islands

Candelaria ❽

Santa Cruz de Tenerife. 🏛 *12,000.*
🚍 ℹ *Calle Antón Guanche 1, (922)
50 04 15.* 🛒 *Sat, Sun.* 🎭 *Nuestra
Señora de la Candelaria (Aug 14–15).*

THIS COASTAL TOWN is famous for its shrine to **Nuestra Señora de la Candelaria**, the Canary Islands' patron saint, whose image is surrounded by flowers and candles in a modern church in the main square. This gaudy Virgin, supposedly washed ashore in pagan times, was venerated before Christianity reached the island. In 1826 a tidal wave returned her to the sea, but a replica draws pilgrims to worship here every August. Outside, stone effigies of Guanche chiefs line the sea wall.

La Laguna ❾

Santa Cruz de Tenerife. 🏛 *130,000.*
🚍 ℹ *Calle Carrera 1, (922) 60 11 00.*
🛒 *daily.* 🎭 *San Benito (Jul 15).*

A BUSTLING university town and former island capital, La Laguna is the second largest settlement on Tenerife.

In its old quarter, best explored on foot, there are many atmospheric squares, historic buildings and several good museums. Most of the sights lie between the bell-towered **Iglesia de Nuestra Señora de la Concepción**, dating from 1502, and the Plaza del Adelantado, on which stand the town hall, a convent (with a fine, traditional balcony), and the elegant **Palacio de Nava**.

Montes de Anaga ❿

Santa Cruz de Tenerife. 🚍 *Santa Cruz
de Tenerife, La Laguna.*

THE RUGGED MOUNTAINS north of Santa Cruz are kept green and lush by a cool, wet climate. They abound with a wide variety of interesting birds and plants, including cactuses, laurels, and tree heathers. Walking the mountain trails is very popular, and maps showing many of the best paths are readily available from the tourist office. A steep road with marker posts climbs up from the village of San Andrés by the beautiful but artificial beach of Las Teresitas. On clear days there are marvellous vistas along the paths, especially from the view points of Pico del Inglés and Bailadero.

Winding down through the laurel forests of Monte de las Mercedes and the valley of Tejina you reach **Tacoronte** with its interesting churches, an ethnographic museum, and a wineshop, where you can sample local wines.

THE CANARY ISLANDS' FIESTAS

Carnival *(Feb/Mar)*, Santa Cruz de Tenerife. One of Europe's biggest carnivals, this grand street party is a lavish spectacle of extravagant costumes and Latin American dance music to rival that of Rio de Janeiro. For years under the Franco regime, Carnival was suppressed for its irreverent frivolity. It begins with the election of a queen of the festivities and builds up to a climax on Shrove Tuesday when there is a large procession. The "funeral" of an enormous mock sardine takes place on Ash Wednesday. Carnival is also celebrated on the islands of Lanzarote and Gran Canaria.

Revelers in Carnival outfits on Tenerife

Corpus Christi *(May/Jun)*, La Orotava (Tenerife). The streets of the town are filled with flower carpets in striking patterns, while the Plaza del Ayuntamiento is covered in copies of works of art, formed from colored volcanic sands.
Descent of the Virgin of the Snows *(Jul, every five years: 2000, 2005)* Santa Cruz de La Palma.
Romería de la Virgen de la Candelaria *(Aug 15)*, Candelaria (Tenerife). Pilgrims come here in the thousands to venerate the Canary Islands' patroness.
Fiesta del Charco *(Sep 7–11)*, San Nicolás de Tolentino (Gran Canaria). People leap into a large saltwater pond to catch mullet.

Large ships moored at the busy port of Santa Cruz de Tenerife

Santa Cruz de Tenerife ⓫

Santa Cruz de Tenerife. 🖼 *200,000.*
✈ 🚢 ➕ *Plaza de España 1, (922) 60 55 92.* 🚍 *Sun.* 🎭 *Carnival (Feb/Mar), Día de la Cruz (May 3), Nuestra Señora del Carmen (Jul 16).*

Tenerife's capital city is an important regional port, with a deepwater harbor suitable for large ships. Its most attractive beach, **Las Teresitas**, lies 8 km (5 miles) to the north. Completely artificial, it was created by importing millions of tons of golden Saharan sand and building a protective reef just offshore. Shaded by palms, backed by mountains, and so far devoid of concrete hotel developments, the result improves on anything nature has bestowed on Tenerife.

Santa Cruz can boast many handsome historic buildings. The hub of the town is around the **Plaza de España**, situated near the harbor. Just off it is the Calle de Castillo, the main shopping street. Its two most noteworthy churches are the **Iglesia de Nuestra Señora de la Concepción**, with parts dating from 1500, and Baroque **Iglesia de San Francisco**.

Particularly interesting is the **Museo Arqueológico**, located in the Palacio Insular, where Guanche mummies grin in glass cases. Inside the museum you can also see the cannon that is alleged to have removed the arm of the British admiral Nelson during an un-

successful raid on the city at the end of the 18th century.

Other attractions include the **Museo de Bellas Artes**, which features old masters as well as modern works. Many of its paintings focus on local events and landscapes. Contemporary sculptures adorn the **Parque Municipal García Sanabria**, a pleasant park with shady paths, laid out in 1926.

In the morning, visit the **Mercado de Nuestra Señora de África**, which combines a bazaar with a food market. Outside stalls sell domestic goods; those inside offer an eclectic mix of live chickens, herbs, spices, and cut flowers. Santa Cruz is especially worth a visit during its flamboyant annual carnival.

🏛 **Museo Arqueológico**
Calle Fuentes Morales. 📞 *(922) 21 30 00.* 🕐 *Tue–Sun.* 🈲 🚫
🏛 **Museo de Bellas Artes**
Calle José Murphy 12. 📞 *(922) 24 43 58.* 🕐 *Mon–Sat.*

The artificial beach of Las Teresitas in Santa Cruz

Regional Food: The Canary Islands

Corn

ALTHOUGH SOMETIMES hard to find, there is a regional cuisine in the Canaries. It combines elements of Guanche cooking with ingredients originally from other continents, such as corn and bananas. A climate of eternal spring provides a wealth of other fruit, and vegetables. The sea supplies many colorful fish, like the purple and yellow *vieja* – or bass – that is eaten with *mojo*, a pounded sauce that varies in its ingredients and color depending on whether coriander or paprika is used. Many dishes are served with *papas arrugadas* (potatoes cooked with their skins in heavily salted water). *Gofio* is a Guanche cornmeal, which is made into porridge and used to thicken stews and to make bread. Desserts include *bienmesabe,* a sweet cream of almonds, egg yolk, and cinnamon.

Sancocho, *parboiled fish best made with* sama, *a type of bass, is often served with sweet and plain potatoes.*

Sama frita con mojo verde *is fried fish served with a sauce blended from garlic, coriander, and vinegar.*

Potaje de berros, *a thick soup, contains watercress, pork ribs, corn on the cob, potatoes, beans, and cumin.*

Conejo al salmorejo, *an appetizing stew made with rabbit and tomato, is best eaten with* papas arrugadas.

Arroz con verduras *is a colorful mixture of rice with chopped peppers, corn, and tomatoes.*

Puchero *is the local saffron-flavored stew, made with chorizo sausage, beans, chickpeas, and potatoes.*

Canary bananas *are the sweet La Gomera variety, small and aromatic. They are made into fritters and tarts; or served with rice and eggs, or meat sauce. Other fruits available are guava, mango, and papaya.*

Dark Canary rum

DRINKS

In the early 17th century the Canary Islands were renowned for their amber-colored Malvasía wine, which is rich, sweet, and highly alcoholic. The best of it is made on Lanzarote. Less potent red and white wines are produced in the Tacoronte-Acentejo region of Tenerife. The Canary Islands also offer a selection of locally made spirits, most notable of which is the excellent white and dark rum (*ron*). Other drinks include liqueurs flavored with coffee, orange, or bananas, and a rough *coñac* (brandy).

Parque Nacional del Teide ❺

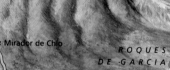

Towering over Tenerife, Mount Teide, surrounded by a wild volcanic landscape, is an awesome sight. Millions of years ago a much larger adjacent cone exploded, leaving behind the devastation of Las Cañadas, a 16-km (10-mile) wide crater, and the smaller volcano, Teide, on its northern edge. Today volcanic material forms a wilderness of weathered, mineral-tinted rocks, ash beds, and lava flows. A single road crosses the plateau of Las Cañadas, passing a parador, cable car station, and visitors' center. Follow the marked paths to see the best of this unique, protected area.

Volcanic Landscapes
The eight-minute cable car ride leaves you 160 m (525 ft) short of Teide's summit. A path through volcanic rubble gives unforgettable views.

Pico del Teide, which is still volcanically active, is Spain's highest summit.

PICO DEL TE

3,718 m
(12,198 ft)

PICO VIEJO

Pico Viejo, a volcanic cone also known as Montaña Chahorra, last erupted in the 18th century.

3,414 m
(11,200 ft)

CHIO

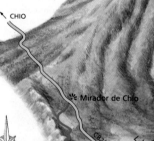

0 kilometers 2

0 miles 1

KEY

▬▬ Road

▬▬ Track

▬ ▬ Footpath

Mirador de Chío

R O Q U E S
D E G A R C I A

Mirador
de La Rulet

C823

L L A N O
D E U C A N C A

Mirador de
Boca Tauce

VILAFLOR

C821

Mi
de

Los Roques de García
These flamboyantly shaped lava rocks near the parador are some of the most photographed in the whole park. The rocks of Los Azulejos, nearby, glitter blue-green because of the copper deposits within them.

WILDFLOWERS

The inhospitable badlands of Las Cañadas are inhabited by some rare and beautiful plants. Many of these are unique to the Canary Islands. Most striking is the tall *Echium wildprettii*, a kind of viper's bugloss, whose red spires reach 2 m (7 ft) in early summer. Other common plants include Teide broom, the distinctive California poppy, and a unique species of violet. The best time of year for flower-spotting is May to June. Displays housed in the visitors' center will help identify them. Don't take any plants away with you: all vegetation within the park is strictly protected and must not be uprooted or picked.

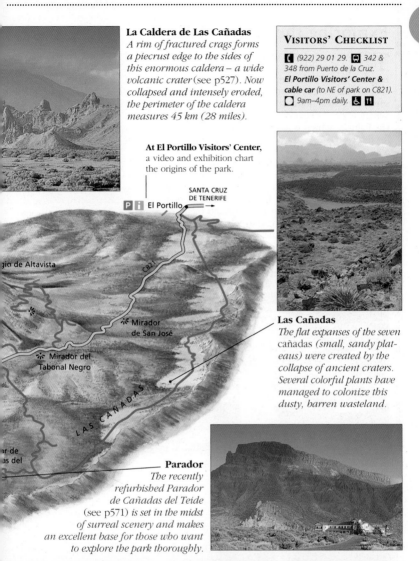

La Caldera de Las Cañadas

A rim of fractured crags forms a piecrust edge to the sides of this enormous caldera – a wide volcanic crater (see p527). *Now collapsed and intensely eroded, the perimeter of the caldera measures 45 km (28 miles).*

At El Portillo Visitors' Center, a video and exhibition chart the origins of the park.

SANTA CRUZ DE TENERIFE

P i El Portillo

gio de Altavista

C821

☀ Mirador de San José

☀ Mirador del Tabonal Negro

LAS CAÑADAS

or de as del

Las Cañadas

The flat expanses of the seven cañadas *(small, sandy plateaus) were created by the collapse of ancient craters. Several colorful plants have managed to colonize this dusty, barren wasteland.*

Parador

The recently refurbished Parador de Cañadas del Teide (see p571) *is set in the midst of surreal scenery and makes an excellent base for those who want to explore the park thoroughly.*

ary mustard
ymbrium
rgaenum)

Teide
allflower
Erysium
parium)

Teide violet
(Viola cheiranthifolia)

Teide viper's bugloss
(Echium wildprettii)

Exploring the Eastern Islands

THE EASTERN PROVINCE of the Canary Islands – Las Palmas – comprises the islands of Gran Canaria, Lanzarote, and Fuerteventura. All feature unusual and spectacular scenery, plenty of sunshine, and excellent sandy beaches, but each has a very different atmosphere. Gran Canaria boasts the only really large town, Las Palmas, which is also the administrative center for the eastern islands. It also offers the biggest resort, Maspalomas, with its Playa del Inglés, which has an unabashed package-tour feel. As a contrast, the long, white beaches of Fuerteventura have been left fairly undeveloped, and it is still possible to find privacy among their sand dunes. Lanzarote also has fine beaches, while its interior is dominated by an eerie volcanic landscape that makes for great excursions.

Corralejo's beach, in the north of Fuerteventura

The marina at Puerto Rico, in southern Gran Canaria

GETTING AROUND

Most people travel from mainland Spain to the eastern islands by air *(see p628)*. The alternative is a long sea crossing from Cádiz *(see p629)*. There are flights between all the islands, except La Gomera. There are also regular interisland ferries. Taxis and public transit are fine within resorts, but expensive over long distances. Cars can be rented on all the islands, usually at airports or ferry terminals. The main roads are well surfaced and fast on the flatter sections, though traffic in Gran Canaria can be heavy in places. A four-wheel drive vehicle is advisable to reach some remoter beaches.

GRAN CANARIA

AGAETE 15

LAS PALMAS DE GRAN CANARIA

TAFIRA 16

17

18 CRUZ DE TEJEDA

SAN NICOLAS DE TOLENTINO

SANTA LUCIA

AGÜIMES

ATLANTICO

PUERTO DE MOGAN 12

13 PUERTO RICO

14 MASPALOMAS

0 kilometers 25

0 miles 10

SIGHTS AT A GLANCE

Agaete **15**
Arrecife **27**
Betancuria **20**
Caleta de Fustes **21**
Corralejo **23**
Costa Teguise **28**
Haría **30**
Jameos del Agua **31**
Maspalomas **14**
Las Palmas de
  Gran Canaria **17**
Parque Nacional de
  Timanfaya **25**

Península de Jandía **19**
Playa Blanca **24**
Puerto del Carmen **26**
Puerto de Mogán **12**
Puerto del Rosario **22**
Puerto Rico **13**
Tafira **16**
Teguise **29**

Tour
Cruz de Tejeda **18**

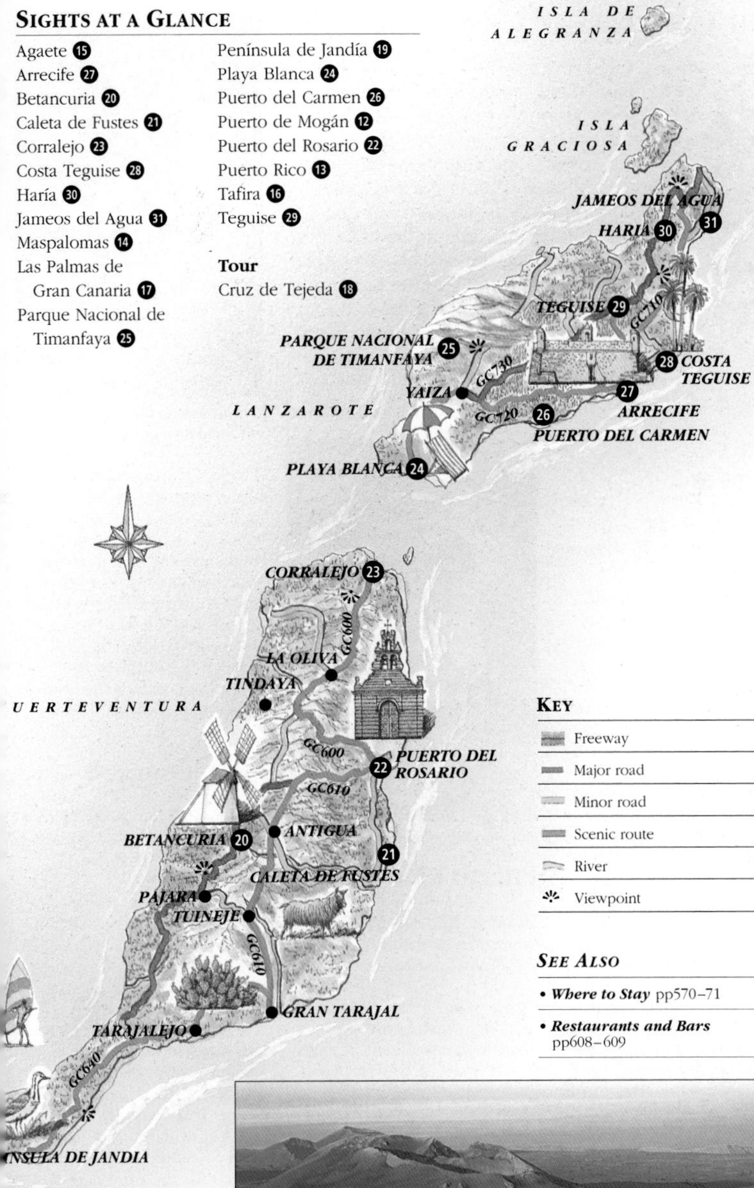

*ISLA DE
ALEGRANZA*

*ISLA
GRACIOSA*

JAMEOS DEL AGUA **31**
HARÍA **30**

TEGUISE **29**

*PARQUE NACIONAL
DE TIMANFAYA* **25**

YAIZA

28 COSTA
TEGUISE
27
ARRECIFE
26
PUERTO DEL CARMEN

LANZAROTE

PLAYA BLANCA **24**

CORRALEJO **23**

LA OLIVA
TINDAYA

UERTEVENTURA

GC600

22 PUERTO DEL
ROSARIO
GC610

BETANCURIA **20**   ANTIGUA

PÁJARA
TUINEJE

21
CALETA DE FUSTES

GC610

GRAN TARAJAL

TARAJALEJO

GC640

NSULA DE JANDÍA

KEY

▬▬	Freeway
▬▬	Major road
▬▬	Minor road
▬▬	Scenic route
⌐	River
⁂	Viewpoint

SEE ALSO

• *Where to Stay* pp570–71

• *Restaurants and Bars*
  pp608–609

Volcanoes of Montañas de Fuego in Parque Nacional de Timanfaya, Lanzarote

Gran Canaria

GRAN CANARIA IS THE MOST POPULAR of the Canary Islands, with over 1.5 million vacationers visiting it each year. The island offers a surprising range of scenery, climate, resorts, and attractions within its compact bounds. Winding roads follow the steep, ruggedly beautiful terrain that rises to a symmetrical cone at the center of the island. Las Palmas, Gran Canaria's capital and port, is the largest city in the Canaries, and Maspalomas/Playa del Inglés, in the south, is one of the biggest resorts in Spain.

Farmer and donkey

Both tourist meccas are packed with high-rise hotels and bungalow complexes, but not far away there is some marvelous scenery to discover.

Vacationers on the golden sands of Puerto Rico beach

Puerto de Mogán ⑫

Las Palmas. 🏠 680. 🛈 Puerto Rico, (928) 56 91 00. 🚢 Fri. 🎉 Virgen del Carmen (Jul).

SITUATED AT THE END of the verdant valley of Mogán, this is one of Gran Canaria's most appealing and success-ful developments - an idyllic spot to many visitors after the brash concrete of Playa del Inglés. Based around a small fishing port, it consists of a villagelike complex of pretty, white, vine-covered houses and a similarly designed hotel built around a marina. Bouti-ques, bars, and restaurants add an ambience without any accompanying rowdiness.

The sandy beach, sheltered between the cliffs, is scarcely big enough for all visitors; a car is recommended to reach more facilities at Maspalomas. Ferries provide a leisurely way to get to nearby resorts.

Sun worshipers in Puerto Rico

Puerto Rico ⑬

Las Palmas. 🏠 1,500. 🛈 Centro Comercial de Puerto Rico, (928) 56 00 29. 🎉 María de Auxiliadora (May).

THE BARREN CLIFFS west of Maspalomas now sprout apartment complexes at every turn. Puerto Rico is an over-

developed resort but has one of the more attractive beaches on the island, a firm crescent of imported sand supplemented by resorts and excellent water sports facilities. It is a great place to learn sailing, scuba-diving, or windsurfing, or just to lie back, relax, and soak up the ultraviolet – Puerto Rico enjoys the best sunshine record in all Spain.

Maspalomas ⑭

Las Palmas. 🏠 36,000. 🚌 🛈 Avda de España, (928) 14 06 64. 🚢 Wed & Sat. 🎉 San Bartolomé (Aug 24).

WHEN THE FAST freeway from Las Palmas airport first drops you off into this bewildering mega-resort, it seems like a homogeneous blur, but gradually three separate communities emerge. **San Agustín**, which is the farthest east, is restrained and sedate compared with the others. It has a series of beaches of dark sand, attrac-tively sheltered by low cliffs and landscaped promenades, and a casino.

The next exit off the coastal highway leads to **Playa del Inglés**, the largest and liveliest resort, a triangle of land jutting into a huge belt of golden sand. Developed since the end of the 1950s, the area is full of giant apartment buildings linked by a maze of roads. Many hotels lack sea views, but most have spacious grounds with swimming pools.

Floral arches decorating a street of apartments in Puerto de Mogán

At night the area pulsates with bright disco lights and flashing neon. There are more than 300 restaurants and over 50 discos in this resort alone.

West of Playa del Inglés the beach undulates into the **Dunas de Maspalomas**. A relieving contrast to the hectic surrounding resorts, these dunes form a nature preserve protected from further development. The western edge of the dunes (marked by a lighthouse) is occupied by a cluster of luxury hotels. Just behind the dunes lies a golf course encircled by bungalow villages.

Package tours are all-inclusive: excursions, water sports, fast food. Relief from beach fatigue comes with go-carts, camel safaris, and amusement centers; these include **Palmitos Park**, with subtropical gardens; and **Sioux City**, a Western theme park.

Palmitos Park
Barranco de los Palmitos. *(928) 14 11 58.* daily.

Sioux City
Cañón del Águila. *(928) 76 25 73.* Tue–Sun.

The rocky shore and steep cliffs of the northeast coast near Agaete

Agaete ⑮

Las Palmas. 5,000. *Calle Antonio de Armas 1, (928) 89 80 02. Fiesta de la Rama (Aug 4).*

THE CLOUDIER northern side of the island is far greener and lusher than the arid south, and banana plantations take up most of the coastal slopes. Agaete, on the northwest coast, a pretty scatter of white houses around a striking rocky bay, is growing into a small resort. Every August Agaete holds the Fiesta de la Rama, a Guanche *(see p523)* rain-making ritual that dates from long before the arrival of the Spanish. An animated procession of villagers bearing green branches heads from the hills above the town down to the coast and into the sea. The villagers beat the water to summon the rain.

Sights in Agaete include the little **Ermita de las Nieves**, containing a fine 16th-century Flemish triptych and model sailing ships, and the **Huerto de las Flores**, a botanical garden. Ask for the key to the garden at the town hall, which is located on the same street.

ENVIRONS: A brief detour inland up along the Barranco de Agaete takes you through a fertile valley of papaya, mango, and citrus trees. North of Agaete are the towns of Guía and Gáldar. Though there is little to see here, both parish churches do contain examples of the religious statuary of the celebrated 18th-century sculptor, José Luján Pérez.

Nearby, toward the north coast, lies the **Cenobio de Valerón**. One of the most dramatic of the local Guanche sights, this cliff face is pockmarked with nearly 300 caves beneath a basalt arch. These are believed to have been hideaways for Guanche priestesses, communal grainstores, and refuges from attack.

♣ Huerto de las Flores
Calle Juan de Armas. Mon–Fri.

Miles of wind-sculptured sand: the dunes at Maspalomas

Tafira 🟤

Las Palmas. 🏠 23,000. 🚌
ℹ️ Jardín Canario, (928) 35 36 04.
📅 San Francisco (Oct).

THE HILLS SOUTHWEST of Las Palmas have long been desirable residential locations. A colonial air still wafts around Tafira's patrician villas. The **Jardín Canario**, a botanical garden founded in 1952, is the main reason for a visit. Plants from all of the Canary Islands can be studied in their own, recreated habitats.

Near La Atalaya lies one of Gran Canaria's most impressive natural sights – the **Caldera de la Bandama**. This is a huge volcanic crater 1,000 m (3,300 ft) wide, best seen from the Mirador de Bandama where you gaze down into the green depression about 200 m (660 ft) deep. Some of the inhabited caves in the **Barranco de Guayadeque**, a valley of reddish rocks to the south, were dug in the late 15th century. A few of them have electricity.

🌿 **Jardín Canario**
Carretera del Centro, Tafira.
📞 (928) 35 36 04. 🕐 daily.

Las Palmas de Gran Canaria 🟤

Las Palmas. 🏠 350,000. 🚌 🚢
ℹ️ Parque de Santa Catalina, (928) 26 46 23. 📅 Carnival (Feb/Mar).

LAS PALMAS IS THE LARGEST city in the Canary Islands. A bustling seaport and industrial city, it sees 1,000 ships docking

Palm trees in a natural setting in the Jardín Canario, Tafira

each month. Las Palmas has faded somewhat from the days when wealthy convalescents flocked here in winter and glamorous liners called in on transatlantic voyages. But it remains a vibrant place to visit.

Las Palmas is a sprawling city built around an isthmus, and its layout can be confusing. The modern commercial shipping area, Puerto de la Luz, takes up the eastern side of the isthmus, which leads to the former island of La Isleta, a sailors' and military quarter. On the other side of the isthmus is the crowded **Playa de las Canteras**, a 3-km (2-mile) long stretch of golden beach. The promenade behind has been built up with bars, restaurants, and hotels.

The town center stretches along the coast from the isthmus. For a pleasant scenic tour, begin in the **Parque Santa Catalina**, near the port. This is a popular, shady square of

Bronze dog at Plaza Santa Ana

cafés and newspaper kiosks. In the leafy residential quarter of Ciudad Jardín is the Parque Doramas and the traditional casino hotel of Santa Catalina.

The **Pueblo Canario** is a tourist enclave where visitors can watch folk dancing, and browse in the craft shops and the small art gallery. All this can be viewed from above by walking uphill toward the Alta- vista district and the Paseo Cornisa.

At the end of town is the Barrio Vegueta, an atmospheric quarter that dates back to the Spanish conquest. At its heart stands the **Catedral de Santa Ana**, begun in 1500. The adjacent **Museo Diocesano de Arte Sacro** contains works of religious art. The square in front is guarded by Canarian dogs in bronze.

Nearby, the **Casa de Colón** is a 15th-century governor's residence where Columbus stayed. A museum dedicated to his voyages displays charts, models, and diary extracts.

Early history can be seen in the **Museo Canario,** which contains Guanche mummies, skulls, pottery, and jewelry.

🏛️ **Museo Diocesano de Arte Sacro**
Calle Espíritu Santo 20. 📞 (928) 31 49 89. 🕐 Mon–Sat. 🎫
🏺 **Casa de Colón**
Calle Colón. 📞 (928) 31 23 84.
🕐 daily.
🏛️ **Museo Canario**
Calle Doctor Chil 25. 📞 (928) 31 56 00. 🕐 daily. 🎫

The Casa de Colón museum, Las Palmas, dedicated to Columbus

Tour of Cruz de Tejeda ⑱

G RAN CANARIA'S mountainous interior makes for an ideal day tour, from any part of the island. Choose a clear day or the views may be obscured. The route from Maspalomas leads through dry ravines of bare rock and cacti, becoming more fertile with altitude. Roads near the central highlands snake steeply through shattered, tawny crags, past caves and pretty villages, to panoramic viewpoints from which you can see Mount Teide *(see pp514–15)* on Tenerife. On the north side, the slopes are much lusher, growing citrus fruits and eucalyptus trees.

White farmhouses en route to Teror

Artenara ②
One of the inhabited caves in this town houses a little church. Another has been converted into an unusual restaurant, the Mesón de la Silla.

LAS PALMAS

Valleseco

Lanzarote

Cuevas Corcho

PINAR DE TAMADABA

GC110

Teror ①
This charming old town has many well-preserved, typical Canary Islands houses. Its church, Nuestra Señora del Pino, is dedicated to Gran Canaria's patron saint.

Cruz de Tejeda ③
In this restaurant-only parador *(see p608)* you can eat Canary Islands specialties while enjoying magnificent mountain views.

Tejeda

C811

C811

Pico de las Nieves ⑤
A meteorological station crowns Gran Canaria's highest peak. At 1,949 m (6,394 ft), it is often chilly up here and it sometimes snows, so take extra clothing.

KEY

▬▬	Tour route
═══	Other roads
☀	Viewpoint
🅿	Parador

0 kilometers 2
0 miles 1

④

TELDE

⑤

Ayacata

C815

MASPALOMAS

Roque Nublo ④
This 60-m (197-ft) high jagged spike of basalt tops a 1,700-m (5,577-ft) peak. Together with nearby Roque Bentayga, it was sacred to the Guanches. It's a stiff climb to the summit.

TIPS FOR DRIVERS

Length: 35–45 km (22–28 miles).
Stopping-off points: popular lunch spots are Mesón de la Silla cave-restaurant in Artenara and Cruz de Tejeda parador.
Note: roads can be narrow with few passing places; sudden patches of cloud or mist may loom without warning.

Fuerteventura

L YING JUST 100 KM (60 MILES) off the Atlantic coast of Morocco, leaf-shaped Fuerteventura is continually battered by coastal winds. It is the second largest of the Canary Islands after Tenerife, and the most sparsely populated: its 30,000 inhabitants are outnumbered by goats. The island used to be densely wooded, but European settlers cut down the timber for shipbuilding; the dry climate and the goats have since reduced the vegetation to parched scrub. It is so dry that water has to be shipped over from the mainland. The only significant revenue is tourism, but the tourist industry is still in its infancy compared with the other main islands. However, visitors are increasing in number as thousands of sun-worshipers flock to more than 150 splendid beaches. The island is popular with water sports fans and nudists.

A herd of goats near the airport on Fuerteventura

Península de Jandía ⑲

Las Palmas. 🚌 Costa Calma, Morro Jable. ⛴ (jetfoil) from Gran Canaria. 🛈 Centro Comercial, Playa de Jandía, (928) 54 07 76.

E XCELLENT BEACHES of pale sand fringe the elongated Jandía peninsula in the south of Fuerteventura. A string of *urbanizaciones* (apartment complexes) now takes up much of the peninsula's shel-tered east coast (Sotavento). **Costa Calma**, a burgeoning cluster of modern complexes, offers the most interesting beaches with long stretches of fine sand interrupted by low cliffs and coves. **Morro Jable**, a fishing village now swamped by new developments, lies at the southern end of a vast, glittering strand. Beyond Morro Jable, the access road dwindles away into a potholed track leading toward the lonely lighthouse at Punta de Jandía.

Expanses of deserted sand, accessible only by four-wheel-drive vehicles, line the westerly windward coast (Barlovento) – too exposed for all but the hardiest beach lovers. Some of the island's best subtropical marine life can be found in this area, however, making it popular with skin divers.

During World War II, Jandía belonged to a German entre-preneur. It was out of bounds to locals and acquired its own mystique. Even today, rumors of spies, submarines, and secret Nazi bases still circulate.

Betancuria ⑳

Las Palmas. 🏠 600. 🏢 🛈 Calle Amador Rodríguez 4, (928) 87 80 92. 🎭 San Buenaventura (Jul 14).

I NLAND, rugged peaks of extinct volcanoes, separated by wide plains, present a scene of austere grandeur. Scattered, stark villages and obsolete windmills occupy the lowlands that are occasionally fertile enough to nurture a few crops or palm trees. Beyond, devoid of vegetation, the hills form stark outlines. From a distance they appear brown and gray, but close up the rocks glow with an astonishing range of mauves, pinks, and ochers. The richness of color in this interior wilderness is at its

The gilded interior of the Iglesia Santa María in Betancuria

most striking at sunset, when a drive can reveal some breathtaking scenes.

Betancuria, built on a small volcano in the center of the island, is named after Jean de Béthencourt, Fuerteventura's 15th-century conqueror, who moved his capital inland to thwart pirates. Nestling in the mountains, this peaceful oasis is now the island's prettiest village. The **Iglesia de Santa María** contains gilded altars, decorated beams, and sacred relics. Ask for the key at the caretaker's house nearby. The **Museo Arqueológico** houses many local artifacts.

ENVIRONS: To the south, the village of **Pájara** boasts a 17th-century church with a curiously decorated doorway. Its design of serpents and strange beasts is believed to be of Aztec in-fluence. Inside, the twin aisles both contain statues: one of a radiant Madonna and Child in white and silver, the other a Virgen de los Dolores in black.

La Oliva, to the north, was the site of the Spanish military headquarters until the 19th century. The Casa de los Coroneles (House of the Colonels) is a faded yellow mansion with a grand façade and hundreds of windows. Inside it has coffered ceilings. The fortified church and the arts center displaying works of Canary Islands artists are also worth a visit.

🏛 **Museo Arqueológico**
Calle Fuentes Morales. 🄲 (922) 21 30 00. 🄾 Tue–Sun. 🈚 🈶

Caleta de Fustes ㉑

Las Palmas. 👥 2,600. 📷 🛈 *Caleta Dorada, El Castillo, (928) 16 32 86.* 📅 *Día del Carmen (Jul 16).*

S OUTH OF Puerto del Rosario, about halfway down the eastern coast of the island, lies Caleta de Fustes. This attractive and tasteful group of low-rise vacation villages surrounds a horseshoe bay of soft, gently sloping sand. The largest complex, El Castillo, takes its name from an 18th-century watchtower situated by the picturesque harbor.

There are many water sports facilities, including diving and windsurfing schools, as well as the Pueblo Majorero, an attractive "village" of shops and restaurants around a central plaza near the beach. These features make Caleta de Fustes one of Fuerteventura's most relaxed and pleasant resorts, popular with all nationalities.

Fishing boats on a beach on the Isla de Lobos, near Corralejo

Puerto del Rosario ㉒

Las Palmas. 👥 14,000. ✈ 📷 🚢 🛈 *Calle Primero de Mayo 37, (928) 85 14 00.* 📅 *El Rosario (Oct 7).*

F UERTEVENTURA'S commercial and administrative capital was founded in 1797. It was originally known as Puerto de Cabras (Goats' Harbor), after a nearby gorge that was once used for watering goats, but was rechristened to freshen up its image in 1957. As Puerto del Rosario is the only large port on Fuerteventura, it is the base for interisland ferries and a busy fishing industry. The town is also enlivened by the presence of the Spanish Foreign Legion, which occupies large barracks here.

Corralejo ㉓

Las Palmas. 👥 4,000. 🚢 🛈 *Plaza Pública, (928) 86 62 35.* 📷 *Mon, Tue, Thu, Fri.* 📅 *Día del Carmen (Jul 16).*

T HIS MUCH-EXPANDED fishing village is now (together with the Jandía peninsula) one of the island's two most important resorts. Its main attraction is a belt of glorious sand dunes stretching to the south, resembling the Sahara in places, and protected as a nature preserve. This designation arrived too late, however, to prevent the construction of two obtrusive hotels right on the beach.

The rest of the resort, mostly consisting of apartments, spills out haphazardly from the town center. The port area is lively, with busy fish restaurants and an efficient ferry service to Lanzarote, 40 minutes away.

Offshore is the tiny Isla de los Lobos, named after the once abundant monk seals (*lobos marinos*). Today, scuba divers, snorkelers, sport fishermen, and surfers claim the clear waters. Glass-bottomed cruise boats take the less adventurous to the island for barbecues and swimming trips.

THE GUANCHES

When Europeans first arrived in the Canary Islands in the late 14th century, they discovered a tall, white-skinned race, who lived in caves and later in small settlements around the edges of barren lava fields. Guanche was the name of one tribe on Tenerife, but it came to be used as the European name for all the indigenous tribes on the islands, and it is the one that has remained. The origins of the Guanches are still unclear, but it is probable that they arrived on the islands in the 1st or 2nd century BC from Berber North Africa. Within 100 years of European arrival the Guanches had been subdued and virtually exterminated by the ruthless conquistadors. A few traces of their culture remain on the islands today.

***Reminders** of the Guanches can be seen in some places in the Canaries. Specimens of their mummified dead, as well as baskets and stone and bone artifacts, are on display in several museums and there are statues of chiefs in Candelaria (see p511) on Tenerife.*

Guanche bowl for preparing gofio (see p513)

A Guanche basket

Lanzarote

THE EASTERNMOST and fourth largest of the Canary Islands is virtually treeless and has a permanent water shortage. Yet many visitors rate Lanzarote the most attractive of all the islands for the vivid shapes and contrasting colors of its volcanic landscapes. Despite low rainfall, carefully tended crops flourish in its black volcanic soil. Locals pride themselves on the way their island has been preserved from the worst effects of tourism; there are no garish billboards, overhead cables, or high-rise buildings. Its present-day image owes much to the artist César Manrique. Touring the spectacular volcanic Timanfaya National Park is a favorite trip.

Wind turbines harnessing Lanzarote's winds for power

Playa Blanca ㉔

Las Palmas. 🚶 4,000. 🚐 🛥️
🛈 Plaza de los Remedios 1, Yaiza,
(928) 83 02 50. 🚌 Wed. 🎇
Nuestra Señora del Carmen (Jul).

THE FISHING VILLAGE origins of this resort are readily apparent around its harbor. Although it has expanded in recent years, Playa Blanca remains an agreeably family-oriented place with some character. It has plenty of cafés and restaurants, shops and bars, and several large hotels. However, the buildings are well dispersed and the resort is rarely noisy at night. Visitors converge here not for nightlife or contrived entertainment, but for relaxing beach vacations. There are one or two good stretches of sand near to the town, but the most enticing lie hidden around the rocky headlands to the east, where the clear, warm sea laps into rocky coves and clothes seem superfluous. **Playa Papagayo** is the best known of these, but a diligent search will probably gain you one all to yourself. A four-wheel drive vehicle is advisable to negotiate the narrow, unsurfaced roads that lead to these beaches.

Parque Nacional de Timanfaya ㉕

Las Palmas. 🛈 Calle García Escámez 157, Arrecife, (928) 80 15 00.
🚌 from Arrecife. 🔘 daily. 🎇

FROM 1730–36 a series of volcanic eruptions took place on Lanzarote. Eleven villages were buried in lava, which eventually spread over 200 sq km (77 sq miles) of Lanzarote's most fertile land. Miraculously, no one was killed, though many islanders subsequently emigrated.

Today, the volcanoes that once devastated Lanzarote provide one of its most lucrative and enigmatic attractions, aptly known as the **Montañas de Fuego** (Fire Mountains). They are part of the Parque Nacional de Timanfaya, established in 1974 to protect a fascinating and important geological record. The entrance to the park lies just north of the small village of Yaiza. Here you can pause and take a 15-minute camel ride up the volcanic slopes for wonderful views across the park. Afterward, you pay the entrance fee and drive through haunting scenery of dark, barren lava cinders

---

CÉSAR MANRIQUE (1920–92)

Local hero César Manrique trained as a painter, and spent time in mainland Spain and New York before returning to Lanzarote in 1968. He campaigned for traditional and environmentally friendly development on the island for the remaining part of his life, setting strict building height limits and color requirements. Dozens of tourist sites throughout the Canaries benefited from his talents and enthusiasm.

César Manrique in 1992

Las Coloradas beach near Playa Blanca in southern Lanzarote

Camel rides from Yaiza across the Montañas de Fuego

topped by brooding red-black volcano cones. Finally, you will reach **Islote de Hilario**. You can park at El Diablo panoramic restaurant. From here, buses take visitors for exhilarating hour-long tours of the desolate, lunarlike landscapes.

Afterward, back at Islote de Hilario, guides will provide graphic demonstrations that this volcano is not extinct but only dormant: brushwood pushed into a crevice bursts instantly into a ball of flame, while water poured into a sunken pipe shoots out in a scorching jet of steam.

The road from Yaiza to the coast leads to the **Salinas de Janubio** where salt is extracted from an old volcano crater. Nearby are the boiling springs of **Los Hervideros** and farther north, at **El Golfo,** an eerie emerald-colored lagoon.

Puerto del Carmen ㉖

Las Palmas. 9,000.
Calle San Antonio 4, (928) 83 36 19.
Nuestra Señora del Carmen (Jul).

Mᴼ **ORE THAN** 60 PERCENT of Lanzarote's tourists stay in this large resort, which now stretches several miles along the seafront. The coastal road carves its way relentlessly through a solid slab of tourist infrastructure: car rental offices, banks, bureaux de change, shops, bars, restaurants, and discos. Behind the roadside arcades lie countless white villas, apartments, and hotels.

Though dense, the buildings are pleasantly designed and unoppressive. All have easy access to a long golden beach, Playa Blanca, which in places

is very wide. Another beach nearby is Playa de los Pocillos. The original village lies west of the port, away from the hustle and bustle of the resort.

Fishing boat in Arrecife port

Arrecife ㉗

Las Palmas. 30,000.
Parque Municipal, (928) 80 15 17.
Sat. San Ginés (Aug 25).

Aᴿ **RRECIFE,** with its modern buildings and lively streets, is the commercial and administrative center of the

island. Despite its modern trappings, the capital retains much of its old charm, with palm-lined promenades, a fine beach, and two small, historic forts. The **Castillo de San Gabriel**, located on a small offshore island accessible by bridge, houses a museum of archaeology. The 18th-century **Castillo de San José**, now a museum of contemporary art, was renovated by César Manrique, and one of his paintings is on display here.

⚓ **Castillo de San Gabriel**
Arrecife. (928) 80 28 84.
Mon–Fri.
⚓ **Castillo de San José**
Puerto de Naos. (928) 81 23 21.
daily. Jan 1, Dec 24.

Costa Teguise ㉘

10 km (6 miles) north of Arrecife.
Arrecife, (928) 80 15 17.

Tᴴ **HIS** RESORT, financed largely by a mining conglomerate, has transformed the arid, low-lying terrain north of Arrecife into an extensive cluster of timeshare accommodations, leisure clubs, and luxury hotels. The contrast between old town Teguise, Lanzarote's former capital, and the exclusive, new Costa Teguise is striking. Fake greenery and suburban lamps line access boulevards amid barren ashlands. Neat white villas line a series of small sandy beaches. The high level of investment has succeeded in attracting some of its intended jet-set clientele. King Juan Carlos also has a villa here.

Umbrellas on the beach, Puerto del Carmen

Iglesia de San Miguel on the main square in Teguise

Teguise 🕗

Las Palmas. 🚶 *9,000.* 🚌 ℹ️ *Calle General Franco 1, (928) 84 50 72.* 🛍️ *Sun.* 🎆 *Día del Carmen (Jul 16), Rancho de Pascua (Dec 24).*

TEGUISE, the island's capital until 1852, is a well-kept, old-fashioned town with wide, cobbled streets and patrician houses grouped around the **Iglesia de San Miguel**. The best time to visit is on a Sunday, when there is a lively handicrafts market and folk dancing. Just outside Teguise, the castle of Santa Bárbara contains the **Museo del Emigrante Canario**, which tells the story of Canarian emigrants to South America.

ENVIRONS: To see more of inland Lanzarote, follow the central road south of Teguise, through the strange farmland of **La Geria**. Black volcanic ash has been scooped into protective, crescent-shaped pits which trap moisture to enable grapes and other crops to flourish. **Mozaga**, one of the main villages in the area, is a major center of wine production. Near Mozaga is the *Monumento al Campesino*, Manrique's *(see p524)* striking modern sculpture dedicated to Lanzarote's farmers.

Halfway between Teguise and Arrecife is the **Fundación César Manrique**. The fascinating former home of the artist incorporates five lava caves. It contains some of his own work and his collection of contemporary art.

🏛 **Museo del Emigrante Canario**
Montaña de Guanapay. 📞 *(928) 84 50 72.* 🕐 *daily.*
🏛 **Fundación César Manrique**
Taro de Tahiche. 📞 *(928) 84 31 38.* 🕐 *daily.*

Haría 🕥

Las Palmas. 🚶 *3,000.* 🚌 ℹ️ *Plaza de la Constitución 1, (928) 83 52 51.* 🎆 *San Juan (Jun 24).*

PALM TREES and white, cube-shaped houses distinguish this picturesque village. It acts as a gateway to excursions round the northern tip of the island. The road to the north gives memorable views over exposed cliffs, and the 609-m (2,000-ft) high Monte Corona.

ENVIRONS: From Manrique's **Mirador del Río** you can see La Graciosa, and the northern-most of the Canary Islands, Alegranza. **Orzola** is a delightful fishing village providing fish lunches as well as boat trips to La Graciosa. To the south are the Mala prickly pear plantations, where cochineal (crimson dye) is extracted from the insects which feed on the plants. Nearby is the **Jardín de Cactus**, a well-stocked cactus garden, which has a stylish restaurant, again designed by Manrique.

🎦 **Mirador del Río**
Haría. 📞 *(928) 80 15 00.* 🕐 *daily.*
🌿 **Jardín de Cactus**
Guatiza. 📞 *(928) 52 93 97.* 🕐 *daily.*

Landscaped pool on top of the caves of Jameos del Agua

Jameos del Agua 🕙

Las Palmas. 📞 *(928) 83 50 10.* 🕐 *daily.* 🎦

AN ERUPTION of the Monte Corona volcano formed the Jameos del Agua lava caves on Lanzarote's northeast coast. In 1965–8, these were landscaped by César Manrique into an imaginative subterranean complex containing a restaurant, nightclub, a swimming pool edged by palm trees, and gardens of oleander and cactus. Steps lead to a shallow seawater lagoon where a rare species of blind white crab, unique to Lanzarote, glows softly in the dim light. An exhibition on volcanology and Canarian flora and fauna also deserves a look. Folk-dancing evenings are regularly held in this unusual setting.

ENVIRONS: Another popular attraction is the nearby **Cueva de los Verdes**, a tube of solidifed lava stretching 6 km (4 miles) underground. Guided tours of the caves are available.

🎦 **Cueva de los Verdes**
Haría. 📞 *(928) 17 32 20.* 🕐 *daily.* 🎦

Volcanic ash swept into crescent-shaped pits for farming, La Geria

Volcanic Islands

THE VOLCANIC ACTIVITY which formed the Canary Islands has created a variety of scenery, from distinctive lava formations to enormous volcanoes crowned by huge, gaping craters. The islands are all at different stages in their evolution. Tenerife, Lanzarote, El Hierro and La Palma are still volcanically active; dramatic displays of flames and steam can be seen in Lanzarote's Montañas de Fuego *(see p524)*. The last eruption was on La Palma in 1971.

Origin of the Islands
The Canaries are situated above faults in the earth's crust, which is always thinner under the oceans than under the continents. When magma (molten rock) rises through these cracks volcanoes are formed.

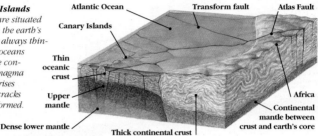

Atlantic Ocean — Transform fault — Atlas Fault — Canary Islands — Thin oceanic crust — Upper mantle — Dense lower mantle — Thick continental crust — Africa — Continental mantle between crust and earth's core

EVOLUTION OF THE CANARY ISLANDS

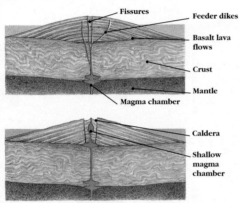

Fissures — Feeder dikes — Basalt lava flows — Crust — Mantle — Magma chamber

Caldera — Shallow magma chamber

Sea level — Exposed solidified magma chamber

1 ***Lanzarote, El Hierro, and La Palma*** are wide, gently sloping shield volcanoes standing on the ocean floor. All of them are composed of basalt formed by a hot, dense magma. The flexible crust is pressed down by the weight of the islands.

2 ***An explosive eruption*** can empty the magma chamber, leaving the roof unsupported. This collapses under the weight of the volcano above to form a depression, or caldera, such as Las Cañadas on Tenerife. There are thick lava flows during this stage of the island's evolution.

3 ***If eruptions cease*** a volcano will be eroded by the action of the sea, and by wind and rain. Gran Canaria's main volcano is in the early stages of erosion, while the volcano on Fuerteventura has already been deeply eroded, exposing chambers of solidified magma.

Rope lava near La Restinga, El Hierro

Pico Viejo crater, next to Mount Teide, Tenerife *(see p514)*

TRAVELERS' NEEDS

WHERE TO STAY

MEDIEVAL CASTLES turned into luxury hotels and mansions converted into youth hostels typify the variety of places to stay in Spain. The tourists who sustain Spain's economy have almost 10,000 establishments to choose from, offering around one million beds. Suites in once-royal palaces are at the top of the scale. Then there are luxury beach hotels on the

Logo for a luxury five-star hotel

Costa del Sol and in the Balearic and the Canary Islands. Visitors can also stay on remote farms, or in villas and old houses rented by the week. For budget travel there are pensions, family-run *casas rurales*, and guest houses, campsites, and shelters with stunning views for mountaineers. Some of the best hotels in all these categories and in every style and price range are listed on pages 536–71.

Hotel de la Reconquista, Oviedo, an 18th-century mansion *(see p539)*

HOTEL GRADING AND FACILITIES

ALL OF SPAIN's hotels are classified into categories and awarded stars by the country's regional tourist authorities. Hotels (indicated by an H on a blue plaque near the hotel door) are awarded from one to five stars. Hostals (Hs) and pensions (P) offer fewer comforts but are correspondingly cheaper than hotels.

Spain's star-rating system reflects the number and range of facilities available – whether the hotel has air conditioning, or an elevator – rather than the level of service.

Most hotels have restaurants that are open to nonresidents. Although hotel-residencias (HR) and hostal-residencias (HsR) do not have dining rooms, some serve breakfast. Among Spain's largest hotel chains are **Grupo Sol-Meliá**, **Grupo Riu**, **NH**, and **TRYP**. Many large tour operators book rooms in Spain's best hotels.

PARADORS

PARADORS are government-run hotels, classified from three to five stars. Spain's first parador opened in the Sierra de Gredos in 1928 *(see p556)*; there is now a wide network of them on the mainland and the islands. They are located close together so that there is never more than a day's drive to the nearest one. The best are in former royal hunting lodges, monasteries, castles, and other monuments; some modern paradors have been custom-built, often in spectacular scenery or in towns of historic interest *(see pp534–5)*.

A parador is not necessarily the best hotel in town, but it can be counted on to

deliver a predictably high level of comfort. The bedrooms are usually spacious and comfortable, and are furnished in a way that varies little from parador to parador.

If you plan to travel in tourist season or stay in the smaller paradors, it is wise to reserve a room. The paradors may be booked through the **Central de Reservas** in Madrid or through their New York agent, **Marketing Ahead**.

PRICES

SPANISH LAW requires all hotel managements to display their prices behind the front desk and in every room. As a rule, the higher a hotel's starrating, the more you pay. Rates for a double room can be as little as 3,000 pesetas a night for a cheap one-star hostal; a five-star hotel will cost more than 20,000 pesetas, but a room price higher than 30,000 pesetas a night is exceptional.

Prices usually vary according to room, region, and season. A suite or a very spacious room, or one with a view, a balcony, or other special feature, may cost more than average. Rural and suburban hotels are generally less expensive than those in the city center. All the prices given on pages 536–71 are based on mid- or tourist-season rates.

Jaén's parador, a modern extension of the medieval castle *(see p565)*

◁ **Madrileños** enjoying afternoon sunshine, drinks, and conversation in the Plaza Mayor

Tourist season generally covers July and August, but in some areas it runs from April to October, and in the Canary Islands it is the winter.

Many of Spain's city hotels charge especially inflated rates for their rooms during major fiestas, such as the April Fair in Seville (see p413), Los Sanfermines in Pamplona (see p128), Carnival in Santa Cruz de Tenerife, and Easter Week (see p34) in many places.

Most hotels quote prices per room and meal prices per person without including VAT (IVA), which is currently 7 percent in most of Spain, but 4 percent in the Canary Islands.

The glass-domed foyer of the Palace Hotel, Madrid (see p553)

BOOKING AND CHECK-IN

OFF-SEASON IN RURAL or small towns it is unlikely that you need to book ahead, but if you plan to travel in tourist season or want to stay in a particular hotel, you should reserve a room by phone or through a travel agent. You will need to reserve if you want a special room: one with a double bed (twin beds are the norm); on the ground floor; away from a noisy main road; or a room with a balcony or a view.

The resort hotels often close from autumn to spring. Before you travel, it is always advisable to check that your preferred hotels will be open at that time of year.

You will not normally be asked for a deposit when you book a hotel room. However, a deposit of 20–25 percent may be requested if you book during a peak period or for a stay of more than a few nights. Send it by credit card or giro in Spain and by credit card or wire transfer from outside the country. If you have to cancel, do so at least a week before the booking date or you may lose all or some of the deposit.

Most hotels will honor a booking only until 8pm unless business is poor. If you are delayed, call the hotel to assure them you are coming.

When you check in you will be asked for your passport or identity card to comply with Spanish police regulations. It will normally be returned to you promptly as soon as your details have been copied.

You are expected to check out of your room by noon on the last day of your stay, or to pay for another night.

PAYING

HOTELS THAT ACCEPT credit cards are listed on pages 536–71. In some large, busy hotels you may be asked to sign a blank credit card slip on arrival. Under Spanish law it is fraudulent to ask you to do this; you should refuse.

Eurocheques are accepted in some hotels, but personal checks are not accepted in Spanish hotels, even if backed by a check guarantee card or drawn on a Spanish bank. Many people pay cash and in some cheap hotels this may be the only payment accepted.

Around 200–300 pesetas is the usual tip for all hotel staff.

The pretty beach of Meliá Salinas Hotel, Lanzarote (see p571)

CASAS RURALES

CASAS RURALES are country houses whose owners accept a few visitors, usually in tourist season. They are most numerous in Asturias, Navarra, Aragón, and Catalonia (where they are called cases de pagès). They are becoming common in Galicia and Cantabria (where they are called casas de labranza), and in Andalusia.

Casas rurales range in style from stately manor houses to small, isolated farms. Some offer bed and breakfast; some an evening meal or full board.

Do not expect hotel service or a long list of facilities in a casa rural. You may, however, be given a friendly welcome and good home cooking, all at a very affordable price.

Book casas rurales directly or through regional associations: **Central de Reservas de Casas Rurales** in Navarra; **RAAR** in Andalusia; **Rutastur** in Asturias; **TURAL** in Aragón; and **Turisvert** in Catalonia.

El Nacimiento, Turre, a charming Andalusian casa rural (see p567)

RENTALS

Villas and vacation flats rented by the week are plentiful along the Spanish coasts. In scenic areas of the countryside there are many *casas rurales* (village and farm houses) available for rent by the day. For more information, contact their regional organizations *(see p531)*. They also take bookings.

In the US, a number of private companies, including **Hometours International, Inc.**, act as agents for owners of apartments and houses. Some other organizations and owners of holiday homes advertise in the travel sections of US Sunday newspapers. Tour operators offer a range of budget accommodation.

The prices for efficiency accommodations vary according to the location, the nature of the property, and the season. An inland four-person villa with a pool can cost under 40,000 pesetas a week; and 160,000 pesetas a week or more if it is on the coast.

An apartment hotel is a new type of accommodation; in Andalusia it is called a *villa turística*. Half hotel, half apartment, it gives guests a choice between cooking your own meals (all rooms have a kitchen) or eating in the hotel restaurant. Holiday villages are similar, often catering to special interests. One example is the village of Ainsa in the mountain sports region of Aragón *(see p547)*, which offers a mix of camping and hostel accommodation, with restaurants and bars.

Typical holiday villas in Lanzarote's Puerto del Carmen, the Canary Islands

YOUTH HOSTELS AND MOUNTAIN REFUGES

To use the network of *albergues juveniles* (youth hostels) in Spain you need to show a YHA (Youth Hostel Association) card from your country or an international card, which you can buy from any hostel. Prices per person for bed and breakfast are lower than hotel prices.

Youth hostels can be booked directly or through the **Red Española de Albergues Juveniles** (Spanish Network of Youth Hostels). Despite the name, there is no age limit.

Mountaineers heading for the more remote areas may use the *refugios* (refuges). These are shelters with a dormitory, cooking facilities, and heating. Some are huts with about six bunks; others are mountain houses with up to 50 beds.

The *refugios* are marked on large-scale maps of mountain areas and national parks. They are administered by the regional mountaineering associations and usually owned by clubs. The **Federación Española de Montañismo** and the local tourist offices will supply their addresses.

La Oliva monastery, Navarra *(see p126)*, welcomes paying guests

MONASTERIES AND CONVENTS

If you have a taste for peace and austerity you may enjoy a night in one of Spain's 150 religious houses where guests are welcome. Most belong to the Benedictine and the Cistercian orders. Room prices are inexpensive. They are not hotels, however; you have to book ahead by writing or by phone; few have private telephones or television. The guests may be asked to tidy their rooms, observe the same strict mealtimes as the monks or nuns, and to help with the washing up. Some convents admit only women and some monasteries only men.

Youth hostel in rustic style on the edge of Cazorla nature reserve, Jaén

CAMPSITES

THERE ARE more than 600 campsites across Spain, mostly on the coasts, but also some outside the major cities and in the most popular areas of countryside. Most campsites have electricity and running water; in addition some also have laundromats, playgrounds, a swimming pool, restaurants, shops, and more.

It is sensible to carry a camping *carnet* (card) with you. This convenient item can be used instead of a passport to check in at campsites, and it also covers you for third-party insurance. *Carnets* are issued in the US by the **Family Campers and RVers Association**.

Every year, the *Guía Oficial de Campings* is published by Turespaña. Information about campsites is available from the **Federación Española de Empresarios de Campings y Ciudades de Vacaciones** (Spanish Camp Site and

Sign for a camp site

Holiday Camp Federation), which also takes bookings. In Spain, camping is permitted only on official sites.

DISABLED TRAVELERS

HOTEL STAFF will be helpful, in general, but few hotels are well equipped for disabled guests. **Servi-COCEMFE** (the Confederación Coordinadora Estatal de Minusválidos Físicos de España) runs a hotel in Madrid for disabled people's groups. Servi-COCEMFE and Viajes 2000 *(see p613)* offer advice on hotels for guests with special needs. The Society for the Advancement of Travel for the Handicapped provides information on Spain. French-based **IHD** (International Help for the Disabled) will arrange help for visitors to the Costa del Sol and Mallorca. **Access to Travel** magazine also provides useful information for the disabled traveler.

View from the Cabina Verónica mountain refuge, Picos de Europa

FURTHER INFORMATION

THE GUIA OFICIAL DE HOTELES is published every spring by Turespaña. It is sold in Spanish bookshops and newsstands and can be consulted in Spanish tourist offices. It lists every pension, hostel, and hotel in Spain and gives their star-rating, their prices, and a resumé of their facilities.

Each *comunidad autónoma* distributes a list of the hotels and other accommodation in its area via the tourist offices.

DIRECTORY

HOTEL CHAINS

Grupo Riu
📞 (971) 49 08 21.
FAX (971) 74 38 98.

Grupo Sol-Meliá
📞 (91) 571 16 16.
FAX (91) 571 49 96.

NH
📞 (93) 412 14 14.
FAX (93) 412 12 02.

TRYP
📞 (91) 315 32 46.
FAX (91) 314 31 56.

PARADORS

Central de Reservas
Calle Requena 3,
28013 Madrid.
📞 (91) 559 00 69.
FAX (91) 559 32 33.

Marketing Ahead
433 Fifth Ave,
New York,
NY 10016.
📞 (212) 686-9213.

RENTALS AND BED AND BREAKFAST

Central de Reservas de Casas Rurales
Calle Espoz y Mina 15,
31002 Pamplona
(Navarra).
📞 (948) 22 93 28.
FAX (948) 21 20 59.

Hometours International, Inc.
P.O.Box 11503
Knoxville,
TN 37939.
📞 (800) 367-4668.

RAAR
Apartado 2035,
04080 Almeria.
📞 (950) 26 50 18.
FAX (950) 27 04 31.

TURAL
22471 Laspaules (Aragón).
📞 (& FAX) (974) 55 40 11.

Turisvert
Plaça Sant Josep Oriol 4,
08002 Barcelona.
📞 (93) 412 69 84.
FAX (93) 317 30 05.

YOUTH HOSTELS

Red Española de Albergues Juveniles
C/ José Ortega y Gasset 71,
28006 Madrid.
📞 (91) 347 77 00.
FAX (91) 401 81 60.

American Youth Hostels
733 15th St. NW,
Suite 840,
Washington, DC 20005.
📞 (202) 783-6161.

MOUNTAIN REFUGES

Federación de Montañismo
C/ Alberto Aguilera 3,
28015 Madrid.
📞 (91) 445 13 82.
FAX (91) 445 14 38.

CAMPING

Family Campers and RVers Association
4804 Transit Road Bldg. #2
Depew, NY 14043.
📞 (716) 668-6242.

Federación de Empresarios de Campings
C/ San Bernardo 97–9,
28015 Madrid.
📞 (91) 448 12 34.
FAX (91) 448 12 67.

DISABLED TRAVELERS

SATH
347 Fifth Ave.
New York, NY 10016.
📞 (212) 447-7284.

IHD (France)
📞 (33) 94 81 61 51.
FAX (33) 94 81 61 43.

Servi-COCEMFE
Calle Eugenio Salazar 2,
28002 Madrid.
📞 (91) 413 80 01.
FAX (91) 416 99 99.

FURTHER INFORMATION

Tourist Office of Spain
666 Fifth Ave.
New York, NY 10103.
📞 (212) 265-8822.
FAX (212) 265 8864.

Spain's Best: Paradors

PARADOR IS AN OLD SPANISH WORD for a lodging place for travelers of respectable rank. In the late 1920s a national network of state-run hotels called paradors was established. Many of the nearly 90 paradors are converted castles, palaces, or monasteries, although some have been custom-built in strategic tourist locations. They are generally well marked, and the prices are comparable with other luxury hotels. All offer a high degree of comfort and service, and all have restaurants offering regional cuisine.

Hotel de los Reyes Católicos, one of the sights of Santiago de Compostela (see p86), may be the world's oldest hotel. It was founded as a hospital in 1499 (see p537).

Hotel de los Reyes Católicos

Parador de León is housed in the Hostal San Marcos, one of Spain's finest Renaissance buildings (see p21). The main hall has a magnificent coffered ceiling (see p556).

Parador de León

Parador de Guadalupe is a 16th-century former hospice for pilgrims; it stands beside a famous monastery in Extremadura (see p560).

Parador de Arcos de la Frontera is situated in one of the archetypal pueblos blancos (white towns). Its wide, semicircular terrace offers panoramic views of the Moorish castle, the Guadalete River, and the rolling farmland beyond (see p563).

Parador de Guadalupe

Parador de Granada

Parador de Arcos de la Frontera

Parador de Granada is a captivating 15th-century convent built in the beautiful gardens of the Alhambra at the instruction of the Catholic Monarchs. Antique Spanish furniture fills the halls and rooms of this atmospheric parador, and an old roofless chapel forms a patio. Advance booking is essential (see p565).

Parador de Sigüenza, *a massive hilltop castle enclosing a large courtyard, was formerly a Visigothic, then a Moorish, fortress. It is approached from the historic town below by a steep cobbled street* (see p559).

Parador de Viella is set in the spectacular Vall d'Arán and surrounded by high peaks. There is ample opportunity for outdoor activity, from skiing to hunting and fishing *(see p547)*.

Parador de Viella

Parador de Sigüenza

Parador de Alcañiz is located in a castle-monastery built by the Knights of Calatrava in the 12th century. Despite its imposing size, the parador has only 12 rooms. The cloister is now a peaceful garden (see p548).

Parador de Alcañiz

| 0 kilometers | 200 |
| 0 miles | 100 |

arador de Cuenca

Parador de Cuenca is housed in the converted 16th-century convent of San Pablo. It enjoys magnificent views of the attractive old town *(see p558)*.

Parador de Cañadas del Teide is a recently refurbished parador situated in the Mount Teide National Park (see pp514–15) on Tenerife. From its terraces there are views of the volcanic landscape (see p571).

'HE CANARY ISLANDS

Choosing a Hotel

T HE HOTELS in this guide have been selected across a wide price range for excellent facilities and location. Many also have a highly recommended restaurant. The chart lists hotels by region, starting in the north; color-coded thumb tabs indicate the regions covered on each page. For more details on restaurants see pages 578–609.

	CREDIT CARDS	NUMBER OF ROOMS	PRIVATE PARKING	SWIMMING POOL	GARDEN OR TERRACE

GALICIA

		CREDIT CARDS	NUMBER OF ROOMS	PRIVATE PARKING	SWIMMING POOL	GARDEN OR TERRACE
ALFOZ: *Pazo Galea.* ⓅⓅ Castro de Ouro, 27776 (Lugo). █ *(982) 55 83 23.* FAX *(982) 55 83 23.* A 19th-century *pazo* (Galician manor house) with a splendid garden. The bedrooms are simple and modern. The owners, a Galician family, operate an original fulling mill and a flour mill as a tourist attraction. ▬		MC V	5	■	●	■
BAIONA: *Villa Sol.* ⓅⓅ C/ Palos de la Frontera 12, 36300 (Pontevedra). █ *(986) 35 56 91.* FAX *(986) 35 67 02.* A family-run hotel in an old country house decorated with antiques. Children are not admitted during tourist season. ▬		MC V	6	■		■
BAIONA: *Parador de Baiona.* ⓅⓅⓅⓅⓅ Carretera de Baiona, 36300 (Pontevedra). █ *(986) 35 50 00.* FAX *(986) 35 50 76.* This parador, built in the style of an old manor house or *pazo*, is located within the walls of Monterreal castle. ▬ TV		AE DC MC V	122	■	●	■
BRIÓN: *Pousada de Rosalía.* Ⓟ Calle Soiglexia, Los Ángeles, 15280 (A Coruña). █ *(981) 88 75 80.* FAX *(981) 88 75 57.* A country house hotel, built of stone and surrounding a cloister. It offers simple accommodations not far from the coast and Santiago de Compostela. There are barbecues by the pool in summer. ▬ TV		AE DC MC V	36	■	●	■
CAMBADOS: *Parador de Cambados.* ⓅⓅⓅ Paseo de Cervantes, 36630 (Pontevedra). █ *(986) 54 22 50.* FAX *(986) 54 20 68.* This parador, on an estuary of the Rías Baixas, occupies a handsome *pazo* built around a large courtyard garden where drinks are served. Galician specialties and local wines are served in the restaurant. ▬ TV		AE DC MC V	63	■		■
CERVO: *Pousada O'Almacén.* Ⓟ Carretera de Sargadelos 2, 27891 (Lugo). █ *(982) 55 78 36.* FAX *(982) 55 78 36.* A restored 18th-century building, once a food storehouse for neighboring hamlets. The best bedrooms look on to the Río Xunco. ▬ TV		DC MC V	7	■		
CORNIDE: *Casa Grande de Cornide.* ⓅⓅⓅ Calo, Teo, 15886 (A Coruña). █ *(981) 80 55 99.* FAX *(981) 80 57 51.* A welcoming small bed-and-breakfast hotel in a renovated house near Santiago de Compostela. It has a library and a garden with two traditional *hórreos* (granaries), and an 18th-century dovecote. ▬ TV		AE DC MC V	7	■	●	■
A CORUÑA: *Ciudad de La Coruña.* ⓅⓅⓅ Paseo de Adormideras, 15002. █ *(981) 21 21 00.* FAX *(981) 22 46 10.* A hotel with views over A Coruña bay and a beach nearby. It has spacious, modern bedrooms and gym and spa facilities. ▬ TV		AE DC MC V	132	■	●	■
A ESTRADA: *Pazo de Leira Herminia.* Ⓟ Calle Carballeira 6, Nigoi, 36684 (Pontevedra). █ *(986) 57 32 00.* FAX *(986) 57 32 00.* A quiet, cozy hotel offering bed and breakfast in a restored, stone-built country house near the source of the Río Liñares. It is a convenient base for visits to the Rías Baixas. ▬			4	■	●	■
FERROL: *Parador de Ferrol.* ⓅⓅ C/ Almirante Fernández Martín, 15401 (A Coruña). █ *(981) 35 67 20.* FAX *(981) 35 67 21.* This spacious parador in the town center is surrounded by gardens. It is decorated with nautical memorabilia of Ferrol's seafaring past. The bedroom windows look out over the harbor. ▬ TV		AE DC MC V	38	■		■
A GUARDA: *Convento de San Benito.* ⓅⓅ Plaza de San Benito, 36780 (Pontevedra). █ *(986) 61 11 66.* FAX *(986) 61 15 17.* A converted 16th-century convent in which the nuns' cells have been transformed into bedrooms for the guests. They surround a small cloister with a palm tree and a stone fountain. ▬ TV		AE DC MC V	24	■		■

Price categories for a standard double room per night, with tax, breakfast, and service included:

ℙ under 8,000 ptas
ℙℙ 8,000–12,000 ptas
ℙℙℙ 12,000–16,000 ptas
ℙℙℙℙ 16,000–20,000 ptas
ℙℙℙℙℙ over 20,000 ptas

CREDIT CARDS
Indicates which credit cards are accepted: *AE* American Express; *DC* Diners Club; *MC* MasterCard/Access; *V* Visa
PARKING
Parking provided by the hotel in a private parking lot or a private garage on the hotel site or very close by. Some hotels charge for use of private parking facilities.
SWIMMING POOL
Hotel pool outdoors unless otherwise stated.
GARDEN
Hotel with garden, courtyard, or terrace, often providing tables for eating outdoors.

		Credit Cards	Number of Rooms	Private Parking	Swimming Pool	Garden or Terrace

NEDA: *Pazo da Merced.* ℙℙℙ
Pazo da Merced, 15510 (A Coruña). ☎ (981) 38 29 00. FAX (981) 38 01 04.
A restored, 17th-century stone manor house with its own chapel, at the head of the Ría de Ferrol. ⛨ TV
Credit Cards: AE DC MC — Rooms: 5 — Private Parking — Swimming Pool — Garden or Terrace

POBRA DE TRIVES: *Pazo Casa Grande.* ℙℙ
Calle Marqués de Trives 17, 32780 (Ourense). ☎ (988) 33 20 66.
A *pousada* (small hotel) in an 18th-century stone manor, with a coat of arms on its central tower. Antiques and old paintings decorate the cozy interior. There is a chapel with a magnificent reredos. ⛨ TV
Credit Cards: AE DC MC V — Rooms: 7 — Garden or Terrace

PONTEVEDRA: *Parador de Pontevedra.* ℙℙℙℙ
Calle Barón 19, 36002. ☎ (986) 85 58 00. FAX (986) 85 21 95.
An elegant parador in a stately manor in the old town. The decor incorporates antiques, gilt mirrors, chandeliers, and tapestries. ⛨ TV
Credit Cards: AE DC MC V — Rooms: 47 — Private Parking — Garden or Terrace

RIBEIRA: *Fonteclara.* ℙℙ
C/ Sta Marina de Ribeira 6, 36685 (Pontevedra). ☎ (986) 68 16 77. FAX (981) 35 11 43.
An old Galician country house of great character, peacefully located in the valley of the Río Ulloa. Visitors are offered bed and breakfast, and a sitting room with an open fireplace. ⛨ ♿
Credit Cards: V — Rooms: 8 — Private Parking — Garden or Terrace

SANTIAGO DE COMPOSTELA: *Hogar San Francisco.* ℙℙ
C/ Campillo de San Francisco 3, 15702 (A Coruña). ☎ (981) 58 16 00. FAX (981) 57 19 16.
A hotel near the cathedral in what was a school for Franciscan friars, with the dining room occupying the former refectory. The bedrooms are simple but bright. ⛨
Credit Cards: AE MC V — Rooms: 70 — Private Parking

SANTIAGO DE COMPOSTELA: *Reyes Católicos.* ℙℙℙℙℙ
Praza do Obradoiro 1, 15705 (A Coruña). ☎ (981) 58 22 00. FAX (981) 56 30 94.
Built under the Catholic Monarchs for poor pilgrims, this 16th-century parador is one of the world's grandest hotels (*see p86*). It is built around four arcaded patios with fountains. ⛨ TV ♿
Credit Cards: AE DC MC V — Rooms: 136 — Private Parking — Garden or Terrace

O SAVIÑAO: *Torre de Vilariño.* ℙ
Calle Fión 47, 27548 (Lugo). ☎ (982) 45 22 60. FAX (982) 45 22 60.
A 17th-century inn converted into a hotel offering bed and breakfast, mainly to tourists following the so-called "Route of the Romanesque." The owners serve food and wine they make themselves. ⛨ TV
Credit Cards: DC V — Rooms: 9 — Private Parking — Swimming Pool — Garden or Terrace

SISÁN-CAMBADOS: *Pazo Carrasqueira.* ℙℙ
Calle Carrasqueira, 36638 (Pontevedra). ☎ (986) 71 00 32. FAX (986) 71 00 32.
A guest house in a rural mansion, with a carved granite staircase and cozy bedrooms on the top floor. Fish, seafood, and Albariño wine (produced on the estate) are served in the dining room. ⛨ TV
Credit Cards: AE MC V — Rooms: 9 — Private Parking — Swimming Pool — Garden or Terrace

A TOXA: *Gran Hotel de La Toja.* ℙℙℙℙℙ
O Grove, 36991 (Pontevedra). ☎ (986) 73 00 25. FAX (986) 73 00 26.
This mansion, built at the end of the 19th century on an island planted with palm and pine trees, is connected to the mainland by an iron bridge. The hotel has a ballroom and a health and fitness center. ⛨ TV
Credit Cards: AE DC V — Rooms: 198 — Private Parking — Swimming Pool — Garden or Terrace

TUI: *Parador de Tui.* ℙℙℙ
Avenida de Portugal, 36700 (Pontevedra). ☎ (986) 60 03 09. FAX (986) 60 21 63.
The public and guest rooms have superb views of the town of Tui and across the Río Miño, which forms the border with Portugal. Local dishes on the menu include eels and oysters. ⛨ TV ♿
Credit Cards: AE DC MC V — Rooms: 34 — Private Parking — Swimming Pool — Garden or Terrace

VERÍN: *Parador de Verín.* ℙℙℙ
Monterrei, 32600 (Ourense). ☎ (988) 41 00 75. FAX (988) 41 20 17.
Verín's parador is on a hilltop, surrounded by lawns and trees, with views across a valley to the medieval castle of Monterrei. Vineyards in the valley supply wines for the hotel restaurant. ⛨ TV
Credit Cards: AE DC MC — Rooms: 23 — Private Parking — Swimming Pool — Garden or Terrace

<table>
<tr><td>

Price categories for a standard double room per night, with tax, breakfast, and service included:

℗ under 8,000 ptas
℗℗ 8,000–12,000 ptas
℗℗℗ 12,000–16,000 ptas
℗℗℗℗ 16,000–20,000 ptas
℗℗℗℗℗ over 20,000 ptas

</td><td>

CREDIT CARDS
Indicates which credit cards are accepted: *AE* American Express; *DC* Diners Club; *MC* MasterCard/Access; *V* Visa
PARKING
Parking provided by the hotel in a private parking lot or a private garage on the hotel site or very close by. Some hotels charge for use of private parking facilities.
SWIMMING POOL
Hotel pool outdoors unless otherwise stated.
GARDEN
Hotel with garden, courtyard, or terrace, often providing tables for eating outdoors.

</td></tr>
</table>

	CREDIT CARDS	NUMBER OF ROOMS	PRIVATE PARKING	SWIMMING POOL	GARDEN OR TERRACE
VILAGARCÍA DE AROUSA: *Pazo O'Rial.* ℗℗℗ Calle El Rial 1, 36600 (Pontevedra). **(** (986) 50 70 11. **FAX** (986) 50 16 76. Wooden beams, tiled floors, and stone walls preserve the character of this old manor; cushions and fine fabrics give comfort. 🔲 TV	AE DC MC V	60	■	●	■
VILLALBA: *Parador de Villalba.* ℗℗℗℗ Valeriano Valdesuso, 27800 (Lugo). **(** (982) 51 00 11. **FAX** (982) 51 00 90. A tiny parador in a medieval octagonal tower with thick walls and narrow windows, entered by a drawbridge. Booking is essential. 🔲 TV	AE DC MC V	6	■		
VILLALONGA: *Pazo El Revel.* ℗℗℗ Camino de la Iglesia 15, 36990 (Pontevedra). **(** (986) 74 30 00. **FAX** (986) 74 33 90. A 17th-century manor house, its façade overgrown with creepers. It has peaceful formal gardens and a colonnaded terrace. 🔲 TV	MC V	22	■	●	■

ASTURIAS AND CANTABRIA

	CREDIT CARDS	NUMBER OF ROOMS	PRIVATE PARKING	SWIMMING POOL	GARDEN OR TERRACE
CANGAS DE ONÍS: *Aultre Naray.* ℗℗ Peruyes, 33547 (Asturias). **(** (98) 584 08 08. **FAX** (98) 584 08 48. There are mountain views from this country house hotel in one of Northern Spain's least-known corners. Every bedroom is different. 🔲 TV	AE MC V	10	■		
CASTROPOL: *Palacete Peñalba.* ℗℗ C/ El Cotarelo, Figueras, 33794 (Asturias). **(** (98) 563 61 25. **FAX** (98) 563 62 47. This hotel in an Art Nouveau mansion built in 1912 by a Gaudí follower has oval balconies, curved staircases, and its original furniture. 🔲 TV	AE DC MC V	13	■		■
COLOMBRES: *La Casona de Villanueva.* ℗℗ Villanueva, Ribadedeva, 33590 (Asturias). **(** (98) 541 25 90. **FAX** (942) 541 25 14. An 18th-century village house, carefully restored in the traditional style, with a peaceful atmosphere. Children under five are not admitted. 🔲	MC V	8	■		
COLOMBRES: *Mirador de La Franca.* ℗℗ Playa de La Franca, Ribadedeva, 33590 (Asturias). **(** (98) 541 21 45. **FAX** (98) 541 21 53. There are magnificent views from the lounge and restaurant of this hotel set back in a rocky cove from La Franca beach. The waters of the bay are safe for water sports and underwater fishing. 🔲 TV	AE DC MC V	50	■		■
COMILLAS: *Casal del Castro.* ℗℗ Calle San Jerónimo, 39520 (Cantabria). **(** (942) 72 00 36. A large, 17th-century house decorated and furnished with antiques. It is on the edge of the town, not far from excellent beaches. 🔲 TV	AE DC MC V	45	■		■
COSGAYA: *Hotel del Oso.* ℗℗ Ctra Potes–Fuente Dé, 39539 (Cantabria). **(** (942) 73 30 18. **FAX** (942) 73 30 36. Surrounded by the mountains of the eastern Picos de Europa, this is a comfortable hotel, very popular with foreign tourists. 🔲	AE DC MC V	17	■	●	
ESCALANTE: *San Román de Escalante.* ℗℗℗℗ Ctra Escalante–Castillo, 39795 (Cantabria). **(** (942) 67 77 45. **FAX** (942) 67 76 43. A hotel in an exquisitely decorated 17th-century house overlooking trees and meadows. Beside it is a Romanesque chapel. 🔲 📋 TV ♿	AE DC MC V	8	■		■
FUENTE DÉ: *Parador de Fuente Dé.* ℗℗ Fuente Dé, 39588 (Cantabria). **(** (942) 73 66 51. **FAX** (942) 73 66 54. This modern building at the foot of the Picos de Europa cable car has pleasant bedrooms and long galleries with huge windows. It is an ideal base for fishing or walking in the mountains. 🔲 TV ♿	AE DC MC V	78	■		■
GIJÓN: *La Casona de Jovellanos.* ℗℗℗ Plaza de Jovellanos 1, 33201 (Asturias). **(** (98) 534 20 24. **FAX** (98) 535 61 51. A small hotel in an 18th-century building overlooking a little square in the old part of the city, and near the San Lorenzo beach. 🔲 TV	AE MC V	16			■

GIJÓN: *Parador Molino Viejo.* Ⓡ Ⓡ Ⓡ
Parque de Isabel la Católica, 33203 (Asturias). 【 (98) 537 05 11. FAX (98) 537 02 33.
A parador in a corner of one of Spain's prettiest parks, in a converted windmill, a type common in Gijón from the 15th to the 18th century. The old watercourse is preserved on the grounds. 🖼 ▤ TV ⟐

			AE	40	■		■
DC							
V							

LIÉRGANES: *Posada del Sauce.* Ⓡ Ⓡ Ⓡ
C/ José Antonio 25, 39722 (Cantabria). 【 (942) 52 80 23. FAX (942) 52 81 17.
This is an imposing 19th-century mountain house in a beautiful village. It has a covered swimming pool, but the bedrooms are rather small. 🖼

AE	50		●	■
MC				
V				

LLANES: *Paraíso.* Ⓡ Ⓡ
Calle Pidal 2, 33500 (Asturias). 【 (98) 540 19 71. FAX (98) 540 25 90.
White marble floors, antique furniture, and a grand piano in the lounge contribute to the kitsch atmosphere of this hotel. It overlooks one of the town's busiest streets, so book a parking space in advance. 🖼 ▤ TV

AE	30	■		
DC				
MC				
V				

LLANES: *La Posada de Babel.* Ⓡ Ⓡ
La Pereda, 33509 (Asturias). 【 (98) 540 25 25. FAX (98) 540 25 25.
The spectacular Picos de Europa tower above this small, family-run hotel. It is partly modern, but has huge, traditional fireplaces, and one bedroom is a converted *hórreo* (grain storeroom). 🖼 TV

| MC | 8 | ■ | | |
| V | | | | |

OVIEDO: *Hotel de la Reconquista.* Ⓡ Ⓡ Ⓡ Ⓡ Ⓡ
Calle Gil de Jaz 16, 33004 (Asturias). 【 (98) 524 11 00. FAX (98) 524 11 66.
A magnificent 18th-century building with a massive stone coat of arms above the main entrance. The public rooms are arranged around several arcaded and balconied courtyards. 🖼 ▤ TV

AE	146			
DC				
MC				
V				

PECHÓN: *Don Pablo.* Ⓡ Ⓡ
Afueras, 39594 (Cantabria). 【 (942) 71 95 00. FAX (942) 71 95 00.
Three houses joined together look like an old, ancestral mansion. The hotel is close to the sea and is family-run, with cozy rooms and a warm atmosphere. The two pretty attic bedrooms are popular. 🖼 TV

AE	30	■		■
DC				
MC				
V				

POTES: *El Jisu.* Ⓡ Ⓡ
Ctra Potes–Camaleño, 39587 (Cantabria). 【 (942) 73 30 38. FAX (942) 73 03 15.
A chalet hotel in the Liébana Valley, with views of the Picos de Europa. The cozy sitting rooms are decorated with antiques. 🖼 TV

| MC | 9 | ■ | | |
| V | | | | |

PRAVIA: *Casa del Busto.* Ⓡ Ⓡ
Plaza del Rey Don Silo 1, 33120 (Asturias). 【 (98) 582 27 71. FAX (98) 582 27 72.
In a beautiful town, and close to a beach, this hotel is in a 16th-century house. It is tastefully furnished with period pieces. The bedrooms overlook a central patio where meals can be served. 🖼 TV

AE	12			
DC				
MC				
V				

QUIJAS: *Hostería de Quijas.* Ⓡ Ⓡ
Calle Barrio Vinueva, 39590 (Cantabria). 【 (942) 82 08 33. FAX (942) 83 80 50.
An 18th-century stone-built mansion on the Santander–Oviedo road, near Torrelavega. It has broad eaves, bay windows, timbered ceilings, and a magnificent garden. The lobby is in the former library. 🖼 TV

AE	33		●	■
DC				
MC				
V				

QUIJAS: *Posada de la Torre de Quijas.* Ⓡ Ⓡ
Calle Barrio Vinueva 76, 39590 (Cantabria). 【 (942) 82 06 45.
This hotel is in a restored, 19th-century stone house with wooden bay windows. It is decorated with farming implements, which give it a rustic atmosphere. The hotel is on a main road. 🖼

AE	12	■		■
DC				
MC				
V				

RIBADESELLA: *Gran Hotel del Sella.* Ⓡ Ⓡ Ⓡ Ⓡ
Calle Ricardo Cangas 2, 33560 (Asturias). 【 (98) 586 01 50. FAX (98) 585 78 22.
The former summer palace of the Marquis of Argüelles now has a new wing and is a family-run hotel. It is on the beach outside town, and has a pool, tennis courts, and vast gardens. 🖼 TV ⟐

AE	82	■	●	■
DC				
MC				
V				

SALAS: *Castillo de Valdés-Salas.* Ⓡ Ⓡ
Plaza de la Campa, 33860 (Asturias). 【 (98) 583 22 22. FAX (98) 583 22 99.
A 16th-century restored castle converted into a simple hotel retaining much of the character of the original building. The local tourist information desk is in the hotel lobby. 🖼 TV

AE	12			■
DC				
MC				
V				

SANTANDER: *Las Brisas.* Ⓡ Ⓡ Ⓡ
Travesía de los Castros 14, 39005 (Cantabria). 【 (942) 27 50 11. FAX (942) 28 11 73.
A homey hotel in a 19th-century white villa close to the popular Sardinero beach. Breakfast can be served on a seaside terrace. 🖼 TV

AE	13	■		
DC				
MC				
V				

Price categories for a standard double room per night, with tax, breakfast, and service included:

- ℙ under 8,000 ptas
- ℙℙ 8,000–12,000 ptas
- ℙℙℙ 12,000–16,000 ptas
- ℙℙℙℙ 16,000–20,000 ptas
- ℙℙℙℙℙ over 20,000 ptas

CREDIT CARDS
Indicates which credit cards are accepted: *AE* American Express; *DC* Diners Club; *MC* MasterCard/Access; *V* Visa
PARKING
Parking provided by the hotel in a private parking lot or a private garage on the hotel site or very close by. Some hotels charge for use of private parking facilities.
SWIMMING POOL
Hotel pool outdoors unless otherwise stated.
GARDEN
Hotel with garden, courtyard, or terrace, often providing tables for eating outdoors.

	CREDIT CARDS	NUMBER OF ROOMS	PRIVATE PARKING	SWIMMING POOL	GARDEN OR TERRACE
SANTANDER: *Hotel Real.* ℙℙℙℙ Paseo Pérez Galdós 28, 39005 (Cantabria). █ *(942) 27 25 50.* **FAX** *(942) 27 45 73.* An elegant, formal hotel, visible on the city's highest hill. It was built late in the 19th century for nobility accompanying the royal family on vacation. The balconies overlook the bay. ▦ ▤ 📺 ♿	AE DC MC V	125	▪		▪
SANTILLANA DEL MAR: *Posada de Santa Juliana.* ℙ Calle Carrera 19, 39330 (Cantabria). █ *(942) 84 01 06.* **FAX** *(942) 84 01 70.* A small guest house located unpromisingly over a souvenir shop, but with charming attic rooms. Guests may eat in a bar across the street. ▦ 📺	AE DC MC V	6			
SANTILLANA DEL MAR: *Altamira.* ℙℙℙ Calle Cantón 1, 39330 (Cantabria). █ *(942) 81 80 25.* **FAX** *(942) 84 01 36.* A town-center hotel in a restored 17th-century palace. The old wooden staircase leads to bedrooms with beams and polished floors. ▦ 📺	AE DC MC V	32			▪
SANTILLANA DEL MAR: *Parador Gil Blas.* ℙℙℙ Plaza Ramón Pelayo 11, 39330 (Cantabria). █ *(942) 81 80 00.* **FAX** *(942) 81 83 91.* This stone mansion, begun in the 15th century, has a pretty patio. Bare walls and tiled floors enhance the medieval atmosphere. ▦ 📺 ♿	AE DC MC V	56	▪		▪
SAN VICENTE DE TORANZO: *Posada del Pas.* ℙℙ Ctra N623 Burgos–Santander, 39699 (Cantabria). █ *(942) 59 44 11.* **FAX** *(942) 59 43 86.* An 18th-century stone mountain house in a green valley on the Santander–Burgos road accommodates this popular hotel. ▦ 📺	AE DC MC V	32	▪	●	▪
SOLARES: *Don Pablo.* ℙℙ Calle General Mola 6, 39710 (Cantabria). █ *(942) 52 21 20.* **FAX** *(942) 52 05 26.* A medieval monastery with an imposing façade and a chapel. The public rooms are spacious and the bedrooms comfortable. ▦ 📺	AE DC MC V	27	▪		
TARAMUNDI: *La Rectoral.* ℙℙℙℙ Taramundi, 33775 (Asturias). █ *(98) 564 67 67.* **FAX** *(98) 564 67 77.* A former priest's house deep in the Asturian countryside has been tastefully converted into a quiet and atmospheric hotel. The ample bedrooms all have views of the surrounding mountains. ▦ ▤ 📺	AE DC MC V	18	▪		▪
BASQUE COUNTRY, NAVARRA, AND LA RIOJA					
ANGUIANO: *Abadía de Valvanera.* ℙ Monasterio de Valvanera, 26323 (La Rioja). █ *(941) 37 70 44.* **FAX** *(941) 37 70 44.* Queen Isabel I stayed in this Benedictine monastery in 1482. The surroundings are beautiful, the rooms simple, and the food good. ▦	AE DC MC V	29	▪		▪
ARGOMÁNIZ: *Parador de Argómaniz.* ℙℙℙ Carretera NI, 01192 (Álava). █ *(945) 29 23 00.* **FAX** *(945) 29 32 87.* Kings have lodged in this 17th-century stone palace. Its location on the slopes of Mount Zabalgaña is peaceful, with good views. ▦ 📺	AE DC MC V	53	▪		▪
AXPE-ATXONDO: *Mendi Goikoa.* ℙℙℙ Calle Barrio de San Juan 33, 48292 (Vizcaya). █ *(94) 682 08 33.* **FAX** *(94) 682 11 36.* Twin stone houses built in the 18th century have been converted into a pleasant hotel in the peaceful heart of the Valle de Atxondo. ▦ ▤	DC MC V	12	▪		
BAKIO: *Hostería del Señorío de Bizkaia.* ℙℙ Calle José María Cirarda 4, 48130 (Vizcaya). █ *(94) 619 47 25.* **FAX** *(94) 619 47 25.* A stone building with wooden balconies houses this hotel. In summer concerts are held in the garden. Bakio beach is nearby. ▦ ▤ 📺 ♿	AE DC MC V	16			▪
BILBAO (BILBO): *Gran Hotel Ercilla.* ℙℙℙℙℙ Calle Ercilla 37–9, 48011 (Vizcaya). █ *(94) 410 20 00.* **FAX** *(94) 443 93 35.* Bilbao's largest hotel is centrally located, comfortable, welcoming, and bustling with life. It has a very good restaurant. ▦ ▤ 📺	AE DC MC V	346	▪		

DONAMARIA: *Donamaria'ko Benta.* ⓅⓅ | V | 5
Barrio Ventas 4, 31750 (Navarra). **☎** *(948) 45 07 08.* **FAX** *(948) 45 09 25.*
This is a small, family-run hotel in a stone-built, Pyrenean mountain
house, with the five bedrooms in an annex. The proprietors create a
pleasant atmosphere and serve excellent food in the restaurant. 🛏 ▤

ELIZONDO: *Casa Urrusca.* Ⓟ | 5
Barrio de Bearzun, 31700 (Navarra). **☎** *(948) 45 21 06.*
This isolated stone farmhouse at the head of a pretty valley is a family
house offering beds and a breakfast of good, fresh, farm food.

EZCARAY: *Albergue de La Real Fábrica.* Ⓟ | AE V | 36
Carretera de Santo Domingo, 20280 (La Rioja). **☎** *(941) 35 44 74.*
This hotel, occupying a restored textile mill in a small town, is an
economical place for a quiet night after walking in the hills. ♿

FITERO: *Gustavo Adolfo Bécquer.* ⓅⓅ | V | 194
C/ Extramuros, Baños de Fitero, 31593 (Navarra). **☎** *(948) 77 61 00.* **FAX** *(948) 77 62 25.*
One of two hotels on the site of the Roman baths, this hotel has a
thermal spring in the basement. Bathing, massage, and many treatments
are available. The hotel also has extensive sports facilities. 🛏 📺

HARO: *Los Agustinos.* ⓅⓅⓅ | AE DC MC V | 62
Calle San Agustín 2, 26200 (La Rioja). **☎** *(941) 31 13 08.* **FAX** *(941) 30 31 48.*
A lounge in a vast, arched chamber hung with tapestries is one of the
highlights of this hotel in a former Augustinian monastery. Another is
the magnificent central patio in the old cloister. 🛏 ▤ 📺 ♿

HONDARRIBIA (FUENTERRABIA): *Pampinot.* ⓅⓅⓅ | AE DC MC V | 8
Calle Nagusia 5, 20280 (Guipúzcoa). **☎** *(943) 64 06 00.* **FAX** *(943) 64 51 28.*
An atmosphere of warmth is achieved by the team of women who run
this hotel in a 16th-century mansion in old Hondarribia. 🛏 ▤ 📺

HONDARRIBIA (FUENTERRABIA): *Parador de Hondarribia.* ⓅⓅⓅⓅ | AE DC MC V | 36
Plaza de Armas 14, 20280 (Guipúzcoa). **☎** *(943) 64 55 00.* **FAX** *(943) 64 21 53.*
This is an elegant parador in the town's restored fortress. Weapons and
other memorabilia of its colorful history adorn the walls. 🛏 📺

LAGUARDIA: *Posada Mayor de Migueloa.* ⓅⓅⓅ | AE MC V | 7
Calle Mayor de Migueloa 20, 01300 (Álava). **☎** *(941) 12 11 75.* **FAX** *(941) 12 10 22.*
A beautiful mansion in the pedestrianized old town. It was built in
1640 and has its original granite walls, beams, and tiled floors. 🛏 ▤ 📺

LECUMBERRI: *Ayestarán.* Ⓟ | V | 91
Calle Aralar 22, 31870 (Navarra). **☎** *(948) 50 41 27.* **FAX** *(948) 50 41 27.*
Part of this family-run hotel, on both sides of the Pamplona–San Sebastián
road, was built in the 1920s. The service is extraordinarily friendly. 🛏 ♿

LOGROÑO: *Herencia Rioja.* ⓅⓅⓅ | AE DC MC V | 83
Calle Marqués de Murrieta 14, 26005 (La Rioja). **☎** *(941) 21 02 22.* **FAX** *(941) 21 02 06.*
A modern hotel near Logroño's historic quarter. It has comfortable,
cheerful bedrooms and a restaurant serving haute cuisine. 🛏 ▤ 📺 ♿

MUNDAKA: *El Puerto.* ⓅⓅ | DC MC V | 11
Calle Portu Kalea 1, 48360 (Vizcaya). **☎** *(94) 687 67 25.* **FAX** *(94) 617 70 64.*
A two-story fisherman's house converted into a simple, cozy
hotel. The windows give views overlooking the sea. 🛏 📺

MUNDAKA: *Atalaya.* ⓅⓅⓅ | AE DC MC V | 15
Paseo de Txorrokopunta 2, 48360 (Vizcaya). **☎** *(94) 687 68 88.* **FAX** *(94) 687 68 99.*
Next to the fishing port, at the mouth of a sea inlet, is this hotel built at
the beginning of the 20th century. It is clean and well-kept, and has small
but pleasant bedrooms, large window galleries, and a garden. 🛏 📺

OLITE: *Casa Zanito.* ⓅⓅ | AE DC MC V | 15
Rua Mayor 16, 31390 (Navarra). **☎** *(948) 74 00 02.*
An unpretentious family-run restaurant-with-rooms in a narrow street
in the lovely old center of a historic town. 🛏 ▤ 📺

OLITE: *Parador de Olite.* ⓅⓅⓅ | AE DC MC V | 43
Plaza de los Teobaldos 2, 31390 (Navarra). **☎** *(948) 74 00 00.* **FAX** *(948) 74 02 01.*
Occupying part of the 15th-century castle and palace of Carlos III, king
of Navarra, this parador has some modern bedrooms. There are some
pricier but atmospheric rooms in the old part of the castle. 🛏 ▤ 📺 ♿

Price categories for a standard double room per night, with tax, breakfast, and service included:

ℙ under 8,000 ptas
ℙℙ 8,000–12,000 ptas
ℙℙℙ 12,000–16,000 ptas
ℙℙℙℙ 16,000–20,000 ptas
ℙℙℙℙℙ over 20,000 ptas

CREDIT CARDS
Indicates which credit cards are accepted: *AE* American Express; *DC* Diners Club; *MC* MasterCard/Access; *V* Visa
PARKING
Parking provided by the hotel in a private parking lot or a private garage on the hotel site or very close by. Some hotels charge for use of private parking facilities.
SWIMMING POOL
Hotel pool outdoors unless otherwise stated.
GARDEN
Hotel with garden, courtyard, or terrace, often providing tables for eating outdoors.

	CREDIT CARDS	NUMBER OF ROOMS	PRIVATE PARKING	SWIMMING POOL	GARDEN OR TERRACE
PAMPLONA (IRUÑA): *Tres Reyes.* ℙℙℙℙ Jardines de la Taconera, 31001 (Navarra). 📞 (948) 22 66 00. FAX (948) 22 29 30. A large modern building between the old and new towns on the edge of the Taconera gardens. The bedrooms have balconies. The services range from a gym and sauna to hairdressing and valet service. 🛏️ 🍽️ 📺 ♿	AE DC MC V	168	■	●	
PUENTE LA REINA: *Mesón del Peregrino.* ℙℙ Ctra Pamplona–Logroño, 31100 (Navarra). 📞 (948) 34 00 75. FAX (948) 34 11 90. A tasteful roadside restaurant-with-rooms in an old stone house near the junction of the two main pilgrim routes to Santiago. 🛏️ 🍽️ 📺 ♿	MC V	16	■	●	■
RONCESVALLES (ORREAGA): *La Posada.* ℙ Carretera de Francia, 31650 (Navarra). 📞 (948) 76 02 25. In 1612 this historic inn opened to cater to pilgrims to Santiago de Compostela. Its austere bedrooms with tiled floors are still a bargain. 🛏️	V	18	■		
SAN SEBASTIÁN (DONOSTIA): *La Galería.* ℙℙℙ Infanta Cristina 1–3, 20008 (Guipúzcoa). 📞 (943) 21 60 77. FAX (943) 21 12 98. A new hotel on Ondarreta beach in a building that dates from the end of the 19th century. It has two charming attic rooms. 🛏️ 📺	MC V	23	■		
SAN SEBASTIÁN (DONOSTIA): *Niza.* ℙℙℙ Calle Zubieta 56, 20007 (Guipúzcoa). 📞 (943) 42 66 63. FAX (943) 42 66 63. A seafront hotel in *belle époque* style on La Concha beach, with sunny bedrooms and a café terrace overlooking the beach. 🛏️ 📺	AE DC MC V	41	■		■
SAN SEBASTIÁN (DONOSTIA): *De Londres y de Inglaterra.* ℙℙℙℙ Calle Zubieta 2, 20007 (Guipúzcoa). 📞 (943) 42 69 89. FAX (943) 42 00 31. A 19th-century palace beautifully situated La Concha beach that was transformed into a hotel in 1902. Monarchs used to stay here for their summer vacations. 🛏️ 🍽️ 📺 ♿	AE DC MC V	145	■		
SAN SEBASTIÁN (DONOSTIA): *Monte Igueldo.* ℙℙℙℙ Paseo del Faro 134, 20008 (Guipúzcoa). 📞 (943) 21 02 11. FAX (943) 21 50 28. Superbly located on Monte Igueldo, this hotel has panoramic views across the city and the bay. It has a rooftop swimming pool. 🛏️ 🍽️ 📺	AE DC MC V	125	■	●	■
SAN SEBASTIÁN (DONOSTIA): *María Cristina.* ℙℙℙℙℙ Paseo República Argentina 4, 20004 (Guipúzcoa). 📞 (943) 42 49 00. FAX (943) 42 67 70. A luxurious, well-situated hotel built in 1912 and decorated in *belle époque* style. It is the site of the annual San Sebastián film festival. 🛏️ 🍽️ 📺	AE DC MC V	136	■		
SANTO DOMINGO DE LA CALZADA: *Parador de Santo Domingo.* ℙℙℙℙ Plaza del Santo 3, 26250 (La Rioja). 📞 (941) 34 03 00. FAX (941) 34 03 25. A hospital founded in the 12th century for pilgrims to Santiago de Compostela has been converted into this parador. It has an imposing lounge divided by arches, and a beautiful carved ceiling. 🛏️ 🍽️ 📺 ♿	AE DC MC V	61	■		■
VITORIA (GASTEIZ): *General Álava.* ℙℙℙ Avenida Gasteiz 79, 01009 (Álava). 📞 (945) 22 22 00. FAX (945) 24 83 95. A modern hotel with comfortable bedrooms in the new town near the Palacio de Congresos. The restaurant serves regional dishes. 🛏️ 🍽️ ♿	AE DC MC V	114	■		
YESA: *Hospedería de Leyre.* ℙℙ Monasterio de Leyre, 31410 (Navarra). 📞 (948) 88 41 00. FAX (948) 88 41 37. This hotel occupies part of an 11th-century monastery, spectacularly located beneath crags in a beautiful landscape. The rooms are plain and clean, and the hotel has a good restaurant. 🛏️ 🍽️	AE DC MC V	29	■		■
ZARAUTZ: *Karlos Arguiñano.* ℙℙℙℙℙ Calle Mendilauta 13, 20800 (Guipúzcoa). 📞 (943) 13 00 00. FAX (943) 13 34 50. An elegant hotel in a stone tower mansion, with views of the sea. It is owned by a TV chef and has an excellent restaurant. 🛏️ 🍽️ 📺	AE DC MC V	12	■		

BARCELONA

OLD TOWN: *Lloret.* **Map 5 A1.**
Rambla de Canaletas 125, 08002. **[** *(93) 317 33 66.* **FAX** *(93) 301 92 83.*
There are views of the city from the foyer of this popular hotel near
the Plaça de Catalunya – but streetside bedrooms can be noisy. The
old building retains many of its original decorative features. 🛏 ▤ TV
| ℗ | AE DC MC V | 52 | | |

OLD TOWN: *Rembrandt.* **Map 5 A2.**
Carrer de Portaferrissa 23, 08002. **[** *(93) 318 10 11.* **FAX** *(93) 318 10 11.*
A clean, homey hotel in the Barri Gòtic, popular with students. A
tiled courtyard is a sitting area. Some bedrooms share bathrooms. 🛏
| ℗ | | 24 | | ▣ |

OLD TOWN: *Toledano.* **Map 5 A1.**
Ramblas 138, 08002. **[** *(93) 301 08 72.* **FAX** *(93) 412 31 42.*
A small hotel near the Plaça de Catalunya, with a lounge overlooking
the Ramblas. The rooms are basic and can be noisy. 🛏 TV
| ℗ | AE DC MC V | 17 | ▣ | |

OLD TOWN: *Atlantis.* **Map 2 F1.**
Carrer de Pelai 20, 08001. **[** *(93) 318 90 12.* **FAX** *(93) 412 09 14.*
This modern, inexpensive hotel is centrally located near the Plaça de
Catalunya. The bedrooms have a range of facilities. 🛏 ▤ TV ♿
| ℗℗ | AE DC MC V | 42 | ▣ | |

OLD TOWN: *España.* **Map 2 F3.**
Carrer de Sant Pau 9–11, 08001. **[** *(93) 318 17 58.* **FAX** *(93) 317 11 34.*
Domènech i Montaner, the outstanding Modernista architect, designed
the lower floor of this hotel. The bedrooms are all modern. 🛏
| ℗℗ | AE DC MC V | 84 | | |

OLD TOWN: *Gaudí.* **Map 2 F3.**
Carrer Nou de la Rambla 12, 08001. **[** *(93) 317 90 32.* **FAX** *(93) 412 26 36.*
A pleasant hotel in a street adjoining the Rambla de Catalunya, near
Gaudí's Palau Güell, with comfortable, well-equipped rooms. 🛏 TV ♿
| ℗℗ | AE DC MC V | 73 | ▣ | |

OLD TOWN: *Jardí.* **Map 2 F3.**
Plaça Sant Josep Oriol 1, 08002. **[** *(93) 301 59 00.* **FAX** *(93) 318 36 64.*
A popular hotel overlooking a leafy square. Some bedrooms have
been renovated and have good views; the others are cheaper. 🛏 TV
| ℗℗ | AE MC V | 38 | | |

OLD TOWN: *Mesón Castilla.* **Map 2 F1.**
Carrer de Valldonzella 5, 08001. **[** *(93) 318 21 82.* **FAX** *(93) 412 40 20.*
A comfortable hotel, if a little old-fashioned, in a building with a
Modernista façade near the Casa de la Caritat arts center. 🛏 ▤ TV
| ℗℗ | AE MC V | 60 | ▣ | ▣ |

OLD TOWN: *San Agustín.* **Map 2 F3.**
Plaça de Sant Agustí 3, 08001. **[** *(93) 318 16 58.* **FAX** *(93) 317 29 28.*
An attractive hotel with a pleasant first-floor lounge and bar looking
across a square. Some bedrooms have Catalan furniture. 🛏 ▤ TV ♿
| ℗℗ | AE DC MC V | 77 | | |

OLD TOWN: *Oriente.* **Map 2 F3.**
Ramblas 45–7, 08002. **[** *(93) 302 25 58.* **FAX** *(93) 412 38 19.*
A former Franciscan friary makes a romantic setting for the Oriente.
The cloister has been converted into a ballroom. Some bedrooms have
balconies overlooking the Ramblas. 🛏 TV
| ℗℗℗ | AE DC V | 142 | | ▣ |

OLD TOWN: *Suizo.* **Map 5 B2.**
Plaça del Ángel 12, 08002. **[** *(93) 310 61 08.* **FAX** *(93) 310 40 81.*
This hotel behind the cathedral has 19th-century Parisian style. The
attic bedrooms with skylights have great character. 🛏 ▤ TV
| ℗℗℗ | AE DC MC V | 51 | ▣ | |

OLD TOWN: *Nouvel.* **Map 5 A1.**
Carrer de Santa Anna 18–20, 08002. **[** *(93) 301 82 74.* **FAX** *(93) 301 83 70.*
In a quiet street off the Ramblas, near the Plaça de Catalunya, this well-
kept, old-style hotel is tastefully decorated and furnished. 🛏 ▤ TV ♿
| ℗℗℗℗ | AE MC V | 54 | | |

OLD TOWN: *Royal.* **Map 5 A1.**
Rambla dels Estudis 117, 08002. **[** *(93) 301 94 00.* **FAX** *(93) 317 31 79.*
This hotel, at the top of the Ramblas, has friendly staff and simple but
elegant rooms with spacious marble bathrooms. 🛏 ▤ TV
| ℗℗℗℗ | AE DC MC V | 108 | ▣ | |

OLD TOWN: *Arts.* **Map 6 E4.**
Carrer de la Marina 19–21, 08005. **[** *(93) 221 10 00.* **FAX** *(93) 221 10 70.*
A modern, superluxurious beachside hotel in one of Spain's tallest
towers. It has a huge swimming pool and a fitness center. 🛏 ▤ TV ♿
| ℗℗℗℗℗ | AE DC MC V | 455 | ▣ | ● | ▣ |

Price categories for a standard double room per night, with tax, breakfast, and service included:

ℙ under 8,000 ptas
ℙℙ 8,000–12,000 ptas
ℙℙℙ 12,000–16,000 ptas
ℙℙℙℙ 16,000–20,000 ptas
ℙℙℙℙℙ over 20,000 ptas

CREDIT CARDS
Indicates which credit cards are accepted: *AE* American Express; *DC* Diners Club; *MC* MasterCard/Access; *V* Visa

PARKING
Parking provided by the hotel in a private parking lot or a private garage on the hotel site or very close by. Some hotels charge for use of private parking facilities.

SWIMMING POOL
Hotel pool outdoors unless otherwise stated.

GARDEN
Hotel with garden, courtyard, or terrace, often providing tables for eating outdoors.

	CREDIT CARDS	NUMBER OF ROOMS	PRIVATE PARKING	SWIMMING POOL	GARDEN OR TERRACE
OLD TOWN: *Colón.* Map 5 B2. ℙℙℙℙ Avinguda de la Catedral 7, 08002. 📞 *(93) 301 14 04.* FAX *(93) 317 29 15.* From the Colón's front windows guests can watch the *sardana*, the traditional Catalan folk dance, performed in the Plaça de la Catedral on Sunday mornings. 🔲 📺	AE DC MC V	147			
OLD TOWN: *Le Meridien.* Map 5 A1. ℙℙℙℙ Ramblas 111, 08002. 📞 *(93) 318 62 00.* FAX *(93) 301 77 76.* An elegant hotel on the Ramblas, popular with rock and movie stars; the Rolling Stones on tour once booked the whole hotel. It has an enormous presidential suite and a business center. 🔲 📺 ♿	AE DC MC V	208	■		
EIXAMPLE: *Felipe II.* Map 3 C4. ℙ Carrer de Mallorca 329, 08037. 📞 *(93) 458 77 58.* A basic, clean hotel in an old apartment block in the Eixample, with a fine antique elevator. Some bedrooms share bathrooms. 🔲 📺		11			
EIXAMPLE: *Gran Vía.* Map 3 A5. ℙℙ Avda Gran Vía de les Corts Catalanes 642, 08007. 📞 *(93) 318 19 00.* FAX *(93) 318 99 97.* A hotel in a late 19th-century building with an aging grandeur, north of the Plaça de Catalunya adjoining the Passeig de Gràcia. 🔲 📺 ♿	AE DC MC V	53	■		
EIXAMPLE: *Catalunya Plaza.* Map 5 A1. ℙℙℙℙ Plaça de Catalunya 7, 08002. 📞 *(93) 317 71 71.* FAX *(93) 317 78 55.* A city-center hotel popular with business people. The 19th-century building has large sitting rooms decorated with frescoes. 🔲 📺	AE DC MC V	46			
EIXAMPLE: *Duques de Bergara.* Map 5 A1. ℙℙℙℙ Carrer de Bergara 11, 08002. 📞 *(93) 301 51 51.* FAX *(93) 317 34 42.* A luxury hotel in an exquisite Modernista building, with its original halls and stairways, near the Plaça de la Catedral. It has spacious, well-furnished bedrooms and modern public rooms. 🔲 📺	AE DC MC V	56			■
EIXAMPLE: *Regente.* Map 3 A4. ℙℙℙℙ Rambla de Catalunya 76, 08008. 📞 *(93) 487 59 89.* FAX *(93) 487 32 27.* A hotel in a Modernista building, with magnificent stained-glass decoration and a small, rooftop pool overlooking Montjuïc. 🔲 📺	AE DC MC V	78	■	●	■
EIXAMPLE: *Rivoli Ramblas.* Map 5 A1. ℙℙℙℙ Rambla dels Estudis 128, 08002. 📞 *(93) 302 66 43.* FAX *(93) 317 50 53.* An elegant hotel on the Ramblas decorated in contemporary style, with spacious bedrooms and city views from a roof terrace. 🔲 📺	AE DC MC V	89	■	●	■
EIXAMPLE: *Claris.* Map 3 B4. ℙℙℙℙℙ Carrer Pau Claris 150, 08009. 📞 *(93) 487 62 62.* FAX *(93) 215 79 70.* Antique rugs and elegant English and French furniture ornament this hotel off the Passeig de Gràcia. It occupies the converted Vedruna Palace and has a private museum of Egyptian art. 🔲 📺 ♿	AE DC MC V	121	■		
EIXAMPLE: *Condes de Barcelona.* Map 3 A4. ℙℙℙℙℙ Passeig de Gràcia 75, 08008. 📞 *(93) 488 22 00.* FAX *(93) 488 06 14.* This Modernista hotel has an impressive pentagonal lobby with a marble floor illuminated by a skylight. Book in advance. 🔲 📺	AE DC MC V	109	■	●	■
EIXAMPLE: *Gran Hotel Calderón.* Map 3 A5. ℙℙℙℙℙ Rambla de Catalunya 26, 08007. 📞 *(93) 301 00 00.* FAX *(93) 317 31 57.* A modern hotel near the Plaça de Catalunya, with spacious, comfortable rooms, indoor and rooftop pools, and a good restaurant. 🔲 📺 ♿	AE DC MC V	252	■	●	■
EIXAMPLE: *Majestic.* Map 3 A4. ℙℙℙℙℙ Passeig de Gràcia 70, 08008. 📞 *(93) 488 17 17.* FAX *(93) 488 18 80.* A hotel in Neo-Classical style in a very chic street (adjoining the Carrer de Valencia). The bedrooms are well equipped and soundproofed. 🔲 📺	AE DC MC V	329	■	●	■

EIXAMPLE: *Ritz*. Map 3 B5. (P)(P)(P)(P)
Avda Gran Via de les Corts Catalanes 668, 08010. ((93) 318 52 00. FAX (93) 318 01 48.
The most elegant of Barcelona's grand hotels, near the Plaça de Catalunya.
The large, luxurious bedrooms are decorated in classic style. 🔒 🍽 TV 🔧
AE DC MC V — 161

FARTHER AFIELD (NORTHWEST): *Gran Derby*. (P)(P)(P)
Loreto 28, 08029. ((93) 322 32 15. FAX (93) 419 68 20.
Attractive suites are the only accommodations offered here. There is no
restaurant; guests may dine in the Hotel Derby across the road. 🔒 🍽 TV
AE DC MC V — 41

FARTHER AFIELD (WEST): *Princesa Sofía*. (P)(P)(P)(P)
Plaça de Pius XII 4, Avda Diagonal, 08028. ((93) 330 71 11. FAX (93) 330 76 21.
A vast, luxury hotel decorated in marble, wood, and bronze, with one
of its several restaurants on the 19th floor, and a nightclub. 🔒 🍽 TV 🔧
AE DC MC V — 506

CATALONIA

ALBONS: *Albons Calm Hotel*. (P)(P)(P)
Ctra Figueres–La Bisbal, 17136 (Girona). ((972) 78 82 99. FAX (972) 78 81 17.
An ultramodern, original hotel in the heart of the Empordà region.
The bathrooms are spectacular and the cooking is excellent. Activities
include underwater swimming, gliding, and horseback riding. 🔒 🍽 TV
AE DC MC V — 32

ANDORRA LA VELLA: *Andorra Park Hotel*. (P)(P)(P)(P)
Les Canals 24 (Andorra). ((07-376) 82 09 79. FAX (07-376) 82 09 83.
One of Andorra's most luxurious hotels, the Andorra Park is modern
and built into a steep, wooded hillside. It has a library, a swimming
pool hewn out of rock, and is next to a department store. 🔒 TV 🔧
AE DC MC V — 40

ARTIES: *Parador Don Gaspar de Portolà*. (P)(P)(P)
Ctra a Baqueira-Beret, 25599 (Lleida). ((973) 64 08 01. FAX (973) 64 10 01.
A modern, warm, comfortable parador, near the Vall d'Arán ski resorts,
ideal for après-ski rest. Beside it is a medieval chapel. 🔒 TV 🔧
AE DC MC V — 52

AVINYONET DE PUIGVENTÓS: *Mas Pau*. (P)(P)(P)
Despoblado, 17500 (Girona). ((972) 54 61 54. FAX (972) 54 63 26.
A beautiful hotel in a 17th-century house, surrounded by wooded
farmland. The bedrooms and suites open onto a garden. 🔒 🍽 TV 🔧
AE DC MC V — 7

BAQUEIRA-BERET: *Royal Tanau*. (P)(P)(P)(P)
Carretera de Beret, 25598 (Lleida). ((973) 64 44 46. FAX (973) 64 43 44.
A luxurious hotel in the Tanau skiing area, with a ski lift to the trails.
It has full après-ski facilities, from whirlpool baths to tanning beds. 🔒 TV
AE MC V — 30

BEGUR (BAGUR): *Aigua Blava*. (P)(P)(P)
Platja de Fornells, 17255 (Girona). ((972) 62 20 58. FAX (972) 62 21 12.
A charming hotel on a small beach in an attractive spot on the
Costa Brava, from which there are marvelous sea views. 🔒 🍽 TV
AE MC V — 85

BOLVIR DE CERDANYA: *Torre del Remei*. (P)(P)(P)(P)
Camí Reial, 17463 (Girona). ((972) 14 01 82. FAX (972) 14 04 49.
An Art Nouveau mansion with a large garden has become a refined
hotel full of comforts such as VCRs in bedrooms. 🔒 🍽 TV
AE DC MC V — 11

CASTELLDEFELS: *Gran Hotel Rey Don Jaime*. (P)(P)(P)(P)
Avenida del Hotel 22, 08860 (Barcelona). ((93) 665 13 00. FAX (93) 665 18 01.
This hotel is in traditional Mediterranean style with arches and white-
washed walls. It is on a hilltop with views of the coast. 🔒 🍽 TV 🔧
AE DC MC V — 240

CASTELLÓ D'EMPÚRIES: *Allioli*. (P)(P)
Urbanització Castell Nou, 17486 (Girona). ((972) 25 03 20. FAX (972) 25 03 00.
A 17th-century Catalan farmhouse with considerable character, just off
the main Rosas–Figueres road. The restaurant is a popular place for
Sunday lunch among the local people. 🔒 🍽 TV 🔧
AE DC MC V — 42

CUBELLES: *Llicorella*. (P)(P)(P)(P)
Carrer Camí de Sant Antoni 101, 08880 (Barcelona). ((93) 895 00 44. FAX (93) 895 24 17.
This elegant hotel has striking sculptures in its garden. Most of the
bedrooms are luxurious, and the restaurant is excellent. 🔒 🍽 TV
AE DC MC V — 15

L'ESPLUGA DE FRANCOLÍ: *Hostal del Senglar*. (P)
Pl de Montserrat Canals 1, 43440 (Tarragona). ((977) 87 01 21. FAX (977) 87 10 12.
A three-story whitewashed hotel with a garden. A delicious menu of
dishes traditional to the area is served in the restaurant. 🔒 TV 🔧
AE DC MC V — 40

For key to symbols see back flap

Price categories for a standard double room per night, with tax, breakfast, and service included:

Ⓟ under 8,000 ptas
ⓅⓅ 8,000–12,000 ptas
ⓅⓅⓅ 12,000–16,000 ptas
ⓅⓅⓅⓅ 16,000–20,000 ptas
ⓅⓅⓅⓅⓅ over 20,000 ptas

CREDIT CARDS
Indicates which credit cards are accepted: *AE* American Express; *DC* Diners Club; *MC* MasterCard/Access; *V* Visa
PARKING
Parking provided by the hotel in a private parking lot or a private garage on the hotel site or very close by. Some hotels charge for use of private parking facilities.
SWIMMING POOL
Hotel pool outdoors unless otherwise stated.
GARDEN
Hotel with garden, courtyard, or terrace, often providing tables for eating outdoors.

	CREDIT CARDS	NUMBER OF ROOMS	PRIVATE PARKING	SWIMMING POOL	GARDEN OR TERRACE
L'ESPLUGA DE FRANCOLÍ: *Masía del Cadet.* ⓅⓅ Les Masies de Poblet, 43449 (Tarragona). (*(977) 87 08 69.* FAX *(977) 87 03 26.* An inexpensive hotel near the monastery of Poblet in a tastefully renovated 15th-century house. The bedrooms are austere and quiet. Traditional Catalan food is served in the restaurant. 🛏 ♿	AE DC MC V	12	■	●	■
LA GARRIGA: *Blancafort.* ⓅⓅⓅⓅ Carrer Banys 59, 08530 (Barcelona). (*(93) 871 46 00.* FAX *(93) 871 57 50.* A 19th-century hotel in a relaxing spa town near Barcelona. There are simple bedrooms and game facilities in the lounges. 🛏 ▤ TV ♿	MC V	52	■	●	■
LA GARRIGA: *La Garriga.* ⓅⓅⓅⓅ Carrer Banys 23, 08530 (Barcelona). (*(93) 871 70 86.* FAX *(93) 871 78 87.* Affluent people from Barcelona have been visiting this spa town for its waters since 1876. Children are not admitted to the hotel. 🛏 ▤ TV	AE MC V	22	■	●	■
GRANOLLERS: *Fonda Europa.* ⓅⓅⓅ Carrer Anselm Clavé 1, 08400 (Barcelona). (*(93) 870 03 12.* FAX *(93) 870 79 01.* This small hotel has been an inn for travelers since 1714. The rooms are on the second floor and are decorated in Art Deco style. 🛏 ▤ TV	AE DC MC V	7			
LLORET DE MAR: *Santa Marta.* ⓅⓅⓅⓅ Platja Santa Cristina, 17310 (Girona). (*(972) 36 49 04.* FAX *(972) 36 92 80.* A modern hotel with tennis courts and other sports facilities on its grounds. It is in a pine wood that extends to a quiet cove. 🛏 ▤ TV	AE DC MC V	78	■	●	■
MONTSENY: *San Bernat.* ⓅⓅⓅ Finca El Cot, 08460 (Barcelona). (*(93) 847 30 11.* FAX *(93) 847 31 02.* A big country house in the Sierra de Montseny, with a façade cloaked in greenery. There are beautiful grounds with lawns and a pond. 🛏 TV	AE DC MC V	20	■		■
PERAMOLA: *Can Boix.* ⓅⓅ Afueras, 25790 (Lleida). (*(973) 47 02 66.* FAX *(973) 47 02 66.* Run by a family of distinguished restaurateurs, this simple, economical hotel is convenient for walking in the Pyrenean foothills. 🛏 ▤ TV ♿	AE DC MC V	69	■	●	■
S'AGARÓ: *Hostal de la Gavina.* ⓅⓅⓅⓅⓅ Plaça de la Rosaleda, 17248 (Girona). (*(972) 32 11 00.* FAX *(972) 32 15 73.* An elegant beach mansion in traditional Mediterranean style with an exclusive feel. It is set in its own estate, with beautiful gardens. 🛏 ▤ TV	AE DC MC V	73	■	●	■
SANTA CRISTINA D'ARO: *Mas Torrellas.* ⓅⓅ Carretera Platja d'Aro, 17246 (Girona). (*(972) 83 75 26.* FAX *(972) 83 75 27.* An 18th-century country house hotel. Its most comfortable bedroom is in a distinctive yellow tower, built at a later date. 🛏 ▤ TV	AE DC MC V	17	■	●	■
SANT PERE DE RIBES: *Els Sumidors.* ⓅⓅ Carretera de Vilafranca, 08810 (Barcelona). (*(93) 896 20 61.* On the southern slope of a hill, with views across the landscape of the fertile Penedès wine region, this rustic 18th-century house has atmosphere and a certain charm, but few comforts. 🛏 TV	MC V	9	■		■
LA SEU D'URGELL: *El Castell.* ⓅⓅⓅ Carretera N260, 25700 (Lleida). (*(973) 35 07 04.* FAX *(973) 35 15 74.* This sumptuous hotel is a low, modern building beneath the medieval castle of Seu d'Urgell. There are impressive views across the mountains of El Cadí, and the ski slopes of Andorra are nearby. 🛏 ▤ TV	AE DC MC V	38	■	●	■
LA SEU D'URGELL: *Parador de La Seu d'Urgell.* ⓅⓅⓅ Carrer Santdomenec 6, 2570 (Lleida). (*(973) 35 20 00.* FAX *(973) 35 23 09.* Only the cloister, now the lounge, remains of a convent that occupied this site close to the 12th-century cathedral of La Seu. The dining room and indoor swimming pool have glass ceilings. 🛏 ▤ TV	AE DC MC V	78	■	●	

SITGES: *La Santa María.* ⓟⓟ | AE DC MC V | 53
Passeig Ribera 52, 08870 (Barcelona). **C** *(93) 894 09 99.* FAX *(93) 894 78 71.*
A cheery modern hotel hidden behind an older, five-story, molded-plaster façade. The restaurant has tables by the seafront. ⌨ ▤ TV ♿

SITGES: *Capri Veracruz.* ⓟⓟⓟ | AE DC MC V | 58
Avinguda de Sofía 13–15, 08870 (Barcelona). **C** *(93) 811 02 67.* FAX *(93) 894 51 88.*
Built in the 1950s near the beach, in one of the quieter parts of Sitges, this hotel has simple bedrooms and a family atmosphere. ⌨ TV

SITGES: *San Sebastián Playa.* ⓟⓟⓟⓟ | AE DC MC V | 51
Carrer Port Alegre 53, 08870 (Barcelona). **C** *(93) 894 86 76.* FAX *(93) 894 04 30.*
This new hotel on the beach near the old part of the town has a very attentive staff and comfortable bedrooms. ⌨ ▤ TV ♿

TAVÉRNOLES: *El Banús.* ⓟ | AE MC V | 6
El Banús, 08519 (Barcelona). **C** *(93) 812 20 91.*
A small, partly 15th-century farmhouse, furnished with Banús family heirlooms, offering basic bedrooms, shared bathrooms, and breakfast.

TARRAGONA: *Lauria.* ⓟⓟⓟ | AE DC MC V | 72
Rambla Nova 20, 43004. **C** *(977) 23 67 12.* FAX *(977) 23 67 00.*
A modern, functional hotel in the town center and close to the sea, with an elegant entrance under balustraded stone stairs. ⌨ ▤ TV

TORRENT: *Mas de Torrent.* ⓟⓟⓟⓟⓟ | AE DC MC V | 30
Afueras, 17123 (Girona). **C** *(972) 30 32 92.* FAX *(972) 30 32 93.*
A superbly converted 18th-century country house in large, terraced gardens. It has magnificent views. ⌨ TV ♿

TORTOSA: *Parador Castillo de La Zuda.* ⓟⓟⓟⓟ | AE DC MC V | 82
Castillo de la Zuda, 43500 (Tarragona). **C** *(977) 44 44 50.* FAX *(977) 44 44 58.*
A medieval castle built by the Moors makes a magnificent hilltop parador with views of the town and the Río Ebro valley. ⌨ ▤ TV

TREDÒS: *Hotel de Tredòs.* ⓟⓟⓟⓟ | MC V | 37
Carretera a Baqueira-Beret, 25598 (Lleida). **C** *(973) 64 40 14.* FAX *(973) 64 43 00.*
Skiers and mountain trekkers find this hotel in the Vall d'Arán a good value. It is built of stone and slate in the local style. ⌨ TV ♿

VIELHA (VIELLA): *Parador Valle de Arán.* ⓟⓟⓟⓟ | AE DC MC V | 135
Carretera del Túnel, 25530 (Lleida). **C** *(973) 64 01 00.* FAX *(973) 64 11 00.*
This modern parador has a semicircular lounge dominated by a large window with magnificent mountain views. ⌨ TV

VILADRAU: *Hostal de la Glòria.* ⓟ | MC V | 28
Carrer Torreventosa 12, 17406 (Girona). **C** *(93) 884 90 34.* FAX *(93) 884 94 65.*
A hotel with a family atmosphere in a traditional Catalan house above the Sierra de Montseny. It is full of copper pots and brass lamps. ⌨ TV

VILANOVA I LA GELTRÚ: *César.* ⓟⓟⓟ | DC MC V | 32
Carrer Isaac Peral 8, 08800 (Barcelona). **C** *(93) 815 11 25.* FAX *(93) 815 67 19.*
This hotel, near the Ribes Roges beach, is owned by two sisters who pay great attention to detail, from the furniture and the fabrics in the bedrooms to the well-known restaurant. ⌨ TV

ARAGÓN

AINSA: *Casa Cambra.* ⓟ | | 17
Morillo de Tou, Ctra Barbastro–Ainsa, 22395 (Huesca). **C** *(& FAX) (974) 50 07 93.*
The hotel is one of three in a formerly abandoned Pyrenean village, rebuilt as a vacation complex with a large campground, restaurants, and bars. The village is a center for almost every mountain sport. ⌨

ALBARRACÍN: *Arabia.* ⓟ | MC V | 21
Calle Bernardo Zapater 2, 44100 (Teruel). **C** *(978) 71 02 12.* FAX *(978) 71 02 37.*
A restored 17th-century school in a picturesque town. Some bedrooms have views of Albarracín's rooftops and its surrounding hills. ⌨ TV

ALBARRACÍN: *Casa de Santiago.* ⓟⓟ | V | 9
Calle Subida a las Torres 11, 44100 (Teruel). **C** *(978) 70 03 16.*
Albarracín's most beautiful hotel, in a restored mansion near the Plaza Mayor. The cozy interior, decorated with lovely printed fabrics, has iron and wood furniture custom made by local craftspeople. ⌨

Price categories for a standard double room per night, with tax, breakfast, and service included: Ⓟ under 8,000 ptas ⓅⓅ 8,000–12,000 ptas ⓅⓅⓅ 12,000–16,000 ptas ⓅⓅⓅⓅ 16,000–20,000 ptas ⓅⓅⓅⓅⓅ over 20,000 ptas	**CREDIT CARDS** Indicates which credit cards are accepted: *AE* American Express; *DC* Diners Club; *MC* MasterCard/Access; *V* Visa **PARKING** Parking provided by the hotel in a private parking lot or a private garage on the hotel site or very close by. Some hotels charge for use of private parking facilities. **SWIMMING POOL** Hotel pool outdoors unless otherwise stated. **GARDEN** Hotel with garden, courtyard, or terrace, often providing tables for eating outdoors.

	CREDIT CARDS	NUMBER OF ROOMS	PRIVATE PARKING	SWIMMING POOL	GARDEN OR TERRACE
ALBARRACÍN: *Albarracín.* ⓅⓅⓅⓅ Calle Azagra, 44100 (Teruel). 📞 (& FAX) (978) 71 00 11. A 16th-century Gothic mansion in a stepped street of medieval houses. The views from the windows are stunning. 🚗 📺	AE DC MC V	43		●	■
ALCAÑIZ: *Parador de Alcañiz.* ⓅⓅⓅⓅ Castillo de Calatravos, 44600 (Teruel). 📞 (978) 83 04 00. FAX (978) 83 03 66. This magnificent 12th-century monastery castle once belonged to the Knights of Calatrava. It is on a hilltop, dominating the town. Its decor is a modern interpretation of medieval castle style. 🚗 ▤ 📺 ♿	AE DC MC V	12	■		■
ALQUÉZAR: *Villa de Alquézar.* Ⓟ Pedro Arnal Cavero 12, 22145 (Huesca). 📞 (974) 31 84 16. FAX (974) 31 84 16. An old house in a medieval village on the Río Vero, near the Sierra de Guara nature preserve. Some rooms have spectacular mountain views. 🚗 📺	MC V	20			■
BENASQUE: *Ciria.* ⓅⓅ Avenida de los Tilos, 22440 (Huesca). 📞 (974) 55 16 12. FAX (974) 55 16 86. An efficient, friendly family runs this Pyrenean hotel. It has cozy attic bedrooms and is economical. There are bicycles for rent. 🚗 📺	AE MC V	34	■		■
BIELSA: *Parador de Bielsa.* ⓅⓅⓅ Valle de Pineta de Bielsa, 22350 (Huesca). 📞 (974) 50 10 11. FAX (974) 50 11 88. A mountain parador beautifully located in wooded country on the edge of Ordesa National Park, across from Monte Perdido. Inside, it is warm and inviting, with leather sofas in a wood-paneled lounge. 🚗 📺	AE DC MC V	34	■		■
CANFRANC-ESTACIÓN: *Santa Cristina de Somport.* ⓅⓅ Ctra de Francia N330, 22880 (Huesca). 📞 (974) 37 33 00. FAX (974) 37 33 10. This hotel is near the Somport Pass, which is on one of the main pilgrim routes from France to Santiago de Compostela. In winter guests can rent skis; in summer the hotel arranges guided mountain walks. 🚗 📺 ♿	AE DC MC V	58	■		■
FUENTESPALDA: *Torre del Visco.* ⓅⓅⓅ Apto de Valderrobres, 44587 (Teruel). 📞 (978) 76 90 15. FAX (978) 76 90 16. A 15th-century semifortified farmhouse in a remote river valley on the Teruel/Tarragona border is run as a hotel by an English couple. Room prices include breakfast and dinner based on produce from their farm. 🚗	V	8	■		■
HUESCA: *Pedro I de Aragón.* ⓅⓅⓅⓅ Calle del Parque 34, 22003. 📞 (974) 22 03 00. FAX (974) 22 00 94. A stylish modern hotel in the city center, bristling with facilities. The bedrooms are soundproofed, and ten have private terraces. 🚗 ▤ 📺	AE DC MC V	130	■	●	■
JACA: *Conde Aznar.* ⓅⓅ Paseo de la Constitución 3, 22700 (Huesca). 📞 (974) 36 10 50. FAX (974) 36 07 97. A simple, hospitable, economical hotel in an old urban mansion on a fashionable avenue. It has a good restaurant serving local dishes. 🚗 📺	AE MC V	24			■
JACA: *Gran Hotel.* ⓅⓅⓅ Paseo de la Constitución 1, 22700 (Huesca). 📞 (974) 36 09 00. FAX (974) 36 40 61. A modern hotel, centrally located next to a park, within reach of the ski slopes around Somport Pass. There is a charge for parking. 🚗 📺	AE DC MC V	165	■	●	■
MORA DE RUBIELOS: *Jaime I.* ⓅⓅ Plaza de la Villa, 44400 (Teruel). 📞 (978) 80 00 92. FAX (978) 80 00 92. A handsome stone building with wooden balconies and simple rooms. The mansion-filled town is on the edge of the Maestrazgo. 🚗 📺	AE DC MC V	35			
NUÉVALOS: *Monasterio de Piedra.* ⓅⓅ Monasterio de Piedra, 50210 (Zaragoza). 📞 (976) 84 90 11. FAX (976) 84 90 54. Beside a nature preserve is this former Cistercian monastery, now a hotel. Among its original details are alabaster window panes. 🚗 📺	AE DC MC V	61	■	●	■

SALLENT DE GÁLLEGO: *Almud.* ℗℗ · DC V · 8
Espadilla 3, 22640 (Huesca). **(** *(& FAX) (974) 48 83 66.*
A charming, homey hotel in the Pyrenees. All rooms are decorated with antiques. The bar is in the former stables in the cellar. 📶 TV

SALLENT DE GÁLLEGO: *Villa de Sallent.* ℗℗ · AE DC MC V · 40
Urbanización El Formigal, 22640 (Huesca). **(** *(974) 49 02 23.* FAX *(974) 49 01 50.*
At the foot of the trails of Formigal ski resort, this family-run hotel is welcoming at dusk. It has open fires and warm bedrooms. 📶 TV 🔶

SOS DEL REY CATÓLICO: *Parador de Sos del Rey Católico.* ℗℗℗ · AE DC MC V · 65
Paseo del Rey Católico, 50680 (Zaragoza). **(** *(948) 88 80 11.* FAX *(948) 88 81 00.*
The parador, at one end of the medieval wall, blends with the town's historic architecture and has fine country views. 📶 TV 🔶

TERUEL: *Parador de Teruel.* ℗℗℗ · AE DC MC V · 60
Ctra a Zaragoza, 44080. **(** *(978) 60 18 00.* FAX *(978) 60 86 12.*
This parador is in leafy surroundings a little outside the city, set back from a main road. It has a pleasant, covered, terrace bar. 📶 TV

TERUEL: *Reina Cristina.* ℗℗℗ · AE DC MC V · 82
Paseo del Ovalo 1, 44001. **(** *(978) 60 68 60.* FAX *(978) 60 53 63.*
The Reina Cristina is a modern, city-center hotel, in easy reach of the main monuments. Some of the bedrooms have terraces. 📶 ▤ TV 🔶

VILLANÚA: *Faus Hütte.* ℗℗ · AE DC MC V · 10
Ctra de Francia, 22870 (Huesca). **(** *(974) 37 81 36.* FAX *(974) 37 81 98.*
This hotel deep in the Pyrenees is owned by a mountain guide. It is a good base for skiing, hiking, and other mountain activities. It is also on the pilgrim's route to Santiago de Compostela. 📶 TV

ZARAGOZA: *Conde de Aranda.* ℗℗℗ · AE DC MC V · 85
Conde de Aranda 48, 50003. **(** *(976) 28 45 00.* FAX *(976) 28 27 17.*
This hotel, not far from the city center, is comfortable and popular with business travelers. 📶 ▤ TV 🔶

ZARAGOZA: *Gran Hotel.* ℗℗℗℗ · AE DC MC V · 140
Calle Joaquín Costa 5, 50001. **(** *(976) 22 19 01.* FAX *(976) 23 67 13.*
Zaragoza's city-center grand hotel was opened in 1929 by Alfonso XIII. It has colonnades and a magnificent domed salon. 📶 ▤ TV

ZARAGOZA: *Tibur.* ℗℗℗ · AE DC MC V · 50
Plaza de la Seo 2 & 3, 50001. **(** *(976) 20 20 00.* FAX *(976) 20 20 02.*
The Tibur is conveniently located in the old heart of the city, with views of the Basílica del Pilar. The bedrooms are well equipped. 📶 ▤ TV 🔶

VALENCIA AND MURCIA

ÁGUILAS: *Carlos III.* ℗℗ · AE DC MC V · 32
Calle Rey Carlos III 22, 30880 (Murcia). **(** *(968) 41 16 50.* FAX *(968) 41 16 58.*
A modern town-center hotel near the beach in a small Murcian resort. The restaurant serves fish, seafood, and other local dishes. 📶 ▤ TV

ALICANTE (ALACANT): *Palas.* ℗℗ · AE DC MC V · 39
Calle Cervantes 5, 03002. **(** *(96) 520 92 11.* FAX *(96) 514 01 21.*
This hotel in an aristocratic mansion built late in the 19th century on the Explanada, near the beach, the harbor, and the city center. 📶 TV

ALICANTE (ALACANT): *Sidi San Juan.* ℗℗℗℗℗ · AE DC MC V · 176
Playa de San Juan, 03540. **(** *(96) 516 13 00.* FAX *(96) 516 33 46.*
A luxury hotel outside Alicante, with access to a beach through gardens. The bedrooms have sea views and there is a health spa. 📶 ▤ TV

ARCHENA: *Termas.* ℗℗℗ · 71
Ctra Balneario, 30600 (Murcia). **(** *(968) 67 01 00.* FAX *(968) 67 10 02.*
Inside, this spa hotel is decorated in a glorious Mudéjar style, with ornate plasterwork, domes, and Moorish arches. Tunnels in the basement are heated by water gushing from the ground. 📶 ▤ TV 🔶

BOCAIRENT: *L'Estació de Bocairent.* ℗℗ · AE DC MC V · 14
Parque de la Estación, 46880 (Valencia). **(** *(96) 290 52 11.* FAX *(96) 290 54 23.*
A small, comfortable hotel set up by the regional tourist board in an old railroad station on the edge of a fascinating medieval town. There are barbecues in summer. 📶 ▤ TV 🔶

Price categories for a standard double room per night, with tax, breakfast, and service included:

Ⓟ   under 8,000 ptas
ⓅⓅ   8,000–12,000 ptas
ⓅⓅⓅ   12,000–16,000 ptas
ⓅⓅⓅⓅ   16,000–20,000 ptas
ⓅⓅⓅⓅⓅ   over 20,000 ptas

CREDIT CARDS
Indicates which credit cards are accepted: *AE* American Express; *DC* Diners Club; *MC* MasterCard/Access; *V* Visa
PARKING
Parking provided by the hotel in a private parking lot or a private garage on the hotel site or very close by. Some hotels charge for use of private parking facilities.
SWIMMING POOL
Hotel pool outdoors unless otherwise stated.
GARDEN
Hotel with garden, courtyard, or terrace, often providing tables for eating outdoors.

	Credit Cards	Number of Rooms	Private Parking	Swimming Pool	Garden or Terrace
CALP: *Venta la Chata.* Ⓟ Carretera de Valencia, 03710 (Alicante). ((96) 583 03 08. An old coaching inn on the main road between Alicante and Valencia. The bedrooms are simple, mixing old and new furniture, and some have terraces looking out on a pretty garden.	DC MC V	17	■		■
CARTAGENA: *Los Habaneros.* Ⓟ Calle San Diego 60, 30202 (Murcia). ((968) 50 52 50. FAX (968) 50 52 54. Located on the edge of the old part of town, this hotel offers comfort at an affordable price. It also has a popular restaurant.	AE DC MC V	65			
CASTELL DE CASTELLS: *Pensión Castells.* Ⓟ Calle San Vicente 18, 03793 (Alicante). ((96) 551 82 54. An old house in an inland village not far from the Costa Blanca. All the rooms are given a loving touch. The British owners offer bed and breakfast, and they take guests walking in the surrounding hills.		4			■
CHULILLA: *Balneario de Chulilla.* Ⓟ Afueras, 46167 (Valencia). ((96) 165 70 13. FAX (96) 165 70 31. This riverside spa hotel is an inexpensive place to stop while exploring the woods and hills of inland Valencia. It has all the facilities for a rest-cure, including a sauna, a gym, tennis courts, and a Jacuzzi.	V	60	■	●	■
DÉNIA: *Rosa.* ⓅⓅ Las Marinas, 03700 (Alicante). ((96) 578 15 73. FAX (96) 578 15 73. A modern white villa close to the beach. It was built and is run by a Parisian expatriate who works hard to please his guests. Rooms have sunny, sheltered, Florentine-style balconies.	MC V	39	■	●	■
ELX: *Huerto del Cura.* ⓅⓅⓅⓅ Porta de la Morera 14, 03203 (Alicante). ((96) 545 80 40. FAX (96) 542 19 10. A secluded hotel in Europe's largest palm tree forest, surrounded by landscaped grounds. The bedrooms are all in Mediterranean-style bungalows. The restaurant is highly regarded.	AE DC MC V	70	■	●	■
FORCALL: *Palau dels Ossets.* ⓅⓅ Plaza Mayor 16, 12310 (Castellón). ((964) 17 75 24. FAX (964) 17 75 56. A tastefully renovated 16th-century mansion on the main square of a quiet village at the heart of El Maestrat. It has wooden beams, tiled floors, and well-equipped bedrooms.	V	20			
FORTUNA: *Balneario.* ⓅⓅ Balneario de Fortuna, 30630 (Murcia). ((968) 68 50 11. FAX (968) 68 50 87. This hotel, used by visitors to a spa, has the atmosphere of a former grand hotel. It has Art Nouveau doors and a grand staircase. The swimming pool is naturally heated.	AE MC V	58	■	●	■
LA MANGA DEL MAR MENOR: *Príncipe Felipe.* ⓅⓅⓅⓅⓅ Hyatt La Manga Club, 30385 (Murcia). ((968) 13 72 34. FAX (968) 13 72 72. A luxurious hotel, part of an exclusive resort complex built in the style of a Spanish village. It is surrounded by palm and olive groves, and has 3 golf courses, 18 tennis courts, and 4 swimming pools.	AE DC MC V	192	■	●	■
MORAIRA: *Swiss Hotel Moraira.* ⓅⓅⓅⓅ Urbanización Club Moraira, 03724 (Alicante). ((96) 574 71 04. FAX (96) 574 70 74. In a development of vacation homes close to the coast is this exclusive hotel. The bedrooms are spacious.	AE DC MC V	25	■	●	■
MORATALLA: *Cenajo.* ⓅⓅ Embalse del Cenajo, 30440 (Murcia). ((968) 72 10 11. FAX (968) 72 06 45. At night, silence descends on this creamy-yellow hotel beside the Cenajo dam, in rural Murcia where few foreign tourists go. Horseback riding is one of many activities available.	MC V	76	■	●	■

MORELLA: *Cardenal Ram.* ℝ — V — 19
Cuesta Suñer 1, 12300 (Castellón). **(** (964) 17 30 85. **FAX** (964) 17 32 18.
A renovated 16th-century mansion with stone arches and beamed ceilings, overlooking the main porticoed street of a historic town. 🚗 TV

MURCIA: *Conde de Floridablanca.* ℝℝ — AE DC MC V — 85
Princesa 18, 30002. **(** (968) 21 46 26. **FAX** (968) 21 32 15.
A comfortable, bargain hotel across the river from the city center, furnished with antiques and decorated with stained glass. 🚗 ▤ TV

MURCIA: *Arco de San Juan.* ℝℝℝ — AE DC MC V — 115
Plaza de Ceballos 10, 30003. **(** (968) 21 04 55. **FAX** (968) 22 08 09.
The restoration of this hotel near the cathedral has won awards. The decor combines contemporary materials with antiques. 🚗 ▤ TV

PENÁGUILA: *Mas de Pau.* ℝℝ — AE MC V — 18
Ctra Alcoi–Penáguila, 03815 (Alicante). **(** (96) 551 31 11. **FAX** (96) 551 31 11.
A 19th-century house in a landscape of almond and olive trees near Alcoi. It has small bedrooms, and some overlook the Sierra Aitana. 🚗 ▤ TV

PEÑÍSCOLA: *Benedicto XIII.* ℝℝ — AE DC MC V — 30
Urbanización Las Atalayas, 12598 (Castellón). **(** (964) 48 08 01. **FAX** (964) 48 95 23.
A white villa in a quiet private estate on a hillside above Peñíscola. Its terraces and arched windows give views of the town. 🚗 TV ♿

PEÑÍSCOLA: *Hostería del Mar.* ℝℝℝℝ — AE DC MC V — 86
Avenida Papa Luna 18, 12598 (Castellón). **(** (964) 48 06 00. **FAX** (964) 48 13 63.
Many of the rooms in this modern beach hotel have sea views. Animated medieval banquets are a house specialty. 🚗 ▤ TV ♿

PUZOL: *Monte Picayo.* ℝℝℝℝ — AE DC MC V — 83
Autopista A7, exit 7, 46530 (Valencia). **(** (96) 142 01 00. **FAX** (96) 142 21 68.
A luxury hotel close to the Valencia bypass but surrounded by gardens, with its own casino and bullring. Some of the bedrooms have a private garden and swimming pool. 🚗 ▤ TV

EL SALER: *Parador de El Saler.* ℝℝℝℝ — AE DC MC V — 58
Avda de los Pinares 151, 46012 (Valencia). **(** (96) 161 11 86. **FAX** (96) 162 70 16.
A modern parador, peacefully situated beside the sea near L'Albufera and surrounded by a famous golf course. 🚗 ▤ TV ♿

VALENCIA: *Ad Hoc.* ℝℝℝ — AE DC MC V — 28
Calle Boix 4, 46003. **(** (96) 391 91 40. **FAX** (96) 391 36 67.
A chic hotel in a renovated, soundproofed, 19th-century building in the historic quarter of the city, near the Río Turia gardens. 🚗 ▤ TV

VALENCIA: *Inglés.* ℝℝℝℝ — AE DC MC V — 62
Calle Marqués de Dos Aguas 6, 46002. **(** (96) 351 64 26. **FAX** (96) 394 02 51.
This convenient city-center hotel is in the old palace of the Dukes of Cardona, next to the National Ceramics Museum. All the bedrooms look onto the street. The restaurant serves Valencian cuisine. 🚗 ▤ TV

VALENCIA: *Reina Victoria.* ℝℝℝℝ — AE DC MC V — 97
Calle Barcas 4, 46002. **(** (96) 352 04 87. **FAX** (96) 352 04 87.
In the city center, near the Plaza del Ayuntamiento, this elegant hotel, built in the late 19th century, has modern bedrooms. 🚗 ▤ TV

LA VILA JOIOSA (VILLAJOYOSA): *El Montíboli.* ℝℝℝℝℝ — AE DC MC V — 53
Partida El Montíboli, 03570 (Alicante). **(** (96) 589 02 50. **FAX** (96) 589 38 57.
This hotel is perched on a low cliff outside the town and looks down on a secluded beach. Each bedroom is different, and each has a terrace with a sea view. 🚗 ▤ TV ♿

XÀBIA (JÁVEA): *Bahía Vista.* ℝℝ — DC MC V — 17
Calle Portichol 76, 03730 (Alicante). **(** (96) 577 04 61. **FAX** (96) 647 09 95.
A small hotel among pine woods at the southern end of Arenales beach. The bedrooms are furnished in wicker and pine, and most have balconies with sea views. 🚗

XÀBIA (JÁVEA): *Parador de Jávea.* ℝℝℝℝ — AE DC MC V — 65
Calle Arenal 2, 03730 (Alicante). **(** (96) 579 02 00. **FAX** (96) 579 03 08.
A parador in the middle of Arenales beach. The dining room looks across the terrace to splendid gardens, and the bedroom balconies have sea views. There are water sports facilities nearby. 🚗 ▤ TV

For key to symbols see back flap

Price categories for a standard double room per night, with tax, breakfast, and service included:

ℙ under 8,000 ptas
ℙℙ 8,000–12,000 ptas
ℙℙℙ 12,000–16,000 ptas
ℙℙℙℙ 16,000–20,000 ptas
ℙℙℙℙℙ over 20,000 ptas

CREDIT CARDS
Indicates which credit cards are accepted: *AE* American Express; *DC* Diners Club; *MC* MasterCard/Access; *V* Visa

PARKING
Parking provided by the hotel in a private parking lot or a private garage on the hotel site or very close by. Some hotels charge for use of private parking facilities.

SWIMMING POOL
Hotel pool outdoors unless otherwise stated.

GARDEN
Hotel with garden, courtyard, or terrace, often providing tables for eating outdoors.

MADRID

	CREDIT CARDS	NUMBER OF ROOMS	PRIVATE PARKING	SWIMMING POOL	GARDEN OR TERRACE
OLD MADRID: *Hostal Buenos Aires*. **Map 1 D1.** ℙ Gran Vía 61, 28013. **(** (91) 542 01 02. **FAX** (91) 542 28 69. A simple, economical hotel, conveniently located on the busy Gran Vía. The public rooms are pleasantly decorated. Each of the bedrooms has its own balcony or small terrace. 🚗 ☰ 📺	AE DC MC V	25			
OLD MADRID: *Inglés*. **Map 5 A1.** ℙℙ Calle de Echegaray 8, 28014. **(** (91) 429 65 51. **FAX** (91) 420 24 23. An economical, family-run hotel with its own garage. The bedrooms facing the street are sunny, but the back rooms are quieter. 🚗 📺	AE DC MC V	58	■		
OLD MADRID: *Regente*. **Map 2 F2.** ℙℙ Mesonero Romanos 9, 28013. **(** (91) 521 29 41. **FAX** (91) 532 30 14. This convenient, centrally located hotel combines new facilities with old-style furniture. 🚗 ☰ 📺	AE DC MC V	145	■		
OLD MADRID: *Carlos V*. **Map 2 E3.** ℙℙℙ Calle Maestro Vitoria 5, 28013. **(** (91) 531 41 00. **FAX** (91) 531 37 61. A city-center hotel in a pedestrian street beside the Puerta del Sol, run by a family. There are interconnecting bedrooms, family rooms, rooms with balconies, and top-floor rooms with sizable sun terraces. 🚗 ☰ 📺	AE DC MC V	67			
OLD MADRID: *Tryp Gran Vía*. **Map 2 F2.** ℙℙℙ Gran Vía 25, 28013. **(** (91) 522 11 21. **FAX** (91) 521 24 24. A chain hotel on one of the city's busiest streets. Some of the furniture is in the style of the 1960s and 1970s. 🚗 ☰ 📺	AE DC MC V	174			
OLD MADRID: *Tryp Rex*. **Map 2 E2.** ℙℙℙℙ Gran Vía 43, 28013. **(** (91) 547 48 00. **FAX** (91) 547 12 38. A chain hotel in an old building between the Plaza del Callao and the Plaza de España, close to a large public parking lot. It has spacious public rooms and well-equipped bedrooms, each with its own safe. 🚗 ☰ 📺	AE DC MC V	144			
OLD MADRID: *Arosa*. **Map 2 F2.** ℙℙℙℙℙ Calle de la Salud 21, 28013. **(** (91) 532 16 00. **FAX** (91) 531 31 27. This centrally located hotel off the Gran Vía and the Puerta del Sol is popular with international and business visitors to Madrid. All the bedrooms are comfortable and well soundproofed. 🚗 ☰ 📺	AE DC MC V	139	■		
OLD MADRID: *Emperador*. **Map 2 E2.** ℙℙℙℙℙ Gran Via 53, 28013. **(** (91) 547 28 00. **FAX** (91) 547 28 17. A popular hotel, ideally placed for exploring the city center. The spacious bedrooms are quiet, in spite of the traffic below. There is a rooftop swimming pool. 🚗 ☰ 📺	AE DC MC V	232	■	●	■
BOURBON MADRID: *Mora*. **Map 5 C2.** ℙℙ Paseo del Prado 32, 28014. **(** (91) 420 15 69. **FAX** (91) 420 05 64. A 1930s hotel with an attractive entrance. Its rooms and facilities are functional, but its prices are low and it is centrally located near the Jardín Botánico and the Prado. 🚗 ☰ 📺	AE DC MC V	62			
BOURBON MADRID: *Palace*. **Map 5 B1.** ℙℙℙℙℙ Plaza de las Cortes 7, 28014. **(** (91) 521 28 57. **FAX** (91) 532 87 76. This gracious *belle époque* hotel with a glass dome and a colonnade has accommodated statesmen and the spy, Mata Hari. The bedrooms are elegant and the service welcoming and efficient. 🚗 ☰ 📺 ♿	AE DC MC V	455	■		■
BOURBON MADRID: *Pintor*. **Map 3 D3.** ℙℙℙℙ Calle Goya 79, 28001. **(** (91) 435 75 45. **FAX** (91) 576 81 57. The lobby of this hotel, in a modern city block off the Plaza de Colón, a stroll from the Parque del Retiro, is in mock-Hawaiian style. 🚗 ☰ 📺	AE MC V	176	■		

BOURBON MADRID: *Reina Victoria.* **Map 5 A1.** ℞℞℞℞
Plaza Santa Ana 14, 28012. **(** (91) 531 45 00. **FAX** (91) 522 03 07.
Ernest Hemingway once lodged in this historic hotel, a graceful edifice and a traditional haunt of bullfighting aficionados. 🖥 ▤ TV ᕦ
Cards: AE, DC, MC, V — Rooms: 201

BOURBON MADRID: *Ritz.* **Map 5 C1.** ℞℞℞℞℞
Plaza de la Lealtad 5, 28014. **(** (91) 521 28 57. **FAX** (91) 532 87 76.
Inaugurated in 1910 as a hotel for aristocrats, the Ritz is still one of Spain's most elegant hotels *(see p274)*. It has an ornate, circular foyer and a terrace garden, and offers musical teas and brunches. 🖥 ▤ TV
Cards: AE, DC, MC, V — Rooms: 158

BOURBON MADRID: *Suecia.* **Map 3 B5.** ℞℞℞℞
Calle del Marqués de Casa Riera 4, 28014. **(** (91) 531 69 00. **FAX** (91) 521 71 41.
Centrally located near the Puerta del Sol, the Suecia has a small, seventh-floor terrace for relaxing and sunbathing. 🖥 ▤ TV
Cards: AE, DC, MC — Rooms: 128

BOURBON MADRID: *Suite Prado.* **Map 5 A1.** ℞℞℞℞
Manuel Fernández y González 10, 28014. **(** (91) 420 23 18. **FAX** (91) 420 05 59.
A stylish apartment hotel of luxurious suites a short distance from the Prado and the Museo Thyssen-Bornemisza. 🖥 ▤ TV
Cards: AE, DC, MC — Rooms: 18

BOURBON MADRID: *Villa Real.* **Map 5 B1.** ℞℞℞℞
Plaza de las Cortes 10, 28014. **(** (91) 420 37 67. **FAX** (91) 420 25 47.
Located close to the Prado, this stylish hotel is housed in an early 19th-century building. The public areas are furnished with reproduction mahogany furniture and embroideries of pastoral scenes. 🖥 ▤ TV
Cards: AE, DC, MC, V — Rooms: 115

BOURBON MADRID: *Wellington.* **Map 4 F4.** ℞℞℞℞℞
Calle de Velázquez 8, 28001. **(** (91) 575 44 00. **FAX** (91) 576 41 64.
A stylish hotel built in the early 1950s close to the Parque del Retiro. It is a meeting place for people interested in bullfighting. 🖥 ▤ TV
Cards: AE, DC, MC, V — Rooms: 288

FARTHER AFIELD (EAST): *Alcalá.* ℞℞℞℞
Calle de Alcalá 66, 28009. **(** (91) 435 10 60. **FAX** (91) 435 11 05.
A hotel with a friendly atmosphere across the street from the Parque del Retiro. The back bedrooms overlook a pretty garden. 🖥 ▤ TV
Cards: AE, DC, MC, V — Rooms: 153

FARTHER AFIELD (EAST): *Colón.* ℞℞℞℞
Calle Doctor Esquerdo 119, 28007. **(** (91) 573 59 00. **FAX** (91) 573 08 09.
A comfortable hotel in a tower block between the Parque del Retiro and the Parque de Roma. It has fitness and business facilities. 🖥 ▤ TV
Cards: AE, DC, MC, V — Rooms: 389

FARTHER AFIELD (NORTH): *Hostal Sil.* **Map 3 A4.** ℞
Calle Fuencarral 95, 28004. **(** (91) 448 89 72. **FAX** (91) 447 48 29.
This comfortable convenient hotel is in a lively part of town, with quality bedroom and bathroom furnishings and low prices. 🖥 ▤ TV
Cards: V — Rooms: 20

FARTHER AFIELD (NORTH): *Mónaco.* **Map 3 B4.** ℞℞
Calle Barbieri 5, 28004. **(** (91) 522 46 30. **FAX** (91) 521 16 01.
The decor of this hotel, formerly Madrid's most famous high-class brothel, is unashamedly kitsch. The bedrooms still have some of their original decadent features. 🖥 ▤ TV
Cards: AE, DC, MC, V — Rooms: 32

FARTHER AFIELD (NORTH): *Serrano.* **Map 4 E1.** ℞℞℞℞
Calle de Marqués de Villamejor 8, 28006. **(** (91) 435 52 00. **FAX** (91) 435 48 49.
The gray façade belies the elegant interior, with some antiques among the furniture. The bedrooms are large and comfortable. 🖥 ▤ TV
Cards: AE, DC, MC, V — Rooms: 34

FARTHER AFIELD (NORTH): *Castellana Intercontinental.* ℞℞℞℞℞
Paseo de la Castellana 49, 28046. **(** (91) 310 02 00. **FAX** (91) 319 58 53.
This hotel in Madrid's commercial center is a favorite with business travelers. Guests can choose between two restaurants. 🖥 ▤ TV ᕦ
Cards: AE, DC, MC, V — Rooms: 313

FARTHER AFIELD (NORTH): *Miguel Angel.* ℞℞℞℞℞
Calle Miguel Angel 31, 28010. **(** (91) 442 81 99. **FAX** (91) 442 53 20.
Beside the Paseo de la Castellana, the Miguel Angel combines modern comfort with classic style. One of its two fine restaurants holds dinner dances until 3am. 🖥 ▤ TV ᕦ
Cards: AE, DC, MC, V — Rooms: 278

FARTHER AFIELD (NORTH): *Santo Mauro.* ℞℞℞℞℞
Calle Zurbano 36, 28010. **(** (91) 319 69 00. **FAX** (91) 308 54 77.
This palace, built in 1894 in one of Madrid's most elegant streets, has housed several embassies. It has a swimming pool beneath a vaulted basement ceiling, and a restaurant occupies the former library. 🖥 ▤ TV ᕦ
Cards: AE, DC, MC, V — Rooms: 36

Price categories for a standard double room per night, with tax, breakfast, and service included:

℗ under 8,000 ptas
℗℗ 8,000–12,000 ptas
℗℗℗ 12,000–16,000 ptas
℗℗℗℗ 16,000–20,000 ptas
℗℗℗℗℗ over 20,000 ptas

CREDIT CARDS
Indicates which credit cards are accepted: *AE* American Express; *DC* Diners Club; *MC* MasterCard/Access; *V* Visa
PARKING
Parking provided by the hotel in a private parking lot or a private garage on the hotel site or very close by. Some hotels charge for use of private parking facilities.
SWIMMING POOL
Hotel pool outdoors unless otherwise stated.
GARDEN
Hotel with garden, courtyard, or terrace, often providing tables for eating outdoors.

	CREDIT CARDS	NUMBER OF ROOMS	PRIVATE PARKING	SWIMMING POOL	GARDEN OR TERRACE
FARTHER AFIELD (NORTH): *Villamagna.* ℗℗℗℗℗ Paseo de la Castellana 22, 28046. (*(91) 587 12 34.* FAX *(91) 575 95 04.* The Villamagna combines 18th-century decor with modern luxury and is ringed by gardens. It is popular with business people. 🖬 ▤ TV ♿	AE DC MC V	182	■		■
FARTHER AFIELD (NORTHEAST): *Conde de Orgaz.* ℗℗℗℗ Avenida Moscatelar 24, 28043. (*(91) 388 40 99.* FAX *(91) 388 00 09.* A modern hotel, with big, comfortable bedrooms, near the airport and the Campo de las Naciones Exhibition Center. 🖬 ▤ TV ♿	AE DC MC V	90	■		
FARTHER AFIELD (NORTHWEST): *Tirol.* ℗℗ Calle de Marqués de Urquijo 4, 28008. (*(91) 548 19 00.* FAX *(91) 541 39 58.* A bargain hotel, conveniently located off the Plaza de España and near the student district. The bedrooms are spacious and clean. 🖬 ▤	MC V	97			
FARTHER AFIELD (NORTHWEST): *Monte Real.* ℗℗℗℗℗ Calle Arroyo Fresno 17, 28035. (*(91) 316 21 40.* FAX *(91) 316 39 34.* Situated in a residential area near the Puerta de Hierro golf course, this imposing modern hotel has a peaceful atmosphere. Its balconies overlook the swimming pool and gardens. 🖬 ▤ TV ♿	AE DC MC V	80	■	●	■
FARTHER AFIELD (SOUTHEAST): *Agumar.* Map 6 F4. ℗℗℗℗ Paseo de Reina Cristina 7, 28014. (*(91) 552 69 00.* FAX *(91) 433 60 95.* A stylish hotel near the big museums, with its own collection of good paintings and carpets from the Real Fábrica de Tapices. 🖬 ▤ TV	AE DC MC V	245	■		
FARTHER AFIELD (SOUTHWEST): *Reyes Católicos.* Map 1 C5. ℗℗℗ Calle del Ángel 18, 28005. (*(91) 365 86 00.* FAX *(91) 365 98 67.* This modern, central hotel is popular and always very busy. Children are made welcome. The bedroom windows are double-glazed for sound-proofing. There are views of the city from the roof terrace. 🖬 ▤ TV	AE DC V	38	■		
MADRID PROVINCE					
ALAMEDA DEL VALLE: *La Posada de Alameda.* ℗℗℗ Calle Grande 34, 28749. (*(91) 869 13 37.* FAX *(91) 869 01 63.* A sensitively restored farmhouse in the tranquil Lozoya valley, about an hour's drive from Madrid. All the bedrooms are well equipped, and some have views of the countryside. Two are in converted silos. 🖬 TV	AE MC V	22	■		■
CHINCHÓN: *Parador de Chinchón.* ℗℗℗℗ Avenida del Generalísimo 1, 28370. (*(91) 894 08 36.* FAX *(91) 894 09 08.* This converted 17th-century monastery has immensely thick walls and is built around an airy green courtyard. Delightful details to look out for include *azulejos (see p420)*, frescoes, and antiques. 🖬 ▤ TV	AE DC MC V	38	■	●	■
RASCAFRÍA: *Santa María de El Paular.* ℗℗℗℗ El Paular, 28741. (*(91) 869 10 11.* FAX *(91) 869 10 06.* This hotel occupies part of a Benedictine monastery in a peaceful corner of the Guadarrama mountains. A *mesón* (bar-restaurant) offers an informal alternative to the dining room. 🖬 TV	AE DC MC V	58	■	●	■
SAN LORENZO DE EL ESCORIAL: *Victoria Palace.* ℗℗℗℗ Calle Juan de Toledo 4, 28200. (*(91) 890 15 11.* FAX *(91) 890 12 48.* A short walk from the 16th-century palace of El Escorial, this stylish and elegant hotel offers magnificent views from the bedrooms. An open fire warms the lounge in winter. 🖬 TV	AE DC MC V	87	■	●	■
TORREJÓN DE ARDOZ: *La Casa Grande.* ℗℗℗℗ Calle Madrid 2, 28850. (*(91) 675 39 00.* FAX *(91) 675 06 91.* This luxurious hotel in a 16th-century house is decorated with antiques that once belonged to the Russian royal family. Catherine the Great is said to have slept in the bed now in the main suite. 🖬 ▤ TV	AE DC MC V	9	■		■

CASTILLA Y LEÓN

AGUILAR DE CAMPOO: *Posada de Santa María la Real.* Ⓟ | V | 18
Avenida Cervera, 34800 (Palencia). (*(979) 12 20 00.*
Part of the Institute of Romanesque Studies is in this monastery; the
hotel entrance is at the back and not marked. The bedrooms are
small and plain, with garden views. The atmosphere is friendly. 🛏 TV

LA ALBERCA: *Las Batuecas.* Ⓟ | V | 24
Carretera de las Batuecas, 37624 (Salamanca). (*(923) 41 51 88.* FAX *(923) 41 50 55.*
On the edge of a pretty village, deep in a green valley, this hotel is a
base for touring the Sierra de la Peña de Francia. It is a stone and wood
building with a first-floor, covered terrace. 🛏 ▤ TV

ASTORGA: *Gaudí.* ⒫⒫ | AE DC MC V | 35
Plaza Eduardo de Castro 6, 24700 (León). (*(987) 61 56 54.* FAX *(987) 61 50 40.*
This stylish hotel is on the same square as Gaudí's Neo-Gothic Bishop's
Palace. The bedrooms overlook the palace and the cathedral. 🛏 TV ♿

AVILA: *Hostería de Bracamonte.* ⒫⒫ | AE MC V | 20
Calle Bracamonte 6, 05001. (*(920) 25 12 80.*
A charming, traditionally Castilian hotel with exposed beams and tiled
floors. It is in a quiet location, close to the cathedral and the town
walls. The bedrooms are attractively decorated. 🛏 TV

AVILA: *Parador de Avila.* ⒫⒫⒫ | AE DC MC V | 61
C/ Marqués de Canales de Chozas 2, 05001. (*(920) 21 13 40.* FAX *(920) 22 61 66.*
A parador in a 15th-century mansion next to Avila's walls. From some
rooms guests can watch storks nest on a gateway in spring. 🛏 ▤ TV

AVILA: *Palacio Valderrábanos.* ⒫⒫⒫⒫ | AE DC MC V | 73
Plaza de la Catedral 9, 05001. (*(920) 21 10 23.* FAX *(920) 25 16 91.*
A spacious, sedate hotel in a stately 15th-century mansion beside the
cathedral. There is a suite in the watchtower. 🛏 ▤ TV

BENAVENTE: *Parador de Benavente.* ⒫⒫⒫⒫ | AE DC MC V | 30
Paseo de Ramón y Cajal, 49600 (Zamora). (*(980) 63 03 00.* FAX *(980) 63 03 03.*
Only the Tower of the Snail remained of Benavente castle in the wake
of Napoleon's troops. As part of the parador, it now accommodates an
extraordinary lounge with a Mudéjar ceiling from a church. 🛏 ▤ TV ♿

EL BURGO DE OSMA: *Virrey II.* ⒫⒫⒫ | AE DC MC V | 52
Calle Mayor 4, 42300 (Soria). (*(975) 34 13 11.* FAX *(975) 34 08 55.*
A lavish hotel near the old town. It is very comfortable, spotlessly clean,
and has efficient, friendly staff and a good restaurant. It makes an
excellent base for exploring the province of Soria. 🛏 TV ♿

BURGOS: *Mesón del Cid.* ⒫⒫⒫ | AE DC MC V | 28
Plaza de Santa María 8, 09003. (*(947) 20 87 15.* FAX *(947) 26 94 60.*
This stylish hotel, across a little square from the cathedral, is dedicated
to the conquering medieval hero, El Cid. 🛏 ▤ TV

BURGOS: *Landa Palace.* ⒫⒫⒫⒫⒫ | MC V | 42
Carretera Madrid–Irún, 09001. (*(947) 20 63 43.* FAX *(947) 26 46 76.*
An extravagant hotel on the city outskirts. The authentic-looking stone
vaults roofing the dining room and the pool are 1960s, not Gothic, but
the medieval tower was transported from a nearby village. 🛏 ▤ TV ♿

CASTRILLO DE LOS POLVAZARES: *Cuca la Vaina.* Ⓟ | V | 7
El Jardín, 24718 (León). (*(987) 69 10 78.* FAX *(987) 69 10 78.*
A quiet, charming hotel occupying a renovated, stylishly decorated
stone house in a well preserved village in the Maragato region. 🛏

CIUDAD RODRIGO: *Parador de Ciudad Rodrigo.* ⒫⒫⒫ | AE DC MC V | 27
Plaza del Castillo 1, 37500 (Salamanca). (*(923) 46 01 50.* FAX *(923) 46 04 04.*
This, the first parador to be installed in a historic building, preserves
some of the atmosphere of a 12th-century castle. The prize suite has
a circular bedroom with a domed roof. 🛏 ▤ TV

COLLADO HERMOSO: *Molino de Río Viejo.* ⒫⒫ | AE V | 7
Carretera N110, 40170 (Segovia). (*(921) 40 30 63.* FAX *(921) 40 30 51.*
A cozy hotel in an old mill among poplars beside the Río Viejo is
a good base for exploring the countryside of Segovia province.
Horses are available for riding. Booking is essential. 🛏

Price categories for a standard double room per night, with tax, breakfast, and service included:

- ℗ under 8,000 ptas
- ℗℗ 8,000–12,000 ptas
- ℗℗℗ 12,000–16,000 ptas
- ℗℗℗℗ 16,000–20,000 ptas
- ℗℗℗℗℗ over 20,000 ptas

CREDIT CARDS
Indicates which credit cards are accepted: *AE* American Express; *DC* Diners Club; *MC* MasterCard/Access; *V* Visa

PARKING
Parking provided by the hotel in a private parking lot or a private garage on the hotel site or very close by. Some hotels charge for use of private parking facilities.

SWIMMING POOL
Hotel pool outdoors unless otherwise stated.

GARDEN
Hotel with garden, courtyard, or terrace, often providing tables for eating outdoors.

	Price	Credit Cards	Number of Rooms	Private Parking	Swimming Pool	Garden or Terrace
COVARRUBIAS: *Arlanza.* Calle Mayor 11, 09346 (Burgos). ((947) 40 64 41. FAX (947) 40 63 59. The Arlanza overlooks a cobbled pedestrian square in a medieval village. It offers simple accommodations in an old building with black beams and a handsome staircase. Mountain food is served, including wild boar.	℗℗	AE DC MC V	38			■
HOYOS DEL ESPINO: *El Milano Real.* Toleo, 05634 (Ávila). ((920) 34 91 08. FAX (920) 34 91 56. A personal touch, a relaxed atmosphere, and silent nights make Milano Real a good vacation hotel. Excursions on horseback are organized along packhorse trails in the picturesque Sierra de Gredos.	℗	DC V	14			
LEÓN: *Alfonso V.* Avenida Padre Isla 1, 24002. ((987) 22 09 00. FAX (987) 22 12 44. This comfortable hotel in the city center has contemporary decor. An extravagant, curving staircase giving some interesting perspectives is its most impressive feature.	℗℗℗℗	AE DC MC V	62			
LEÓN: *Parador de León.* Plaza de San Marcos 7, 24001. ((987) 23 73 00. FAX (987) 23 34 58. This parador is in the Hostal San Marcos, a former convent and one of Spain's loveliest Renaissance buildings. It has a magnificent hall with a coffered ceiling, and luxurious old and modern bedrooms.	℗℗℗℗℗	AE DC MC V	229	■		■
NAVARREDONDA DE GREDOS: *Parador de Gredos.* Sierra de Gredos, 05132 (Ávila). ((920) 34 80 48. FAX (920) 34 82 05. Inaugurated in 1928 by Alfonso XIII, this was the first parador in Spain. It is set in a beautiful pine forest in the Sierra de Gredos. It is restful and a good base for exploring the surrounding mountains.	℗℗℗	AE DC MC V	77			■
PEDRAZA DE LA SIERRA: *El Hotel de la Villa.* Calle Calzada 5, 40172 (Segovia). ((921) 50 86 51. FAX (921) 50 86 53. No two bedrooms in this charming hotel are alike. All are exquisitely decorated with floral wallpapers and furnished with antiques, four-poster beds, and cozy armchairs.	℗℗℗	AE DC MC V	24	■		
PEDRAZA DE LA SIERRA: *La Posada de Don Mariano.* Calle Mayor 14, 40172 (Segovia). ((921) 50 98 86. FAX (921) 50 98 86. It is hard to nominate the best hotel in this lovely village. Don Mariano and the Hotel de la Villa are the work of the same decorator. Every room looks like something out of a decorating magazine.	℗℗℗	AE DC MC V	18			
PONFERRADA: *El Temple.* Avenida de Portugal 2, 24400 (León). ((987) 41 00 58. FAX (987) 42 35 25. El Temple's façade is a replica of the town's Templar castle. The decor evokes the Middle Ages with antiques and stone walls.	℗℗℗	AE DC MC V	114	■		■
SALAMANCA: *Las Torres.* Plaza Mayor 26, 37002. ((923) 21 21 00. FAX (923) 21 21 01. The restaurant of this hotel overlooks Salamanca's magnificent Plaza Mayor. Guests can take advantage of many extras, from a rapid valet service to complimentary toiletries.	℗℗℗	AE DC MC V	44			■
SALAMANCA: *Rector.* Paseo del Rector Esperabé 10, 37008. ((923) 21 84 82. FAX (923) 21 40 08. The façade looks old, but the hotel was built in the 1940s by an architect who specialized in reproducing old styles. Inside, leather sofas and stained glass suggest restrained elegance.	℗℗℗℗	AE DC MC V	13	■		
SALAMANCA: *Gran Hotel.* Plaza Poeta Iglesias 3, 37001. ((923) 21 35 00. FAX (923) 21 35 00. A hotel with spacious, quiet bedrooms near the spectacular Plaza Mayor, popular with bullfighters and their entourages.	℗℗℗℗℗	AE DC MC V	137			■

SANTA MARÍA DE HUERTA: *Santa María de Huerta.* ⓅⓅⓅ | MC V | 40
Carretera NII, 42260 (Soria). ((975) 32 70 11. FAX (975) 32 70 11.
Beside the Santa María de Huerta monastery is this former parador,
now a private hotel, with hand-painted bedroom furniture. Guests can
walk, fish, and cycle in the area. 🛏 ▤ TV &

SANTA MARÍA DE MAVE: *Hostería El Convento.* Ⓟ | AE MC V | 25
Santa María de Mave, 34422 (Palencia). ((979) 12 36 11. FAX (979) 12 54 92.
Just off the N661 south of Aguilar is this family-run hotel in a former
convent in pretty countryside. Several public areas have decorative
stonework. Traditional Castilian food is served in the restaurant. 🛏

SANTO DOMINGO DE SILOS: *Tres Coronas de Silos.* ⓅⓅ | AE MC V | 16
Plaza Mayor 6, 09610 (Burgos). ((947) 39 00 47. FAX (947) 39 00 65.
This modest inn in an 18th-century mansion dominates the village square,
with an arched doorway and a proud coat of arms. Bare stone walls
and seasoned wood lend atmosphere to the interior. 🛏

SEGOVIA: *Infanta Isabel.* ⓅⓅⓅ | AE DC MC V | 29
Plaza Mayor, 40001. ((921) 44 31 05. FAX (921) 43 32 40.
A modern hotel in *fin de siècle* style, complemented by traditional
Segovian decor. The bedrooms are cozy. 🛏 ▤ TV

SEGOVIA: *Los Linajes.* ⓅⓅⓅ | AE DC MC V | 55
Calle Doctor Velasco 9, 40003. ((921) 46 04 75. FAX (921) 46 04 79.
Hidden behind an ancient half-timbered, red-brick façade is a modern
hotel that steps eight levels down the hillside beside the city walls.
The higher your room level, the better the view. 🛏 TV &

SEGOVIA: *Parador de Segovia.* ⓅⓅⓅⓅⓅ | AE DC MC V | 113
Carretera de Valladolid, 40003. ((921) 44 37 37. FAX (921) 43 73 62.
This luxury parador has been strategically sited just outside Segovia so
that guests can enjoy magnificent views of the city while sunbathing in
the gardens. Facilities include a gym and an indoor pool. 🛏 ▤ TV &

SIGUERUELO: *Posada de Sigueruelo.* ⓅⓅ | V | 6
Calle Badén 40, 40590 (Segovia). ((921) 50 81 35.
Breakfast and dinner are included in the room price of this rural house.
The owners organize riding, cycling, walking, and canoeing. 🛏

SOLOSANCHO: *Sancho de Estrada.* ⓅⓅ | AE DC MC V | 12
Castillo de Villaviciosa, 05130 (Ávila). ((920) 29 10 82. FAX (920) 29 10 82.
The medieval castle of Villaviciosa, built to defend the Roman roads
over the Sierra de Gredos, has been restored. There are coats of
arms and other medieval touches in the bedrooms. 🛏 TV

SORIA: *Parador de Soria.* ⓅⓅⓅ | AE DC MC V | 34
Parque del Castillo, 42005. ((975) 21 34 45. FAX (975) 21 28 49.
The image and examples of the work of the Spanish poet Antonio
Machado decorate the walls of this parador in a hilltop park. It over-
looks the wooded Duero valley. 🛏 TV

VALLADOLID: *Lasa.* ⓅⓅ | AE MC V | 62
Calle Acera de Recoletos 21, 47004. ((983) 39 02 55. FAX (983) 30 25 61.
A renovated 19th-century apartment building in the city center. The
bedrooms are double glazed to reduce street noise. 🛏 ▤ TV

VILLAFRANCA DEL BIERZO: *Parador de Villafranca.* ⓅⓅⓅ | AE DC MC V | 40
Avenida de Calvo Sotelo, 24500 (León). ((987) 54 01 75. FAX (987) 54 00 10.
This rural parador has well-kept gardens and an attractive dining room.
The town was founded by French pilgrims and is traditionally a stop
on the pilgrimage route to Santiago de Compostela. 🛏 TV

ZAMORA: *Hostería Real de Zamora.* ⓅⓅ | AE MC V | 18
Cuesta de Pizarro 7, 49027. ((980) 53 45 45. FAX (980) 53 45 45.
The Inquisition once occupied this 16th-century mansion beside the
city wall and near the Río Duero. Now it is an affordable hotel with
a pretty courtyard at its center. Basque cooking is served. 🛏 TV

ZAMORA: *Parador de Zamora.* ⓅⓅⓅⓅⓅ | AE DC MC V | 52
Plaza de Viriato 5, 49001. ((980) 51 44 97. FAX (980) 53 00 63.
A city-center parador in a Renaissance mansion. From a magnificent
courtyard bordered by carved stone pillars, stone stairs lead to a
sunny gallery furnished with antiques and potted plants. 🛏 ▤ TV &

For key to symbols see back flap

Price categories for a standard double room per night, with tax, breakfast, and service included:

Ⓟ under 8,000 ptas
ⓅⓅ 8,000–12,000 ptas
ⓅⓅⓅ 12,000–16,000 ptas
ⓅⓅⓅⓅ 16,000–20,000 ptas
ⓅⓅⓅⓅⓅ over 20,000 ptas

CREDIT CARDS
Indicates which credit cards are accepted: *AE* American Express; *DC* Diners Club; *MC* MasterCard/Access; *V* Visa
PARKING
Parking provided by the hotel in a private parking lot or a private garage on the hotel site or very close by. Some hotels charge for use of private parking facilities.
SWIMMING POOL
Hotel pool outdoors unless otherwise stated.
GARDEN
Hotel with garden, courtyard, or terrace, often providing tables for eating outdoors.

	CREDIT CARDS	NUMBER OF ROOMS	PRIVATE PARKING	SWIMMING POOL	GARDEN OR TERRACE

CASTILLA-LA MANCHA

ALARCÓN: *Parador de Alarcón.* ⓅⓅⓅⓅ
Avda Amigos de los Castillos 3, 16213 (Cuenca). 【 *(969) 33 03 15.* FAX *(969) 33 03 03.*
A medieval fortress stunningly located above the Júcar valley, on the edge of the plains of La Mancha. The lounge and dining room are vaulted chambers with thick walls. 🔲 ▤ TV

| AE DC MC V | 13 | ▪ | | ▪ |

ALBACETE: *Los Llanos.* ⓅⓅⓅⓅ
Avenida de España 9, 02002. 【 *(967) 22 37 50.* FAX *(967) 23 46 07.*
A modern hotel overlooking a verdant park. It has a disco, bingo, a hair salon, and a giant video screen in the TV room. 🔲 ▤ TV

| AE DC MC V | 102 | ▪ | | |

ALBACETE: *Parador de Albacete.* ⓅⓅⓅ
Carretera N301, 02000. 【 *(967) 50 93 43.* FAX *(967) 22 60 92.*
A custom-built parador with shady terraces and a pool, decorated with ox yokes and other rural implements. 🔲 ▤ TV

| AE DC MC V | 70 | ▪ | ● | ▪ |

ALMAGRO: *Almagro.* ⓅⓅⓅ
Carretera de Bolaños, 13270 (Ciudad Real). 【 *(926) 86 00 11.* FAX *(926) 86 06 18.*
This chain hotel in the new town is a two-story brick building with a balcony. It offers business services and bicycles for rent. 🔲 ▤ TV 🔧

| AE DC MC V | 50 | ▪ | | ▪ |

ALMAGRO: *Parador de Almagro.* ⓅⓅⓅⓅ
Ronda de San Francisco 31, 13270 (Ciudad Real). 【 *(926) 86 01 00.* FAX *(926) 86 01 50.*
One of Spain's most charming paradors is in a 16th-century convent. Most bedrooms look onto one of 14 courtyards. A lace maker works in one courtyard, keeping the town's tradition alive. 🔲 ▤ TV

| AE DC MC V | 55 | ▪ | ● | ▪ |

AYNA: *Felipe II.* Ⓟ
Avenida Manuel Carrera 9, 02125 (Albacete). 【 *(967) 29 50 83.* FAX *(967) 29 51 12.*
The semicircular layout of this modern, family-run hotel in the mountains of Albacete allows every bedroom to have a balcony with a panoramic view of the town and the valley. 🔲 TV

| | 42 | ▪ | | |

BALLESTEROS DE CALATRAVA: *Palacio de la Serna.* Ⓟ
Calle Cervantes 18, 13432 (Ciudad Real). 【 *(926) 84 22 08.* FAX *(926) 84 22 24.*
An 18th-century farm on the plains of La Mancha, in a mix of Castilian and modern styles. It is quiet and comfortable. There are excursions on horseback and on mountain bikes into the nearby hills. 🔲 ▤ TV 🔧

| V | 15 | ▪ | | ▪ |

BETETA: *Los Tilos.* Ⓟ
Extrarradio, 16870 (Cuenca). 【 *(969) 31 80 98.* FAX *(969) 31 82 99.*
This traditional whitewashed country house, near a mineral spring in the beautiful Serranía de Cuenca, offers basic, affordable rooms. It is popular with hikers and nature lovers. Regional food is served. 🔲 TV

| AE DC V | 24 | ▪ | | ▪ |

CUENCA: *Posada de San José.* ⓅⓅ
Calle Julián Romero 4, 16001. 【 *(969) 21 13 00.* FAX *(969) 23 03 65.*
An original, charming hotel run by a Canadian-Spanish couple in a historic building in the old part of town. It is curiously labyrinthine and lovingly decorated with antiques and frescoes. 🔲

| AE DC MC V | 30 | | | ▪ |

CUENCA: *La Cueva del Fraile.* ⓅⓅⓅ
Carretera Cuenca–Buenache, 16001. 【 *(969) 21 15 71.* FAX *(969) 25 60 47.*
In a green valley outside Cuenca, this hotel is built around a white patio. It has tennis courts and bicycles for rent. 🔲 TV

| AE DC MC V | 63 | ▪ | ● | ▪ |

CUENCA: *Leonor de Aquitania.* ⓅⓅⓅ
Calle San Pedro 58–60, 16001. 【 *(969) 23 10 00.* FAX *(969) 23 10 04.*
Hunting trophies are displayed in the lobby of this hotel in the old part of town. The bedrooms are welcoming and cozy, and some have views of the gorge of the Río Huécar. 🔲 ▤ TV

| AE MC V | 49 | | | |

CUENCA: *Parador de Cuenca.* ℗℗℗℗ — AE DC MC V — 62
Hoz del Huécar, 16001. 【 (969) 23 23 20. FAX (969) 23 25 34.
The 16th-century convent of San Pablo, on the opposite side of the Río Huécar from the city, is an elegant parador. Cuenca's famous old hanging houses *(see p367)* can be seen from the bedrooms. 🔒 ▤ TV

GUADALAJARA: *España.* ℗ — MC V — 40
Calle Teniente Figueroa 3, 19001. 【 (949) 21 13 03. FAX (949) 21 13 05.
A family-run hotel in a 19th-century mansion in the center of the city. The modernized interior is lightened by touches of originality, such as a mural on the staircase. The staff can advise on sightseeing. 🔒 TV 🅰

MANZANARES: *Parador de Manzanares.* ℗℗℗ — AE DC MC V — 50
Ctra Madrid–Cádiz, 13200 (Ciudad Real). 【 (926) 61 04 00. FAX (926) 61 09 35.
In one of the main cities of La Mancha's principal wine region, this parador is a base for exploring Don Quixote country. 🔒 ▤ TV

OROPESA: *Parador de Oropesa.* ℗℗℗℗ — AE DC MC V — 48
Plaza del Palacio 1, 45560 (Toledo). 【 (925) 43 00 00. FAX (925) 43 07 77.
The Sierra de Gredos forms a backdrop to this medieval fortress rising above a plain of olive groves and vineyards. It has plenty of modern comforts, including a Jacuzzi in one bedroom. 🔒 ▤ TV

OSSA DE MONTIEL: *Albamanjón.* ℗℗ — DC MC V — 8
Laguna de San Pedro 16, 02611 (Albacete). 【 (926) 69 90 48. FAX (96) 588 88 32.
This modern complex in a mix of local and Andalusian style is the best hotel on the Lagunas de Ruidera, La Mancha's string of attractive turquoise lakes. It is decorated with tiles and climbing plants. 🔒 TV

PASTRANA: *Colegio San Buenaventura.* ℗℗ — MC V — 2
Calle Adolfo Martín-Gamero 20, 19100 (Guadalajara). 【 (949) 37 00 21.
A 16th-century school of sacred music in a town in the Alcarria has become a tasteful guest house offering bed and breakfast. 🔒 🅰

PASTRANA: *Hospedería Real de Pastrana.* ℗℗ — AE MC V — 27
Convento del Carmen, 19100 (Guadalajara). 【 (& FAX) (949) 37 10 60.
A hotel in a wing of the Monasterio del Carmen, founded by St. Teresa of Avila, with simple, quiet rooms. On one side is the valley of the Río Tajo and on the other the picturesque town of Pastrana. 🔒 ▤ TV 🅰

PUERTO LÁPICE: *Aprisco de Puerto Lápice.* ℗ — DC MC V — 17
Carretera Madrid–Cádiz, 13650 (Ciudad Real). 【 (& FAX) (926) 57 61 50.
An economical overnight stop next to a popular, often crowded restaurant on the Madrid–Andalusia road. The lounge has a rustic decor and is crammed with ornaments, including a boar's head. 🔒

SIGÜENZA: *Parador de Sigüenza.* ℗℗℗℗ — AE DC MC V — 81
Plaza del Castillo, 19250 (Guadalajara). 【 (949) 39 01 00. FAX (949) 39 13 64.
Sigüenza's massive castle overlooks the town from a hilltop. Its former VIP guests include the Catholic Monarchs *(see pp52–3)*. It is furnished in regal style, and the bedrooms surround a courtyard. 🔒 ▤ TV 🅰

TALAVERA DE LA REINA: *Beatriz.* ℗℗ — AE DC MC V — 161
Avenida de Madrid 1, 45600 (Toledo). 【 (925) 80 76 00. FAX (925) 81 58 08.
A modern hotel on the town's edge, on the road from Madrid. In the cellar is a fallout shelter built by the owner. 🔒 ▤ TV 🅰

TOLEDO: *La Almazara.* ℗ — AE DC MC V — 21
Carretera Toledo-Argés, 45080. 【 (925) 22 38 66. FAX (925) 25 05 62.
This 16th-century country house hotel is high on a wooded hilltop outside Toledo and has a magnificent view. Obliging and informal staff compensate for simple bedrooms and limited facilities. 🔒 🅰

TOLEDO: *Hostal del Cardenal.* ℗℗℗ — AE DC MC V — 27
Paseo de Recaredo 24, 45004. 【 (925) 22 49 00. FAX (925) 22 29 91.
Now a historic hotel next to the city walls, this 18th-century mansion was formerly the residence of the archbishop of Toledo. It has splendid sculpted ceilings and pretty brick courtyards. 🔒 ▤ TV

TOLEDO: *Pintor El Greco.* ℗℗℗ — AE DC MC V — 33
Calle Alamillos del Tránsito 13, 45002. 【 (925) 21 42 50. FAX (925) 21 58 19.
A 17th-century house in Toledo's former Jewish quarter has been discreetly extended behind the original façade and patio. Wrought iron and traditional ceramics add character to the hotel. 🔒 ▤ TV 🅰

				CREDIT CARDS	NUMBER OF ROOMS	PRIVATE PARKING	SWIMMING POOL	GARDEN OR TERRACE

Price categories for a standard double room per night, with tax, breakfast, and service included:

℗   under 8,000 ptas
℗℗   8,000–12,000 ptas
℗℗℗   12,000–16,000 ptas
℗℗℗℗   16,000–20,000 ptas
℗℗℗℗℗   over 20,000 ptas

CREDIT CARDS
Indicates which credit cards are accepted: *AE* American Express; *DC* Diners Club; *MC* MasterCard/Access; *V* Visa
PARKING
Parking provided by the hotel in a private parking lot or a private garage on the hotel site or very close by. Some hotels charge for use of private parking facilities.
SWIMMING POOL
Hotel pool outdoors unless otherwise stated.
GARDEN
Hotel with garden, courtyard, or terrace, often providing tables for eating outdoors.

Entry	Cards	Rooms	Parking	Pool	Garden
TOLEDO: *Parador de Toledo.* ℗℗℗ Cerro del Emperador, 45002. 📞 *(925) 22 18 50.* FAX *(925) 22 51 66.* There is a spectacular view of Toledo from the terrace of this parador on the brow of a hill overlooking the city. The hotel is popular with sightseers and photographers, so book in advance. 🛏 📧 TV	AE DC MC V	76	■	●	
TRAGACETE: *El Gamo.* ℗ Plaza de los Caídos 2, 16150 (Cuenca). 📞 *(969) 28 90 08.* FAX *(969) 28 92 28.* A bargain restaurant-with-rooms in a peaceful village among hills and woods in the Serranía de Cuenca, near the Río Cuervo's source. 🛏	MC V	35			
VALDEPEÑAS: *Meliá El Hidalgo.* ℗℗℗ Ctra Madrid–Cádiz, 13300 (Ciudad Real). 📞 *(926) 31 30 88.* FAX *(926) 31 33 36.* A roadside motel built in the 1960s in a landscape of vineyards. The rooms are in large, bright bungalows, each with its own parking space and direct access to the swimming pool. 🛏 📧 TV ♿	AE DC MC V	54	■	●	■

EXTREMADURA

Entry	Cards	Rooms	Parking	Pool	Garden
BADAJOZ: *Río.* ℗℗℗ Avenida Adolfo Díaz Ambrona 13, 06006. 📞 *(924) 27 26 00.* FAX *(924) 27 38 74.* A comfortable, modern hotel in the city center. As well as all the standard facilities it has a bingo hall and a solarium. 🛏 📧 TV	AE DC MC V	85	■	●	■
CÁCERES: *Parador de Cáceres.* ℗℗℗℗ Calle Ancha 6, 10003. 📞 *(927) 21 17 59.* FAX *(927) 21 17 29.* A small parador in the converted 14th-century Palace of Torreorgaz. Inside it is a labyrinth of stairs, doors, patios, and corridors. 🛏 📧 TV	AE DC MC V	31	■		
CÁCERES: *Meliá Cáceres.* ℗℗℗℗℗ Plaza de San Juan 11, 10003. 📞 *(927) 21 58 00.* FAX *(927) 21 40 70.* This 16th-century mansion beside the city walls has been renovated by a hotel chain. Some of the bedrooms have vaulted ceilings. 🛏 📧 TV	AE DC MC V	86	■		
GUADALUPE: *Hospedería del Real Monasterio.* ℗℗ Plaza de Juan Carlos I, 10140 (Cáceres). 📞 *(927) 36 70 00.* FAX *(927) 36 71 77.* The *hospedería* is part of the 16th-century Franciscan monastery which dominates Guadalupe. Many of the rooms that surround the stone courtyard were originally monks' cells. 🛏 📧	MC V	47			■
GUADALUPE: *Parador de Guadalupe.* ℗℗℗ C/ Marqués de la Romana 12, 10140 (Cáceres). 📞 *(927) 36 70 75.* FAX *(927) 36 70 76.* A pilgrim's hospice in the 16th century, this parador has a central court-yard planted with citrus trees. The rooms in the modern annex are spacious, but those in the old building are more popular. 🛏 📧 TV	AE DC MC V	40	■	●	■
JARANDILLA DE LA VERA: *Parador de Jarandilla.* ℗℗℗ Avenida de García Prieto 1, 10450 (Cáceres). 📞 *(927) 56 01 17.* FAX *(927) 56 00 88.* This imposing 15th-century castle, where the Emperor Charles V stayed for a year, has been modernized without losing its medieval feel. It has rose gardens, a tennis court, and a children's play area. 🛏 📧 TV	AE DC MC V	53	■	●	■
JEREZ DE LOS CABALLEROS: *Tryp Los Templarios.* ℗℗ Carretera de Villanueva, 06380 (Badajoz). 📞 *(924) 73 16 36.* FAX *(924) 75 03 38.* A modern hotel named after the Knights Templar, who played an important part in the history of the area. All the bedrooms have views over the valley. A wide terrace surrounds the pool. 🛏 📧 TV	AE DC MC V	49	■	●	■
LOSAR DE LA VERA: *Antigua Casa del Heno.* ℗ Finca Valdepimienta, 10460 (Cáceres). 📞 *(927) 19 80 77.* A simple old stone farmhouse surrounded by oak trees and meadows. It offers bed and breakfast and is most popular in the spring, when the cherry trees come into blossom. 🛏	V	8	■		

LOSAR DE LA VERA: *Hostería Fontivieja.* Ⓟ | MC V | 12
Calle Mártires 11, 10460 (Cáceres). (927) 57 01 08.
A small, family-run hotel in a peaceful olive grove outside the town.
Two bedrooms have terraces with views of the countryside. 🛏 ▤ 📺

MALPARTIDA DE PLASENCIA: *Montfragüe.* ⓅⓅ | AE MC V | 40
Cruce Ctra Navalmoral, 10680 (Cáceres). (927) 45 91 36. FAX (927) 40 40 73.
A modern hotel in easy striking distance of Plasencia and Montfragüe
nature preserve. The bedrooms are simple but spacious. 🛏 ▤ 📺

MÉRIDA: *Emperatriz.* ⓅⓅ | AE MC V | 41
Plaza de España 19, 06800 (Badajoz). (924) 31 31 11. FAX (924) 31 33 05.
An austere-looking, 16th-century granite mansion on the main square,
with a cloistered courtyard and a bar in the cellar. Bedrooms with
balconies overlooking the square can be noisy during the day. 🛏 ▤ 📺

MÉRIDA: *Tryp Medea.* ⓅⓅ | AE DC MC V | 126
Avenida de Portugal, 06800 (Badajoz). (924) 37 24 00. FAX (924) 37 30 20.
The semicircular shape of this modern hotel near the ancient Roman
bridge suggests an ancient theater. The hotel has two swimming pools
(one indoors), a gym, a sauna, and a squash court. 🛏 ▤ 📺 ♿

MÉRIDA: *Parador de Mérida.* ⓅⓅⓅⓅ | AE DC MC V | 82
Plaza de la Constitución 3, 06800 (Badajoz). (924) 31 38 00. FAX (924) 31 92 08.
A converted 17th-century Baroque convent on a shady square. Roman
columns, inscriptions in Arabic, and Visigothic capitals have been
preserved. The lounge is in a former chapel. 🛏 ▤ 📺 ♿

ORELLANA LA VIEJA: *Castillo de Orellana.* Ⓟ | AE V | 70
Cerro de la Herrería, 06740 (Badajoz). (924) 86 70 02. FAX (924) 86 70 40.
An economical vacation complex on the shores of the Orellana reservoir,
a swimming and picnicking spot in pretty countryside. 🛏 ▤ 📺 ♿

PLASENCIA: *Alfonso VIII.* ⓅⓅⓅ | AE DC MC V | 57
Avenida Alfonso VIII 32, 10600 (Cáceres). (927) 41 02 50. FAX (927) 41 80 42.
A modern hotel, centrally located near the Parque de la Isla (where
there is a swimming pool), with a very attentive staff. 🛏 ▤ 📺

TRUJILLO: *Mesón La Cadena.* Ⓟ | AE MC V | 8
Plaza Mayor 8, 10200 (Cáceres). (927) 32 14 63.
This restaurant-with-rooms in an attractive granite house on the main
square offers a less expensive alternative to the parador. The bedrooms,
decorated with textiles made locally, are on the third floor. 🛏 ▤

TRUJILLO: *Parador de Trujillo.* ⓅⓅⓅⓅ | AE DC MC V | 46
Plaza Santa Beatriz de Silva, 10200 (Cáceres). (927) 32 13 50. FAX (927) 32 13 66.
This charming parador, built in the 1980s, incorporates parts of a 16th-
century convent, including the former cloister. The parador is within
walking distance of Trujillo's sights, but away from its noise. 🛏 ▤ 📺

ZAFRA: *Huerta Honda.* ⓅⓅⓅ | AE MC DC V | 45
Avenida López Asme 30, 06300 (Badajoz). (924) 55 41 00. FAX (924) 55 25 04.
Many regular guests feel this hotel offers accommodations as good as
the parador next door. The restaurant is also a good value. 🛏 ▤ 📺

ZAFRA: *Parador de Zafra.* ⓅⓅⓅⓅ | AE DC MC V | 45
Pl del Corazón de María 7, 06300 (Badajoz). (924) 55 45 40. FAX (924) 55 10 18.
This castle with round towers was built in the 15th century on the
ruins of a Moorish fortress. A beautiful staircase leads from the courtyard, with an arcaded gallery, to the bedrooms. 🛏 ▤ 📺

SEVILLE

EL ARENAL: *La Rábida.* **Map 3 B1.** ⓅⓅ | AE DC MC V | 104
Calle Castelar 24, 41001. (95) 422 09 60. FAX (95) 422 43 75.
This hotel in one of several old palaces on residential streets near the
cathedral has a few modern bedrooms. Its beautiful public rooms are
built around two courtyards, one with a stained-glass roof. 🛏 ▤ 📺

EL ARENAL: *Simón.* **Map 3 B2.** ⓅⓅ | AE DC MC V | 29
Calle García de Vinuesa 19, 41001. (95) 422 66 60. FAX (95) 456 22 41.
A central hotel in an 18th-century mansion built around a pretty patio
planted with ferns. The bedrooms vary in size and quality. Some have
balconies overlooking the street. 🛏 ▤

For key to symbols see back flap

Price categories for a standard double room per night, with tax, breakfast, and service included:

- ℗ under 8,000 ptas
- ℗℗ 8,000–12,000 ptas
- ℗℗℗ 12,000–16,000 ptas
- ℗℗℗℗ 16,000–20,000 ptas
- ℗℗℗℗℗ over 20,000 ptas

CREDIT CARDS
Indicates which credit cards are accepted: *AE* American Express; *DC* Diners Club; *MC* MasterCard/Access; *V* Visa

PARKING
Parking provided by the hotel in a private parking lot or a private garage on the hotel site or very close by. Some hotels charge for use of private parking facilities.

SWIMMING POOL
Hotel pool outdoors unless otherwise stated.

GARDEN
Hotel with garden, courtyard, or terrace, often providing tables for eating outdoors.

	CREDIT CARDS	NUMBER OF ROOMS	PRIVATE PARKING	SWIMMING POOL	GARDEN OR TERRACE
EL ARENAL: *Álvarez Quintero.* **Map 3 C1.** ℗℗℗℗ Calle Álvarez Quintero 9–13, 41004. ℂ *(95) 422 12 98.* FAX *(95) 456 41 41.* Although it is surrounded by the city's star sights, this hotel's regulars are business people. Behind a Sevillian mansion façade is a remodeled interior. Wines from the hotel's own bodegas are served. 🔁 ▤ 📺	AE DC MC V	40	■		■
EL ARENAL: *Taberna del Alabardero.* **Map 3 B1.** ℗℗℗℗ Calle Zaragoza 20, 41001. ℂ *(95) 456 06 37.* FAX *(95) 456 36 66.* An exquisite restaurant-with-rooms occupying a 19th-century mansion. The house is built around a central courtyard illuminated by a stained-glass roof. There are cozy bedrooms on the top floor. 🔁 ▤ 📺 ⅍	AE DC MC V	7	■		
SANTA CRUZ: *Las Casas de la Judería.* **Map 3 D2.** ℗℗℗ Callejón de las Dos Hermanas 7, 41004. ℂ *(95) 441 51 50.* FAX *(95) 442 21 70.* Less a hotel, more a labyrinth of suites, some with a private terrace. This is a peaceful place to rest, away from the city rush. 🔁 ▤ 📺 ⅍	AE DC MC V	31	■		■
SANTA CRUZ: *Hostería del Laurel.* **Map 3 C2.** ℗℗℗ Plaza de los Venerables 5, 41004. ℂ *(95) 422 02 95.* FAX *(95) 421 04 50.* A hotel in a small square near the Hospital de los Venerables. The lobby is in a covered courtyard, reached through an inn hung with hams and garlic. The rooms are simple but spacious. 🔁 ▤ 📺	AE DC MC V	21			■
SANTA CRUZ: *Murillo.* **Map 6 E4.** ℗℗℗ Calle Lope de Rueda 7 & 9, 41004. ℂ *(95) 421 60 95.* FAX *(95) 421 96 16.* A pleasant, reasonably priced hotel in an old building off Plaza Alfaro, a short walk from the cathedral. Book well ahead for Holy Week and the April Fair. The management also rents apartments nearby. 🔁 ▤	AE DC MC V	57			
SANTA CRUZ: *Doña María.* **Map 3 C2.** ℗℗℗℗ Calle Don Remondo 19, 41004. ℂ *(95) 422 49 90.* FAX *(95) 421 95 46.* This hotel is in a street running alongside the Palacio Arzobispal. Its terrace and swimming pool overlook the Giralda. Guests can choose from bedrooms decorated in a variety of styles. 🔁 ▤ 📺 ⅍	AE DC MC V	68	■	●	■
FARTHER AFIELD (LA MACARENA): *Baco.* **Map 2 E5.** ℗℗℗ Plaza Ponce de León 15, 41003. ℂ *(95) 456 50 50.* FAX *(95) 456 36 54.* An old house has been transformed into a modern hotel in Sevillian style. A spiral staircase ascends from the lobby; the quieter back bedrooms overlook patios with tiles and potted plants. 🔁 ▤ 📺	AE DC MC V	25			■
FARTHER AFIELD (LA MACARENA): *Patio de la Cartuja.* **Map 1 C4.** ℗℗℗ Calle Lumbreras 8 & 10, 41002. ℂ *(95) 490 02 00.* FAX *(95) 490 20 56.* A group of old houses has been converted into this hotel in La Macarena. It offers apartments of excellent quality at very competitive prices and a tranquil atmosphere in a busy city. 🔁 ▤ 📺	AE DC MC V	33	■		
FARTHER AFIELD (LA MACARENA): *San Gil.* **Map 2 D4.** ℗℗℗℗ Calle Parras 28, 41002. ℂ *(95) 490 68 11.* FAX *(95) 490 69 39.* A beautiful early 20th-century mansion classed as one of Seville's 100 most important buildings. It has spacious, beautifully furnished rooms and a peaceful garden with palm trees and an old cypress. 🔁 ▤ 📺 ⅍	AE DC MC V	39	■	●	■
FARTHER AFIELD (PARQUE MARÍA LUISA): *Alfonso XIII.* **Map 3 C3.** ℗℗℗℗℗ Calle San Fernando 2, 41004. ℂ *(95) 422 28 50.* FAX *(95) 421 60 33.* Elegance and appropriately formal service are assured in Seville's grand hotel, built in Neo-Mudéjar style. Inside there are chandeliers and statuary; outdoors there are palm trees. 🔁 ▤ 📺 ⅍	AE DC MC V	149	■	●	■
FARTHER AFIELD (SOUTH): *Ciudad de Sevilla.* **Map 4 D5.** ℗℗℗℗ Avenida Manuel Siurot 25, 41013. ℂ *(95) 423 05 05.* FAX *(95) 423 85 39.* Behind its old façade, this hotel, away from the center, is modern. It has large, bright rooms and a rooftop swimming pool. 🔁 ▤ 📺 ⅍	AE DC MC V	94	■	●	■

ANDALUSIA

ALCALÁ DE GUADAIRA: *Hotel Oromana.* ₧₧₧
Avenida de Portugal, 41500 (Sevilla). 【 (& FAX) (95) 568 64 00.
On the edge of town, within easy reach of Seville, the Oromana is shaded by pines. It is run by a team of women who are happy to cater to families with children and to the disabled.
AE MC V — 30

ALMERÍA: *Torreluz IV.* ₧₧₧
Plaza Flores I, 04001. 【 (& FAX) (950) 23 47 99.
A stylish, city-center hotel with a spiral staircase and a rooftop pool. The Torreluzs II and III, sister hotels nearby, are cheaper.
AE DC MC V — 100

ARACENA: *Sierra de Aracena.* ₧₧
Gran Via 21, 21200 (Huelva). 【 (959) 12 61 75. FAX (959) 12 62 18.
This quiet hotel is in the center of the attractive town of Aracena. The rooms in the back overlook the town's castle.
AE DC MC V — 43

ARACENA: *Finca Buen Vino.* ₧₧₧₧₧
Los Marines, 21293 (Huelva). 【 (& FAX) (959) 12 40 34.
A stylish modern villa on a hilltop at the heart of a wooded nature preserve. This is a private home open to guests, and it has an informal atmosphere. Cordon bleu cooking is served by candlelight.
AE DC MC V — 4

ARCOS DE LA FRONTERA: *Cortijo Faín.* ₧₧₧
Carretera de Algar, 11630 (Cádiz). 【 (& FAX) (956) 70 11 67.
This 17th-century farmhouse stands majestically in an grove of olive trees. The rooms are furnished with antiques, and some have old brass bedsteads. A swimming pool is hidden among the olive trees.
AE MC V — 9

ARCOS DE LA FRONTERA: *Parador de Arcos de la Frontera.* ₧₧₧
Plaza del Cabildo, 11630 (Cádiz). 【 (956) 70 05 00. FAX (956) 70 11 16.
A fine mansion, formerly a magistrate's house, on the main square. Its terrace overhangs a precipice and has spectacular views.
AE DC MC V — 24

AYAMONTE: *Riu Palace.* ₧₧₧₧
Playa de Isla Canela, 21470 (Huelva). 【 (959) 47 71 24. FAX (959) 47 71 70.
With its three pools, one for children, the beachside Riu Palace is more a summer resort than a hotel. The hotel is on Isla Canela near the Portuguese border, close to the Algarve.
AE DC MC V — 350

BAENA: *Hotel Zambudio.* ₧
Carretera Baena–Zuheros, 14850 (Córdoba). 【 (& FAX) (957) 67 08 37.
An inn near Baena with views of the hills around Zuheros. It is quiet, comfortable, and economical.
AE MC V — 11

BAEZA: *Hospedería Fuentenueva.* ₧₧
Paseo Arca del Agua 11, 23440 (Jaén). 【 (953) 74 31 00. FAX (953) 74 32 00.
This Renaissance town has an unusual hotel in a converted women's prison, run by a cooperative of five young hoteliers. The rooms are in excellent taste; there is a quiet lounge with a domed ceiling.
AE DC MC V — 12

BENAOJÁN: *Molino del Santo.* ₧₧
Calle Barriada Estación, 29370 (Málaga). 【 (95) 216 71 51. FAX (95) 216 73 27.
This converted water mill in the hills near Ronda is a relaxing, sunny spot with an attractive swimming pool. The British owners are a mine of tourist information. They keep mountain bikes for guests to rent.
AE DC MC V — 12

BUBIÓN: *Villa Turística de Bubión.* ₧₧₧
Calle Barrio Alto, 18412 (Granada). 【 (958) 76 31 11. FAX (958) 76 31 36.
This minivillage is in the distinct building style of the Alpujarras, with flat roofs and tall chimneys. You can cook in your kitchen or eat in the restaurant. Horseback riding and hiking are arranged.
AE DC MC V — 43

CARMONA: *Parador de Carmona.* ₧₧₧
Calle Alcázar, 41410 (Sevilla). 【 (95) 414 10 10. FAX (95) 414 17 12.
This clifftop parador was built as a fortress by the Moors and became the palace of the Christian king, Pedro the Cruel. Historic Carmona is a good base for exploring Seville province.
AE DC MC V — 63

CARMONA: *Casa de Carmona.* ₧₧₧₧₧
Plaza de Lasso 1, 41410 (Sevilla). 【 (95) 414 33 00. FAX (95) 414 37 52.
This 16th-century converted palace, decorated in a blend of modern and period styles, has been featured in design magazines.
AE DC MC V — 30

Price categories for a standard double room per night, with tax, breakfast, and service included:

- ℙ under 8,000 ptas
- ℙℙ 8,000–12,000 ptas
- ℙℙℙ 12,000–16,000 ptas
- ℙℙℙℙ 16,000–20,000 ptas
- ℙℙℙℙℙ over 20,000 ptas

CREDIT CARDS
Indicates which credit cards are accepted: *AE* American Express; *DC* Diners Club; *MC* MasterCard/Access; *V* Visa

PARKING
Parking provided by the hotel in a private parking lot or a private garage on the hotel site or very close by. Some hotels charge for use of private parking facilities.

SWIMMING POOL
Hotel pool outdoors unless otherwise stated.

GARDEN
Hotel with garden, courtyard, or terrace, often providing tables for eating outdoors.

	CREDIT CARDS	NUMBER OF ROOMS	PRIVATE PARKING	SWIMMING POOL	GARDEN OR TERRACE
CASTELLAR DE LA FRONTERA: *Casa Convento La Almoraima.* ℙℙℙ Finca La Almoraima, 11350 (Cádiz). ☎ (956) 69 30 02. ☎ FAX (956) 69 32 14. One of Europe's largest country estates (now in public ownership) surrounds this hotel. The house was built by the Dukes of Medinaceli in the 17th century and used by them as a hunting lodge. 🅿 ☰	AE DC MC V	17	■	●	■
CASTILLEJA DE LA CUESTA: *Hacienda de San Ygnacio.* ℙℙℙℙ Calle Real 194, 41950 (Sevilla). ☎ (95) 416 04 30. FAX (95) 416 14 37. A 17th-century Andalusian farmhouse built around a patio planted with palms. The dining room was once an olive oil mill. 🅿 ☰ TV	AE DC MC V	17	■	●	■
CAZALLA DE LA SIERRA: *Las Navazuelas.* ℙ Apartado 14, 41370 (Sevilla). ☎ (95) 488 47 64. FAX (95) 488 47 64. The rooms in this charming, family-run farmhouse are furnished with handworked fabrics. Staying here gives visitors a rare opportunity to experience living in an authentic Andalusian *cortijo* (farmstead). 🅿	MC V	8	■		■
CAZALLA DE LA SIERRA: *Hospedería La Cartuja.* ℙℙ Carretera Cazalla–Constantina, 41370 (Sevilla). ☎ (& FAX) (95) 488 45 16. An old monastery has been eccentrically rehabilitated by its crusading owner as a refuge for artists. The walls are hung with their paintings. Organic produce from the farm is used in the cooking. 🅿	MC V	11	■	●	■
CAZORLA: *Molino de la Fárraga.* ℙ Apartado 1, 23470 (Jaén). ☎ (953) 72 12 49. A 200-year-old mill, recently renovated, near the Plaza Santa María, is a relaxing stop. An annex can be rented as an efficiency apartment. 🅿		5		●	■
CAZORLA: *Parador de Cazorla.* ℙℙℙℙ Cazorla 23470 (Jaén). ☎ (953) 72 70 75. FAX (953) 72 70 77. The forests and mountains of the Sierra de Cazorla, a major Andalusian nature preserve, are the superb setting for this modern parador. 🅿 TV	AE DC MC V	33	■	●	
CÓRDOBA: *Maestre.* ℙ Plazuela de Maimónides 3, 14004. ☎ (957) 42 03 35. FAX (957) 47 53 95. Near the Mezquita in the center of Córdoba, this is a simple, very economically priced hotel with basic modern amenities. 🅿 ☰ ♿	AE DC MC V	26	■		
CÓRDOBA: *Occidental.* ℙℙℙ Calle Poeta Alonso Bonilla 7, 14012. ☎ (957) 40 04 40. FAX (957) 40 04 39. This is a modern hotel in a residential suburb in the north of the city, with coffered ceilings and handsome brass lanterns. 🅿 ☰ TV ♿	AE DC MC V	153	■	●	
CÓRDOBA: *Alfaros.* ℙℙℙ Calle Alfaros 18, 14001. ☎ (957) 49 19 20. FAX (957) 49 22 10. In a busy street, but soundproofed against traffic noise, Alfaros has three attractive courtyards in Neo-Mudéjar style. 🅿 ☰ TV ♿	AE DC MC V	133	■	●	
DÚRCAL: *Cortijo la Solana.* ℙ La Solana Alta 3, 18650 (Granada). ☎ (& FAX) (958) 78 05 75. A country house with extensive grounds in a little-known valley in the mountains of Granada, offering bed and breakfast only.		4			■
ECIJA: *Platería.* ℙ Calle Garcilópez 1–A, 41400 (Sevilla). ☎ (95) 483 50 10. FAX (95) 483 50 10. This hotel is in the former silversmiths' quarter and is named after it. Its large, cool rooms are relaxing in the searing summer heat. 🅿 ☰ TV ♿	AE DC MC V	18			
GIBRALTAR: *The Rock.* ℙℙℙℙℙ 3 Europa Road. ☎ (9567) 730 00. FAX (9567) 735 13. Trading on old-fashioned colonial style and service, Gibraltar's first five-star hotel is elevated above the town and harbor and has views across the bay. Many celebrities have stayed here. 🅿 ☰ TV	AE DC MC V	141	■	●	

GRANADA: *Reina Cristina.* ₧₧
Calle Tablas 4, 18002. ☎ *(958) 25 32 11.* FAX *(958) 25 57 28.*
A glass-covered courtyard and a handsome balustrade are preserved in this 19th-century mansion, once a hiding place of the poet García Lorca *(see p31)*. The rooms are small but comfortable. 🛏 ▤ TV ♿
Cards: AE DC MC V — *Rooms:* 42

GRANADA: *América.* ₧₧₧
Calle Real de la Alhambra 53, 18009. ☎ *(958) 22 74 71.* FAX *(958) 22 74 70.*
This cozy, affordable, family-run hotel beside the Alhambra is on the same street as Granada's parador. In summer, home cooking is served in a plant-filled courtyard. Always book well in advance. 🛏 ▤
Cards: AE DC MC V — *Rooms:* 13

GRANADA: *Alhambra Palace.* ₧₧₧₧
Calle Peña Partida 2 & 4, 18009. ☎ *(958) 22 14 68.* FAX *(958) 22 64 04.*
A gloriously kitsch mock-Moorish building on the same hill as the Alhambra. A superb terrace has views of old Granada. 🛏 ▤ TV ♿
Cards: AE DC MC V — *Rooms:* 140

GRANADA: *Parador de Granada.* ₧₧₧₧
Calle Real de la Alhambra, 18009. ☎ *(958) 22 14 41.* FAX *(958) 22 22 64.*
This elegant parador in the Alhambra gardens was once a convent. For a room in such a spot you must book months ahead. 🛏 ▤ TV ♿
Cards: AE DC MC V — *Rooms:* 36

GUALCHOS: *La Posada.* ₧₧₧
Plaza de la Constitución 3 & 4, 18614 (Granada). ☎ *(& FAX) (958) 65 60 34.*
This is primarily a restaurant, with a few cozy rooms scattered around an interesting old building. It is on the square of an unspoiled village in the hills above Granada's coast. 🛏
Cards: MC V — *Rooms:* 9

JAÉN: *Parador de Jaén.* ₧₧₧₧
Carretera del Castillo, 23001. ☎ *(953) 23 00 00.* FAX *(953) 23 09 30.*
From this castle-parador above Jaén there are spectacular views of the Sierra Morena. With its dimly lit corridors, small arched windows, huge doors, and suits of armor, it retains a medieval atmosphere. 🛏 ▤ TV
Cards: AE DC MC V — *Rooms:* 45

LOJA: *La Bobadilla.* ₧₧₧₧₧
Finca La Bobadilla, 18300 (Granada). ☎ *(958) 32 18 61.* FAX *(958) 32 18 10.*
Looking rather like a labyrinthine Andalusian village, surrounded by its own grounds, this is one of the most luxurious hotels in Europe. Guests can take part in a wide range of sports and activities. 🛏 ▤ TV
Cards: AE DC MC V — *Rooms:* 60

MÁLAGA: *Don Curro.* ₧₧₧
Calle Sancha de Lara 7, 29015. ☎ *(95) 222 72 00.* FAX *(95) 221 59 46.*
The exterior may not be attractive, but inside, this hotel is charming and comfortable, with a friendly, welcoming atmosphere. 🛏 ▤ TV
Cards: AE DC MC V — *Rooms:* 105

MARBELLA: *El Fuerte.* ₧₧₧₧
Avenida El Fuerte, 29600 (Málaga). ☎ *(95) 286 15 00.* FAX *(95) 282 44 11.*
El Fuerte was the first hotel built in Marbella, and it is still one of the best. Some rooms have mountain views and others look out to sea. The hotel has a heated, glassed-in pool and a fitness center. 🛏 ▤ TV
Cards: AE DC MC V — *Rooms:* 263

MARBELLA: *Marbella Club Hotel.* ₧₧₧₧₧
Blvr Príncipe von Hohenlohe, 29600 (Málaga). ☎ *(95) 282 22 11.* FAX *(95) 282 98 84.*
An exclusive, low-rise, beachside complex between Marbella and Puerto Banús. There are two pools, one indoors, and subtropical gardens with a choice of places to eat and relax. 🛏 ▤ TV
Cards: AE DC MC V — *Rooms:* 129

MAZAGÓN: *Parador de Mazagón.* ₧₧₧₧
Ctra Huelva–Matalascañas, 21130 (Huelva). ☎ *(959) 53 63 00.* FAX *(959) 53 62 28.*
A modern parador on the Huelva coast, between a large, sandy beach and a pine forest. It is in a good location for visiting the wildlife preserve of Doñana National Park nearby. 🛏 ▤ TV ♿
Cards: AE DC MC V — *Rooms:* 43

MIJAS: *Club Puerta del Sol.* ₧₧₧
Ctra Fuengirola–Mijas, 29650 (Málaga). ☎ *(95) 248 64 00.* FAX *(95) 248 54 62.*
An elegant, low, U-shaped hotel on a foothill of the Sierra de Mijas. From its gardens, pool, and terraces there is an impressive view of Fuengirola and the coast. It has tennis courts and a gym. 🛏 ▤ TV ♿
Cards: AE DC MC V — *Rooms:* 130

MOJÁCAR: *Parador de Mojácar.* ₧₧₧₧
Playa de Mojácar, 04638 (Almería). ☎ *(950) 47 82 50.* FAX *(950) 47 81 83.*
The architecture of this custom-built parador on the dry, sunny coast of Almería echoes that of the dazzling white cube houses in nearby Mojácar. There are facilities for water sports. 🛏 ▤ TV ♿
Cards: AE DC MC V — *Rooms:* 98

For key to symbols see back flap

<table>
<tr><td>

Price categories for a standard double room per night, with tax, breakfast, and service included:

Ⓟ under 8,000 ptas
ⓅⓅ 8,000–12,000 ptas
ⓅⓅⓅ 12,000–16,000 ptas
ⓅⓅⓅⓅ 16,000–20,000 ptas
ⓅⓅⓅⓅⓅ over 20,000 ptas

</td><td>

CREDIT CARDS
Indicates which credit cards are accepted: *AE* American Express; *DC* Diners Club; *MC* MasterCard/Access; *V* Visa
PARKING
Parking provided by the hotel in a private parking lot or a private garage on the hotel site or very close by. Some hotels charge for use of private parking facilities.
SWIMMING POOL
Hotel pool outdoors unless otherwise stated.
GARDEN
Hotel with garden, courtyard, or terrace, often providing tables for eating outdoors.

</td></tr>
</table>

	CREDIT CARDS	NUMBER OF ROOMS	PRIVATE PARKING	SWIMMING POOL	GARDEN OR TERRACE
NERJA: *Hostal Avalón.* Ⓟ Calle Punta Lara, 29780 (Málaga). ☎ (95) 252 06 98. This small hotel above the coast road just outside Nerja has a friendly atmosphere, pleasant, clean bedrooms – all but one with views of the sea – and an informal lounge with comfortable sofas. 🛏		8	■		
OJÉN: *Refugio de Juanar.* ⓅⓅ Sierra Blanca, 29610 (Málaga). ☎ (95) 288 10 00. FAX (95) 288 10 01. A hunting lodge has been converted into this tranquil, cozy hotel. It is in the Sierras de Ojén, the wooded hills behind Marbella, a region of wildlife interest. The restaurant specializes in regional cooking. 🛏 📺	AE DC MC V	23	■	●	■
ORGIVA: *Taray.* ⓅⓅ Ctra Tablate–Albuñol,18400 (Granada). ☎ (958) 78 45 25. FAX (958) 78 45 31. A hotel in a garden of lawns and olive and orange trees. The bedrooms are large enough to be small apartments. The hotel is in good walking country, and horseback riding is arranged for guests. 🛏 📋 📺 ♿	AE DC MC V	15	■	●	■
PALMA DEL RÍO: *Hospedería de San Francisco.* ⓅⓅ Avenida Pío XII 33, 14700 (Córdoba). ☎ (957) 71 01 83. FAX (957) 71 07 32. Built in the 15th century as a Franciscan monastery, this hotel has some bedrooms in former monks' cells. They have hand-painted sinks and bedcovers woven by nuns. Meals are served in the cloister. 🛏 📋 📺	MC V	17	■		■
PECHINA: *Balneario de Sierra Alhamilla.* ⓅⓅ Pechina, 04259 (Almería). ☎ (950) 31 74 13. FAX (950) 16 02 57. This spa hotel in peaceful hills has been restored to its 18th-century glory. There are Roman baths in the basement and, nearby, a naturally heated swimming pool. 🛏 📺 ♿	AE MC V	24	■	●	■
PINOS GENIL: *Labella María.* Ⓟ Carretera Sierra Nevada, 18191 (Granada). ☎ (958) 48 87 46. FAX (958) 48 87 26. A modern, family-run hotel, just outside Granada, that is well placed for visiting the city or the Sierra Nevada. The rooms are comfortable and airy. Some are large enough for a family of four. 🛏 📋 📺 ♿	AE DC MC V	24	■		
PRADO DEL REY: *Cortijo Huerta Dorotea.* Ⓟ Ctra Vilamartín–Ubrique, 11660 (Cádiz). ☎ (956) 72 42 91. FAX (956) 72 42 89. On a hill surrounded by olive trees, near the white town of Prado del Rey, is this new hotel, run by a cooperative. Guests can choose rooms or log cabins. Riding is one leisure activity available. 🛏 📋 📺	AE DC MC V	7	■		■
EL PUERTO DE SANTA MARÍA: *Monasterio San Miguel.* ⓅⓅⓅⓅ Calle Larga 27, 11500 (Cádiz). ☎ (956) 54 04 40. FAX (956) 54 26 04. An elegant, rather luxurious hotel, well placed for visits to Cádiz and Jerez de la Frontera. It has a faintly monastic atmosphere, recalling the former function of this Baroque building. 🛏 📋 📺 ♿	AE DC MC V	150	■	●	■
EL ROCÍO: *Puente del Rey.* ⓅⓅ Avenida Canaliega, 21750 (Huelva). ☎ (959) 44 25 75. FAX (959) 44 20 70. A country hotel on the edge of Doñana National Park. It is reasonably comfortable. Horseback riding and excursions are arranged. 🛏 📋 📺 ♿	AE DC MC V	185	■	●	■
RONDA: *Reina Victoria.* ⓅⓅⓅⓅ Calle Jerez 25, 29400 (Málaga). ☎ (95) 287 12 40. FAX (95) 287 10 75. The Reina Victoria, perched on the edge of a cliff, has spectacular views. It was Ronda's grand hotel until the parador was built. 🛏 📋 📺 ♿	AE DC MC V	89	■	●	■
RONDA: *Parador de Ronda.* ⓅⓅⓅⓅⓅ Plaza España, 29400 (Málaga). ☎ (95) 287 75 00. FAX (95) 287 81 88. Perched on the edge of Ronda's famous cliff, yet close to the town center, this modern, custom-built parador has stunning views over the gorge, especially from the top floor suites. 🛏 📋 📺 ♿	AE DC MC V	79	■	●	■

SAN JOSÉ: *San José.* ⓅⓅⓅ
Calle Correo, 04118 (Almería). 【 *(950) 38 01 16.* 🖷 *(950) 38 00 02.*
A gaudy color scheme, eccentric furnishings, and a parrot lend charm
to this hotel. It is near the beach in a small, developing resort, and
close to the Cabo de Gata nature preserve. 🛏 📺
MC V — 8

SANLÚCAR DE BARRAMEDA: *Los Helechos.* ⓅⓅ
Plaza Madre de Dios 9, 11540 (Cádiz). 【 *(956) 36 13 49.* 🖷 *(956) 36 96 50.*
Decorated with tiles and potted plants, Los Helechos is a stylish, relaxing
hideaway. Visits to Doñana National Park are arranged. 🛏 🍽 📺
AE DC MC V — 56

SANLÚCAR LA MAYOR: *Hacienda de Benazuza.* ⓅⓅⓅⓅⓅ
Virgen de las Nieves, 41800 (Sevilla). 【 *(95) 570 33 44.* 🖷 *(95) 570 34 10.*
Parts of this old hilltop house are said to be 1,000 years old. It is now
a luxury hotel, furnished in traditional Andalusian style. It has several
suites, three restaurants, a game preserve, and a heliport. 🛏 🍽 📺 ♿
AE DC MC V — 44

SAN ROQUE: *La Solana.* ⓅⓅ
Ctra Cádiz–Málaga N340, 11360 (Cádiz). 【 *(956) 78 02 36.* 🖷 *(953) 78 02 36.*
A useful stop en route to or from the Tangier ferry, this pleasant small
hotel in a 200-year-old house is set back from the freeway in its
own grounds. The 12 rooms and 6 suites are all different. 🛏 📺
AE V — 18

SIERRA NEVADA: *Santa Cruz.* ⓅⓅ
Ctra Sierra Nevada, 18160 (Granada). 【 *(958) 48 48 00.* 🖷 *(958) 48 48 06.*
From the windows and balconies of this high-altitude hotel guests can
contemplate the snowy peaks of the lovely Sierra Nevada. Open fires
make the modern building cozy in winter. 🛏 📺 ♿
AE DC MC V — 66

TARIFA: *Hurricane.* ⓅⓅⓅ
Carretera N340, 11380 (Cádiz). 【 *(956) 68 49 19.* 🖷 *(956) 68 03 29.*
Tarifa is a mecca for windsurfers, and the Hurricane is a temple to the
sport and to physical fitness. It is an imaginative, open-plan building
in subtropical gardens. There are views across the sea to Africa. 🛏
AE DC MC V — 33

TORREMOLINOS: *Hotel Miami.* Ⓟ
Calle Aladino 14, 29620 (Málaga). 【 *(95) 238 52 55.*
The Miami, between Torremolinos and Málaga, gives welcome respite
from the Costa del Sol's modern developments. It has whitewashed
walls, tiles, iron grilles, balconies, and potted plants. 🛏
— 26

TREVÉLEZ: *Mesón La Fragua.* Ⓟ
Calle San Antonio 4, 18417 (Granada). 【 *(958) 85 86 26.* 🖷 *(958) 85 86 14.*
This *mesón* (inn) is in what claims to be the highest village in Spain.
There are great views of the valley from the rooftop terrace. The
rooms vary considerably in size and character. 🛏 📺
MC V — 14

TURRE: *El Nacimiento.* Ⓟ
Cortijo El Nacimiento, 04639 (Almería). 【 *(950) 52 80 90.*
This remote and lovely old house is run by a friendly couple. They
offer bed and breakfast, serving organic produce from their farm.
— 4

TURRE: *Finca Listonero.* ⓅⓅ
Cortijo Grande, 04639 (Almería). 【 *(950) 47 90 94.* 🖷 *(950) 47 90 94.*
This hotel is in a restored farmhouse in the country near Mojácar. The
breakfasts are generous; home-grown vegetables are served at meals.
MC V — 5

ÚBEDA: *Palacio de La Rambla.* ⓅⓅⓅ
Plaza del Marqués 1, 23400 (Jaén). 【 *(953) 75 01 96.* 🖷 *(953) 75 02 67.*
A 17th-century mansion run by its aristocratic owner as a small, central,
exclusive hotel. The rooms, furnished with heirlooms, enclose a patio
thought to be by the Renaissance architect Vandelvira. 🛏 🍽 📺 ♿
AE MC V — 8

ÚBEDA: *Parador de Úbeda.* ⓅⓅⓅⓅ
Plaza Vázquez de Molina 1, 23400 (Jaén). 【 *(953) 75 03 45.* 🖷 *(953) 75 12 59.*
Presiding over Úbeda's monumental central square, this parador is in
a former 16th-century aristocratic residence. Blue and white tiles adorn
the façade, and the house surrounds a pretty courtyard. 🛏 🍽 📺
AE DC MC V — 31

ZUHEROS: *Zuhayra.* Ⓟ
Calle Mirador 10, 14870 (Córdoba). 【 *(957) 69 46 93.* 🖷 *(957) 69 45 34.*
The principal charm of this simple hotel is its location in a white town
on the edge of a range of high hills. The building imitates the style of
the noble mansion it replaced. Silence reigns at night. 🛏 ♿
AE DC MC V — 18

For key to symbols see back flap

		CREDIT CARDS	NUMBER OF ROOMS	PRIVATE PARKING	SWIMMING POOL	GARDEN OR TERRACE

Price categories for a standard double room per night, with tax, breakfast, and service included:

℗ under 8,000 ptas
℗℗ 8,000–12,000 ptas
℗℗℗ 12,000–16,000 ptas
℗℗℗℗ 16,000–20,000 ptas
℗℗℗℗℗ over 20,000 ptas

CREDIT CARDS
Indicates which credit cards are accepted: *AE* American Express; *DC* Diners Club; *MC* MasterCard/Access; *V* Visa
PARKING
Parking provided by the hotel in a private parking lot or a private garage on the hotel site or very close by. Some hotels charge for use of private parking facilities.
SWIMMING POOL
Hotel pool outdoors unless otherwise stated.
GARDEN
Hotel with garden, courtyard, or terrace, often providing tables for eating outdoors.

THE BALEARIC ISLANDS

	CREDIT CARDS	NUMBER OF ROOMS	PRIVATE PARKING	SWIMMING POOL	GARDEN OR TERRACE
FORMENTERA, ES PUJOLS: *Sa Volta.* ℗℗ Calle Miramar 94, 07871. 📞 *(971) 32 81 25.* FAX *(971) 32 82 28.* An inexpensive, family-run hotel in a modern three-story building within walking distance of the beach in one of Formentera's main resorts. Each bedroom has its own terrace. 🔲 📺	AE DC MC V	25			▣
IBIZA (EIVISSA), IBIZA TOWN: *Hostal La Marina.* ℗ Calle Barcelona 7, 07800. 📞 *(971) 31 01 72.* FAX *(971) 31 39 11.* An old hotel, modernized inside but with much of its 1862 decoration. Airy front bedrooms overlook the harbor. Breakfast is not served. 🔲	AE DC MC V	47			▣
IBIZA (EIVISSA), IBIZA TOWN: *El Palacio.* ℗℗℗℗℗ Calle de la Conquista 2, 07800. 📞 *(971) 30 14 78.* FAX *(971) 39 15 81.* A theme hotel in the old town, with Marilyn Monroe penthouse suites, public rooms hung with movie memorabilia, and Hollywood Boulevard-style hand prints in the secluded garden. 🔲 📄 📺	AE DC MC V	7			▣
IBIZA (EIVISSA), SANT ANTONI: *Pikes.* ℗℗℗℗℗ Camino Sa Vorera, 07820. 📞 *(971) 34 22 22.* FAX *(971) 34 23 12.* A chic hotel in a tastefully restored mansion on a hill planted with pines. Celebrities sometimes stay here. 🔲 📄	AE DC MC V	24	▣	●	▣
IBIZA (EIVISSA), SANT MIQUEL: *Hacienda Na Xamena.* ℗℗℗℗℗ Apto 423, Urb Na Xamena, 07080. 📞 *(971) 33 45 00.* FAX *(971) 33 45 14.* There are stunning views from the bedrooms of this modern clifftop hotel built above a pretty, rocky cove, and from the elegant sun terrace surrounding the swimming pool. 🔲 📄 📺	AE DC MC V	63	▣	●	▣
IBIZA (EIVISSA), SANTA EULÀRIA D'ES RIU: *Les Terrasses.* ℗℗℗ Apto 1235, Carretera de Santa Eulària, 07600 📞 *(& FAX) (971) 33 26 43.* A country house decorated simply but beautifully in Ibizan style, painted white, blue, and yellow. Each room is individually decorated. There are quiet corners inside and out to sit and read or relax. 🔲 📄	MC V	7	▣	●	▣
MALLORCA, ANDRATX: *Villa Italia.* ℗℗℗℗℗ Camino Sant Carles 13, Port d'Andratx, 07157. 📞 *(971) 67 40 11.* FAX *(971) 67 33 50.* A pink, Florentine-style villa built in the 1920s by an eccentric Italian millionaire for his lover. Inside there are stucco ceilings, marble floors, and columns with Roman capitals. 🔲 📄 📺	AE DC MC V	16		●	▣
MALLORCA, BANYALBUFAR: *Sa Baronía.* ℗ Calle Sa Baronía 16, 07191. 📞 *(971) 61 81 46.* FAX *(971) 61 81 46.* A family-run hotel built as a modern extension to a 17th-century baronial tower. It is in a small village on the island's unspoiled northwest coast. All the bedrooms have terraces with sea views. 🔲	V	30	▣	●	▣
MALLORCA, BANYALBUFAR: *Mar i Vent.* ℗℗ Calle Mayor 49, 07191. 📞 *(971) 61 80 00.* FAX *(971) 61 82 01.* A hospitable hotel perched on a terrace above a rocky cove. The bedrooms in the annex are large and quiet. 🔲	MC V	23	▣	●	▣
MALLORCA, DEIÀ: *La Residencia.* ℗℗℗℗℗ Finca Son Canals, 07179. 📞 *(971) 63 90 11.* FAX *(971) 63 93 70.* Two magnificently restored 16th-century manors on the outskirts of Deià have been made into an elegant hotel. Most bedrooms have four-poster beds, and all have traditional Spanish furniture. 🔲 📄	AE DC MC V	64	▣	●	▣
MALLORCA, ESCORCA: *Santuari de Lluc.* ℗ Santuari de Lluc, 07315. 📞 *(971) 51 70 25.* FAX *(971) 51 70 96.* The Santuari de Lluc, high in the Tramuntana mountains, is accessible only by car. The simple bedrooms are in the monastery buildings. 🔲 ♿	MC V	97	▣	●	▣

MALLORCA, PALMA DE MALLORCA: *Born.*　　　　　　　　　ⓅⓅ | AE | 29 | | | ■
Calle Sant Jaume 3, 07012. █ *(971) 71 29 42.* **FAX** *(971) 71 86 18.* | MC
The Marquis of Ferrandell's town mansion, built in the 16th century | V
and restored in the 18th, makes a splendid hotel. It has a typical
Mallorcan courtyard with palms and a grand staircase. 🛏 🗐 TV

MALLORCA, POLLENÇA: *Illa d'Or.*　　　　　　　　　　　Ⓟ Ⓟ Ⓟ | AE | 119 | | | ■
Paseo de Colón 265, 07470. █ *(971) 86 51 00.* **FAX** *(971) 86 42 13.* | DC
Built in the 1930s for elite Northern Europeans to summer on the | MC
island, the hotel retains its original furniture and atmosphere. 🛏 🗐 TV | V

MALLORCA, POLLENÇA: *Formentor.*　　　　　　　　Ⓟ Ⓟ Ⓟ Ⓟ Ⓟ | AE | 127 | ■ | ● | ■
Playa de Formentor, 07470. █ *(971) 86 53 00.* **FAX** *(971) 86 51 55.* | DC
The visitors' book of this luxury hotel in a beautiful spot on the | MC
island's northwest tip is signed by writers, opera singers, movie stars, | V
and the Dalai Lama. There is a health and beauty center. 🛏 🗐 TV

MALLORCA, RANDA: *Es Recó de Randa.*　　　　　　　　Ⓟ Ⓟ Ⓟ | MC | 14 | ■ | ● | ■
Font 13, 07629. █ *(971) 66 09 97.* **FAX** *(971) 66 25 58.* | V
A restaurant-with-rooms in an old stone house in a quiet village at
the foot of the Puig de Randa mountain. There are views of the village
and the mountains from some of the bedroom windows. 🛏 🗐 TV

MALLORCA, SES SALINES: *Es Turó.*　　　　　　　　　Ⓟ Ⓟ Ⓟ | AE | 10 | ■ | ● | ■
Ses Salines, 07640. █ *(971) 64 95 31.* **FAX** *(971) 64 95 48.* | DC
Rural calm, tasteful comfort, and timeless Mallorcan life are brought | MC
together in this hotel in an old farmhouse. It contains a small museum | V
of local life and is surrounded by olive and almond orchards. 🛏 TV &

MALLORCA, SÓLLER: *Ca N'Aí.*　　　　　　　　　Ⓟ Ⓟ Ⓟ Ⓟ | AE | 11 | ■ | ● | ■
Camí de Son Puça 48, 07100. █ *(971) 63 24 94.* **FAX** *(971) 63 18 99.* | DC
An old Mallorcan house built into the side of Sóller valley, which is | MC
covered with orange and palm trees. Inside, the decor is refined. The | V
service has a personal touch and the cooking is excellent. 🛏 🗐 &

MALLORCA, VALLDEMOSSA: *Vistamar.*　　　　　Ⓟ Ⓟ Ⓟ Ⓟ | AE | 16 | ■ | ● | ■
Ctra de Valldemossa–Andratx, 07170. █ *(971) 61 23 00.* | DC
This is a peaceful clifftop hotel in a villa built early in the 20th century. | MC
The bedrooms, furnished with antiques, overlook a courtyard. Chopin | V
and George Sand made the nearby monastery famous. 🛏 TV

MENORCA, CIUTADELLA: *Hostal Residencia Ciutadella.*　　　Ⓟ | AE | 17 | | |
Calle San Eloy 10, 07760. █ *(971) 38 34 62.* **FAX** *(971) 38 35 69.* | DC
Just a few minutes' walk from the Plaça des·Borne, this simple, modern | MC
hotel offers bargain accommodations. The rooms are | V
plainly furnished and spotless. Simple meals are served in the bar. 🛏

MENORCA, CIUTADELLA: *Patricia.*　　　　　　　　Ⓟ Ⓟ Ⓟ | AE | 44 | ■ | ● |
Paseo San Nicolás 90–92, 07760. █ *(971) 38 55 11.* **FAX** *(971) 48 11 20.* | DC
A modern, cream-colored chain hotel with white bay windows | MC
on one of the town's main avenues, near the harbor. 🛏 🗐 TV | V

MENORCA, MAÓ: *Capri.*　　　　　　　　　　　　　Ⓟ Ⓟ | AE | 75 | | |
Calle San Esteban 8, 07703. █ *(971) 36 14 00.* **FAX** *(971) 35 08 53.* | DC
This is a central hotel in a modern, five-story building close to shopping, | MC
the harbor, and the beach. Most bedrooms have a terrace. 🛏 🗐 TV | V

MENORCA, MAÓ: *Del Almirante.*　　　　　　　　　　Ⓟ Ⓟ | | 40 | ■ | ● | ■
Carretera de Villacarlos, 07780. █ *(971) 36 27 00.* **FAX** *(971) 36 27 04.*
Built in the 18th century in classic Georgian style, this house became
the home of Admiral Lord Collingwood, a friend of Admiral Nelson.
The hotel has a new wing built around the swimming pool. 🛏 &

MENORCA, MAÓ: *Mirador des Port.*　　　　　　　Ⓟ Ⓟ Ⓟ | AE | 70 | | ● | ■
Calle Dalt Villanova 1, 07700. █ *(971) 36 00 16.* | MC
A modern, comfortable hotel at the western end of town with a view | DC
across the harbor. Many bedrooms have shuttered terraces – ideal for | V
summer evenings. There is a stylish designer bar downstairs. 🛏 🗐 TV

MENORCA, MAÓ: *Port Mahón.*　　　　　　　Ⓟ Ⓟ Ⓟ Ⓟ Ⓟ | AE | 82 | | ● | ■
Fort de L'Eau 13, 07701. █ *(971) 36 26 00.* **FAX** *(971) 35 10 50.* | DC
Housed in an attractive red and white colonial-style building, this hotel | MC
looks over Maó harbor. Its grounds include wide terraces and a | V
curving swimming pool surrounded by lawns. 🛏 🗐 TV &

For key to symbols see back flap

Price categories for a standard double room per night, with tax, breakfast, and service included:

Ⓟ under 8,000 ptas
ⓅⓅ 8,000–12,000 ptas
ⓅⓅⓅ 12,000–16,000 ptas
ⓅⓅⓅⓅ 16,000–20,000 ptas
ⓅⓅⓅⓅⓅ over 20,000 ptas

CREDIT CARDS
Indicates which credit cards are accepted: *AE* American Express; *DC* Diners Club; *MC* MasterCard/Access; *V* Visa
PARKING
Parking provided by the hotel in a private parking lot or a private garage on the hotel site or very close by. Some hotels charge for use of private parking facilities.
SWIMMING POOL
Hotel pool outdoors unless otherwise stated.
GARDEN
Hotel with garden, courtyard, or terrace, often providing tables for eating outdoors.

	CREDIT CARDS	NUMBER OF ROOMS	PRIVATE PARKING	SWIMMING POOL	GARDEN OR TERRACE

THE CANARY ISLANDS

FUERTEVENTURA, ANTIGUA: *El Castillo.* ⓅⓅ
Caleta de Fuste, 36610. 【 *(928) 16 31 00.* FAX *(928) 16 30 46.*
The attractive apartments in this village-style complex have direct access to a beach curving around a gentle bay, and to a central plaza of shops, cafés, and restaurants. A popular location for water sports. 🖥 ♿
AE DC MC V — 390 · ● ·

FUERTEVENTURA, CORRALEJO: *Tres Islas.* ⓅⓅⓅⓅⓅ
Grandes Playas, 35660. 【 *(928) 53 57 00.* FAX *(928) 53 58 58.*
All the bedrooms of this spacious hotel have balconies facing the ocean. There are two huge pools set among the gardens. 🖥 ▤ TV ♿
AE DC MC V — 365 · ● ·

FUERTEVENTURA, COSTA CALMA: *Fuerteventura Playa.* ⓅⓅⓅ
Urb Cañada del Río, Polígono C1, 35627. 【 *(928) 54 73 44.* FAX *(928) 54 70 97.*
The two wings of this hotel curve around gardens and pools. It is in a secluded spot with direct access to the beach. All the bedrooms are large, with balconies overlooking the ocean. 🖥 ▤ TV ♿
AE MC V — 300 · ● ·

LA GOMERA, PLAYA DE SANTIAGO: *Jardín Tecina.* ⓅⓅⓅⓅ
Lomada de Tecina, 38811. 【 *(922) 89 50 50.* FAX *(922) 89 51 88.*
Its many facilities make this complex in the hills behind the Playa de Santiago virtually a self-contained resort. A cliffside elevator takes guests down to the beach club. 🖥 ▤ ♿
AE MC V — 434 · ● ·

LA GOMERA, SAN SEBASTIÁN: *Parador de San Sebastián.* ⓅⓅⓅ
San Sebastián de La Gomera, 38800. 【 *(922) 87 11 00.* FAX *(922) 87 11 16.*
On a clifftop above La Gomera's main town and port, this parador is in traditional style, with pitched ceilings. The bedrooms have dark wood fittings and tiled bathrooms, and there are tropical gardens. 🖥 TV
AE DC MC V — 42 · · ·

GRAN CANARIA, AGAETE: *Princesa Guayarmina.* Ⓟ
Los Berrazales, 35480. 【 *(928) 89 80 09.* FAX *(928) 89 85 25.*
A small, plain hotel in the mountains. The simply furnished rooms overlook a tropical valley. It is an excellent value and has a friendly staff. 🖥
— 27 · ● ·

GRAN CANARIA, MASPALOMAS: *Maspalomas Oasis.* ⓅⓅⓅⓅⓅ
Playa de Maspalomas 3, 35106. 【 *(928) 14 14 48.* FAX *(928) 14 11 92.*
This quiet hotel is in a prime spot by the dunes. The guests are stylishly accommodated in split-level suites with spacious bedrooms. The staff is efficient and pleasant. 🖥 ▤ TV
AE DC MC V — 334 · ● ·

GRAN CANARIA, LAS PALMAS: *Imperial Playa.* ⓅⓅⓅ
Calle Ferreras 1, 35008. 【 *(928) 46 88 54.* FAX *(928) 46 94 42.*
A smart, comfortable business hotel in a modern building overlooking Las Canteras beach, close to the port and shops. 🖥 ▤ TV
AE DC MC V — 142

GRAN CANARIA, LAS PALMAS: *Santa Catalina.* ⓅⓅⓅⓅ
Calle León y Castillo 227, 35005. 【 *(928) 24 30 40.* FAX *(928) 24 27 64.*
An long-established hotel in a large park. It is a traditional building of the Canary Islands, with carved wooden balconies and a colonial atmosphere. There is an opulent casino. 🖥 ▤ TV
AE DC MC V — 200 · ● ·

GRAN CANARIA, PLAYA DEL INGLÉS: *Parque Tropical.* ⓅⓅⓅⓅ
Avenida de Italia 1, 35100. 【 *(928) 77 40 12.* FAX *(928) 76 81 37.*
An attractive hotel in local style with comfortable rooms, direct access to the beachfront, and good sports facilities. Book ahead. 🖥
AE DC MC V — 235 · ● ·

GRAN CANARIA, PUERTO DE MOGÁN: *Club de Mar.* ⓅⓅⓅ
Puerto de Mogán, 35138. 【 *(928) 56 50 66.* FAX *(928) 56 54 38.*
Pretty buildings with rooms and apartments are ranged around a small bay with a sandy beach and a marina. There are pleasant grounds, a swimming pool, and lively local bars. 🖥 ▤ TV.
AE MC V — 56 · ● ·

EL HIERRO, FRONTERA: *Punta Grande.* ⓅⓅ

4

Las Puntas, 38911. 🄲 *(922) 55 90 81.* FAX *(922) 55 90 81.*
Guests are charmed to find themselves in the world's smallest hotel,
as listed in *The Guinness Book of Records*: four bedrooms and a sitting
room converted from what was once a customs store. 🛏

EL HIERRO, VALVERDE: *Parador El Hierro.* ⓅⓅⓅ

AE	47
DC	
MC	
V	

Valverde, 38910. 🄲 *(922) 55 80 36.* FAX *(922) 55 80 86.*
Black cliffs are the backdrop for this modern, tiled-roof hotel on an
isolated beach. It is attractively decorated and quiet, with an informal,
intimate atmosphere. A good base for a hiking vacation. 🛏 ♿

LANZAROTE, ARRECIFE: *Lancelot.* Ⓟ

AE	113
DC	
MC	
V	

Avenida Mancomunidad 9, 35500. 🄲 *(928) 80 50 99.* FAX *(928) 80 50 39.*
A stylish new hotel beside a beach of soft, pale sand. Coral reefs lie just
offshore. There are good restaurants in the hotel and the town. 🛏 📺

LANZAROTE, COSTA TEGUISE: *Meliá Salinas.* ⓅⓅⓅⓅ

AE	310
DC	
MC	
V	

Urbanización Costa Teguise, 35509. 🄲 *(928) 59 00 40.* FAX *(928) 59 03 90.*
A vast atrium with central water gardens and ornamental plants is the
focus of this contemporary hotel. It offers big, restful bedrooms,
boutiques, sports facilities, and an attractive beach. 🛏 ▤ 📺 ♿

LANZAROTE, PUERTO DEL CARMEN: *Los Fariones.* ⓅⓅⓅ

AE	249
DC	
MC	
V	

Calle Roque del Oeste 1, 35510. 🄲 *(928) 51 01 75.* FAX *(928) 51 02 02.*
A secluded hotel on an attractive beach. It is relaxing and comfortable,
with spacious bedrooms and a good range of facilities. 🛏 📺 ♿

LANZAROTE, YAIZA: *Lanzarote Princess.* ⓅⓅⓅ

AE	449
DC	
MC	
V	

Avenida Playa Blanca 35570. 🄲 *(928) 51 71 08.* FAX *(928) 51 70 11.*
A resort hotel, popular with families. It is cool and light, with split-level
areas ornamented with water gardens. There is a large pool. 🛏 ▤ ♿

LA PALMA, BARLOVENTO: *La Palma Romántica.* ⓅⓅ

AE	41
MC	
V	

Calle Las Llanadas, 38726. 🄲 *(922) 18 62 21.* FAX *(922) 18 64 00.*
Nestling into a hillside high above the sea is this light, airy hotel with
spacious rooms. It has an indoor pool, a sauna, and a solarium. 🛏

TENERIFE, LOS CRISTIANOS: *Estefanía.* ⓅⓅⓅ

AE	32
MC	
V	

Carretera de Arona, 38660. 🄲 *(922) 75 16 97.* FAX *(922) 75 15 93.*
A hotel in the hills behind the Playa de las Américas, with luxurious
bedrooms and a cool, stylish decor. 🛏 ▤ 📺

TENERIFE, LA OROTAVA: *Parador de Cañadas del Teide.* ⓅⓅ

AE	23
DC	
MC	

Apto de Correos 15, Cañadas del Teide, 38300. 🄲 *(922) 38 64 15.* FAX *(922) 38 23 52.*
There are views of Mount Teide from this modern parador that
looks like an Alpine chalet. It is inside the national park, and is
a useful center from which to explore this volcanic region. 🛏 📺

TENERIFE, PLAYA DE LAS AMÉRICAS: *Jardín Tropical.* ⓅⓅⓅⓅ

AE	315
DC	
MC	
V	

Urbanización San Eugenio, 38660. 🄲 *(922) 75 01 00.* FAX *(922) 75 28 44.*
In the heart of the resort, with access to the beachfront, this is an
imaginative modern hotel with turrets and tiled patios. 🛏 ▤ 📺

TENERIFE, PUERTO DE LA CRUZ: *Monopol.* ⓅⓅ

AE	100
DC	
MC	
V	

Calle Quintana 15, 38400. 🄲 *(922) 38 46 11.* FAX *(922) 37 03 10.*
An old-style, family-run hotel with a plant-filled patio with wooden
balustrades. The bedrooms are modern and spacious, and there is a
basement restaurant. The staff is smart and efficient. 🛏

TENERIFE, PUERTO DE LA CRUZ: *Botánico.* ⓅⓅⓅⓅ

AE	282
DC	
MC	
V	

Calle Richard J Yeoward, 38400. 🄲 *(922) 38 14 00.* FAX *(922) 38 15 04.*
The sea is some distance away from this restful hotel near the Botanic
Gardens, but it offers excellent leisure facilities. 🛏 ▤ 📺 ♿

TENERIFE, SANTA CRUZ DE TENERIFE: *Náutico.* ⓅⓅⓅ

AE	40
DC	
MC	
V	

Calle Profesor Peraza 13, 38001. 🄲 *(922) 24 70 66.* FAX *(922) 24 72 76.*
A small, modern building behind the port, close to a bus stop for Las
Teresitas beach. The small café serves a good Spanish breakfast. 🛏 📺

TENERIFE, VILAFLOR: *Alta Montaña.* ⓅⓅ

AE	12
DC	
MC	
V	

Calle Morro del Cano 1, 38613. 🄲 *(922) 70 90 49.* FAX *(922) 70 90 49.*
A small, homey hotel with spectacular views. It is run by a friendly
Belgian couple who serve organic food in their restaurant. ♿

For key to symbols see back flap

RESTAURANTS AND BARS

ONE OF THE JOYS of eating out in Spain is the sheer sociability of the Spanish. Family and friends, often with children in tow, can be seen eating out from early in the day until after midnight.

Spanish food has a regional bias. Traditional restaurants originated as taverns and tapas bars serving dishes based on local produce. Spain also has

Wall tile advertising a Barcelona restaurant

its fair share of top-quality gourmet restaurants, notably in the Basque Country.

The restaurants listed on pages 578–609 have been selected for their food and conviviality. Pages 574–7 illustrate some of the best tapas and drinks; and each of the book's five regional sections includes features on the area's unique food and wines.

Bodegas are bars that specialize in wines and do not often serve food

RESTAURANTS AND BARS

THE CHEAPEST and quickest places to eat are the bars and cafés that serve tapas. Some bars, however, especially *pubs* (late-opening bars for socializing) serve no food.

Family-run *bar-restaurantes*, *ventas*, *posadas*, *mesones*, and *fondas* – all old words for the different types of inn – serve inexpensive, sit-down meals. *Chiringuitos* are beachside bars. They open only during the summer season.

Spain's top restaurants tend to be clustered in the Basque Country, Galicia, Barcelona, Catalonia, and Madrid.

Most restaurants close one day a week, some for lunch or dinner only, and most for an annual vacation. They also close on some public holidays. The main closing times of the restaurants on pages 578–609 are listed at the end of each entry. Always check these opening times, however, when calling to book a table.

EATING HOURS IN SPAIN

THE SPANISH often have two breakfasts *(desayunos)*. The first is a light meal of biscuits or toast with olive oil or butter and jam and *café con leche* (coffee with milk). A more substantial breakfast may follow between 10 and 11am, perhaps in a café. This may consist of a savory snack, such as a *bocadillo* (sandwich) with sausage, ham, or cheese, or a thick slice of *tortilla de patatas* (potato omelette). Fruit juice, coffee, or beer are the usual accompaniments.

From about 1pm people will stop in the bars for a beer or a *copa* (glass) of wine with tapas. By 2pm those who can will have arrived home from work for *la comida* (lunch), which is the main meal of the day. Others will choose to have lunch in a restaurant.

The cafés, *salones de té* (tea rooms), and *pastelerías* (pastry shops) fill up by about 5:30 or

Decoration, Barcelona bar

6pm for *la merienda* (tea) of sandwiches, pastries, or cakes, with coffee, tea, or juice. Snacks like *churros* (fried batter sticks) can also be bought from stalls.

By 7pm, bars are crowded with people having tapas with sherry, wine, or beer. In Spain *la cena* (dinner or supper), begins at about 9pm. Restaurants sometimes begin their evening service earlier for tourists. In summer, however, Spanish families and groups of friends often do not sit down to eat until as late as midnight. At weekend lunchtimes, especially in the summer, you may find that restaurants are filled by large and noisy family gatherings.

HOW TO DRESS

A JACKET AND TIE are rarely required, but the Spanish dress well, especially for city restaurants. Day dress is casual in beach resorts, but shorts are frowned on in the evenings.

The parador restaurant in Pedraza de la Sierra, Segovia *(see p595)*

Sidewalk tables outside a cafeteria, in Cadaqués on the Costa Brava

READING THE MENU

ASIDE FROM TAPAS, perhaps the cheapest eating options in Spanish restaurants are the fixed-price *platos combinados* (meat or fish with vegetables and, usually, french fries) and the *menú del día*. A *plato combinado* is offered by less expensive places. Most restaurants – but not all – offer an inexpensive, fixed-price *menú del día*, normally of three courses, but with little choice. Some gourmet restaurants offer a *menú de degustación* with a choice of six or seven of the head chef's special dishes.

The Spanish word for menu is *la carta*. It starts with *sopas* (soups), *ensaladas* (salads), *entremeses* (hors d'oeuvres), *huevos y tortillas* (eggs and omelettes), and *verduras y legumbres* (vegetable dishes).

Main courses are *pescados y mariscos* (fish and shellfish) and *carnes y aves* (meat and poultry). Daily specials are chalked on a board or clipped to menus. Paella and other rice dishes may be served as the first course. A useful rule is to follow rice with meat, or start with *serrano* ham or salad and then follow with a paella.

Desserts are called *postres* in Spanish. All restaurants offer fresh fruit (the usual dessert in Spain), but otherwise the range of *postres* is generally poor. The better restaurants offer a limited choice, perhaps *natillas* (custard) and *flan* (crème caramel). Gourmet restaurants have more creative choices.

Vegetarians are rather poorly catered to in Spain. Some vegetable, salad, and egg dishes will be vegetarian, but may contain pieces of ham or fish, so ask before you order.

All eating places welcome children and will serve small portions if requested.

Las Torres de Ávila *(see p185)*, a distinctive Barcelona bar

WINE CHOICES

DRY FINO WINES are perfect with shellfish, *serrano* ham, olives, soups, and most first courses. Main courses are commonly accompanied by wines originating from Ribera del Duero, Rioja, Navarra, or Penedès. A typical bar might serve wines from Valdepeñas or the local vineyards. Oloroso wines *(see p577)* are often ordered as a *digestif*.

SMOKING

IN FINE RESTAURANTS customers are offered *puros* (cigars) with their coffee and brandy. Many people in Spain smoke and very few restaurants have no-smoking areas or tables.

PRICES AND PAYING

IF YOU ORDER from *la carta* in a restaurant, your check can soar way above the price of the *menú del día*, especially if you order pricey items such as fresh seafood, fish, or *ibérico* ham *(see p438)*. If there is an expensive fish like sole or swordfish at a bargain price, it may be frozen. Sea bass and other popular fish and shellfish, such as jumbo shrimp, lobster, and crab, are priced by weight.

La cuenta (the check) includes service and perhaps a small cover charge. Prices on menus do not include seven percent VAT *(IVA)*, which is usually added when the bill is totaled. The Spanish rarely tip restaurant staff more than five percent, often just rounding up the bill.

Checks are rarely used in Spain. Traveler's checks are usually accepted, but you may be given a poor rate of exchange. The major credit cards and international direct debit cards (ATM) are now accepted in most restaurants. Do not expect to pay by credit card in smaller eating or drinking places like tapas bars, cafés, village *mesones*, roadside *ventas*, pubs, or bodegas.

WHEELCHAIR ACCESS

SINCE RESTAURANTS are rarely designed for wheelchairs, phone in advance (or ask the hotel staff to call) to check on access to tables and toilets.

Early 20th-century decor in a Madrid bar

Choosing Tapas

Tapas, sometimes called pinchos, are small snacks that originated in Andalusia in the 19th century to accompany sherry. Stemming from a bartender's practice of covering a glass with a saucer or *tapa* (cover) to keep out flies, the custom progressed to a chunk of cheese or a few olives being placed on a platter to accompany a drink. Once free of charge, tapas usually have to be paid for nowadays. Choose from a range of appetizing varieties, from cold meats or cheeses to elaborately prepared hot dishes of seafood, meat, or vegetables.

Dry fino sherry

Fritura de pescado *is a mixture of fried fish and seafood served with lemon. It includes red mullet, squid, and baby hake or other available fresh fish.*

Albondigas *(meatballs) are a hearty tapa and may be served with a zesty tomato sauce.*

Jamón serrano, *salt-cured ham dried in mountain* (serrano) *air, can be served unadorned in chunks* (tacos) *or in thin slices* (lonchas)*. This basic tapas dish is often accompanied by bread.*

Gambas a la plancha *is a simple but flavorful dish of whole grilled unpeeled shrimp.*

Tortilla a la española *is the ubiquitous thick Spanish omelette, a tasty dish of onion and potato, bound together with seasoned eggs. It is served in wedges or small squares.*

Mejillones a la marinera *is a dish of mussels cooked in a tasty sauce of sautéed onion and garlic, white wine, olive oil, lemon juice, and parsley.*

Banderillas *canapés skewered toothpicks. Popular ingredients include marinated f and vegetables, hard-boil eggs, shrimp, gherkins, a olives. The entire cana should be eaten at once, blend the flavors togeth*

Almendras fritas *(fried salted almonds) are a common snack, since almond trees grow in many parts of Spain. Pistachios* (pistachios)*, salted peanuts* (cacahuetes)*, and sunflower seeds* (pipas) *can also be ordered to accompany a drink.*

Pollo al ajillo, *a widely available tapa, consists of small pieces of chicken (often wings or legs) browned in oil and then gently simmered in an appetizing garlic-flavored sauce.*

Ensaladilla rusa (Russian salad) is cold dish of tuna, shrimp, potatoes, carrots, and peas coated with mayonnaise. It may be topped with peppers or eggs.

Chorizo, a popular sausage that is flavored with garlic and paprika, is usually eaten cold, but some kinds are fried and served hot.

Patatas bravas is a piquant dish of potatoes fried in oil and coated in a spicy tomato sauce flavored with onion, garlic, white wine, parsley, and red chili peppers. The bite-sized morsels are both delicious and filling.

Olives are common tapas and come in several varieties. Gordals are fat Seville olives. Manzanillas may be pitted and stuffed with anchovies, almonds, or pimientos. Some olives are marinated in herbs and oil or vinegar.

Salpicón de mariscos is a luxurious cold salad consisting of an assortment of fresh seafood, including lobster, crab, and shrimp, with chopped tomatoes. The salad is coated in a zesty vinaigrette flavored with onion and red peppers.

Calamares fritos are squid rings that have been dusted with flour before being deep fried in olive or vegetable oil. They are served garnished with a slice of lemon.

Ensalada de pimientos rojos is a colorful cold salad of roasted red peppers and tomatoes. The juices from the roasting are combined with olive oil and vinegar to make a delicious sauce for the salad.

Queso manchego, sheep's cheese from La Mancha (see p321), is Spain's most popular cheese. It comes served with bread in either a mild, semisoft form (semicurado) or, when left to age, a tangy mature form (curado).

TAPAS BARS

Even a small village will have at least one bar where the locals go to enjoy drinks, tapas, and conversation with friends. On Sundays and holidays, the favorite places are packed with whole families enjoying the fare. In larger towns it is customary to move from bar to bar, sampling the specialties of each. A tapa is a single serving, whereas a *ración* serves two or three. *Bocadillos*, sandwiches filled with the same ingredients as tapas, can also be ordered. Tapas are generally eaten standing at the bar rather than sitting at a table, for which a surcharge is usually made.

Friends gathered for conversation and a selection of tapas in a local bar

What to Drink in Spain

S PAIN IS ONE OF THE WORLD'S largest wine-producing countries and many fine wines are made here, particularly reds in La Rioja and sherry in Andalusia. Many other beverages – both alcoholic and nonalcoholic – are served in bars and cafés, which provide an important focus for life in Spain. Spaniards are also great coffee drinkers. In the summer months a tempting range of cooling drinks is on offer, in addition to beer, which is always available. Brandy and a variety of liqueurs, such as *anís*, are drunk as aperitifs and *digestifs*, as is chilled pale gold fino sherry.

Customers enjoying a drink at a terrace café in Seville

Hot chocolate

A plate of *churros* (batter sticks)

Café con leche

Camomile

Lime flower

HOT DRINKS

C AFE CON LECHE is a large half-and-half measure of milk and coffee; *café cortado* is an espresso with a splash of milk; *café solo* is a black coffee. Hot chocolate is also popular and is often served with *churros* (batter sticks). Herbal teas include *manzanilla* (camomile) and *tila* (linden flower).

COLD DRINKS

I N MOST SPANISH TOWNS and cities it is safe to drink the tap water, but people generally prefer to buy bottled mineral water, either still *(sin gas)* or sparkling *(con gas)*. Besides soft drinks, a variety of other thirst-quenching summer beverages is available, including *horchata (see p243)*, a sweet, milky drink made from ground *chufas* (earth almonds). Another popular refreshing drink is *leche merengada* (iced milk with sweet meringue floating in it). *Gaseosa*, fizzy lemonade, can be drunk either on its own or as a mixer, usually with wine. *Zumo de naranja natural* (freshly squeezed orange juice) is an excellent thirst quencher.

Horchata, made from *chufas*

Sparkling and still mineral water

SPANISH WINE

Wine has been produced in Spain since pre-Roman times, and there is great variety available today, including famous types such as Rioja. The key standard for the industry is the *Denominación de Origen* (DO) classification, a guarantee of a wine's origin and quality. *Vino de la Tierra* is a classification of wines below that of DO in which over 60 percent of the grapes come from a specified region. *Vino de Mesa*, the lowest category, covers basic unclassified wines. For more detailed information on Spain's principal wine producing regions, refer to the following pages: Northern Spain *(see pp74–5)*, Eastern Spain *(see pp192–3)*, Central Spain *(see pp322–3)*, and Southern Spain *(see pp402–3)*.

Penedès white wine

Rioja red wine

Sparkling wine (cava)

SPIRITS AND LIQUEURS

S PANISH BRANDY, which comes mainly from the sherry bodegas in Jerez, is known as *coñac*. Most bodegas produce at least three different labels and price ranges. Magno is a good middle-shelf brandy; top-shelf labels are Lepanto and Larios. *Anís*, which is flavored with anise, is a popular liqueur. *Pacharán*, made from sloes, is sweet and is also anise flavored. Licor 43 is a vanilla liqueur. Ponche is brandy that has been aged and flavored with herbs.

Anís

Pacharán

Licor 43

Ponche

BEER

M OST SPANISH BEER *(cerveza)* is bottled lager, although you can sometimes find it on draft. Popular brands include San Miguel, Cruzcampo and Águila. To order a glass of beer in a bar ask for *una caña*. Alcohol-free lager *(cerveza sin alcohol)* is also available in most bars in Spain.

Bottled beers

SHERRY

S HERRY IS PRODUCED in bodegas in Jerez de la Frontera (Andalusia) and in nearby towns Sanlúcar de Barrameda and El Puerto de Santa María *(see pp402–3)*. Although not officially called sherry, similar kinds of wine are produced in Montilla near Córdoba. Pale fino is dry and light and excellent as an apéritif. Amber amontillado (aged fino) has a strong, earthy taste while oloroso is full-bodied and ruddy.

Two brands of fino sherry

Red wine and lemonade

Sangria

MIXED DRINKS

S ANGRIA IS A refreshing mixture of red wine, *gaseosa* (lemonade) and other ingredients including chopped fruit and sugar. Wine diluted with lemonade is called *vino con gaseosa*. Another favorite drink is *Agua de Valencia*, a refreshing blend of *cava* (sparkling wine) and orange juice. Young people will often order the popular *cubalibres*, coke with rum or gin.

Cubalibre **Vino con gaseosa**

HOW TO READ A WINE LABEL

If you know what to look for, the label will provide a key to the wine's flavor and quality. It will bear the name of the wine and its producer or bodega *(see p619)*, its vintage if there is one, and show its *Denominación de Origen* (DO) if applicable. Wines labeled *cosecha* are recent vintages and are less expensive, while *crianza* and *reserva* wines are aged a minimum of two or three years – part of that time in oak casks – and therefore more expensive. Table wine *(Vino de Mesa)* may be *tinto* (red), *blanco* (white) or *rosado* (rosé). *Cava* is a sparkling wine made by the *méthode champenoise* in specified areas of origin.

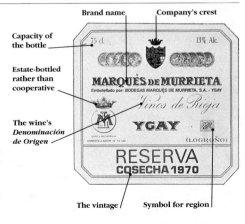

Brand name — Company's crest
Capacity of the bottle
Estate-bottled rather than cooperative
The wine's *Denominación de Origen*
The vintage — Symbol for region

Choosing a Restaurant

THE RESTAURANTS in this guide have been selected across a wide range of price categories for their good value, exceptional food and interesting location. This chart lists the restaurants by region, starting with Galicia. Use the color-coded thumb tabs, which indicate the regions covered on each page, to guide you to the relevant section of the chart.

	Price	CREDIT CARDS	TAPAS BAR	FIXED-PRICE MENU	GOOD WINE LIST	OUTDOOR TABLES
GALICIA						
BAIONA: *Moscón*. Calle Alférez Barreiro 2 (Pontevedra). ((986) 35 50 08. Galician cuisine including a tasty fish *caldeirada* (casserole) spiced with paprika. The harbor view makes for a pleasant dining experience. ▤ ⓖ	℗℗	AE DC MC V			●	
BETANZOS: *La Casilla*. Avenida de Madrid 90 (A Coruña). ((981) 77 01 61. This old stone house by the roadside is famous throughout Spain for its omelettes. You can admire the garden from the terrace. ● *Mon.* ⓖ	℗	V		■	●	■
BUEU: *A Centoleira*. Playa de Beluso 28 (Pontevedra). ((986) 32 08 96. Choose your own lobster from the aquarium or try the hake with clams accompanied by a good Albariño wine. ● *Mon & Oct.* ▤	℗℗	AE DC MC V	●		●	
A CORUÑA: *La Penela*. Plaza de María Pita 12. ((981) 20 92 00. Simple, unpretentious dining both indoors and out. The roast veal, Spanish omelette, and Galician-style monkfish are specialties. ● *Sun.* ▤	℗	AE DC MC V			●	■
A CORUÑA: *Casa Pardo*. Calle Novoa Santos 15. ((981) 28 00 21. This tavern by the fishing port is famous for its monkfish, prepared in various ways. The blackberry crème caramel is also popular. ● *Sun.* ▤	℗℗	AE DC MC V		■	●	
O GROVE: *Crisol*. Calle Hospital 10–12 (Pontevedra). ((986) 73 00 29. A variety of seafood and shellfish dishes is served here, using first-class ingredients. The dining room overlooks the sea. ▤	℗℗℗	AE MC V		■	●	
A GUARDA: *Anduriña*. Calle Calvo Sotelo 48 (Pontevedra). ((986) 61 11 08. Watch the fishing boats bring in their catch as you enjoy fresh hake, turbot, or a fish casserole in this port-side restaurant. ▤ ⓖ	℗℗	AE DC MC V	●		●	■
LUGO: *Alberto*. Calle Cruz 4. ((982) 22 83 10. Award-winning chef Alberto García's delicacies include beef entrecôte served in a green turnip sauce and sea bass with baby eels. ● *Sun.* ▤	℗℗	AE DC MC V	●	■	●	
LUGO: *Verruga*. Calle Cruz 12. ((982) 22 98 55. This restaurant offers a wide variety of seafood from its own hatchery. Try the red peppers stuffed with crab meat and the delicious home-made *filloas* (crêpes) prepared in different ways. ● *Mon.* ▤ ⓖ	℗℗℗	AE DC MC V	●	■	●	
OURENSE: *Pingallo*. Rúa San Miguel 6. ((988) 22 00 57. Wholesome home cooking, with Galicia's trademark dish of *lacón con grelos* (turnip greens with ham). Try the tasty cutlets of beef or kid. ⓖ	℗	AE MC V	●	■	●	■
OURENSE: *San Miguel*. Rúa San Miguel 12–14. ((988) 22 12 45. Innovative Galician cuisine specializing in seafood dishes. Try the sea bass in crayfish sauce or the fresh oysters and cockles. ● *Tue.* ▤	℗℗℗	AE DC MC V	●	■	●	
PADRÓN: *Casa Ramallo*. Calle Castro 5, Rois (A Coruña). ((981) 80 41 80. Home-grown vegetables and hearty fish casseroles are served in this rustic house. The *xobiña guisada* is a tasty casserole of sardines with potatoes and tomatoes. The homemade desserts are delicious. ● *Mon.* ▤	℗℗	AE DC MC V			●	■

Price categories for a three-course evening meal for one, including a half-bottle of house wine, tax, and service: ℗ under 3,000 ptas ℗℗ 3,000–4,500 ptas ℗℗℗ 4,500–6,000 ptas ℗℗℗℗ over 6,000 ptas	**TAPAS BAR** In addition to the main dining room, there is a bar serving tapas *(see p574–5)* and *raciones* (larger portions). **FIXED-PRICE MENU** A good-value, fixed-price menu is offered at lunch, dinner, or both, usually with three courses. **GOOD WINE LIST** Denotes a wide range of good wines, or a more specialized selection of local wines. **OUTDOOR TABLES** Facilities for eating outdoors, on a terrace, or in a garden or courtyard, often with a good view.				

		CREDIT CARDS	TAPAS BAR	FIXED-PRICE MENU	GOOD WINE LIST	OUTDOOR TABLES
PONTEVEDRA: *Doña Antonia.* ℗℗℗ Calle Soportales, Plaza de la Herrería 4. ((986) 84 72 74. Contemporary European cuisine in a refined setting overlooking the lovely Plaza de la Herrería. The warm monkfish salad and the nougat ice cream with hazelnuts and pistachios are favorites. ● *Sun.* ▤		MC V			●	
SAN SALVADOR DE POYO: *Casa Solla.* ℗℗℗ Avenida Sineiro 5 (Pontevedra). ((986) 87 28 84. Specialties of this elegant restaurant, housed in a lovely old *pazo* (manor house), include lobster salad with tomato vinaigrette and sea bass served on a bed of leeks. ▤ &		AE DC MC V			●	■
SANTIAGO DE COMPOSTELA: *Nixon.* ℗℗ Calle Santiago de Chile 15 (A Coruña). ((981) 53 15 31. Good home cooking, based on local recipes. The house specialties are river salmon, prepared in various ways, and sirloin steak. Try the *filloas* (crêpes) for dessert. Well-stocked wine cellar. ● *Sun.* ▤		AE V		■	●	
SANTIAGO DE COMPOSTELA: *Toñi Vicente.* ℗℗℗℗ Avenida Rosalía de Castro 24 (A Coruña). ((981) 59 41 00. Worshippers of Galician haute cuisine flock faithfully to Toñi's culinary temple. The marinated sea bass salad and the hake cooked in a shell of potato are just two of her creations. ● *Sun.* ▤ &		AE DC MC V		■	●	
SANXENXO: *La Taberna de Rotilio.* ℗℗℗℗ Avenida del Puerto (Pontevedra). ((986) 72 02 00. Located in the cellar of the hotel, this smart restaurant has gained fame for its innovative approach to Galician cuisine. The chef's creations include a monkfish *caldeirada*, an all-time favorite. ● *Mon & mid Dec–mid Jan.* ▤		AE DC MC V		■	●	
VEDRA: *Roberto.* ℗℗℗ Calle San Julián de Sales (A Coruña). ((981) 51 17 69. With an emphasis on fish and vegetables, Roberto Crespo uses home-grown produce to create interesting dishes such as sea bass with turnip greens. In the garden is a 300-year-old magnolia tree.		AE MC V	●	■	●	■
VERÍN: *Gallego.* ℗℗ Carretera N525, Albarellos de Monterrei (Ourense). ((988) 41 82 02. Enjoy traditional Galician recipes, including a wide variety of seafood and shellfish, in this bright dining room with views of the countryside. ▤ &		AE DC MC V	●	■	●	■
VIGO: *El Castillo.* ℗℗℗ Parque del Castro (Pontevedra). ((986) 42 11 11. There is a stunning view of Vigo and the ria from this elegant hilltop restaurant, which specializes in grilled fish and meat. ● *Mon.* ▤		AE DC MC V		■		
VILAGARCÍA DE AROUSA: *El Lagar.* ℗℗ Pazo Sobrán, Villajuan de Arosa (Pontevedra). ((986) 50 09 09. Situated in a large 11th-century *pazo* (manor house), this building is reputedly older than the cathedral of Santiago de Compostela. Informal dining with good regional cooking. &		AE MC V	●	■		
VILAGARCÍA DE AROUSA: *Chocolate.* ℗℗℗ Avenida de Cambados 151 (Pontevedra). ((986) 50 11 99. Manolo Cores, a local personality and master of the grill, offers a balanced selection of seafood and meat. He is proud to tell you that his wife's savory cockle pies with sweet corn are unbeatable. ● *Sun.* ▤ &		AE MC V			●	
VILLAFRAMIL: *La Villa.* ℗ Carretera Oviedo–A Coruña (Lugo). ((982) 12 30 01. This charming 300-year-old village house has been artfully restored and specializes in traditional regional food. The hake served with caviar and the tender Galician veal are recommended. ● *Tue.*		AE DC MC V		■	●	■

Price categories for a three-course evening meal for one, including a half-bottle of house wine, tax, and service:

- Ⓟ under 3,000 ptas
- ⓅⓅ 3,000–4,500 ptas
- ⓅⓅⓅ 4,500–6,000 ptas
- ⓅⓅⓅⓅ over 6,000 ptas

TAPAS BAR
In addition to the main dining room, there is a bar serving tapas *(see p574–5)* and *raciones* (larger portions).

FIXED-PRICE MENU
A good-value, fixed-price menu is offered at lunch, dinner, or both, usually with three courses.

GOOD WINE LIST
Denotes a wide range of good wines, or a more specialized selection of local wines.

OUTDOOR TABLES
Facilities for eating outdoors, on a terrace, or in a garden or courtyard, often with a good view.

ASTURIAS AND CANTABRIA

	Price	Credit Cards	Tapas Bar	Fixed-Price Menu	Good Wine List	Outdoor Tables
AVILÉS: *Real Balneario de Salinas.* Calle Juan Sitges 3, Salinas (Asturias). (98) 551 86 13. This lovely restaurant in the seaside resort of Salinas is owned by a prestigious Avilés restaurateur. The emphasis of the seasonal menu is on seafood, and the baby eels are the house specialty. 🍽 ♿	ⓅⓅⓅ	AE MC V		■	●	■
CANGAS DE ONÍS: *La Cabaña.* Calle Susierra 34 (Asturias). (98) 594 00 84. A popular grill room with a wood fire where suckling pig and baby lamb are roasted to perfection. Finish with cheese or apple pie. ● Thu. 🍽 ♿	Ⓟ	AE DC MC V		■		
CASTAÑEDA: *Hostería de Castañeda.* Calle Villabañez (Cantabria). (942) 59 81 13. After seeing the nearby caves at Puente Viesgo, relax in the converted stables of this 17th-century farmhouse. Enjoy the wild boar stew with *fines herbes* or the sirloin steak with mushrooms. 🍽 ♿	ⓅⓅ	AE DC MC V	●		●	
CASTRO URDIALES: *Mesón del Marinero.* Calle Correría 23 (Cantabria). (942) 86 00 05. This listed historic building houses a stylish seafood restaurant. The portions are generous, and its proximity to the fishing port is evident in the freshness of the produce. Excellent wine list.	ⓅⓅⓅ	AE DC MC V	●	■	●	
CASTROPOL: *El Risón.* Calle del Puerto (Asturias). (98) 563 50 65. Delightful rustic house with a terrace by the banks of the Eo River where you can savor authentic Asturian cuisine. The shellfish crêpes *(frixuelos)* and sea bass in white Albariño wine are delicious. ● Mon & Feb.	Ⓟ	AE DC MC V	●	■	●	■
COMILLAS: *El Capricho de Gaudí.* Barrio de Sobrellano (Cantabria). (942) 72 03 65. Antoni Gaudí's whimsical architectural wonder provides a unique setting for this sophisticated restaurant. The salmon in anchovy cream and the turbot with garlic sprouts are recommended. ● Mon & mid Jan–mid Feb. 🍽	ⓅⓅⓅ	AE DC MC V		■	●	■
COSGAYA: *Mesón del Oso.* Carretera Potes–Fuente Dé (Cantabria). (942) 73 30 18. Delightful country hotel and restaurant by the Río Deva with splendid views of the Picos de Europa. The veal steaks and *cocido lebaniego* (a rich stew with chickpeas and pork) are local specialties. ● Jan–mid Feb.	ⓅⓅ	DC MC V		■	●	■
CUDILLERO: *Mariño.* Playa de la Concha de Artedo (Asturias). (98) 559 01 86. The fish casseroles, *calderadas*, are this restaurant's specialty. A typical dish is *curadillo* (a member of the shark family) served in sauce. ♿	ⓅⓅ	AE DC MC V	●	■	●	
ESCALANTE: *San Román de Escalante.* Carretera Escalante–Castillo (Cantabria). (942) 67 77 28. This lovely old mountain house, set in gardens with a 12th-century chapel, is the elegant setting for French-style cuisine. ● mid Dec–mid Jan. 🍽 ♿	ⓅⓅⓅ	AE DC MC V	●	■	●	■
LAREDO: *Risco.* Calle la Arenosa 2 (Cantabria). (942) 60 50 30. Book a table by one of the large panoramic windows with wonderful views of the bay and savor a hake stew with potatoes and clams in *salsa verde* (a garlic and parsley sauce), or cod prepared with fried red peppers.	ⓅⓅⓅⓅ	AE DC MC V	●		●	■
LASTRES: *El Cafetín.* Calle Matemático Pedrayes (Asturias). (98) 585 00 85. Fresh sea produce is served together with regional specialties such as *pote asturiano* (a stew made with white beans and sausage meat). ● Wed.	Ⓟ	DC MC V	●	■		■

Luarca: *Villa Blanca.*   ℗℗   AE DC MC V
Avenida de Galicia 25–27 (Asturias). [(98) 564 10 79.
Try your hand at pouring cider in the rustic bar and then enjoy the *pitu de aldea* (chicken served with peas and small potatoes). ▤ ♿

Oviedo: *El Raitán.*   ℗℗   AE DC MC V
Plaza de Trascorrales 6 (Asturias). [(98) 521 42 18.
Discover the variety of Asturian cuisine with the nine-course lunchtime *menú de degustación*, served by waiters in regional costume. ● Sun. ▤

Potes: *Martín.*   ℗   AE V
Calle Roscabao, Urbanización Ivana (Cantabria). [(942) 73 02 33.
Authentic regional cooking including the hearty *cocido lebaniego* (a stew with chickpeas and pork) and peppers stuffed with local Treviso cheese. There are great views of the countryside from the dining room. ● Jan. ♿

Prendes: *Casa Gerardo.*   ℗℗   AE MC V
Carretera N632 (Asturias). [(98) 588 77 97.
This delightful restaurant reputedly serves the best *fabada* – a rich stew with white beans and black pudding – in all of Spain. ● Mon. ▤ ♿

Puente Arce: *El Molino.*   ℗℗℗   AE DC MC V
Carretera Nacional (Cantabria). [(942) 57 50 55.
Esthetically and gastronomically, this has to be the finest dining experience in the area. Housed in a converted mill, it offers sophisticated Cantabrian cuisine, with romantic views of the river. ● Mon. ♿

Ramales de la Victoria: *Río Asón.*   ℗℗℗   AE DC MC V
Calle Barón de Adzaneta 17 (Cantabria). [(942) 64 61 57.
Off the beaten tourist track hides one of Cantabria's best restaurants. The salmon is caught in the nearby Río Asón, and the seasonal menu will delight even the most sophisticated of palates. ● Mon & Jan. ▤ ♿

Reinosa: *Vejo.*   ℗℗   AE DC MC V
Avenida de Cantabria 83 (Cantabria). [(942) 75 17 00.
Tender veal is this modern restaurant's specialty. The sirloin with foie gras and truffles is delectable, and the Cantabrian cheese board will give you an idea why this region is renowned for its dairy products.

Santander: *Bodega del Riojano.*   ℗℗   AE DC MC V
Calle Río de la Pila 5 (Cantabria). [(942) 21 67 50.
This colorful bodega is as famous for its decorative wine barrels, painted by Spanish artists, as it is for its delicious food. The stuffed red peppers are said to be "the best in the world." Good selection of tapas. ▤

Santander: *Zacarías.*   ℗℗   AE DC MC V
Calle Hernán Cortés 38 (Cantabria). [(942) 21 23 33.
Featuring authentic Cantabrian dishes, this popular restaurant and lively tapas bar will give you a complete taste of regional specialties. ▤ ♿

Taramundi: *El Mazo.*   ℗   AE DC MC V
Cuesta de la Rectoral (Asturias). [(98) 564 67 60.
This old rectory house offers simple home cooking in an enchanting rural setting. Sirloin steak with local Cabrales blue cheese is one example. ▤

BASQUE COUNTRY, NAVARRA, AND LA RIOJA

Aoiz: *Beti Jai.*   ℗℗   MC V
Calle Santa Agueda 2 (Navarra). [(948) 33 60 52.
Old town house in the main square with views of the river, serving authentic Navarrese cuisine. The sheep's tripe *(menudicos)*, pig's feet, and the homemade sponge cake are local specialties. ▤

Azpeitia: *Kiruri Jatetxea.*   ℗℗   AE DC MC V
Barrio de Loiola 23 (Guipúzcoa). [(943) 81 56 08.
Enjoy the Guridi family's traditional Basque dishes such as *txangurro* (spider crab baked and served in the shell) or *lubina al txacoli* (sea bass cooked in the local white wine). ▤ ♿

Bilbao (Bilbo): *Zortziko.*   ℗℗℗℗   AE DC MC V
Calle Alameda Mazarredo 17 (Vizcaya). [(94) 423 97 43.
Contemporary haute cuisine served in a beautiful and elegant building, declared a historic monument. The menu is seasonal and the creative Basque elaborations are sublime. ● Sun. ▤

Price categories for a three-course evening meal for one, including a half-bottle of house wine, tax, and service:

℗ under 3,000 ptas
℗℗ 3,000–4,500 ptas
℗℗℗ 4,500–6,000 ptas
℗℗℗℗ over 6,000 ptas

TAPAS BAR
In addition to the main dining room, there is a bar serving tapas *(see p574–5)* and *raciones* (larger portions).
FIXED-PRICE MENU
A good-value, fixed-price menu is offered at lunch, dinner, or both, usually with three courses.
GOOD WINE LIST
Denotes a wide range of good wines, or a more specialized selection of local wines.
OUTDOOR TABLES
Facilities for eating outdoors, on a terrace, or in a garden or courtyard, often with a good view.

	CREDIT CARDS	TAPAS BAR	FIXED-PRICE MENU	GOOD WINE LIST	OUTDOOR TABLES
CINTRUÉNIGO: *Maher.* ℗℗℗ Calle Ribera 19 (Navarra). ☎ (948) 81 11 50. Innovative cuisine is impeccably presented in this basement restaurant. Asparagus pudding, rice with hare, and suckling lamb ribs in a delicious mushroom sauce are all house specialties. 🍽	AE DC MC V	●	■	●	
EGÜES: *Mesón Egües.* ℗℗℗ Carretera de Aoiz (Navarra). ☎ (948) 33 00 81. Enjoy excellent meat and fish in this cozy restaurant with a rustic atmosphere. Specialties include turbot, chargrilled steaks, and delicious fresh foie gras. Good homemade desserts. ● Mon. 🍽 ♿	AE DC MC V			●	
ELORRIO: *Nico.* ℗℗ Plaza Arbol de Guernika 4 (Vizcaya). ☎ (94) 682 04 69. This old Vizcayan house with wooden beams and rustic decor is a popular eating spot serving simple yet tasty cooking. ● Mon & Aug.	MC V		■		
ESTELLA (LIZARRA): *Navarra.* ℗℗ Calle Gustavo de Maeztu 16, Los Llanos (Navarra). ☎ (948) 55 10 69. Traditional regional cuisine is served in this grand house, with tiles depicting Navarra's former kings. The *blanca de navarra* (a lemon and honey ice cream, served with fresh cream and nuts) is superb. ● Mon. 🍽	AE MC V	●	■	●	■
EZCARAY: *Echaurren.* ℗℗ Calle Héroes del Alcázar 2 (La Rioja). ☎ (941) 35 40 47. One of La Rioja's emblematic restaurants, run by the delightful Paniego family. The region's superlative vegetables are cooked to perfection, and there is a great variety of Rioja and Albariño wines. ● Nov. 🍽 ♿	AE DC MC V		■		
GALDÁCANO: *Aretxondo.* ℗℗℗ Calle Elexalde 20 (Vizcaya). ☎ (94) 456 76 71. One of the region's best restaurants, this is a veritable showcase of sophisticated Basque cooking, and well worth the drive of 10 km (6 miles) from Bilbao. Reservations are advised. ● Mon. 🍽 ♿	AE MC V		■	●	
GETARIA: *Elkano.* ℗℗℗℗ Calle Herrerita 2 (Guipúzcoa). ☎ (943) 14 06 14. Pedro Arregui is famous for his grilled fish dishes. The squid served with its own ink and the turbot are both excellent. The best Basque brand of *txacoli* wine – Txomín Echaniz – is also available here. 🍽 ♿	AE DC MC V			●	■
HARO: *Terete.* ℗℗ Calle Lucrecia Arana 17 (La Rioja). ☎ (941) 31 00 23. This ancient wood-burning oven has been roasting lamb since 1877. Sit at the long wooden tables and savor the Riojan specialties, accompanied by a bottle of house wine. ● Mon. 🍽 ♿	V		■	●	
HONDARRIBIA (FUENTERRABIA): *Sebastián.* ℗℗ Calle Mayor 9–11 (Guipúzcoa). ☎ (943) 64 01 67. A lovely 16th-century house in the historic part of town serving Basque-French cuisine. Game dishes are available in season. ● Mon & Nov. ♿	AE DC MC V		■		
KORTEZUBI: *Lezika.* ℗℗ Barrio Basondo 8, Santimamiñe (Vizcaya). ☎ (94) 625 29 75. Close to the Santimamiñe caves is this delightful 18th-century country house serving traditional Basque cuisine, such as hake in *salsa verde*, and red beans with ham and sausage. Good selection of wines. 🍽 ♿	AE DC MC V	●	■	●	■
LAGUARDIA: *Posada Mayor de Migueloa.* ℗℗℗ Calle Mayor de Migueloa 20 (Álava). ☎ (941) 12 11 75. The elegant and beautifully restored 17th-century palace of Viana now houses one of La Rioja's best restaurants. The roast lamb and the Riojan potatoes *(a la riojana)* are just two of the specialties. 🍽 ♿	AE DC MC V	●	■	●	■

LASARTE: *Martín Berasategui.* ⓅⓅⓅ
Calle Loidi 4 (Guipúzcoa). **(** *(943) 36 64 71.*
One of the area's leading restaurants, in a converted farmhouse. The cold
potato soup with smoked bacon is just one of Martín's creations. He will
also design a menu to fit your budget. ● *Mon.* 目 ⑤
AE DC MC V

LEKEITIO: *Mesón Arropain.* ⓅⓅⓅ
Carretera de Marquina, Arropain, Ispaster (Vizcaya). **(** *(94) 684 03 13.*
A rustic farmhouse with an emphasis on seafood. Grilled turbot, baked
crayfish, and spider crab are all specialties. The homemade *cuajada*
(a curd pudding) is typical of the region. ● *Wed & mid Dec–mid Jan.* ⑤
AE DC MC V

LOGROÑO: *El Cachetero.* ⓅⓅ
Calle Laurel 3 (La Rioja). **(** *(941) 22 84 63.*
Home-style local cuisine is served in this cozy restaurant. The vegetable
dishes are excellent, and it is also a good place to try roast kid. Desserts
include *arroz con leche* (rice pudding). ● *Sun & mid Jul–mid Aug.* 目 ⑤
DC MC V

OIARTZUN: *Zuberoa.* ⓅⓅⓅⓅ
Calle Iturriotz Auzoa 8 (Guipúzcoa). **(** *(943) 49 12 28.*
Another of Spain's best restaurants, Zuberoa is set in a lovely 600-year-old
farmhouse. The Arbelaitz brothers maintain a consistent level of culinary
artistry, and their foie gras with chickpea sauce is a classic. ● *Mon.* 目 ⑤
AE DC MC V

PAMPLONA (IRUÑA): *Sarasate.* ⓅⓅ
Carretera de Irún, Olave (Navarra). **(** *(948) 33 08 20.*
This farmhouse just outside Pamplona serves great food at affordable
prices. Grilled dishes are the specialty, and you can try their *guisado de
toro* (bull stew) just after the Sanfermines bull-running fiesta. ● *Mon.* ⑤
MC V

PAMPLONA (IRUÑA): *Alhambra.* ⓅⓅⓅ
Calle Bergamín 7 (Navarra). **(** *(948) 24 50 07.*
Typical Navarrese cooking is served in this welcoming restaurant. The
artichokes, the truffle and vegetable purée, and the mushroom risotto
are all delicious appetizers. Good selection of local wines. ● *Sun.* 目 ⑤
AE DC MC V

PASAI DONIBANE: *Casa Cámara.* ⓅⓅ
Pasajes de San Juan 79 (Guipúzcoa). **(** *(943) 52 36 99.*
Choose your own live lobster from the aquarium or try the baked
spider crab as you admire panoramic sea views. ● *Mon.* ⑤
MC V

PUENTE LA REINA: *Mesón el Peregrino.* ⓅⓅⓅ
Carretera Pamplona–Logroño (Navarra). **(** *(948) 34 00 75.*
This charming country inn provides a peaceful setting to enjoy refined,
regional cuisine. Savor veal cheeks in an onion sauce and finish off with
a white chocolate mousse. ● *Mon.* 目
MC V

SAN SEBASTIÁN (DONOSTIA): *Akelaré.* ⓅⓅⓅⓅ
Paseo Padre Orcolaga 56, Barrio de Igueldo (Guipúzcoa). **(** *(943) 21 20 52.*
A Spanish gastronomic temple with spectacular views of rolling hills
that plunge into the sea. To savor the chef's star dishes, try the
seven-course *menú de degustación.* Proper attire only. ● *Mon & Feb.* 目 ⑤
AE DC MC V

SAN SEBASTIÁN (DONOSTIA): *Arzak.* ⓅⓅⓅⓅ
Calle Alto del Miracruz 21 (Guipúzcoa). **(** *(943) 27 84 65.*
According to many gourmets, this is Spain's best restaurant. Master chef
Juan Mari Arzak's international reputation for innovative Basque cuisine,
rewarded with three Michelin stars, is well deserved. ● *Mon & Nov.* 目 ⑤
AE DC MC V

TAFALLA: *Túbal.* ⓅⓅ
Plaza de Navarra 6 (Navarra). **(** *(948) 70 08 52.*
This historic building has 18 balconies overlooking the square. Try the
crêpes filled with borage, a traditional Navarrese vegetable. ● *Mon.* 目 ⑤
AE DC MC V

VIANA: *Borgia.* ⓅⓅⓅ
Calle Serapio Urra (Navarra). **(** *(948) 64 57 81.*
A small restaurant in the historic part of town with an interesting seasonal
menu. The artichokes with foie gras served on a bed of watercress, and
the lamb marinated in herbs with a gin sauce are specialties. ● *Sun & Aug.*
AE DC MC V

VITORIA (GASTEIZ): *Dos Hermanas.* ⓅⓅⓅ
Madre Vedruna 10 (Álava). **(** *(945) 13 29 34.*
Classic regional cooking with a seasonal menu. The tuna served on a
bed of peppers and the oxtail stew are both delicious. ● *Sun.* 目 ⑤
AE DC MC V

<table>
<tr><td rowspan="2">

Price categories for a three-course evening meal for one, including a half-bottle of house wine, tax, and service:

Ⓟ under 3,000 ptas
ⓅⓅ 3,000–4,500 ptas
ⓅⓅⓅ 4,500–6,000 ptas
ⓅⓅⓅⓅ over 6,000 ptas

</td></tr>
</table>

	TAPAS BAR In addition to the main dining room, there is a bar serving tapas *(see p574–5)* and *raciones* (larger portions). FIXED-PRICE MENU A good-value, fixed-price menu is offered at lunch, dinner, or both, usually with three courses. GOOD WINE LIST Denotes a wide range of good wines, or a more specialized selection of local wines. OUTDOOR TABLES Facilities for eating outdoors, on a terrace, or in a garden or courtyard, often with a good view.	CREDIT CARDS	TAPAS BAR	FIXED-PRICE MENU	GOOD WINE LIST	OUTDOOR TABLES
VITORIA (GASTEIZ): *Ikea.* ⓅⓅⓅ Portal de Castilla 27 (Álava). [(945) 14 47 47. José Ramón Berriozabal masterfully combines traditional Basque cuisine with a French influence. The hake fillet in *salsa verde* is a classic dish. The foie gras terrine and the Bresse pigeon are both exquisite. ● *Mon.* ▤	AE DC MC V		■	●	

BARCELONA

	CREDIT CARDS	TAPAS BAR	FIXED-PRICE MENU	GOOD WINE LIST	OUTDOOR TABLES
OLD TOWN: *Agut.* **Map 5 A3.** Ⓟ Carrer Gignàs 16. [(93) 315 17 09. Painters used to exchange their artwork for a hearty, honest Catalan meal here. Nowadays the specialties include an eggplant terrine and succulent blood-red steaks from Girona. ● *Aug.* ▤	MC V		■	●	
OLD TOWN: *Cal Pep.* **Map 5 B3.** Ⓟ Plaça de les Olles 8. [(93) 310 79 61. According to some seafood fanatics, Pep's *pescado frito* (fried fish) is the best in the world! Other recommended dishes include clams with ham, fried baby squid, and crayfish with onion. ● *Sun & Aug.* ▤	AE DC MC V	●			
OLD TOWN: *Egipte.* **Map 2 F2.** Ⓟ Carrer Jerusalem 3. [(93) 317 74 80. This lively place, once a monks' residence, serves Mediterranean specialties, and salt cod prepared in ten different ways. ▤	AE DC MC V		■	●	
OLD TOWN: *Les Quinze Nits.* **Map 5 A3.** Ⓟ Plaça Reial 6. [(93) 317 30 75. Conveniently located, this attractive restaurant draws a young crowd and offers good Catalan dishes at reasonable prices. ▤ ⬛	AE DC MC V		■	●	■
OLD TOWN: *Romesco.* **Map 2 F3.** Ⓟ Carrer de Sant Pau 28. [(93) 318 93 81. A popular spot just off the Ramblas with home-style cooking, a lively atmosphere, and unbeatable prices. The house specialty is *frijoles* (a Cuban dish of rice, black beans, fried banana, and eggs). ● *Sun & Jul.*		●	■		
OLD TOWN: *Amaya.* **Map 5 A1.** ⓅⓅ Ramblas 24. [(93) 302 10 37. This classic, popular Basque-Catalan restaurant offers a good selection of tapas at the bar and half portions of many dishes that appear on the encyclopedic menu. Fantastic wine list. ▤	AE DC MC V	●	■	●	
OLD TOWN: *Can Culleretes.* **Map 5 A2.** ⓅⓅ Carrer Quintana 5. [(93) 317 64 85. The city's oldest restaurant, established in 1786, serves traditional Catalan dishes such as *pica pica de pescado* (a seafood medley). ● *Mon & Jul.* ▤ ⬛	AE DC MC V		■	●	
OLD TOWN: *Can Majó.* **Map 5 B5.** ⓅⓅ Carrer de l'Almirall Aixada 23. [(93) 221 54 55. This renowned seafood restaurant in Barceloneta serves great rice dishes such as a peeled shellfish paella, and *suquet* (a delicious hot fish and potato stew). Extensive wine list. ● *Mon.* ▤ ⬛	AE DC MC V		■	●	
OLD TOWN: *Los Caracoles.* **Map 5 A3.** ⓅⓅ Carrer Escudellers 14. [(93) 302 31 85. Bustling restaurant in the Barri Xinès (Chinese Quarter) serving simple dishes such as paella, suckling lamb, and chicken roasted on a spit. ▤	AE DC MC V	●			
OLD TOWN: *Fonda Senyor Parellada.* **Map 5 B3.** ⓅⓅ Carrer de la Argenteria 37. [(93) 310 50 94. With wooden benches, old chandeliers, and candlesticks on the tables, this atmospheric restaurant is a great choice for authentic, reasonably priced Catalan cuisine. ● *Sun.* ▤ ⬛	AE DC MC V			●	

OLD TOWN: *Reial Club Marítim de Barcelona*. **Map 5 A4.** ⓟⓟ | MC V
Moll d'Espanya. ⓒ *(93) 221 62 56.*
Classic nautical club restaurant with spectacular views of the port. The elaborate cuisine includes dishes such as eggplant terrine with goat cheese, and fish with apples and a cider sauce. ▤

OLD TOWN: *Casa Leopoldo*. **Map 2 F3.** ⓟⓟⓟ | AE DC V
Carrer de Sant Rafael 24. ⓒ *(93) 441 30 14.*
This delightful restaurant, set in old stables and a carriage house, has been in the family since 1929, and the menu, featuring good quality regional dishes, has altered little since then. Good service. ● *Mon & Aug.* ▤ ⓑ

OLD TOWN: *Llevataps*. **Map 5 B4.** ⓟⓟⓟ | AE DC MC V
Plaça Pau Vila. ⓒ *(93) 221 24 33.*
Overlooking the marina, this modern restaurant is decorated with corkscrews and offers seven different fixed-price menus. ▤ ⓑ

OLD TOWN: *Set Portes*. **Map 5 B3.** ⓟⓟⓟ | AE DC MC V
Passeig de Isabel II 14. ⓒ *(93) 319 29 50.*
This lavishly decorated restaurant is reminiscent of an elegant Parisian café. Specialties include eleven different types of paella, and delicious homemade cannelloni. Efficient service and a good wine list. ▤ ⓑ

OLD TOWN: *Talaia Mar*. **Map 6 E5.** ⓟⓟⓟⓟ | AE DC MC V
Anexo Torre Mapfre, Carrer de la Marina 16. ⓒ *(93) 221 90 90.*
This stunning, sleek, circular shaped restaurant, with views of the marina, offers extremely good food. The menu varies with the season. You can order half portions *(pica pica)* of most dishes. ▤ ⓑ

EIXAMPLE: *Roig Robí*. **Map 3 A2.** ⓟⓟⓟ | AE DC MC V
Carrer de Séneca 20. ⓒ *(93) 218 92 22.*
Small, intimate restaurant offering authentic Catalan cuisine, with a lovely interior courtyard for summer. The terrines, fresh salads, and any of the rice or seafood dishes are bound to please. ● *Sun.* ▤ ⓑ

EIXAMPLE: *El Tragaluz*. **Map 3 A3.** ⓟⓟⓟ | AE DC MC V
Passeig Concepció 5. ⓒ *(93) 487 06 21.*
Two different dining concepts are offered here: the second floor serves fast food, and the third has contemporary Mediterranean cuisine. The restaurant's logo is by graphic designer Javier Mariscal. ▤

EIXAMPLE: *La Venta*. ⓟⓟⓟ | AE DC MC V
Plaça Doctor Andreu. ⓒ *(93) 212 64 55.*
At the foot of Tibidabo is this attractive restaurant. The glass covered terraces are open in summer and provide a bright, greenhouse setting in winter, with views of the city. Catalan-French cuisine. ● *Sun.* ▤ ⓑ

FARTHER AFIELD (NORTHWEST): *Chicoa*. ⓟⓟ | AE MC V
Carrer d'Aribau 73. ⓒ *(93) 453 11 23.*
A haven for lovers of salt cod, with more than ten different preparations of the celebrated *bacallà*. As well as many other seafood and meat dishes, there is a good Penedès rosé house wine. ● *Sun & Aug.* ▤ ⓑ

FARTHER AFIELD (NORTHWEST): *Giardinetto Notte*. **Map 3 A2.** ⓟⓟ | AE DC MC V
Carrer Granada del Penedès 22. ⓒ *(93) 218 75 36.*
Mediterranean and Italian dishes are served in this romantic setting. Try the homemade pasta with a bottle of Catalan wine. ● *Sun & Aug.* ▤

FARTHER AFIELD (NORTHWEST): *Tiro Mimet*. ⓟⓟ | AE MC V
Carrer de Sant Marius 22. ⓒ *(93) 211 77 66.*
The cuisine here can best be described as Catalan-French. Hot and cold duck livers are served as well as a wide variety of mushrooms and game in season. Good selection of Catalan wines and *cavas*. ● *Sun & Aug.* ▤

FARTHER AFIELD (NORTHWEST): *La Balsa*. ⓟⓟⓟ | AE DC MC V
Carrer de Infanta Isabel 4. ⓒ *(93) 211 50 48.*
There are great views of Barcelona from the terrace of this restaurant. The Catalan cuisine includes an excellent goose liver as an appetizer. ● *Sun.*

FARTHER AFIELD (NORTHWEST): *Botafumeiro*. **Map 3 A2.** ⓟⓟⓟⓟ | AE DC MC V
Carrer Gran de Gràcia 81. ⓒ *(93) 218 42 30.*
Fine quality seafood and Galician specialties are served in this stylish restaurant. The shellfish dishes are served in generous portions, and the desserts are mouthwatering. Extensive wine list. ● *Aug.* ▤ ⓑ

For key to symbols see back flap

<table>
<tr><td>

Price categories for a three-course evening meal for one, including a half-bottle of house wine, tax, and service:

ℙ under 3,000 ptas
ℙℙ 3,000–4,500 ptas
ℙℙℙ 4,500–6,000 ptas
ℙℙℙℙ over 6,000 ptas

</td><td>

TAPAS BAR
In addition to the main dining room, there is a bar serving tapas (see p574–5) and raciones (larger portions).
FIXED-PRICE MENU
A good-value, fixed-price menu is offered at lunch, dinner, or both, usually with three courses.
GOOD WINE LIST
Denotes a wide range of good wines, or a more specialized selection of local wines.
OUTDOOR TABLES
Facilities for eating outdoors, on a terrace, or in a garden or courtyard, often with a good view.

</td></tr>
</table>

	CREDIT CARDS	TAPAS BAR	FIXED-PRICE MENU	GOOD WINE LIST	OUTDOOR TABLES
FARTHER AFIELD (NORTHWEST): *Jaume de Provença.* ℙℙℙ Carrer de Provença 88. ((93) 430 00 29. The bold and innovative chef's original and creative Catalan cuisine has established his restaurant as among the city's finest. Despite the business-like decor, the food is excellent and the service attentive. ● Mon & Aug. 🍽	AE DC MC V		■	●	
FARTHER AFIELD (WEST): *Peixerot.* Map 1 B1. ℙℙℙ Torre Catalunya, Carrera de Tarragona 177. ((93) 424 69 69. First-class seafood predominates on the menu of this comfortable, modern restaurant. Great rice dishes and shellfish. 🍽	AE DC MC V	●		●	
FARTHER AFIELD (WEST): *Neichel.* ℙℙℙℙ Beltrán i Rózpide 16. ((93) 203 84 08. European haute cuisine with Catalan touches is served in one of the city's most prestigious establishments. It has an excellent selection of cheese and over 300 wine labels. ● Sun & Aug. 🍽 &	AE DC MC V		■	●	
CATALONIA					
ANDORRA LA VELLA: *Borda Estevet.* ℙℙ Carretera de la Comella 2 (Andorra). ((07-376) 86 40 26. This old country house, decorated in rustic style, is still used for the traditional practice of drying tobacco from the nearby fields. Ask for the meat *a la llosa* (brought to you on a hot slate). 🍽 &	AE MC V			●	
ALTAFULLA: *Faristol.* ℙ Carrer de Sant Martí 5 (Tarragona). ((977) 65 00 77. Wine was once made in this delightful 18th-century house, now decorated with antiques. Try the the superb chocolate mousse. ● Oct–May: Mon–Thu.	DC MC V	●		●	■
ARENYS DE MAR: *Hispania.* ℙℙℙℙ Carrer Real 54, Carretera NII (Barcelona). ((93) 791 04 57. Authentic Catalan cuisine that has won accolades from near and far. The classic clam *suquet*, similar to a fricassee, and the *crema catalana* (a rich caramel custard) are both delicious. ● Tue & Oct. 🍽	AE DC MC V			●	
ARTIES: *Casa Irene.* ℙℙℙ Hotel Valarties, Calle Mayor 3 (Lleida). ((973) 64 43 64. Located in a picturesque village, this restaurant offers wonderful, French-influenced food and three *menús de degustación*. 🍽 &	AE DC MC V		■	●	
BERGA: *Sala.* ℙℙ Passeig de la Pau 27 (Barcelona). ((93) 821 11 85. Classic Catalan dishes are offered here, many of which feature mushrooms. Game is available in season. ● Mon. 🍽 &	AE DC MC V		■	●	
BLANES: *Can Patacano.* ℙℙ Passeig del Mar 12 (Girona). ((972) 33 00 02. Delightful family-run establishment serving good, affordable, fresh seafood and shellfish. Catalan specialties include the fish and potato *suquet*. 🍽 &	DC MC V		■	●	
BOLVIR DE CERDANYA: *Torre del Remei.* ℙℙℙℙ Camí Reial (Girona). ((972) 14 01 82. This stunning palace surrounded by gardens has been impeccably restored and now houses an elegant restaurant and hotel. The chef will delight you with his gourmet dishes and superb wine selection. 🍽	AE DC MC V		■	●	■
CALAFELL: *Giorgio.* ℙℙ Carrer Ángel Guimerá 4 (Tarragona). ((977) 69 11 59. Delicious Italian food with homemade pasta, bread, and desserts, served on a terrace overlooking the sea. The lasagne is legendary, but be sure to reserve, because there are only ten tables. &			■	●	■

CAMBRILS: *Joan Gatell-Casa Gatell.* ⓅⓅⓅ
Passeig Miramar 26, Cambrils Port (Tarragona). (*(977) 36 00 57.*
Seafood is the specialty of this establishment. The rice dishes, shellfish, and lobster casserole are all first class. ● *Mon & mid Dec–mid Jan.* 🗏 &

	AE			
	DC	■	●	■
	MC			
	V			

CASTELL-PLATJA D'ARO: *Joan Piqué.* ⓅⓅⓅ
Barri de Crota 3 (Girona). (*(972) 81 79 25.*
Lovely, 14th-century *masía* (farmhouse), decorated in keeping with the period, serving innovative cuisine of the Empordà region. The frogs' legs served with celery in a pesto sauce is one example. ● *Tue & Nov.* 🗏 &

	AE			
	DC	■	●	■
	MC			
	V			

FIGUERES: *Ampurdán.* ⓅⓅⓅ
Hotel Ampurdán, Carretera NII (Girona). (*(972) 50 05 62.*
Gourmets congregate here to enjoy Josep Mercader's legendary cuisine. The fresh broad beans with mint and the salt cod with a garlic mousseline are both exquisite. Delightful terrace for dining in the summer. 🗏 &

	AE			
	DC	■	●	■
	MC			
	V			

GIRONA: *El Celler de Can Roca.* ⓅⓅⓅ
Carretera Taialá 40. (*(972) 22 21 57.*
The capital's best restaurant, where Juan Roca creates imaginative dishes such as lamb stuffed with sweetbreads and cinnamon. ● *Sun.* 🗏 &

	AE			
	DC	■	●	
	MC			
	V			

LLEIDA: *Forn del Nastasi.* ⓅⓅ
Carrer Salmerón 10. (*(973) 23 45 10.*
Excellent regional cuisine including chargrilled vegetables *(escalivada)* and snails *a la llauna* (baked in the oven). ● *Mon.* 🗏 &

	AE			
	DC		●	
	MC			
	V			

LLORET DE MAR: *El Trull.* ⓅⓅⓅ
Ronda Europa, Cala Canyellas (Girona). (*(972) 36 49 28.*
Rustic dining room with marine motifs where you can choose your lobster from the aquarium and then watch it sizzle on the open grill. The *arrosat* (pasta prepared with seafood) is also a good choice. 🗏 &

	AE			
	DC	■	●	■
	MC			
	V			

MARTINET: *Boix.* ⓅⓅⓅ
Carretera N260 (Lleida). (*(973) 51 50 50.*
A famous Catalan restaurant, located on the banks of the Río Segre, serving roast leg of lamb so tender you can eat it with a spoon. ● *Tue.* 🗏

	AE			
	DC	■	●	■
	MC			
	V			

PERALADA: *Castell de Peralada.* ⓅⓅⓅ
Casino Castell de Peralada (Girona). (*(972) 53 81 25.*
Dine in the incomparable medieval setting of this castle and try any of the dishes of the Empordà region and the castle's own wine. 🗏

	AE			
	MC	■	●	■
	V			

REUS: *El Pa Torrat.* ⓅⓅ
Avinguda Reus 24, Castellvell del Camp (Tarragona). (*(977) 85 52 12.*
Good, regional home cooking with dishes such as roast rabbit with *alioli* (a garlic mayonnaise) and stuffed *calamares* (squid). ● *Tue.* 🗏 &

	AE			
	MC	■	●	
	V			

ROSES: *El Bulli.* ⓅⓅⓅⓅ
Cala Montjoi (Girona). (*(972) 15 04 57.*
Considered by many to be one of Spain's best restaurants and perhaps one of Europe's most beautiful, El Bulli is a must on any gourmet's itinerary. Expensive, but definitely worth the treat. ● *mid Oct–mid Mar.*

	AE			
	DC	■	●	■
	MC			
	V			

SANT CARLES DE LA RÀPITA: *Miami Can Pons.* ⓅⓅ
Avinguda Constitució 35 (Tarragona). (*(977) 74 05 51.*
Good quality Catalan cooking is served here by the Pons family. The *suquet* and the *crema catalana* are just two of the specialties. ● *Feb.* 🗏

	AE			
	DC	■	●	
	MC			
	V			

SANT CELONI: *El Racó de Can Fabes.* ⓅⓅⓅⓅ
Carrer de Sant Joan 6 (Barcelona). (*(93) 867 28 51.*
Santi Santamaría is considered one of Spain's best chefs, and this delightful country restaurant is a gastronomic paradise. The ever changing seasonal menu combines many kinds of fresh regional produce. ● *Mon.* 🗏 &

	AE			
	DC	■	●	
	MC			
	V			

SANT FELIÚ DE GUIXOLS: *Can Toni.* ⓅⓅ
Carrer Garrofers 54 (Girona). (*(972) 32 10 26.*
Enjoy traditional cooking of the Empordà region here. Many dishes include mushrooms when in season (September–March). ● *Tue.* 🗏 &

	AE	●		
	DC		■	●
	MC			
	V			

SANT SADURNI D'ANOIA: *El Mirador de les Caves.* ⓅⓅⓅ
Carretera Sant Sadurni–Ordal, Subirats (Barcelona). (*(93) 899 31 78.*
The duck with a foie gras and truffle sauce is one of the superb dishes served here. Guests can enjoy views over the Penedès vineyards. 🗏 &

	AE			
	DC	■	●	
	MC			
	V			

Price categories for a three-course evening meal for one, including a half-bottle of house wine, tax, and service:

℗ under 3,000 ptas
℗℗ 3,000–4,500 ptas
℗℗℗ 4,500–6,000 ptas
℗℗℗℗ over 6,000 ptas

TAPAS BAR
In addition to the main dining room, there is a bar serving tapas *(see p574–5)* and *raciones* (larger portions).
FIXED-PRICE MENU
A good-value, fixed-price menu is offered at lunch, dinner, or both, usually with three courses.
GOOD WINE LIST
Denotes a wide range of good wines, or a more specialized selection of local wines.
OUTDOOR TABLES
Facilities for eating outdoors, on a terrace, or in a garden or courtyard, often with a good view.

		CREDIT CARDS	TAPAS BAR	FIXED-PRICE MENU	GOOD WINE LIST	OUTDOOR TABLES
LA SEU D'URGELL: *El Castell.* Carretera N260 (Lleida). (*(973) 35 07 04.* At the foot of Seu d'Urgell castle, surrounded by beautiful countryside, lies this idyllic hotel-restaurant serving modern Catalan cuisine. The wine list will delight even sophisticated wine lovers. ● *mid Jan–mid Feb.* 目 ら	℗℗℗	AE DC MC V		■	●	
SITGES: *EL Velero.* Passeig de la Ribera 38 (Barcelona). (*(93) 894 20 51.* A seaside restaurant whose creations include sole fillets on a bed of mushrooms and crab sauce, and lobster with a chickpea sauce. 目 ら	℗℗	AE DC MC V		■		
TARRAGONA: *El Merlot.* Carrer Caballers 6. (*(977) 22 06 52.* Situated in the old part of town, this restaurant serves Mediterranean cuisine based on first-class local produce. Specialties include game dishes (available in season) and homemade desserts. ● *Mon & Feb.* 目	℗℗℗	DC MC V		■	●	■
VALLS: *Masía Bou.* Carretera Lleida (Tarragona). (*(977) 60 04 27.* Many interesting dishes are on the menu. The specialty is *calçotadas* (onions charred over embers, served with *romesco* sauce). ● *Tue.* 目 ら	℗℗	AE DC MC V	●	■	●	■
VIC: *Floriac.* Carretera Manresa–Vic, Collsuspina (Barcelona). (*(93) 887 09 91.* A 16th-century *masía* (farmhouse) surrounded by woods, serving regional cuisine. The game dishes, available in winter, are excellent. ● *Tue.*	℗℗	AE MC V	●	■	●	
VILAFRANCA DEL PENEDÈS: *Airolo.* Rambla Nostra Senyora 10 (Barcelona). (*(93) 892 17 98.* Over 250 varieties of Penedès wine accompany the seasonal menu that includes duck served with *millefeuille* and eggplant. ● *Mon & Aug.* 目 ら	℗℗℗	AE DC MC V		■	●	

ARAGÓN

		CREDIT CARDS	TAPAS BAR	FIXED-PRICE MENU	GOOD WINE LIST	OUTDOOR TABLES
AINSA: *Bodegas del Sobrarbe.* Plaza Mayor 2 (Huesca). (*(974) 50 02 37.* Get a taste of medieval history in the vaulted wine cellar of this 11th-century house. Typical Pyrenean dishes include game and *ternasco* (tender suckling lamb roasted on a wood fire). ● *mid Dec–mid Mar.*	℗℗	AE DC MC V		■	●	
ALCAÑIZ: *Meseguer.* Avenida del Maestrazgo 9 (Teruel). (*(978) 83 10 02.* Popular for its updated home cooking at reasonable prices, Félix Meseguer's menu includes a delicious vegetable stew (*menestra*), and white beans with partridge. Good local wines. ● *Sun.* 目 ら	℗℗	AE DC MC V	●	■		
BARBASTRO: *Flor.* Calle Goya 3 (Huesca). (*(974) 31 10 56.* Seasonal menu with fresh produce from the fertile Vero valley and an excellent wine cellar. The baked hake with garlic and the salad of tomato, fresh cheese, and local black olives are recommended. 目 ら	℗℗	AE DC MC V		■		
BIESCAS: *Casa Ruba.* Calle Esperanza 18–20 (Huesca). (*(974) 48 50 01.* The Ruba family has been serving traditional Aragonese dishes here since 1884. This delightful mountain hotel offers game dishes in season and delicious mushroom and vegetable savory pies. ● *Oct–Nov.* 目 ら	℗℗	V	●	■		
BORJA: *La Bóveda del Mercado.* Plaza del Mercado 4 (Zaragoza). (*(976) 86 82 51.* Carefully restored 16th-century wine cellar where you can enjoy original dishes using Jewish and Arab recipes as a base. The *delicias de sartén* (fried pastry with anise and cinnamon) is one example. ● *Mon & Feb.*	℗	MC V			●	

CANTAVIEJA: *Buj.*   ℙℙ
Avenida del Maestrazgo 6 (Teruel). 📞 *(964) 18 50 33.*
A simple, family-run restaurant by the roadside. The stuffed potatoes and
mushroom soup are always on the menu due to popular demand.
Game dishes are available in season. Open for lunch only. ● *Feb.* &

CARIÑENA: *La Rebotica.*   ℙ
Calle San José 3 (Zaragoza). 📞 *(976) 62 05 56.*
Try any of the 58 varieties of local Cariñena wine available in this
converted village pharmacy. Most of the recipes are elaborated with
wine, such as the suckling pig sirloin in a white wine sauce. ● *Mon.*

ESQUEDAS: *Venta del Sotón.*   ℙℙ
Carretera Tarragona–San Sebastián (Huesca). 📞 *(974) 27 02 41.*
This wayside inn is one of Aragón's leading restaurants, with a creative
cuisine including local specialties and excellent grilled dishes. ● *Mon.* 📋

HUESCA: *Las Torres.*   ℙℙℙ
Calle María Auxiliadora 3. 📞 *(974) 22 82 13.*
The Abadía brothers offer an interesting seasonal menu with innovative
flourishes. The crisp grouper served on a bed of pig's feet, with a
raisin and pine nut sauce, should give you an idea. ● *Sun.* 📋 &

LA IGLESUELA DEL CID: *Casa Amada.*   ℙ
Calle Fuente Nueva 10 (Teruel). 📞 *(964) 44 33 73.*
Straightforward regional cooking, a simple setting, and affordable prices
ensure a steady crowd. Try the walnut crème caramel for dessert. 📋 &

JACA: *La Cocina Aragonesa.*   ℙℙ
Calle Cervantes 5 (Huesca). 📞 *(974) 36 10 50.*
One of the best restaurants in the area, serving elaborate regional cuisine.
In winter, the partridge stuffed with foie gras or the wild boar meatballs
can be enjoyed around the fireplace. ● *Wed.* 📋

NUÉVALOS: *Reyes de Aragón.*   ℙ
Hotel Monasterio de Piedra (Zaragoza). 📞 *(976) 84 90 11.*
Typical Aragonese cuisine is offered in this 12th-century monastery
set in a beautiful nature preserve. The trout, fresh from the monastery's
own fish farm, served with a ham and almond sauce, is delicious. 📋 &

RUBIELOS DE MORA: *Portal del Carmén.*   ℙℙ
Calle Glorieta 2 (Teruel). 📞 *(978) 80 41 53.*
A former Carmelite monastery with a delightful cloister, specializing in
regional food. The salmon and trout are from the nearby fish farms and
the *tocinillo de cielo* (a candied egg yolk dessert) is heavenly. ● *Thu.* &

SENEGÜÉ: *Casbas.*   ℙ
Carretera a Francia (Huesca). 📞 *(974) 48 01 49.*
A restaurant with a large wood fire where skiers and hikers congregate
for a hearty meal. The typical mountain dessert of aged wine with sliced
peaches is a very popular choice. ● *Sep.* 📋 &

TERUEL: *La Menta.*   ℙℙ
Calle Bartolomé Esteban 10. 📞 *(978) 60 75 32.*
One of the best restaurants in the area, offering an original menu with
Basque and Catalan influences. The delicious *pastel ruso* – a traditional
cake from Aragón – is made with egg yolks and almonds. ● *Sun.* 📋 &

UNCASTILLO: *Casa Sierra.*   ℙℙ
Calle Mediavilla 71 (Zaragoza). 📞 *(976) 67 94 81.*
Simple yet tasty regional dishes, such as dried white beans with olive
oil, and *migas a la pastora* (breadcrumbs with grapes). ● *Dec–Feb.*

ZARAGOZA: *La Rinconada de Lorenzo.*   ℙℙ
Calle la Salle 3. 📞 *(976) 55 51 08.*
Typical Aragonese cuisine is served here, such as *migas con jamón*
(breadcrumbs with ham) and *ternasco al horno* (roast lamb). The
homemade desserts include *higos con nueces* (figs with nuts). 📋 &

ZARAGOZA: *Gayarre.*   ℙℙℙ
Carretera del Aeropuerto. 📞 *(976) 34 43 86.*
Lovely house with a pretty garden, just outside the city. The menu is
seasonal with an emphasis on regional vegetables such as borage, which
are used in a variety of salads. Good service and wine list. ● *Mon.* 📋 &

	CREDIT CARDS			
Cantavieja				●
Cariñena	MC V		■	●
Esquedas	AE DC MC V	●		● ■
Huesca	AE DC MC V		■	●
La Iglesuela del Cid	AE MC V		■	
Jaca	AE MC V		■	●
Nuévalos	AE DC MC V		■	●
Rubielos de Mora	AE DC MC V		■	● ■
Senegüé	AE DC MC V	●		●
Teruel	AE DC MC V			●
Uncastillo	DC MC V		■	●
Zaragoza (La Rinconada)	AE DC MC V	●		●
Zaragoza (Gayarre)	AE DC MC V		■	●

Price categories for a three-course evening meal for one, including a half-bottle of house wine, tax, and service:

Ⓟ under 3,000 ptas
ⓟⓟ 3,000–4,500 ptas
ⓟⓟⓟ 4,500–6,000 ptas
ⓟⓟⓟⓟ over 6,000 ptas

TAPAS BAR
In addition to the main dining room, there is a bar serving tapas (see p574–5) and raciones (larger portions).
FIXED-PRICE MENU
A good-value, fixed-price menu is offered at lunch, dinner, or both, usually with three courses.
GOOD WINE LIST
Denotes a wide range of good wines, or a more specialized selection of local wines.
OUTDOOR TABLES
Facilities for eating outdoors, on a terrace, or in a garden or courtyard, often with a good view.

	Credit Cards	Tapas Bar	Fixed-Price Menu	Good Wine List	Outdoor Tables
ZARAGOZA: *La Venta del Cachirulo.* ⓟⓟⓟ Autovía de Logroño (Zaragoza). 【 (976) 33 16 74. A large, elegantly decorated Aragonese house. The beef cutlet is brought to you on a bed of glowing salt embers allowing you to grill it to perfection. There is a wide variety of vegetable dishes. 🍽 ♿	AE DC MC V			●	

VALENCIA AND MURCIA

	Credit Cards	Tapas Bar	Fixed-Price Menu	Good Wine List	Outdoor Tables
ALICANTE (ALACANT): *Dársena.* ⓟⓟ Paseo del Puerto. 【 (96) 520 75 89. With 50 different rice dishes on the menu, you might be hard pressed to choose. The generous portions are served in individual paella pans. 🍽	AE DC MC V		■	●	■
ALICANTE (ALACANT): *Delfín.* ⓟⓟ Explanada de España 12. 【 (96) 521 49 11. Overlooking the harbor, the Delfín offers formal and informal dining areas, both serving imaginative Mediterranean cuisine. Try one of the rice dishes or the sea bass in a puff pastry crust with a lobster mousse. 🍽 ♿	AE DC MC V		■	●	
ALTEA: *Raco de Toni.* ⓟⓟ Calle de la Mar 127 (Alicante). 【 (96) 584 17 63. Regional food including rice dishes and locally caught fish is served in this simple, cozy restaurant. The rice with salt cod and vegetables and the anchovies stuffed with peppers are two of the specialties. ● Nov. 🍽 ♿	AE DC MC V	●	■	●	
BENIDORM: *La Palmera-Casa Paco Nadal.* ⓟ Avenida Penetración, Rincón de Loix (Alicante). 【 (96) 585 32 82. Agreeable place just outside Benidorm offering regional specialties. Of the 15 rice dishes, the rice with monkfish and clams is especially good. 🍽 ♿	AE DC MC V		■	●	■
BENIDORM: *El Molino.* ⓟⓟ Carretera Alicante–Valencia (Alicante). 【 (96) 585 71 81. Thousands of wine bottles decorate this restaurant, where chef Ivan serves traditional fare including *nayuscas* (grilled crêpes filled with ham and caviar). ● Mon & mid Feb–mid March. 🍽 ♿	AE DC MC V			●	■
BENIMANTELL: *L'Obrer.* ⓟ Carretera de Alcoi 27 (Alicante). 【 (96) 588 50 88. A rustic-style restaurant, decorated with locally made ceramics. Enjoy roast lamb, followed by one of the homemade desserts. ● Fri & Jul. 🍽 ♿	AE MC V			●	
BENISSANO: *Levante.* ⓟⓟ Calle Virgen del Fundamento 15 (Valencia). 【 (96) 278 07 21. You can't leave Valencia without trying the excellent paellas here, cooked over a wood fire. One of the region's largest and best wine cellars is also at your disposal. Open for lunch only. ● Tue & mid Jul–mid Aug. 🍽 ♿	AE MC V			●	
BUÑOL: *Venta L'Home.* ⓟⓟ Carretera NIII Madrid–Valencia, Ventamina exit (Valencia). 【 (96) 250 35 15. A 17th-century coaching inn now housing a delightful restaurant decorated with rustic touches. Great Valencian cuisine such as rabbit with honey or lamb with olives. Good local wines. 🍽 ♿	AE DC MC V	●	■	●	
CASTELL DE GUADALEST: *Venta la Montaña.* ⓟ Carretera de Alcoi 9, Benimantell (Alicante). 【 (96) 588 51 41. A picturesque mountain inn decorated with antique farming implements where wholesome dishes, such as the typical *olleta de trigo* (a broth made with pork, vegetables, and wheat), are served. ● Mon. 🍽 ♿	AE DC MC V		■	●	
CASTELLÓ DE LA PLANA: *La Tasca del Puerto.* ⓟⓟⓟ Avenida del Puerto 13, El Grao (Castellón). 【 (964) 28 44 81. Specialties include rice dishes, *fideuà* (noodles), and *calderetas* (fish casseroles). There are good views of the harbor and sea. ● Mon. 🍽 ♿	AE DC MC V		■	●	■

COCENTAINA: *L'Escaleta.*
Avenida País Valenciano 119 (Alicante). (96) 559 21 00.
This basement restaurant, tastefully decorated with tiles and old brass
items, serves imaginative dishes such as fillets of sole with *cava*. Excellent
desserts – try the minted pears with honey ice cream. ● *Mon.* ▤ ♿

ⓅⓅ	AE DC MC V		■	●		

CULLERA: *Casa Salvador.*
L'Estany de Cullera (Valencia). (96) 172 01 36.
Sited on a pretty inlet of a lake *(estany)*, this restaurant in two cottages
serves 20 different rice dishes and fish specialties. Some of the fish are
caught in the lake, and the vegetables are home-grown. ▤ ♿

ⓅⓅ	AE DC MC V	●	■	●	■	

ELX: *Mesón El Granaíno.*
Calle José María Buch 40 (Alicante). (96) 546 01 47.
The bar is very popular, offering more than 30 different tapas. The
dining room, decorated in traditional Andalusian style, serves regional and
southern dishes. The wine cellar contains over 5,000 bottles. ● *Sun.* ▤

ⓅⓅ	AE DC MC V	●	■	●		

FORCALL: *Mesón de la Vila.*
Plaza Mayor 8 (Castellón). (964) 17 11 25.
Enjoy affordable regional dishes in the vaulted basement of this
15th-century building, which was once the town hall. Try the rabbit,
served with either truffles or white snails from the region. ▤

Ⓟ	AE DC MC V	●	■	●		

GANDIA: *Gamba.*
Carretera Nazaret–Oliva, Gandía-Playa (Valencia). (96) 284 13 10.
Although you can't see the sea, the fish and shellfish are fresh from
the fishermen's nets. The set menu *(menú dirigido)* offers shellfish
and a rice or pasta dish. Open for lunch only. ● *Mon & Nov.* ▤ ♿

ⓅⓅⓅ	AE DC MC V		■	●	■	

MORAIRA: *Girasol.*
Carretera Moraira–Calp (Alicante). (96) 574 43 73.
Joachim Koerper's innovative Mediterranean cuisine has won over
gourmets throughout Europe and is perfectly complemented by the
refined decoration of this seaside villa. ● *Mon & Feb.* ▤ ♿

ⓅⓅⓅⓅ	AE DC MC V		■	●	■	

MORELLA: *Casa Roque.*
Calle Segura Barreda 8 (Castellón). (964) 16 03 36.
Diners come from near and far to savor Roque Gutiérrez's famous lamb
stuffed with truffles. Or try the duck with red wine and bitter orange
essence, and the mushrooms served with truffles. ● *Mon & Feb.*

ⓅⓅ	AE DC MC V		■	●		

MURCIA: *Las Cocinas del Cardenal.*
Plaza del Cardenal Belluga 7. (968) 21 13 10.
In this restaurant you can opt for the fixed-price menu with a great
variety of dishes, or enjoy excellent tapas at the bar. ● *Mon.* ▤

ⓅⓅ	AE MC V	●	■	●	■	

MURCIA: *Hispano.*
Calle Arquitecto Cerdán 7. (968) 21 61 52.
Regional cooking, including *caldero marinero del Mar Menor* (a typical
seafood casserole). The vegetable paella and the gilthead (fish) cooked
in salt are also delicious. Good selection of regional wines. ▤ ♿

ⓅⓅⓅ	AE DC MC V	●	■	●		

ORIHUELA: *Casa Corro.*
Palmeral de San Antón (Alicante). (96) 530 29 63.
A popular family-run establishment serving typical dishes such as *arroz
con costra* (baked rice with a crust) and a hearty stew with meatballs. ▤

Ⓟ	MC V	●	■	●		

POLOP DE LA MARINA: *Ca l'Angeles.*
Calle Gabriel Miró 35 (Alicante). (96) 587 02 26.
Eat in one of three dining rooms, with wooden beams and rustic decor.
Dishes include roast baby kid with almonds. ● *Tue & mid Jun–mid Jul.* ▤ ♿

ⓅⓅ	MC V		■	●		

SANTA POLA: *Batiste.*
Avenida Pérez Ojeda 6, Playa de Poniente (Alicante). (96) 541 14 85.
Reasonably priced seafood and shellfish, as well as delicious rices, such as
arroz a banda (fish risotto), are featured on the menu of this classic
restaurant. The sea bass in puff pastry is also a specialty. ▤ ♿

ⓅⓅ	AE DC MC V		■	●	■	

TORREVIEJA: *Cabo Roig.*
Urbanización Cabo Roig, Playas de Orihuela (Alicante). (96) 676 02 90.
Perched on top of the cliff with magnificent views of the Costa Blanca,
Cabo Roig offers a great variety of seafood and rice dishes. The ancient
watchtower houses a collection of over 20,000 bottles of wine.

ⓅⓅⓅ	AE DC MC V		■	●	■	

		CREDIT CARDS	TAPAS BAR	FIXED-PRICE MENU	GOOD WINE LIST	OUTDOOR TABLES

Price categories for a three-course evening meal for one, including a half-bottle of house wine, tax, and service:

ℙ under 3,000 ptas
ℙℙ 3,000–4,500 ptas
ℙℙℙ 4,500–6,000 ptas
ℙℙℙℙ over 6,000 ptas

TAPAS BAR
In addition to the main dining room, there is a bar serving tapas *(see p574–5)* and *raciones* (larger portions).
FIXED-PRICE MENU
A good-value, fixed-price menu is offered at lunch, dinner, or both, usually with three courses.
GOOD WINE LIST
Denotes a wide range of good wines, or a more specialized selection of local wines.
OUTDOOR TABLES
Facilities for eating outdoors, on a terrace, or in a garden or courtyard, often with a good view.

VALENCIA: *La Rosa.* ℙℙ
Avenida del Neptuno 70. ☏ *(96) 371 20 76.*
Typical beachside restaurant with around 30 different rice dishes and a good assortment of fresh fish and shellfish. Open for lunch only. 📋 ♿

CREDIT CARDS	TAPAS BAR	FIXED-PRICE MENU	GOOD WINE LIST	OUTDOOR TABLES
AE MC V			●	▪

VALENCIA: *Albacar.* ℙℙℙ
Calle Sorní 35. ☏ *(96) 395 10 05.*
Enjoy innovative cuisine in attractive surroundings. Try the warm salad of fish with tarragon vinaigrette, and finish with the excellent homemade apple *millefeuille* with ice cream. ● *Sun & mid Aug–mid Sep.*

CREDIT CARDS	TAPAS BAR	FIXED-PRICE MENU	GOOD WINE LIST	OUTDOOR TABLES
AE DC MC V			●	

VINARÒS: *El Langostino de Oro.* ℙℙℙ
Calle San Francisco 31. ☏ *(964) 45 12 04.*
Carefully selected seafood menu, including seafood *suquet*. The rice dishes and the *fideus rosetjats* (specially prepared noodles) are also very popular, and the homemade date tart, excellent. ● *Mon.* 📋 ♿

CREDIT CARDS	TAPAS BAR	FIXED-PRICE MENU	GOOD WINE LIST	OUTDOOR TABLES
AE DC MC V		▪	●	

MADRID

OLD MADRID: *La Bola Taberna.* **Map 2 D2.** ℙ
Calle de la Bola 1. ☏ *(91) 547 69 30.*
A true bastion of the *cocido madrileño*, this restaurant dates back to 1870. Since then, little has changed in the preparation of the hearty stew, made with chickpeas and sausage and served at lunch only. ● *Sun.* 📋 ♿

CREDIT CARDS	TAPAS BAR	FIXED-PRICE MENU	GOOD WINE LIST	OUTDOOR TABLES
		▪	●	

OLD MADRID: *Casa Patas.* **Map 5 A2.** ℙ
Calle Cañizares 10. ☏ *(91) 369 04 96.*
Known for its flamenco shows in the evening, Casa Patas is also an original place to eat in the heart of Old Madrid. Well-stocked tapas bar and unbeatable fixed-price menu. ● *Sun & Aug.* 📋 ♿

CREDIT CARDS	TAPAS BAR	FIXED-PRICE MENU	GOOD WINE LIST	OUTDOOR TABLES
AE DC MC V	●	▪	●	

OLD MADRID: *Casa Ciriaco.* **Map 1 C4.** ℙℙ
Calle Mayor 84. ☏ *(91) 548 06 20.*
A traditional tavern near the Royal Palace, renowned for its *gallina en pepitoria* (a chicken stew with eggs and saffron). ● *Wed & Aug.* 📋 ♿

CREDIT CARDS	TAPAS BAR	FIXED-PRICE MENU	GOOD WINE LIST	OUTDOOR TABLES
DC MC V	●	▪	●	

OLD MADRID: *Botín.* **Map 2 E4.** ℙℙℙ
Calle de Cuchilleros 17. ☏ *(91) 366 42 17.*
Reputedly the oldest restaurant in the world, dating back to 1725. The original wood-burning oven is still used to cook the traditional Castilian roast lamb and suckling pig. Reasonable fixed-price menu. 📋

CREDIT CARDS	TAPAS BAR	FIXED-PRICE MENU	GOOD WINE LIST	OUTDOOR TABLES
AE DC MC V		▪	●	

OLD MADRID: *Lhardy.* **Map 2 F3.** ℙℙℙℙ
Carrera de San Jerónimo 8. ☏ *(91) 521 33 85.*
Established in 1839 and conserving its true character with chandeliers, mirrors, and dark wood paneled walls, this restaurant serves what is is arguably the most classic *cocido madrileño*. 📋

CREDIT CARDS	TAPAS BAR	FIXED-PRICE MENU	GOOD WINE LIST	OUTDOOR TABLES
AE DC MC V	●	▪	●	

BOURBON MADRID: *Champagnería Gala.* **Map 5 B2.** ℙ
Calle Moratín 22. ☏ *(91) 429 25 62.*
Admire the indoor patio and chandeliers and enjoy a generous set menu with Catalan specialties at an unbelievably reasonable price. ● *Aug.* 📋

CREDIT CARDS	TAPAS BAR	FIXED-PRICE MENU	GOOD WINE LIST	OUTDOOR TABLES
	●	▪		▪

BOURBON MADRID: *Hylogui.* **Map 5 A1.** ℙ
Calle Ventura de la Vega 3. ☏ *(91) 429 73 57.*
This traditional restaurant attracts families for Sunday lunch. The long menu includes typical dishes such as *callos a la madrileña* (tripe in a spicy tomato sauce). Service is efficient. ● *Aug.* 📋 ♿

CREDIT CARDS	TAPAS BAR	FIXED-PRICE MENU	GOOD WINE LIST	OUTDOOR TABLES
AE MC V	●	▪	●	

BOURBON MADRID: *Teatriz.* **Map 4 E3.** ℙℙ
Calle Hermosilla 15. ☏ *(91) 577 53 79.*
A restaurant in the stalls of an old theater, with a cocktail bar on the stage. Italian-inspired food, such as a salmon and sole *carpaccio*. ● *Aug.* 📋 ♿

CREDIT CARDS	TAPAS BAR	FIXED-PRICE MENU	GOOD WINE LIST	OUTDOOR TABLES
AE DC MC V	●	▪	●	

BOURBON MADRID: *Al Mounia*. Map 4 D4. ⓅⓅⓅ
Calle de Recoletos 5. ☎ *(91) 435 08 28.*
Madrid's finest Moroccan restaurant serving authentic couscous and *tajine*
(lamb stew). If you have room, there is the rich house dessert, made with
honey, almonds, and orange blossom water. ● *Sun, Mon & Aug.* ▤ ♿

	AE		▦	●	
	DC				
	MC				
	V				

BOURBON MADRID: *Alkalde*. Map 4 E3. ⓅⓅⓅ
Calle Jorge Juan 10. ☎ *(91) 576 33 59.*
Call ahead for Basque specialties in the dining room or at the lively tapas bar.
The spider crab soup, the *chipirones* (small squid cooked in its ink), and
the clams in a white wine, onion, and garlic sauce are all good. ● *Aug.* ▤

	AE	●			
	DC				
	MC				
	V				

BOURBON MADRID: *La Giralda*. Map 4 E4. ⓅⓅⓅ
Calle Claudio Coello 24. ☎ *(91) 576 40 69.*
Andalusian cuisine is served in a restaurant decorated in Moorish style.
Try the *pescado frito* (an assortment of fried fish) or any grilled fish. ▤ ♿

	AE	●	▦	●	
	DC				
	MC				
	V				

BOURBON MADRID: *Paradis*. Map 5 B1. ⓅⓅⓅ
Calle Marqués de Cubas 14. ☎ *(91) 429 73 03.*
Part of a successful Catalan chain, offering high quality Mediterranean
cuisine. The grilled vegetables and the rice dishes make delicious appetizers;
they can be followed by any of the fresh fish. ● *Sun & Aug.* ▤ ♿

	AE	●			
	DC				
	MC				
	V				

BOURBON MADRID: *El Amparo*. Map 4 E4. ⓅⓅⓅⓅ
Callejón de Puigcerdá 8. ☎ *(91) 431 64 56.*
New Basque cuisine in what many consider to be Madrid's nicest setting,
with a skylight that lets you gaze up at the stars. The tuna mousse with
lobster and parsley oil is just one creation. ● *Sun & Aug.* ▤

	AE			●	
	MC				
	V				

BOURBON MADRID: *Viridiana*. Map 6 D1. ⓅⓅⓅⓅ
Calle Juan de Mena 14. ☎ *(91) 523 44 78.*
Innovative Spanish cuisine complemented by an encyclopedic wine list
is offered in this restaurant decorated with stills from Luis Buñuel's film
Viridiana. The creative menu changes frequently. ● *Sun & Aug.* ▤

	AE			●	
	V				

FARTHER AFIELD (EAST): *La Taberna de la Daniela*. ⓅⓅ
Calle General Pardiñas 21. ☎ *(91) 575 23 29.*
A short but well-chosen menu is offered at this restaurant. The only thing
served for lunch is *cocido madrileño*, or you can choose from a wide
range of tapas at the bar. Good homemade desserts. ● *Aug.* ▤

	V	●			

FARTHER AFIELD (NORTH): *Casa Ricardo*. Ⓟ
Calle Fernando El Católico 31. ☎ *(91) 447 61 19.*
This typical Spanish bar offers good, home-style dishes. The oxtail
soup is delicious, as are the baby squid prepared in their own ink. ▤ ♿

	MC			●	
	V				

FARTHER AFIELD (NORTH): *La Barraca*. Map 3 A5. ⓅⓅ
Calle de la Reina 29. ☎ *(91) 532 71 54.*
Over ten different Valencia-style rice dishes and paellas are offered here,
made with first class ingredients. Good homemade desserts. ▤

	AE		▦	●	
	DC				
	MC				
	V				

FARTHER AFIELD (NORTH): *El Puchero*. Map 3 A2. ⓅⓅ
Calle de Larra 13. ☎ *(91) 445 05 77.*
Popular, unfussy restaurant offering hearty, home-style cooking. The baby
broad beans with ham, the roast suckling pig, and the game stews are
legendary, as are the cantankerous waitresses. ● *Sun & Aug.* ▤

	AE			●	
	MC				
	V				

FARTHER AFIELD (NORTH): *Goizeko Kabi*. ⓅⓅⓅⓅ
Calle Comandante Zorita 37. ☎ *(91) 533 01 85.*
Traditional Basque cuisine served in a refined setting. Excellent fresh
produce and seafood are the basis of the chef's creations. Good wine
list and delectable desserts. ● *Sun.* ▤ ♿

	AE			●	
	DC				
	MC				
	V				

FARTHER AFIELD (NORTH): *Jockey*. Map 4 D2. ⓅⓅⓅⓅ
Calle Amador de los Ríos 6. ☎ *(91) 319 10 03.*
Among Madrid's top five restaurants, frequented by gourmets and
celebrities, Jockey offers a seasonal menu. Excellent poultry and game
dishes and a superb wine list. Proper attire only. ● *Sun & Aug.* ▤ ♿

	AE			●	
	DC				
	MC				
	V				

FARTHER AFIELD (NORTH): *Zalacaín*. ⓅⓅⓅⓅ
Calle Álvarez de Baena 4. ☎ *(91) 561 48 40.*
Considered to be Madrid's finest restaurant, Zalacaín lives up to its
reputation with a luxurious setting, attentive service, and above all
delicious Basque-oriented cuisine. Proper attire only. ● *Sun & Aug.* ▤ ♿

	AE		▦	●	▦
	DC				
	MC				
	V				

For key to symbols see back flap

Price categories for a three-course evening meal for one, including a half-bottle of house wine, tax, and service:

Ⓟ under 3,000 ptas
ⓅⓅ 3,000–4,500 ptas
ⓅⓅⓅ 4,500–6,000 ptas
ⓅⓅⓅⓅ over 6,000 ptas

TAPAS BAR
In addition to the main dining room, there is a bar serving tapas *(see p574–5)* and *raciones* (larger portions).
FIXED-PRICE MENU
A good-value, fixed-price menu is offered at lunch, dinner, or both, usually with three courses.
GOOD WINE LIST
Denotes a wide range of good wines, or a more specialized selection of local wines.
OUTDOOR TABLES
Facilities for eating outdoors, on a terrace, or in a garden or courtyard, often with a good view.

	CREDIT CARDS	TAPAS BAR	FIXED-PRICE MENU	GOOD WINE LIST	OUTDOOR TABLES
FARTHER AFIELD (NORTHEAST): *Sacha.* ⓅⓅⓅ Calle Juan Hurtado de Mendoza 11. 【 (91) 345 59 52. Decorated like a cozy bistro, this restaurant serves specialties such as partridge with rice and mushrooms. ● *Sun & Aug.* 🍴 ⅙	AE DC MC V			●	■
FARTHER AFIELD (NORTHEAST): *Cabo Mayor.* ⓅⓅⓅⓅ Calle Juan Ramón Jiménez 37. 【 (91) 350 87 76. One of Madrid's finest seafood restaurants with Cantabrian-Navarrese cuisine. Try the delicious fresh pasta and shrimp salad or the monkfish with mushrooms. Excellent wines and desserts. ● *Sun.* 🍴	AE DC MC V	●	■	●	■
FARTHER AFIELD (NORTHEAST): *El Olivo.* ⓅⓅⓅⓅ Calle General Gallegos 1. 【 (91) 359 15 35. Top of the line Mediterranean cuisine, with olive oil as the underlying culinary theme. The owner will advise you on which of the 40 different olive oils will best accompany your meal. ● *Sun & Mon.* 🍴	AE DC MC V		■	●	
FARTHER AFIELD (SOUTHWEST): *Malacatín.* **Map 2 E5.** Ⓟ Calle de la Ruda 5. 【 (91) 365 52 41. This old bar in the center of the Rastro has only one item on the menu: *cocido madrileño.* It has to be ordered a day in advance, and is served in three separate stages. The price includes wine and dessert. ● *Sun.* 🍴		●	■		
FARTHER AFIELD (SOUTHWEST): *Casa Lucio.* **Map 2 D5.** ⓅⓅⓅ Calle Cava Baja 35. 【 (91) 365 32 52. This historic tavern serves Castilian specialties. The fried eggs with potatoes are exquisite and the rice pudding renowned. ● *Aug.* 🍴	AE DC MC V	●		●	
FARTHER AFIELD (SOUTHWEST): *Gure-Etxea.* **Map 1 C4.** ⓅⓅⓅ Plaza de la Paja 12. 【 (91) 365 61 49. Quality Basque cooking in a vaulted dining room. The *piperrada,* made with scrambled eggs, red peppers, green beans, and ham, goes well with the sharp white Basque wine, *txacoli.* ● *Sun & Aug.* 🍴 ⅙	AE DC MC V		■	●	
MADRID PROVINCE					
ARANJUEZ: *Casa Pablo.* ⓅⓅ Calle Almíbar 42. 【 (91) 891 14 51. A centrally located tavern offering solid home cooking. Try the pheasant with grapes or the fresh asparagus and strawberries. ● *Aug.* 🍴 ⅙	AE MC V	●	■	●	
CHINCHÓN: *Mesón de la Virreina.* ⓅⓅ Plaza Mayor 28. 【 (91) 894 00 15. Traditional Castilian food, including *sopa castellana* (a garlic soup with chickpeas) and classic roast lamb, is prepared in this 16th-century building. The local *anís* makes an excellent *digestif.* 🍴 ⅙	AE DC V MC	●	■	●	■
MORALZARZAL: *El Cenador de Salvador.* ⓅⓅⓅⓅ Avenida de España 30. 【 (91) 857 77 22. Many gourmets make the trek from Madrid to Moralzarzal just for the pleasure of dining in this lovely chalet. The exquisite seasonal cooking is bound to delight even the most refined taste buds. ● *Mon.* 🍴 ⅙	AE DC MC V		■	●	■
PATONES DE ARRIBA: *El Poleo.* ⓅⓅⓅ Travesía del Arroyo 1–3. 【 (91) 843 21 01. This picturesque town with slate roofed houses boasts a wonderful restaurant offering Navarrese-style cuisine. Open Fri–Sun only. ● *Aug.* 🍴	AE DC MC V	●		●	■
SAN LORENZO DE EL ESCORIAL: *Taberna La Cueva.* ⓅⓅ Calle San Antón 4. 【 (91) 890 15 16. Juan de Villanueva, architect of the Prado, designed this 18th-century inn whose specialties include the *huevos a la cueva* (fried eggs and ham served in a nest of straw potatoes). ● *Mon.*		●	■	●	

CASTILLA Y LEÓN

ARANDA DE DUERO: *Mesón La Villa.*
Plaza Mayor 3 (Burgos). (947) 50 10 25.
High-quality regional cooking with a great variety of Castilian dishes,
such as pickled partridge, sweetbreads with mushrooms, and *menestra de
verduras* (vegetable stew). Impressive selection of local wines. ● Mon.

ARÉVALO: *Asador La Cubas.*
Calle Figones 9 (Ávila). (920) 30 01 25.
This converted wine cellar with clay casks embedded in the walls offers
delicious suckling lamb and pig roasted in the wood-burning oven, and
tasty regional desserts such as sweet custard fritters *(leche frita).*

ASTORGA: *La Peseta.*
Plaza de San Bartolomé 3 (León). (987) 61 72 75.
A family-run restaurant with a tradition for hearty, healthy cooking. Try
the rabbit and potato stew accompanied by a local Bierzo wine.

ÁVILA: *Mesón del Rastro.*
Plaza del Rastro 1. (920) 21 12 18.
Authentic regional dishes are offered in this truly Castilian restaurant
nestled in the city wall. The *Judías de El Barco de Ávila* (dried white
beans served in a thick sauce with chorizo) is an all-time favorite.

BURGOS: *Casa Ojeda.*
Calle Vitoria 5. (947) 20 90 52.
The city's most traditional restaurant serving classic dishes such as roast
suckling lamb and *morcilla* (a black blood sausage) with red peppers.
There is an extensive choice of Ribera del Duero and La Rioja wines.

COVARRUBIAS: *El Galín.*
Plaza de Doña Urraca 4 (Burgos). (947) 40 30 15.
The Galín is a simple, busy restaurant in the main square, preparing
succulent baby lamb and other hearty regional dishes such as *olla
podrida* (a thick, bean based broth). Good tapas bar. ● Tue & Sep.

FRÓMISTA: *Hostería de Los Palmeros.*
Plaza San Telmo 4 (Palencia). (979) 81 00 67.
This ancient inn on the Road to Santiago has been agreeably restored.
The menu offers good Castilian dishes including baby pigeon casserole
and *tocinillo de cielo* (sweet candied egg yolks) for dessert.

LA GRANJA DE SAN ILDEFONSO: *Hilaria.*
Carretera Valladolid–Madrid, Valsaín (Segovia). (921) 47 02 92.
The owners of this family-run restaurant still use an original recipe for
their white bean stew. Good roast suckling lamb and pig. ● Mon.

LEÓN: *Mesón Leonés del Racimo de Oro.*
Calle Caño Vadillo 2. (987) 25 75 75.
Enjoy traditional cooking in the stables of a 16th-century inn. In winter
there are game dishes and stews, such as the *cocido leonés* (a hearty broth
of chickpeas, potatoes, bacon, blood sausage, and cabbage). ● Tue.

MEDINACELI: *Las Llaves.*
Plaza Mayor 13 (Soria). (975) 32 63 51.
A small, cozy restaurant decorated with antiques, in the center of windy
Medinaceli. The lentil stew with curry and the oven-cooked veal stew
are just two of the specialties. ● Mon & mid Jan–mid Feb.

PALENCIA: *Casa Damián.*
Calle Ignacio Martínez de Azcoitia 9. (979) 74 46 28.
A reliable restaurant with provincial specialties including a fresh *menestra
de verduras* and delicious *buñuelos* (sweet fritters). ● Mon & Aug.

PEDRAZA DE LA SIERRA: *Hostería Pintor Zuloaga.*
Calle Matadero 1 (Segovia). (921) 50 98 35.
Located in a former Inquisition house, this restaurant serves traditional
Castilian fare such as roast pork, lamb, and hearty stews. ● Tue.

PONFERRADA: *Azul-Montearenas.*
Carretera NVI Madrid–A Coruña (León). (987) 41 70 12.
Simple, home-style cooking is prepared in this restaurant with mountain
views. Try the chard filled with shrimp and monkfish.

For key to symbols see back flap

Price categories for a three-course evening meal for one, including a half-bottle of house wine, tax, and service:

℗ under 3,000 ptas
℗℗ 3,000–4,500 ptas
℗℗℗ 4,500–6,000 ptas
℗℗℗℗ over 6,000 ptas

TAPAS BAR
In addition to the main dining room, there is a bar serving tapas *(see p574–5)* and *raciones* (larger portions).
FIXED-PRICE MENU
A good-value, fixed-price menu is offered at lunch, dinner, or both, usually with three courses.
GOOD WINE LIST
Denotes a wide range of good wines, or a more specialized selection of local wines.
OUTDOOR TABLES
Facilities for eating outdoors, on a terrace, or in a garden or courtyard, often with a good view.

		CREDIT CARDS	TAPAS BAR	FIXED-PRICE MENU	GOOD WINE LIST	OUTDOOR TABLES
QUINTANA DE RANEROS: *Bodega El Cercao.* Calle de la Bodega 4, Finca El Cercao (León). 【 *(987) 28 01 28.* This huge 17th-century wine cellar is one long maze of underground passages and rustic dining rooms. Enjoy any of the traditional dishes, such as *morcilla* (blood sausage) with locally grown red Bierzo peppers.	℗℗	AE DC MC V	●	■	●	■
SALAMANCA: *Río de la Plata.* Plaza del Peso 1. 【 *(923) 21 90 05.* A tiny, popular restaurant next to the Plaza Mayor, serving a great variety of fresh fish and Castilian dishes, all of superb quality. ◗ *Mon & Jul.* ▤	℗℗℗	AE MC V	●	■		
SANTA MARÍA DE MAVE: *Hostería El Convento.* Santa María de Mave (Palencia). 【 *(979) 12 36 11.* This ancient Benedictine monastery on the banks of the Río Pisuerga now houses an inn serving traditional Castilian fare, including lamb roasted in a wood-burning oven and *sopa castellana* (a rich garlic soup). 🛦	℗℗	AE MC V	●	■		■
SANTO DOMINGO DE SILOS: *Casa Emeterio.* Hotel Tres Coronas de Silos, Plaza Mayor 6 (Burgos). 【 *(947) 39 00 47.* After admiring the monastery you can relax in the rustic dining room of this large, 18th-century house and enjoy good, regional cooking. 🛦	℗℗	AE MC V	●	■	●	
SEGOVIA: *Mesón de Cándido.* Plaza del Azoguejo 5. 【 *(921) 42 81 03.* Don't leave town without visiting Mesón de Cándido, *the* place to eat in Segovia. The restaurant has good views of the Roman aqueduct and serves local specialties such as roast lamb and suckling pig. ▤ 🛦	℗℗	AE DC MC V	●		●	■
SEPÚLVEDA: *Cristóbal.* Calle Conde de Sepúlveda 9 (Segovia). 【 *(921) 54 01 00.* Enjoy impressive views of the Duratón gorges as you dine on traditional hearty stews and, reputedly, the best roast lamb in the region. ◗ *Tue.* ▤	℗℗	AE DC MC V	●	■	●	
TORDESILLAS: *El Torreón.* Calle Dimas Rodríguez 11 (Valladolid). 【 *(983) 77 01 23.* Specializing in first class grilled meats, El Torreón has a reproduction of the Convento de Santa Clara's beautiful ceiling. Reservations advised. ▤	℗℗℗	AE DC MC V			●	
TORO: *Casa Lorenzo.* Puerta del Mercado 21 (Zamora). 【 *(980) 69 11 53.* Typical Zamoran dishes, including peppers stuffed with cod, and baked asparagus with smoked salmon. Try the potent local wine. ◗ *Sep.* ▤ 🛦	℗℗	AE DC MC V	●	■		
TORRECABALLEROS: *El Rancho de la Aldegüela.* Carretera N110 (Segovia). 【 *(921) 40 10 46.* A country house with rustic decor serving regional specialties such as *revuelto de morcilla* (scrambled eggs with blood sausage). ◗ *Mon.*	℗℗	AE DC V	●	■	●	■
VALLADOLID: *La Fragua.* Paseo de Zorrilla 10. 【 *(983) 33 87 85.* The rich garlic soup, lamb casserole with white wine and spring vegetables, and the veal stew are all proof that this is a truly Castilian restaurant. Fish is a specialty too. Great tapas bar. ◗ *Mon & Aug.* ▤ 🛦	℗℗℗	AE DC MC V	●		●	■
VILLAFRANCA DEL BIERZO: *La Charola.* Carretera NVI Madrid–A Coruña (León). 【 *(987) 54 00 95.* A family-run restaurant by the side of the road, serving generous portions of regional dishes. Simple, reliable, and inexpensive. ▤ 🛦	℗	AE DC MC V	●	■	●	
ZAMORA: *Pizarro.* Cuesta de Pizarro 7. 【 *(980) 53 45 45.* Once used as an Inquisition palace, this 16th-century building serves regional and Basque specialties such as sole with anchovy sauce. 🛦	℗℗	AE MC V		■	●	■

CASTILLA-LA MANCHA

ALBACETE: *Nuestro Bar.* ⓅⓅ
Calle Alcalde Conangla 102. ☎ *(967) 22 72 15.*
The dining room serves regional dishes and a *menú de degustación* which includes specialties of La Mancha such as *gazpacho manchego* (a rich game stew thickened with biscuits). Great tapas bar. ● *Jul.* 目
AE DC MC V

ALMAGRO: *El Corregidor.* ⓅⓅ
Calle Jerónimo Ceballos 2 (Ciudad Real). ☎ *(926) 86 06 48.*
This delightful old house, with many dining rooms and a central patio, is one of Castilla-La Mancha's prettiest restaurants. Creative, regional cuisine including the town's specialty, pickled eggplant. ● *Mon.* 目
AE DC MC V

ALMANSA: *Mesón de Picelín.* ⓅⓅ
Calle Norias 10 (Albacete). ☎ *(967) 34 00 07.*
Considered by many to be one of the region's best restaurants. You can try authentic regional dishes including their famous *gazpacho manchego* made with chicken, rabbit, and partridge. ● *Mon & Aug.* 目 ♿
AE DC MC V

BETETA: *Hotel Los Tilos.* Ⓟ
Extrarradio (Cuenca). ☎ *(969) 31 80 98.*
A simple, unfussy hotel restaurant serving typical mountain dishes, such as onion soup, venison stew, and *morteruelo* (a mixed game pâté). ♿
AE MC V

BRIHUEGA: *Asador El Tolmo.* ⓅⓅ
Avenida de la Constitución 26 (Guadalajara). ☎ *(949) 28 04 76.*
The traditional Castilian decor is in keeping with the cuisine, which includes roast kid, beans with partridge, and homemade desserts. 目 ♿
MC V

CIUDAD REAL: *Gran Mesón.* ⓅⓅ
Ronda de Ciruela 34. ☎ *(926) 22 72 39.*
Ample fixed menu with regional specialties such as *gachas* (gruel), *pisto* (a vegetable mix), suckling pig, and local cheese and wines. 目 ♿
AE MC V

CUENCA: *Marlo.* ⓅⓅ
Calle Colón 59. ☎ *(969) 21 11 73.*
Fish and shellfish feature predominantly on the modern menu here, and there are also good meat dishes. Try the stuffed partridge, the fillet steak in a cheese sauce, or the eggplant and cheese pie. 目
AE MC V

CUENCA: *Mesón Casas Colgadas.* ⓅⓅⓅ
Calle Canónigos. ☎ *(969) 22 35 09.*
Dine above the gorge in one of Cuenca's famous hanging houses *(see p367).* Great views and great regional cuisine, including game dishes, make this an experience not to miss. 目
AE DC MC V

GUADALAJARA: *Minaya.* ⓅⓅ
Calle Mayor 23. ☎ *(949) 21 22 53.*
A wonderful 16th-century palace with period furniture. The short seasonal menu has an emphasis on grilled meats and roast kid. ● *Sun.* 目
AE MC V

GUADALAJARA: *Amparito Roca.* ⓅⓅⓅ
Calle de Toledo 19. ☎ *(949) 21 46 39.*
This pleasantly decorated house offers traditional Spanish cuisine with innovative touches. The venison sirloin served in a mushroom sauce and the scrambled eggs with potato and salmon are examples. ● *Sun.* 目 ♿
MC V

JADRAQUE: *El Castillo.* ⓅⓅ
Carretera de Soria (Guadalajara). ☎ *(949) 89 02 54.*
After visiting the castle, stop here for delicious roast kid or any of the other classic Castilian dishes prepared in this typical *mesón* (inn).
AE DC MC V

MANZANARES: *Mesón Sancho.* Ⓟ
Calle Jesús del Perdón 26 (Ciudad Real). ☎ *(926) 61 10 16.*
This simple, down-to-earth restaurant serves typical, robust dishes such as garlic soup, *duelos y quebrantos* (scrambled eggs with pork), and rabbit *a la manchega* (in a sauce), washed down with local wine. 目 ♿
AE MC V

LAS PEDROÑERAS: *Las Rejas.* ⓅⓅⓅ
Avenida de Brazil (Cuenca). ☎ *(967) 16 10 89.*
Spain's garlic capital also has a first class restaurant with an appetizing seasonal menu and an unforgettable garlic soup. Many dishes feature regional produce. Try the fresh *manchego* cheese salad. ● *Mon.* 目 ♿
AE DC MC V

<table>
<tr><td colspan="2">
Price categories for a three-course evening meal for one, including a half-bottle of house wine, tax, and service:

₧ under 3,000 ptas
₧₧ 3,000–4,500 ptas
₧₧₧ 4,500–6,000 ptas
₧₧₧₧ over 6,000 ptas
</td></tr>
</table>

		CREDIT CARDS	TAPAS BAR	FIXED-PRICE MENU	GOOD WINE LIST	OUTDOOR TABLES

TAPAS BAR
In addition to the main dining room, there is a bar serving tapas *(see p574–5)* and *raciones* (larger portions).
FIXED-PRICE MENU
A good-value, fixed-price menu is offered at lunch, dinner, or both, usually with three courses.
GOOD WINE LIST
Denotes a wide range of good wines, or a more specialized selection of local wines.
OUTDOOR TABLES
Facilities for eating outdoors, on a terrace, or in a garden or courtyard, often with a good view.

		CREDIT CARDS	TAPAS BAR	FIXED-PRICE MENU	GOOD WINE LIST	OUTDOOR TABLES
PUERTO LÁPICE: *Venta del Quijote.* ₧₧ Autovía de Andalucía (Ciudad Real). ▐ *(926) 57 61 10.* Set in the heart of Don Quixote territory, this legendary inn evokes Cervantes' masterpiece. Sit around the pebbled courtyard and enjoy any of the Manchegan specialties or have tapas at the bar. ⬥	AE DC MC V	●	■	●	■
SIGÜENZA: *El Motor.* ₧ Avenida Juan Carlos (Guadalajara). ▐ *(949) 39 08 27.* As well as the typical roast suckling pig and lamb you can also try the fried breadcrumbs *(migas)*, or the garlic soup *(sopa castellana)*. ▤ ⬥	AE MC V	●	■	●	
TALAVERA DE LA REINA: *Antonio.* ₧ Avenida de Portugal 8 (Toledo). ▐ *(925) 80 40 17.* A bar serving good quality tapas at reasonable prices and a dining room offering great regional food make this place very popular. ▤ ⬥	AE DC MC V	●	■	●	
TOLEDO: *Hostal del Cardenal.* ₧₧ Paseo de Recaredo 24. ▐ *(925) 22 08 62.* Once the summer residence of Cardinal Lorenzana, this 18th-century palace retains its beautiful garden, enclosed by the city walls. It serves garlic soup, suckling pig, and the famous Toledo *mazapán* (marzipan). ▤	AE DC MC V		■	■	■
TOLEDO: *La Lumbre.* ₧₧ Calle Real de Arrabal 3. ▐ *(925) 22 03 73.* A lovely old house with wooden beams, next to the Puerta de Bisagra. The meat dishes, such as roast suckling pig and lamb, are especially good, and there is delicious *manchego* cheesecake for dessert. ● *Sun.* ▤	AE MC V		■	●	
TOLEDO: *Adolfo.* ₧₧₧ Calle de Granada 6. ▐ *(925) 22 73 21.* Set in the heart of Toledo's Jewish quarter, the Adolfo, with its tiles, columns, antiques, and a wonderful 15th-century Mudéjar coffered ceiling, serves game in winter and fresh trout from the Río Tajo. ▤ ⬥	AE DC MC V	●	■	●	
TRAGACETE: *El Gamo.* ₧ Plaza de los Caídos 2 (Cuenca). ▐ *(969) 28 90 08.* This mountain inn has a simple, family run restaurant where you can try home-style cooking, such as venison stew and *morteruelo.* ⬥	MC V		■		■
VALDEPEÑAS: *Baviera.* ₧ Calle 6 de Junio 30 (Ciudad Real). ▐ *(926) 32 40 84.* A centrally located restaurant serving authentic cuisine of La Mancha. The *galianos* (a typical dish made with game) and the mountain rabbit with garlic are two specialties. Good selection of Valdepeñas wines. ● *Tue.* ▤	AE DC MC V	●	■	●	
VILLALBA DE LA SIERRA: *Nelia.* ₧₧ Ruta de la Ciudad Encantada (Cuenca). ▐ *(969) 28 10 21.* A wood and stone restaurant on the banks of the Río Júcar. The wild boar meatballs, the marinated venison, and the vegetables in puff pastry are all superb. Good Valdepeñas wines. ● *Wed & mid Jan–mid Feb.* ▤ ⬥	AE MC V	●	■	●	■

EXTREMADURA

		CREDIT CARDS	TAPAS BAR	FIXED-PRICE MENU	GOOD WINE LIST	OUTDOOR TABLES
ALMENDRALEJO: *Nando.* ₧ Calle Ricardo Romero 12 (Badajoz). ▐ *(924) 66 12 71.* The dining room serves generous portions of rice with rabbit, *judiones* (locally grown beans prepared with pig's knuckle or partridge), and fresh fish. Good tapas bar for trying local specialties. ● *Sun.* ▤	AE MC V	●	■		
BADAJOZ: *Los Gabrieles.* ₧ Calle Vicente Barrantes 21. ▐ *(924) 22 00 01.* Regional cooking including roast lamb and *revuelto mixto*, composed of scrambled eggs, mushrooms, shrimp, and white truffles. ▤ ⬥	AE DC MC V	●	■		

BADAJOZ: *Aldebarán.*
Avenida de Elvas, Urbanización Guadiana. 【 (924) 27 42 61.
One of Badajoz province's finer restaurants, with elaborate cuisine in an elegant setting. Creations include the pickled Iberian pork salad, ravioli filled with mushrooms and liver, and pigeon in wine sauce. ● *Sun.* 🍽 ⓑ

	AE		■	●	
	DC				
	MC				
	V				

CÁCERES: *El Figón de Eustaquio.*
Plaza de San Juan 12–14. 【 (927) 24 81 94.
Simple restaurant in the historic part of town where you can sample genuine Extremaduran cooking such as trout *a la extremeña* (stuffed with ham) and the house soup of tomato with poached egg. 🍽 ⓑ

	AE		■	●	
	DC				
	MC				
	V				

CÁCERES: *Atrio.*
Avenida de España 30. 【 (927) 24 29 28.
Innovative, contemporary cuisine offset by elegant decor in Cáceres' most sophisticated restaurant. The tender venison fillets served with muscat grapes and pears is just one of the chef's creative combinations. ⓑ

	DC		■	●	
	V				

GUADALUPE: *Hospedería del Real Monasterio.*
Plaza de Juan Carlos 1 (Cáceres). 【 (927) 36 70 00.
Owned by the Franciscan order, this restaurant offers simple regional cooking. The tomato soup, the roast kid, and the *migas extremeñas* (breadcrumbs with pork) are all recommended. ● *mid Jan–mid Feb.* 🍽

	MC		■	●	■
	V				

GUADALUPE: *Mesón El Cordero.*
Calle Alfonso Onceno 27 (Cáceres). 【 (927) 36 71 31.
Regional specialties are served in the cozy wood paneled dining room. Enjoy the fresh vegetable *menestra* (stew) or the partridge casserole as you admire the view of the mountains. ● *Mon & mid Sep–mid Oct.* 🍽 ⓑ

	AE		■		
	MC				
	V				

JARANDILLA DE LA VERA: *Cueva de Puta Parió.*
Calle Francisco Pizarro 8 (Cáceres). 【 (927) 56 03 92.
A lively and popular tavern with good regional dishes including tomato soup and lamb casserole, and locally produced house wine. ● *Mon.* 🍽

	AE	●			
	DC				
	MC				
	V				

JEREZ DE LOS CABALLEROS: *La Ermita.*
Calle Doctor Benítez 9 (Badajoz). 【 (924) 73 14 76.
This 17th-century chapel converted into a wine cellar now houses a restaurant serving local dishes. Sample the partridge stew or the typical *revuelto de espárragos* (made with scrambled eggs and asparagus tips). ⓑ

	V	●			■

LOSAR DE LA VERA: *Carlos V.*
Avenida de Extremadura 45 (Cáceres). 【 (927) 57 06 36.
Home cooking and lovely views of the mountains and the Tiétar valley. The *revuelto con criadillas de tierra* (scrambled eggs with white truffles), the roast kid, and the steaks are all house specialties. 🍽 ⓑ

	AE	●	■	●	
	MC				
	V				

MÉRIDA: *Nicolás.*
Calle Félix Valverde Lillo 13 (Badajoz). 【 (924) 31 96 10.
You might want to visit the small brick wine cellar for an apéritif before digging into the regional specialties such as the delicious lamb with plums or the pork sirloin with peppers. Pretty garden and terrace. 🍽

	AE	●		●	
	DC				
	MC				
	V				

MÉRIDA: *Parador de Mérida.*
Plaza de la Constitución 3 (Badajoz). 【 (924) 31 38 00.
This lovely old convent now houses a parador and a restaurant well worth a visit. Savor regional specialties such as Extremaduran cheeses, cold meats, and the *caldereta de cordero* (lamb casserole). 🍽 ⓑ

	AE	●	■	●	■
	DC				
	MC				
	V				

PLASENCIA: *Alfonso VIII.*
Avenida Alfonso VIII 32 (Cáceres). 【 (927) 41 02 50.
Creative cuisine, relying heavily on local produce and updated traditional recipes. Try the kid stew or the Iberian ham. 🍽 ⓑ

	AE		■	●	
	DC				
	MC				
	V				

PLASENCIA: *El Rincón Extremeño.*
Calle Vidrieras 8 (Cáceres). 【 (927) 41 11 50.
Traditional Plasencian dishes including frogs in *salsa verde*, lizard (in season), and more "usual" fare such as suckling pig. Be sure to try the raspberry, cheese, and honey dessert called *Tío Pichu.* 🍽 ⓑ

	AE	●	■		
	DC				
	MC				
	V				

PUEBLA DE LA REINA: *Mesón La Jara-Casa Andrés.*
Calle Luis Chamizo 14 (Badajoz). 【 (924) 36 00 05.
This charming *mesón* has become a sanctuary of authentic regional food. Those with stamina can try the 14-course meal. ● *Mon.* 🍽

	DC	●	■	●	■
	MC				
	V				

For key to symbols see back flap

<table>
<tr><td colspan="2">

Price categories for a three-course evening meal for one, including a half-bottle of house wine, tax, and service:

Ⓟ under 3,000 ptas
ⓅⓅ 3,000–4,500 ptas
ⓅⓅⓅ 4,500–6,000 ptas
ⓅⓅⓅⓅ over 6,000 ptas

</td></tr>
</table>

TAPAS BAR
In addition to the main dining room, there is a bar serving tapas *(see p574–5)* and *raciones* (larger portions).
FIXED-PRICE MENU
A good-value, fixed-price menu is offered at lunch, dinner, or both, usually with three courses.
GOOD WINE LIST
Denotes a wide range of good wines, or a more specialized selection of local wines.
OUTDOOR TABLES
Facilities for eating outdoors, on a terrace, or in a garden or courtyard, often with a good view.

	CREDIT CARDS	TAPAS BAR	FIXED-PRICE MENU	GOOD WINE LIST	OUTDOOR TABLES
TRUJILLO: *Mesón La Troya.* Ⓟ Plaza Mayor 10 (Cáceres). 【 *(927) 32 13 64.* A typical *mesón* dating back to the 16th century, serving regional food in hearty portions. The *migas* (breadcrumbs) with pork, the dried white beans in sauce, and the lamb in its own juice are all recommended. ▤	V	●	■	●	■
TRUJILLO: *Pizarro.* ⓅⓅ Plaza Mayor 13 (Cáceres). 【 *(927) 32 02 55.* The decor in this restaurant has changed little since it opened before the Spanish Civil War. Enjoy traditional dishes such as tomato soup with figs and grapes, and chicken stuffed with truffles. ● *Tue.* ▤	MC V		■	●	
ZAFRA: *Barbacana.* ⓅⓅ Hotel Huerta Honda, Avenida López Asme 30 (Badajoz). 【 *(924) 55 41 00.* This 16th-century house, finely decorated with antiques, provides a lovely backdrop for good regional and Basque cuisine, including roast suckling lamb with rosemary, and fillet of hake with clams. ● *Mon.* ▤	MC V		■	●	
SEVILLE					
EL ARENAL: *Bodegón Torre del Oro.* **Map 3 B2.** ⓅⓅ Calle Santander 15. 【 *(95) 422 08 80.* This combined bar and dining room specializes in *raciones*. Try the *garbanzos con espinacas* (chickpeas with spinach), *puntillitas* (tiny grilled cuttlefish), or the *punta de solomillo* (fillet tip). ⚵	AE DC MC V	●	■		■
EL ARENAL: *Enrique Becerra.* **Map 3 B1.** ⓅⓅ Calle Gamazo 2. 【 *(95) 421 30 49.* This plush restaurant-bar attracts well-heeled customers for aperitifs and meals. Besides a fine selection of fish and meat dishes, the daily specials feature Andalusian home-style cooking. ● *Sun.* ▤	AE DC MC V	●	■	●	
EL ARENAL: *El Burladero.* **Map 3 B1.** ⓅⓅⓅ Hotel Colón, Calle Canalejas 1. 【 *(95) 422 29 00.* Decorated with bullfighting memorabilia, this restaurant offers caviar and filet mignon as well as local dishes such as *puchero* (meat-in-a-pot). ▤ ⚵	AE DC MC V	●	■		
EL ARENAL: *La Isla.* **Map 3 B2.** ⓅⓅⓅ Calle Arfe 25. 【 *(95) 421 26 31.* An attractive, centrally located restaurant featuring superb seafood: turbot, bream, and delicacies such as *percebes* (sea barnacles). ● *Mon & Aug.* ▤	AE DC MC V	●		●	
SANTA CRUZ: *Las Meninas.* **Map 3 D1.** Ⓟ Calle Santo Tomás 3. 【 *(95) 422 62 26.* Hearty food and good prices make this a popular place. A variety of excellent local dishes, such as braised bull's tail, chowder of chickpeas and cod, and gazpacho may be on the menu. ▤	AE DC MC V	●	■	●	■
SANTA CRUZ: *Casa Robles.* **Map 3 C1.** ⓅⓅ Calle Álvarez Quintero 58. 【 *(95) 456 32 72.* Right in the heart of Seville, this lively place has three small dining rooms. Fish is a specialty – fried, baked, or with rice – and there is an excellent choice of fresh shellfish. Good meat dishes and tapas. ▤	AE DC MC V	●	■	●	■
SANTA CRUZ: *Corral del Agua.* **Map 3 C2.** ⓅⓅ Callejón del Agua 6. 【 *(95) 422 48 41.* Dine on the cool patio in a lee of the Reales Alcázares gardens. The menu emphasizes seasonal specialties, carefully prepared and served. ● *Sun.*	AE DC MC V		■		■
SANTA CRUZ: *Hostería del Laurel.* **Map 3 C2.** ⓅⓅ Plaza de los Venerables 5. 【 *(95) 422 02 95.* Rustic decoration, with wooden barrels and colorful wall tiles. Try local specialties: *serrano* ham and *tortilla de patatas* (potato omelette). ▤ ⚵	AE DC MC V	●	■	●	■

SANTA CRUZ: *Mesón Don Raimundo.* **Map 3 C1.** 	(P)(P) AE DC MC V
Calle Argote de Molina 26. 【 *(95) 422 33 55.*
This restaurant is set in a 17th-century convent and decorated with ceramics and tapestries. Traditional Andalusian cuisine, based on game from the marshes of the Guadalquivir, as well as seafood dishes. 🍴 ♿

SANTA CRUZ: *La Albahaca.* **Map 3 D2.** 	(P)(P)(P) AE DC MC V
Plaza de Santa Cruz 12. 【 *(95) 422 07 14.*
This 1920s mansion furnished with 17th-century antiques makes a fine setting to enjoy good Basque-influenced food. ● Sun. 🍴 ♿

SANTA CRUZ: *Egaña Oriza.* **Map 3 C3.** 	(P)(P)(P)(P) AE DC MC V
Calle San Fernando 41. 【 *(95) 422 72 11.*
Tucked against the walls of the Alcázar gardens is this stylish place. Fish is a specialty, and both the meat dishes and desserts are superb. ● Sun. 🍴

FARTHER AFIELD (WEST): *Río Grande.* **Map 3 B3.** 	(P)(P) AE DC MC V
Calle Betis. 【 *(95) 427 83 71.*
Terrific location, where you can enjoy the gazpacho or the *rabo de toro* (braised bull's tail) on a terrace overlooking the Guadalquivir. 🍴 ♿

FARTHER AFIELD (WEST): *Ox's.* **Map 3 C3.** 	(P)(P)(P) AE DC MC V
Calle Betis 61. 【 *(95) 427 62 75.*
A small and intimate *asador* (grill room) specializing in grilled meats. Clams with artichokes and *angulas* (tiny baby eels) are specialties. 🍴 ♿

ANDALUSIA

ALJARAQUE: *Las Candelas.* 	(P)(P) AE DC MC V
Carretera Huelva–Punta Umbria (Huelva). 【 *(959) 31 84 33.*
An attractive restaurant with a rustic dining room serving fine local seafood and excellent meat dishes. ● Sun. 🍴

ALMERÍA: *Rincón de Juan Pedro.* 	(P) AE DC MC V
Calle Federico Castro 2. 【 *(950) 23 58 19.*
Andalusian meat and seafood specialties, and local dishes such as *trigo a la cortijera* (a stew with wheat berries, meat, and sausage). ● Mon. 🍴 ♿

ALMERÍA: *Bellavista.* 	(P)(P) AE DC MC V
Calle Llanos del Alquián. 【 *(950) 29 71 56.*
This restaurant outside the city offers top quality fish and shellfish prepared in various ways. It is also a good place to try baby kid. 🍴

ALMERÍA: *Club de Mar.* 	(P)(P) AE DC MC V
Calle Muelle 1. 【 *(950) 23 50 48.*
Enjoy fresh fish and shellfish right on the seafront. The *bullabesa* (Spanish bouillabaisse) and *fritura* (mixed fried fish) are specialties. 🍴

ALMUÑÉCAR: *Playa Cotobro.* 	(P)(P) MC V
Calle Bajada del Mar 1 (Granada). 【 *(958) 63 18 02.*
The food here has a French touch, with specialties such as pastry with shrimp and leeks, and anglerfish gratin with spinach. ● Mon.

ANTEQUERA: *La Espuela.* 	(P) AE DC MC V
Plaza de Toros (Málaga). 【 *(95) 270 26 76.*
Uniquely situated in a bullring, this restaurant prepares Andalusian dishes including the town specialty, *porra* (a thick gazpacho). ♿

BAEZA: *Juanito.* 	(P)(P) V
Avenida Arca del Agua (Jaén). 【 *(953) 74 00 40.*
Right in the heart of the olive belt, Juanito offers a selection of olive oils to accompany your meal. Specialties include spinach casserole. 🍴

BAEZA: *Andrés de Vandelvira.* 	(P)(P)(P) AE DC MC V
Calle San Francisco 14 (Jaén). 【 *(953) 74 81 30.*
Located in a 16th-century monastery built by Andrés de Vandelvira, Jaén's Renaissance architect, this restaurant serves typical regional food: *cardos* (cardoons, a type of artichoke) in a cream sauce, and partridge salad. 🍴

LOS BARRIOS: *Mesón El Copo.* 	(P)(P)(P) AE DC MC V
Calle Almadraba 2, Palmones (Cádiz). 【 *(956) 67 77 10.*
Dine on superb seafood, from fried anchovies to lobster and sea bass. Order a few shellfish dishes *para picar* (to share as a starter) and follow with the *dorada al horno* (bream casserole with potatoes). ● Sun. 🍴

<table>
<tr><td colspan="2">

Price categories for a three-course evening meal for one, including a half-bottle of house wine, tax, and service:

Ⓟ under 3,000 ptas
ⓅⓅ 3,000–4,500 ptas
ⓅⓅⓅ 4,500–6,000 ptas
ⓅⓅⓅⓅ over 6,000 ptas

</td><td colspan="5">

TAPAS BAR
In addition to the main dining room, there is a bar serving tapas (see p574–5) and raciones (larger portions).
FIXED-PRICE MENU
A good-value, fixed-price menu is offered at lunch, dinner, or both, usually with three courses.
GOOD WINE LIST
Denotes a wide range of good wines, or a more specialized selection of local wines.
OUTDOOR TABLES
Facilities for eating outdoors, on a terrace, or in a garden or courtyard, often with a good view.

</td></tr>
<tr>
<th colspan="2"></th>
<th>CREDIT CARDS</th>
<th>TAPAS BAR</th>
<th>FIXED-PRICE MENU</th>
<th>GOOD WINE LIST</th>
<th>OUTDOOR TABLES</th>
</tr>

<tr><td colspan="2">

BAILÉN: *Zodíaco.*   ⓅⓅ
Carretera Madrid–Cádiz (Jaén). 【 (953) 67 10 58.
Cold soups, such as *ajo blanco* (white garlic) with almonds, feature on the menu in summer. Other specialties include the *revuelto* (scrambled eggs with ham, asparagus, shrimp, and young eels) and partridge. 🍴 ♿

</td><td>AE
DC
MC
V</td><td></td><td>■</td><td></td><td></td></tr>

<tr><td colspan="2">

BUBIÓN: *Villa Turística de Bubión.*   Ⓟ
Calle Barrio Alto (Granada). 【 (958) 76 31 11.
This restaurant in the Alpujarras serves typical mountain food such as *plato alpujarreño* (potatoes with eggs, sausage, ham, and pork loin). 🍴 ♿

</td><td>AE
DC
MC
V</td><td></td><td>■</td><td></td><td>■</td></tr>

<tr><td colspan="2">

CÁDIZ: *La Costera.*   ⓅⓅ
Calle Doctor Fleming 8. 【 (956) 27 34 88.
Fish dominates the menu at this restaurant, but the meat dishes are also good. You can order tapas at the bar or on the lovely terrace. 🍴 ♿

</td><td>AE
DC
MC
V</td><td>●</td><td></td><td>●</td><td>■</td></tr>

<tr><td colspan="2">

CÁDIZ: *Ventorillo del Chato.*   ⓅⓅ
Carretera Cádiz–San Fernando. 【 (956) 25 00 25.
This old rustic inn offers seafood, venison, and a stew of the day such as *berza* (vegetable and sausage) or *menudo* (tripe). ● Sun. 🍴 ♿

</td><td>AE
DC
MC
V</td><td></td><td>■</td><td>●</td><td></td></tr>

<tr><td colspan="2">

CÁDIZ: *El Faro.*   ⓅⓅⓅ
Calle San Félix 15. 【 (956) 21 10 68.
Classic restaurant with a warm atmosphere. The menu, a superb blend of modern and traditional dishes, changes daily but always features local seafood, as in the *tortillitas de camarones* (fritters of tiny shrimp). 🍴 ♿

</td><td>AE
DC
MC
V</td><td>●</td><td>■</td><td>●</td><td></td></tr>

<tr><td colspan="2">

CÓRDOBA: *Federación de Peñas.*   Ⓟ
Calle Conde y Luque 8. 【 (957) 47 54 27.
Inexpensive local food. Try the *rabo de toro* (braised bull's tail), a house specialty, or the *cardos* (cardoons) with clams. ● mid Jan–mid Feb. ♿

</td><td>MC
V</td><td>●</td><td>■</td><td></td><td>■</td></tr>

<tr><td colspan="2">

CÓRDOBA: *Almudaina.*   ⓅⓅ
Jardines de los Santos Mártires 1. 【 (957) 47 43 42.
Once the palace of Bishop Leopold of Austria, this mansion serves typical dishes from the Sierra Morena, including venison and boar. 🍴

</td><td>AE
DC
MC
V</td><td></td><td>■</td><td>●</td><td></td></tr>

<tr><td colspan="2">

CÓRDOBA: *El Churrasco.*   ⓅⓅ
Calle Romero 16. 【 (957) 29 08 19.
The specialty here is charcoal grilled meat, but vegetable dishes such as *salmorejo* (a thick tomato soup served with crisp wafers of eggplant) are also good. Sip an aperitif in the wine cellars a few doors away. ● Aug. 🍴

</td><td>AE
DC
MC
V</td><td></td><td>■</td><td>●</td><td></td></tr>

<tr><td colspan="2">

CÓRDOBA: *Taberna Pepe de la Judería.*   ⓅⓅ
Calle Romero 1. 【 (957) 20 07 44.
Sit in the dining rooms festooned with photos of notable customers and try the gazpacho or the *flamenquín* (fried rolls of veal and ham). 🍴 ♿

</td><td>AE
DC
MC
V</td><td>●</td><td></td><td></td><td>■</td></tr>

<tr><td colspan="2">

CÓRDOBA: *El Blasón.*   ⓅⓅⓅ
Calle José Zorilla 11 (Córdoba). 【 (957) 48 06 25.
The ground-floor café in this charming old house, situated near Córdoba's main shopping area, is an ideal place for light meals. 🍴

</td><td>AE
DC
MC
V</td><td>●</td><td>■</td><td>●</td><td>■</td></tr>

<tr><td colspan="2">

CÓRDOBA: *Caballo Rojo.*   ⓅⓅⓅ
Calle Cardenal Herrero 28 (Córdoba). 【 (957) 47 53 75.
A lovely restaurant offering traditional dishes, including many adapted from Moorish and Sephardic recipes. Enjoy lamb with honey or *Sefardi* salad of wild mushrooms, asparagus, roasted peppers, and salt cod. 🍴 ♿

</td><td>AE
DC
MC
V</td><td></td><td>■</td><td>●</td><td></td></tr>

<tr><td colspan="2">

ESTEPONA: *La Alborada.*   ⓅⓅ
Puerto Deportivo de Estepona (Málaga). 【 (95) 280 20 47.
This dockside eatery serves excellent paella and other rice dishes, such as *arroz a la banda* (fish risotto), plus fish and steaks. ● Wed & Nov. ♿

</td><td>AE
DC
MC
V</td><td></td><td></td><td></td><td>■</td></tr>

</table>

FUENGIROLA: *Portofino.* ₧₧   AE DC MC V
Edificio Perla 1, Paseo Marítimo (Málaga). ((95) 247 06 43.
This seafront restaurant is popular for its friendly service and good
Italian food, such as the fish and shellfish brochette. ● Mon. 目 &

GRANADA: *Las Brasas.* ₧
Calle Generalife 54, Cenes de la Vega. ((958) 48 60 35.
Besides steaks, try the *plato alpujarreño* (with its red and black sausages),
or the *patatas arrugadas* (fried potatoes with garlic). ● Wed & Aug. &

GRANADA: *Casa Bienvenido.* ₧   DC MC V
Calle Cádiz–San José 1, Monachil. ((958) 50 05 03.
Home style cooking, using vegetables and meat grown on the farm.
The daily specials include lentils with rice and sausages. ● Mon. 目 &

GRANADA: *Don Giovanni.* ₧
Avenida de Cádiz 65. ((958) 81 87 51.
It is hard to beat Don Giovanni's prices for oven baked pizzas and the
wide variety of pastas, meat dishes, and salads. ● Mon. &

GRANADA: *Chikito.* ₧₧   AE DC MC V
Plaza Campillo 9. ((958) 22 33 64.
Built on the site of a café where Lorca and his contemporaries used to
meet, Chikito serves broad beans with ham and Sacromonte omelettes
as specialties. Try the *piononos* (anise-scented cake). ● Wed. 目 &

GRANADA: *Mirador de Morayma.* ₧₧   AE MC V
Calle Pianista García Carillo 2. ((958) 22 82 90.
Situated in the Albaicín with views of the Alhambra, this restaurant
specializes in typical dishes of Granada, such as *remojón* (a salad of
oranges and codfish) and *choto albaicinero* (kid fried with garlic). 目

GRANADA: *Velázquez.* ₧₧   AE DC MC V
Calle Emilio Orozco 1. ((958) 28 01 09.
The ambience here is warm and the food imaginative, with modern
interpretations of such Moorish dishes as *bstella* (a meat pastry with pine
nuts and almonds), and savory almond cream soup. ● Sun & Aug. 目 &

GRANADA: *Ruta del Veleta.* ₧₧₧   AE DC MC V
Carretera Sierra Nevada 50, Cenes de la Vega. ((958) 48 61 34.
The decor, with typical Alpujarran textiles and ceramic jugs, goes
well with the traditional cuisine – roast baby kid and good seafood. 目

HUELVA: *El Estero.* ₧₧   AE DC MC V
Avenida Martín Alonso Pinzón 13. ((959) 25 65 72.
A good, centrally located restaurant, serving local fare. Enjoy *chocos con
babas* (cuttlefish and beans) or sole stuffed with oysters. ● Sun. 目 &

ISLA CRISTINA: *Casa Rufino.* ₧   AE DC MC V
Avenida de la Playa (Huelva). ((959) 33 08 10.
A popular beachside place whose *el tonteo* menu (for four) consists of
eight different fish in sauces, including anglerfish in raisin sauce. &

JABUGO: *Mesón Sánchez Romero Carvajal.* ₧   V
Carretera San Juan del Puerto (Huelva). ((959) 12 15 15.
Fine Jabugo hams are made here, and the adjoining bar-restaurant is a
good place to sample them. Besides dishes featuring ham and sausage,
try the fresh *ibérico* pork dishes, such as *presa de paletilla al mesón.* 目 &

JAÉN: *Casa Vicente.* ₧₧   MC V
Calle Francisco Martín Mora 1. ((953) 23 28 16.
Vicente serves typical dishes from Jaén – lamb stew, spinach casserole,
artichokes in sauce – in a classic setting with a central patio. 目 &

JEREZ DE LA FRONTERA: *Gaitán.* ₧₧   AE DC MC V
Calle Gaitán 3 (Cádiz). ((956) 34 58 59.
Gaitán's innovative chef combines Basque and Andalusian influences
to create dishes such as hake confit with roasted vegetables and bay,
and breast of chicken with foie gras and pine nuts. 目

JEREZ DE LA FRONTERA: *La Mesa Redonda.* ₧₧   AE DC MC V
Calle Manuel de la Quintana 3 (Cádiz). ((956) 34 00 69.
A charming small restaurant, where the dedication to fine cooking is very
much in evidence. Try the *mojama* (cured tuna) as an appetizer. ● Sun. 目 &

Price categories for a three-course evening meal for one, including a half-bottle of house wine, tax, and service: Ⓟ under 3,000 ptas ⓅⓅ 3,000–4,500 ptas ⓅⓅⓅ 4,500–6,000 ptas ⓅⓅⓅⓅ over 6,000 ptas	**TAPAS BAR** In addition to the main dining room, there is a bar serving tapas *(see p574–5)* and *raciones* (larger portions). **FIXED-PRICE MENU** A good-value, fixed-price menu is offered at lunch, dinner, or both, usually with three courses. **GOOD WINE LIST** Denotes a wide range of good wines, or a more specialized selection of local wines. **OUTDOOR TABLES** Facilities for eating outdoors, on a terrace, or in a garden or courtyard, often with a good view.	**CREDIT CARDS**	**TAPAS BAR**	**FIXED-PRICE MENU**	**GOOD WINE LIST**	**OUTDOOR TABLES**

	Credit Cards	Tapas Bar	Fixed-Price Menu	Good Wine List	Outdoor Tables
LOJA: *La Finca.* ⓅⓅⓅⓅ Hotel La Bobadilla, Autovía Granada–Seville (Granada). 【 (958) 32 18 61. Worth a detour off the *autovía*, this exceptional restaurant is a place for fine dining. The chef makes creative use of fresh vegetables, capon, and pork grown on the farm, game (in season), and seafood. 🍴	AE DC MC V		■	●	■
MÁLAGA: *Marisquería Santa Paula.* ⓅⓅ Avenida de los Guindos, Barriada Santa Paula. 【 (95) 223 65 57. One of Málaga's traditional seafood bars, Santa Paula serves a great *fritura* (mixed fish fry) and *mariscada* (selection of shellfish). 🍴 ♿	AE DC MC V	●	■	●	■
MÁLAGA: *Mesón Astorga.* ⓅⓅ Calle Gerona 11. 【 (95) 234 68 32. Creative flair using Málaga's superb local produce makes this restaurant popular. Try the fried eggplant drizzled with molasses, or the salad of fresh tuna with sherry vinegar dressing. Lively tapas bar. ◐ Sun. 🍴 ♿	AE DC MC V	●		●	■
MANILVA: *Macues.* ⓅⓅ Puerto de la Duquesa (Málaga). 【 (95) 289 03 95. At this restaurant, with its covered terrace overlooking the yacht harbor, your fish will be brought around for inspection before it is cooked. Fish baked in salt is a specialty, and the meat is good too. ◐ Mon & Feb. 🍴 ♿	AE DC MC V			●	■
MARBELLA: *Triana.* ⓅⓅ Calle Gloria 11 (Málaga). 【 (95) 277 99 62. An intimate restaurant, right in the center of Marbella's old town, specializing in Valencia-style rice dishes. Apart from paella, there is *caldoso con langosta* (soupy rice with lobster). ◐ Mon & mid Jan–Mar. 🍴	AE DC MC V				
MARBELLA: *Santiago.* ⓅⓅⓅ Paseo Marítimo 5 (Málaga). 【 (95) 277 43 39. This is probably the best place for seafood on the Costa del Sol. On any day, there might be 40 to 50 fish and shellfish dishes, including paella, and good meat dishes such as pig and suckling lamb. ◐ Nov. 🍴 ♿	AE DC MC V		■	●	■
MARBELLA: *Toni Dalli.* ⓅⓅⓅ El Oasis, Carretera de Cádiz (Málaga). 【 (95) 277 00 35. This lovely white palace flanked by palms, right on the beach, makes for a great night out. The Italian-influenced food includes homemade pastas, meat, and fish. Live music is sometimes provided by Toni himself. ♿	AE DC MC V			●	■
MARBELLA: *La Hacienda.* ⓅⓅⓅⓅ Urbanización Hacienda Las Chapas, Ctra Cádiz (Málaga). 【 (95) 283 12 67. Set in a gracious villa, the restaurant has gardens with sea views. The food – Andalusian with French touches – includes specialties such as guinea fowl with raisin sauce, and game in season. ◐ mid Nov–mid Dec. ♿	AE DC MC V		■	●	■
MARBELLA: *La Meridiana.* ⓅⓅⓅⓅ Camino de la Cruz (Málaga). 【 (95) 277 61 90. Situated in Marbella's rarefied heights, La Meridiana has a canopied garden room and adjoining patio bar. The menu features dishes such as swordfish *carpaccio*, artichokes with foie gras, and game in season. ◐ Jan. 🍴 ♿	AE DC MC V		■	●	■
MIJAS: *El Mirador.* ⓅⓅ La Alcazaba, Plaza de la Constitución (Málaga). 【 (95) 259 00 97. In this picturesque hill town there are regrettably few good restaurants. However, this one has great sea views and offers excellent meat dishes and Valencia-style paella. ◐ Tue. 🍴 ♿	AE DC MC V				■
MOTRIL: *Tropical.* ⓅⓅ Avenida Rodríguez Acosta 23 (Granada). 【 (958) 60 04 50. Both seafood, such as bass with *ajo verde* (green garlic), and meat, such as *choto a la brasa* (roast baby kid), are specialties here. ◐ Sun & Jun. 🍴	AE DC MC V		■		

PALMA DEL RÍO: *Hospedería de San Francisco.* ℗℗ MC V
Avenida Pio XII 33 (Córdoba). (957) 71 01 83.
Dine in the cloisters of this out-of-the-way former monastery. The ever-changing menu features superb Basque specialties. ● *Sun.* ▤

EL PUERTO DE SANTA MARÍA: *Las Bóvedas.* ℗℗ AE DC MC V
Monasterio de San Miguel, Calle Larga 27 (Cádiz). (956) 54 04 40.
Dine in style under the vaulted brick ceilings of a former monastery. Fish and shellfish are specialties, as is the dessert *tocino de cielo* ("heavenly bacon"), made from egg yolks by nuns. ▤ &

EL PUERTO DE SANTA MARÍA: *El Faro del Puerto.* ℗℗℗ AE DC MC V
Carretera de Rota (Cádiz). (956) 87 09 52.
The menu here offers refined interpretations of modern dishes. Not to be missed are the desserts, especially the oloroso sherry ice cream. ▤ &

LA RÁBIDA: *Hostería de la Rábida.* ℗℗ MC V
Paraje de la Rábida (Huelva). (959) 35 03 12.
This restaurant, beside the 14th-century monastery where Christopher Columbus once stayed, has good meat and seafood specialties. ▤

RONDA: *Pedro Romero.* ℗ AE DC MC V
Calle Virgen de la Paz 18 (Málaga). (95) 287 11 10.
Facing Ronda's graceful bullring, this restaurant serves well-prepared country food. Try the rabbit with thyme or the braised bull's tail. ▤ &

SAN FERNANDO: *Venta Vargas.* ℗℗ AE MC V
Avenida Puente Zuazo (Cádiz). (956) 88 16 22.
This popular small town eatery has lots of flamenco atmosphere. Order *raciones* of classics such as *aliñadas* (potato salad). ● *Mon.* ▤ &

SAN ROQUE: *Los Remos en Villa Victoria.* ℗℗℗ AE DC MC V
Ctra San Roque–La Línea, Gibraltar Campamento (Cádiz). (956) 69 84 12.
Housed in a restored mansion with Mediterranean decor, this restaurant serves exquisite dishes, with a focus on first-rate seafood. A sampling menu includes shrimp fritters and sea nettles. ● *Sun.* ▤ &

SANLÚCAR DE BARRAMEDA: *Casa Bigote.* ℗℗ AE DC MC V
Bajo de Guía (Cádiz). (956) 36 26 96.
At the mouth of the Río Guadalquivir, this typical sailors' *taberna* is the place to sample *langostinos de Sanlúcar* (large, sweet, striped shrimp) and fresh fish from the day's catch, such as baby eels. ● *Sun.* ▤ &

SANLÚCAR LA MAYOR: *La Alquería.* ℗℗℗ AE DC MC V
Hacienda de Benazuza, Virgen de las Nieves (Sevilla). (95) 570 33 44.
The chef at this beautiful country hacienda offers a choice of innovative and simple dishes, all based on quality produce. ● *mid Jul–Sep.* ▤

TORREMOLINOS: *Bar Restaurante Casa Juan.* ℗ AE DC MC V
Calle Mar 14, La Carihuela (Málaga). (95) 238 41 06.
A popular beachfront restaurant offering favorites such as fish baked in salt and *fritura malagueña* (mixed fish fry). ● *Jan.* ▤ &

TORREMOLINOS: *Frutos.* ℗℗ AE DC MC V
Urbanización Los Álamos, Carretera a Cádiz (Málaga). (95) 238 14 50.
The *grande dame* of Costa del Sol restaurants, serving superb meat and fish. Enjoy suckling pig and follow with *arroz con leche* (rice pudding). ▤

VERA: *Terraza Carmona.* ℗℗ AE DC MC V
Calle Manuel Giménez 1 (Almería). (950) 39 07 60.
The specialties here are excellent seafood and unusual regional dishes such as *gurullos con conejo* (pasta with rabbit). ● *Mon.* ▤ &

THE BALEARIC ISLANDS

FORMENTERA, ES PUJOLS: *Sa Palmera.* ℗ AE MC V
Playa Es Pujols. (971) 32 83 56.
Freshly caught seafood is served at this seafront restaurant. Try the mixed fish paella or the shellfish casserole *(zarzuela de mariscos).* ● *Nov–Jan.* &

IBIZA (EIVISSA), IBIZA TOWN: *Ca'n Alfredo.* ℗ AE DC MC V
Paseo Vara de Rey 16. (971) 31 12 74.
Regional cuisine is served in this popular establishment. Choose from numerous rice dishes or the *borrida de ratjada* (ray stew). ● *Mon.* ▤ &

Price categories for a three-course evening meal for one, including a half-bottle of house wine, tax, and service:

- Ⓟ under 3,000 ptas
- ⓅⓅ 3,000–4,500 ptas
- ⓅⓅⓅ 4,500–6,000 ptas
- ⓅⓅⓅⓅ over 6,000 ptas

TAPAS BAR
In addition to the main dining room, there is a bar serving tapas (see p574–5) and raciones (larger portions).

FIXED-PRICE MENU
A good-value, fixed-price menu is offered at lunch, dinner, or both, usually with three courses.

GOOD WINE LIST
Denotes a wide range of good wines, or a more specialized selection of local wines.

OUTDOOR TABLES
Facilities for eating outdoors, on a terrace, or in a garden or courtyard, often with a good view.

	Price	CREDIT CARDS	TAPAS BAR	FIXED-PRICE MENU	GOOD WINE LIST	OUTDOOR TABLES
IBIZA (EIVISSA), IBIZA TOWN: *El Cigarral.* Calle Fray Vicente Nicolás 9. (971) 31 12 46. A family-run restaurant where the menu changes according to what is fresh in the market. Delicious grilled steaks and fish, complemented by one of the largest selections of wines in Ibiza. ● mid Aug–mid Sep. ▤ ♿	ⓅⓅ	AE DC MC V			●	
IBIZA (EIVISSA), SANT ANTONI: *Sa Capella.* Carretera Can Germà. (971) 34 00 57. Housed in a former chapel, this restaurant offers an international menu, including good fish and steaks. Open for dinner only. ● Nov–Apr. ♿	ⓅⓅⓅ	DC MC V	●		●	
IBIZA (EIVISSA), SANT JOSEP: *Cana Joana.* Carretera Ibiza–Sant Josep. (971) 80 01 58. One of the island's most interesting gastronomic offerings. The seasonal menu, with Catalan and Mediterranean influences, includes dishes such as *pan palles* (toasted bread with tomato and olive oil). ● Nov–Jan. ♿	ⓅⓅⓅ	AE MC V			●	▪
IBIZA (EIVISSA), SANTA EULÀRIA D'ES RIU: *Doña Margarita.* Paseo Marítimo. (971) 33 06 55. A port-side restaurant offering fresh fish, perfectly prepared, and a delicious yogurt mousse with raspberry sauce as dessert. ● Nov. ▤ ♿	ⓅⓅ	AE DC MC V			●	▪
IBIZA (EIVISSA), SANTA GERTRUDIS: *Ca'n Pau.* Carretera de Sant Miquel. (971) 19 70 07. Rustic Ibizan *masía* (farmhouse) serving good Catalan cuisine. Tender roast kid, quail with cabbage, and rabbit are a few of the house specialties, and there is a good selection of Catalan wines. ● Mon. ♿	ⓅⓅ	AE MC V			●	▪
MALLORCA, ALCÚDIA: *Mesón Los Patos.* Carretera Sa Pobla–Alcúdia. (971) 89 02 65. An agreeably decorated family restaurant with a garden and a children's playground. Simple and traditional Mallorcan dishes, including *arroz brut* (a soupy rice served with meat). ● Tue & mid Jan–Feb. ▤ ♿	ⓅⓅ	AE V	●	▪	●	▪
MALLORCA, CALA D'OR: *Port Petit.* Avenida Cala Llonga. (971) 64 30 39. Enjoy creative Mediterranean cuisine overlooking the marina. The salmon and monkfish *carpaccio* and the turbot in a mustard sauce are classics, along with the rich chocolate fondue. Open for dinner only. ● Nov–Apr.	ⓅⓅ	AE DC MC V			●	▪
MALLORCA, CALA RATJADA: *Ses Rotges.* Calle Rafael Blanes 21. (971) 56 31 08. This lovely old stone mansion, surrounded by palm trees and azaleas, is an ideal setting for sophisticated dining on French cuisine prepared using local produce. Good local wines. ● Dec–Feb. ♿	ⓅⓅⓅ	AE DC MC V		▪	●	▪
MALLORCA, DEIÀ: *Bens d'Avall.* Urbanización Costa Deià. (971) 63 23 81. Perched on top of a cliff, this restaurant offers wonderful views of the coastline. Traditional regional recipes are given modern touches, creating dishes such as shrimp *carpaccio* with pesto and Parmesan. ● Nov–Mar. ♿	ⓅⓅ	AE DC MC V		▪	●	▪
MALLORCA, DEIÀ: *El Olivo.* Hotel la Residencia, Finca Son Canals. (971) 63 90 11. One of the island's best restaurants, with delightful decor and views of the mountains. Delicious *nouvelle cuisine* incorporating Mediterranean influences, with dishes such as lamb baked with olives. ▤ ♿	ⓅⓅⓅⓅ	AE DC MC V		▪	●	▪
MALLORCA, INCA: *Celler Ca'n Amer.* Calle Pau 39. (971) 50 12 61. This wonderful old wine cellar is now home to one of the island's most authentic regional dishes, *sopa mallorquina* (made with bread and braised vegetables). Good rice dishes and roast suckling pig. ● Sun. ▤	ⓅⓅ	AE MC V			●	

MALLORCA, PAGUERA: *La Gran Tortuga.* ⓅⓅ
Aldea Cala Fornells 1. 【 *(971) 68 60 23.*
There is a great sea view from the terrace, where you can try homemade
foie gras or monkfish stuffed with smoked salmon in a spinach sauce.
The atmosphere is agreeable and the service efficient. ● *Mon & Dec–Jan.*

AE DC MC V

MALLORCA, PALMA DE MALLORCA: *Ca'n Carlos.* Ⓟ
Calle del Agua 5. 【 *(971) 71 38 69.*
Old Balearic recipes have been revived, providing diners with an
authentic version of the islands' food. The oven-roasted suckling lamb
and the grouper with cabbage are just two examples. ● *Sun.* ▤

AE DC MC V

MALLORCA, PALMA DE MALLORCA: *Porto Pí.* ⓅⓅ
Calle Garita 25. 【 *(971) 40 00 87.*
This elegant old house, surrounded by gardens, is an ideal spot to savor
creative Mediterranean cuisine using first-class ingredients. ● *Sun.* ▤

MC V

MALLORCA, POLLENÇA: *Celler Ca Vostra.* ⓅⓅ
Carretera Alcúdia–Port de Pollença. 【 *(971) 86 55 46.*
This former wine bar is still decorated with wine barrels. Typical local
food, with fresh fish and *escudella* (a vegetable stew). ● *Wed.* ▤ ♿

AE MC V

MALLORCA, PORT D'ANDRATX: *Layn.* ⓅⓅ
Calle Almirante Riera Alemany 19. 【 *(971) 67 18 55.*
This restaurant has its own fishing boat to ensure the freshest of sea fare.
There are also meat specialties including roast suckling pig and beef
with cabbage. Views of the sea from the terrace. ● *Mon & mid Dec–Jan.*

AE DC MC V

MALLORCA, PORT D'ANDRATX: *Miramar.* ⓅⓅ
Avenida Mateo Bosch 22. 【 *(971) 67 16 17.*
A family-run restaurant with views of the marina, offering good seafood
and impeccable service. Specialties include *arroz negro* (black rice, made
with squid's ink) and shrimp in rock salt. ● *Mon & mid Dec–mid Jan.*

AE DC MC V

MALLORCA, SÓLLER: *El Guía.* ⓅⓅ
Calle Castañer 2. 【 *(971) 63 02 27.*
People come from near and far for El Guía's artichokes stuffed with
spinach. Good, tasty, home cooking at excellent prices. ▤ ♿

AE DC MC V

MALLORCA, SON SERVERA: *S'Era de Pula.* ⓅⓅ
Carretera Son Servera–Capdepera. 【 *(971) 56 79 40.*
A rustic Mallorcan country house in a peaceful spot with mountain
views. The interesting mix of continental and local cuisine features
dishes such as cod with crystallized garlic. ● *Mon & mid Jan–mid Mar.* ▤ ♿

AE DC MC V

MENORCA, CIUTADELLA: *Ca's Quintu.* ⓅⓅ
Plaza de Alfonso III 4. 【 *(971) 38 10 02.*
This centrally located restaurant serves traditional Menorcan food, with an
emphasis on fresh fish. Try the house specialty, *caldera de langosta*
(lobster casserole) or *caldera de mariscos* (the shellfish version). ▤ ♿

AE MC V

MENORCA, CIUTADELLA: *Casa Manolo.* ⓅⓅⓅ
Calle Marina 117. 【 *(971) 38 00 03.*
A lively restaurant in the harbor with a delightful terrace overlooking
the marina. Regional seafood dishes including a selection of grilled
Menorcan fish, rice with seafood, and lobster casserole. ▤ ♿

AE DC MC V

MENORCA, FORNELLS: *Es Cranc.* ⓅⓅⓅ
Calle Escoles 31. 【 *(971) 37 64 42.*
This establishment deserves the reputation it has throughout the island
for the freshness and preparation of its seafood. The lobster *caldereta* and
the succulent grilled shrimp are two examples. ● *Wed & Dec–Feb.* ▤ ♿

MC V

MENORCA, MAÓ: *Jágaro.* ⓅⓅ
Moll de Levant 334. 【 *(971) 36 23 90.*
Enjoy an excellent view of the harbor from this restaurant where seafood
dishes predominate in the summer and hearty stews in the winter. The
potato pie and almond pie are popular choices for desserts. ♿

AE DC MC V

MENORCA, ES MERCADAL: *Ca'n Aguedet.* ⓅⓅ
Calle Lepanto 23–30. 【 *(971) 37 53 91.*
Authentic Menorcan dishes such as rabbit with figs, cuttlefish with shrimp
and pine nuts, and *arroz de tierra* (a rice and meat dish dating back to
Moorish times). Try a wine from the proprietor's own vineyard. ▤

AE DC MC V

For key to symbols see back flap

	CREDIT CARDS	TAPAS BAR	FIXED-PRICE MENU	GOOD WINE LIST	OUTDOOR TABLES

Price categories for a three-course evening meal for one, including a half-bottle of house wine, tax, and service:

Ⓟ under 3,000 ptas
ⓅⓅ 3,000–4,500 ptas
ⓅⓅⓅ 4,500–6,000 ptas
ⓅⓅⓅⓅ over 6,000 ptas

TAPAS BAR
In addition to the main dining room, there is a bar serving tapas (see p574–5) and raciones (larger portions).
FIXED-PRICE MENU
A good-value, fixed-price menu is offered at lunch, dinner, or both, usually with three courses.
GOOD WINE LIST
Denotes a wide range of good wines, or a more specialized selection of local wines.
OUTDOOR TABLES
Facilities for eating outdoors, on a terrace, or in a garden or courtyard, often with a good view.

THE CANARY ISLANDS

	CREDIT CARDS	TAPAS BAR	FIXED-PRICE MENU	GOOD WINE LIST	OUTDOOR TABLES
FUERTEVENTURA, PUERTO DEL ROSARIO: *Benjamín.* Ⓟ Calle León y Castillo 139. 【 *(928) 85 17 48.* Innovative Canary Islands cooking relying exclusively on local produce. The potatoes with *mojo* (a spicy sauce), the goat cheese, and sorbet made from prickly pear fruit are all recommended. ● Sun.			■	●	
FUERTEVENTURA, PUERTO DEL ROSARIO: *La Casa del Jamón.* Ⓟ La Asomada. 【 *(928) 53 00 64.* Decorated like a traditional Spanish *mesón*, this family-run restaurant offers a mix of Basque and regional dishes including roast kid and a tasty variety of cheeses and Iberian cold meats. ● Sep. ⑤	AE DC MC V			●	
LA GOMERA, SAN SEBASTIÁN DE LA GOMERA: *Casa del Mar.* Ⓟ Avenida Fred Olsen 2. 【 *(922) 87 12 19.* Simple seafood dishes are served in this family-style restaurant close to the harbor. You can have fish in a stew, in a paella, or grilled. ● Sun.	AE DC MC V	●			
GRAN CANARIA, CRUZ DE TEJEDA: *Hostería Cruz de Tejeda.* ⓅⓅ Cruz de Tejeda. 【 *(928) 66 60 50.* Gran Canaria's famed parador restaurant dominates the lovely central mountains. Try the traditional roast kid or rabbit terrine, and the delicious *bienmesabe* (almond cake) with ice cream for dessert. ⑤	AE DC MC V	●	■	●	■
GRAN CANARIA, MASPALOMAS: *Orangerie.* ⓅⓅⓅⓅ Hotel Palm Beach, Avenida Oasis. 【 *(928) 14 08 06.* A lush, tropical setting where you can dine on creative, stylish cuisine either indoors or out. Open for dinner only. ● Thu & Sun. ▤	AE DC MC V		■	●	■
GRAN CANARIA, LAS PALMAS: *Casa Carmelo.* ⓅⓅ Paseo de las Canteras 2. 【 *(928) 46 90 56.* The sleek upstairs dining room gives a grandstand view of Las Palmas' superb seafront, which is particularly beautiful at night. The emphasis here is on chargrilled meat and fresh local fish. ▤	AE DC MC V		■	●	
GRAN CANARIA, LAS PALMAS: *Mesón La Cuadra.* ⓅⓅ Calle General Mas de Gaminde 32. 【 *(928) 24 33 80.* Choose from either the tempting variety of tapas at the bar, or the truly "home-grown" menu. The proprietor's own farm produces the tender suckling lamb, the goat cheese, and the milk curd dessert. ● Mon. ▤ ⑤	AE DC MC V	●	■	●	
GRAN CANARIA, PLAYA DEL INGLÉS: *Tenderete II.* ⓅⓅ Avenida Tirajana 5. 【 *(928) 76 14 60.* Typical Canary Islands cooking with an emphasis on fresh seafood. The fish prepared in rock salt and the *potaje de berros* (watercress broth) are house specialties. Try the locally grown *manga* (similar to mango). ▤ ⑤	AE DC MC V	●		●	■
GRAN CANARIA, SANTA BRÍGIDA: *Las Grutas de Artiles.* ⓅⓅ Las Meleguinas. 【 *(928) 64 05 75.* A restaurant set in caves, offering authentic Canary Islands specialties and grilled meat. The gardens and swimming pool are ideal for children.	AE DC MC V	●	■	●	■
GRAN CANARIA, VEGA DE SAN MATEO: *Museo Cho-Zacarías.* Ⓟ Avenida de Tinamar. 【 *(928) 66 06 27.* Old farmers' cottages provide a unique setting for this restaurant. The traditional Canary Islands menu features *cherne* (a local fish) served in a coriander sauce, and watercress broth. Open for lunch only. ● Mon.	AE MC V			●	■
EL HIERRO, LA RESTINGA: *Casa Juan.* Ⓟ Calle Juan Gutiérrez Monteverde 23. 【 *(922) 55 80 02.* Local families flock to this inexpensive, no frills restaurant. Delicious fresh fish such as *vieja* and *cherne*, accompanied by a *mojo* sauce.		●			

LANZAROTE, ARRECIFE: *Castillo de San José.*   Ⓟ Ⓟ
Castillo de San José. 【 *(928) 81 23 21.*
A converted 16th-century fortress, now housing a contemporary art
gallery and restaurant. Enjoy international and regional specialties
as you admire the art on the walls and the views of the harbor.

	AE			
	MC			
	V			

LANZAROTE, COSTA TEGUISE: *Mesón La Jordana.*   Ⓟ Ⓟ
Centro Comercial de Lanzarote, Lanzarote Bay. 【 *(928) 59 03 28.*
A popular and attractive spot where you can sample local fare given a
French touch. Try the fresh *cherne* or the roast kid. ● *Sun & Sep.* ▤

	AE			●	▪
	MC				
	V				

LANZAROTE, PUERTO DEL CARMEN: *Colón.*   Ⓟ Ⓟ
Centro Comercial Mata Gorda. 【 *(928) 51 25 54.*
Decorated in traditional style, this restaurant serves international and
regional cuisine. The menu includes fresh duck foie gras and fish
dishes of the highest quality. Excellent wine list. &

	AE			●	▪
	DC				
	MC				
	V				

LANZAROTE, YAIZA: *Casa Salvador.*   Ⓟ
Avenida Playa Blanca. 【 *(928) 51 70 25.*
Located right on the beach, this establishment serves freshly caught fish
and shellfish, as well as good grilled steaks and paellas.

	AE	●		●	▪
	DC				
	MC				
	V				

LANZAROTE, YAIZA: *La Era.*   Ⓟ Ⓟ
Calle El Barranco 3. 【 *(928) 83 00 16.*
La Era is set in one of the few old country houses to survive the island's
volcanic eruptions of 1730 to 1736. Enjoy regional specialties such as
lamb, kid, or lentil stew in one of the pretty, rustic dining rooms.

	AE	●	▪	●	
	DC				
	MC				
	V				

LA PALMA, SANTA CRUZ DE LA PALMA: *Chipi Chipi.*   Ⓟ
Calle Juan Mayor 42. 【 *(922) 41 10 24.*
Just 6 km (3.5 miles) out of town, this restaurant, with dining rooms
around a pretty patio, specializes in grilled meats and local dishes such
as chickpea soup. Good selection of island wines. ● *Wed, Sun & Oct–Nov.* &

	AE	●	▪	●	▪
	MC				
	V				

TENERIFE, ADEJE: *El Patio.*   Ⓟ Ⓟ Ⓟ Ⓟ
Hotel Jardín Tropical, Urbanización San Eugenio. 【 *(922) 75 01 00.*
An enchanting setting for a special evening out. The lovely, flower-filled
patio is ideal for balmy summer nights. Imaginative, modern dishes are
created using local produce. Open for dinner only. ▤

	AE		▪	●	▪
	DC				
	MC				
	V				

TENERIFE, LA OROTAVA: *Los Corales.*   Ⓟ Ⓟ
Carretera General del Norte 130, Santa Úrsula. 【 *(922) 30 19 18.*
Genuine Canary Islands food with creative flourishes and wonderful
views of the valley. The meat or fish *carpaccio* and the traditional
conejo en salmorejo (rabbit terrine) are recommended. ● *Mon.* &

	AE			●	
	DC				
	MC				
	V				

TENERIFE, PUERTO DE LA CRUZ: *Mi Vaca y Yo.*   Ⓟ
Calle Cruz Verde 3. 【 *(922) 38 52 47.*
A typical Canary Islands house, in the old part of town, agreeably
decorated with plants. There is a lively atmosphere in which to enjoy
a seafood paella or the house specialty, lobster casserole. ● *Jun.* &

	AE			●	▪
	DC				
	MC				
	V				

TENERIFE, PUERTO DE LA CRUZ: *Magnolia "Felipe el Payés."*   Ⓟ Ⓟ Ⓟ
Avenida Marqués de Villanueva del Prado. 【 *(922) 38 56 14.*
Assured Catalan cooking, including the traditional *pan con tomate* (bread
with tomato) and *suquet* (fish stew), served in a flamboyant modern
dining room or in the gardens. ▤ &

	AE		▪	●	▪
	DC				
	MC				
	V				

TENERIFE, SANTA CRUZ DE TENERIFE: *Café del Príncipe.*   Ⓟ
Plaza del Príncipe de Asturias. 【 *(922) 27 88 10.*
Sample any of the good local dishes in this pretty restaurant that
overlooks the square in the center of town. ● *Mon & Jun.* &

	MC	●	▪	●	▪
	V				

TENERIFE, SANTA CRUZ DE TENERIFE: *El Coto de Antonio.*   Ⓟ Ⓟ Ⓟ
Calle General Goded 13. 【 *(922) 27 21 05.*
Excellent regional specialties are served in this simple restaurant near the
bullring. The black potato salad, with salt cod, peppers, and olive oil, and
the *vieja* in a coriander sauce are favorites among the clientele. ▤ &

	AE			●	
	DC				
	MC				
	V				

TENERIFE, TEGUESTE: *El Drago.*   Ⓟ Ⓟ
Urbanización San Gonzálo 1. 【 *(922) 54 30 01.*
This delightful 18th-century farmhouse provides a rustic setting for
excellent Canary Islands cooking, including traditional watercress broth,
puchero (vegetable and meat broth), and fish casserole. ● *Mon & Aug.* &

	AE		▪	●	
	DC				
	MC				
	V				

SURVIVAL
GUIDE

PRACTICAL INFORMATION

Old street signs

Spain has finally begun to market itself beyond the attractions of its coastline, and now has a solid tourist information infrastructure. There are national tourist offices in every large city, and regional offices in the smaller towns. All offer help with finding accommodation, restaurants, and activities in their area. August is Spain's main vacation month. Many businesses close for the whole month, and roads are very busy at the beginning and end of this period. At any time of year, try to find out in advance whether your visit coincides with local fiestas, because although these are attractions, they often entail widespread closings. It is a good idea to plan leisurely lunches, as most of Spain stops from 2pm to 5pm.

A bilingual Basque/Castilian reserved parking sign

LANGUAGE

THE MAIN LANGUAGE of Spain, *Castellano* (Castilian), is spoken by almost everyone. There are three main regional languages: Catalan, spoken in Catalonia, *Gallego* (Galician) in Galicia, and *Euskera* (Basque) in the Basque Country. Variants of Catalan are spoken in the Valencia region and also in the Balearic Islands.

People who speak English are often employed in places that deal with tourists.

MANNERS

THE SPANISH greet and say goodbye to strangers at bus stops, and in elevators, shops and other public places. They often talk to people they do not know. People shake hands when introduced and whenever they meet. Women usually kiss on both cheeks when they meet, and friends and family members may kiss or embrace briefly.

VISAS AND PASSPORTS

VISAS ARE NOT required for citizens of EU countries, Iceland, or Norway.

A list of entry requirements, which is available from Spanish embassies, specifies 35 other countries, including New Zealand, Canada, and the US, whose nationals do not need to apply for a visa if visiting Spain for less than 90 days. Thereafter they may apply to the *Gobierno Civil* (a local government office) for an extension. You usually need proof of employment or of sufficient funds to support yourself during a long stay.

Visitors from other countries, including Australia, must obtain a valid visa before traveling.

If you intend to stay for a long time in Spain, you should contact your nearest Spanish embassy several months in advance about your needs.

TAX-FREE GOODS AND CUSTOMS INFORMATION

NON-EU (EUROPEAN UNION) residents can reclaim *IVA* (VAT) (Value Added Tax – VAT or sales tax) on single items worth over 15,000 pesetas bought in shops displaying a "Tax-free for Tourists" sign. (Food, drink, tobacco, cars, motorbikes, and medicines are exempt.) You pay the full price and ask the sales assistant for a *formulario* (tax exemption form). On leaving Spain, you ask customs to stamp your

formulario (this must be within six months of the purchase). You receive the refund by mail or on your credit card account.

Banco Exterior branches at Barcelona, Madrid, Málaga, Mallorca, Oviedo, Santander, and Seville airports will give refunds on *formularios* stamped by customs.

TOURIST INFORMATION

ALL MAJOR CITIES and towns have *oficinas de turismo*. They will provide town maps, lists of hotels and restaurants, information about the locality, and details of activities and events for tourists.

There is a **Spanish National Tourist Office** in several large cities abroad.

OPENING HOURS

MOST MONUMENTS and museums close on Mondays. On other days they generally open from 10am to 2pm, close from 2pm to 5pm, and, in some cases, reopen from 5pm to 8pm. Churches may follow these opening hours or be open only for services. Admission is charged for most museums and monuments.

In smaller towns it is common for churches, castles, and other sights to be kept locked. The key, available to visitors on request, will be lodged with a caretaker in a neighboring house, in the town hall, or perhaps with the owners of the local bar.

OFICINA DE TURISMO   *i*

Spanish tourist office sign with distinctive "i" logo

◁ **The old town of Ibiza enclosed by its 16th-century walls, seen from the harbor**

Students enjoy reduced admission fees to many museums and galleries

FACILITIES FOR THE DISABLED

S PAIN'S NATIONAL association for the disabled, the Confederación Coordinadora Estatal de Minusválidos Físicos de España (COCEMFE), has a tour company, Servi-COCEMFE *(see p533)*, that publishes guides to facilities in Spain and will help plan a vacation to individual requirements.

Tourist offices and the social services departments of town halls can provide information on local conditions and facilities. A travel agency, **Viajes 2000**, specializes in vacations for the disabled, and **The Society for the Advancement of Travel for the Handicapped, Inc.** provides travel information for the disabled.

COCEMFE sign for disabled access

SPANISH TIME

S PAIN IS SIX HOURS ahead of Eastern Standard Time (EST) and Eastern Daylight Time. The Canary Islands are five hours ahead. Spain uses the 24-hour (military) clock, so 1pm = 13:00.

La madrugada is the very early hours of the morning. *Mañana* (morning) lasts until the late Spanish lunch time at about 2pm, and *mediodía* (midday) is the middle of the afternoon, about 1–4pm. *La tarde* is the late afternoon as well as the evening.

STUDENT INFORMATION

H OLDERS OF THE International Student Identity Card (ISIC) are entitled to benefits such as discounts on travel and reduced entrance charges to museums and galleries. Information is available from all national student organizations and, in Spain, from the local government-run **Centros de Información Juvenil (CIJ)** in large towns. **Turismo y Viajes Educativos (TIVE)** specializes in student travel.

ELECTRICAL ADAPTERS

S PAIN'S ELECTRICITY supply is 220 volts, but the 125-volt system still operates in some old buildings. Plugs for both have two round pins. A three-tier standard travel converter enables you to use appliances from abroad on both supplies. Heating appliances should be used only on 220 volts.

CONVERSION CHART

US Standard to metric
1 inch = 2.54 centimeters
1 foot = 30 centimeters
1 mile = 1.6 kilometers
1 ounce = 28 grams
1 pound = 454 grams
1 US quart = 0.947 liter
1 US gallon = 3.6 liters

Metric to US Standard
1 millimeter = 0.04 inch
1 centimeter = 0.4 inch
1 meter = 3 feet 3 inches
1 kilometer = 0.6 mile
1 gram = 0.04 ounce
1 kilogram = 2.2 pounds
1 liter = 1.1 US quarts

Personal Security and Health

I N SPAIN, AS IN MOST EUROPEAN countries, rural areas are generally safe, but certain parts of cities are subject to petty crime. Carry cards and money in a belt and never leave anything visible in your car when you park it.

If you are ill, Spanish pharmacists are qualified to advise and sometimes to prescribe. Emergency phone numbers vary from region to region. The most important ones are given on the opposite page. If you lose your documents, contact your consulate or the local police.

Spanish pharmacy sign

IN AN EMERGENCY

O NLY THE *Policía Nacional* operate a nationwide emergency phone number. Call it even if you need some other service, and they will assist you in getting help. Telephone directories list local emergency numbers under *Servicios de Urgencia,* and they appear on tourist maps and leaflets.

For emergency medical treatment call the Cruz Roja (Red Cross), look under *Ambulancias* in the phone book, or go to a hospital emergency room *(Urgencias).*

Sign identifying a Cruz Roja (Red Cross) emergency treatment center

provide an official translation before they will reimburse you. Travelers may wish to take out additional, private insurance against the cost of any emergency hospital care, doctor's fees, and returning you to the US. If you have private travel insurance, make sure you have your policy with you when requesting

medical assistance. You may be expected to pay up front for treatment and be reimbursed at a later date.

PHARMACIES

S PANISH PHARMACISTS have wide responsibilities. They can advise, and, in some cases, prescribe without consulting a doctor. In a non-emergency a *farmacéutico* is a good

person to see first. It is easy to find one who speaks English.

The *farmacia* sign is a green or red illuminated cross. Those open at night in a town are listed in the windows of all the local pharmacies. Do not confuse them with *perfumerías,* which sell toiletries only.

PERSONAL SECURITY

V IOLENT CRIME is rare in Spain, but visitors should avoid walking alone in poorly lit areas. Wear a bag or camera across your body, not on your shoulder. Men occasionally make complimentary remarks *(piropos)* to women in public, particularly in the street. This is an old custom and not intended to be intimidating.

SPANISH POLICE

T HERE ARE ESSENTIALLY three types of police in Spain. The *Guardia Civil* (National Guard) mainly police rural areas. Their uniform is olive green, but there are local and regional variations. They impose fines for traffic offences.

The *Policía Nacional,* who wear a blue uniform, operate in towns with a population of more than 30,000. The *Policía Nacional* have been replaced with a regional force, the *Ertzaintza,* in the Basque country, and with the *Mossos d'Esquadra* in Catalonia. These can be distinguished by their respective red and blue berets.

The *Policía Local,* also called *Policía Municipal* or *Guardia Urbana,* dress in blue. They operate independently in each town and also have a separate branch for city traffic control.

All three services will direct you to the relevant authority in the event of an incident requiring police help.

MEDICAL TREATMENT

V ISITORS FROM THE US should check with their insurance carriers before leaving home to be sure they are covered. Many medical facilities will require that you pay for your treatment in full at time of service. Be sure to get an itemized bill for your carrier. In some cases, insurance companies require that you

Guardia Civil   **Policía Nacional**   **Policía Local**

EMERGENCY NUMBERS

Policía Nacional
℃ *091 (nationwide).*

Fire Department (Bomberos)
℃ *080 (Madrid, Barcelona, Seville).*

Ambulance: (Red Cross, Cruz Roja)
℃ *522 22 22 (Madrid).*
℃ *300 20 20 (Barcelona).*
℃ *435 01 35 (Seville).*

For emergency services outside these cities, consult the local telephone directory.

LEGAL ASSISTANCE

SOME INSURANCE POLICIES cover legal costs, for instance after an accident. If you are not covered, telephone your nearest consulate for the name of a reputable lawyer.

You can also contact the *Colegio de Abogados* (lawyers' association) of the nearest town or city for advice on obtaining legal help locally.

If you need an interpreter, consult the *Páginas Amarillas (Yellow Pages)* telephone directory for the region under *Traductores* or *Intérpretes*. Both *Traductores Oficiales* and *Traductores Jurados* are qualified to translate legal or official documents.

PERSONAL PROPERTY

TRAVEL INSURANCE is there to protect you financially from the loss or theft of your property, but it is always best to take obvious precautions against loss and theft.

If you have to carry large sums of money with you, take traveler's checks and, if you have two credit cards, do not carry them together. Never leave a bag or handbag unattended anywhere, and do not put down a purse or handbag on the tabletop in a café.

The moment you discover a loss or theft, report it to the local police station. To claim insurance you must do this immediately, as many companies give you only 24 hours. Ask the police for a *denuncia*

Patrol car of the Policía Nacional, Spain's main urban police force

Policía Local patrol car, mainly seen in small towns

Cruz Roja (Red Cross) ambulance

The emergency number on the side of fire engines varies regionally

(written statement), which you need to make a claim. If your passport was one of the items stolen, or if you lose it, report it to your consulate.

RESTROOMS

PUBLIC PAY-TOILETS are rare in Spain. Department stores are often good places to try, as are bars and restaurants where you are a customer. On freeways, there are restrooms at service stations. You may have to ask for a key *(la llave)*, not only at the service stations but also in some bars in country areas. It is best to bring your own tissues, too. The term generally used for toilets in Spain is *los servicios*.

OUTDOOR HAZARDS

SPAIN is prey every summer to forest fires fanned by winds and fueled by bone-dry vegetation. Be sensitive to fire hazards and use car ashtrays. Broken glass can start a fire so be careful to take your empty bottles away with you.

The sign *coto de caza* in woodland areas identifies a hunting preserve where you must follow the country codes. *Toro bravo* means "fighting bull" – do not approach. A *camino particular* sign indicates a private driveway.

If you are climbing or hiking go properly equipped and let someone know when you expect to return.

Banking and Local Currency

YOU MAY ENTER SPAIN with any amount of money, but if you intend to export more than one million pesetas, you should declare it. Eurocheques are widely accepted in Spain. Traveler's checks may be exchanged at banks, *cajas de cambio* (bureaux de change), some hotels, and some shops. Banks generally offer the best exchange rates. The best exchange may be offered on your credit or direct debit (ATM) card, which may be used in cash dispensers displaying the appropriate sign.

24-hour cash dispenser

BANKING HOURS

SPANISH BANKS are beginning to extend their opening hours, but expect extended hours only at large central branches in the big cities.

As a rule of thumb, banks are open from 8am to 2pm on weekdays. Some open until 1pm on Saturdays. Most close on Saturdays in August; in the south they also close on Saturdays from May to September.

Bureau de change

CHANGING MONEY

MOST BANKS have a foreign exchange desk with the sign *Cambio* or *Extranjero*. Always take your passport as ID for any transaction.

You can draw up to 50,000 pesetas on major credit cards at a bank. If you bank with **Barclays** or **NatWest**, it is possible to cash a check in the usual way at one of their branches in Spain.

Bureaux de change, with the sign *Caja de Cambio* or "Change," invariably charge higher rates of commission than banks, but they are often open after hours. They are commonly found in the tourist areas of Spanish towns and cities.

Cajas de Ahorro (savings banks) also exchange money. They open from 8:30am to 2pm on weekdays and also on Thursday afternoons from 4:30pm to 7:45pm.

CHECKS AND CARDS

TRAVELER'S CHECKS can be purchased at American Express, Thomas Cook, or your bank. All are accepted in Spain. If you exchange AmEx checks at an AmEx office, commission is not charged. You can purchase checks in pesetas from any bank.

You can write a check in pesetas using Eurocheques, which may also be used to change money at a bank. You must show your Eurocard or Mastercard and your passport.

The most widely accepted card in Spain is the **Visa** card. **Mastercard** (Access)/Eurocard and **American Express** are also useful currency. The major banks will allow cash withdrawals on credit cards.

When you pay for goods or services with a card, cashiers will usually pass your card through a reading machine. Sometimes, however, you will be asked to punch your PIN into a small keypad attached to the machine.

Credit card reader with PIN keypad

CASH DISPENSERS

IF YOUR CARD is linked to your home bank account, you can use it with your PIN to withdraw money from cash dispensers. These are widespread and nearly all take Visa or Mastercard (Access) cards.

When you enter your PIN, instructions are displayed in English, French, German, and Spanish. These days, many dispensers are inside buildings and to gain access you will have to run your card through a door-entry system.

Cards with Cirrus and Maestro logos can also be widely used to withdraw money from cash machines.

CURRENCY

THE CURRENCY of Spain is the peseta, usually abbreviated to "pta," or "ptas." It is common to speak of *duros* in popular speech (1 *duro* is 5 pesetas). *Cinco* (5) *duros* equal 25 pesetas and *mil* (1,000) *duros* is 5,000 pesetas. Sales clerks giving change often round the figure up or down to the nearest 5 pesetas.

Spanish coins are often a source of confusion. For only nine denominations, 58 different coins are in circulation. However, many of these are now being phased out, and from January 1997 only coins minted after 1986 will be in use. (The almost worthless 1-peseta and 2-peseta coins will be removed from circulation.)

The seven denominations of coin that will be in circulation after 1997 will be easy to distinguish by shape and color, but the designs will change each year. A 200-peseta coin minted in 1992 shows King Juan Carlos and his son Prince Felipe on one side, and the statue of a bear in Madrid's Puerta del Sol on the other; paintings by Velázquez and Goya appear on the 1994 coin.

A 2,000-peseta coin, minted in silver to commemorate Spain's presidency of the EU Council of Ministers in 1996 is available as a collectors' item. One side shows the Royal Palace in Madrid and the other has the King's head.

1,000 pesetas

2,000 pesetas

Bank Notes
Spanish bank notes are in four denominations. The 1,000-peseta note (two designs, both in green), is the smallest, followed by the 2,000-peseta note (pink), the 5,000-peseta note (ocher with brown and purple), and the 10,000-peseta note (blue).

5,000 pesetas

10,000 pesetas

Coins
Spanish coins, shown here at actual size, are in denominations of 5 ptas, 10 ptas, 25 ptas, 50 ptas, 100 ptas, 200 ptas, and 500 ptas. The 500-pta, 100-pta, 25-pta, and 5-pta coins are all a dull gold. The 200-pta, 50-pta, and 10-pta coins are all silvered.

5 pesetas   **10 pesetas**   **25 pesetas**

50 pesetas   **100 pesetas**   **200 pesetas**   **500 pesetas**

Shopping

SHOPPING IN SPAIN is a pleasurable activity, particularly if you approach it in a leisurely way, punctuating it with frequent breaks for coffee. In small, family-run shops especially, people will go out of their way to fulfill your smallest request. Markets sell the freshest of produce, and quality wines can be found at almost any grocer. Leatherwork is still highly regarded among Spain's many traditional crafts. Spanish design has come to the forefront in both fashion and decor. Below is a size conversion chart for clothes and shoes, and suggestions to help you make the most of shopping in Spain.

A drinking vessel or glass *porrón*

Fresh produce in a market in Pollença (Mallorca)

OPENING HOURS

SHOPS USUALLY open at 10am, close at 2pm and reopen from 5pm to 8pm. Bakeries and bars generally open earlier, at around 8am. Hypermarkets and department stores stay open over lunchtime.

Markets are held in the morning only. In some regions Sunday trading is just limited to the bakeries, *pastelerías*, and newspaper kiosks, but in many vacation resorts stores open on Sunday.

Fans are still in daily use as well as being costume accessories

PAYING

CASH AND CREDIT CARDS are the usual methods of payment in Spain. Checks are rarely accepted. Visitors can reclaim the *IVA* (VAT) charged on all purchases except food, drink, motor vehicles, and medicines *(see p612)*. Money-changing and currency are explained on pages 616–17.

LARGER SHOPS

THE HIPERMERCADOS ("superstores") are outside towns and can often be found by following *centro comercial* signs. The best known are Alcampo, Continente, and PRYCA.

Spain's leading department store is El Corte Inglés. It has branches in all cities, and most of the larger regional towns.

Major sales are advertised by the word *Rebajas* displayed in shop windows.

SPECIALTY SHOPS

SPECIALTY SHOPS often represent generations of family business. *Panaderías* (also called *hornos*) are bakeries selling bread, *bollos* (sweet buns), and rolls. Cakes and pastries are sold in *pastelerías;* many sell chocolates, as well. You buy fresh meat from a *carnicería*, but for the best cold meats go to a *charcutería*, which also sells cheese. *Charcuterías* are often found in or near markets. *Pescaderías* sell fish and shellfish, although the best fish is often sold on market stands.

For fruit and vegetables, a *frutería* or *verdulería* will have better produce, because they stock only what is in season.

Hardware stores are called *ferreterías*. *Librerías* are in fact bookstores, not libraries, and *papelerías* are stationers.

Anything you buy as a *regalo* (gift) will be gift-wrapped on request. When you buy flowers from a *florestería*, the clerk will expect to arrange them.

MARKETS

EVERY LARGE TOWN has a daily market *(mercado)*, open from 9am to 2pm. Small towns have one or more market days a week. This guide lists market days for all towns featured.

Markets usually have the best fresh produce, but they sell all types of food, including *frutos secos* (dried fruits) and seasonal produce, such as mushrooms, soft fruit, and game. There are also usually other types of goods on sale, such as flowers, hardware, and clothes.

Antique and flea markets *(rastros)* are held everywhere in Spain, but the largest is in Madrid *(see p292)*.

Display of hand-painted ceramics in Toledo

REGIONAL PRODUCTS

Spanish REGIONAL specialties are often a better value when bought where they are made. Each region produces its own type of sausage. In Burgos, for example, *morcilla* (blood sausage) is made, and a fiery red chorizo comes from Guijelo, Extremadura. Andalusia is renowned for olives and olive oil and Galicia for its cheeses.

Seasonal delicacies include *rovellons* (huge golden mushrooms) in Catalonia and tiny fiery peppers, *pimientos de Padrón*, in Galicia.

Some crafts originated with the Moors, such as the *azulejos* (ceramic tiles) of Andalusia. Paterna and Manises near Valencia, and Talavera de la Reina in Castilla-La Mancha are towns famous for their ceramics.

Lace from the villages of the Sierra de Gata in Extremadura and Galicia's Costa do Morte is prized. Carved fiddles and clogs are Cantabrian crafts. Spanish crafts, such as guitars, fans, and flamenco shoes, are sold in major cities.

Basketware is sold in all parts of Spain

WINE AND OTHER BEVERAGES

Wine IS SOLD in groceries and supermarkets, but only specialty dealers can do justice to Spain's many grape-growing areas. Local wines can be bought by the liter at either a town or village shop (bodega), or directly from the vineyard (also called a bodega), but you need an appointment to visit.

Spain's most famous grape-growing regions are La Rioja and Navarra *(see pp74–5)*; Penedés, where *cava* (sparkling wine) is produced *(see pp192–3)*; Valdepeñas *(see pp322–3)*; Ribera del Duero *(see pp322–3)*; and Jerez, the sherry region *(see pp402–3)*.

Among the many Spanish liqueurs are *Pacharán (see p577)*, made from sloes, and *licor de bellota*, from acorns.

A range of olives, some flavored with herbs, on a market stall

HOUSEHOLD AND KITCHEN GOODS

Department STORES have a good selection of household goods, but the *ferreterías* (small hardware stores) often have the more authentic selection. Traditional pottery, such as red clay *cazuelas* (dishes) that can be used in the oven and on the stove are cheap. Paella pans have always been made of iron or enamel, but now come in stainless steel or with nonstick finishes. Table linen is often a bargain on market stalls. Spanish lighting design is widely admired and sold in *lampisterías*. Traditional wrought-iron goods, such as candlesticks and door hardware, are always popular.

CLOTHING AND SHOES

The LARGER CITIES naturally offer the widest selection of clothing stores, but Spanish designer labels can be found even in the smaller towns.

If you wish to purchase an item that needs altering, it is still usual for shops to offer the services of a seamstress for a very modest fee. Most can be persuaded to return your item within two days.

Leather shoes and accessories can be inexpensive, and there is a wide range in terms of quality and price. It is the practice in mid-range shops for customers to choose from the selection in the window and give the sales assistant the code number indicated and your *talla* (size). If you want an all-leather shoe, look for *cuero*, the hide label mark. Leather clothes are also good quality and well designed.

SIZE CHART

For Australian sizes follow British and American convention.

Women's dresses, coats and skirts

Spanish	40	42	44	46	48	50	52 (size)
British	8	10	12	14	16	18	20 (size)
American	6	8	10	12	14	16	18 (size)

Women's shoes

Spanish	36	37	38	39	40	41
British	3	4	5	6	7	8
American	5	6	7	8	9	10

Men's suits

Spanish	44	46	48	50	52	54	56	58 (size)
British	34	36	38	40	42	44	46	48 (inches)
American	34	36	38	40	42	44	46	48 (inches)

Men's shirts (collar size)

Spanish	36	38	39	41	42	43	44	45 (cm)
British	14	15	$15^{1}/_{2}$	16	$16^{1}/_{2}$	17	$17^{1}/_{2}$	18 (inches)
American	14	15	$15^{1}/_{2}$	16	$16^{1}/_{2}$	17	$17^{1}/_{2}$	18 (inches)

Men's shoes

Spanish	39	40	41	42	43	44	45	46
British	6	7	$7^{1}/_{2}$	8	9	10	11	12
American	7	$7^{1}/_{2}$	8	$8^{1}/_{2}$	$9^{1}/_{2}$	$10^{1}/_{2}$	11	$11^{1}/_{2}$

Communications

TELEFONICA, THE SPANISH telecommunications company, has improved its service since it was digitized in 1995, and the state monopoly is to be removed in 1998. Public telephones are easy to find, and most operate with a card or coins, but international calls have a high charge.

The postal service, Correos, is identified by a crown insignia in red or white on a yellow background. Registered mail and telegrams can be sent from all Correos offices (see pp622–3). They sell stamps as well, but most people buy them from state-run *estancos* (tobacconists). There are no public phones in Correos offices.

Logo of the Spanish telecom system

USING A COIN AND CARD TELEPHONE

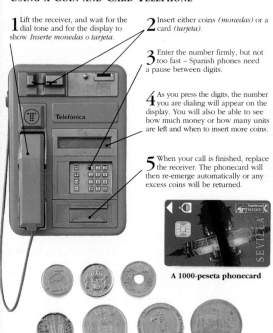

1 Lift the receiver, and wait for the dial tone and for the display to show *Inserte monedas o tarjeta*.

2 Insert either coins *(monedas)* or a card *(tarjeta)*.

3 Enter the number firmly, but not too fast – Spanish phones need a pause between digits.

4 As you press the digits, the number you are dialing will appear on the display. You will also be able to see how much money or how many units are left and when to insert more coins.

5 When your call is finished, replace the receiver. The phonecard will then re-emerge automatically or any excess coins will be returned.

A 1000-peseta phonecard

Denominations of pesetas accepted in coin-operated telephones

TELEPHONING IN SPAIN

AS WELL AS PUBLIC telephone boxes *(cabinas)*, there are nearly always pay phones in bars. Both types take coins of 5, 25, and 100 pesetas. There will be a high minimum connection charge, especially for international calls, so make sure that you have plenty of change at the ready.

Phonecards are far more convenient and can be bought at newsstands and *estancos*. Some phones are equipped with multilingual electronic instruction displays.

There are public telephone offices called *locutorios* where you can make a call and pay for it afterward. They are usually quieter than phone booths, and you do not need coins. Telefónica runs the official ones, which are the cheapest type; private ones, often located in shops, are pricier.

There are four charge brackets for international calls: EU countries; non-EU European countries and Northwest Africa; North and South America; and the rest of the world. With the exception of local calls, using

USEFUL SPANISH DIALING CODES

- To make a call within a province, dial the number directly.
- To call another province, first dial the area code (beginning with 9; e.g. Madrid 91). Area codes are listed in the A-K phone book or obtained from directory assistance.
- To make an international call, dial 07, wait for the tone, then dial the country code, the area code and the number.
- Country codes are: US and Canada 1; UK 44; Eire 353; France 33; Australia 61; New Zealand 64. (It may be necessary to omit the initial digit of the destination's area code.)

- For operator/directory service, dial 003.
- For international directories, dial 025.
- To make a reversed-charge (collect) call within the EU, dial 900 99 00 followed by the country code; to the US or Canada, dial 900 99 00 followed by 11 or 15 respectively. Numbers for other countries can be found in the front of the A-K telephone directory under *Modalidades del Servicio Internacional*.
- To report technical problems, dial 002.
- For the speaking clock dial 093, for the weather 094, for a wake-up call 096.

the telephone system can be expensive, especially from a hotel, which may add a surcharge. A call from a *cabina* or a *locutorio* costs 35 percent more than one made from a private phone in someone's home. Collect calls made to EU countries may be dialed directly, but most other collect calls must be made through the operator.

The Spanish dialing code system works on a provincial basis, with each area code prefixed by the number 9. For example, Barcelona is 93. When dialing from outside Spain, you omit the 9. The international code for Spain is always 34 so, to get through to Barcelona, you dial 34 3.

Phone numbers in Spanish cities generally have seven digits, but in smaller towns and in country areas they have six.

Public telephone booth, easily visible in a city street

TELEVISION AND RADIO

TELEVISION ESPAÑOLA, Spain's state television company, broadcasts two channels that are called TVE1 and TVE2.

Several of the *comunidades* (*see pp622–3*) have their own publicly owned television channels that broadcast in the language of the region.

There are three national independent television stations: Antena 3, Tele-5 (Telecinco), and Canal+ (Canal Plus). Some Canal+ programs are available

Spanish daily papers

Spanish magazines

only on payment of a subscription for a station decoder.

Most foreign films shown on Spanish television (and in theaters) are dubbed, and subtitled films are listed as *V.O. (versión original).*

Several satellite channels, such as CNN, Eurosport, and Cinemanía, can be received throughout Spain.

The state radio station is Radio Nacional de España. Radio Clásico and Radio 2 broadcast music.

Some stations in tourist areas rebroadcast BBC World Service programs in English. They are: Radio Mijas; Coastline Radio in Torrox; Onda Cero Radio in Marbella and Tenerife; Radio Maspalomas in Gran Canaria; and Sunshine Capital Radio in Palma de Mallorca.

NEWSPAPERS AND MAGAZINES

NEWSSTANDS in the town centers often stock periodicals in English. The newspapers available on publication day are the *International Herald Tribune, USA Today,* the *Financial Times,* and the *Guardian International.* Other English-language and European titles are on sale, but usually not until a day after they have been published.

The European newspaper and popular weekly news magazines such as *Time, Newsweek,* and *The Economist* are readily available throughout the country. The most

Logo of Radio Nacional de España

widely read of the Spanish newspapers, in descending number of sales, are *El País, El Mundo, ABC,* and *La Vanguardia* (in Catalonia). *El Mundo* is oriented more toward features and aimed at a younger market than the other three, which cover international news more thoroughly. Weekly listings magazines for arts and events are published in Barcelona (*see p184*), Madrid (*see p306*), and Seville. They are the *Guía del Ocio* in Barcelona and Madrid, and *El Giraldillo* in Seville. Several other cities also have listings magazines.

Local newspapers in Spanish, such as *Levante* in Valencia and *La Gaceta de Canarias* in the Canary Islands, are a useful source of information on local and regional events.

Foreign-language periodicals are published by expatriates in Madrid and in the country's main tourist areas. Examples in English include *Sur* on the Costa del Sol, the *Costa Blanca News,* and the *Mallorca Daily Bulletin.* One of the longest-running magazines is *Lookout.* Published in Fuengirola, it features in-depth reports covering all aspects of life in Spain.

A *prensa* (press) sign identifies a newsstand

POSTAL SERVICE

CORREOS, the postal service in Spain, is rather slow. Mail sent to an address in the city where it is posted can take three to four days to arrive, and a national or international delivery may take more than a week. Send any urgent or important post by *urgente* (express) or *certificado* (registered) mail. To be sure of fast delivery it is wise to use a private courier.

Shops with this sign sell stamps

Mail can be registered and telegrams sent from all Correos offices. However, it is much more convenient to buy stamps for letters and postcards from an *estanco* (tobacconist). Postal rates fall into four price bands: the EU; the rest of Europe; the US; and the rest of the world. Packages have to be weighed and stamped by Correos, and must be securely tied with string or a charge may be made at the counter to have them sealed by a clerk.

The main Correos offices open 8am–9pm from Monday to Friday and 9am–7pm on Saturday. Branches in the suburbs of cities and in villages open 9am–2pm from Monday to Friday and 9am–1pm on Saturday.

Standard issue postage stamps

ADDRESSES

HERE, THE HOUSE number follows the name of the street. The floor of an apartment building comes after a hyphen. Therefore 4-2° means an apartment on the second floor of number four. Postcodes have five digits, the first two being the province number.

SPAIN'S LOTTERIES

Lottery fever is greater in Spain than in any other European country. The Lotería Nacional runs prize draws most Saturdays, plus a few special ones, the *extraordinarios*, of which the biggest is El Gordo ("the Fat One") at Christmas *(see p39)*. It is common to buy a *décimo* (one-tenth of a number), rather than a full ticket. Bettors can also try their luck with the ONCE lottery, which has drawings daily, the Thursday Lotería Primitiva, and the Bono-loto, with four draws a week.

ONCE lottery booth

LETTERS AND FAXES

LETTERS MAILED at a central post office usually arrive more quickly than if posted in a postbox *(buzón)*. Postboxes in cities are yellow pillar boxes; in towns and villages they are usually small, wall-mounted postboxes. Poste restante letters should be addressed care of the *Lista de Correos* and the town. You can collect them from main post offices. To send and receive money by mail ask for a *giro postal*.

When dealing with businesses in Spain, it is best to phone or fax. The mail tends to be used only as a last resort. There are fax facilities in some *locutorios (see p620)* and in hotels and many private shops. Look for a *telefax* sign.

Spanish mailbox

LOCAL GOVERNMENT

SPAIN is one of Europe's most decentralized states. Many powers have been devolved to the 17 regions, *comunidades autónomas*, which have their own elected parliaments. These regions have varying degrees of independence from Madrid, with the Basques and Catalans enjoying the most autonomy. The *comunidades* provide some services – such as the promotion of tourism – which were once carried out by central government.

The country is subdivided into 50 provinces, each with its *diputación* (council). The affairs of each of the Balearic and Canary islands are run by an island council.

Every town, or group of villages, is administered by an *ayuntamiento* (town council – the word also means town hall) which is supervised by an elected *alcalde* (mayor) and a team of councillors.

Murcia's town hall *(ayuntamiento or casa consistorial)*

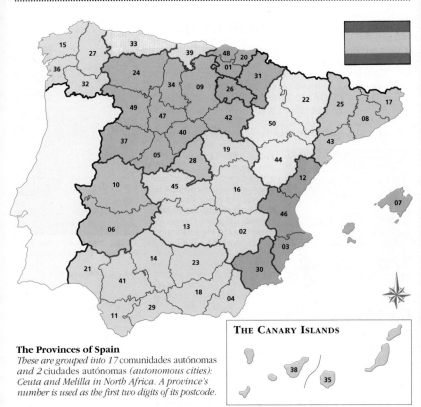

The Provinces of Spain

These are grouped into 17 comunidades autónomas and 2 ciudades autónomas (autonomous cities): Ceuta and Melilla in North Africa. A province's number is used as the first two digits of its postcode.

THE CANARY ISLANDS

THE COMUNIDADES OF SPAIN AND THEIR PROVINCES

NORTHERN SPAIN

Galicia
15 A Coruña
27 Lugo
32 Ourense
36 Pontevedra

Asturias   **Cantabria**
33 Asturias
39 Cantabria

Basque   **Navarra**   **La Rioja**
Country
Basque Country (Euskadi)
01 Álava
20 Guipúzcoa
48 Vizcaya
Comunidad Foral de Navarra
31 Navarra
La Rioja
26 La Rioja

EASTERN SPAIN

Catalonia
08 Barcelona
25 Lleida
17 Girona
43 Tarragona

Aragón
22 Huesca
44 Teruel
50 Zaragoza

Valencia   Murcia
Comunidad Valenciana
03 Alicante
46 Valencia
12 Castellón
Murcia
30 Murcia

CENTRAL SPAIN

Madrid
28 Comunidad de Madrid

Castilla-La Mancha
02 Albacete
13 Ciudad Real
16 Cuenca
19 Guadalajara
45 Toledo

Extremadura
06 Badajoz
10 Cáceres

Castilla y León
05 Ávila
09 Burgos
24 León
34 Palencia
37 Salamanca
40 Segovia
42 Soria
47 Valladolid
49 Zamora

SOUTHERN SPAIN

Andalusia
04 Almería
11 Cádiz
14 Córdoba
18 Granada
21 Huelva
23 Jaén
29 Málaga
41 Sevilla

SPAIN'S ISLANDS

The Balearic Islands (Islas Baleares)
07 Baleares

The Canary Islands (Islas Canarias)
35 Las Palmas
38 Santa Cruz de Tenerife

Sports and Outdoor Activities

SPAIN IS ONE OF EUROPE'S most geographically diverse countries. Its mountain ranges, woodlands, and deltas are all fertile ground for scenic tours and sports vacations as alternatives to a break on the beach. It also has a full calendar of seasonal and annual events and activities *(see pp36–9)*. Tourist offices will provide lists of leisure and sporting activities in their region. These pages give an idea of the range of activities there is to choose from.

A game of golf on a course on Ibiza in the Balearic Islands

SPECIAL INTEREST TRIPS

ALL SPANISH tourist offices provide details of special interest holidays. Cooking, wine, and painting vacations, and tours led by professional historians and archaeologists, are all increasingly popular. There is a wide choice for nature lovers and photographers, particularly in Spain's many national parks.

Information about courses in Spanish language and culture is provided by the **Instituto Cervantes** (Spanish Institute) in New York.

GOLF AND TENNIS

SPAIN NOW HAS an abundance of golf courses, some with activities for nongolfers. The **Real Federación Española de Golf** will give locations and more detailed information.

In most tourist areas there are tennis courts for rent by the hour, and some hotels have tennis courts for their guests *(see pp536–71)*. Travel agents arrange tennis vacations for enthusiasts. For more information contact the **Real Federación Española de Tenis**.

WALKING, CYCLING, AND HORSEBACK RIDING

MANY tour operators now specialize in outdoor holidays. The **Federación Hípica Española** and Spanish tourist offices have information on horseback riding and pony trekking in most regions.

The road to Santiago de Compostela *(see pp78–9)* is Spain's most famous walk and some national parks *(see pp26–7)* have spectacular routes for hiking. Picturesque minor roads in many regions of Spain are excellent for bicycle touring.

Walking along the Río Cares in the Picos de Europa in Asturias

MOUNTAIN SPORTS

SPAIN'S MOST POPULAR resorts for downhill skiing are in the Vall d'Aran in Catalonia *(see pp200–201)*, and in the Sierra Nevada, near Granada *(see p461)*. Downhill skiing is often possible in the Sierra de Guadarrama north of Madrid, and there is cross-country skiing in other mountain areas.

Every region of this mountainous country has a climbing association. The **Federación Española de Montañismo** will supply details. This national organization has information about climbing and many other mountain sports.

AIR SPORTS

A PRIVATE pilot's licence is valid in Spain for up to six months. The **Federación Nacional de Deportes Aéreos** will send information about Spanish airfields and clubs where visitors can practice flying *(vuelo)*, gliding *(vuelo sin motor)*, and parachuting *(salto en paracaídas)*.

The organization also gives information on places where tourists can go ballooning *(volar en globo)*, hang gliding *(ala delta)*, and paragliding *(parapente)*. Parts of Castilla y León and Castilla-La Mancha are recognized internationally as excellent places for hang gliding, and the Valle de Abdalajís, north of Málaga, is well known for paragliding.

Paragliding above the Vall d'Aran in the eastern Pyrenees

White-water rafting in the Spanish Pyrenees

WATER SPORTS

THERE IS WHITE WATER RAFTING and canoeing on rivers in Catalonia, Aragón and many other regions of Spain. Sort, a village set in the Catalonian Pyrenees, is one of Europe's prime river sports resorts.

Boating, sailing, and windsurfing are very popular. The tourist offices at the coastal resorts of the mainland and in the islands give information about local rental of boats and sailboards. Experienced . windsurfers head for Tarifa *(see p 444)*, whose windswept location has made it one of Europe's windsurfing capitals.

Information on sailing is available from the **Federación Española de Vela**.

Those beaches, marinas, and ports that meet strict European standards of cleanliness and safety are permitted to fly a *bandera azul* (blue flag).

Windsurfing off Fuerteventura in the Canary Islands

HUNTING AND FISHING

CONTACT THE **Federación Española de Naturismo**, or coastal tourist offices for the location of nudist beaches.

Fly-fishing in the rivers of Castilla y León, famous for their trout

FIELD SPORTS

IF YOU WANT TO HUNT or shoot in Spain you must first apply for a licence and be properly insured. To obtain a licence you apply to the *comunidad* (regional government) of the area where you want to hunt. The fees tend to be high.

Permits for river or ocean fishing for any length of period from one day to one year, and for fishing competitions, are issued by the *comunidades*. The **Federación Española de Caza** (for hunting) and the **Federación Española de Pesca** (for fishing) give information on where each different field sport is permitted, dates of open seasons, and advice on licences. Travel agents and hotels specializing in hunting and fishing trips will obtain licences for clients.

TRAVEL INFORMATION

SPAIN HAS AN INCREASINGLY EFFICIENT transportation system. All the major cities have airports, and flights from all over the globe arrive at those of Madrid and Barcelona. Both the road and rail networks were greatly improved during the 1980s and in preparation for the Olympics and Expo in 1992 *(see p65)*. Intercity rail ser-

➤ **aeropuerto**

Sign for an airport

vices are efficient, but buses are a faster and more frequent option between smaller towns. In much of rural Spain, however, public transport is limited, and a car is the most practical solution for getting around. Ferries connect mainland Spain with the UK, North Africa, and the Balearic and Canary islands.

Duty-free shopping at Barcelona's El Prat airport

ARRIVING BY AIR

SPAIN IS SERVED by many international airlines. **Iberia** has direct flights daily into Madrid from New York, Miami, and Los Angeles, as well as direct flights to many destinations in Spain from Montreal and Toronto. Of the several US airlines serving Spain, **Continental** and **American** have direct flights to Madrid from Newark and Miami respectively. **Delta** and **TWA**

have direct flights to both Madrid and Barcelona.

There are no airlines operating direct flights between Spain and Australasia. Iberia also has scheduled daily flights into Madrid and Barcelona from all major western European cities and once or twice weekly from most large eastern European cities. **British Airways** and **Virgin Atlantic** offer scheduled flights to many cities in Spain from the UK.

BARAJAS AIRPORT, MADRID

Madrid's airport is 13 km (8 miles) from the city center. The international terminal (which is connected to the domestic terminal) is illustrated here. Arrivals are on the ground floor; departures, check in, and boarding on the first floor. A shuttle bus runs every 12 minutes to the center of Madrid, stopping at six stops, the most central of which are Calle de Velázquez and Plaza de Colón. Alternatively, you can take a taxi (allow half an hour to the center) or, at much greater expense, a chauffeur-driven car.

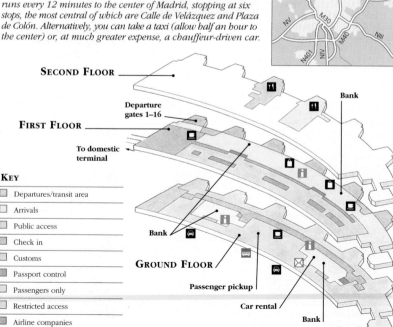

SECOND FLOOR

Departure gates 1–16

FIRST FLOOR

To domestic terminal

Bank

Bank

KEY

- ☐ Departures/transit area
- ☐ Arrivals
- ☐ Public access
- ☐ Check in
- ☐ Customs
- ☐ Passport control
- ☐ Passengers only
- ☐ Restricted access
- ☐ Airline companies

Bank

GROUND FLOOR

Passenger pickup

Car rental

Bank

INTERNATIONAL AIRPORTS

R EGULAR international services operate from Madrid and Barcelona. The busiest international airports for scheduled and charter flights in Spain are marked on the map on pages 10–11.

Palma de Mallorca, Tenerife Sur, Las Palmas de Gran Canaria, Málaga, Lanzarote, Ibiza, Alicante, Fuerteventura, and Menorca handle large amounts of seasonal tourist traffic; at peak summer vacation time these airports are often very crowded. Details of public transportation to and from Spain's most important airports are on page 628.

The Balearic and Canary islands have international airports, except for Hierro, which has a domestic one, and La Gomera, which has no airport at all. Both Melilla and Ceuta are served by domestic flights only.

Iberia plane on the apron of Seville airport

AIR FARES

A PEX/SUPER APEX fares offer the best deals on scheduled flights to Spain, but they must be purchased well in advance; some require minimum stays, and all are subject to penalty clauses. It is well worth scouring the small ads in the Travel Section of newspapers for discount charters and discounted scheduled flights to Spain.

Fares tend to vary greatly during the year, but generally the most expensive periods are during the summer months and over the Christmas and Easter holidays.

CAR RENTAL

M ANY TRAVEL AGENTS and car rental firms will organize special fly-drive packages that enable you to book a flight and have a rental car waiting at the airport of your destination. This is cheaper and involves fewer formalities than renting a car on arrival.

EL PRAT AIRPORT, BARCELONA

Barcelona's airport is 12 km (7 miles) from the city center. Terminal A handles international arrivals and foreign airlines' departures. Terminals B and C are for departures on Spanish airlines and arrivals from European Union countries. Trains to the Plaça de Catalunya in the city center leave every 30 minutes. For intercity rail services get off at Sants mainline station. There is also a shuttle bus, the Aerobús, running every 15 minutes, that will also leave you in Plaça de Catalunya.

FIRST FLOOR — Terminal C

Terminal B

Terminal A

GROUND FLOOR

Bank

Car rental

KEY

- Departures
- Arrivals
- Public access
- Check in
- Customs
- Passport control
- Passengers only
- Restricted access

Car rental

Passenger pickup

Bank

Car rental

Bank

Insignia of Spain's national airline

DOMESTIC FLIGHTS

Most of Spain's domestic flights have traditionally been operated by **Iberia** and **Aviaco**, its affiliated airline. In recent years, however, this monopoly has been broken to encourage competition. The two main alternative carriers are **Air Europa** and **Spanair**.

The most frequent shuttle service is the Puente Aéreo, run between Barcelona and Madrid by Iberia. It flies every 15 minutes at peak business times, hourly at other times. A ticket machine allows passengers to buy tickets up to 15 minutes before a flight departs. When a flight is full, waiting passengers are always offered a seat on the next available shuttle. The flight usually takes 50 minutes.

Aviaco, Air Europa, and Spanair services between Madrid and the regional capitals are not as frequent as the Puente Aéreo, but their prices are usually slightly lower. They operate in a similar way to

Apex tickets: the earlier the booking is made, the greater the discount. The cheapest ticket, which must be booked a week in advance, can save up to one-third of the full price. Flights to the provincial cities usually operate in the morning and evening. They can be expensive, costing as much as 20,000 pesetas for a one-way trip. Pressure from the intercity rail services may eventually result in lower air fares.

Flights to the Balearic and Canary islands, and island-

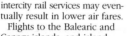

Ticket machine

hopping flights between them, are operated by two Iberia-affiliated companies: **Binter**, and an air charter company, **Viva**. Travel agencies often offer a variety of special deals on domestic flights, which may include one night or more in a hotel. These deals are advertised in the Spanish press.

Some flights from domestic airports are billed as international flights but they do not go directly to foreign destinations. Instead, they stop en route at Madrid or Barcelona.

The departure concourse in Seville Airport

AIRPORT	ℂ INFORMATION	DISTANCE TO CITY CENTER	PUBLIC TRANSIT TIME TO CITY CENTER
Alicante	(96) 691 90 00	15 km (9 miles)	Bus: 20 mins
Barcelona	(93) 478 50 00	15 km (9 miles)	Rail: 20 mins Bus: 25 mins
Bilbao	(94) 486 93 00	10 km (6 miles)	Bus: 30 mins
Madrid	(91) 305 83 43	15 km (9 miles)	Bus: 30 mins
Málaga	(95) 204 88 38	10 km (6 miles)	Rail: 15 mins Bus: 20 mins
Palma de Mallorca	(971) 78 90 00	9 km (5.5 miles)	Bus: 30 mins
Las Palmas de Gran Canaria	(928) 57 90 00	20 km (12 miles)	Bus: 30 mins
Santiago de Compostela	(981) 54 75 00	10 km (6 miles)	Bus: 30 mins
Seville	(95) 444 90 23	8 km (5 miles)	Rail: 15 mins Bus: 30 mins
Tenerife Sur – Reina Sofía	(922) 75 92 00	69 km (43 miles) to Santa Cruz	Bus: 60 mins
Valencia	(96) 370 95 00	8 km (5 miles)	Rail: 20 mins Bus: 30 mins

ARRIVING BY SEA

FERRIES connect the Spanish mainland to the Balearic and Canary islands, to North Africa, and to the UK. All the important routes are served by car ferries. It is wise to make an advance reservation, especially in summer.

Two routes link Spain with the UK. **Brittany Ferries** sails between Plymouth in the UK and Santander in Cantabria; and **P&O European Ferries** sails from Portsmouth into Santurce harbor, near Bilbao in the Basque Country. The crossings take over 24 hours. Each ship has cabins, chairs to sleep on, a restaurant, cafés, and a cinema. Discos are sometimes held on board.

FERRIES TO THE ISLANDS

FREQUENT CROSSINGS run from Barcelona and Valencia on the mainland to the three main Balearic islands. The crossings, on **Trasmediterránea** ferries, take about eight hours. The same company also operates frequent interisland services; and small operators take day-trippers (passengers only) from Ibiza to Formentera. Storms are rare in this part of the Mediterranean and crossings are, therefore, usually calm and comfortable.

Trasmediterránea operates a weekly service from Cádiz in Andalusia to the main ports of the Canary Islands – Las Palmas de Gran Canaria and Santa Cruz de Tenerife. Crossings normally take 39 hours.

Ferry in port at Los Cristianos (Tenerife) in the Canary Islands

Car ferries link the islands with each other. Trasmediterránea also runs passengers-only services between the islands of Gran Canaria, Tenerife, and Fuerteventura, and between Tenerife and La Gomera.

The ferries to Spain's islands have cabins, cafés, restaurants, bars, shops, movies, pools, and sunbathing decks for the summer. They are also fitted with elevators and facilities for people with special needs, and they even have kennels. A variety of entertainment, such as films and discos, is provided on the long crossing from the mainland to the Canary Islands.

Trasmediterránea Ferries logo

FERRIES TO AFRICA

TRASMEDITERRANEA operates ferries daily to the Spanish territories in North Africa: from Málaga and Almería to Melilla, and from Algeciras to Ceuta. Ferries also cross to Tangier in Morocco from Algeciras.

Trasmediterránea car ferry to the Balearic Islands in Barcelona harbor

Traveling by Train

Logo of the Spanish national railways

THE SPANISH STATE RAILROAD, **RENFE** *(Red Nacional de Ferrocarriles Españoles),* operates a service that is continually improving, particularly between cities. The fastest intercity services are called the TALGO and the AVE – their names are acronyms for the high-speed, luxury trains that run on these routes. *Largo recorrido* (long-distance) and *regionales y cercanías* (regional and local) trains are notoriously slow, many stopping at every station. They are much cheaper than the high-speed trains, but can take hours longer.

ARRIVING BY TRAIN

THERE ARE SEVERAL routes to Spain from France. The main western route runs from Paris through Hendaye in the Pyrenees to San Sebastián. The eastern route from Paris runs via Cerbère and Port Bou to Barcelona. The trains from London, Brussels, Amsterdam, Geneva, Zurich, and Milan all reach Barcelona via Cerbère. At Cerbère there are connections with the TALGO and the *largo recorrido* (long-distance) services to Valencia, Málaga, Seville and Madrid, and other major destinations. If you book a sleeper on the TALGO from Paris, you travel to your destination without having to change trains.

EXPLORING BY TRAIN

SPAIN OFFERS many options for train travelers. In the last ten years, the TALGO high-speed services have belied Spain's reputation for inefficiency, and it is now possible to travel the long distances between the main cities extremely quickly. Ticket prices compare very favorably with the cost of high-speed train fares in many other countries in Europe. AVE is the efficient high-speed rail service between Madrid and Seville via Córdoba. The full journey normally takes just under three hours.

The *largo recorrido* (long-distance) trains are so much slower you usually need to travel overnight. You can

AVE high-speed trains at Estación de Santa Justa in Seville

choose between a *cochecama* (compartment with two *camas* or beds) or a *litera*, one of six seats in a compartment which converts into a bunk bed. You reserve these when booking and pay a supplement. You should book at least a month in advance, but bear in mind that it is difficult to change a ticket you have paid for.

Regionales y cercanías (the regional and local services) are frequent and very cheap. You buy the tickets from machines on the station.

Some cities have more than one station. In Madrid the major stations for regional and long-distance trains are Atocha, Chamartín, and Norte. The AVE runs from Atocha, the TALGO from all three. Sants and Francia are Barcelona's two principal stations. In Seville, Santa Justa is the only station for regional and international services.

Logo for a high-speed rail service

RENFE INFORMATION AND RESERVATIONS

Madrid
℡ *(91) 328 90 20.*

Barcelona
℡ *(93) 490 02 02.*

Seville
℡ *(95) 454 02 02.*

Credit Card Bookings
℡ *(91) 374 38 24.*

REGIONAL RAILROADS

ET
℡ *(943) 45 01 31.*

FEVE
℡ *(98) 534 24 15.*

FF CC
℡ *(93) 205 15 15.*

FGV
℡ *(96) 347 37 50.*

Iberrail
℡ *(93) 310 15 12.*

FARES

SPANISH RAILROADS offer a ten percent discount on specified days to encourage people to travel. They are called *días azules* (blue days) and are indicated in the timetables in blue.

Fares for rail travel in Spain are structured according to the speed and quality of the service. Tickets for the TALGO and AVE are most expensive.

Interrail tickets for people under 26, and Eurodomino tickets for people over 26, are available from major travel agencies in Europe and from RENFE ticket offices in Spain. Always take proof of your identity when booking.

Iberrail holidays offer rail-plus-hotel deals for traveling between Spanish cities at very economical prices.

REGIONAL RAILWAYS

THREE OF THE *comunidades autónomas* have regional rail companies. Catalonia and Valencia each has its own *Ferrocarrils de la Generalitat:*

SPAIN'S PRINCIPAL RENFE NETWORK

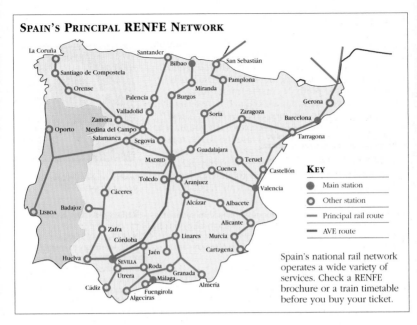

KEY

● Main station
○ Other station
— Principal rail route
— AVE route

Spain's national rail network operates a wide variety of services. Check a RENFE brochure or a train timetable before you buy your ticket.

respectively the **FF CC** and the **FGV**; and the Basque Country has the **ET** *(Eusko Trenbideak)*.

Iberrail markets tickets for two special trains similar to the Orient Express. One is the Al Andalus Expres, which tours Andalusia, stopping at Seville, Córdoba, Granada, Jerez and Ronda. The other is the Transcantábrico, run by **FEVE** *(Ferrocarriles de Vía Estrecha)*, which leaves San Sebastián to travel the length of Spain's north coast, ending its journey in Santiago de Compostela. Passengers travel in style in 14 antique cars built between 1900–30 since restored.

The regional tourist offices publicize unusual rail services, such as the narrow-gauge lines to Inca and Sóller in Mallorca.

RESERVATIONS

Talgo, AVE, and any other tickets for *largo recorrido* travel by train may be booked and bought at any of the major railroad stations from the *taquilla* (ticket office). They are also sold by all travel agents in Spain, who will charge a commission. RENFE tickets are sometimes sold by travel agents in other countries. Telephone reservations may be made directly to all RENFE

Ticket machine for local and regional lines

ticket offices using a credit card number. A booking may be made or a special pass purchased as long as 59 days ahead of travel. Tickets for local and regional services are purchased from the station *taquilla*. In larger stations they can be bought from ticket machines, but these accept only coins. Tickets for *cercanías* (local services) cannot be reserved. For a one-way trip ask for *ida* and for a round trip ask for *ida y vuelta*.

TIMETABLES

RENFE TIMETABLES change in May and October each year. They are not very easy to obtain outside Spain, but your travel agent will be able to provide the correct times of trains for your journey. In Spain timetables are available from RENFE offices. Most come in the form of leaflets and are broken down into the various types of journey: intercity, *largo recorrido*, and *regionales*. C*ercanías* timetables are posted on boards at local railroad stations.

Atocha, one of Madrid's largest mainline railroad stations

Traveling by Road

Spain's fastest roads are its *autopistas*. They are normally divided highways and are subsidized by *peajes* (tolls). *Autovías* are similar but have no tolls. The *carretera nacional* is the countrywide network of main roads or highways with the prefix N. Smaller minor roads are generally less well kept but are often a more leisurely and enjoyable way to see rural areas of Spain. These pages tell you how to use the roads, tolls, and parking meters, how to buy gas, and explain important driving regulations.

Red de Carreteras del Estado

CARRETERA   N-110

Sign for national highway N110

Cambio de sentido (U-turn)
300 m (330 yd) ahead

Arriving by Car

Many people drive to Spain via the French freeways. The most direct routes across the Pyrenees, using the freeways, pass through Hendaye on the western flank and Port Bou in the east. Other, rather more tortuous routes may be used, from Toulouse through the Vall d'Aran, for instance. From the UK there are car ferries from Plymouth to Santander and from Portsmouth to Bilbao in northern Spain *(see p629)*.

What to Take

Visitors driving vehicles from other countries need no special documentation in Spain. You should just make sure you have all the relevant papers from your country of origin: your driver's license, vehicle registration document, and insurance. Your insurance company should be able to arrange an overseas extension of your car insurance. To rent a car in Spain you need to show only a current driver's license, however, it is generally recommended that you obtain an international driver's license to facilitate dealing with traffic officials in case of problems.

The headlights of right-hand drive vehicles will have to be adjusted or deflected. This is done with stickers that can be bought at ferry ports and on ferries. You risk on-the-spot fines if you do not carry a red warning triangle, spare light bulbs, and a first-aid kit.

In winter you should carry chains if you intend to drive in mountain areas. In summer, it is a good idea to take drinking water with you if you are traveling in a remote area.

Buying Gas

In Spain *gasolina* (gas) and *gasóleo* (diesel) are priced by the liter. *Gasolina sin plomo* (unleaded gas) is available everywhere. All cost more at the *autopista* service stations. Self-service stations, where you fill up yourself, are common. You must wait for service if there are attendants. They will ask *¿cuánto?* (how much?); you should reply *lleno* (fill the tank) or specify an amount in pesetas: *dos mil pesetas por favor*. Small stations do not all accept credit cards. If you use your credit card to pay at a freeway service station you will be asked to show your passport or ID. Modern pumps sometimes operate by credit card. You run your card through the machine, press the buttons to indicate the amount of fuel you want in pesetas, and then serve yourself.

Rules of the Road

Most traffic regulations and warnings to motorists are represented on signs by easily recognized symbols. But Spain has a few road rules and signs that may be unfamiliar to some drivers from other countries.

To turn left at a busy junction or across oncoming traffic you may have to turn right first and cross a main road, often by way of traffic lights, a bridge, or an underpass. If you are going the wrong way on a freeway or a main road with a solid white line, you are allowed to turn around where you see a sign for a *cambio de sentido*.

At any crossing you must yield to the right unless a sign indicates otherwise. It is compulsory always to wear seat belts if they are fitted in front and rear seats. Oncoming drivers may flash their headlights at you to mean "you go," "danger," "your lights are on unnecessarily," or (most often) "speed trap ahead."

60

Speed limit 60 km/h (37 mph)

Pedestrian crossing sign

A filling station run by a leading chain with branches throughout Spain

SPEED LIMITS AND FINES

SPEED LIMITS on the roads in Spain for cars without trailers are as follows:
• 120 km/h (75 mph) on *autopistas* (toll highways).
• 100 km/h (62 mph) on *autovías* (non-toll freeways).
• 90 km/h (56 mph) on *carreteras nacionales* (main roads) and *carreteras comarcales* (secondary roads).
• 60 km/h (37 mph) in built-up areas.

Speeding fines are imposed on the spot at the rate of 1,000 pesetas for every kilometer per hour over the limit. Fines for other traffic offenses (such as turning the wrong way into a one-way street) depend on the severity of the offense and the whim of a police officer.

Tests for drunk driving and fines for drivers over the blood alcohol legal limit, which is 80 mg per milliliter, are now imposed frequently throughout the country.

Blue *antopista* (highway) sign for motorists approaching the A6

FREEWAYS

SPAIN HAS more than 2,000 km (1,240 miles) of *autopistas*, and many more are planned. They are toll roads and they are rather expensive to use. The long-distance tolls are calculated per kilometer and the rate varies from region to region. Among the busiest and most expensive are the A7 along the south coast to Alicante and the A68 Bilbao-Zaragoza *autopista*.

There are service stations every 40 km (25 miles) or so along the *autopistas*, marked by a blue and white parking sign (P) or a sign indicating the services available. About 1 km (550 yd) from a service station, a sign indicates the distance to the next one and lists its services. Most have fuel, toilets, a shop for maps,

Driving through the Sierra Nevada along one of Europe's highest roads

coffee, and snacks, and a café that serves full meals.

Emergency telephones occur every 2 km (1.25 miles) along the *autopistas*.

USING AUTOPISTA TOLLS

IF YOU ARE TRAVELING a long distance on the *autopista* you pick up a ticket from a toll booth *(peaje)* as you enter and give it up at a booth as you exit. Your toll will be calculated according to the distance you have covered. Over some short stretches of freeways near to cities a fixed price is charged. Tolls can be paid either in cash or by credit card.

You must join one of three lanes at the *peaje* leading to different booths. Do not drive into *telepago*, a credit system for which you need a sticker on your windshield. *Automático* has machines for you to pay by credit card or with exactly the right coins. In *manual* an attendant in the booth takes your ticket and your money.

PEAJE TOLL

Autopista toll booths ahead

The *peaje manual* lane, with attendant

OTHER ROADS

CARRETERAS NACIONALES, Spain's highways, have black and white signs and are designated N *(Nacional)* plus a number. Those with Roman numerals (NIII) start at the Puerta del Sol, Madrid. The distance from the Kilometer Zero mark in the Puerta del Sol *(see p262)* appears on kilometer markers. Those with ordinary numbers (N6) have kilometer markers giving the distance from the provincial capital. Some *carreteras nacionales* are divided highways, but most are two-lane roads and can be slow. They tend to be least busy at lunch time, from 2–5pm, when many truck drivers stop for lunch.

Autovías are new roads built in recent years to freeway standard to replace N roads. They have blue signs similar to *autopista* signs. Because they have no tolls they are busier than *autopistas*.

Carreteras comarcales, secondary roads, have a number preceded by a letter C. Other minor roads have numbers preceded by letters representing the name of the province such as the LE 1313 in Lleida. On any road in winter, look out for signs indicating whether a mountain pass ahead is open *(abierto)* or closed *(cerrado)*.

CAR RENTAL

As well as the international car rental companies, a few Spanish companies, such as **Atesa**, operate nationwide. You can probably negotiate the best deal with an international company from home. There are also fly-drive and other package deals, including car rental. Fly-drive, an option for two or more travelers, can be arranged by travel agents.

There are car rental desks at airports and offices in the large towns. Alternatively, if you wish to rent a car locally for, say, a week or less, you can arrange it with a local travel agent. A rental car is called a *coche de alquiler*.

For chauffeur-driven cars in Spain, **Avis** offer deals for major cities. Rental cars prices and conditions vary according to the region and locality.

Some of the leading car rental companies operating in Spain

MAPS

Foldout road maps can be obtained at airports, on the ferries, and from tourist offices. The Spanish Ministry of Transportation publishes a comprehensive road map in book form, the *Mapa Oficial de Carreteras*. Campsa, the oil company, publishes the *Guía Campsa*, a road map and restaurant guide in one book. Michelin publishes a useful series of maps (440–448, with orange covers) at a scale of 1:400,000 (1 cm:4 km), which cover Spain in eight sections, including the islands. They are sold at bookshops and gas stations all over Spain.

A series of more detailed maps at 1:200,000 for cycling, walking, and other uses is published by Plaza y Janés. Military maps at scales of 1:50,000 and 1:100,000 are available from many large bookstores in the US and from specialty bookshops and

City taxis with their logo and official numbers

some local bookshops in Spain. Tourist offices in towns and cities usually have a free street map of the town showing the principal sights.

There are detailed street maps of central Barcelona on pages 176–81, of Madrid on pages 298–303, and of Seville on pages 430–33 of this guide.

PARKING

The hours for which drivers have to pay for parking in Spain are 8am until 2pm and 4pm until 8pm on Mondays to Saturdays.

As a rule, you may not park where the pavement edge is painted yellow or where a no parking sign is displayed. Occasionally there is a no parking sign on both sides of a city street, one saying "1–15" and the other "16–30." This means that you can park on one side of the street only for the two weeks indicated on the sign.

In the cities, non-metered, on-street parking is generally hard to find, but there are blue pay-and-display parking spaces. To use them you buy a ticket from the machine and display it on the inside of your windshield. The cost varies, but averages about 200 pesetas per hour. You can usually park at the same spot for up to two hours. The penalties for infringements vary from town to town.

Major cities have many large underground parking lots. You collect a ticket when you enter, keep it, and pay the attendant as you drive out.

A parking ticket machine

No parking at any time of day

TAXIS

There is no central system for taxis in Spain. Every city and/or region has its own design and rates for its taxis. All will display a green light if they are free. Most taxis are metered, and at the start of the journey a minimum fee will be shown on the meter. In smaller villages the taxi service may well be run by a resident driving an unmetered private car. Ask at the hotel desk or in a nearby shop for the name and number of a local driver. It is best to negotiate a price for the trip before you set off.

In the cities there are taxi ranks at the airports, the railroad and bus stations and usually in the main shopping areas. Tips of 50–100 pesetas will be acceptable.

ROAD CONDITIONS AND WEATHER FORECASTS

To hear recorded road and traffic information call the national toll-free number for **Información de Tráfico de Carreteras**. This service is in Spanish only. Ask your hotel receptionist to call for you if you need a translation. The RAC offers route-planning services tailored to individual requirements, which may include current road conditions. The weather information service, **Teletiempo Nacional**, gives forecasts for the regions and provinces, as well as the national weather. It also provides information on maritime and mountain conditions.

ARRIVING BY BUS

OFTEN THE CHEAPEST WAY to reach and travel around Spain is by bus. **Eurolines** operates routes throughout Europe and runs daily services to Madrid and Barcelona.

If you are traveling from the UK to Spain, buses depart from London Victoria Coach Station. The journey to both cities take about 24 hours. Check with your travel agent for other options or departures from other cities.

TRAVELING AROUND SPAIN BY BUS

THERE IS NO Spanish national bus company, but private regional companies operate routes around the country. The largest bus tour company, **Autocares Juliá**, which acts as an agent for Eurolines in Spain, offers itineraries, bus tours, and sightseeing trips nationwide. Other bus companies operate in particular regions – Alsina Graells, for instance, covers most of the south and east of Spain. Tickets and information for long-distance travel are available at all main bus stations and from travel

CYCLING

Cycling is popular in Spain, and there are bicycles for rent in most tourist spots but there are few bike lanes, even in towns. Bicycles may be carried on *cercanías* trains after 2pm on Fridays until the last train on Sunday night, on any *regional* train

Bicycle touring, a popular activity

with a baggage car, and on all long-distance overnight trains. If you need to take your bicycle long-distance at other times, you should check it in an hour before the train departs. You may have to send it as luggage and pay a baggage charge based on its weight. It might not travel with you, so you will have to collect it when it arrives.

Alsina Graells, a regional bus service

agents but they cannot always be booked in advance. In Madrid there are several bus stations. The biggest of them are **Estación Sur**, which serves the whole of Spain; **Terminal Auto Res**, serving Valencia, Extremadura and Andalusia; and **Terminal Continental Auto**, for destinations in the north.

LOCAL BUSES

LOCAL BUS routes and timetables are posted at bus terminals and stops. You pay on the bus or buy strips of ten tickets called *billetes bonabús* from *estancos* (tobacconists).

Indicators for Seville's circular bus routes

General Index

Acknowledgments

DORLING KINDERSLEY would like to thank the following people whose contributions and assistance have made the preparation of this book possible.

MAIN CONTRIBUTORS
JOHN ARDAGH is a journalist and writer, and the author of several books on modern Europe.

DAVID BAIRD, resident in Andalusia from 1971 to 1995, is the author of *Inside Andalusia*.

VICKY HAYWARD, a writer, journalist, and editor, lives in Madrid, and has traveled extensively in Spain.

ADAM HOPKINS is an indefatigable travel writer and author of *Spanish Journeys: A Portrait of Spain*.

LINDSAY HUNT has traveled widely and has contributed to several Eyewitness Travel Guides.

NICK INMAN writes regularly on Spain for books and magazines.

PAUL RICHARDSON is the author of *Not Part of the Package*, a book on Ibiza, where he lives.

MARTIN SYMINGTON is a regular contributor to the *Daily Telegraph*. He also worked on the *Eyewitness Travel Guide to Great Britain*.

NIGEL TISDALL, contributor to the *Eyewitness Travel Guide to France*, is the author of the *Insight Pocket Guide to Seville*.

ROGER WILLIAMS has contributed to Insight Guides on Barcelona and Catalonia, and was the main contributor to the *Eyewitness Travel Guide to Provence*.

ADDITIONAL CONTRIBUTORS
Mary Jane Aladren, Pepita Aris, Emma Dent Coad, Rebecca Doulton, Harry Eyres, Josefina Fernández, Anne Hersh, Nick Rider, Mercedes Ruiz Ochoa, David Stone, Clara Villanueva, Christopher Woodward, Patricia Wright.

ADDITIONAL ILLUSTRATIONS
Arcana Studio, Richard Bonson, Louise Boulton, Martine Collings, Brian Craker, Jared Gilbey (Kevin Jones Associates), Paul Guest, Steven Gyapay, Claire Littlejohn.

ADDITIONAL PHOTOGRAPHY
Tina Chambers, Geoff Dann, Phillip Dowell, Mike Dunning, Neil Fletcher, Steve Gorton, Frank Greenaway, Derek Hall, Colin Keates, Alan Keohane, Dave King, D Murray, Cyril Laubsouer, Stephen Oliver, J Selves, Mathew Ward.

CARTOGRAPHY
Lovell Johns Ltd (Oxford), ERA-Maptec Ltd.

DESIGN AND EDITORIAL ASSISTANCE
Rosemary Bailey, Vicky Barber, Teresa Barea, Gretta Britton, Peter Casterton, Elspeth Collier, Carey Combe, Jonathan Cox, Martin Cropper, Linda Doyle, Des Hemsley, Michael Lake, Erika Lang, Rebecca Lister, Sarah Martin, Jane Oliver, Mike Osborn, Malcolm Parchment, Anna Streiffert, Helen Townsend, Phoebe Todd-Naylor, Andy Wilkinson.

PROOFREADER
Stewart J. Wild.

INDEXER
Hilary Bird.

SPECIAL ASSISTANCE
DORLING KINDERSLEY would like to thank all the regional and local tourist offices, *ayuntamientos*, shops, hotels, restaurants and other organizations throughout Spain for their invaluable help. Particular thanks are also due to Dr. Giray Ablay (University of Bristol); María Eugenia Alonso and María Dolores Delgado Peña (Museo Thyssen-Bornemisza); Ramón Álvarez (Consejería de Educación y Cultura, Castilla y León); Señor Ballesteros (Santiago de Compostela Tourist Office); Carmen Brieva, Javier Campos and Luis Esteruelas (Spanish Embassy, London); Javier Caballero Arranz; Fernando Cañada López; The Club Taurino of London; Consejería de Turismo, Castilla-La Mancha; Consejería de Turismo and Consejería de Cultura, Junta de Extremadura; Mònica Colomer and Montse Planas (Barcelona Tourist Office); María José Docal and Carmen Cardona (Patronato de Turismo, Lanzarote); Edilesa; Klaus Ehrlich; Juan Fernández, Lola Moreno and others at El País-Aguilar; Belén Galán (Centro de Arte Reina Sofía); Amparo Garrido; Adolfo Díaz Gómez (Albacete Tourist Office); Professor Nigel Glendinning (Queen Mary and Westfield College, University of London); Pedro Hernández; Insituto de Cervantes, London; Victor Jolín (SOTUR); Joaquim Juan Cabanilles (Servicio de Investigación Prehistórica, Valencia); Richard Kelly; Mark Little (Lookout Magazine); Carmen López de Tejada and Inma Felipe (Spanish National Tourist Office, London); Caterine López and Ana Roig Mundi (ITVA); Julia López de la Torre (Patrimonio Nacional, Madrid); Lovell Johns Ltd (Oxford); Josefina Maestre (Ministerio de Agricultura, Pesca y Alimentación); Juan Malavia García and Antonio Abarca (Cuenca Tourist Office); Mario (Promoción Turismo, Tenerife); Janet Mendel; Javier Morata (Acanto Arquitectura y Urbanismo. Madrid); Juan Carlos Murillo; Sonia Ortega and Bettina Krücken (Spain Gourmetour); Royal Society for the Protection of Birds (UK); Alícia Ribas Sos; Katusa Salazar-Sandoval (Fomento de Turismo, Ibiza); María Ángeles Sánchez and Marcos; Ana Sarrieri (Departamento de Comercio, Consumo y Turismo, Gobierno Vasco); Klaas Schenk; María José Sevilla (Foods From Spain); The Sherry Institute of Spain (London); Anna Skidmore (Fomento de Turismo, Mallorca); Philip Sweeney; Rupert Thomas; Mercedes Trujillo and Antonio Cruz Caballero (Patronato de Turismo, Gran Canaria); Gerardo Uarte (Gobierno de Navarra); Fermín Unzue (Dirección General de Turismo, Cantabria); Puri Villanueva.

ARTWORK REFERENCE
Sr. Joan Bassegoda, Catedral Gaudí (Barcelona);
José Luis Mosquera Muller (Mérida); Jorge
Palazón, Paisajes Españoles (Madrid).

PHOTOGRAPHY PERMISSIONS
THE PUBLISHER would like to thank the following
for their kind assistance and permission to
photograph at their establishments:
© Patrimonio Nacional, Madrid; Palacio de la
Almudaina, Palma de Mallorca; El Escorial,
Madrid; La Granja de San Ildefonso; Convento
de Santa Clara, Tordesillas; Las Huelgas Reales,
Burgos; Palacio Real, Madrid; Monasterio de las
Descalzas; Bananera "El Guanche S.L."; Museo
Arqueológico de Tenerife-OACIMC del Excmo.
Cavildo Insular de Tenerife; Asociación de
Encajeras de Acebo-Cáceres; Museo de Arte
Abstracto Español, Cuenca; Fundación Juan
March; Pepita Alia Lagartera; Museo Naval de
Madrid; © Catedral de Zamora; Museo de
Burgos; Claustro San Juan de Duero, Museo
Numantino, Soria; San Telmo Museoa Donostia-
San Sebastián; Hotel de la Reconquista, Oviedo;
Catedral de Jaca; Museo de Cera, Barcelona;
Museu D'Història de la Ciutat, Barcelona;
© Capitol Catedral de Lleida; Jardí Botànic
Marimurtra, Estació Internacional de Biologia
Mediterrània, Girona; Museo Arqueológico
Sagunto (Teatro Romano-Castillo); Museo
Municipal y Ermita de San Antonio de la Florida,
Madrid. Also all the other churches, museums,
hotels, restaurants, shops, galleries, and sights
too numerous to thank individually.

PICTURE CREDITS
Key: t=top; tl=top left; tlc=top left center; tc=top
center; trc=top right center; tr=top right; cla=center
left above; ca=center above; cra=center right
above; cl=center left; c=center; cr=center right;
clb=center left below; crb=center right below;
cb=center below; bl=bottom left; br=bottom right;
b=bottom; bc=bottom center; bcl=bottom center
left; bcr=bottom center right; (d)=detail.

Every effort has been made to trace the copyright
holders. Dorling Kindersley apologizes for any
unintentional omissions and would be pleased,
in such cases, to add an acknowledgement in
future editions.

Works of art have been published with the
permission of the following copyright holders:
Dona i Ocell Joan Miró © ADAGP, Paris & DACS,
London 172tl; *Guernica* Pablo Ruiz Picasso
1937 © DACS 1996 289cb; *Morning* George Kolbe
© DACS 1996; *Peine de los Vientos* Eduardo
Chillida 118b; Various works by Joaquín Sorolla ©
DACS 1996 295t; *Rainy Taxi* Salvador Dalí
© DEMART PRO ARTE BV/DACS 1996 205tr;
Tapestry of the Foundation Joan Miró 1975 ©
ADAGP, Paris & DACS, London; *Three Gypsy Boys*
© Joan Rebull 1976 140bl.

The publisher would like to thank the following
individuals, companies, and picture libraries for their
kind permission to reproduce their photographs:
ACE PHOTO AGENCY: Bob Masters 22b; Mauritius
19t; Bill Wassman 306b; AISA ARCHIVO
ICONOGRAFICO, BARCELONA: 18t, 32bl, 42l, 44ca,
44cb, 45bl, 45br, 46ca, 46cb, 47tl, 48cla, 48bl(d),
50bl, 50br, 50 cla, 50–51, 51cl, 51cra, 51bl, 52bl,
57br, 61tr, 63tl, 63b, 264t, 293b, 337bl, 405bl,
405br, 406cl, 465 br; Biblioteca Nacional, Madrid
Felipe V Luis Meléndez 67bl; Catedral de Sevilla
Ignacio de Loyola Alonso Vázquez 120bl(d);
Camilo José Cela Álvaro Delgado 1916 © DACS
1996 31br (d); *La Tertulia del Pombo* José
Gutiérrez Solana 1920 © DACS 1996 289t;
Museo de América, Madrid *Vista de Sevilla*
Alonso Sánchez Coello 54cb; Museo de Bellas
Artes, Seville *Sancho Panza y El Rucio* Moreno
Carbonero 56ca; Museo de Bellas Artes, Valencia
Ecce Homo Juan de Juanes 242br; Museo Frankfurt
La Armada 55tl; Museo de Historia de México
Hernán Cortés S.E. Colane 54bl(d); Museo
Histórico Militar, San Sebastián *Guerra Carlista*
59br(d); Museo Lázaro Galdiano, Madrid *Lope de
Vega* Caxes 280tr; Museo Nacional del Teatro
Poster for "Yerma" (FG Lorca) Juan Antonio
Morales y José Caballero © DACS 1996 31tr;
Museo del Prado, Madrid *La Rendición de Breda*
Diego Velázquez 57cb, *El Tres de Mayo de 1808
en Madrid* Francisco de Goya y Lucientes 58-
59(d), *La Reina María Luisa* María Francisco de
Goya 58cla, *Carlos IV* Francisco de Goya 67bc, *Los
Borrachos* Diego de Velázquez 282t, *Saturno
devorando a un hijo* Francisco de Goya 284tr, *El
Descendimiento* Van der Weyden 285b; Real
Academia de Bellas Artes de San Fernando,
Madrid *El Sueño del Caballero* Antonio de Pereda
56–57(d); AKG, London: 63cr; ALLSPORT: Stephen
Munday 38cr; AQUILA: Adrian Hoskins 200cla,
200clb; Mike Lane 325clb; James Pearce 195bl;
ARXIU MAS: 32br, 33bl, 47crb, 52tl, 53cl, 53br(d);
Museo del Prado, Madrid *Felipe II* Sánchez Coello
66br(d); Patrimonio Nacional 55cl,55b(d).

BIOFOTOS: Heather Angel 76cla, 76bl; BRIDGEMAN
ART LIBRARY: *St. Dominic enthroned as Abbot*
Bartolomé Bermejo 284tl; Index/Museo del Prado,
Madrid *Auto-da-fé in the Plaza Mayor* Francisco
Rizi 264c; Musée des Beaux Artes, Berne *Colossus
of Rhodes* Salvador Dalí 1954 DEMART PRO ARTE
BV/DACS 1996 29tr; Museo del Prado, Madrid
Charles IV and his Family Francisco de Goya y
Lucientes 29cb, *The Adoration of the Shepherds* El
Greco 282tc, *The Annunciation* Fra Angelico
282cb, *The Clothed Maja* Francisco de Goya y
Lucientes 283t, *The Naked Maja* Francisco de
Goya y Lucientes 283ca, *The Three Graces* Peter
Paul Rubens 283cb, *The Martydom of St. Philip*
José de Ribera 283b; Museo Picasso, Barcelona
Las Meninas, Infanta Margarita Pablo Ruiz
Picasso 1957 © DACS 1996 28tl; *Children On the
Beach* Joaquin y Bastida Sorolla © DACS 1996
285t; Phoenix Galleries, London *Rooftops, Fortna
Luxt, Majorca* Frederick Gore 8-9; MICHAEL
BUSSELLE: 197r, 199b, 200t.

CENTRO DE ARTE REINA SOFIA: *Bertsolaris* Zubiaurre
© DACS 1996 121cb, *Paisaje de Cadaqués*

Salvador Dalí 1923 © DEMART PRO ARTE BV/DACS 1996 288cb, *Accidente* Ponce de León 288b; CEPHAS: Mick Rock 25bl, 38t, 74t, 192tr, 192cl, 193tr, 322tr, 402tr, 403br, 403cr; Roy Stedall 403tr; COCOMFE: 613b; BRUCE COLEMAN: Eric Crichton 194tr; José Luis González Grande 195tr; Werner Layer 325tl; Andy Purcell 27ca; Hans Reinhard 76crb; Norbert Schwirtz 195tl; Colin Varndell 195crb; DEE CONWAY: 407cl, 407cr; SYLVIA CORDAIY PHOTO LIBRARY: Chris North 34tl; JOE CORNISH: 24ca, 328, 346b, 354tr; GIANCARLO COSTA: 33bc; COVER: Genin Andrada 36b, 39b; Angel Bocalandro 624tl; Austin Catalan 64bl; Juan Echeverria 27cra, 37br, 521bl; Pepe Franco 182c; Quim Llenas 121ca, 305tl; Matías Nieto 39c; José R Platón 624tr; F J Rodríguez 121bl.

J D DALLET: 65tr,440tl, 575br.

EDEX: 47bl, 387b; EDILESA: 334b; EL DESEO: Pedro Almodóvar 295b; PACO ELVIRA: 26crb; EMI: Hispavox 358b; EQUIPO 28: 407t; ET ARCHIVE: 48br; EUROPA PRESS: 19c, 64tl, 65ca; MARY EVANS PICTURE LIBRARY: 9t, 52cla, 59bl, 69t, 133r, 187t, 255r, 264bl, 317, 397r, 447b, 479, 529t, 611r; Explorer 406t; EYE UBIQUITOUS: James Davis Travel Photography 17t, 208br.

FIRO FOTO: 153c; 509t; FOTOTECA: IFEMA: Philipe Imbault 304br; FUNDACION CÉSAR MANRIQUE: 524br; FUNDACION COLECCION THYSSEN-BORNEMISZA: *Madonna of Humility* Fra Angelico 173t, *La Virgen del Árbol* Petrus Christus 278tr, *Harlequin with a mirror* Pablo Ruiz Picasso 1923 © DACS 1996 278c, *Hotel Room* © Edward Hopper 1931 278bl, *Portrait of Baron HH Thyssen-Bornemisza* © Lucian Freud 1981–82 278br, *Venus y Cupido* Peter Paul Rubens (after 1629) 279tl, *Saint Jerome in the Wilderness* Tiziano c.1575 279tr, *Santa Casilda* Francisco de Zurbarán 1640–1645 279c, *Autumn Landscape in Oldenburg* Karl Schmidt-Rottluff 1907 © DACS 1996 279b; FUNDACIO JOAN MIRO, BARCELONA: *Flama en L'espai i dona nua* Joan Miró 1932 © ADAGP, Paris and DACS, London 1996 168t.

GODO FOTO: 210b, 211t, 215t, 239b, 245t, 315bl; RONALD GRANT ARCHIVE: *For a Few Dollars More* © United Artists 476b.

ROBERT HARDING PICTURE LIBRARY: 15t, 137tr, 156ca, 168b, 169b, 239t, 293t, 487br; Julia Bayne 186–187; Nigel Blythe 15b, 145c; Bob Cousins 22clb; Robert Frerck 439tr; James Strachan 270tl; MARIA VICTORIA HERNANDEZ: 509b; HULTON DEUTSCH COLLECTION: 62b, 373br.

IBERDIAPO: Triangle 500–501; THE IMAGE BANK, London: Andra Pistolesi 170; Mark Romanelli 136bl; Mathew Weinreb 157b; IMAGES COLOUR LIBRARY: 629b; A.G.E Fotostock 24tr, 25t, 26cra, 26ca, 26br, 32tr, 33ca, 36c, 38cl, 118b, 164, 183t, 183c, 201br, 223ca, 223br, 304t, 307c, 325cla, 331 tr, 403cl, 406br, 442b, 473t, 507t, 533tr, 625c, 625b; Horizon International 32-33, 136cb; INCAFO: J A Fernández & C De Noriega 71bl, 121br; Juan

Carlos Muñoz 378b, 473b; A Ortega 26bl; INDEX: 30tl, 44c, 44b, 45c, 45cb, 46tl, 49b, 50cra, 52br (d), 55tr, *Los Moriscos suplicando al rey Felipe III* 57c, 60–61, 61b, 63 cl, *Carlos I* 66tc, 66 bl, 67br, 467ca; Bridgeman, London 54cra; CCJ 19b;X Correa 44tl; *Garrote Vil* José Gutiérrez Solana 1931 © DACS 1996 61clb(d); Galería del Ateneo, Madrid *Lucio Anneo Seneca* Villodas 46cla (d); Galeria Illustres Catalonia, Barcelona *Joan Prim I Prats* J Cusachs 59ca(d); Image *José Zorilla* 31bl; Instituto Valencia de Don Juan, Madrid *Carlos V* Simón Bening 55crb; Iranzo 52cra; Mithra 48clb, 54br (d), 60tl; Museo de América, Madrid *Indio Yumbo y Frutas Tropicales* 55cra; Museo Lázaro Galdiano, Madrid *Lope de Vega* Anonymous 30c, *Félix Lope de Vega* Francisco Pacheco 56br(d); Museo Municipal, Madrid *Fiesta en la Plaza Mayor de Madrid* Juan de la Corte 57tl; Museo del Prado, Madrid *Ascensión de un globo Montgolfier en Madrid* Antonio Carnicero 58cra(d), *José Moreño Conde de Floridablanca* Francisco de Goya 58br(d), *Flota del Rey Carlos III de España* A Joli 59t(d); National Maritime Museum, Greenwich *Batalla de Trafalgar* Chalmers 58cb; A Noé 52cb; Palacio del Senado, Madrid *Alfonso X "El Sabio"* Matías Moreno 30b(d), *Rendición de Granada* Francisco Pradilla 52–53(d); Patrimonio Nacional 47br; Private Collection, Madrid *Pedro Calderón de la Barca* Antonio de Pereda 57bl(d); Real Academia de Bellas Artes de San Fernando, Madrid *San Diego de Alcalá dando de comer a los pobres* Bartolomé Esteban Murillo 57ca(d), *Fernando VII* Francisco de Goya 67tl(d), *Isabel* II 67tc, *Self Portrait* Francisco de Goya 229b; A Tovy 65cb; NICK INMAN: 194bc, 612t, 615cb, 622tr, 631b; INSTITUT TURISTIC VALENCIÀ: 235br.

CÉSAR JUSTEL: 335b.

ANTHONY KING: 281t.

L'ESTARTIT TOURIST BOARD: 207c; LIFE FILE PHOTOGRAPHIC: 207c; Tony Abbott 324cla; Xavier Catalan 137cb; Emma Lee 137cra, 402tl, 635tr; NEIL LUKAS: 440cb, 440b.

MAGNUM: S Franklin 64cb; Jean Gaumy 64br, 65tl; JOHN MILLER: 196l, 478–479, 481cb, 505r, 514b, 519b, 524t, 525b; MUSEO ARQUEOLOGICO DE VILLENA: 44–45; MUSEU NACIONAL D'ART DE CATALUNYA: Museu d'Art Modern *El Tombant del Loing* Alfred Sisley 151t; MUSEO NACIONAL DEL PRADO: *El Jardín de las Delicias* 282b; MUSEU ARQUEOLOGIC DE BARCELONA: 167c; MUSEU PICASSO BARCELONA: *Auto Retrato* Pablo Ruiz Picasso 1899–1900 © DACS 1996 148b; *Las Meninas* Pablo Ruiz Picasso 1957 © DAC S 1996 149b.

NATURPRESS: Oriol Alamany 27bl; J L Calvo & J R Montero 325crb; José Luis Grande 441b; Walter Kwaternik 26clb, 27bc, 324cra, 325cra; Francisco Márquez 441cb, 398bl; Aurelio Martín 27br, Sebastián Martín 325bc; José A Martínez 76tr, 324clb, 324crb; © NATIONAL MARITIME MUSEUM: 54–55; Network: Bilderberg/W Kunz 403tl; NHPA:

Laurie Campbell 76cra; Stephen Dalton 77cl; Vicente García Canseco 27cla; Manfred Daneggar 76br, 77br; NATURAL SCIENCE PHOTOS: Nigel Charles 104tl; C Dani & I Jeske 100b, 325br; J Plant 222cb; Richard Revels 324br; Brian Sutton 324bl; W Tarboton 324tl; P & S Ward 222br.

OMEGA FOTO: 106tl, Manuel Pinilla 38b, 119b; ORONOZ: 4, 29br, 32 cl, 33br, 43b, 45t, 46b, 49t, 49clb, 49crb, 50tl, 50cb, 51t, 51br, 54tl, 54cla, 56cb, 61tl, 64ca, 65c, 78tl, 108t, 295cr, 337br, 345br, 352b, 416bl, 423bl, 443tl, 455t, 456l, 465bl; Biblioteca Nacional, Madrid *Isabel la Católica* Luis Madrazo 66tl(d); *El Espíritu de los Pájaros o Pájaros Volando* Eduardo Chillida 1953 © DACS 1996 289b; Iglesia Santo Tomé, Toledo *El Entierro del Conde de Orgaz* El Greco 28ca; *Portrait II* Joan Miró 1938 © ADAGP, Paris and DACS, London 1996 288t; Monasterio Santa Maria, Barcelona *Virgen con Niño* Ferrer Bassa 28clb(d); Museo de Bellas Artes, Cádiz *San Bruno en Éxtasis* Zurbarán 443tr; Museo Casa Gredo, Toledo *Carlos II* Miranda Correño 66tr(d); Museo del Ejército, Madrid *Isabel II* Madrazo 58tl; Museo Municipal de Bellas Artes, Tenerife *Retrato de Boabdil o Abu Abdala* 53tr(d); Museo Nacional de Escultura, Valladolid *Natividad* Berruguete 349tr; Museo Naval, Madrid *Desembarco de Colón* José Garnelo 53tl; Museo Naval Laminas, Madrid *Carabelas de Colón* Monleón 53bl(d); Museo del Prado, Madrid *El Salvador* José de Ribera 28crb, *Las Meninas o Familia de Felipe V* Diego Velázquez 28–29, *Felipe III* Pedro A Vidal 56bl, *Felipe V* 58bl, *Guernica* Pablo Ruiz Picasso 1937 © DACS 1996, 62–63, *Felipe IV* Diego Velázquez 66bc(d), *Bodegón* Zurbarán 284b, *David Vencedor de Goliat* Caravaggio 285c; Palacio Moncloa *Interior de la Catedral de Santiago* Villaamil Pérez 78–79; *Mujer en Azul* Pablo Ruiz Picasso 1901 © DACS 1996 288ca; Private Colection, Palma *Oleo Sobre Lienzo* Joan Miró 1932 © ADAGP, Paris and DACS, London 29ca; Real Academia de Bellas Artes de San Fernando *Fray Pedro Machado* Zurbarán 271tr.

PANOS PICTURES: Adrian Evans 64–65; JOSÉ M PÉREZ DE AYALA: 26cr, 440tr, 440ca, 441t, 441ca; THE PHOTOGRAPHERS LIBRARY: 499tr; PICTURES COLOUR LIBRARY: 18b, 26tr, 158-159, 248b, 398cl; PRISMA 60ca , 61crb, 62ca, 62cb, 63tr, 93t, 136br, 229c, 240t, 307t, 435, 492br, 508cl, 515clb, 515cb, 515crb, 515bl, 519t, 527bl, 527br; *Franco* Aguiar 67tr; *El ingenioso hidalgo Don Quixote de la Mancha* 1605 Ricardo Balaca 377br; Diputación de Madrid *Francisco Bahamonde Franco* Enrique Segura 62tl; Domenech & Azpiliqueta 114t; Albert Heras 182b; Marcel Jaquet 507b, 517b; Hans Lohr 459b; *Los Niños de la Concha* Bartolomé Esteban Murillo 29bl(d); Museo de Arte Moderno, Barcelona *Pío Baroja* Ramón Casas 60cb(d); Museo de Bellas Artes, Bilbao *Condesa Mathieu de Noailles* Ignacio Zuloaga y Zubaleta © DACS 1996 114b; Museo de Bellas Artes, Zaragoza *Príncipe de Viana* José Moreno Carbonero 126b (d); Mateu 185c; Palacio del Senado, Madrid *Alfonso XIII* Aquino © DACS 1996 67cr; Patrimonio Nacional Palacio de Riofrío, Segovia: 60br; *Auto Retrato* Pablo Ruiz Picasso 1907 © Succession Picasso DACS 1996 61ca; Marta Povo 626t; Real Academia de Bellas Artes de San Fernando, Madrid *Las Bodas de Camacho* José Moreno Carbonero 31tl(d), *Procession of the Flagellants* Francisco de Goya 264br(d); *Emilio Castelar* Joaquin Sorolla © DACS 1996 60bl. REX FEATURES: Sipa Press 205cb; © ROYAL MUSUEM OF SCOTLAND: Michel Zabé 43t.

MARIA ÁNGELES SANCHEZ: 34tr, 35b, 39t, 75t, 94cl, 14l, 280tl, 294b, 369c, 387tr, 508t, 508cr, 508b, 512c, 523t; SCIENCE PHOTO LIBRARY: Geospace 10l; 6 TOROS 6: 33cb; SPANISH TOURIST BOARD: 245c; SPECTRUM COLOUR LIBRARY: 132–133, 136tr, 528–529; STOCKPHOTOS, Madrid: Marcelo Brodsky 36t; Campillo 625t; Heinz Hebeisen 37bl; Mikael Helsing 624b, 314tl; David Hornback 17b; Javier Sánchez 314tl; Werner Otto Reisefotografie 629t; JAMES STRACHAN: 281b, 292t, 292c, 294t; TONY STONE WORLDWIDE: Doug Armand 16b; Jon Bradley 304bl; Robert Everts 422ca.

VISIONS OF ANDALUCÍA: Michelle Chaplow 406–407; JD Dallet 379tr; VU: Christina García Rodero 2–3, 16c, 34b, 35c, 35t, 128cl, 246–247, 350l, 413cr.

CHARLIE WAITE: 116–117, 470–471; WERNER FORMAN ARCHIVE: Museo de Arte Hispanomusulmán 48t; Museum of Catalan Art, Barcelona 326tl; National Maritime Museum, Greenwich 48cr; ALAN WILLIAMS: 74b; PETER WILSON: 254–255, 272, 444b, 445c, 451t, 457t; WORLD PICTURES: 305c, 488t;

ZEFA: 1.

Front endpaper: All special photography except JOE CORNISH cbl; JOHN MILLER tr; SPECTRUM COLOUR LIBRARY ca; PETER WILSON cbr.

Jacket: All special photography except INDEX: spine cb; ORONOZ front cbl; ZEFA: front t.

Phrase Book

IN AN EMERGENCY

Help!	¡Socorro!	soh-**koh**-roh
Stop!	¡Pare!	**pah**-reh
Call a doctor!	¡Llame a un médico!	**yah**-meh ah **oon** meh-dee-koh
Call an ambulance!	¡Llame a una ambulancia!	**yah**-meh ah **oonah** ahm-boo-**lahn**-thee-ah
Call the police!	¡Llame a la policía!	**yah**-meh ah lah poh-lee-**thee**-ah
Call the fire department!	¡Llame a los bomberos!	**yah**-meh ah lohs bohm-**beh**-rohs
Where is the nearest telephone?	¿Dónde está el teléfono más próximo?	**dohn**-deh ehs-**tah** ehl teh-**leh**-foh-noh mahs prohx-ee-moh
Where is the nearest hospital?	¿Dónde está el hospital más próximo?	**dohn**-deh ehs-**tah** ehl ohs-pee-tahl mahs prohx-ee-moh

COMMUNICATION ESSENTIALS

Yes	Sí	see
No	No	noh
Please	Por favor	pohr fah-**vohr**
Thank you	Gracias	**grah**-thee-ahs
Excuse me	Perdone	pehr-**doh**-neh
Hello	Hola	**oh**-lah
Goodbye	Adiós	ah-dee-**ohs**
Good night	Buenas noches	**bweh**-nahs **noh**-chehs
Morning	La mañana	lah mah-**nyah**-nah
Afternoon	La tarde	lah **tahr**-deh
Evening	La tarde	lah **tahr**-deh
Yesterday	Ayer	ah-**yehr**
Today	Hoy	oy
Tomorrow	Mañana	mah-**nya**-nah
Here	Aquí	ah-**kee**
There	Allí	ah-**yee**
What?	¿Qué?	keh
When?	¿Cuándo?	**kwahn**-doh
Why?	¿Por qué?	pohr-**keh**
Where?	¿Dónde?	**dohn**-deh

USEFUL PHRASES

How are you?	¿Cómo está usted?	**koh**-moh ehs-**tah** oos-**tehd**
Very well, thank you.	Muy bien, gracias.	mwee bee-**ehn grah**-thee-ahs
Pleased to meet you.	Encantado de conocerle.	ehn-kahn-**tah**-doh deh koh-noh-**thehr**-leh
See you soon.	Hasta pronto.	ahs-tah **prohn**-toh
That's fine.	Está bien.	ehs-**tah** bee-**ehn**
Where is/are . . . ?	¿Dónde está/están . . . ?	**dohn**-deh ehs-**tah**/ehs-**tahn**
How far is it to . . . ?	Cuántos metros/ kilómetros hay de aquí a . . . ?	**kwahn**-tohs meh-trohs/kee-**loh**-meh-trohs **eye** deh ah-**kee** ah
Which way to . . . ?	¿Por dónde se va a . . . ?	pohr **dohn**-deh seh **bah** ah
Do you speak English?	¿Habla inglés?	**ah**-blah een-**glehs**
I don't understand	No comprendo	noh kohm-**prehn**-doh
Could you speak more slowly please?	¿Puede hablar más despacio por favor?	**pweh**-deh ah-**blahr** mahs dehs-pah-thee-oh pohr fah-**vohr**
I'm sorry.	Lo siento.	loh see-**ehn**-toh

USEFUL WORDS

big	grande	**grahn**-deh
small	pequeño	peh-**keh**-nyoh
hot	caliente	kah-lee-**ehn**-teh
cold	frío	**free**-oh
good	bueno	**bweh**-noh
bad	malo	**mah**-loh
enough	bastante	bahs-**tahn**-teh
well	bien	bee-**ehn**
open	abierto	ah-bee-**ehr**-toh
closed	cerrado	thehr-**rah**-doh
left	izquierda	eeth-key-**ehr**-dah
right	derecha	deh-**reh**-chah
straight ahead	todo recto	toh-doh **rehk**-toh
near	cerca	**thehr**-kah
far	lejos	**leh**-hohs
up	arriba	ah-**ree**-bah
down	abajo	ah-**bah**-hoh
early	temprano	tehm-**prah**-noh
late	tarde	**tahr**-deh
entrance	entrada	ehn-**trah**-dah
exit	salida	sah-**lee**-dah
toilet	lavabos, servicios	lah-**vah**-bohs, sehr-**bee**-thee-ohs
more	más	mahs
less	menos	**meh**-nohs

SHOPPING

How much does this cost?	¿Cuánto cuesta esto?	**kwahn**-toh **kwehs**-tah **ehs**-toh
I would like . . .	Me gustaría . . .	meh goos-ta-**ree**-ah
Do you have?	¿Tienen?	tee-**yeh**-nehn
I'm just looking.	Sólo estoy mirando, gracias.	**soh**-loh ehs-**toy** mee-**rahn**-doh **grah**-thee-ahs
Do you take credit cards?	¿Aceptan tarjetas de crédito?	ah-**thehp**-tahn tahr-**heh**-tahs deh **kreh**-dee-toh
What time do you open?	¿A qué hora abren?	ah keh oh-rah **ah**-brehn
What time do you close?	¿A qué hora cierran?	ah keh oh-rah thee-**ehr**-rahn
This one.	Éste.	**ehs**-teh
That one.	Ése.	**eh**-seh
expensive	caro	**kahr**-oh
cheap	barato	bah-**rah**-toh
size, clothes	talla	**tah**-yah
size, shoes	número	**noo**-mehr-oh
white	blanco	**blahn**-koh
black	negro	**neh**-groh
red	rojo	**roh**-hoh
yellow	amarillo	ah-mah-**ree**-yoh
green	verde	**behr**-deh
blue	azul	ah-**thool**
antique shop	la tienda de antigüedades	lah tee-**ehn**-dah deh ahn-tee-gweh-**dah**-dehs
bakery	la panadería	lah pah-nah-deh-**ree**-ah
bank	el banco	ehl **bahn**-koh
book shop	la librería	lah lee-breh-**ree**-ah
butcher's	la carnicería	lah kahr-nee-theh-**ree**-ah
cake shop	la pastelería	lah pahs-teh-leh-**ree**-ah
drug store	la farmacia	lah fahr-**mah**-thee-ah
fish market	la pescadería	lah pehs-kah-deh-**ree**-ah
greengrocer's	la frutería	lah froo-teh-**ree**-ah
grocery	la tienda de comestibles	lah tee-**yehn**-dah deh koh-mehs-**tee**-blehs
hairdresser	la peluquería	lah peh-loo-keh-**ree**-ah
market	el mercado	ehl mehr-**kah**-doh
newsstand	el kiosko de prensa	ehl kee-**ohs**-koh deh **prehn**-sah
post office	la oficina de correos	lah oh-fee-**thee**-nah deh **kohr**-reh-ohs
shoe store	la zapatería	lah thah-pah-teh-**ree**-ah
supermarket	el supermercado	ehl soo-pehr-mehr-**kah**-doh
tobacco shop	el estanco	ehl ehs-**tahn**-koh
travel agency	la agencia de viajes	lah ah-**hehn**-thee-ah dee bee-ah-hehs

SIGHTSEEING

art gallery	el museo de arte	ehl moo-**seh**-oh deh **ahr**-teh
cathedral	la catedral	lah kah-teh-**drahl**
church	la iglesia	lah ee-**gleh**-see-ah
	la basílica	lah bah-**see**-lee-kah
garden	el jardín	ehl hahr-**deen**
library	la biblioteca	lah bee-blee-oh-**teh**-kah
museum	el museo	ehl moo-**seh**-oh
tourist information	la oficina de turismo	lah oh-fee-**thee**-nah deh too-**rees**-moh
town hall	el ayuntamiento	ehl ah-yoon-tah-mee-**ehn**-toh
closed for vacation	cerrado por vacaciones	thehr-**rah**-doh pohr bah-kah-thee-**oh**-nehs
bus station	la estación de autobuses	lah ehs-tah-thee-**ohn** deh owtoh-**boo**-sehs
railroad station	la estación de trenes	lah ehs-tah-thee-**ohn** deh **treh**-nehs

STAYING IN A HOTEL

Do you have a vacant room?	¿Tienen una habitación libre?	tee-**eh**-nehn oo-nah ah-bee-tah-thee-**ohn lee**-breh
double room	habitación doble	ah-bee-tah-thee-**ohn doh**-bleh
with double bed	con cama de matrimonio	kohn **kah**-mah deh mah-tree-**moh**-nee-oh
twin room	habitación con dos camas	ah-bee-tah-thee-**ohn** kohn dohs **kah**-mahs
single room	habitación individual	ah-bee-tah-thee-**ohn** een-dee-vee-doo-**ahl**
room with a bath	habitación con baño	ah-bee-tah-thee-**ohn** kohn **bah**-nyoh
shower	ducha	**doo**-chah
porter	el botones	ehl boh-**toh**-nehs
key	la llave	lah **yah**-veh
I have a reservation.	Tengo una habitación reservada.	tehn-goh **oo**-na ah-bee-tah-thee-**ohn** reh-sehr-**bah**-dah

EATING OUT

Do you have a table for . . .?	¿Tienen mesa para . . .?	tee-**eh**-nehn meh-sah pah-**rah**
I want to reserve a table.	Quiero reservar una mesa.	kee-eh-roh reh-sehr-**bahr** oo-nah **meh**-sah
The check please.	La cuenta por favor.	lah **kwehn**-tah pohr fah-**vohr**
I am a vegetarian	Soy vegetariano/a	soy beh-heh-tah-ree-**ah**-no/na
waitress/	camarera/	kah-mah-**reh**-rah
waiter	camarero	kah-mah-**reh**-roh
menu	la carta	lah **kahr**-tah
fixed-price menu	menú del día	meh-**noo** dehl **dee**-ah
wine list	la carta de vinos	lah **kahr**-tah deh **bee**-nohs
glass	un vaso	oon **bah**-soh
bottle	una botella	oo-nah boh-**teh**-yah
knife	un cuchillo	oon koo-**chee**-yoh
fork	un tenedor	oon teh-neh-**dohr**
spoon	una cuchara	oo-nah koo-**chah**-rah
breakfast	el desayuno	ehl deh-sah-**yoo**-noh
lunch	la comida/ el almuerzo	lah koh-**mee**-dah/ ehl ahl-**mwehr**-thoh
dinner	la cena	lah **theh**-nah
main course	el primer plato	ehl pree-**mehr plah**-toh
appetizers	los entremeses	lohs ehn-treh-**meh**-sehs
dish of the day	el plato del día	ehl **plah**-toh dehl **dee**-ah
coffee	el café	ehl kah-**feh**
rare	poco hecho	**poh**-koh **eh**-choh
medium	medio hecho	**meh**-dee-oh **eh**-choh
well done	muy hecho	mwee **eh**-choh

MENU DECODER

al horno	ahl **ohr**-noh	baked
asado	ah-**sah**-doh	roast
el aceite	ah-**thee**-eh-teh	oil
las aceitunas	ah-theh-**toon**-ahs	olives
el agua mineral	**ah**-gwa mee-neh-**rahl**	mineral water
sin gas/con gas	seen gas/kohn gas	still/sparkling
el ajo	**ah**-hoh	garlic
el arroz	ahr-**rohth**	rice
el azúcar	ah-**thoo**-kahr	sugar
la carne	**kahr**-neh	meat
la cebolla	theh-**boh**-yah	onion
la cerveza	thehr-**beh**-thah	beer
el cerdo	**thehr**-doh	pork
el chocolate	choh-koh-**lah**-teh	chocolate
el chorizo	choh-**ree**-thoh	red sausage
el cordero	kohr-**deh**-roh	lamb
el fiambre	fee-**ahm**-breh	cold meat
frito	**free**-toh	fried
la fruta	**froo**-tah	fruit
los frutos secos	**froo**-tohs **seh**-kohs	nuts
las gambas	**gahm**-bahs	shrimp
el helado	eh-**lah**-doh	ice cream
el huevo	oo-**eh**-voh	egg
el jamón serrano	hah-**mohn** sehr-**rah**-noh	cured ham

el jerez	heh-**rehz**	sherry
la langosta	lahn-**gohs**-tah	lobster
la leche	**leh**-cheh	milk
el limón	lee-**mohn**	lemon
la limonada	lee-moh-**nah**-dah	lemonade
la mantequilla	mahn-teh-**kee**-yah	butter
la manzana	mahn-**thah**-nah	apple
los mariscos	mah-**rees**-kohs	seafood
la menestra	meh-**nehs**-trah	vegetable stew
la naranja	nah-**rahn**-hah	orange
el pan	pahn	bread
el pastel	pahs-**tehl**	cake
las patatas	pah-**tah**-tahs	potatoes
el pescado	pehs-**kah**-doh	fish
la pimienta	pee-mee-**yehn**-tah	pepper
el plátano	**plah**-tah-noh	banana
el pollo	**poh**-yoh	chicken
el postre	**pohs**-treh	dessert
el queso	**keh**-soh	cheese
la sal	sahl	salt
las salchichas	sahl-**chee**-chahs	sausages
la salsa	**sahl**-sah	sauce
seco	**seh**-koh	dry
el solomillo	soh-loh-**mee**-yoh	sirloin
la sopa	**soh**-pah	soup
la tarta	**tahr**-tah	pie/cake
el té	teh	tea
la ternera	tehr-**neh**-rah	beef
las tostadas	tohs-**tah**-dahs	toast
el vinagre	bee-**nah**-greh	vinegar
el vino blanco	**bee**-noh **blahn**-koh	white wine
el vino rosado	**bee**-noh roh-**sah**-doh	rosé wine
el vino tinto	**bee**-noh **teen**-toh	red wine

NUMBERS

0	cero	**theh**-roh
1	uno	**oo**-noh
2	dos	dohs
3	tres	trehs
4	cuatro	**kwa**-troh
5	cinco	**theen**-koh
6	seis	says
7	siete	**see**-eh-teh
8	ocho	**oh**-choh
9	nueve	**nweh**-veh
10	diez	dee-**ehth**
11	once	**ohn**-theh
12	doce	**doh**-theh
13	trece	**treh**-theh
14	catorce	kah-**tohr**-theh
15	quince	**keen**-theh
16	dieciséis	dee-eh-thee-**seh-ees**
17	diecisiete	dee-eh-thee-see-**eh**-teh
18	dieciocho	dee-eh-thee-**oh**-choh
19	diecinueve	dee-eh-thee-**nweh**-veh
20	veinte	**beh**-een-teh
21	veintiuno	beh-een-tee-**oo**-noh
22	veintidós	beh-een-tee-**dohs**
30	treinta	**treh**-een-tah
31	treinta y uno	treh-een-tah ee **oo**-noh
40	cuarenta	kwah-**rehn**-tah
50	cincuenta	theen-**kwehn**-tah
60	sesenta	seh-**sehn**-tah
70	setenta	seh-**tehn**-tah
80	ochenta	oh-**chehn**-tah
90	noventa	noh-**vehn**-tah
100	cien	thee-**ehn**
101	ciento uno	thee-**ehn**-toh **oo**-noh
102	ciento dos	thee-**ehn**-toh **dohs**
200	doscientos	dohs-thee-**ehn**-tohs
500	quinientos	khee-nee-**ehn**-tohs
700	setecientos	seh-teh-thee-**ehn**-tohs
900	novecientos	noh-veh-thee-**ehn** tohs
1,000	mil	meel
1,001	mil uno	meel **oo**-noh

TIME

one minute	un minuto	oon mee-**noo**-toh
one hour	una hora	oo-na **oh**-rah
half an hour	media hora	**meh**-dee-a **oh**-rah
Monday	lunes	**loo**-nehs
Tuesday	martes	**mahr**-tehs
Wednesday	miércoles	mee-**ehr**-koh-lehs
Thursday	jueves	hoo-**weh**-vehs
Friday	viernes	bee-**ehr**-nehs
Saturday	sábado	**sah**-bah-doh
Sunday	domingo	doh-**meen**-goh

BARCELONA TRANSIT MAP

The metro is the quickest way of getting around Barcelona. It runs from 5:30am–11pm on weekdays; 6:30am–11:30pm on Sundays and public holidays. In the stations the lines are identified by number and color; platform signs display the name of the last station on the line. You can buy a one-trip ticket (*billete*) or a discounted, ten-trip *tarjeta*: the T-1, which is valid for the metro only; or the T-2, which is valid for the metro and the buses. Tickets for the interconnecting FF CC suburban rail network, which runs from the city center out to the airport and to Barcelona's environs, and for the funiculars, must be purchased separately.

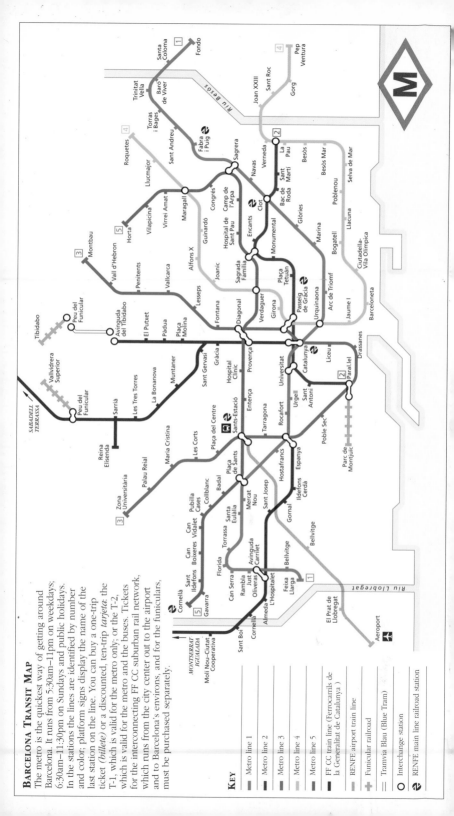

KEY

- Metro line 1
- Metro line 2
- Metro line 3
- Metro line 4
- Metro line 5
- FF CC train line (Ferrocarrils de la Generalitat de Catalunya)
- RENFE airport train line
- Funicular railroad
- Tramvia Blau (Blue Tram)
- O Interchange station
- RENFE main line railroad station